Decoding the Ethics Code

Fourth Edition

To my husband Gary, who lovingly supported my ethical quests; my children Brian and Erica, who taught me how to combine responsibility with care; and to the memory of my parents, Helen and Norman Burg, who taught me by example the importance of moral values.

Decoding the Ethics Code

A Practical Guide for Psychologists

Fourth Edition

Celia B. Fisher

Center for Ethics Education,
Fordham University

Los Angeles | London | New Delhi
Singapore | Washington DC | Melbourne

FOR INFORMATION:

SAGE Publications, Inc.
2455 Teller Road
Thousand Oaks, California 91320
E-mail: order@sagepub.com

SAGE Publications Ltd.
1 Oliver's Yard
55 City Road
London, EC1Y 1SP
United Kingdom

SAGE Publications India Pvt. Ltd.
B 1/I 1 Mohan Cooperative Industrial Area
Mathura Road, New Delhi 110 044
India

SAGE Publications Asia-Pacific Pte. Ltd.
3 Church Street
#10-04 Samsung Hub
Singapore 049483

Acquisitions Editor: Lara Parra
Editorial Assistant: Morgan Shannon
Production Editor: Veronica Stapleton Hooper
Copy Editors: Paula L. Fleming and Doug McNair
Typesetter: C&M Digitals (P) Ltd.
Proofreader: Susan Schon
Indexer: Jeanne R. Busemeyer
Cover Designer: Candice Harman
Marketing Manager: Katherine Hepburn

Printed in the United States of America

Library of Congress Cataloging-in-Publication Data

Names: Fisher, Celia B., author.

Title: Decoding the ethics code : a practical guide for psychologists / Celia B. Fisher, Center for Ethics Education, Fordham University.

Description: Fourth edition. | Los Angeles : SAGE, [2016] | Includes bibliographical references and index.

Identifiers: LCCN 2015044697 | ISBN 978-1-4833-6929-7 (pbk. : alk. paper)

Subjects: LCSH: Psychologists—Professional ethics. | Psychology—Moral and ethical aspects.

Classification: LCC BF76.4.F57 2016 | DDC 174/.915—dc23
LC record available at http://lccn.loc.gov/2015044697

This book is printed on acid-free paper.

20 21 22 23 24 10 9 8 7 6 5 4

Brief Contents

Detailed Contents

Preface

Welcome to the fourth edition of *Decoding the Ethics Code: A Practical Guide for Psychologists.* This edition retains the format and critical content of the previous editions. The interval between this and the first edition has demonstrated the durability of the current American Psychological Association's (APA's) Ethical Principles of Psychologists and Code of Conduct first published in 2002 and amended in 2010 (APA, 2002a, 2010a). During the past 14 years, the field has witnessed new insights into how the Ethics Code can be applied to ethical decision making in the science and practice of psychology and faced new challenges for its application to emerging moral debates.

The success of the earlier editions encouraged the decision to retain the user-friendly format of the book. For this edition, all chapters have been revised to ensure that they reflect the most current status of scientific and professional theory, practices, and debate across all facets of ethical decision making. The wisdom of the more recent articles and chapters, incorporated into this fourth edition, sheds new light on the application and continued relevance and vitality of the Ethics Code to moral discourse and practical challenges characterizing the dynamic and thriving discipline of psychology.

Additions and New Features

One motivation for producing a fourth edition was to incorporate the wealth of knowledge generated by more than 200 articles and chapters written on the relevance of the APA Ethics Code for research and practices since the earlier edition. New topics addressed in this edition include the expansion of web-based services into all aspects of psychological practice and research, the new interprofessional competencies required by psychologists' participation in the Affordable Care Act (ACA) and by advances in evidence-based practices, human rights considerations raised anew by the APA's independent investigation into psychologists' participation in military interrogations and this activity's implications for the globalization of psychology, the continued growth of the self-care movement as a means of maintaining competence, expanding applications of multicultural competence to the rights and welfare of sexual and gender minorities, implications of case law for the role of religious beliefs in practice and training, and updated application of the Health Insurance Portability and Accountability Act of 1996 (HIPAA) and changes in federal regulations for research.

A second motivation for this edition was to respond to requests from students and early career professionals to emphasize specific applications of Ethics Code standards that might be of immediate import to the unfamiliar professional and scientific challenges they were or would soon be confronting in internships, postdoctoral research fellowships, consulting and industrial–organizational positions, and teaching. This edition includes expanded and updated "Need to Know" sections and new "Digital Ethics" sections integrated throughout the chapters to help alert students and early-career psychologists to specific strategies for applying the Ethics Code to traditional and new arenas of ethical science and practice.

A final motivation for writing a fourth edition was to update the ethical decision-making model based on current advances in the field and provide readers with opportunities to apply the model, described in Chapter 3, to pressing ethical questions and case analyses. Such opportunities are presented in a section titled "Chapter Cases and Discussion Questions" at the end of each chapter. This volume continues to include an appendix with 10 detailed case studies accompanied by relevant, thought-provoking questions and suggested readings. These cases encourage ethical analysis that integrates multiple standards described across the chapters and sensitivity to context and relational responsibilities, analysis and sensitivity that lead to the responsible conduct of psychological research and practice.

The Goals of This Book

The primary purpose of this book is to provide graduate students, early-career and seasoned psychologists, consumers of psychological services, and professionals in related scientific and professional disciplines with a practical guide to the meaning and applicability of the APA's Ethical Principles of Psychologists and Code of Conduct. The book seeks to place into practical perspective the format, choice of wording, aspirational principles, and enforceable standards of the code. It provides in-depth discussions of the rationale behind and application of each ethical standard to the broad spectrum of scientific, teaching, and professional roles and activities of psychologists. It gives clear examples of behaviors that would be in compliance with or in violation of enforceable standards.

The fourth edition of *Decoding the Ethics Code: A Practical Guide for Psychologists* is also intended to assist psychologists in effectively using the Ethics Code's principles and standards to conduct their work activities in ethically responsible ways, to avoid ethical violations, and to preserve and protect the fundamental rights and welfare of those with whom they work. By incorporating the most recent scholarship on ethical issues in psychology and by addressing topical issues in the field, this fourth edition continues the vision of the earlier editions in providing psychologists with the information and decision-making skills they need to apply the Ethics Code to the constantly changing scientific, professional, and legal realities of the discipline.

How to Use This Book

This book was written to provide an in-depth, yet easily accessible, guide to applying the Ethical Principles of Psychologists and Code of Conduct (APA, 2010c) to psychologists' everyday ethical decision making. The book has several features designed to provide easy reference to a wide range of information and practical guidance on each component of the APA Ethics Code.

How the Book Is Organized

The APA Ethics Code consists of the Introduction and Applicability section, the Preamble, 5 General Principles, and 10 specific sections putting forth enforceable standards for ethical conduct. Although the chapters of this book are organized around the format of the Ethics Code, the book does not have to be read from cover to cover. Each chapter and the discussion of each standard are designed to stand on their own. Cross-references to other parts of the code are provided when they are helpful to ethical decision making. The book is organized around 13 chapters.

Chapter 1. A Code of Ethics for Psychology: How Did We Get Here?

Chapter 1 presents an introduction to the history, goals, controversies, major advances, and revision strategies associated with the APA Ethics Code since its inception over half a century ago. It contains specific examples of the innovations and challenges characterizing the process of creating the current Ethics Code, including the 2010 amendments to the Code that increased psychologists' obligation to protect human rights. It familiarizes readers with the value of the Ethics Code to the profession and the public. This chapter also explains the format and distinctive features of the Code and where to find Ethics Code Standards that apply to different activities in which psychologists are engaged.

Chapter 2. The Introduction and Applicability Section, Preamble, and General Principles: What Do They Mean?

Chapter 2 provides a guide to the practical meaning of the Ethics Code's Introduction and Applicability section, Preamble, and General Principles. It includes discussion of to whom and what activities the Ethics Code applies; the rationale and meaning of the language used in the Ethics Code; the relationship among the Ethics Code, APA guidelines, and the rules and procedures for enforcement of the code; the relevance of the Ethics Code to sanctions applied by other professional bodies and state licensure boards as well as to litigation; and the meaning and practical significance of the General Principles.

Chapter 3. The APA Ethics Code and Ethical Decision Making

The Ethical Principles and Standards provide critical guidance for ethical decision making, but there is no set formula for resolving the complex ethical challenges psychologists will confront over the course of their careers. Chapter 3 discusses the importance of ethical commitment, ethical awareness, and ethical decision making to good and rightly practiced professional and scientific psychology. It elucidates the role of moral character and moral frameworks in the ability to prepare for, identify, and resolve ethical challenges and illustrates a step-by-step decision-making strategy to assist psychologists in applying the Ethics Code to new and emerging areas of psychology as the discipline continues to evolve.

Chapters 4 to 13. Enforceable Standards

Chapters 4 to 13 provide in-depth explanations and practical examples of how to apply the 151 enforceable standards. The chapter titles correspond to the titles of the 10 sections on enforceable standards in the Ethics Code: (1) Resolving Ethical Issues, (2) Competence, (3) Human Relations, (4) Privacy and Confidentiality, (5) Advertising and Other Public Statements, (6) Record Keeping and Fees, (7) Education and Training, (8) Research and Publication, (9) Assessment, and (10) Therapy.

Chapter Cases and Discussion Questions

Ethical decision making in psychology requires a commitment to do what is right; an awareness of Ethics Code principles and standards, relevant laws, and institutional policies; and the flexibility and sensitivity to the context, role responsibilities, and stakeholder expectations unique to each work endeavor. New to this fourth edition is the inclusion of cases and discussion questions at the end of chapters 3–13. These are designed to assist the reader in applying ethical issues, standards, and guidelines specific to each chapter to real-world ethical dilemmas.

Supplements and Appendix

The companion website at **study.sagepub.com/fisher4e** provides password-protected instructor resources including a test bank and PowerPoint slides, and open-access student resources including additional case studies with discussion questions as well as links to the current version of the APA Ethical Principles of Psychologists and Code of Conduct. Appendix A provides 10 additional case studies designed to assist the reader in applying the Ethics Code and the ethical decision-making steps presented in Chapter 3 to the diversity of work settings and responsibilities of psychologists. While the cases and discussion questions provided at the end of each chapter draw readers' attention to dilemmas tied directly to topics covered in the chapter, these 10 additional case studies are written broadly to require consideration of Ethics Code standards described across chapters. Accompanying the cases are updated lists of suggested readings and discussion questions designed to place in vivid relief the moral principles underlying ethical conflicts, guide readers in generating and evaluating alternative courses of action, and stimulate creative strategies to resolve dilemmas responsibly. Continuously updated links to the APA guidelines online are available at **study.sagepub.com/fisher4e.**

Hot Topics

This edition updates the popular *Hot Topic* sections at the end of Chapters 3 to 13, which provide in-depth analysis of current areas of ethical concern in the science and practice of psychology:

- The Ethical Component of Self-Care: Chapter 3
- Human Rights and Psychologists' Involvement in Assessments Related to Death Penalty Cases: Chapter 4
- Multicultural Ethical Competence: Chapter 5
- Goodness-of-Fit Ethics for Informed Consent to Research and Treatment Involving Adults With Impaired Decisional Capacity: Chapter 6
- Confidentiality and Involvement of Parents in Mental Health Services for Children and Adolescents: Chapter 7
- Avoiding False and Deceptive Statements in Scientific and Clinical Expert Testimony: Chapter 8
- Managing the Ethics of Managed Care: Chapter 9
- Ethical Supervision of Trainees in Professional Psychology Programs: Chapter 10
- Informational Risk and Disclosure of Genetic Information to Research Participants: Chapter 11
- The Use of Assessments in Expert Testimony: Implications of Case Law and the Federal Rules of Evidence: Chapter 12
- Ethical Issues for the Integration of Religion and Spirituality in Therapy: Chapter 13

Digital Ethics

A new addition to the chapters in this edition is brief sections describing ethical practices and decision-making strategies for activities that involve telecommunication technologies, which are continuously evolving. These technologies include synchronous (in real time) and asynchronous (communication outside of real time) web-based research and services, telephone and video conferencing, email and text messaging, online chat rooms and bulletin boards, social media, and mobile applications. In this volume, digital ethics are applied to the use of these technologies in psychotherapy, health promotion, team-based services, assessment, research, education, supervision, advertising and marketing, individual and organizational consultation, record keeping, and billing.

Chapter	Page	Standard	Digital Ethics Sections
5	82	2.01a	Competence in Basic Knowledge of Electronic Modalities
5	90	2.01e	Competence in the Use of Telepsychology
5	101	2.04	Navigating the Online Search for Evidence-Based Practices
6	117	3.01	Use of Internet Searches for Evaluation of Student Applicants
6	122	3.04	Avoiding Harm in Telepsychology Services
6	138	3.05	Professional Boundaries and Self-Disclosure Over the Internet
6	157	3.10a	Consent via Electronic Transmission
7	173	4.01	Cybersecurity Is a Two-Way Street
7	182	4.02	Should Psychologists Search the Internet for Information on Clients/Patients, Students, Employees, and Others With Whom They Work?
7	197	4.06	Consultation Over the Internet
9	229	6.01	HIPAA Regulations on Email and Texting With Clients/Patients and Other Professionals
9	230	6.01	Electronic Health Records (EHR) in Interprofessional Organizations
9	236	6.02a	Deleting Electronic Protected Health Information (PHI)
9	237	6.02a	Record Keeping in the Cloud
9	238	6.02a	HIPAA and Internet-Based Document Sharing
9	242	6.04	Fees for Telehealth Services
9	245	6.04	Submitting Claims for Telehealth Services
9	247	6.04d	Third-Party Reimbursement for Telehealth Services
10	261	7.01	Online Distance Education
10	267	7.04	Disclosure of Student Personal Information Through Social Media
10	272	7.06	Use of Technology for Supervision
11	287	8.02	Confidentiality and Informed Consent for Facebook-Based Research

Chapter	Page	Standard	Digital Ethics Sections
11	292	8.02	Documentation of Informed Consent for Internet Research
11	308	8.05	Determining Public Versus Private Information
11	319	8.08	Debriefing for Online Studies
12	345	9.01	Use of Mobile Phones for Treatment Adherence Monitoring
12	349	9.02	Internet-Mediated Assessments
12	363	9.04	Client/Patient Requests for Electronic Records
12	380	9.09b	Security and Interpretation of Online Testing
13	396	10.01	Discussion of Confidentiality Risks in Telepsychology
13	397	10.01	Setting an Internet Search and Social Media Policy During Informed Consent
13	399	10.01	Child Assent and Parental Permission for Online Therapies
13	401	10.01	State Laws Regulating Use of Telehealth Services
13	406	10.02	Telepsychology Involving Family Members
13	408	10.03	Setting Internet Use Policies for Group Therapy
13	420	10.10	Terminating Telepsychology Services

Need to Know

Chapters also contain brief sections highlighting critical information and strategies for applying the Ethics Code to traditional and new arenas of psychological science and practice that often require immediate ethical attention.

Chapter	Page	Standard	Digital Ethics Sections
2	23	—	What to Do When You Receive an Ethics Complaint
3	42	—	"Why Good Students Go Bad"
3	43	—	Ethical Competence and Ethical Planning
4	57	1.01	Reasonable Expectations for Awareness of Misuse

(Continued)

(Continued)

Chapter	Page	Standard	Digital Ethics Sections
4	60	1.02	The 2015 Independent Review Relating to APA Ethics Guidelines, Security Interrogations, and Torture
4	66	1.03	Resolving Ethical Conflicts Through Organizational Advocacy
4	72	1.05	Consultation on Misconduct
5	85	2.01	Critical Self-Reflection and Personal and Professional Bias
5	86	2.01b	Guidelines for Psychological Practice With Transgender and Gender-Nonconforming People (TGNC)
5	91	2.01e	Expert and Fact Witnesses
5	93	2.01e	Treatment of Alleged Child Victims
5	96	2.02	Provision of Emergency Services to Forensic Examinees
5	108	2.06b	Seeking Personal Psychotherapy
5	109	2.06b	Stressors During Graduate and Postdoctoral Training
6	116	3.01	Can Religious Beliefs Exempt Students From Supervised Treatment of Specific Clients/Patients?
6	126	3.04	When HMOs Refuse to Extend Coverage
6	126	3.04	How to Detect Harm in Psychotherapy and Counseling
6	129	3.04	Clinical Equipoise and Evaluating Risk in Randomized Clinical Trials
6	132	3.05	Ethical "Hot Spots" of Combined Therapy
6	142	3.05	Avoiding Harmful Multiple Relationships in Embedded Communities
6	155	3.09	Essential Skills for Interprofessional Models of Primary Care
6	158	3.10	Ethically Appropriate Child and Adolescent Assent Procedures
6	160	3.10a	Re-consent for Use of Stored Data When Minor Participants Reach Adulthood

Chapter	Page	Standard	Digital Ethics Sections
6	161	3.10a	Working With Involuntary Clients
7	189	4.05	Are Therapists Required to Report Abuse Already Under Investigation?
7	191	4.05b	Assessing Duty-to-Warn Obligations
7	193	4.05b	Suicide Helpline Assessment and Disclosure Policies
7	195	4.05b	Disclosure in Response to Nonsuicidal Self-Injury in Adolescents and Young Adults
8	217	5.04	Working With the Media
8	218	5.06	HIPAA Marketing Prohibitions
9	227	6.01	Unexpected Contacts With Clients/Patients
9	232	6.01	Evolving Codes for Biopsychosocial Services
9	233	6.01	Avoiding Conversion of Treatment Records to Educational Records
9	253	6.07	Fees and Group Practice
10	260	7.01	Competency Benchmarks in Professional Psychology
10	263	7.02	Language-Matching Training Experiences
10	267	7.04	Supervision of Trainees With Disabilities
10	268	7.05a	Ethical Criteria for Mandatory Personal Psychotherapy (MPP)
11	282	8.01	Proposed Changes to Federal Regulations
11	283	8.01	Submitting Successful IRB Proposals
11	286	8.02	When Does Informed Consent Begin and End?
11	289	8.02	Legal Challenges to the Certificate of Confidentiality
11	290	8.02	NIH Points to Consider for Research Involving Adults With Cognitive Impairments
11	301	8.03	Consent to Digital Archives
11	314	8.06	When Are Research Inducements Coercive?
11	327	8.10	Program Evaluation, Policy Studies, and Accountability
11	334	8.14	Procedures for Sharing and Using "Big Data"

(Continued)

(Continued)

Chapter	Page	Standard	Digital Ethics Sections
12	343	9.01	Assessment in Child Protection Matters
12	351	9.02	Assessment of Dementia
12	359	9.03a	Informed Consent for Forensic Assessments Requested by an Examinee's Attorney
12	364	9.04	Access to Forensic Records
12	373	9.06	Sexual and Gender Minority (SGM) Parents and Determination of Child Custody
12	378	9.08	When to Use Obsolete Tests
13	393	10.01	Informed Consent With Suicidal Patients
13	402	10.01	Expanded Informed Consent for Psychologists With Prescriptive Authority
13	420	10.10	Abandonment Considerations

Discussion of Ethical Standards

Most of the enforceable standards in the Ethics Code were written broadly so they would apply to psychologists in varied roles and work contexts. As much as possible, this book attempts to explain the overriding purpose of each standard, help readers understand the implications of critical terminology, provide examples of the range of psychological activities to which the standard applies, and offer suggestions for ethical dos and don'ts quickly identified by these icons.

Psychological Activity and Work Setting Icons

The Ethics Code is divided into six general sections representing ethical standards that apply to a broad spectrum of psychological activities and four more sections putting forth ethical rules explicitly for teaching, research, assessment, and therapy. The document itself, however, does not provide a precise way to locate standards directly relevant to other common work roles and settings. To help readers quickly navigate the Ethics Code for direct application to work roles that do not have special sections in the code, this book has icons that are strategically placed before the discussion of each standard in which such activities are mentioned for the following areas of psychology.

This icon alerts readers that the standard is particularly relevant to psychologists who apply the science and practice of psychology to enhance human well-being and performance in organizational and work settings, and in interprofessional health care settings. This includes consulting, personnel screening and promotion, marketing research, employee counseling, executive coaching, and research on job or organization effectiveness. Throughout the Ethics Code, the term *organizational client* refers to organizations to which the psychologist provides the services described above, whereas the term *client/patient* refers to individuals receiving therapy or other health services. This icon also signals readers that the standard is relevant to interprofessional work and quality improvement research conducted within integrated care systems now arising from the Affordable Care Act (ACA), including patient-centered medical homes (PCMH) and accountable care organizations (ACO).

This icon indicates that the standard applies to work involving forensic, court-ordered, or other activities relevant to the legal system, including forensic examinations, expert testimony, testimony as a fact witness, research on a psychologal issue, trial behavior consultation, or court-ordered or other forensic mental health services.

When readers see this icon, it means that the standard is related to research about the schooling process, consultative services to schools, or delivery of psychological services to children, adolescents, and families to assess, remediate, or otherwise address school performance and related psychological skills or vulnerabilities.

This icon indicates that a standard is particularly relevant to psychological practice, research, training, or policy formation in military, criminal justice, correctional facilities, police work, or other public service settings.

This icon highlights standards relevant to psychologists' involvement with regulations regarding record keeping and billing in the context of health maintenance organizations (HMOs), managed care organizations (MCOs), the Affordable Care Act, Medicaid, and Medicare.

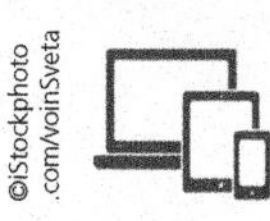

This icon draws readers' attention to standards that explicitly mention or for which examples are given for research or services using the Internet, telephone, fax machines, videoconferencing, computerized services, social media, mobile health applications, or other forms of electronic transmission.

This icon alerts readers to standards that are particularly relevant to psychological services that include prescription privileges, the conduct of research on psychopharmacological medications and agents, or psychologists' involvement with psychopharmaceutical companies.

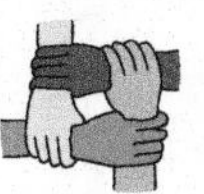

This icon highlights standards that explicitly address factors associated with age, gender, gender identity, race, ethnicity, culture, national origin, religion, sexual orientation, gender identity, disability, language, or socioeconomic status. It also signifies when the text offers examples for more broadly worded standards that illustrate attention to group and individual differences.

This icon draws readers' attention to compliance with standards that will be affected by or must take into account HIPAA regulations. (See "A Word About HIPAA," below.)

The special areas for which icons were selected are not exhaustive of the work contexts covered in this book but represent common areas outside of teaching, research, assessment, and therapy that have their own sections in the Ethics Code.

Don't forget: Although there are special sections in the code on teaching, research, assessment, and therapy, the standards within the first six general sections apply to all of these activities.

A Word About HIPAA

In 1996, Congress enacted the Health Insurance Portability and Accountability Act (HIPAA) in response to the increasing costs associated with transmitting health records lacking standardized formatting across providers, institutions, localities, and states. Recognizing that uniform standards for creating, transmitting, and storing health care records would require additional patient protections, Congress included in HIPAA regulations standards giving patients greater access to and control of their records (http://aspe.hhs.gov/admnsimp/p1104191.htm). The Ethics Code Task Force (ECTF) responsible for the major revision leading to the current Ethics Code was aware that the scope and detail of HIPAA regulations would change the nature of health care practice and research in the United States. The ECTF sought to ensure that ethical standards would reflect sensitivity to and avoid inconsistency with the new HIPAA regulatory landscape.

HIPAA has three components: (1) *privacy standards* for the use and disclosure of individually identifiable private health information (Privacy Rule, effective April 14, 2003), (2) *transaction standards* for the electronic exchange of health information (Transaction Rule, effective October 16, 2003), and (3) *security standards* to protect the creation and maintenance of private health information (Security Standards, effective April 21, 2003; compliance date April 21, 2005). The security standards were modified by the Omnibus Rule (2013) in an effort to harmonize HIPAA with rules promulgated by the Health Information Technology for Economic and Clinical Health (Department of Health and Human Services, 2009) and the Genetic Information Nondiscrimination Act (GINA, 2008).

Protected Health Information (PHI) and Covered Entities

HIPAA regulations apply to *protected health information* (PHI), defined as oral, written, typed, or electronic individually identifiable information related to (a) a person's past, present, or future physical or mental health; (b) provision of health care to the person; or (c) past, present, or future payment for health care. For health information to come under the definition of PHI, it must be created by the following *covered entities:* a health plan, a health care clearinghouse, or a health care provider who transmits any health information in electronic form in connection with financial or administrative activities related to health care. Educational records covered by the Family Educational Rights and Privacy Act of 1974, employment records held by a covered entity in its role as employer, and de-identified records (in which all individually identifiable information has been removed) are *not* considered PHI. Covered entities may engage *business associates* to carry out their health care activities (e.g., billing services, web hosting, technology services, accounting services), and they may share PHI with a business associate if they receive satisfactory assurance that the business associate will use the information only for the purposes for which the associate was engaged by the covered entity, will safeguard the information from misuse, and will help the covered entity comply with some of the covered entity's duties under the Privacy Rule.

Definition of Electronic Media (160.103)

HIPAA regulations refer to PHI created, recorded, or stored electronically, including but not limited to computer hard drives, removable/transportable flash drives, or other digital memory media. HIPAA also pertains to any transmission media used to exchange information already created or stored electronically, including the Internet, extranet, or intranet; leased lines; dial-up lines; and private networks, as well as to the physical movement of removable/transportable electronic storage media. Certain transmissions, including via paper, facsimile, and voice (e.g., telephone), are not considered to be transmissions via electronic media if the information being exchanged did not exist in electronic form immediately before the transmission.

HIPAA Protections and Requirements

The HIPAA rules protect individually identifiable health information through regulations that

- standardize the format of electronically transmitted records related to individually identifiable health information;
- secure the electronic transaction and storage of individually identifiable health information;
- limit the use and release of individually identifiable health information, including honoring client/patient requests to restrict disclosure to health plans if services are paid in cash;
- increase patient control of use and disclosure of private health information;
- increase patients' access to their health records, including the right to receive electronic copies of their health information;
- establish legal accountability and penalties for unauthorized use and disclosure and violation of transaction and security standards for covered entities and business associates;
- identify public health and welfare needs that permit use and disclosure of individually identifiable health information without patient authorization;
- strengthen limitations on use and disclosure of protected health information (PHI) for marketing, fund-raising, and sale of PHI to third parties;
- prohibit most health plans from using or disclosing genetic information for underwriting purposes;
- create a system of tiered financial civil penalties if the violation is considered more willful and not promptly fixed (HHS can deem a violation affecting multiple patients to be separate violations).

What Do Covered Entities Need to Do to Comply With HIPAA?

Under HIPAA, covered entities must (a) provide information to patients about their privacy rights and the covered entity's privacy practices, called a *notice of privacy practices;* (b) permit patient access to records and upon patient request provide an *accounting of disclosures* of PHI made to others over the past 6 years; (c) obtain patient *authorization* for use and disclosures to others in a manner and for purposes specified in the regulations; (d) implement clear privacy procedures for electronic transmission and storage of PHI; (e) designate a *privacy officer;* (f) implement security procedures that prevent unauthorized access to health records; (g) train and ensure that employees comply with privacy, transaction, and security procedures; (h) reasonably ensure that business associates, individual contractors, consultants, collection agencies, third-party payors, and researchers with whom PHI is shared comply with privacy and transaction rules; and (i) attempt to correct violations by these other entities if they occur or cease the relationship.

Notice of Privacy Practices

Prior to beginning treatment or treatment-relevant assessments or randomized clinical trials in which health care is provided, HIPAA-covered entities must provide patients with a *Notice of Privacy Practices* that describes the psychologist's policies for use and disclosure of PHI, the clients'/patients' rights regarding their PHI under HIPAA, and the provider's obligations under the Privacy Rule. In most instances, the notice will be given to prospective clients/patients at the same time as informed consent is obtained since the notice provides information relevant to the scope and limits of confidentiality. The Notice (or a summary alerting clients/patients to the availability of the full document) must also be posted in a clear and prominent location in the psychologist's office.

Right to an Accounting of Disclosures

The HIPAA Privacy Rule provides an individual with the right to receive a listing, known as an *accounting of disclosures,* that provides information about when a covered entity has disclosed the individual's PHI to others not listed in the Notice of Privacy Practices. Under HITECH, clients/patients also have a right to receive information about disclosures made through a covered entity's electronic health record for purposes of carrying out treatment, payment, and health care operations.

Authorization to Release Information

HIPAA requires that covered entities obtain written valid authorization from the individual or his or her personal representative prior to releasing PHI. The authorization must include a specific description of information to be disclosed, specific identification of the person or class of persons who can make the authorization and to whom information may be disclosed, a description of the purpose and use of the disclosure, an expiration date, and a signature. In addition, when appropriate release and authorizations are obtained, the HIPAA Privacy Rule requires that covered entities share only the *minimum amount of information necessary* for billing agencies, other covered entities, and non–health provider internal staff to perform their roles.

Minimum Necessary

When disclosing or requesting PHI, a covered entity must make reasonable efforts to limit the information to the *minimum necessary* to accomplish the intended purpose of the use, disclosure, or request. This requirement does not apply to disclosures to another health care provider for treatment or to the individual client/patient, disclosures required by law, or disclosures for other purposes under the HIPAA regulation. Under HIPAA, psychologists have the responsibility to determine the "minimum necessary" information they must provide to insurance companies for coverage of care. However, health insurers are not prohibited from denying care or payment if they maintain that the minimum information provided is insufficient to determine whether the proposed care is necessary (http://store.apapractice.org/files/HIPAA_Final_Rule_July_2013.pdf).

Privacy Officer

Under HIPAA, "covered entities" must designate a "privacy officer" to oversee and ensure that HIPAA-compliant privacy procedures are developed and implemented. This requirement is "scalable," in that what is required differs depending on whether a psychologist is in solo practice, directing a group practice, or administering a large institutional program.

Are Researchers Affected by HIPAA?

Intervention research that creates, uses, or discloses PHI will come under HIPAA. This includes research-generated information that is placed in a participant's health records or otherwise used for treatment, if the study related to treatment is paid for by the participant's health insurance or the researcher or the institution at which the intervention is conducted is a covered entity. In such instances, researchers may be considered *business associates* who are directly liable for compliance with certain HIPAA Privacy and Security Rules requirements. Researchers who are not themselves collecting health relevant data but who plan to use in their research or consulting services PHI created by a covered entity must provide to the covered entity written assurance that they will comply with HIPAA standards. HIPAA often will not apply to health-related data generated solely for research purposes, even if a covered entity has hired the psychologist to conduct the research, if the data will not be shared with participants or third parties, will not be included in participants' health records, and will not be collected on behalf of a covered entity. Similarly, an external or independent IRB is not a business associate regulated under HIPAA simply by virtue of its performing research review approval and continuing oversight functions for a covered entity who has permitted or hired a researcher to collect or use PHI or non-PHI-related data.

Are Industrial–Organizational or Consulting Psychologists Affected by HIPAA?

HIPAA does not apply to data collected by consulting and industrial–organizational psychologists who administer psychological tests solely for the purpose of training, employment, promotion, or quality assurance.

The Patient Protection and Affordable Care Act (ACA)

Continued refinement and implementation of the Patient Protection and Affordable Care Act (ACA; Pub. L. 111-148, 2010) will continue to redefine the landscape of health care delivery systems in the United States. The law focuses on ensuring wider access to health care through mandated enrollment in health plans supported by government financial assistance for those who qualify. It also seeks to promote the delivery of efficient, cost-effective, and quality services through expanded coverage of preventive services, evidence-based treatments, and provider accountability (Koh & Sebelius, 2010; Orszag & Emanuel, 2010). Psychology is included as a health care profession under the law; it appears in sections on research and evaluation, and psychological services are specifically described for several patient populations (Rozensky, 2014a, 2014b).

Interprofessional Organizations

Currently, two types of interprofessional organizations, the accountable care organization (ACO) and the patient-centered medical home (PCMH), are key components of the law's emphasis on delivery of efficient, safe, and cost-effective services. These—and other interprofessional organizations that will most likely emerge in the next decade—represent a transition from the traditional medical model of symptom- and illness-based episodic care to a more patient-centered, comprehensive, continuous, and team-based system that includes psychologists in the provision of proactive, preventive, and chronic medical care management across the life span (APA, 2014). This reflects the increasing behavioral health integration requirements for medical staff to work with behavioral health care providers and to communicate the availability of behavioral health care to patients. As detailed in sections of this book, the increased involvement of psychologists in all aspects of team-based health care bring benefits as well as the ethical obligation to acquire certain competencies to do the following:

- Identify and resolve ethical conflicts in ways that reflect an understanding of role responsibilities in patient-centered primary care organizations and the ethical and legal responsibilities of team members from other health care professions (Standards 1.03, Conflicts Between Ethics and Organizational Demands; 1.04, Informal Resolution of Ethical Violations; 1.05, Reporting Ethical Violations).

- Acquire the training appropriate to competently engage in coordinated care services and identify appropriate evidence-based practices for team-based primary care (Standards 2.01, Boundaries of Competence; 2.04, Bases for Scientific and Professional Judgments).
- Develop and communicate to patients the nature of individual practitioner and team-based confidentiality policies (Standards 4.01, Maintaining Confidentiality; 4.02, Discussing the Limits of Confidentiality).
- Acquire the expertise needed to engage in treatment management consultations in response to requests for assistance by other health providers (Standards 3.09, Cooperation With Other Professionals; 4.06, Consultations).
- Create and maintain records that document continuously evolving categories of health services and treatment outcomes and appropriately bill for reimbursement for team-based services (Standards 6.01, Documentation of Professional and Scientific Work and Maintenance of Records; 6.04, Fees and Financial Arrangements).
- Design, implement, and evaluate the efficiency, quality, and cost-effectiveness of biobehavioral and team-based services within organizations (Standard 8.04, Client/Patient, Student, and Subordinate Research Participants).
- Select and interpret assessment instruments appropriate for screening and targeted interventions to help prevent and manage chronic disease and interpret results to both patients and medical team members (Standards 9.01, Bases for Assessments; 9.06, Interpreting Assessment Results; 9.10, Explaining Assessment Results).
- Provide appropriate informed consent procedures for patients receiving services within ACO and PCMH organizations consistent with models of patient-centered shared decision making (Standards 3.10, Informed Consent; 9.03, Informed Consent in Assessments; 10.01, Informed Consent to Therapy; 10.02, Therapy Involving Couples or Families; 10.03, Group Therapy).

Acknowledgments

The American Psychological Association's (APA) Ethical Principles of Psychologists and Code of Conduct is the product of an extraordinary process of revisions built on APA's 60-year tradition of applying a group dynamics approach to create a living code of conduct with which psychologists can identify and that they can use in their everyday professional and scientific decisions (Hobbs, 1948). I was privileged to chair the APA Ethics Code Task Force (ECTF) responsible for developing, implementing, and completing in 2002 the revision that, with the addition of language on human rights amended in 2010, is today's current code (APA, 2010a, 2010c). The ECTF mission was to create a process and product that reflected the values of the discipline and that would assist APA members in meeting ethical challenges in the new millennium.

The ECTF was composed of remarkable individuals representing the public and the diverse constituencies within APA. Each member was committed to developing an ethics code that would reflect the ideals and merit the trust of psychologists and consumers.

Over its 5-year journey, the ECTF continuously sought member input on the revision process through critical incident surveys; calls for member comments; and open meetings encouraging lively exchange among the ECTF, APA members, and observers from APA constituencies. ECTF members brought to the revision process their professional, ethical, and scientific expertise. But perhaps more important, they demonstrated a special ability to listen to member concerns and a unique willingness to challenge their own ethical preconceptions. I greatly benefited from the wisdom and friendship of the following ECTF members: Peter Appleby, Bruce Bennett, Laura Brown, Linda F. Campbell, Nabil El-Ghoroury, Dennis J. Grill, Jessica Henderson Daniel, Samuel J. Knapp, Gerald P. Koocher, Marcia Moody, Peter E. Nathan, Thomas D. Oakland, Mary H. Quigley, Julia M. Ramos-Grenier, Abigail Sivan, Steven N. Sparta, Elizabeth Swenson, Melba J. T. Vasquez, and Brian Wilcox.

The ECTF had a dedicated and talented APA staff navigating the revision process through what often felt like a voyage through the Scylla and Charybdis of seven Ethics Code drafts. Stan Jones as Director of the Ethics Office and later ECTF consultant was a treasure trove of knowledge about the history of past APA ethics codes and ethics adjudication. In the middle of the revision process, Steve Behnke dived into the role of Director of the Ethics Office with a perfect combination of scholarly expertise, administrative acumen, and personal warmth.

Debbie Felder, Revision Coordinator, was ECTF's gatekeeper, librarian, scribe, grammarian, minutes keeper, and schedule maker, and she performed many other essential roles with a competence and commitment remarkable to find in a single individual. Nathalie Gilfoyle, APA General Counsel, continuously helped clarify the legal parameters and challenges of the ECTF's work, nurturing the construction of standards sensitive to but not dictated by law. Along with Lindsay Childress Beatty, then Deputy General Counsel, Nathalie made sure that the ECTF was up-to-date on continuously evolving federal regulations.

As chair of the ECTF, I also benefited from the support and guidance of the APA board of directors, committee chairs, and division representatives. I am particularly grateful to Charles Brewer, Pat Bricklin, Jean Carter, Stuart Cooper, Pat DeLeon, Mike Honaker, Norine Johnson, Deirdre Knapp, Ron Levant, Russ Newman, Katherine Nordal, Ruth Paige, Stuart Pizer, Norma Simon, and Phil Zimbardo and to the more than 1,300 APA members who shared their kudos and concerns with the task force.

This fourth edition of *Decoding the Ethics Code: A Practical Guide for Psychologists* has also benefited from the wisdom of many. Adam Fried, assistant director of the Fordham University Center for Ethics Education, has been a rich resource of knowledge and advice for this fourth edition. I would also like to record my indebtedness to Carolyn Funke for her editorial assistance, as well as the many Fordham University graduate students who provided valuable feedback on each edition and continue to teach me about new and emerging ethical arenas. I am fortunate to have had the guidance and support of SAGE associate director, Reid Hester; acquisitions editor Lara Parra; editorial assistant Morgan Shannon; and eLearning editor Lucy Berbeo as well as the assistance of project editor Veronica Stapleton Hooper and copy editors Paula Fleming and Doug McNair of Fleming Editorial Services. My husband, Gary, read each draft of the book and, as he did with the first edition, dramatically reduced the number of paragraph-length sentences in the final draft. I am also grateful to my daughter Erica for providing the title for this book and to both my children, Brian and Erica, and my son-in-law, Steven Battle, for their love and support.

Publisher's Acknowledgments

SAGE wishes to acknowledge the valuable contributions of the following reviewers.

Jeffrey S. Ashby, Georgia State University

Linda L. Bacheller, Barry University

Tom J. Brian, The University of Tulsa

Agatha E. Carroo, North Carolina Central University

Lisa DeMarni Cromer, The University of Tulsa

Ida Dickie, Spalding University

Richard P. Halgin, University of Massachusetts Amherst

Tamara Coder Mikinski, University of Kansas

Thomas Plante, Santa Clara University and Stanford University School of Medicine

Linda Carter Sobell, Nova Southeastern University

About the Author

Celia B. Fisher, PhD, Director of the Fordham University Center for Ethics Education and the Marie Ward Doty University Chair and Professor of Psychology, served as Chair of the American Psychological Association's (APA's) Ethics Code Task Force responsible for the 2002 revision of the APA Ethical Principles of Psychologists and Code of Conduct that, with the addition of language on human rights amended in 2010, is today's current code. She currently serves as Chair of the Ethics Code Task Force for the American Public Health Association and Director of the NIDA-funded Fordham University HIV and Drug Abuse Prevention Research Ethics Institute. She has served as Chair of the Environmental Protection Agency's Human Subjects Research Board, the New York State Board for Licensure in Psychology, the National Task Force on Applied Developmental Science, and the Society for Research in Child Development (SRCD) Committee for Ethical Conduct in Child Development Research and the SRCD Common Rule Task Force. Dr. Fisher was also a member of the APA Ethics Committee, the National Institute of Mental Health (NIMH) Data Safety and Monitoring Board, the Institute of Medicine (IOM) Committee on Clinical Research Involving Children, the IOM Committee on Ethical Review and Oversight Issues in Research Involving Standard of Care Interventions, the National Academies' Committee on Revisions to the Common Rule for the Protection of Human Subjects in Research in the Behavioral and Social Sciences, and the Department of Health and Human Services Secretary's Advisory Committee on Human Research Protections (SACHRP), for which she cochaired the SACHRP Subcommittee on Research Involving Children, of the NIH Societal and Ethical Issues in Research Study Section. She is currently a member of the External Advisory Board for the NIH Adolescent Brain and Cognitive Development Study. She also served as the founding director of the Fordham University Doctoral Program in Applied Developmental Psychology and as cofounding editor of the journal *Applied Developmental Science.* She is the recipient of the 2010 Lifetime Achievement Award for Excellence in Human Research Protection and a Fellow of the American Association for the Advancement of Science.

Dr. Fisher has written commissioned papers on research ethics with mentally impaired and vulnerable populations for President Clinton's National Bioethics Advisory Commission, for NIMH on points for consideration in the ethical conduct of suicide research and research involving children and adolescents, and for the National Institute on Drug Abuse (NIDA) on HIV education, treatment, and referrals for research participants. She cochaired the national conference on Research Ethics for Mental Health Science Involving Ethnic Minority Children and Youth (*American Psychologist,* December 2002), cosponsored by the APA and NIMH, and the first National Conference on Graduate Education in Applied Developmental Science (*Journal of Applied Developmental Psychology,* 1993).

Dr. Fisher has coedited 8 books and authored more than 200 scholarly chapters and empirical articles on cognitive and social development across the life span and on research and professional ethics, with special emphasis on the rights of racial/ethnic minorities, sexual- and gender-minority youth, children and adults with impaired decision making, and socially marginalized populations. With support from the National Institute for Child Health and Human Development (NICHD), she has studied how to assess and enhance the abilities of adults with developmental disabilities to consent to research and is currently working on a project to develop research ethics–training modules for American Indian and Native Alaskan community-engaged researchers. With funding from the National Science Foundation (NSF) and the National Institutes of Health (NIH), she has developed research ethics instructional materials for undergraduates, graduate students, senior scientists, and institutional review boards. She has developed assessment instruments to evaluate how teenagers and parents from different racial/ethnic backgrounds prepare for and react to racial discrimination and examined the validity of child abuse assessment techniques in institutional and forensic settings. With support from the NSF, NIDA, and the National Center for Research Resources (NCRR), she has partnered with culturally diverse community members and frontline researchers conducting community-based research to understand their perspectives on the ethics of adolescent risk research and research involving adults involved in street drug use and related HIV risk. With support from the National Institute of Neurological Disorders and Stroke (NINDS) and the Office of Research Integrity, she has developed and validated measures assessing mentoring behaviors and departmental climates nurturing the responsible conduct of research in psychology graduate programs. Her research on intervention programs to reduce college students' drinking behaviors has been supported by the Department of Education and the National Institute on Alcohol Abuse and Alcoholism (NIAAA). She is also coprinciple investigator on a National Institute for Minority Health Disparities grant to examine ethical issues in HIV research involving sexual and gender minority youth.

PART I

Introduction and Background

CHAPTER 1

A Code of Ethics for Psychology

How Did We Get Here?

In a field so complex, where individual and social values are yet but ill defined, the desire to play fairly must be given direction and consistency by some rules of the game. These rules should do much more than help the unethical psychologist keep out of trouble; they should be of palpable aid to the ethical psychologist in making daily decisions.

—Hobbs (1948, p. 81)

Beginnings

The American Psychological Association (APA) has had more than six decades of experience constructing and revising an ethics code that strives to reflect both the aspirations and practical aspects of ethical decisions made by members of the profession. The creation and each subsequent revision of the APA Ethics Code has been driven by the desire for standards that would encourage the highest endeavors of psychologists, ensure public welfare, promote sound relationships with allied professions, and further the professional standing of the discipline (Hobbs, 1948).

Discussions within APA regarding the need for an ethics code in psychology arose in response to an increase in professional activity and public visibility of its members before and after World War II. During this period, the societal value of the still young discipline of psychology was evidenced as psychologists developed group tests to help the armed services quickly determine the draft eligibility of young men in wartime and provided mental health services to hospitalized soldiers when they returned home. In 1947, the first APA Committee on Ethical Standards for Psychologists was appointed. The committee, chaired by Edward Tolman, wanted to create a code of ethics for psychologists that would be more than a document with an imposing title (Hobbs, 1948). The members were committed to producing professional standards that would provide psychologists with a set of values and practical techniques for identifying and resolving moral problems.

To achieve these goals, a second committee chaired by Nicholas Hobbs decided to draw on the knowledge of the field to create a process of developing a code that would "be effective in modifying human behavior" (Hobbs, 1948, p. 82). According to Hobbs, "This is an old and familiar task to psychologists, their very stock in trade, in fact. The only difference here is that human behavior means specifically the behavior of psychologists" (p. 82). Drawing on the knowledge of group processes during that period, the committee conceived the task of developing ethical standards as one of group dynamics (Hobbs, 1948). The process chosen was the critical incident method (Flanagan, 1954), a technique that involved asking the members of the APA to describe a situation they knew of firsthand, in which a psychologist made a decision having ethical implications, and to indicate the ethical issues involved.

After reviewing more than 1,000 such incidents submitted by APA members, the committee identified major ethical themes emerging from the incidents that focused on psychologists' relationships with and responsibilities to others, including patients, students, research participants, and other professionals. Many of the incidents reflected the political climate of the postwar period, including confrontations between academic freedom and McCarthyism and dilemmas faced by psychologists working in industry asked to design tests for the purpose of maintaining racial segregation in the workforce. As different segments of the code were created, drafts were submitted to the membership for critique and revision. A final draft was adopted by the APA in 1952 and published in 1953.

The Purpose of an Ethics Code

At the time of the adoption of the first Ethics Code, continual review and revision based on the experience and perspectives of members was seen as integral to maintaining the value of the Code for both the profession and the public (Adkins, 1952). Each revision of the Ethics Code has been driven by the evolving roles and responsibilities of psychologists within a constantly changing sociocultural, economic, political, and legal landscape. As a result, the Ethics Code of the APA has undergone 10 revisions since 1953, guided by the following objectives.

Establishing the Integrity of a Profession

One purpose of an ethics code is to help establish and maintain the viability of a profession. An ethics code reflects a collective decision that a profession is better off when ethical standards are not based solely on individual assessments of what is or what is not morally acceptable. Adoption of a set of core values that reflect consensus among members of a discipline distinguishes psychology as a "community of common purpose" and enhances public confidence in individuals who have been trained to meet the profession's ethical standards (Callahan, 1982; Frankel, 1996; Seitz & O'Neill, 1996). Acceptance of an identified set of core values by individual psychologists across the broad spectrum of psychological activities also helps protect the integrity of the profession by focusing the attention of individual psychologists on their responsibilities and duties to others and setting the expectation that all members of the profession have a stake in behaving by the rules.

A core value of the discipline of psychology, as articulated in the Preamble of the current Ethics Code, is the welfare and protection of the individuals and groups with whom psychologists work.

Education and Professional Socialization

A second purpose of an ethics code is its professional socialization function. A document reflecting the profession's values and standards provides a guide to what psychologists should reasonably expect of themselves and one another. A code can be conceived as an enabling document that acts as a support and guide to individual psychologists in their efforts to resolve ethical dilemmas (Frankel, 1996; Sinclair, Poizner, Gilmour-Barrett, & Randall, 1987). A code of ethics also serves to deter psychologists from engaging in unethical conduct before a problem develops by specifically proscribing what the profession has identified as unethical behaviors (Fisher & Younggren, 1997). In addition, it assists faculty and supervisors in communicating the values of the profession to graduate students and to new PhDs with limited professional experience.

Public Trust

A third purpose of an ethics code is to gain public trust by demonstrating that psychologists are members of a responsible and substantial profession with high standards. A code can serve a public relations value by being seen as a contract with society to act in consumers' best interest. A professional ethics code also provides standards against which the public can hold psychologists accountable. It thus offers a means by which members of the public can draw on norms prescribed by the profession itself to evaluate the conduct of scientists, educators, consultants, and practitioners with whom they interact.

Enforcement Value

A profession that demonstrates it can monitor itself is less vulnerable to external regulation. Therefore, a fourth purpose of an ethics code is to provide a clear statement of the types of behaviors considered ethical violations to guide psychologists in avoiding such behaviors, to assist consumers in making ethical complaints, and to ensure that such complaints can be adjudicated clearly and fairly by the APA and other organizations (Fisher & Younggren, 1997). The APA Ethics Code also serves as a guide for licensing boards, courts, and other institutions for the evaluation of the responsible conduct of psychology and is thus a means of avoiding capricious standards set by nonpsychologists. In addition, the Ethics Code can help psychologists defend their decisions to courts, institutions, or government agencies that would encourage them to go against the values of the profession.

Aspirational Principles and Enforceable Standards

At its heart, an ethics code should reflect the moral principles underlying the values of the profession. For most professions, ethical behaviors are generally those that fulfill the fundamental moral obligations to do good, to do no harm, to respect others, and to treat all individuals honestly and fairly. For some, statements of general principles are sufficient to guide the ethical behavior of persons devoted to the ideals of their profession. For others, however, statements describing specific types of behaviors that meet these ideals are necessary to maximize the code's utility and to provide a means of evaluating its efficacy (Schur, 1982).

The form in which ethical guidelines are written will determine whether an ethics code is an aspirational or enforceable document. Although all codes should have a foundation in moral principles, the document can take one of three forms. An aspirational code is composed of statements of broadly worded ideals and principles that do not attempt to define with any precision right and wrong behaviors. An educational code combines ethical principles with more explicit interpretations that can help individual professionals make informed decisions in morally ambiguous contexts. An enforceable code includes a set of standards that specifically describe behaviors required and proscribed by the profession and is designed to serve as a basis for adjudicating grievances (Frankel, 1996).

The original APA Ethics Code, and the seven revisions that followed up to 1990, gradually combined statements of aspirational principles with general guidelines and enforceable standards for ethical behavior. During this period, the increasingly legalistic reaction of consumers and psychologists involved in charges of ethical violations raised concerns about the fairness of subjective interpretations of such broadly worded principles and standards. Moreover, a rise in the number of appeals to decisions made by the APA Ethics Committee and regulatory bodies (e.g., state licensing boards) that relied on the APA Ethics Code for their disciplinary procedures suggested that adjudicatory decisions based on the existing format would be increasingly difficult to enforce and thus a disservice to the APA membership (Bersoff, 1994). Accordingly, to strengthen both the enforceability and credibility of APA ethical guidelines, the 1992 Ethics Code represented a radical change from its predecessors in both structure and content. For the first time, clear distinctions were made between aspirational principles that articulated foundational values of the discipline and specific decision rules; the latter were articulated in 180 distinct ethical standards that would be subject to enforcement by the APA, other organizations, and licensing boards that adopted them (Canter, Bennett, Jones, & Nagy, 1994).

The current Ethics Code (APA, 2010c), first approved in 2002 and with two standards revised in 2010, maintains the distinction between aspirational principles and enforceable standards. Over the 5-year revision process to develop the current Code, the Ethics Code Task Force (ECTF), chaired by Celia B. Fisher, drew on the transparent and inclusive process pioneered for the 1953 code. The task force conducted a critical incident member survey and received continuous input from observers representing a broad spectrum of scientific and professional APA divisions, through open member forums at APA annual meetings, and via calls for comments from APA members and other stakeholders (see Fisher, 2003b, for a more detailed summary of this process). Major trends influencing the revisions leading to the current Code included (a) the growth of health maintenance organizations (HMOs) and their increased influence on the provision of health services; (b) the advent of Internet-mediated research and practice and the use of other electronic media; (c) greater sensitivity to the needs of culturally and linguistically diverse populations in research and practice; (d) increasing participation of psychologists in the legal system; (e) the sea change from paternalistic to autonomy-based public attitudes toward access to health records; (f) federal regulations affecting industries, organizations, the health care field, research practices, and educational institutions; and (g) recognition of the continually evolving legal landscape of ethics adjudication and federal regulation of science and health practices.

The 2010 Amendments: The Controversy Over Psychologists' Involvement in Inhumane Military Interrogations

Over the past several decades, APA has issued statements against psychologists' involvement in torture (e.g., American Psychiatric Association & APA, 1985; APA Council of Representatives, 1986). However, concern heightened over the adequacy of these statements as information surfaced regarding psychologists' post-9/11 participation in inhumane military interrogations during the "war on terror" (Lewis, 2004). To address these concerns, the APA convened the Presidential Task Force on Ethics and National Security (APA Presidential Task Force, 2005), and this was followed by a resolution of the APA Council of Representatives (2006). Although both the report and the resolution prohibited participation of members in torture and other cruel, inhumane, and degrading treatment or punishment, they made the controversial claim that it was consistent with the APA Ethics Code for psychologists to serve in consultative roles to interrogation and information-gathering processes for national security–related purposes.

As more information came to light from the congressional investigation into the alleged role of psychologists in developing harsh interrogation programs for the Central Intelligence Agency (CIA; Risen, 2014; Steele & Morlin, 2007), many APA members questioned whether a consultative role can be morally distinguished from involvement in torture if the tactic is used in the psychologist's presence or with the psychologist's awareness, or is based on techniques the psychologist has developed for the purpose of interrogation. While there was little disagreement that military psychologists were highly qualified to assess detainees' mental health during or following inhumane interrogations, once the George W. Bush administration had determined that such interrogations were lawful, some forcefully argued that any psychological activity conducted in a setting in which prisoners were subjected to harsh interrogation or not afforded basic human rights—such as the right to an attorney, to habeas corpus, and to refuse to self-incriminate—should be ethically prohibited irrespective of whether it was considered lawful (APA, 2015d; Olson, Soldz, & Davis, 2008).

As detailed more fully in Chapter 4 of this volume and in the investigative report commissioned by APA (APA, 2015d), this controversy extended to the wording of Standard 1.02, Conflicts Between Ethics and Law, Regulations, or Other Governing Legal Authority, and Standard 1.03, Conflicts Between Ethics and Organizational Demands. Some argued that the language in these standards could be interpreted as permitting psychologists to follow laws permitting torture and other violations of human rights if conflicts between the Ethics Code and these laws (or similar organizational policies) could not be resolved. On June 1, 2010, the APA voted to amend the language of these two standards to make clear that when there is a conflict between ethics and law or between ethics and organizational demands, psychologists are prohibited from "engaging in activities that would justify or defend violating human rights" (APA, 2010b, 2010c, 2015d).

Format and Distinctive Features of the APA Ethics Code

Why Does the Ethics Code Separate General Principles From Enforceable Standards?

The General Principles provide a conceptual framework that expresses the aspirational values of the common community of psychologists and the behavioral rules articulated in the standards flow from these principles. They impart core moral values reflecting the highest ideals of the profession: promoting the welfare and protecting the rights of others, doing no harm, and acting faithfully and responsibly with integrity and fairness. The principles themselves are not enforceable but represent the ideals shaping the standards, which are enforceable.

The 151 standards differ from the principles in that, because they are cast in behaviorally specific language, they can be enforced by the APA Ethics Committee and other state or professional organizations that adopt the Code. The explicit statements of ethical conduct in these standards provide APA members with sufficient due notice of the behaviors required and prohibited by the APA, support members' ability to defend their ethical actions, and increase the APA's success in sustaining decisions by the APA Ethics Committee in court, thus strengthening both the enforceability and credibility of APA's ethical oversight procedures.

General and Area-Specific Standards

The Ethics Code includes six general standard sections that apply to all psychological activities: (1) Resolving Ethical Issues, (2) Competence, (3) Human Relations,

(4) Privacy and Confidentiality, (5) Advertising and Other Public Statements, and (6) Record Keeping and Fees. These standards are worded broadly to apply to the spectrum of scientific and professional work performed by psychologists. There are four additional sections reflecting specialized activities of psychologists: (1) Education and Training, (2) Research and Publication, (3) Assessment, and (4) Therapy.

Are Standards Relevant to Teaching, Research, Assessment, and Therapy Restricted to Their Specific Sections in the Code?

No! Standards within the first six general sections apply to *all* psychological activities.

Where Are Standards That Apply to Activities in Forensic Psychology?

Forensic psychologists engage in a wide range of activities, including assessment, treatment, teaching, research, consultation, and public statements. In these activities, they must conform to the relevant general and area-specific standard sections throughout the Ethics Code. Forensic or court-related work activities are explicitly mentioned in Standards 2.01f, Boundaries of Competence; 3.05c, Multiple Relationships; 3.10c, Informed Consent; 9.01a, Bases for Assessments; 9.03c, Informed Consent in Assessments; 9.04b, Release of Test Data; 9.10, Explaining Assessment Results; 9.11, Maintaining Test Security; and 10.02b, Therapy Involving Couples or Families.

The forensic icons and case illustrations throughout this book are meant to assist in quickly identifying standards applicable to forensic work. Hot Topics at the end of Chapters 8 and 12 provide in-depth analysis of the relevance of Ethics Code standards to testimony given by psychologists in legal settings. The Hot Topic at the end of Chapter 4 provides readers with an opportunity to examine the relevance of the human rights language in Standard 1.02, Conflicts Between Ethics and Law, Regulations, and Other Governing Legal Authority, to forensic assessment of intellectual disability in death penalty cases.

Where Are Standards That Apply to Work With and Within Organizations?

Psychologists working in industry, consulting, or delivering services to other organizations should refer to Standard 3.11, Psychological Services Delivered To or Through Organizations. This standard lists the information that must be provided to organizational clients beforehand and, when appropriate, to those directly affected by the organizational services psychologists provide (e.g., employees). Other standards that explicitly refer to work for or within organizations include Standards 1.03, Conflicts Between Ethics and Organizational Demands; 3.07, Third-Party Requests for Services; 5.01, Avoidance of False or Deceptive Statements; 8.05,

Dispensing With Informed Consent for Research; and 9.03, Informed Consent in Assessments. As with other areas of specialization, the broadly worded enforceable standards are relevant to and should be carefully read by consulting, organizational, and industrial psychologists. The industrial–organizational icons and case illustrations throughout this book are meant to assist in quickly identifying standards applicable to organizational settings.

Where Are Standards That Apply to Psychologists' Involvement With Health Maintenance Organizations (HMOs)?

Psychologists' involvement with HMOs is addressed in standards throughout the Ethics Code. The implications of HMOs for standards on record keeping and fees are discussed in Chapter 9 of this book, followed by a Hot Topic devoted to the application of the Ethics Code to billing and contractual arrangements with HMOs, "Managing the Ethics of Managed Care." Involvement with HMOs is also relevant to standards on privacy and confidentiality (Standards 1.03, Conflicts Between Ethics and Organizational Demands; 3.07, Third-Party Requests for Services) and standards on informed consent (Standards 3.10, Informed Consent; 8.02, Informed Consent to Research; 9.03, Informed Consent in Assessments; 10.01, Informed Consent to Therapy). The HMO icons and case illustrations throughout this book are meant to assist in quickly identifying standards applicable to work involving HMOs.

Where Are Standards That Apply to Psychologists' Responsibilities Under the Affordable Care Act (ACA) and Their Involvement in Integrated Care Settings?

Psychologists' responsibilities under the ACA and ethical challenges emerging in the new interprofessional patient-centered medical care facilities are covered by multiple standards in the Ethics Code. The competencies required for psychologists' involvement in interprofessional group practices, primary and integrated care settings, and other health care and research opportunities provided by the ACA are discussed in Chapter 5 of this book under Standards 2.03, Maintaining Competence and 2.04, Bases for Scientific and Professional Judgments. Working in interprofessional environments is also relevant to Standard 3.09, Cooperation With Other Professionals (Chapter 6), Standard 4.02, Discussing the Limits of Confidentiality (Chapter 7), Standards 6.01, Documentation of Professional and Scientific Work and Maintenance of Records, and 6.04, Fees and Financial Arrangements (Chapter 9). Also pertaining to these professional obligations are requirements for preparing students for practice and research in primary care settings (Standard 7.01, Design of Education and Training Programs, Chapter 10) and for conducting quality improvement in health care settings (Standard 8.04, Client/Patient, Student, and Subordinate Research Participants, Chapter 11). The organizational icons throughout this book are meant to assist in quickly identifying standards applicable to work in these settings.

Are the Standards Relevant to Psychologists Working in the Military, Law Enforcement, and Correctional Facilities?

Military and correctional psychologists engage in a range of psychological activities, including treatment, assessment, research, and consultation, and their work is addressed in relevant standards across the Ethics Code. As detailed in this chapter and in Chapter 4, military and correctional contexts often raise unique ethical challenges when the requirements of the Ethics Code are in conflict with laws and organizational policies (Standards 1.02, Conflicts Between Ethics and Law, Regulations, or Other Governing Legal Authority; 1.03, Conflicts Between Ethics and Organizational Demands). The balancing of dual roles as officer and psychologist (Standard, 3.05, Multiple Relationships) is discussed in Chapter 6 and related issues regarding confidentiality (Standards 4.01, Maintaining Confidentiality; 4.02, Discussing the Limits of Confidentiality) in Chapter 7. The broadly worded enforceable standards are relevant to and should be carefully read by psychologists in the military and other areas of public service. The military/correctional psychology icons throughout this book are meant to assist in quickly identifying standards and case examples applicable to these contexts. The value of self-care for military as well as other psychologists is discussed in Hot Topic "The Ethical Component of Self-Care" in Chapter 3.

Is Sufficient Attention Given to Responsibilities of Administrators of Psychology Programs and Psychology Faculty?

The Ethics Code devotes a separate section to standards designed to highlight responsibilities of university administrators and faculty and to strengthen protections for students. Relevant standards include 7.01, Design of Education and Training Programs; 7.02, Descriptions of Education and Training Programs; 7.04, Student Disclosure of Personal Information; 7.06, Assessing Student and Supervisee Performance; 7.05a and b, Mandatory Individual or Group Therapy; 7.07, Sexual Relationships With Students and Supervisees; 8.04, Client/Patient, Student, and Subordinate Research Participants; and 8.12c, Publication Credit. The relevance of enforceable standards to supervision and training is also covered in Hot Topic "Ethical Supervision of Trainees" in Chapter 10 and Case 7, "Handling Disparate Information for Evaluating Trainees," in Appendix A.

Does the Ethics Code Specifically Address Internet and Other Electronically Mediated Research and Services?

The past two decades have witnessed an expansion and evolution in psychology's use of the Internet, mobile phones, and other electronic media for behavioral telehealth, psychological assessment, consulting, video conferencing, public statements, and research. Throughout each section of the Code, the broadly worded enforceable standards are applicable to these activities and do not require specific reference to the medium in which research or services are conducted. Use of the Internet and other electronically mediated forms relevant to research or services is explicitly mentioned in four standards: 3.10a, Informed Consent; 4.02c, Discussing the Limits of Confidentiality; 5.01a, Avoidance of False or Deceptive Statements; and 5.04, Media Presentations. In addition, throughout this volume, applications of standards to electronic media appear in "Digital Ethics" features. To quickly locate discussions in this book on how other enforceable standards should be applied to work using electronic media, readers can look for the electronic media icon.

Informed Consent for Research, Assessment, and Therapy

Informed consent is seen by many as the primary means of ensuring the rights and welfare of those with whom psychologists work. Informed consent is designed to ensure that research participants and clients/patients are provided with sufficient information to rationally and voluntarily decide whether they wish to participate in research or to receive psychological services. The general standard on informed consent provides direction on the nature of information that must be included in all informed consent procedures and steps that must be taken to protect the rights of children and adults with cognitive impairments who are legally unable to provide consent (Standard 3.10, Informed Consent). The Hot Topic in Chapter 6 of this book examines specific applications of informed consent standards to adults with impaired decisional capacity. Additional standards lay out information required for basic and intervention research; psychological assessments relevant to mental health, forensic, and employment contexts; and individual and multiperson therapies, as well as additional consent safeguards for therapies for which generally recognized techniques and procedures have not been established (Standards 8.02, Informed Consent to Research; 8.03, Informed Consent for Recording Voices and Images in Research; 9.03, Informed Consent in Assessments; 10.01, Informed Consent to Therapy; 10.02, Therapy Involving Couples or Families; 10.03, Group Therapy).

Dispensing With Informed Consent

In some instances, informed consent is not necessary or is unfeasible as a means to protect the rights and welfare of those with whom psychologists work. The Ethics Code provides specific descriptions of situations in which the requirement for informed consent may be waived and the additional steps needed to ensure individuals are treated with respect and concern for their welfare. These standards reflect enhanced sensitivity to naturalistic, neuropsychological, forensic, school, and industrial–organizational contexts in which psychologists provide services, conduct research, or administer assessments, including anonymous research surveys, assessments to determine decisional capacity, emergency treatment, and assessment or treatment mandated by law (Standards 3.10a, Informed Consent; 8.05, Dispensing With Informed Consent for Research; 9.03a, Informed Consent in Assessments; and 10.01, Informed Consent to Therapy).

Are There Ethical Standards Specific to Issues of Individual and Cultural Diversity?

Principal D, Justice, and Principal E, Respect for People's Rights and Dignity, are reflected in enforceable standards designed to ensure the fair treatment of all individuals and groups regardless of age, gender, gender identity, race, ethnicity, culture, national origin, religion, sexual orientation, disability, language, or socioeconomic status. Psychologists must obtain the necessary competencies to work effectively with diverse populations and are prohibited from engaging in unfair discrimination or harassment based on any of these characteristics (Standards 2.01b, Competence; 3.01, Unfair Discrimination; 3.02, Sexual Harassment; 3.03, Other Harassment). They must provide informed consent information and administer assessments appropriate to an individual's language competence and use assessment techniques whose validity and reliability have been established with members of the population tested (Standards 3.10, Informed Consent; 9.02, Use of Assessments). These issues are also covered in the Hot Topics "Multicultural Ethical Competence" (Chapter 5) and "Ethical Issues for the Integration of Religion and Spirituality in Therapy" (Chapter 13); the discussion of discrimination based on a practitioner's religious beliefs (Standard 3.01, Unfair Discrimination, Chapter 6); and a summary of new guidelines prohibiting the use of "conversion therapy" for gay, lesbian, bisexual, and transgender persons (Standard 2.04, Bases for Scientific and Professional Judgments, Chapter 5). The diversity icon helps readers locate discussions in this book on how other standards should be applied to individual and group differences.

What Is the Distinction Between the APA Ethics Code and Specific APA Guidelines?

The Introduction and Applicability section of the Ethics Code recommends that members refer to guidelines adopted or endorsed by scientific and professional psychological organizations as materials that may be useful in applying the Ethics Code to everyday activities. Specific APA guidelines to which psychologists may refer are not listed in the current Code. The reason for this decision is that APA guidelines are frequently revised or become outdated and, in some instances, older guidelines are inconsistent with standards in the current Ethics Code and prevailing psychological science and practice. Professional and scientific guidelines are essential to ethical practice. As indicated earlier, the language of the Ethics Code is intentionally broad to be as applicable as possible to the wide range of activities that psychologists perform. Guidelines help psychologists place the standards in the context of their field of expertise. Guidelines will be cited throughout this book to illustrate best ethical practices in a given area. Continuously updated links to APA guidelines are provided at http://study.sagepub.com/fisher4e.

Under the Ethics Code, Are Psychologists Obligated to Report Ethics Code Violations of Others?

When psychologists learn about a potential violation by another psychologist, they must attempt to resolve it informally by bringing it to the attention of the other psychologist if a resolution appears appropriate and the confidentiality rights of a research participant, client/patient, organizational client, or others are not violated (Standard 1.04, Informal Resolution of Ethical Violations). However, Standard 1.05, Reporting Ethical Violations, requires psychologists to formally report an ethical violation if it has or is likely to result in substantial harm, informal resolution is not appropriate, and the reporting would not violate confidentiality rights. This standard does not apply to psychologists retained to review another psychologist's ethical conduct.

The integrity of the APA adjudication of ethics complaints is jeopardized when psychologists make "frivolous" complaints, and Standard 1.07, Improper Complaints, prohibits filing an ethics complaint with reckless disregard for or willful ignorance of facts that would disprove the allegation. The Ethics Code also prohibits psychologists from penalizing persons based solely on their having made or been the subject of an ethics complaint (Standard 1.08, Unfair Discrimination Against Complainants and Respondents). This standard is often relevant to situations that arise in whistle-blowing, discrimination, and sexual harassment cases.

CHAPTER 2

The Introduction and Applicability Section, Preamble, and General Principles

What Do They Mean?

> *Psychologists are committed to increasing scientific and professional knowledge of behavior and people's understanding of themselves and others and to the use of such knowledge to improve the condition of individuals, organizations, and society. Psychologists respect and protect civil and human rights and the central importance of freedom of inquiry and expression in research, teaching, and publication. They strive to help the public in developing informed judgments and choices concerning human behavior.*
>
> —Ethical Principles of Psychologists and Code of Conduct (APA, 2010b)

The 2010 Ethics Code begins with the Introduction and Applicability section, followed by the Preamble and a set of five General Principles that reflect the underlying values and ideals of the discipline.

The remainder of the code is composed of 151 enforceable standards that describe required, prohibited, and permitted behaviors. This chapter highlights the implications for ethical conduct of the Introduction and Applicability section, Preamble, and General Principles.

Understanding the Introduction and Applicability Section and the Preamble

To Whom Does the Ethics Code Apply?

Membership in the APA commits members and student affiliates to comply with the standards of the Ethics Code. Many psychology programs adopt the Ethics Code into their faculty and student policies, and portions of the Ethics Code are integrated into state laws, rules, and regulations governing the licensed practice of psychology.

To What Does the Ethics Code Apply?

The answer to this question is all activities, all persons, all settings, and all communication contexts that are conducted, encountered, or used in one's role as a psychologist.

- *Activities* include, but are not limited to, clinical, counseling, and school practice; research; teaching and supervision; public service and policy development; program design, implementation, and evaluation; construction, administration, and interpretation of assessment instruments; organizational consulting; forensic activities; and administration.
- *Persons* include individual clients/patients, research participants, and students; children and adults of all ages; individuals with or without mental disorders; individuals with disabilities; persons of diverse cultural and language backgrounds and different sexual orientations; individuals within families, groups, and organizations; medical and social service providers; attorneys; and other professionals.
- *Settings* include military bases, schools, research laboratories, universities, private or group practice offices, business organizations, hospitals, integrated care systems and patient-centered medical homes, managed care companies, the courts, private and public social services programs, government agencies, and public spaces where research or intervention is carried out.
- *Communication contexts* include research, consultation, and the delivery of services in person or via post, telephone, fax, Internet, mobile phone, television, radio, and other electronic transmissions.

Psychologists should be aware that the Introduction and Applicability section clearly states that lack of awareness or misunderstanding of any part of the Ethics Code is not itself a defense to a charge of unethical conduct.

Professional Versus Personal Activities

The Ethics Code applies only to psychologists' activities that are part of their scientific, educational, professional, or consulting roles. The Code does not apply to the purely private conduct of psychologists, although the APA may take action against a member after his or her conviction for a felony, whether or not it directly resulted from activities performed in the member's role as a psychologist.

In some situations, distinctions between professional and personal activities may appear ambiguous. For example, if a psychology professor has a personal web page that includes racist comments, will these comments be relevant to his professional role if some of his students have access to this page? If a counseling psychologist criticizes the professionalism of a school psychologist during a parent meeting at her children's school, will other parents perceive her statements as at least partially professional? Pipes, Holstein, and Aguirre (2005) suggested some questions that may help psychologists determine when their personal actions overlap their role as a psychologist and thus are subject to the Ethics Code:

- Is the behavior linked to a role played by psychologists?
- Does the behavior, on its face, seem at least partially professional?
- Is there a high probability that those with whom the psychologist works will be affected?
- Does the action threaten the professional credibility of the psychologist or the discipline of psychology?

Professional Versus Personal Values

Actions that are contrary to the Ethics Code principles and standards can arise when psychologists apply values that may be virtuous in personal relationships to professional contexts in which the same values may be harmful (Knapp, Handelsman, Gottlieb, & VandeCreek, 2013). For example, the personal values of family caring and connectedness may lead a clinical child psychologist to believe it ethically appropriate to agree to a request from her brother to help set up a behavioral management program for his daughter who has been diagnosed with pervasive developmental disorder. An understanding of professional values would alert the psychologist to the potential harm of adding a professional relationship to her close personal relationship with her brother and his family and lead to the more ethical decision to provide an appropriate referral (Principle B, Fidelity and Responsibility; Standard 3.04, Avoiding Harm; Standard 3.05, Multiple Relationships).

At the same time, displacing a set of personal values with mechanical and narrow interpretations of specific ethical standards and laws can lead to thoughtless or unethical responses in the context of the complex moral issues encountered by psychologists across the full spectrum of role responsibilities. For example, a research psychologist specializing in ethnographic studies of youth gangs who has just learned from a participant about the planned murder of another youth might apply a strict interpretation of Standard 4.01, Maintaining Confidentiality, to dictate a decision not to alert the youth or law enforcement, rather than the more nuanced moral evaluation called for by Principle A, Beneficence and Nonmaleficence and Standard 4.05, Disclosures.

To best ensure psychologists appropriately balance professional and personal values, Handlesman and colleagues (Anderson & Handelsman, 2010, 2013; Handelsman, Gottlieb, & Knapp, 2005) recommended that training in the discipline of psychology must help students integrate new professional and scientific values with their preexisting moral values in ways that promote the adoption and internalization of the unique ethical responsibilities and social roles expected of psychologists. This issue is further addressed in the discussion of aspirational principles later in this chapter and the treatment of virtues in Chapter 3.

What Is the Relevance of Specific Language Used in the Ethics Code?

To fulfill the Ethics Code's professional, educational, public, and enforcement goals, the language of the Ethics Code needs (a) to have the clarity necessary to provide adequate notice of behaviors that would be considered code violations, (b) to be applicable across many multifaceted roles and responsibilities of psychologists, and (c) to enhance and not impede good scientific and professional practice. The language of the Ethics Code must be specific enough to provide guidance yet general enough to allow for critical thinking and professional judgment.

This section includes some general guidance for interpreting the language of the Ethics Code. The implications of specific terminology for specific standards are addressed in greater detail in relevant chapters.

Due Notice

Adjudicatory decisions based on an ethics code remain vulnerable to overturn on appeal if defendants can argue they had no forewarning that specific behaviors were ethical violations (Bersoff, 1994). For example, language in enforceable standards requiring psychologists to be "alert to," "to guard against," or "to respect" certain factors is problematic because the behaviors expected by these terms remain undefined and are thus vulnerable to subjective interpretation by psychologists, consumers, and ethics committees. Accordingly, the language of the enforceable standards in the Ethics Code was crafted to describe the behaviors that are required and those that are proscribed in a manner that readers would reasonably understand.

Applicability Across Diverse Roles and Contexts

Psychologists teach, conduct research, provide therapy, administer and interpret psychological tests, consult to business, provide legal testimony, evaluate school programs, serve in public service sectors and the military, and take on a multitude of scientific and professional roles. An enforceable ethics code for psychologists must therefore be worded broadly enough to ensure that (a) standards apply across a broad range of activities in which psychologists are engaged; (b) role-specific standards are clearly presented as such; and (c) standards do not compromise scientific, practice, or consulting activities through inattention to or inconsistencies with the constantly changing realities of professional and legal responsibilities.

This requirement, viewed alongside the need for language providing due notice, means that some standards reflecting generally accepted ethical values in one work area were not included in the current Ethics Code because they could not be worded in such a way as to prevent undue burden on psychologists working in another area. For example, the Ethics Code Task Force (ECTF) struggled with appropriate wording for a general "honesty" standard within the Human Relations section that would reflect the aspirational principle of integrity. However, such a general standard had to be abandoned because it risked prohibiting ethically acceptable practices such as paradoxical therapy and deception research. The principle of integrity is reflected in more circumscribed standards, including Standards 5.01, Avoidance of False or Deceptive Statements; 5.02, Statements by Others; 6.06, Accuracy in Reports to Payors and Funding Sources; and 8.10, Reporting Research Results. For additional discussion of this issue, readers may wish to refer to the Hot Topic in Chapter 8 on avoiding false and deceptive statements in scientific and clinical expert testimony.

The Use of Modifiers

A modifier is a word or phrase that qualifies the meaning of an ethical rule. Modifiers in the Ethics Code include terms such as *appropriate, potentially, to the extent feasible,* and *attempt to.* An explanation of the use of modifiers is provided in the Introduction and Applicability section of the Code. The use of modifiers is necessary in standards that are written broadly to allow for professional judgment across a wide range of psychological activities and contexts. For example, the term *feasible* in a standard permits psychologists to evaluate whether factors within the specific context in which they are working justify delaying or not implementing behaviors required by a particular standard. Modifiers are also used to eliminate injustice or inequality that would occur without the modifier. For example, a modifier such as *appropriate* signals that the behaviors required to comply with a standard can vary with the psychological characteristics of the persons involved, psychologists' roles, or specific situational demands. A modifier such as the term *relevant* is used in standards to guard against language that would create a rigid rule that would be quickly outdated. Below are three examples of the use of modifiers:

- Standard 10.01a, Informed Consent to Therapy, requires psychologists to obtain informed consent from clients/patients as early as is feasible in the therapeutic relationship. The phrase *as early as is feasible* provides decisional latitude when fully informed consent during an initial therapy session may not be possible or clinically appropriate. A client/patient may be experiencing acute distress that requires immediate psychological intervention and for which informed consent procedures may be clinically contraindicated. As another example, psychologists may need to wait for feedback from a client's/patient's HMO before consent discussions regarding fees can be completed.

- Standard 3.10b, Informed Consent, requires that for persons who are legally incapable of giving informed consent, psychologists "provide an appropriate explanation." The term *appropriate* indicates that the nature of the explanation will vary depending on, among other factors, the person's developmental level, cognitive capacities, mental status, and language preferences and proficiencies.
- Under Standard 2.01c, Boundaries of Competence, psychologists planning to engage in activities new to them must undertake relevant education, training, supervised experience, consultation, or study. By including the term *relevant,* this standard can continue to be applied to new roles, new techniques, and new technologies as they emerge over time.

What Is "Reasonable"?

In the Introduction and Applicability section, the term *reasonable* is defined as the "prevailing professional judgment of psychologists engaged in similar activities in similar circumstances, given the knowledge the psychologist had or should have had at the time." The use of this term serves two functions. It prohibits psychologists from exercising idiosyncratic ethical judgments inconsistent with the prevailing values and behaviors of members of the profession. In doing so, it provides other psychologists and recipients of psychological services, students, and research participants a professional standard against which to judge psychologists' ethical behaviors. At the same time, by requiring that criteria for compliance or violation of an Ethical Standard be judged against the prevailing practices of peers, the use of the term *reasonable* guards against unrealistic or unfair expectations of responsible conduct. The wording enables psychologists to launch a legitimate defense of their actions based on current best practices in the field and documentation of efforts to resolve problems in an ethical manner. The examples below illustrate these two applications of the term *reasonable:*

- Standard 4.07, Use of Confidential Information for Didactic or Other Purposes, prohibits psychologists from disclosing in public statements confidential and personally identifiable information about those with whom they work unless they have taken "reasonable steps to disguise the person or organization." The term *reasonable* recognizes that despite steps to protect confidentiality that would be considered ethically acceptable by other psychologists (i.e., the use of pseudonyms; disguising gender, ethnicity, age, setting, and business products), persons to whom the statements refer may recognize (or erroneously attribute the description to) themselves or others may be privy to information not under the psychologist's control that leads to identification.
- Standard 2.05, Delegation of Work to Others, requires that psychologists who delegate work to employees, supervisees, research or teaching assistants, interpreters, or others "take reasonable steps to authorize only those responsibilities

that such persons can be expected to perform competently on the basis of their education, training, or experience, either independently or with the level of supervision being provided." In this case, a psychologist who asked a secretary who spoke the same language as a client/patient to serve as an interpreter during an assessment would not have taken steps considered *reasonable* in the prevailing view of the profession. On the other hand, a psychologist who hired an interpreter based on an impressive set of credentials in mental health evaluation would not be in violation if the interpreter had fabricated the credentials.

"Client/Patient" and "Organizational Client"

Throughout the Ethics Code, the combined term *client/patient* refers to individual persons to whom a psychologist is providing treatment, intervention, or assessment services. The term *organizational clients, organizations,* or *clients* refers to organizations, representatives of organizations, or other individuals for whom the psychologist is providing consultation, organization or personnel evaluations, test development, research, forensic expertise, or other services that do not involve a treatment, intervention, or diagnostic professional relationship with the person to whom services are provided. For example, a bank hired a psychologist to provide counseling services to employees who had experienced trauma during a recent robbery. In this context, the bank was the psychologist's "client" or "organizational client," and the employees who sought the psychologist's counseling services were the clients/patients. To further illustrate this distinction, readers can compare the use of the term *client* in Standard 3.11, Psychological Services Delivered To or Through Organizations, with the use of the term *client/patient* in Standard 10.01, Informed Consent to Therapy.

How Is the Ethics Code Related to APA Ethics Enforcement?

The APA Ethics Committee investigates complaints against APA members alleging violations of the APA Ethics Code that was in effect at the time the conduct occurred. The APA Ethics Committee Rules and Procedures detail the ethics enforcement process and can be obtained online at http://www.apa.org/ethics/code.committee-2016.aspx. Below is a brief summary of these rules and procedures.

Ethics Complaints

Complaints to the Ethics Committee may be brought by APA members or nonmembers or initiated by members of the Ethics Committee (*sua sponte* complaints) within specified time periods. A complaint may be dismissed prior to review by the Ethics Committee if it does not meet jurisdictional criteria or if, on preliminary review, the Ethics Office director and the Ethics Committee chair or their designees fail to find grounds for action. If the Ethics Committee does have jurisdiction and the complaint provides grounds for action, the case is opened, violations of specific Ethical Standards are charged, and an investigation is begun. The psychologist against whom the complaint is made receives a charge letter and is given an opportunity to provide the committee with comment and materials regarding the allegations.

Failure of the respondent to cooperate with the Ethics Committee is itself an ethical violation (APA Ethics Code Standard 1.06, Cooperating With Ethics Committees; see Chapter 4). However, in response to a request by a respondent, the committee may proceed or stay the ethics process if the respondent is involved in civil or criminal litigation or disciplinary proceedings in other jurisdictions. Psychologists who do not wish to contest the allegations may submit to the APA an offer of "resignation while under investigation."

Sanctions

The Ethics Committee reviews the materials and resolves to either dismiss the case or recommend one of the following actions:

- *Reprimand.* A reprimand is given when a violation was not of a kind likely to cause harm to another person or to cause substantial harm to the profession and was not otherwise of sufficient gravity as to warrant a more severe sanction.
- *Censure.* The Ethics Committee may issue a censure if the violation was of a kind likely to cause harm to another person but not likely to cause substantial harm to another person or to the profession and was not otherwise of sufficient gravity as to warrant a more severe sanction.
- *Expulsion.* A member can be expelled from the APA when the violation was of a kind likely to cause substantial harm to another person or the profession or was otherwise of sufficient gravity as to warrant such action.
- *Stipulated resignation.* Contingent on execution of an acceptable affidavit and approval by the Board of Directors, members may be offered a stipulated resignation following a committee finding that they committed a violation of the Ethics Code or failed to show good cause why they should not be expelled.

The Ethics Committee may also issue directives requiring the respondent to (a) cease and desist from an activity, (b) obtain supervision or additional training or education, (c) be evaluated for and obtain treatment if appropriate, or (d) agree to probationary monitoring.

A psychologist who has been found in violation of the Ethics Code may respond to the recommendation by requesting an independent case review or, in the case of expulsion, an in-person proceeding before a formal hearing committee.

Notification

The director of the Ethics Office informs the respondent and the complainant of the final disposition in a matter, provides to the APA membership on an annual basis the names of individuals who have been expelled and those who have resigned from membership while under investigation, and informs the APA Council of Representatives in confidence who received a stipulated resignation and who resigned from membership while under investigation. The Board of Directors or the Ethics Committee may also determine that additional notification is necessary to protect the APA or the public or to maintain APA standards. The Ethics Office director may also notify state boards, affiliated state and regional associations, the American Board of Professional Psychology (ABPP), the Association of State and Provincial Psychology Boards, the Council for the National Register of Health Service Providers in Psychology, and other appropriate parties. In addition, the APA may provide such information to any person who submits a request about a former member who has lost membership because of an ethical violation.

Show Cause Procedure

The Ethics Committee can also take action against a member if a criminal court, licensing board, or state psychological association has already taken adverse action against the member. The rationale for such actions can go beyond a violation of the Ethics Code and can include conviction of a felony or revocation of state licensure.

How Is the Ethics Code Related to Sanctions by Other Bodies?

The APA Ethics Code is widely used by other bodies regulating the ethical science and practice of psychology. It is intended to be applied by the APA Ethics Committee and by other bodies that choose to adopt specific standards. The Introduction and Applicability section states,

> Actions that violate the standards of the Ethics Code may also lead to the imposition of sanctions on psychologists or students whether or not they are APA members by bodies other than APA, including state psychological associations, other professional groups, psychology boards, other state or federal agencies, and payors for health services.

In contrast to the Ethical Standards, as stated in the General Principles section, the aspirational principles of the Ethics Code are not intended to represent specific obligations or be the basis for imposing sanctions.

Across the country, the Ethics Code is adopted in its entirety or in part in statute by more than half the state boards responsible for licensing the practice of psychology. Insurance companies regularly require psychologists applying or reapplying for professional liability policies to reveal whether they have been the recipient of an ethics complaint or been found in ethical violation by a professional organization, state board, or state or federal agency. Many insurance companies retain the right to raise rates or cancel policies depending on the nature of the violation. In addition, the APA Ethics Committee may notify other bodies and individuals of sanctions it imposes for ethical violations. For information on the procedures for filing, investigating, and resolving ethics complaints, readers should refer to the Rules and Procedures of the APA Ethics Committee at http://www.apa.org/ethics/code/committee.aspx.

Need to Know: What to Do When You Receive an Ethics Complaint

Although the number of complaints is low, receiving a formal inquiry or complaint from a licensing board, ethics committee, or other institutional body can be a stressful experience. Koocher & Keith-Spiegel (2013) provided the following excellent advice for how to handle such complaints.

First, gather facts to determine the nature of the complaint and whether it is a formal or informal charge, the jurisdictional authority and rules and procedures of the body handling the complaint, and procedures for responding and the consequences of failing to respond (Standards 1.04, Informal Resolution of Ethical Violations; 1.05, Formal Resolution of Ethical Violations; 1.06, Cooperating With Ethics Committees).

Second, do not respond to the complaint without a clear written explanation of the charges against you. Do not contact the complainant directly, and if the complainant is a client/patient, ensure that you are provided with a waiver to disclose confidential information (Standards 1.06, Cooperating With Ethics Committees; 4.01, Maintaining Confidentiality). Obtain consultation and, if appropriate, legal advice prior to responding or providing materials.

Third, in most cases, psychologists are expected to respond personally to an inquiry, even when they have retained the services of an attorney. In crafting a response, assess the credibility of the charge. Limit your response in writing or in person to the scope of the inquiry and provide appropriate documentation. If you have committed the offense, begin and document remediation actions immediately if possible (e.g., supervision or training to increase competencies in scientific or professional ethics or other competencies).

Fourth, understand the professional, legal, and economic consequences of any offered settlement, "consent decree," sanction, or other resolution that is not a full dismissal of charges and seek additional professional or legal consultation.

How Is the APA Ethics Code Related to Law?

Civil Litigation

The Introduction and Applicability section clearly states that the Ethics Code is not intended to be a basis of civil liability: "Whether a psychologist has violated the Ethics Code standards does not by itself determine whether the psychologist is legally liable in a court action, whether a contract is enforceable, or whether other legal consequences occur." However, psychologists should be aware that it seems highly unlikely that such a disclaimer would have any legally binding effect. Compliance with or violation of the Ethics Code may be admissible as evidence in some legal proceedings, depending on the circumstances. Similarly, although the Ethics Code states that using the General Principles as a representation of obligations or to apply sanctions distorts the meaning and purpose of the aspirational principles, attorneys may introduce into litigation the General Principles or Ethical Standards as evidence of the ethical values, requirements, or prohibitions of the discipline.

Compliance With Law

Law does not dictate ethics, but sensitivity to law protects the integrity of the profession. Whereas few standards require psychologists to comply with the law, many standards were written to minimize the possibility that compliance with the Ethics Code would be in conflict with state laws and federal regulations. Those standards that require compliance with the law include the following:

- Work-related discrimination, Standard 3.01, Unfair Discrimination
- Obtaining consent from legally authorized persons for individuals legally incapable of giving such consent, Standard 3.10b, Informed Consent
- Legal prohibitions against disclosure of confidential information, Standards 4.05a and b, Disclosures
- Creation, storage, and disposal of records, Standard 6.01, Documentation of Professional and Scientific Work and Maintenance of Records
- Fee practices, Standard 6.04a, Fees and Financial Arrangements
- Care and use of animals in research, Standard 8.09, Humane Care and Use of Animals in Research
- Legal and contractual obligations, Standard 9.11, Maintaining Test Security

Throughout this volume, the applicability of ethical standards to compliance with federal regulations governing the creation and protection of health care records, third-party payments, and the conduct of research are described. Although there are no specific Ethical Standards for which a criminal conviction is a violation, the Introduction and Applicability section and the APA Rules and Regulations clearly state that the APA may take action against a member after his or her conviction of a felony, including expulsion from the organization.

Conflicts Between Ethics and Law, Regulations, or Other Governing Legal Authority

In applying the Ethics Code to their scientific and professional work, psychologists may find relevant laws, regulations, or other governing legal authority that conflicts with the Ethical Standards. As articulated in the Introduction and

Applicability section, psychologists must comply with the Ethics Code if it establishes a higher standard of conduct than is required by law. When an Ethical Standard is in direct conflict with law, regulations, or other governing legal authority, psychologists must make known their commitment to the Ethics Code and take steps to resolve the conflict in a responsible manner in keeping with basic principles of human rights. If the conflict is unresolvable via such means, psychologists are permitted to adhere to the legal requirements, but only if such adherence *cannot* be used to justify or defend violation of human rights (Standard 1.02, Conflicts Between Ethics and Law, Regulations, or Other Governing Legal Authority). See also the section on "The 2010 Amendments: The Controversy Over Psychologists' Involvement in Inhumane Military Interrogations" (Chapter 1) and the section "Psychology and Human Rights" and the Hot Topic "Human Rights and Psychologists' Involvement in Assessments Related to Death Penalty Cases" (Chapter 4).

General Principles

> *Ethics are principles of action based on a commonly accepted system of values, and agreement upon these principles and values must be reached before progress toward an acceptable code can be expected.*
>
> —Bixler and Seeman (1946, p. 486)

"A genuine and practical code of ethics . . . stems from a philosophy as well as a need" (Bixler & Seeman, 1946, p. 486). The moral values from which the APA Ethical Standards stem are articulated in five General Principles. These principles are aspirational, intended to inspire psychologists toward the highest ethical ideals of the profession. Unlike the Ethical Standards, they do not represent specific or enforceable behavioral rules of conduct. The General Principles articulate the moral vision of psychology's common community of purpose. Although psychologists must strive to act in accordance with all the principles, the moral priority of any one principle will be determined by the specific ethical problem. The principles are therefore listed in alphabetical order and are not hierarchically organized.

The General Principles help guide psychologists' decision making by providing an analytic framework from which to identify those Ethical Standards that are appropriate to the situation at hand. Each enforceable standard reflects one or more of these principles. Below, each principle is described, and examples are provided of standards in which the principle ideals are embedded.

Principle A: Beneficence and Nonmaleficence

Principle A reflects psychologists' dual obligation to strive to do good and avoid doing harm. As articulated in the Preamble and in Principle A, psychologists strive to do good by promoting the welfare of others; treating people and animals humanely; increasing scientific and professional knowledge of behavior and people's understanding of themselves; and improving the condition of individuals, organizations, and society. Examples of standards reflecting the principle of beneficence include Standards 2.02, Providing Services in Emergencies; 3.09, Cooperation With Other Professionals; 8.09, Humane Care and Use of Animals in Research; and 8.14, Sharing Research Data for Verification. Principle A represents the joint influences of beneficence and nonmaleficence in recognition that in rightly practiced psychology, individuals may be harmed without being wronged. For example, to preserve academic standards and to ensure grading fairness, teaching psychologists may be obligated to give a student a poor or failing grade. Similarly, disclosing confidential information to protect a client/patient, student, or research participant from self-harm or from harming others may have moral priority over protecting that individual's privacy rights (see Standard 4.05, Disclosures). To maximize good and minimize harm, Principle A also calls for psychologists to be alert to and guard against personal problems that could lead to exploitation or harm to individuals or organizations with whom they work (see Standard 2.06, Personal Problems and Conflicts).

Throughout the enforceable standards of the Ethics Code, psychologists are expected to avoid harm by maintaining competence, guarding against behaviors that would lead to exploitation of those with whom they work, minimizing intrusions on privacy in reports or consultations with colleagues, providing opinions and reports based only on information or techniques sufficient to substantiate findings, and terminating therapy when the client/patient is likely to be harmed by continued services (Standards 2.01, Competence; 2.03, Maintaining Competence; 3.04, Avoiding Harm; 3.05, Multiple Relationships; 3.08, Exploitative Relationships; 9.01, Bases for Assessments; and 10.10, Terminating Therapy). Psychologists are also required to minimize harm by taking steps to ameliorate harms caused by misuse of their work (Standard 1.01, Misuse of Psychologists' Work). For additional information, readers may refer to the Hot Topic in Chapter 7, on disclosures and confidentiality relevant to parental involvement in mental health services for children and adolescents, and in Chapter 10, on ethical supervision of trainees.

Principle B: Fidelity and Responsibility

Fidelity reflects faithfulness of one human being to another (Ramsey, 2002). In psychology, such faithfulness includes promise keeping; discharge and acceptance of fiduciary responsibilities; and appropriate maintenance of scientific, professional, and teaching relationships. Psychologists recognize their responsibility to obtain and maintain high standards of competence in their own work and to be concerned about the ethical compliance of their colleagues.

Developing a professional identity as a psychologist is a critical step toward understanding how to conduct oneself in a professional manner, to infuse the values of the profession in the conduct of psychological research and practice, to accept responsibility for one's professional actions, and to resolve situations that challenge professional values and integrity in one's own work and the work of others (APA, 2012f; Nash, Khatri, Cubic, & Baird, 2013; Standards 1.01, Misuse of Psychologists' Work, 1.04, Informal Resolution of Ethical Violations, 1.05, Reporting Ethical Violations).

The nature of the competencies and responsibilities of psychologists to individuals, organizations, and communities will be determined by the specific scientific or professional relationship. For example, forensic psychologists have distinctive professional obligations and duties that arise through relationships established by those who retain their services (e.g., defense or prosecuting attorneys, insurers, the court) and by those with whom they interact (e.g., examinees, collateral contacts; APA, 2013e). Similarly, psychologists working in organizations established under the Affordable Care Act (ACA), such as Accountable Care Organizations (ACO) or Patient-Centered Medical Homes (PCMH), need to comport themselves in a manner consistent with the operations and culture of integrated primary care settings and at the same time display the knowledge, values, and skills of a psychologist (Nash et al., 2013). Many of the standards on competence discussed in Chapter 5 reflect the aspirations articulated in Principle B.

In fulfilling the ideals expressed in Principle B, psychologists seek to meet their responsibilities by avoiding conflicts of interest that would jeopardize trust or lead to exploitation or harm. They also consult with other professionals when necessary (see, e.g., Standards 3.05, Multiple Relationships; 3.06, Conflict of Interest; and 3.09, Cooperation With Other Professionals). The fiduciary and professional obligations to which Principle B asks psychologists to aspire are also reflected in the standards on resolving ethical issues (Chapter 4), record keeping and fees (Chapter 9), and education and training (Chapter 10). Readers may also wish to refer to Standard 8.01, Institutional Approval, for a discussion on submitting research proposals to institutional review boards (IRBs) in Chapter 11, as well as the Hot Topics on psychological assessments and the rules of evidence (Chapter 12) and on the integration of religion and spirituality in therapy (Chapter 13).

Principle C: Integrity

Maintaining integrity in psychological activities requires honest communication; truth telling; promise keeping; and accuracy in the science, teaching, and practice of psychology. It involves refraining from making professional commitments that cannot be met and avoiding or correcting misrepresentations of one's work. In following Principle C, psychologists do not steal, cheat, or engage in fraud or subterfuge. These ideals are evidenced in Standards 5.01, Avoidance of False or Deceptive Statements; 6.04, Fees and Financial Arrangements; and 8.10, Reporting Research Results.

Psychologists advertising their services on websites or other media have an ethical responsibility greater than do non-healthcare professionals to present information clearly, because many potential consumers of psychological services do not have the knowledge or experience to understand their own treatment needs or evaluate the legitimacy of claims made. Such individuals may be particularly vulnerable to persuasion or exploitation (Standards 3.08, Exploitive Relationships; 5.01, Avoidance of False or Deceptive Statements). Consistent with Principle C, psychologists offering expert opinions in legal proceedings need to recognize the adversarial nature of the legal system and treat all participants and weigh all data, opinions, and rival hypotheses impartially (Standards for Forensic Psychology; APA, 2013e).

When serving as expert or fact witnesses, providing educational services, or disseminating the results of research, psychologists present their findings objectively and dispassionately, provide all relevant material, and offer reasonable alternative interpretations in an unbiased and impartial manner. For further discussion, refer to the Hot Topics on avoiding false and deceptive statements in expert testimony (Chapter 8) and the ethics of managed care (Chapter 9).

In some scientific and professional relationships, deception may be justified to maximize knowledge gained or the welfare of individuals served. As articulated in Standard 8.07, Deception in Research, in each instance, psychologists have a serious obligation to evaluate whether deception is warranted, to decide whether negative consequences outweigh the benefits to participants or society, and to correct any mistrust or harm that arises from the use of such techniques.

Principle D: Justice

Principle D calls for psychologists to strive to provide all people with fair, equitable, and appropriate access to treatment and the benefits of scientific knowledge. Psychologists endeavor to be aware of and guard against their own biases and the prejudices of others that may condone or lead to unjust practices. These ideals are reflected in Standards 1.08, Unfair Discrimination Against Complainants and Respondents; 3.01, Unfair Discrimination; 3.02, Sexual Harassment; and 3.03, Other Harassment. Readers may also wish to refer to the Hot Topics on human rights and psychological assessment in death penalty cases (Chapter 4) and multicultural ethical competence (Chapter 5).

Principle D calls for psychologists to select procedures and services that meet the needs of those with whom they work, recognizing that existing social and economic inequities may require different but comparable scientific and professional techniques. For example, when conducting assessments, psychologists must be cognizant of the fact that fairness and accessibility are fundamental issues in testing that require the unobstructed opportunity for all examinees to demonstrate their standing on the construct(s) being tested through population-sensitive and valid instruments (AERA, APA, & NCME, 2014).

Consideration of Standard 2.04, Bases for Scientific and Professional Judgments also helps ensure that individuals and populations are treated fairly by emphasizing the importance of evidence-based practices and requiring psychologists to avoid subjective biases in designing research questions, administering tests, and selecting therapeutic approaches. Additional enforceable standards reflecting the values of fairness articulated in Principle D include 7.06, Assessing Student and Supervisee Performance; 8.04, Client/Patient, Student, and Subordinate Research Participants; 9.01, Bases for Assessments; and 10.02, Therapy Involving Couples or Families.

Principle E: Respect for People's Rights and Dignity

Principle E calls for psychologists to "respect the dignity and worth of all people, and the rights of individuals to privacy, confidentiality, and self-determination." Standards requiring informed consent to research, assessment, and therapy (Standards 3.10,

8.02, 9.03, and 10.01) reflect respect for the autonomous decision making articulated in Principle E. Psychologists must also be attentive to the circumstances of individuals who may have limited capacity for autonomous decision making and take the extra precautions necessary to safeguard these individuals' rights and welfare. This responsibility is specifically addressed in Standard 3.10b, Informed Consent. Readers may also wish to refer to the Hot Topic on informed consent involving adults with impaired decisional capacity (Chapter 6) and sections on the informational risk of genetic testing and research involving children and adolescents in Chapter 11.

Psychologists are aware of and respect cultural, individual, and role differences, including those based on age, gender, gender identity, race, ethnicity, culture, national origin, religion, sexual orientation, disability, language, and socioeconomic status. They ensure that they are familiar with the scientific and professional knowledge relevant to these differences and acquire the competencies necessary to perform their roles effectively. Psychologists strive to be aware of and eliminate from their work the effect of their own and others' prejudices. Exemplar standards reflecting the ideal of respect for individual differences are Standards 2.01, Boundaries of Competence; 3.01, Unfair Discrimination; and 9.01, Bases for Assessments.

Principle E also addresses psychologists' duty to protect the rights of individuals to determine what personal information will be shared and with whom and psychologists' responsibility to protect test results from unauthorized use. This ideal is embedded in standards on privacy and confidentiality (Chapter 7), as well as Standards 6.02, Maintenance, Dissemination, and Disposal of Confidential Records of Professional and Scientific Work; 7.04, Student Disclosure of Personal Information; and 10.03, Group Therapy. Readers may also refer to the Hot Topic "Confidentiality and Involvement of Parents in Mental Health Services for Children and Adolescents" in Chapter 7.

In accordance with Principle E, psychologists conducting psychological assessments should take appropriate steps to ensure test takers' rights to information about the purpose of a test prior to test administration, when appropriate, so that test results accurately reflect the abilities, diagnosis, or competencies that are the purpose of the assessment. Psychologists should also be aware of their ethical and legal responsibility to provide test takers appropriate access to their test results. This principle is reflected throughout the standards on assessment (Chapter 12).

Chapter Cases and Ethics Discussion Questions

According to the APA Ethics Code, "if neither law nor the Ethics Code resolves an issue, psychologists should consider other professional materials and the *dictates of their own conscience,* as well as seek consultation with others within the field when this is practical." The APA Ethics Code makes clear that one's values may, in conjunction with other professional guidance and professional consultation, play a role in professional decision making. What are the risks of exclusively following the dictates of one's personal views and values in making ethical decisions in professional research or practice?

Dr. Shue is a faculty member in a doctoral psychology program. She is sitting in the faculty–student lounge and overhears two graduate students making derogatory, heterosexist comments about another student in the program. Does she have a professional obligation to intervene in the students' "private" discussion? Are there ethical reasons she should not intervene? Should she discuss her observations with other faculty?

A research psychologist is testing whether a combination of standard behavioral therapy and a standard psychopharmaceutical treatment to prevent alcohol cravings is more effective than either approach alone for individuals diagnosed with alcohol use disorder. Discuss how different ethical theories might be applied to determine whether randomly assigning patients to one of the three conditions (standard behavior therapy, psychopharmaceutical treatment, or a combination of both) is ethically justified.

CHAPTER 3

The APA Ethics Code and Ethical Decision Making

The APA's Ethics Code provides a set of aspirational principles and behavioral rules written broadly to apply to psychologists' varied roles and the diverse contexts in which the science and practice of psychology are conducted. The five aspirational principles described in Chapter 2 represent the core values of the discipline of psychology that guide members in recognizing in broad terms the moral rightness or wrongness of an act. As an articulation of the universal moral values intrinsic to the discipline, the aspirational principles are intended to inspire right actions but do not specify what those actions might be. The ethical standards that will be discussed in later chapters of this book are concerned with specific behaviors that reflect the application of these moral principles to the work of psychologists in specific settings and with specific populations. In their everyday activities, psychologists will find many instances in which familiarity with and adherence to specific Ethical Standards provide adequate foundation for ethical actions. There will also be many instances in which (a) the means by which to comply with a standard are not readily apparent, (b) two seemingly competing standards appear equally appropriate, (c) application of a single standard or set of standards appears consistent with one aspirational principle but inconsistent with another, or (d) a judgment is required to determine whether exemption criteria for a particular standard are met.

The Ethics Code is not a formula for solving these ethical challenges. Psychologists are not moral technocrats simply working their way through a decision tree of ethical rules. Rather, the Ethics Code provides psychologists with a set of aspirations and broad general rules of conduct that psychologists must interpret and apply as a function of the unique scientific and professional roles and relationships in which they are embedded. Successful application of the principles and standards of the Ethics Code involves a conception of psychologists as active moral agents committed to the good and just practice and science of psychology. Ethical decision making thus involves a commitment to applying the Ethics Code and other legal and professional standards to construct rather than simply discover solutions to ethical quandaries (APA, 2012f).

This chapter discusses the ethical attitudes and decision-making strategies that can help psychologists prepare for, identify, and resolve ethical challenges as they continuously emerge and evolve in the dynamic discipline of psychology. An opportunity to apply these strategies is provided in the cases at the end of each chapter and the 10 case studies presented in Appendix A.

Ethical Commitment and Virtues

> *The development of a dynamic set of ethical standards for psychologists' work-related conduct requires a personal commitment and lifelong effort to act ethically; to encourage ethical behavior by students, supervisees, employees, and colleagues; and to consult with others concerning ethical problems.*
>
> —APA (2010b, Preamble)

Ethical commitment refers to a strong desire to do what is right because it is right (Josephson Institute of Ethics, 1999). In psychology, this commitment reflects a moral disposition and emotional responsiveness that move psychologists to creatively apply the APA's Ethics Code principles and standards to the unique ethical demands of the scientific or professional context.

The desire to do the right thing has often been associated with moral virtues or moral character, defined as a disposition to act and feel in accordance with moral principles, obligations, and ideals—a disposition that is neither principle bound nor situation specific (Beauchamp & Childress, 2001; MacIntyre, 1984). Virtues are dispositional habits acquired through social nurturance and professional education that provide psychologists with the motivation and skills necessary to apply the ideals and standards of the profession (see, e.g., Hauerwas, 1981; Jordan & Meara, 1990; May, 1984; National Academy of Sciences, 1995; Pellegrino, 1995). Fowers (2012) described virtues as the cognitive, emotional, dispositional, behavioral, and wisdom aspects of character strength, which motivates and enables us to act ethically out of an attachment to what is good.

Focal Virtues for Psychology

Virtue ethics can provide psychologists a more personal and therefore more effective foundation from which to approach ethical issues, and it helps offset an overreliance on conformity to rules that may be inconsistent with the aspirational principles of the discipline (Anderson & Handelsman, 2013; Kitchener & Anderson, 2011). Many moral dispositions have been proposed for the virtuous professional (Beauchamp & Childress, 2001; Keenan, 1995; MacIntyre, 1984; May, 1984). For disciplines such as psychology, in which codes of conduct dictate the general parameters but not the context-specific nature of ethical conduct, conscientiousness, discernment, and prudence are requisite virtues.

- A *conscientious* psychologist is motivated to do what is right because it is right, diligently tries to determine what is right, makes reasonable attempts to do the right thing, and is committed to lifelong professional growth.
- A *discerning* psychologist brings contextually and relationally sensitive insight, good judgment, and appropriately detached understanding to determine what is right.
- A *prudent* psychologist applies practical wisdom to ethical challenges, leading to right solutions that can be realized given the nature of the problem and the individuals involved.

The virtues considered most salient by members of a profession will vary with differences in role responsibilities. The asymmetrical power relationship and the client's/patient's vulnerability in the provision of mental health services requires virtues of benevolence, care, empathy, emotional self-restraint and monitoring, and compassion (Ivey, 2014). Prudence, discretion, and trustworthiness have been considered salient in scientific decision making. Scientists who willingly and consistently report procedures and findings accurately are enacting the virtue of honesty (Fowers, 2012). Fidelity, integrity, and wisdom are moral characteristics frequently associated with teaching and consultation. The Standards for Forensic Psychology (APA, 2013e) encourages forensic practitioners to act with reasonable diligence and promptness in managing their workloads so they can provide agreed upon and reasonably anticipated services across all work activities. The virtue of self-care enables psychologists to maintain appropriate competencies under stressful work conditions (see the Hot Topic "The Ethical Component of Self-Care" at the end of this chapter).

Openness to Others

"Openness to the other" has been identified as a core virtue for the practice of multiculturalism (Fowers & Davidov, 2006). Openness is characterized by a personal and professional commitment to applying a multicultural lens to our work motivated by a genuine interest in understanding others rather than reacting to a new wave of multicultural "shoulds" (Gallardo, Johnson, Parham, & Carter, 2009). It reflects a strong desire to understand how culture is relevant to the identification and resolution of ethical challenges in research and practice, to explore cultural differences, to respond to fluid definitions of group characteristics, to recognize the realities of institutional racism and other forms of discrimination on personal identity and life opportunities, and to creatively apply the profession's ethical principles and standards to each cultural context (Aronson, 2006; Fisher, 2015; Fowers & Davidov, 2006; Hamilton & Mahalik, 2009; Neumark, 2009; Riggle, Rostosky, & Horne, 2010; Sue & Sue, 2003; Trimble, 2009; Trimble & Fisher, 2006).

Openness may also be a core virtue for practicing in the primary care interprofessional organizations created by the Affordable Care Act, where the psychologists' role extends beyond providing patient services to include making contributions to integrated teams of health care professionals. Nash et al. (2013) have proposed a "primary care ethic" that reflects a guiding philosophy or set of values characterized by openness, appreciation, and willingness to engage as a psychologist in the interprofessional primary care environment. It reflects (a) a respect and appreciation for contributions by professionals from other disciplines; (b) a desire to integrate disciplinary perspectives; (c) a valuing of collaborative relationships and a willingness to cultivate and maintain them; and (d) a willingness to initiate clear, open, and constructive interprofessional communication.

Can Virtues Be Taught?

No course could automatically close the gap between knowing what is right and doing it.

—Pellegrino (1989, p. 492)

Some have argued that psychology professors cannot change graduate students' moral character through classroom teaching and therefore ethics education should focus on understanding the Ethics Code rather than instilling moral dispositions to right action. Without question, however, senior members of the discipline, through teaching and through their own examples, can enhance the ability of students and young professionals to understand the centrality of ethical commitment to ethical practice. At the same time, the development of professional moral character is not to simply know about virtue but to become good (Scott, 2003). Beyond the intellectual virtues transmitted in the classroom and modeled through mentoring and supervision, excellence of character can be acquired through habitual practice (Begley, 2006). One such habit for the virtuous graduate student and seasoned psychologist is a commitment to lifelong learning and practice in the continued development of moral excellence.

Some moral dispositions can be understood as derivative of their corresponding principles (Beauchamp & Childress, 2001). Drawing on the five APA General Principles, Table 3.1 lists corresponding virtues.

Ethical Awareness and Moral Principles

In the process of making decisions regarding their professional behavior, psychologists must consider this Ethics Code, in addition to applicable laws and psychology board regulations.

—APA (2010b, Introduction)

Lack of awareness or misunderstanding of an ethical standard is not itself a defense to a charge of unethical conduct.

—APA (2010b, Introduction)

Ethical commitment is just the first step in effective ethical decision making. Good intentions are insufficient if psychologists fail to identify the ethical situations to which they should be applied. Psychologists found to have violated Ethical Standards or licensure regulations have too often harmed others or damaged their own careers or the careers of others because of ethical ignorance. Conscientious psychologists understand that identification of situations requiring ethical attention depends on familiarity and understanding of the APA Ethics Code, relevant scientific and professional guidelines, laws and regulations applicable to their specific work-related activities, and an awareness of relational obligations embedded within each context.

Moral Principles and Ethical Awareness

To identify a situation as warranting ethical consideration, psychologists must be aware of the moral values of the discipline. Although the Ethics Code's General Principles are not exhaustive, they do identify the major moral ideals of psychology as a field. Familiarity with the General Principles, however, is not sufficient for good ethical decision making. Psychologists also need the knowledge, motivation, and coping skills to detect when situations call for consideration of these principles and attempt to address these issues when and if possible before they arise (Crowley & Gottlieb, 2012; Tjeltveit & Gottlieb, 2010; see also the Hot Topic "The Ethical Component of Self-Care" at the end of this chapter). Table 3.1 identifies types of ethical awareness corresponding to each General Principle.

Table 3.1 Principles, Virtues, and Ethical Awareness

APA General Principles	Corresponding Virtues	Corresponding Ethical Awareness
Principle A: Beneficence and Nonmaleficence	Compassionate, humane, nonmalevolent, prudent	Psychologists should be able to identify what is in the best interests of those with whom they work, when a situation threatens the welfare of individuals, and the competencies required to achieve the greatest good and avoid or minimize harm.
Principle B: Fidelity and Responsibility	Faithful, dependable, conscientious, committed to professional growth	Psychologists should be aware of their obligations to the individuals and communities affected by their work, including their responsibilities to the profession and obligations under the law.
Principle C: Integrity	Honest, reliable, self-aware, genuine	Psychologists should know what is possible before making professional commitments and be able to identify when it is necessary to correct misconceptions or mistrust.

(Continued)

Table 3.1 (Continued)

APA General Principles	Corresponding Virtues	Corresponding Ethical Awareness
Principle D: Justice	Judicious, fair, open to complexity and ambiguity	Psychologists should be able to identify individual or group vulnerabilities that can lead to exploitation and recognize when a course of action would result in or has resulted in unfair or unjust practices.
Principle E: Respect for People's Rights and Dignity	Respectful, considerate	Psychologists must be aware of special safeguards necessary to protect the autonomy, privacy, and dignity of members of the diverse populations with whom psychologists work.

Ethical Awareness and Ethical Theories

Ethical theories provide a moral framework to reflect on conflicting obligations. Unfortunately, ethical theories tend to emphasize one idea as the foundation for moral decision making, and illustrative problems are often reduced to that one idea. Given the complexity of moral reality, these frameworks are probably not mutually exclusive in their claims to moral truth (Steinbock, Arras, & London, 2003). However, awareness of the moral frameworks that might help address an ethical concern can also help clarify the values and available ethical choices (Beauchamp & Childress, 2001; Fisher, 1999; Kitchener, 1984).

Deception Research: A Case Example for the Application of Different Ethical Theories

Since Stanley Milgram (1963) published his well-known obedience experiments, the use of deception has become normative practice in some fields of psychological research and a frequent source of ethical debate (Baumrind, 1964, 1985; Fisher & Fyrberg, 1994). Researchers using deceptive techniques intentionally withhold information or misinform participants about the purpose of the study, the methodology, or roles of research confederates (Sieber, 1982). Deception is still widely practiced within experimental social psychology and in sexual health behavior and health care research (Kirschner et al., 2010; Miller, Gluck, & Wendler, 2008; Wong et al., 2012). By its very nature, the use of deception in research creates what Fisher (2005a) has termed the *consent paradox*: obtaining 'informed consent' under conditions in which participants are not truly informed.

On the one hand, intentionally deceiving participants about the nature and purpose of a study conflicts with Principle C: Integrity and Principle E: Respect for People's Rights and Dignity and with enforceable standards requiring psychologists to obtain fully informed consent of research participants prior to study initiation (Standards 3.10, Informed Consent; 8.02, Informed Consent to Research; 9.03, Informed Consent in Assessments; 10.01, Informed Consent to Therapy).

On the other hand, the methodological rationale for the use of deception is that some psychological phenomena cannot be adequately understood if research participants are aware of the purpose of the study. Thus by approximating the naturalistic contexts in which everyday behaviors take place, deception research can reflect Principle A: Beneficence and Nonmaleficence and Principle B: Fidelity and Responsibility by enhancing the ability of psychologists to generate scientifically and socially useful knowledge that might not otherwise be obtained. For example, deception has been used to study the phenomenon of "bystander apathy effect," the tendency for people in the presence of others to observe but not help a person who is a victim of an attack, medical emergency, or other dangerous condition (Latane & Darley, 1970). In such experiments, false emergency situations are staged without the knowledge of the research participants, whose reactions to the "emergency" are recorded and analyzed.

Standard 8.07, Deception in Research (as well as federal regulations governing participant protections) permits deception under limited conditions. However, its use remains ethically controversial. Below we present a case example of a deception study with discussion of how different ethical theories might lead to different conclusions about the moral acceptability of deceptive research. Readers should refer to Chapter 11 for a more in-depth discussion of Standard 8.07, Deception in Research.

CASE EXAMPLE

The Gaffe Study (Gonzales, Pederson, Manning, & Wetter, 1990)

This experiment was conducted to examine whether undergraduate males and females differ in their explanations for an embarrassing incident and whether the severity of their mistake would influence their explanations. Undergraduate students were "invited" to help researchers develop a video for a future study on how people form impressions. Each student participated in a taped discussion with another student in which they either were interviewed or were the interviewer. They were not told the true purpose of the study or that the other "student" was actually a confederate of the research team. Participants were then told to place their belongings on a table. As they did so, the experimenter pulled a hidden string attached to a strategically placed cup of colored water, which spilled onto what appeared to be the confederate's bag. For half the participants, only papers were in the tote bag (low-severity incident) while for the other half an expensive camera was in the tote bag (high-severity incident). Immediately after the cup spilled, the confederate exclaimed, "Oh no, my stuff!" followed by "What happened?" The experimenter had turned on the video so that participants' nonverbal responses (e.g., hand to face, head shaking), instrumental behaviors (e.g., attempts to empty the bag), and verbal responses (e.g., "I'm sorry" or "I didn't do it") could be analyzed. See Fisher and Fyrberg (1994) to learn how introductory students evaluated the ethics of this study.

Ethical Theories

Deontology or Kantian Ethics

Deontology has been described as "absolutist," "universal," and "impersonal" (Kant, 1785/1959). It prioritizes absolute obligations over consequences. In this moral framework, ethical decision making is the rational act of applying universal principles to all situations irrespective of specific relationships, contexts, or consequences. This approach reflects Immanuel Kant's conviction that ethical decisions cannot vary or be influenced by special circumstances or relationships. Rather, Kant stipulated that an ethical decision is only morally justified if a rational person believes the act resulting from the decision should be universally followed in all situations. This is called the *categorical imperative.* For Kant, respect for the worth of all persons was one such universal principle. A course of action that results in a person being used simply as a means for others' gains would be ethically unacceptable.

With respect to deception in research, from a deontological perspective, since we would not believe it moral to intentionally deceive individuals across a variety of other contexts, neither the potential benefits to society nor the effectiveness of participant debriefing (informing participants about the true nature of the study after their participation is completed) for a particular deception study can morally justify intentionally deceiving persons about the purpose or nature of the study. Further, from a Kantian perspective, deception in research is not ethically permissible, since intentionally disguising the nature of the study for the goals of research violates the moral obligation to respect each participant's intrinsic worth by undermining that individual's right to make rational and autonomous informed consent decisions regarding participation (Fisher & Fyrberg, 1994).

Utilitarianism or Consequentialism

Utilitarian theory prioritizes the consequences (or utility) of an act over the application of universal principles (Mill, 1861/1957). From this perspective, an ethical decision is situation specific and must be governed by a risk–benefit calculus that determines which act will produce the greatest possible balance of good over bad consequences. An "act utilitarian" makes an ethical decision by evaluating the consequences of an act for a given situation. A "rule utilitarian" makes an ethical decision by evaluating whether following a general rule in all similar situations would create the greater good. Like deontology, utilitarianism is impersonal: It does not take into account interpersonal and relational features of ethical responsibility. From this perspective, psychologists' obligations to those with whom they work can be superseded by an action that would produce a greater good for others.

A psychologist adhering to act utilitarianism might decide that the potential knowledge about social behavior during an embarrassing situation generated by this deception study could produce benefits for many members of society, thereby justifying the minimal risk of harm that the embarrassment might cause and the violation of autonomy rights based on the absence of true informed consent for only a few research participants. A rule utilitarian might decide against the use of deception in all research studies because the unknown benefits to society do not outweigh the potential harm to the discipline of psychology if society began to see it as an untrustworthy science.

Communitarianism

Communitarian theory assumes that right actions derive from community values, goals, traditions, and cooperative virtues. It considers the common good, community values and goals, and cooperative virtues as fundamental to ethical decision making (MacIntyre, 1989; Melchert, 2015; Walzer, 1983). Communitarianism is often contrasted with liberal individualism, an ethical theory that privileges the individual over the group and identifies individual autonomy, privacy, property, free speech, and freedom of religion as the cornerstones of a civil society, thus elevating individual over group rights (Beauchamp & Childress, 2001; Dworkin, 1977). Although all forms of communitarianism support ethical decisions that improve the health and welfare of members of the community, some forms value group welfare over individual rights and reject the deontological categorical imperative that ethical decisions have universal application across different communities.

Whereas utilitarianism asks whether a policy will produce the greatest good for all individuals in society, communitarianism asks whether a policy will promote the kind of community we want to live in (Steinbock et al., 2003). For example, from a communitarian perspective, the competent practice of psychology cannot be defined simply in terms of individual interpretations of ethical standards but rather must be consistently evaluated and affirmed through interdependent and communal dialogue and support among members of the field (Johnson, Barnett, Elman, Forrest, & Kaslow, 2013).

The challenge to a communitarian perspective is the question of which community values should be represented in ethical decision making. Drawing on the principle of justice, Fisher and her colleagues have argued that the values of a majority may not reflect the needs or values of a more vulnerable minority within a community. For this reason, scientific, intervention, or policy decisions made in response to majority values may result in or perpetuate health disparities and other inequities suffered by marginal groups (Fisher, 1999, 2011; Fisher et al., 2002; Fisher & Wallace, 2000). For example, sensitivity to "who is the community" is particularly important when psychologists are consulting with community "representatives" in the design and evaluation of social or educational programs. Restricting consultation to community leaders and program administrators may result in programs that fail to adequately serve the members most in need.

Research psychologists who believe deception research is ethically justified can be conceived as members of a scientific community of shared values that has traditionally assumed (a) the pursuit of knowledge is a universal good, (b) the results of deception research are intrinsically valuable, and (c) consideration for the practical consequences of research will inhibit scientific progress (Fisher, 1999; Sarason, 1984; Scarr, 1988). The historical salience of these shared values may be implicitly reflected, at least in part, in the acceptance of deception research in the APA Ethics

Code (Standard 8.07, Deception in Research) and in current federal regulations (Department of Health and Human Services [DHHS], 2009). However, little is known about the extent to which the "community of research participants" shares the scientific community's valuing of deception methods. The participant community may instead place greater value on their right to determine whether they will be exposed to specific research risks and benefits and on society's need to perceive scientists as members of a trustworthy profession.

Relational Ethics

Relational ethics, originating out of feminist ethics or an ethics of care, sees a commitment to act on behalf of persons with whom one has a significant relationship as central to ethical decision making. This moral theory rejects the primacy of universal values of deontology and the cost–benefit calculus of utilitarianism in favor of relationally specific obligations (Baier, 1985; Brabeck, 2000; Fisher, 1999, 2000, 2004). It also rejects communitarianism's emphasis on group norms and instead stresses the importance of the uniqueness of individuals embedded in relationships. Relational ethics focuses our attention on power imbalances and supports efforts to promote equality of power and opportunity for women and other marginalized groups (Brabeck & Brabeck, 2012; Sechzer & Rabinowitz, 2008). It underscores the value of understanding the point of view, needs, and expectations of clients/patients, research participants, and others as a means of enhancing psychologists' own moral development and ethical decision making (Fisher, 2000; Noddings, 1984).

In relational ethics, responsiveness to research participants and psychologists' awareness of their own boundaries, competencies, and obligations are the foundation of ethics-in-science decision-making (Fisher, 1999, 2002a, 2004, 2011). From a relational perspective, in the absence of dialogue with prospective participants, the psychologists designing the "Gaffe" study, by virtue of their training and institutional positions, may have overestimated the scientific validity and value of the study and underestimated undergraduates' stress, discomfort, and sense of disempowerment during the study and following debriefing (Fisher & Fyrberg, 1994). Thus, relational ethics would view this study as a violation of investigators' obligations of interpersonal trust to participants and as reinforcing power inequities by permitting faculty members to deprive undergraduates of information that might affect their decision to participate.

Ethical Absolutism, Ethical Relativism, and Ethical Contextualism

Psychologists with high levels of ethical commitment and awareness are often stymied by moral complexities that surface when individuals or cultural communities with whom they work hold values that are or appear to be distinctly different from the Ethics Code aspirational principles, contrary to evidence-based "right" clinical outcomes, or inconsistent with federal regulations and professional guidelines for protecting the rights and welfare of research participants. Such dilemmas can be framed in three different ways.

The first, termed "ethical absolutism," adopts the universal perspective of the deontic position and rejects the influence of culture on the identification and resolution of ethical problems in a manner that can lead to a one-size-fits-all form of ethical problem solving. However, psychologists who adopt an absolutist stance misconceive the discipline of psychology as an impartial helping or scientific profession whose values and techniques are universally related to the essential humanity of those with whom we work (Fisher, 1999; Koenig & Richeson, 2010). For example, drawing on Principle C, Integrity, a psychologist who has learned that a child client has a genetic marker for a serious adult onset disorder may believe it is his ethical duty to share this information with the child, without considering other moral positions, including the child's right to have one's future options kept open until one is old enough to make one's own life choices (Millum, 2014).

In sharp contrast, "ethical relativism," often associated with some forms of utilitarianism and communitarianism, denies the existence of universal or common moral values characterizing the whole of human relationships, proposing instead that how ethical problems are identified and resolved is unique to each particular culture or community. This can result in confusing what "is" for what "ought" to be (Melchert, 2015). For example, this stance runs the risk of condoning client or organizational behaviors, beliefs, and attitudes that reflect systemic cultural injustices or cultural values such as racism, heterosexism, or misogyny that are iatrogenic to a client's mental health or the well-being of employees or those whom organizations serve (Cassidy, 2013; Fisher, 2014; Knapp & VandeCreek, 2007).

Ethical contextualism, variously known as cross-cultural ethics or moral realism, blends the two approaches and assumes that moral principles such as beneficence, integrity, social justice, and respect for people's rights and dignity are or should be universally valued across diverse contexts and cultures, but the expression of an ethical problem and the right actions to resolve it can be unique to the cultural context (Fisher, 1999, 2000, 2014; Korchin, 1980; Macklin, 1999; Melchert, 2015). This position is reflected in the *Universal Declaration of Ethical Principles for Psychologists* (International Union of Psychological Science, 2008), which includes an articulation of ethical contextualism in its recognition that these value principles may be expressed in different ways in different communities and cultures and that respect for different customs and beliefs should be limited only when they seriously contravene "the dignity of persons or peoples or causes serious harm to their well-being." Consistent with the relational or feminist ethics framework, psychologists taking a contextual stance are motivated to understand how ethical values may be differentially expressed across different cultural contexts and to identify when group acceptance of a norm is inconsistent with a basic universal morality.

CASE EXAMPLE

Working With a Client With Racist Attitudes and Behaviors

Psychotherapists may wrestle with ethical principles guiding treatment of clients/patients with impulse control or cognitive or emotional disorders whose symptomatology includes expressions of racist attitudes and behaviors. Consider the case of a client who has been suspended from work for continued harassment of and threats against his Hispanic coworkers.

Psychologists applying an ethical absolutist position might jump to the conclusion that since racism and intolerance are universally morally reprehensible, the client has no regard for right and wrong or the feelings of others and thus is suffering not only from possible impulse control disorders but also from the more character-based antisocial or paranoid personality disorder.

By contrast, those holding a relativist position might decide that the best approach would be to treat the mental health problem as distinct from the client's prejudicial attitudes because of their belief that psychologists should be accepting of their clients' socially constructed values.

Approaching this dilemma from an ethical contextual perspective, psychologists would base their treatment plan on the assumption that, given intolerant beliefs driving the client's behavior are inconsistent with basic moral values, the crucial task for the psychologist is to understand the meaning and function of the racist attitudes and behaviors as they relate to the client's mental health problems and address both the racism and mental health conditions during treatment.

Ethical Competence

Too often, psychologists approach ethics as an afterthought to assessment or treatment plans, research designs, course preparation, or groundwork for forensic or consulting activities. Ethical planning based on familiarity with ethical standards, professional guidelines, state and federal laws, and organizational and institutional policies should be seen as integral rather than tangential to psychologists' work.

Need to Know: "Why Good Students Go Bad"

Burkholder & Burkholder (2014) identified four ethical pitfalls that often lead students to commit ethical violations:

- Beliefs that the Ethics Code is optional or only applies to "bad" people
- Personal characteristics, such as mental health and substance abuse disorders, that distract from a focus on learning how to integrate ethics into professional activities

- Poor advisement or supervision or misguidance, leading to deficient preparation and training
- Overenthusiasm, pressure to achieve high grades, or rushing to complete training requirements that leads to a blurring of appropriate boundaries, taking inadequate steps to protect confidentiality, or taking other ethical shortcuts in science or practice

Ethical Planning

Ethical commitment and well-informed ethical planning will reduce but not eliminate ethical challenges that emerge during the course of psychologists' work. Ideally, ethical competence should be "preventive." A working understanding of ethical theories, Ethics Code principles and standards, scientific and professional guidelines, laws, and organizational policies should help psychologists anticipate situations that require ethical planning before a problem occurs.

Need to Know: Ethical Competence and Ethical Planning

Obtaining the competencies necessary to recognize when a situation requires ethical decision making is a daunting task for graduate students, early career professionals, and seasoned professionals (Moffett, Becker, & Patton, 2014). To limit mistakes that can be made when facing unexpected ethical challenges, whenever psychologists begin new professional or scientific work, they should do the following:

- Evaluate their role responsibilities and ensure they have the competencies required to fulfill these roles
- Identify the potential psychological, social, or legal vulnerabilities of those with whom they will work
- Become familiar with commonly established ethical procedures for the type of activities in which they will be engaged, the populations with whom they will work, and the work setting
- Develop a plan to readily draw on the ethical standards, professional guidelines, organizational policies, and laws that should guide their decision making if unanticipated ethical situations arise and identify colleagues who can provide consultation

Competence and Ethical Decision Making

Ethical competence is also necessary to identify unanticipated situations that require ethical decision making. Ethical problems often arise when two or more principles or standards appear to be in conflict, when unexpected events occur, or in response to unforeseen reactions of those with whom a psychologist works. There is no ethical menu from which the right ethical actions can simply be selected. Many ethical challenges are unique in time, place, and persons involved. The very process of generating and evaluating alternative courses of action helps place in vivid relief the moral principles underlying such conflicts and stimulates creative strategies that may resolve or eliminate them.

Ethical decisions are neither singular nor static. They involve a series of steps, each of which will be determined by the consequences of previous steps. Evaluation of alternative ethical solutions should take a narrative approach that sequentially considers the potential risks and benefits of each action. Understanding of relevant laws and regulations as well as the nature of institutions, companies, or organizations in which the activities will take place is similarly essential for adequate evaluation of the reactions and restraints imposed by the specific ethical context.

Ethical Standards

Familiarity with the rules of conduct set forth in the Ethical Standards enables psychologists to take preventive measures to avoid the harms, injustices, and violations of individual rights that often lead to ethical complaints. For example, psychologists familiar with the standards on confidentiality and disclosure discussed in Chapter 7 will take steps in advance to (a) develop appropriate procedures to protect the confidentiality of information obtained during their work-related activities; (b) appropriately inform research participants, clients/patients, organizational clients, and others in advance about the extent and limitations of confidentiality; and (c) develop specific plans and lists of appropriate professionals, agencies, and institutions to be used if disclosure of confidential information becomes necessary.

Guidelines

Good ethical planning also involves familiarity with guidelines for responsible practice and science. The APA and other professional and scientific organizations publish guidelines for responsible practice appropriate to particular psychological activities. Guidelines, unlike ethical standards, are essentially aspirational and unenforceable. As a result, compared with the enforceable Ethics Code standards, guidelines can include recommendations for and examples of responsible conduct with greater specificity to role, activity, and context. For example, Standard 2.01, Boundaries of Competence, requires psychologists to limit their services to populations and areas within their boundaries of competence, but as a general standard it does not specify what such competencies are in different work contexts. By contrast, guidelines such as those for multicultural education, training, research, practice, and organizational change (APA, 2003) describe the specific areas of training, education, or supervision that psychologists must have to perform their jobs competently. The Guidelines for the Evaluation of Dementia and Evaluation of Age-Related Cognitive Change (APA, 2012d) provide a list of necessary competencies, including memory changes associated with normative aging and the broad range of medical, pharmacological, and mental health disorders (e.g., depression) that can influence cognition in older adults. The crafters of guidelines developed by APA constituencies usually attempt to ensure that their recommendations are consistent with the most current APA Ethics Code. However, readers should be alert to instances in which the 2010 Ethics Code renders some guideline recommendations adopted prior to 2010 obsolete. Specific Guidelines are discussed throughout this book where their relevance to ethical standards can be applied. Continuously updated links to APA guidelines are provided at http://study.sagepub.com/fisher4e.

Laws, Regulations, and Policies

Another important element of information gathering is identifying and understanding applicable laws, government regulations, and institutional and organizational policies that may dictate or limit specific courses of action necessary to resolve an ethical problem. There are state and federal laws and organizational policies governing patient privacy, mandated reporting for child abuse and neglect and elder abuse, research with humans and animals, conduct among military enlistees and officers, employment discrimination, conflicts of interest, billing, and treatment. For example, practicing psychologists need to be familiar with rules and procedures under the Health Insurance Portability and Accountability Act (HIPAA). Those working in schools must understand privacy rights protections under the Family Education Rights and Privacy Act (FERPA). Psychologists involved in forensically relevant activities must also be familiar with continuing evaluation of rules of evidence governing expert testimony, and research psychologists need to know the Department of Health and Human Services Part 46 Protection of Human Subjects. The relevance of these laws to the science and practice of psychology is discussed throughout this volume.

As discussed in Chapter 2, only a handful of Ethical Standards require psychologists to adhere to laws or institutional rules. However, choosing an ethical path that violates law, institutional rules, or company policy can have serious consequences for psychologists and others. Laws and policies should not dictate ethics, but familiarity with legal and organizational rules is essential for informed ethical decision making. When conflicts between ethics and law arise, psychologists consider the consequences of the decision for stakeholders, use practical wisdom to anticipate and take preventive actions for complications that can arise, and draw on professional virtues to help identify the moral principles most salient for meeting professional role obligations (Knapp, Gottlieb, Berman, & Handelsman, 2007).

Stakeholders

Ethical decision making requires sensitivity to and compassion for the views of the affected individuals. Discussions with stakeholders can clarify the multifaceted nature of an ethical problem, illuminate ethical principles that are in jeopardy of being violated or ignored, and alert psychologists to potential unintended consequences of specific action choices. In research, this means enhancing external validity and the generalizability of findings by understanding the realities of participants' lives. To this end, psychologists draw on the perspectives of prospective participants to ensure that the research design and procedures reflect their values and merit their trust. Psychologists also consult with other community stakeholders to ensure reasonable steps are taken to avoid community harm that may arise following dissemination of research results (Fisher, 1999, 2004, 2015).

In assessment, attention to stakeholder perspectives requires consideration of how examinees' understanding of the purpose of a test and their trust in the integrity of the testing process may facilitate or hinder test validity. It can also include considering how the way in which a client's assessment report is written may affect family members or other third parties. In therapy, stakeholder sensitivity entails attending to clients'/patients' responses to treatment and modifying approaches based on such feedback rather than simply categorizing failure to respond as a form of resistance or other weakness on the part of the client/patient. Sensitivity also requires understanding that family caretakers of children or mentally impaired adults and other professionals providing services in schools, organizations, or integrated health care systems can be affected by or have an effect on treatment outcomes.

By taking steps to understand the concerns, values, and perceptions of clients/patients, research participants, family members, organizational clients, students, IRBs or corporate compliance officers, and others with whom they work, psychologists can avoid making decisions that would be ineffective or harmful (Fisher, 1999, 2000).

Steps in Ethical Decision Making

A number of psychologists have proposed excellent ethical decision-making models to guide the responsible conduct of psychological science and practice (e.g., Barnett, Zimmerman, & Walfish, 2014; Canter et al., 1994; Handelsman et al., 2005; Kitchener & Anderson, 2011; Koocher & Keith-Spiegel, 2008; Newman, Gray, & Fuqua, 1996; Rest, 1983; Staal & King, 2000). A six-step model is proposed that draws on these models and the importance of ethical commitment, awareness, and competence:

Step 1: Through a sustained professional commitment to doing what is right, develop the skills to identify when a situation raises ethical issues. This commitment includes (a) continuous reflection on the personal versus professional values and potential conflicts of interest influencing reactions to ethical dilemmas and (b) ongoing implementation of appropriate self-care strategies to guard against the influence of occupational stress.

Step 2: Consider the relevant APA Ethics Code General Principles and Ethical Standards and scientific and professional guidelines as well as organizational policies.

Step 3: Determine whether there are local, state, and federal laws specific to the ethical situation. Identify also the procedures required to be in compliance with these laws and the consequences of legal action for the welfare of individuals with whom the psychologist works and relevant third parties.

Step 4: Make efforts to understand the perspective of different stakeholders who will be affected by and who will affect the outcome of the decision. These efforts should help illuminate aspects of the dilemma that are related to power, privilege, and sociopolitical oppression.

Step 5: Apply Steps 1 to 4 to generate ethical alternatives. Assess the competencies required to implement each alternative and consult with colleagues if necessary. Consider how different ethical theories might prioritize each alternative. Select the alternative that best fulfills one's obligations under the Ethics Code and has the greatest likelihood of protecting the rights and welfare of those who will be affected.

Step 6: Monitor and evaluate the effectiveness of the course of action. Modify and continue to evaluate the ethical plan if feasible and necessary.

The cases at the end of each chapter and the 10 case studies in Appendix A provide readers with the opportunity to creatively apply the ethical decision-making model described above and the knowledge they gain in reading chapters throughout this book to ethical challenges across a broad range of psychological work. The next section provides an example of how the six ethical decision-making steps can be applied to an ethical dilemma.

CASE EXAMPLE

An Example of Ethical Decision Making

Dr. Ames conducts individual and group therapy for young adults with dual diagnosis (substance dependence and anxiety disorders) whom she sees in her private practice. Although Dr. Ames was careful not to enter into the group those of her patients who were friends, partners, or relatives, she has recently learned that two group members (James and Angela) have started to date one another. In her next individual therapy session, Angela excitedly tells Dr. Ames that she is pregnant and is planning to move in with James, the father of her baby. When asked if she has seen a doctor, Angela replies that she does not have health insurance and has nothing to worry about since neither she nor James has any diseases. Dr. Ames knows from previous individual sessions with James that he is HIV positive. She asks Angela's permission to speak with James about their new situation, and Angela agrees. During his next session, James tells Dr. Ames that he does not plan to tell Angela that he is HIV positive because she would leave him. He also angrily reminds Dr. Ames that she is "sworn to secrecy" because she promised that everything he told her, except child abuse or hurting someone, would be confidential.

Step 1: Ethical Commitment. Dr. Ames is committed to doing the right thing. She thinks of herself as honest, judicious, respectful, and compassionate. She struggles with her desire to maintain James' confidentiality about his HIV status and her concern about the health risks to Angela and her pregnancy. She recognizes that as a new mother herself, she places a high value on the importance of parental responsibility for an infant's health and welfare, and her new parental status is influencing her reaction to Angela's disclosure. Since her return from a maternity leave, she has been diligent in instituting self-care strategies to address the dual stressors of work and new parenthood.

Step 2: Relevant ethical principles, standards, guidelines, and organizational policies. Dr. Ames reviews the Ethics Code standards. She realizes that because two of her group therapy patients have unexpectedly entered into a romantic relationship discussed only in their individual sessions that she is confronting an unforeseen potentially harmful multiple relationship (Standard 3.05b, Multiple Relationships). She realizes that her concerns regarding the health risks to Angela and her baby and her conflict over maintaining James' confidentiality can potentially compromise her objectivity and effectiveness in performing her job. According to Standard 3.05b, she must take reasonable steps to resolve the problem with due regard for the best interests of all the affected persons.

Dr. Ames also recognizes that while it is important to protect James' confidentiality (Standard 4.01, Maintaining Confidentiality), the Ethics Code permits her to disclose confidential information to protect others from harm (Standard 4.05, Disclosures). She had thought that her informed consent procedure was consistent with ethical standards, since she did inform James and all her individual and group clients/patients of her legal obligation to report child abuse and the possibility that disclosure could also occur to protect others from harm (Standard 4.02, Discussing the Limits of Confidentiality). However, although she was prepared to address issues of group members fraternizing outside of group, she did not anticipate that this type of situation would arise, and she is unsure about the answers to the following questions. Should James' decision to intentionally keep his HIV status secret and to continue to have unprotected sex with Angela be considered "harm" to another person? Did the consent language adequately inform Dr. Ames' clients/patients that the risk of transmitting HIV would meet the criteria for disclosure (Standards 10.01, Informed Consent to Therapy; 10.03, Group Therapy)?

Dr. Ames also reviews the Ethics Code's aspirational principles. She recognizes that she has a fiduciary responsibility to both James and Angela that rests on establishing relationships of trust (Principle B: Fidelity and Responsibility) and worries that the therapeutic alliance with James may be jeopardized if she discloses his HIV status to Angela and that her therapeutic alliance with Angela may be compromised if she is perceived to be colluding with James in a secret that could be harmful to the health of Angela and her baby (Principle A: Beneficence and Nonmaleficence, Principle C: Integrity, and Principle E: Respect for People's Rights and Dignity).

Step 3: Federal, state, and civil law. Dr. Ames consults with legal counsel at her state psychological association and discovers that her state does not have a "duty to protect" law requiring clinicians to take steps to protect identified others from harm (see Chapter 7), nor does it impose criminal penalties on people living with HIV who know their HIV status and potentially expose others to HIV. In addition, her state's mandatory child abuse–reporting laws do not extend to pregnancy. Her state does not have a prohibition against a mental health professional revealing a client's HIV status to a third party if there is a high risk of transmission to this third party. HIPAA also permits disclosure of information to protect against serious harm to others. However, the attorney also informs her that if she disclosed such information, she might incur legal liability under a variety of civil laws.

Step 4: Stakeholders. Dr. Ames consults with medical colleagues regarding the probability that James will transmit the virus to Angela and the risks to the fetus and learns that infectivity rates are highly variable, ranging from 1 per 1,000 to 1 per 3 contacts, that mother to child transmission is 15% to 30% and occurs mostly in the last trimester, and that diagnosis and treatment during pregnancy can reduce perinatal transmission (Centers for Disease Control and Prevention, 2015). She also speaks to the prenatal department of the community clinic and finds out that health care providers there routinely provide pregnant women with information regarding HIV risk protection and available HIV testing. To ensure that she is sensitive to the cultural context from which James' and Angela's reactions to her decision may be embedded, she also consults with staff in the community outreach department. Some staff express the belief that the risk of HIV is well-known in the community and that Angela is responsible for protecting herself. Others believe that James is violating community standards and that he has therefore given away his right to confidentiality (see Fisher et al., 2009). Still others point out that Dr. Ames may lose the trust of the rest of her group therapy members if she violates James' confidentiality (Standard 10.03, Group Therapy). Through all of these discussions, Dr. Ames is careful not to reveal the identities of James and Angela (Standard 4.06, Consultations).

Step 5: Generating alternatives and selecting a course of action. Dr. Ames begins to contemplate alternative actions. From a Kantian/deontic perspective, by not disclosing the HIV risk information to Angela, she would fulfill her confidentiality commitment to James, on which his autonomous consent to participate was based. At the same time, Kant's idea of humanity as an end in itself might support taking steps to protect Angela and her fetus from harm. From a utilitarian perspective, the importance of protecting Angela and her fetus from a potentially life-threatening health risk must be weighed against the unknown probability of HIV infection to Angela and her fetus as well as Angela's reaction to the disclosure. Dr. Ames also considers what type of decision would preserve the trust she has developed with her other group therapy clients/patients. The advisory board consultation suggested that there was not a broadly shared common moral perspective that would suggest a specific communitarian or multicultural approach to the problem. From a relational ethics perspective, failing to disclose the information to Angela might perpetuate the powerlessness and victimization of women. At the same time, disclosure might undermine Angela's autonomy if in fact she is aware of HIV risk factors in general and knows or suspects James' HIV positive status.

Dr. Ames decides that she will not at this point disclose James' HIV status to Angela. She concludes that her promise of confidentiality to James is explicitly related to his agreement to participate in treatment, while her sense of obligation to protect Angela from James' behavior is not related to Angela's agreement to participate in individual therapy. The feedback Dr. Ames received from community outreach staff suggests that Angela is most likely aware of the general risks of HIV transmission among drug users, and some of Angela's comments in Dr. Ames' notes from previous sessions reinforce this inference. In addition, Dr. Ames' visit to the clinic indicated that there are community health services that routinely advise pregnant women about these risks and provide HIV testing. Dr. Ames decides that at her next individual session with Angela, and during subsequent sessions, she will encourage her to visit the free prenatal clinic for HIV testing, as well as discuss sexual health, related prenatal risks, and the value of prenatal care. She will also tell James of her decision not to disclose his HIV status to Angela at this time, continue to encourage him to do so, and provide him with written information regarding prenatal HIV risk and safer sexual practices.

Step 6: Monitoring. Dr. Ames will monitor and evaluate the effectiveness of her course of action. During sessions, she will keep apprised of whether Angela visits the prenatal clinic, including whether Angela is tested for HIV. She will also monitor whether James gains the confidence to reveal his HIV status to Angela, especially as Angela enters her third trimester. If Angela remains unaware of her risk, Dr. Ames will ask the couple to come in for a joint session and prepare James in advance for how the information will be shared. In addition, Dr. Ames will continue to evaluate whether the unexpected multiple relationship with James and Angela compromises her ability to maintain objectivity in her individual and group sessions with them and seek consultation if necessary. Dr. Ames also reflects on the adequacy of the criteria she has been using to determine the composition of therapy groups and begins to develop (a) more detailed screening procedures for her individual clients that can identify individuals who may be more prone to romantic or other types of involvement with group members and (b) a plan for referring such clients to another group therapist when appropriate.

Doing Good Well

Ethical decision making in psychology requires flexibility and sensitivity to the context, role responsibilities, and stakeholder expectations unique to each work endeavor. At their best, ethical choices reflect the reciprocal interplay between psychological activities and interpretation of ethical standards in which each is continuously informed and transformed by the other. The specific manner in which the APA Ethics Code General Principles and Ethical Standards are applied should reflect a "goodness of fit" between ethical alternatives and the psychologist's professional role, work setting, and stakeholder needs (Fisher, 2002b, 2003c; Fisher & Goodman, 2009; Fisher & Ragsdale, 2006; Masty & Fisher, 2008). Envisioning the responsible conduct of psychology as a process that draws on psychologists' human responsiveness to those with whom they work and their awareness of their own boundaries, competencies, and obligations will sustain a profession that is both effective and ethical.

Ethics requires self-reflection and the courage to analyze and challenge one's values and actions. Ethical practice is ensured only to the extent that there is a personal commitment accompanied by ethical awareness and active engagement in the ongoing construction, evaluation, and modification of ethical actions. In their commitment to the ongoing identification of key ethical crossroads and the construction of contextually sensitive ethical courses of action, psychologists reflect the highest ideals of the profession and merit the trust of those with whom they work.

HOT TOPIC

The Ethical Component of Self-Care

The professional practice of psychology can be rewarding as well as stressful. Psychological treatment often involves working with clients/patients who express acute or chronic suicidality, engage in self-harm, are victims of abuse or assault, or are coping with the death of loved ones or with their own chronic or fatal disease. Clinicians treating veterans or others with posttraumatic stress disorder (PTSD) are regularly assessing and treating patients struggling with repetitive aggressive or homicidal episodes that may place the client/patient, their family, and the treating psychologist in physical danger (Voss Horrell, Holohan, Didion, & Vance, 2011). Those treating survivors of sexual abuse by family members or strangers may find their clients' experiences have a personal impact on their own worldview and life meaning (Courtois, 2015).

The Emotional Toll of Professional Practice

The emotional toll and precarious nature of this work makes psychologists vulnerable to occupational stress, including emotional exhaustion, depersonalization, and a feeling of lack of personal accomplishment. These outcomes can in turn lead to burnout, overcompensating efforts to "save" clients/patients or participants, boundary violations, and other behaviors that impair job performance (APA Committee on Colleague Assistance, 2006; Lee, Lim, Yang, & Lee, 2011; Webb, 2011). For example, military psychologists with extended deployments to war zones who practice in life-threatening contexts risk direct trauma-related distress and vicarious distress working with traumatized military personnel (W. B. Johnson et al., 2011; Johnson, Bertschinger, Snell, & Wilson, 2014). Psychologists working with patients or research participants who graphically describe child or partner abuse, homelessness and hunger, drug abuse and violence, or death and dying may also experience vicarious or secondary trauma, guilt, or a sense of powerlessness for which there is little institutional support (Fisher, True, Alexander, & Fried, 2013; Mailloux, 2014; McGourty, Farrants, Pratt, & Cankovic, 2010; Simmons & Koester, 2003). Psychologists who have a client/patient die from suicide, accident, or fatal disease may not recognize or receive social support for their own grief reactions (Doka, 2008).

Psychologists conducting clinical research requiring strict adherence to manualized treatment protocols and those working in schools, military hospitals, or correctional facilities may experience the painful feelings and psychological disequilibrium that characterizes moral distress—lack of

(Continued)

(Continued)

professional control to do what they believe is right (Corely, 2002; Fried & Fisher, in press) in response to institutional constraints on caseload, resources, use of evidence-based practices (EBPs), up-to-date assessment instruments, or trained personnel (Maltzman, 2011; O'Brien, 2011; Voss Horrell et al., 2011). School psychologists working in underpopulated rural settings may experience stressors associated with isolation when they feel detached from both the surrounding community and their professional community (Edwards & Sullivan, 2014). Or in response to work-related stressors, psychologists may develop compassion fatigue or begin to process client/patient experiences on a purely cognitive level, a syndrome W. B. Johnson et al. (2011) described as "empathy failure."

"Wounded Healer"

Competent treatment of fatally ill, violent, or suicidal clients/patients may require extensive patient contact, behavioral monitoring, interactions with family members, and significant flexibility in identifying appropriate treatment strategies. Not surprisingly, many ethical dilemmas for psychologists working with these patients revolve around decisions regarding maintaining an appropriate balance between personal and professional boundaries (e.g., Standards 3.04, Avoiding Harm; 3.05, Multiple Relationships; 7.07, Sexual Relationships with Students and Supervisees; and 10.05, Sexual Intimacies with Current Therapy Clients/Patients).

Working in emotionally charged therapeutic contexts can lead to work-related exhaustion, a sense of urgency, and worries that may compromise competent therapeutic decisions (Standard 2.06, Personal Problems and Conflicts). Practitioners who have little or no preparation for treating post-traumatic phenomena may overrespond by engaging in rescue behaviors that blur appropriate professional boundaries or underrespond by distancing, blaming, or responding aggressively to the client, thereby causing additional interpersonal damage (Courtois, 2015). On the other hand, such experiences can lead to unique professional growth. Jackson (2001) introduced the term *wounded healer* to describe how the emotional experience of working with such clients/patients can serve to eventually enhance psychologists' therapeutic endeavors. Voss Horrell et al. (2011) have described similar positive developments in compassion satisfaction and posttraumatic growth in response to the challenges of treating veterans with PTSD.

Mindfulness-Based Stress Reduction

Research and clinical scholarship on the potential for and diminished work competence associated with burnout, social isolation, compassion fatigue, depression, and vicarious traumatization among psychologists working with high-risk populations have led to a widening endorsement of self-care practices as an essential ethical tool in ensuring competence in psychological work (APA, 2012f). Discerning when stress becomes impairment is difficult in the present moment (Barnett, 2008) and thus requires a proactive approach to self-care that mitigates the effect of stressors on professional competence (Tamura, 2012).

One such approach is mindfulness-based stress reduction (MBSR; Kabat-Zinn, 1993) as adapted for the practice of psychology. MBSR is rapidly becoming a popular approach for maintaining appropriate competencies under stressful work conditions. MBSR is a technique for enhancing emotional competence through attention to present-moment inner experience without judgment. It is seen as an effective means of reducing emotional reactions toward and identification with clients'/patients' problems that can lead to therapeutic deficits (Christopher & Maris, 2010; Davis &

Hayes, 2011; Shapiro, Brown, & Biegel, 2007). Several recent studies have demonstrated positive effects of MBSR training on counseling skills and therapeutic relationships, including distribution of self-care educational materials in graduate courses and modeling and mentoring self-care habits in supervisory relationships (Christopher, Christopher, Dunnagan, & Schure, 2006; McCollum & Gehart, 2010).

Practical Guidelines for Self-Care

While there are empirical studies on effective approaches such as MBSR for maintaining and developing the competencies required, several psychologists have generously shared their own experiences and hard-earned professional insights on personal and professional approaches to such challenging cases (Barnett, Cornish, Goodyear, & Lichtenberg, 2007; Bearse, McMinn, Seegobin, & Free, 2013; O'Brien, 2011; Tamura, 2012; Webb, 2011).

Specific self-care strategies for competent practice include the following:

- Minimize risks posed by the social isolation of working in individualized therapeutic settings through formal (peer consultation or supervision) and informal (professional conferences, lunch with peers) activities.
- Schedule activities that are not work related and develop daily strategies for transitioning from work life to home life.
- Develop healthy habits of eating, sleeping, and exercise.
- Set appropriate boundaries for work-related activities such as beginning and ending sessions on time and limiting work-related phone calls or emails to specific times of the day or early evening.
- Diversify work activities and/or caseload.
- Utilize personal psychotherapy as a means of addressing psychological distress and enhancing professional competence through increased self-awareness, self-monitoring, and emotional competence.

Preparing Psychology Trainees for Work-Related Risks and Self-Care

Self-care strategies should be included in graduate education and training and encouraged as lifelong learning techniques (Bamonti et al., 2014; Barnett & Cooper, 2009). Trainees and young professionals may be particularly susceptible to stressors associated with clinical work, especially when programs have not provided training in self-awareness and self-regulation techniques to balance self and other interests and because they lack experience in maintaining emotional competence (Andersson, King, & Lalande, 2010; Shapiro et al., 2007; Tamura, 2012). W. B. Johnson et al. (2011) proposed that psychologists acknowledge the ethical obligation to routinely assess their colleagues' performance. This is especially important in graduate and internship programs in which students may rely on peer and faculty reactions as measures of their own competence. Programs should thus strive to create a culture of community competence that encourages trainees to recognize themselves as vulnerable to work-related stress and reduced competence, to recognize personal and professional dysfunction, and to develop professional self-care habits that support emotional and professional competence. Developing such a culture will require a shift from the current reactive self-care training climate to a proactive and preventive professional one with a focus on wellness and responsibility to self and others (Bamonti et al., 2014).

Chapter Cases and Ethics Discussion Questions

A primary care medical center (PCMC) hires an organizational psychologist to help reduce patient complaints about conflicting diagnoses and treatment recommendations from different members of the interdisciplinary team. Discuss the types of professional virtues or moral dispositions that would be most important to nurture in a program designed to improve the performance of treatment staff.

A psychologist is treating a client with explosive anger disorder who has been in several fights with gang members in his neighborhood. The client has expressed a desire to purchase a firearm as protection against the gang. The state has just enacted a law requiring mental health professionals to file a report with a firearm background check database if the client threatens harm to themselves or others. Discuss how different ethical theories might lead to different decisions about whether reporting the client is ethically justified. (Readers may wish to refer to Kangas and Calvert, 2014.)

A graduate teaching assistant (GTA) has repeatedly cancelled the undergraduate experimental psychology lab section she is teaching and was late grading students' final papers. The professor responsible for the class was aware the GTA was having trouble keeping up with her graduate coursework and, as a result, had taken on some of the GTA's responsibilities during the semester. The professor is required to complete an end-of-semester GTA evaluation. A poor evaluation can contribute to the GTA losing her assistantship. Discuss how the perspectives and interests of different stakeholders should be considered as the professor decides what to include on the evaluation form.

PART II

Enforceable Standards

CHAPTER 4

Standards for Resolving Ethical Issues

1. Resolving Ethical Issues

1.01 Misuse of Psychologists' Work

If psychologists learn of misuse or misrepresentation of their work, they take reasonable steps to correct or minimize the misuse or misrepresentation.

Psychologists have professional and scientific responsibilities to society and to the specific individuals, organizations, and communities with whom they work to ensure that their work products are not misused or misrepresented. Psychologists cannot reasonably be expected to anticipate all the ways in which their work can be wrongly used. Thus, Standard 1.01 of the APA Ethics Code (APA, 2010b) focuses on corrective action that must be taken when psychologists learn that others have misused or misrepresented their work. To remedy misuse, psychologists can write letters to or speak with interested parties, request retraction of misrepresentations, or discuss with appropriate persons the corrective measures to be taken.

> ✓ A school psychologist completed a report summarizing her assessment of a child whose test results did not meet diagnostic criteria for serious emotional disturbance. Several days later, she learned that the principal of her school, who desired to fill a special education quota, had forwarded to the superintendent of schools only those parts of the assessment report that could be interpreted as confirming the student as having a serious emotional disturbance. The psychologist asked the principal to send the entire report, explaining the ethical issues involved (Standard 1.03, Conflict Between Ethics and Organizational Demands).

- ☑ A research psychologist learned that a special interest group had sent a listserv mailing for financial contributions that misquoted and misrepresented the psychologist's writings as supporting the group's cause. The psychologist contacted the group and asked it to cease sending this email to other potential contributors and to email a correction to the listserv recipients.
- ☑ A health psychologist who had developed a commercially marketed instrument for assessing environmental and psychosocial risks for children diagnosed with asthma discovered that the company responsible for test scoring had miskeyed some of the items. The psychologist contacted the company and requested that it (a) immediately correct the error for future use, (b) rescore tests that had been subject to the miskeying, and (c) send practitioners who had used the scoring service the rescored test results with a letter of explanation.

The phrase *reasonable steps* in Standard 1.01 recognizes that despite their best efforts in some instances, psychologists may not be in a position to ensure that their requests to correct misuse are followed. For example, if the research psychologist whose work had been misrepresented did not have access to the listserv and if the group refused requests for retraction, short of a civil suit, the psychologist would have few corrective options. In other instances, it may not be possible or appropriate to actively seek a correction. For example, during a trial, attorneys may phrase questions that, by their nature, distort or otherwise lead to misrepresentation of a psychologist's testimony. In such instances, it is ethically appropriate for psychologists at the time of their testimony to (a) rely on existing corrective mechanisms (i.e., asking the judge to permit the psychologist to provide clarification; responding as fully as possible to a related question during cross-examination) or (b) refrain from corrective actions when an attempt to remedy the misrepresentation would violate the rules of the court or the legal rights of a complainant or defendant (see Standard 2.01f, Boundaries of Competence). Psychologists should always document the corrective efforts made to remedy known misuse or misrepresentations.

Need to Know: Reasonable Expectations for Awareness of Misuse

Frequently, psychologists will not be aware that their work has been misrepresented, and in such cases, inaction on their part would not be an ethical violation. However, when it is reasonable to expect that psychologists would be aware of misuse or misrepresentation of their work, a claim of ignorance would not be an acceptable defense against a charge of violation of this standard (Canter et al., 1994; Standard 3.04, Avoiding Harm). The following case (although involving a psychiatrist) illustrates a situation in which it would be reasonable to expect

(Continued)

(Continued)

awareness of the misuse of one's work. In 2001, Dr. Robert Spitzer presented a paper at a psychiatry meeting describing a telephone survey of gay and lesbian patients who reported that participation in "reparative therapy" had successfully reoriented them to heterosexuality. The paper was immediately seized on as supporting evidence by groups who believed sexual orientation was a choice and by politicians to argue against civil unions. Dr. Spitzer was aware of these responses to his paper, as well as serious methodological flaws in his research, but he convinced a colleague who was a journal editor to publish the article without its undergoing the traditional peer review. It was not until 2012 that Dr. Spitzer wrote the gay community an apology for the harm that had resulted from misinterpretation of his work (Carey, 2012).

1.02 Conflicts Between Ethics and Law, Regulations, or Other Governing Legal Authority

If psychologists' ethical responsibilities conflict with law, regulations, or other governing legal authority, psychologists clarify the nature of the conflict, make known their commitment to the Ethics Code, and take reasonable steps to resolve the conflict consistent with the General Principles and Ethical Standards of the Ethics Code. Under no circumstances may this standard be used to justify or defend violating human rights.

As highlighted in Chapter 3, to ethically navigate conflicting obligations, psychologists must have sufficient understanding of the Ethics Code standards and be familiar with laws and regulations relevant to their activities as psychologists (APA, 2012f). Standard 1.02, amended in 2010 (APA, 2010c), addresses instances in which the requirements of the Ethics Code may conflict with judicial authority, with state or federal laws, or with regulations governing the activities of psychologists working in the military, correctional facilities, or other areas of public service. Standard 1.02 requires that psychologists take action when conflicts between the Ethics Code and laws, regulations, or governing legal authority arise. Specific steps that may be taken include informing appropriate authorities of the conflict, explaining the rationale for the Ethics Code standard, and recommending ways to resolve the conflict consistent with General Principles and Ethical Standards.

⊘ A research psychologist had recently completed an intervention study designed to improve mother–infant interaction patterns of teen parents. All interactions were videotaped for coding. The psychologist received a request from Child Protective Services (CPS) for the videotapes of a participant whom CPS was currently investigating for charges of child neglect. In consultation with her university attorney, the psychologist sent a letter to CPS respectfully refusing to release the tapes. The letter explained the confidentiality that had been promised to all participants and her obligation to protect participant confidentiality under the Ethics Code (Standard 4.01, Protecting Confidentiality; Standard 8.02, Informed Consent to Research).

- A correctional psychologist refused a request from the prison warden to draw upon his therapy sessions with a prisoner to help the warden recommend punishment for the prisoner after he had gotten into a fight with a fellow inmate. The psychologist explained to the warden that to do so could violate several ethical standards, including 1.01, Misuse of Psychologists' Work; 3.05, Multiple Relationships; and 4.01, Maintaining Confidentiality.

When a Conflict Cannot Be Resolved

Standard 1.02 also recognizes that legal and regulatory authorities may not always respond to specific steps taken or recommended by psychologists to resolve conflicts between ethics and law. When reasonable actions taken by psychologists do not resolve the conflict, they are permitted to make a conscientious decision to comply with the legal or regulatory authority under circumstances in which their actions cannot be used to justify or defend violating human rights (Trestman, 2014).

The permissive portion of the standard recognizes that in some contexts, when legal ethics and professional ethics conflict, each may be equally defensible in terms of moral principles. For example, in some instances, a judicial review requested by a psychologist in response to a court order may determine that full release of confidential therapy notes is required to protect the legal right of a defendant or plaintiff to a fair trial. In such situations, Principle D: Justice is in conflict with Principle E: Respect for People's Rights and Dignity, and Standard 1.02 permits psychologists to draw upon ethical decision-making strategies, as described in Chapter 3, to decide whether to obey or disobey the court order.

In other instances, emergencies that arise in correctional settings or war zones may require psychologists whose ordinary role is to provide treatment to take on a temporary enforcement role to prevent clients/patients or others from physical harm. In such situations, Principle A: Beneficence and Nonmaleficence may be in conflict with Principle B: Fidelity and Responsibility and Standard 3.05, Multiple Relationships. Standard 1.02 allows psychologists to make a reasoned decision regarding whether engaging or refraining from such roles is ethically justified as long as their actions do not contribute to or justify violations of human rights.

It is important to note that Standard 1.02 does *not* require compliance with law. The intentional absence of such a requirement reflects the APA's long-standing commitment to the value of civil disobedience in response to unjust laws. Relatedly, psychologists should not assume that Standard 1.02 waives their obligation to adhere to other standards of the Ethics Code when laws are unjust. To the contrary, as described in the next section, the 2010 amended language to Standard 1.02

makes clear that the participation of psychologists in an activity that can be used by others to justify or defend violations of human rights, even when lawful, is a violation of the APA Ethics Code.

Psychology and Human Rights

The language of Standard 1.02 approved by APA Council in August 2002 did not contain the last sentence prohibiting psychologists from following the law when their professional activities could be used to justify or defend violating human rights. As in the illustrations above, the original intent of this standard was to recognize that in some situations, laws requiring psychologists to disclose confidential information or assume a dual role, while inconsistent with specific Ethics Code standards, may nonetheless meet APA aspirational principles. However, following the 2002 Ethics Code adoption, APA members became increasingly aware of reports that psychologists were actively involved in the psychologically and physically harsh interrogations of post-9/11 detainees thought to be a threat to national security (Lewis, 2004; Steele & Morlin, 2007). Such techniques included waterboarding and sensory deprivation, which under international law were and continue to be considered torture (United Nations, 1984).

When legal interpretations by the George W. Bush administration indicated that such acts did not meet the definition of torture and thus were legally permitted in military and other government interrogations, it became apparent to many APA members that the absence of a clear prohibition against violations of human rights language in Standard 1.02 could be misinterpreted as "ethically" justifying the use of such harsh interrogation practices under the law. Many members who wanted APA to issue a policy specifically prohibiting psychologists from engaging in these practices were disappointed when the APA issued the Presidential Task Force on Ethics and National Security (PENS) report (APA, 2005) and a subsequent Council of Representatives resolution (APA, 2006) claiming that the participation of psychologists in a consulting role for harsh interrogations declared legal by the White House was consistent with the Ethics Code (Olson et al., 2008). After much controversy within the organization, in 2010 the APA Council of Representatives amended the language of the Code to make clear that psychologists' ethical duties supersede their legal obligations when their activities contribute in any way to a violation of human rights. The APA is also considering a proposed change to Ethics Code Standard 3.04, Avoiding Harm, that would explicitly prohibit psychologists from participation in any activities related to torture or cruel, inhuman, or degrading treatment or punishment. (For additional information, see the "Need to Know" feature below and APA 2010c, 2015d.)

Need to Know: The 2015 Independent Review Relating to APA Ethics Guidelines, Security Interrogations, and Torture

In 2014, the APA board of directors commissioned Mr. David Hoffman of the Sidley Austin law firm to conduct a thorough and independent review of allegations of a relationship between the APA and Bush administration related to the use of abusive interrogation techniques during the War on Terror (APA, 2015d; Risen, 2014). The report found undisclosed coordination between some APA officials and Department of Defense psychologists that had resulted in less restrictive ethical guidance for military psychologists in national security settings and provided a justification of abusive interrogation techniques. The findings were extremely troubling and required action, resulting in the termination and resignation of several APA staff members. The report's findings also led to a new resolution by the APA Council of Representatives at the August 2015 annual meeting (https://www.apa.org/independent-review/psychologists-interrogation.pdf). The resolution does the following:

- Prohibits psychologists from participating in conducting, supervising, assisting, facilitating, or being in the presence of any national security interrogations for any military or intelligence agency or private contractors
- Redefines the term *cruel, inhumane, or degrading treatment or punishment* to be in accordance with the United Nations Convention Against Torture rather than with the 1994 US Reservations to this treaty, "which were co-opted by the Bush administration to justify harsh interrogation techniques"
- Clarifies that psychologists can only provide services in detention or other settings in which torture and other cruel inhuman or degrading treatment or punishment is occurring if they are working directly for persons being detained or for an independent third party seeking to protect human rights

Psychology and International Declarations on Human Rights

The Standard 1.02 prohibition against any activities that may be used to justify or defend violation of human rights, whether or not they are legally sanctioned, highlights the critical intersections between the ethical responsibilities of psychologists and the international human rights movement. Under the United Nation's Universal Declaration of Human Rights and the International Covenant on Economic, Social and Cultural Rights (United Nations, 1948, 1966), governments and their citizenry have a duty to respect the dignity of all human beings and promote and ensure all people's right to life, liberty, and security of persons; freedom from torture or other inhumane punishment; the right to the highest attainable standard of physical and mental health; and conditions that ensure medical service is provided in the event of sickness.

In her 2012 address to the 30th International Congress of Psychology, United Nations high commissioner for human rights Navi Pillay (2012) described how the objectives of psychology and human rights converge. First, psychologists recognize that failure to protect human rights has adverse consequences for health, as exemplified in cases of domestic violence, child abuse, and government-sanctioned torture. Conversely, protection of human rights can enhance psychological well-being. Second, psychologists are aware that mental health activities themselves may violate human rights in settings in which people are involuntarily hospitalized for mental illness based on invalid assessments and subjected to procedures that do not respect their right to personal liberty and security. Conversely, rehabilitation efforts by mental health professionals can help individuals who have been the victims of human rights violations enjoy their freedom and opportunities.

> ✓ A psychologist sought to study PTSD among Somali refugees. In some of the tribal communities in which these individuals had lived, it was customary for male relatives to provide permission for women's participation in any medical or other types of research. Based on current federal regulations and National Bioethics Advisory Committee recommendations (NBAC, 2001), the IRB approved seeking initial male permission followed by each female participant's independent informed consent. However, the investigator quickly realized that women whose male relatives had approved the study were too frightened to refuse participation. The psychologist decided that the IRB-approved consent procedures would unintentionally contribute to the violation of these women's human right to voluntarily participate and did not conduct the study. (See also Standard 8.02, Informed Consent to Research.)

1.03 Conflicts Between Ethics and Organizational Demands

If the demands of an organization with which psychologists are affiliated or for whom they are working are in conflict with this Ethics Code, psychologists clarify the nature of the conflict, make known their commitment to the Ethics Code, and take reasonable steps to resolve the conflict consistent with the General Principles and Ethical Standards of the Ethics Code. Under no circumstances may this standard be used to justify or defend violating human rights.

Organizational norms assist organizations in meeting their obligations through regulating the behavior of board members, business managers, hospital and school administrators, employees, and others who provide services for the organization. The function of an organization determines these norms and often requires psychologists to adopt a role that is different from a healing role (Allen, 2013). Unlike scientific and professional norms in psychology, organizational norms in many instances prioritize the needs or welfare of the organization over those of the individual. This emphasis does not necessarily result in an ethical dilemma. For example, to meet its productivity requirements, a company may ask a psychologist to develop performance tests for specific positions and use the results of the tests to retain or fire employees who do not meet performance criteria. If the company relies on the psychologist's expertise to develop a valid, reliable, and culturally fair test and the nature and purpose of the test are explained to employees, then the demands of the organization and the Ethics Code do not conflict

Standards 3.01, Unfair Discrimination; 3.11b, Psychological Services Delivered To or Through Organizations; 9.02, Use of Assessments; 9.05, Test Construction.

However, psychologists working in or with organizations may encounter company policies, plans, or procedures that conflict with the Ethics Code. For example, an organization that wished to eliminate employees with seniority as a cost-cutting strategy might ask a psychologist to develop a performance test that would be difficult for many older employees to pass. Such a test would be in violation of Principle D: Justice and Standards 3.01, Unfair Discrimination; 9.02, Use of Assessments; and 9.05, Test Construction. In such situations, Standard 1.03 requires that psychologists inform the organization of the nature of the conflict and the ways in which policies or activities violate the Ethics Code, take actions to resolve the conflict in a manner consistent with Ethics Code standards, and refrain from acceding to organization demands since doing so would violate the human rights of employees. The standard specifically requires psychologists to make known their commitment to the Ethics Code in communications with the organization.

- ⊘ An industrial–organizational psychologist recently employed by a company to handle employment testing discovered that the organization used a test for pre-employment screening for which there was no documented evidence that test scores could be validly applied to the competencies required for the job (Standard 9.02b, Use of Assessments). The psychologist notified the employer of the problem and recommended that use of the test be suspended until a more suitable pre-employment screening process could be identified and validated. The psychologist provided a specific, realistic plan for helping the employer move toward an ethical and legally defensible applicant-screening process.
- ⊘ A superintendent of schools asked a counseling psychologist whose job it was to provide career and academic counseling to high school students in the school district to take on an added role as the Title IX officer designated to evaluate and enforce school rules regarding student–student and faculty–student sexual harassment. The psychologist explained that the dual assignment could compromise her ability to effectively conduct either role because it was likely that some students who came to the psychologist for counseling about sexual harassment would need to appear before the psychologist in her Title IX role to press for or defend against sexual harassment charges (Standard 3.05, Multiple Relationships).

The phrase *to the extent feasible* recognizes that despite reasonable efforts by psychologists, an organization may refuse to change a policy that is inconsistent with the Ethics Code. However, the Ethics Code does not accept the "exceptionalist" argument that psychologists working for businesses or other organizations can abandon their ethical responsibilities and moral agency as members of the discipline of psychology when their actions will deprive individuals of their human rights (Candilis & Neal, 2014). Consider for example the situation described above, in which an employer wanted to use a test biased against long-term employees. Psychologists who despite reasonable efforts were unable to convince the organization to change its position would be in violation of Standard 1.03 if they agreed to design and/or administer the instrument that would deprive employees of their right to equal protection against discrimination (United Nations, 1948; Standards 3.01, Unfair Discrimination; 3.04, Avoiding Harm; 3.06, Conflict of Interest; 9.2, Use of Assessments; 9.05, Test Construction).

☒ A psychologist was hired by an HMO to implement preexisting company criteria for mental health services claims. During a utilization review, she noticed that company policy on the use of psychopharmacological medications in the absence of conjoint psychotherapy was counter to recently published evidence-based practice guidelines for the disorder under review and believed that the policy was potentially harmful to patients (Standards 2.04, Bases for Scientific and Professional Judgments; 3.04, Avoiding Harm). The psychologist drew the company's attention to the problem and the relevant APA Ethical Standards, but the HMO management refused to change the policy without a full review of alternative policies. The psychologist agreed to use the preexisting criteria.

☒ A psychologist working for an HMO was asked to develop evidence-based utilization standards for a specific class of mental health disorders. On the basis of current research, he recommended that individuals diagnosed as having this class of disorders receive psychopharmacological medications and conjoint psychotherapy. During a review of the first draft of the psychologist's recommendations, his employer told him that conjoint psychotherapy would significantly diminish the profitability of plans covering the disorder and asked the psychologist to remove the recommendation from the final draft of the report. The psychologist did not attempt to discuss with his employer the ethical issues associated with approving for reimbursement what was known to be inadequate treatment (Standards 2.04, Bases for Scientific and Professional Judgments; 3.04, Avoiding Harm) and simply agreed to change his recommendation in the final report.

Psychologists should not assume that Standard 1.03 waives their obligation to adhere to other standards in this Ethics Code. For example, a psychologist who implemented a health care organization's policy to increase revenue by providing unwarranted treatment to Medicaid patients could be charged with Medicaid fraud and a violation of Standards 6.04b, Fees and Financial Arrangements, and 9.01a, Bases for Assessments, even if the psychologist brought the unethical nature of the policy to the organization's attention (see Acuff et al., 1999).

☒ A recently hired school psychologist discovered that district-mandated test batteries for suspected learning disabilities were outdated, were inconsistent with current professional standards, and violated the intent of special education laws that require tests to be selected in light of the unique characteristics of the individual child. She reasoned that as a new hire, it would be professionally risky to raise this issue with the district school psychology supervisor and decided to do her best for the children using the district's test battery (see Standard 9.02a, Use of Assessments; Jacob & Hartshorne, 2007)

⊘ A prescribing psychologist was employed by a nursing home to assess the psychological status and psychopharmacology needs of residents. She noticed that the excessive job demands placed on nurses' aides were resulting in limited and restrictive patient care. It further promoted an overuse of medications for patient sedation, which in turn was contributing to patients' loss of independent functioning and deterioration of cognitive and other functional capacities. The psychologist recognized that current financial difficulties at the nursing home precluded the hiring of additional nurses' aides. When she approached the institutional director with her concerns about the overmedication, she offered to provide training sessions for the nurses' aides in behavioral techniques that would help reduce patient agitation and encourage greater patient functional independence without adding to the aides' work responsibilities. The director agreed with her recommendation.

Human Rights and Organizational Consulting

Social inequalities embedded within organizations and social institutions are most often the driving force behind human rights violations (Farmer, 2003). A commitment to human rights within organizational settings places new ethical obligations on psychologists that may require uncovering and recommending changes in institutionally entrenched rights violations of which organizational stakeholders may or may not be aware (M. A. Fisher, 2014). It calls upon psychologists working in or consulting to organizations to reevaluate how their work may unintentionally condone organizational practices that justify violation of human rights and are currently prohibited by APA Ethical Standards. Such practices include unfair discrimination against complainants and respondents (Standard 1.08); unfair discrimination based on age, gender, gender identity, race, ethnicity, and other group characteristics (Standard 3.01); provision of psychological services delivered to or through organizations (Standard 3.11); and use of assessment techniques whose validity and reliability have not been established for members of the population tested (Standard 9.02b; APA, 2010b).

Psychologists working in and consulting to organizations must address the needs of multiple stakeholders who differ in terms of power and privilege, for example, administrators, employees, supervisors, and executives (D'Andrea & Daniels, 2010). To help organizations develop fair and just procedures that address institutional bias and meet the needs of all organizational members, psychologists should consider the following actions (see also Fisher, 2015):

- Draw on multicultural knowledge and sensitivity and principles of fairness and social justice to identify organizational policies that condone or justify human rights violations (Romney, 2008; Whealin & Ruzek, 2008).

- Avoid recommendations for organizational change that are grounded solely in the needs and worldview of executives (Romney, 2008).
- Assist organizations in recognizing that to overcome embedded biases requires intervention at the individual (e.g., staff), the organizational (e.g., executive, board of directors), and the larger community level (e.g., policy makers, stockholders; Griffith et al., 2007).
- Help organizations adapt to and use diversity to maintain or improve effectiveness by providing equal access and opportunity (Sue, 2008).

Need to Know: Resolving Ethical Conflicts Through Organizational Advocacy

When a conflict between ethics and organizational demands arise, Standard 1.03 requires psychologists to clarify the conflict and take steps to resolve it. However, psychologists receive little training in how to change the norms of organizations in which they work. Organizational advocacy is a process by which psychologists can influence organizational change by linking desired goals to the organization's vision, mission, and core values. To be effective, before an ethics crisis arises, psychologists should position themselves as key stakeholders in the mission and continuous improvement of the organization. This can be accomplished by embedding themselves in strategic discussions or on key committees so the psychologists can understand the organizational and social realities that potentiate and constrain improvement. They will also have the opportunity to demonstrate how the psychological perspective can support others' views and facilitate change that helps the organization achieve its goals (see Hill, 2013).

Commercially Funded Research

Advances in training programs in neuropsychology, psychopharmacology, and pharmacotherapy have been accompanied by increased participation of psychologists in research on psychoactive and central nervous system medications, drugs, and chemicals. Growing involvement in the empirical assessment of psychotropic medications is likely to be paralleled by increased funding for research psychologists from pharmaceutical companies. Psychologists who are unfamiliar with private industry sponsorship of research may be unprepared for the ethical challenges that arise. While conflict-of-interest dilemmas have been spotlighted in the media and scholarly journals (see Standard 3.06, Conflict of Interest), university-affiliated research psychologists may find themselves experiencing the type of conflict between ethics and organizational demands described in Standard 1.03 when the research sponsor attempts to control the dissemination of research findings.

It should not be surprising that conflicts between ethics and organizations may arise when psychologists' research results are inconsistent with the commercial interests of the company funding their study. When unanticipated risks to participants emerge during a clinical trial, psychologists are obligated to take appropriate steps to minimize such risks (Standard 3.04, Avoiding Harm). Such steps may involve actions the sponsor company objects to, including informing the IRB (Standard 8.01, Institutional Approval), terminating or modifying the study, or informing participants about new adverse events that may influence their willingness to continue in the research (see Standards 3.04, Avoiding Harm; 8.02, Informed Consent to Research). Sponsors may also attempt to prevent publication of data that jeopardize the marketability of their product; they may even exert pressure on psychologists to falsify results (Standard 8.10, Reporting Research Results).

When faced with conflicts between ethics and organizational demands, Standard 1.03 requires that psychologists explain to the sponsor their ethical obligations under the Ethics Code, including their commitment to participant protection and the responsible conduct of research. In so doing, they must develop a plan and take actions to resolve the conflict in a manner that permits adherence to the code. Psychologists and their universities should also be alert to research contracts that include nondisclosure or confidentiality agreements that create additional barriers to resolution of such conflicts.

The highly publicized dispute between university medical school researcher Nancy Olivieri and the commercial sponsor of her research illustrates the type of conflict between ethics and organizations that research psychologists may increasingly face and the ethical problems that can emerge when researchers and their universities fail to ensure that grants from private companies do not carry stipulations that could lead to Ethics Code violations.

CASE EXAMPLE

Conflict Between Ethics and Research Sponsor Demands

Dr. Olivieri received a grant from a private drug manufacturer to begin short-term clinical trials of deferiprone, a drug thought to reduce iron overload in patients with thalassemia. To obtain the grant, she signed a confidentiality agreement stating she would not publish the findings of the trials without prior approval of the company. Following success of the short-term trial, she received a second grant from the manufacturer for a larger-scale study (for which she did not sign a confidentiality agreement). As the research progressed, the data suggested that deferiprone either failed to reduce iron levels or increased them. Against the wishes of the sponsor, she notified the University Research Ethics Board of the findings, and the patients were given revised consent forms telling them of the newly suspected risks. Within 72 hours, the sponsor terminated the trials and warned that the company would use legal remedies if Olivieri told patients, regulatory agencies, or the scientific community about her concerns. Expressing her ethical obligation to her research participants and to the medical science community, Olivieri discussed the risks with each participant and published the results. Although lauded for her actions by the scientific community, she spent years in litigation with the company and her university. For additional information on this case, readers should refer to Olivieri (2003) and Thompson, Baird, and Downie (2001).

1.04 Informal Resolution of Ethical Violations

When psychologists believe that there may have been an ethical violation by another psychologist, they attempt to resolve the issue by bringing it to the attention of that individual, if an informal resolution appears appropriate and the intervention does not violate any confidentiality rights that may be involved. (See also Standard 1.02, Conflicts Between Ethics and Law, Regulations, or Other Governing Legal Authority, and Standard 1.03, Conflicts Between Ethics and Organizational Demands.)

Professional and scientific misconduct by psychologists can harm coworkers, distort the public's ability to make decisions informed by knowledge generated by members of the profession, and harm the profession itself by instilling public distrust. When an ethical violation by another psychologist occurs, members of the profession are in the best position to recognize the violation and select a course of action that could ameliorate harm or prevent further violations. Standards 1.04 and 1.05 underscore the responsibility of psychologists to be concerned about and, when appropriate, address the scientific or professional misconduct of their colleagues (Principle B: Fidelity and Responsibility).

Standard 1.04 requires psychologists to attempt an informal resolution when they suspect an ethical violation has occurred that could be adequately addressed through discussion with and subsequent remedial actions by the violating psychologist. In such instances, psychologists should discuss the violation with the offending psychologist to confirm whether misconduct has actually occurred and, if appropriate, recommend corrective steps and ways to prevent future ethical violations. The following are examples of psychologists appropriately initiating an informal resolution when they become aware of misconduct by another psychologist:

- ✓ A psychologist with no prior education, training, or supervised experience in neuropsychological assessment began to incorporate a number of such instruments into a battery of tests for elderly clients (Standard 2.01a, Boundaries of Competence). After a colleague brought her lack of training to her attention, an informal resolution was achieved when the psychologist agreed to obtain appropriate training in neuropsychological assessment before continuing to use such techniques.
- ✓ A psychologist working with a non-English-speaking psychotherapy client asked the client's son to serve as an interpreter during sessions. The psychologist agreed to use an independent translator after being approached by a colleague who explained that he was jeopardizing the value of the treatment by using an untrained interpreter and potentially jeopardizing the mother–son relationship (Standard 2.05, Delegation of Work to Others).
- ✓ A consulting psychologist hired to help management plan for a shift in organizational structure planned to take stock options in partial payment for the work. When a colleague pointed out that this might impair her

objectivity and expose the company to harm (Standard 3.06, Conflict of Interest), the psychologist agreed to discuss alternative compensation with the organization.

- In a job application, a psychologist claimed as a credential for health service delivery a degree earned from an educational institution that was neither regionally accredited nor a basis for state licensure. When another psychologist pointed out the unethical nature of this behavior (Standard 5.01c, Avoidance of False or Deceptive Statements), the psychologist agreed to send a letter to the potential employer clarifying the nature of the degree.
- A professor of psychology had not established a timely or specific process for providing feedback to and evaluating student performance (Standard 7.06, Assessing Student and Supervisee Performance). After discussions with the department chair, the professor agreed to develop such a system.
- An assistant professor of psychology began data collection without submitting a research proposal to the university's IRB (Standard 8.01, Institutional Approval). After a senior faculty member brought this to the psychologist's attention, the researcher agreed to submit an IRB application and to cease data collection contingent on IRB approval.
- A psychologist working in a hospital had entered identifiable confidential information into a database available to other staff members (Standard 6.02b, Maintenance, Dissemination, and Disposal of Confidential Records of Professional and Scientific Work). When another psychologist working at the hospital pointed out the problem, the psychologist agreed to use a password and other procedures for protecting the information.

Informal Resolutions in Interprofessional Settings

As psychologists increasingly work as behavioral health providers in integrated care settings created through the Affordable Care Act (ACA), they may be approached by other providers seeking assistance for emotional distress or personal problems. Such requests raise ethical questions regarding whether the impairment is jeopardizing the welfare of patients at the site and the extent to which psychologists have an ethical responsibility to report such behaviors (Kanzler, Goodie, Hunter, Glotfelter, & Bodart, 2013b). At the beginning of their employment, psychologists should become familiar with site rules and procedures for reporting impaired practitioners and, if such formal guidance does not exist, ask how such incidents are handled. As part of the interdisciplinary team, psychologists can also work with colleagues to establish guidelines that clarify professional boundaries among staff and limits of confidentiality when colleagues are alerted to impairments harmful to patient welfare.

Implications of HIPAA

Psychologists should be aware that the Health Insurance Portability and Accountability Act Final Rule (2013) also requires that health care professionals take reasonable steps to mitigate any harmful effects of unlawful disclosure of protected health information (PHI) by an employee or business associate of which they are aware (see "A Word About HIPAA" in the preface to this book).

When an Informal Resolution Is Not Feasible

Standard 1.04 recognizes that in some instances, an informal resolution may not be feasible. For example, previous attempts to discuss ethical problems with the offending psychologist may have been ineffective, or the offending psychologist may have left the position in which he or she had committed the violation or be otherwise inaccessible. In addition, psychologists should not attempt an informal resolution if to do so would violate an individual's confidentiality rights.

> ✓ During a session at the university counseling center, a graduate student complained that her psychology professor required students to discuss their sexual history in a required experiential group (Standard 7.04, Student Disclosure of Personal Information). The student did not want anyone in the program to know she was receiving counseling. Although the counseling psychologist knew that the professor might be violating Standard 7.04, the psychologist did not attempt to resolve the issue because to do so would have placed the confidentiality of the counseling relationship at risk (Standard 4.01, Maintaining Confidentiality).

Peer Review

Journal editors or psychologists reviewing manuscripts or grant proposals may come across information in the submitted materials that suggests a potential ethical violation. For example, an initial reading of the manuscript might lead a reviewer to suspect that the data, presented as original in the manuscript, have been previously published in another journal (a violation of Standard 8.13, Duplicate Publication of Data). In such cases, the reviewer should alert the editor, who in turn can request from the author written clarification of the source and originality of the data and copies of previous publications if appropriate. Suspected plagiarism or data fabrication in a submitted manuscript or grant proposal may be similarly handled through a journal editor or grant program officer in situations in which there is sufficient uncertainty about whether a violation has occurred (Standards 8.10, Reporting Research Results; 8.11, Plagiarism).

If the violation is not resolved through or appropriate for informal resolution, a formal complaint may be made; however, psychologists need to investigate the confidentiality and proprietary rights of the submitted materials within the context of the specific review process. For example, editors of APA journals who have good cause to believe that an ethical violation has occurred are required to report the matter to the chief editorial adviser and the APA journal's senior director, even if the manuscript has been rejected (APA, 2006, Policy 1.05). By contrast, some publishing companies, especially those that publish journals in multiple disciplines, may not have formal policies in place for reporting suspected ethical violations for submitted manuscripts. In such cases, editors and reviewers should consult with the publisher's legal office to clarify reporting responsibilities and limitations. In most instances, whether or not confidentiality rights prohibit making a formal complaint to the APA or other ethics committees, reviewers may be asked to document for a journal or grant committee the factual basis of their concerns (see also Standard 1.07, Improper Complaints).

1.05 Reporting Ethical Violations

> If an apparent ethical violation has substantially harmed or is likely to substantially harm a person or organization and is not appropriate for informal resolution under Standard 1.04, Informal Resolution of Ethical Violations, or is not resolved properly in that fashion, psychologists take further action appropriate to the situation. Such action might include referral to state or national committees on professional ethics, to state licensing boards, or to the appropriate institutional authorities. This standard does not apply when an intervention would violate confidentiality rights or when psychologists have been retained to review the work of another psychologist whose professional conduct is in question. (See also Standard 1.02, Conflicts Between Ethics and Law, Regulations, or Other Governing Legal Authority.)

Standard 1.05 requires psychologists to report ethical violations committed by another psychologist only if the violation has led to or has the potential to lead to substantial harm and informal resolution is unsuccessful or inappropriate. The extent to which most ethical violations have or are likely to cause substantial harm will depend on the professional or scientific context and the individuals involved. As a rule of thumb, behaviors likely to cause substantial harm are of a kind similar to sexual misconduct, insurance fraud, plagiarism, and blatant intentional misrepresentation (APA, 2010b, Section 5.3.5.1.1).

Standard 1.05 also offers nonbinding examples of available reporting options, including filing a complaint with the APA or one of its state affiliates if the offending psychologist is a member of that organization, referring the case to a state licensing board if the ethical violation also violates state law, or filing a complaint with the appropriate committee in the institution or organization at which the offending psychologist works. As does Standard 1.04, Standard 1.05 prioritizes the protection of confidentiality over the duty to report an ethical violation.

> ⊘ A psychology professor reviewing an assistant professor's promotion application materials discovered that the faculty member had several publications that plagiarized articles written by a senior colleague (8.11, Plagiarism). The psychologist presented the evidence to the chair of the department.
>
> *(Continued)*

(Continued)

The chair and the professor informed the faculty member that they had discovered the plagiarism and would be forwarding the information to the university committee on ethical conduct and, if the committee found that plagiarism had occurred, would inform the journal in which the articles were published.

⊘ A client told a psychologist about the sexual misconduct of another psychologist with whom the client had previously been in psychotherapy (Standard 10.05, Sexual Intimacies With Current Therapy Clients/Patients). Judging that it was clinically appropriate, the psychologist discussed with the client the unethical nature of the previous therapist's behavior and the available reporting options. The psychologist, respecting the client's request to keep the sexual relationship confidential, did not pursue reporting the violation (Standard 4.01, Maintaining Confidentiality).

Need to Know: Consultation on Misconduct

Psychologists may be retained to help an organization, the courts, or an individual evaluate whether the actions of a psychologist have violated the Ethics Code. Standard 1.05 preserves the ability of members of the discipline to provide expert opinion on the ethical conduct of their peers by exempting from the reporting requirement psychologists hired to review the ethical activities of another psychologist.

1.06 Cooperating With Ethics Committees

Psychologists cooperate in ethics investigations, proceedings, and resulting requirements of the APA or any affiliated state psychological association to which they belong. In doing so, they address any confidentiality issues. Failure to cooperate is itself an ethics violation. However, making a request for deferment of adjudication of an ethics complaint pending the outcome of litigation does not alone constitute noncooperation.

A profession that demonstrates that it can monitor itself promotes public confidence in the services of its members. Thus, an ethics code must enable professional organizations to effectively adjudicate ethics complaints. Membership in the APA and its affiliated state psychological associations brings with it a commitment to adhere to the Ethical Standards of the profession. To ensure the validity and viability of APA ethics adjudication, Standard 1.06 requires that when called on to do so, psychologists cooperate with APA and state-affiliated ethics investigations, proceedings, and resulting requirements. One question repeatedly raised is whether requiring cooperation with an ethics committee when a complaint has been brought against a psychologist violates the Fifth Amendment right against self-incrimination. The answer to this question is no. Unlike state licensing boards and other government and judicial agencies, professional organizations are not bound by the Fifth Amendment.

Standard 1.06 recognizes that when a complaint is brought against a psychologist, the ability to respond in full to an ethics committee's request for information may be limited by confidentiality responsibilities, detailed in Chapter 7.

> ⊘ A patient submitted a complaint to the APA charging a neuropsychologist with misinterpreting the results of an assessment battery, leading to an inaccurate diagnosis and subsequent denial of disability (Standards 3.04, Avoiding Harm; 9.06, Interpreting Assessment Results). To fully respond to the complaint, the psychologist needed to obtain the patient's written release so that the psychologist could submit to the ethics committee the test report and other information about the patient relevant to the complaint. Despite reasonable efforts, the patient refused to sign the release. The psychologist provided the APA Ethics Committee documentation of his requests to the client and her written refusal as well as a statement indicating how the client's refusal placed confidentiality limitations on his ability to fully respond to the committee's request.

Standard 1.06 permits psychologists to request that an APA or affiliated state psychological association ethics committee delay adjudication of a complaint pending the outcome of litigation related to the complaint. If, however, the ethics committee declines such a request, failure to cooperate will be considered a violation of Standard 1.06. Readers may also wish to refer to the section on APA Ethics Enforcement in Chapter 2.

1.07 Improper Complaints

Psychologists do not file or encourage the filing of ethics complaints that are made with reckless disregard for or willful ignorance of facts that would disprove the allegation.

The filing of frivolous complaints intended solely to harm the respondent undermines the educative, adjudicative, and public protection purposes of the Ethics Code. Unfounded and revengeful complaints can taint a scientific or professional career, lead to unfair denial of professional liability insurance or hospital privileges (because some insurers ask if a complaint has been made), incur costly legal fees for a respondent, and dilute public trust in the profession. Feelings of hostility and intent to do harm may accompany a valid complaint against psychologists who have acted unethically. However, the language of this standard was crafted to focus on the complaining psychologist's disregard for available information that would disprove the allegation rather than on the personal motives underlying the complaint.

Examples of improper complaints to the APA Ethics Committee often involve academic colleagues, business rivals, or psychologists with opposing forensic roles who attempt to misuse the ethics adjudication process as a means of defeating a competitor rather than addressing wrongful behavior or who attempt to dilute a complaint against them through a countercomplaint. Standard 1.07 is violated if psychologists making a complaint had access to information refuting the accusation—whether or not they availed themselves of such information.

☒ Two academic psychologists, well-known for conducting methodologically rigorous research on the validity of children's eyewitness testimony, were often asked to serve as forensic experts on opposing sides in criminal cases. The defense attorney who had retained one of the psychologists for a highly publicized child abuse case was concerned that a recent article published by the opposing psychologist would be potentially damaging to the defendant's case. At the attorney's urging, the psychologist submitted a complaint to the APA Ethics Committee claiming that the opposing psychologist had fabricated the data. The psychologist based her complaint only on the fact that the data seemed "too good to be true" (see also Standard 3.06, Conflict of Interest).

Member groups of psychologists involved in adversarial proceedings are increasingly recognizing the need to address improper complaints. For example, the American Academy of Clinical Neuropsychology (2003) has made the following recommendations for ethical and professional bodies considering ethical complaints made against neuropsychologists involved in adversarial proceedings: (a) Ethical complaints should be examined after the resolution of related adversarial proceedings, (b) investigators should consider the motivation of those making the complaints, (c) investigative board members should be from different geographical regions and should have no prior relationships with those involved in the complaints and have expertise in clinical neuropsychology, and (d) multiple unfounded complaints against the same psychologists should not be used to substantiate unethical practices where none exist.

The discipline of psychology and the public benefit from psychologists monitoring the ethical activities of other psychologists, but both are damaged when the Ethics Code is misused as a weapon to harass or otherwise harm members of the profession.

1.08 Unfair Discrimination Against Complainants and Respondents

Psychologists do not deny persons employment, advancement, admissions to academic or other programs, tenure, or promotion, based solely upon their having made or their being the subject of an ethics complaint. This does not preclude taking action based upon the outcome of such proceedings or considering other appropriate information.

Situations arise in which employees, colleagues, students, or student applicants accuse others or are accused of sexual harassment or other forms of professional misconduct. Standard 1.08 protects the rights of individuals to make ethical complaints without suffering unfair punitive actions from psychologists responsible for their employment, academic admission, or training. The standard also protects the rights of those accused of unethical behaviors to pursue their career paths pending resolution of a complaint. Some highly publicized cases of whistle-blowing have illustrated how premature punitive actions against those who make complaints or those who are the subjects of complaints can hamper the ability of a profession or an organization to monitor itself and can violate the rights of those accused to have a fair hearing (Lang, 1993; Needleman, 1993; Sprague, 1993). The Ethics Code makes clear that psychologists have a responsibility to be concerned about the ethical compliance of their colleagues' scientific and professional conduct (Principle B: Fidelity and Responsibility and Standards 1.04, Informal Resolution of Ethical Violations; 1.05, Reporting Ethical Violations). Standard 1.08 supports the implementation of this obligation by prohibiting unfair discrimination against those who make ethics complaints.

☒ A psychology department voted to deny doctoral candidacy to a student in the department's master's program solely because she had filed a still pending sexual harassment complaint against a member of the faculty.

Standard 1.08 also recognizes that not all complaints have a basis in fact or rise to the threshold of an ethics violation. Therefore, the standard prohibits psychologists from unfair discrimination against individuals who have been accused of, but not found to have committed, an ethical violation.

☒ A client accused a member of a group practice of misrepresenting the fee for psychotherapy. Fearful of additional litigation, regardless of whether the psychologist was ultimately found innocent or guilty, the other group members asked the psychologist to leave the practice.

The use of the term *solely* in the first sentence of Standard 1.08 permits complainants or respondents to be denied employment, professional or academic advancement, or program admission for reasons unrelated to the complaint or for reasons based on the outcome of the complaint.

- An assistant professor accused of student sexual harassment had a documented history of poor student teaching evaluations, which, independent of the sexual harassment accusation, was sufficient to support a denial of promotion to associate professor.
- A psychologist who accused a colleague of insurance fraud was found to have fabricated the evidence used against the colleague. The psychologist was fired from the group practice (Standard 1.07, Improper Complaints).

HOT TOPIC

Human Rights and Psychologists' Involvement in Assessments Related to Death Penalty Cases

In 2010, following intense controversy over the involvement of psychologists in military interrogations at US detention centers such as Guantanamo Bay and Abu Ghraib, the APA amended its Ethics Code Standard 1.02, Conflicts Between Ethics and Law, Regulations, or Other Governing Legal Authority. The amended language made clear that psychologists were prohibited from engaging in activities, however lawful, that would "justify or defend violating human rights." The broad language of this modified standard raises new questions for ethical analysis of psychologists' participation in another kind of controversial legal proceeding: death penalty cases.

Court Rulings

Forensic psychologists—those with specialty training in psychological evaluation, treatment, or consultation relevant to legal proceedings—have been increasingly involved in death penalty cases since the Supreme Court in *Gregg v. Georgia* (1976) ruled that capital sentencing must be tailored to the individual offense and the person who committed it. In practice, this has meant that during the sentencing phase of a capital case, courts must consider psychological factors that might influence a jury's recommendation for execution or life imprisonment, such as whether the defendant is capable of understanding the State's reason for execution or is likely to engage in future violent behavior (DeMatteo, Murrie, Anumba, & Keesler, 2011).

The need for psychological assessment in capital cases intensified in 2002 when the Supreme Court decided that use of the death penalty for defendants with mental retardation is unconstitutional (*Atkins v. Virginia,* 2002). Consequently, prosecutors cannot bring a capital case against a defendant accused of murder if a forensic psychologist or other mental health expert gives the defendant a diagnosis of mental retardation. (It is important to note that some but not all states' laws have begun to incorporate terms such as *intellectual development disorder* [IDD] to be more consistent with the *DSM-5* (American Psychiatric Association, 2013; *Hall v. Florida,* 2014). Similarly, the more recent *Panetti v. Quarterman* (2007) decision prohibits execution of criminal defendants sentenced to death if assessments indicate they do not understand the reason for their imminent execution. As a result of these decisions, in capital cases, psychologists' expertise plays an essential role in determining the legal grounding on which a defendant may be tried for a capital offense and sentenced to death.

Legal Flaws in Death Penalty Cases

Within the profession, psychologists' involvement in capital cases has drawn ethical debate as new evidence of the flaws in the death penalty process has come to light (Birgden & Perlin, 2009). As of December 2015, at least 156 innocent people placed on death row in the United States since 1973 have been released (http://www.deathpenaltyinfo.org/innocence-list-those-freed-death-row/). Moreover, still unknown is the number of innocent persons who have been on death row for years or executed. Consistent findings that racial minorities and defendants from lower socioeconomic levels are more likely to receive a death sentence than white and middle-class defendants further underscore the inequities and unfairness of capital punishment procedures (Glaser, Martin, & Kahn, 2015; Jacobs, Qian, Carmichael, & Kent, 2007; http://www.aclu.org/race-and-death-penalty/). Additionally, the fallibility of eyewitness testimony, long documented by research psychologists, is increasingly recognized by law enforcement agencies and the courts as a serious threat to fair conviction procedures (Liptak, 2011). That innocent people in the United States are being put to death or waiting on death row is indisputable.

Responding to these inequities, in 2001, the APA issued a statement calling upon US jurisdictions not to carry out the death penalty until localities develop policies and procedures that can be shown through psychological and other social science research to ameliorate capital case procedural flaws associated with incompetent counsel, inadequate investigative services, police and prosecutors withholding exculpatory evidence, and selection of conviction-prone jurors (APA, 2001). Only a few states thus far have instituted such a moratorium.

Fallibility of Psychological Tests in Capital Cases

The inherent fallibility of psychological tests may also contribute to arbitrariness and inequities in death penalty proceedings. Most test scores indicating cognitive disability and other psychological disorders are based on probabilities—the likelihood someone has a mental disorder is determined by the degree to which his or her score is similar to the scores of others diagnosed with the disorder.

In *Atkins*, the Supreme Court did not define mental retardation, charging states to identify their own definitions. This has created potential inequities in diagnosis. First, although there is general agreement that a diagnosis of mental retardation/intellectual and developmental disability (MRIDD) requires an individual to have demonstrated prior to age 18 a combination of below-average general intellectual ability and lack of adaptive skills necessary for independent daily living (American Psychiatric Association, 2013), in law and forensic psychology there is variability across states on the specific legal definition of mental retardation (for an excellent review, see Wood, Packman, Howell, & Bongar, 2014). Second, mental health practitioners disagree about whether an IQ (intelligence quotient) score of 70 should be an absolute cutoff point for MRIDD, the relative weight that should be given to IQ scores versus adaptive functioning in reaching a diagnosis, and the validity and reliability of IQ scores over time (Cunningham & Tassé, 2010; Everington & Olley, 2008).

Socioeconomic and Cultural Inequities

Socioeconomic disadvantage constitutes a third factor contributing to diagnostic fallibility; many defendants raised in economically and educationally disadvantaged neighborhoods were never evaluated for mental retardation prior to age 18, and their childhood school and medical records may be sparse. Lack of childhood psychological assessment can lead to the default position that these defendants do not meet mental retardation criteria and can therefore be charged with a capital offense. Fourth, cultural bias of psychological tests used in death penalty cases continues to

(Continued)

(Continued)

be a source of concern within the profession (Perlin & McClain, 2009). Many tests available to evaluate overall intelligence, adaptive behavior, and psychological disorders related to aggression are based on test scores of white, English-speaking, US-born, and middle-class populations. Accordingly, in capital cases, MRIDD and violence risk may be systematically over- or underdiagnosed in poorly educated individuals or those lacking proficiency in English.

Predicting Future Acts of Violence

Finally, during death penalty sentencing, forensic psychologists are often asked to provide expert testimony on whether the defendant is likely to engage in future violent acts. Psychological tests for violence risk are also probabilistic, and research consistently shows that psychologists and other forensic practitioners cannot predict future dangerousness with any certainty, particularly because context-appropriate base rate data are only beginning to be developed (Bersoff, DeMatteo, & Foster, 2012; DeMatteo et al., 2011; Sorensen & Cunningham, 2010). Jury predictions are similarly unreliable (Gillespie, Smith, Bjerregaard, & Fogel, 2014). Juries are more likely to arrive at a death sentence when defendants have a diagnosed mental illness, based on the unfounded belief that individuals with psychological disorders are inherently more prone to future violence (Cunningham & Reidy, 2002).

In summary, a diagnosis of MRIDD and a prediction that an individual will commit future violence are, at best, probabilistic and, at worst, subject to test bias and state and practitioner idiosyncrasies. By contrast, the decisions presented to and determined by a court are absolute: A defendant has or does not have mental retardation, is or is not likely to be violent in the future, is or is not guilty, and should or should not be sentenced to death.

Does Forensic Psychologists' Involvement in Capital Cases "Justify or Defend Violating Human Rights"?

Even as Americans continue to disagree about whether the death penalty in itself violates human rights, the unwarranted and inequitable killing of innocent persons by their government is a flagrant violation of the basic rights of individuals to life and liberty (Dieter, 2011).

As in the debate over psychologists' involvement in military interrogations, some might argue that the psychological assessment is neutral and does not determine whether a judge or jury will sentence a prisoner to death. However, given the current documented flaws in death penalty procedures, psychologists' contribution to legal decisions concerning competency and predictions of future violence places the defendant at the mercy of an imperfect and unjust system. Others might argue that despite the inexactitude of current diagnostic techniques, participation of well-trained forensic psychologists enhances the accuracy of mental health–based legal decisions and that to prohibit their services in capital proceedings would only lead to capricious and unprofessional assessments conducted by those without appropriate training. To be sure, the probabilistic nature of forensic assessments does not override their importance and usefulness to the courts. The US legal system affords defendants and prisoners basic protections that can rectify flawed evaluations or jury decisions, including the right to appeal, the right to receive psychological treatment and ongoing psychological evaluations, and the possibility of entering new evidence into consideration following conviction. However, in capital cases, the usual human rights protections for continued evaluation and appeals can be cut short by death.

Moral questions about forensic psychologists' participation in capital punishment cases bear striking similarity to issues that drove the heated controversy over psychologists' participation in harsh military interrogations. The APA has taken a moral stance against psychologists' participation in military activities that justify human rights violations. It may be time to do the same for the death penalty, an inequitable legal process whose inconsistencies lethally violate the human rights of defendants in capital cases.

Adapted from Fisher, C. B. (2013). Human rights and psychologists' involvement in assessments related to death penalty cases. *Ethics & Behavior, 23*(1), 58–61.

Chapter Cases and Ethics Discussion Questions

A psychologist employed as a mental health professional in an interdisciplinary primary care medical center (PCMC) becomes aware that the prescribing psychiatrists with whom she works are disproportionately classifying lower-income ethnic minority clients as meeting criteria for psychotic disorders and prescribing antipsychotic medications. The director of her department is pressuring her to develop behavioral management plans based on these classifications. However, her psychological assessments of many of these patients do not confirm the psychotic classification, and she believes the behavioral management plans will not adequately address the patients' mental health needs. She is concerned that the PCMC may be motivated by higher rates of insurance reimbursement for these types of diagnosis. Is she in violation of the Ethics Code if she complies with this PCMC policy? If so, what actions might she take to be in compliance with the Code?

You are a student in a clinical psychology doctoral program. You and a fellow student have an externship at a veteran's mental health facility. You have repeatedly seen the other student smoking marijuana a few blocks from the clinic before he comes in for his clinic hours. What are your ethical responsibilities in this situation? Who are the stakeholders who will be affected by any decision you make?

The chair of a psychology department receives a complaint from a faculty member accusing another colleague in the department of plagiarizing his work. After a preliminary investigation by the department's executive committee, the chair tells the faculty member that there is no evidence supporting his complaint. The faculty member accuses the department of bias favoring the colleague, who brings in a significant amount of grant money, and begins to publicly levy these accusations against his colleague on the university website and professional listservs. Which Ethics Code standards might guide the chair in taking steps to address this problem?

CHAPTER 5

Standards on Competence

2. Competence

2.01 Boundaries of Competence

(a) Psychologists provide services, teach, and conduct research with populations and in areas only within the boundaries of their competence, based on their education, training, supervised experience, consultation, study, or professional experience.

Psychologists benefit those with whom they work and avoid harm through the application of knowledge and techniques gained through education, training, supervised experience, consultation, study, or professional experience in the field (Principle A: Beneficence and Nonmaleficence). Competence is the linchpin enabling psychologists to fulfill other ethical obligations required by the APA Ethics Code (APA, 2010b). Under Standard 2.01a, psychologists must refrain from providing services, teaching, or conducting research in areas in which they have not had the education, training, supervised experience, consultation, study, or professional experience recognized by the discipline as necessary to conduct their work competently.

- Psychologists with doctoral degrees from programs solely devoted to research should not provide therapy to individuals without obtaining additional education or training in practice fields of psychology.
- Graduates of counseling, clinical, or school psychology programs should not conduct neuropsychological assessments unless their programs, internships, or postdoctoral experiences provided specialized training in those techniques.
- Psychologists should not offer courses or professional workshops if their graduate education, training, or continued study is insufficient to provide students with fundamental knowledge and concepts of the topics or areas to be taught.

- Psychologists without applicable training in job-related counseling and assessment should not offer executive-coaching services (Anderson, Williams, & Kramer, 2012).
- Forensic psychologists should not offer opinions on children's ability to testify if they have not obtained requisite knowledge of developmental processes related to recollection of facts, susceptibility to leading questions, understanding of court procedures, and emotional and behavioral reactions to legal proceedings.
- Psychologists should not suggest to clients/patients that they alter their psychotropic medication regimen unless they have specialized training as a prescribing psychologist.

Specialties, Certifications, and Professional and Scientific Guidelines

Determinations of whether psychologists are engaged in activities outside the boundaries of their competence will vary with current and evolving criteria in the relevant field. For example, the Council of Specialties in Professional Psychology currently recognizes 13 "specialty areas" defined in terms of the education, training, and competencies required to provide distinctive configurations of services for specified problems and populations (http://cospp.org/specialties/).

As noted in the Introduction and Applicability section of the Ethics Code and discussed in Chapters 1 and 3 of this book, psychologists are encouraged to refer to materials and guidelines endorsed by scientific and professional psychological organizations to help identify competencies necessary for adherence to Standard 2.01a.

- According to the Specialty Guidelines for Forensic Psychology (APA, 2013e), when providing information about the legal process, forensic psychologists do not provide legal advice or opinions; rather they explain to parties that legal information is not the same as legal advice and encourage parties to consult with an attorney for guidance regarding relevant legal issues.
- According to the Guidelines for Child Custody Evaluation in Law Proceedings (APA, 2010), custody evaluation requires specialized knowledge of psychological assessments for children, adults, and families; child and family development and psychopathology; the impact of divorce on children; applicable legal standards; and, in some instances, expertise on child abuse and neglect, domestic violence, or parental mental or physical illness (see also Guidelines for the Practice of Parenting Coordination [APA, 2012e]).
- According to the Guidelines for the Evaluation of Dementia and Age-Related Cognitive Decline (APA, 2012d), psychologists who provide evaluations for dementia and age-related cognitive decline must have education, training, experience, or supervision in clinical interviews and neuropsychological testing and training in the areas of gerontology, neuropsychology, rehabilitation psychology, neuropathology, psychopharmacology, and psychopathology in older adults.

- The Guidelines for Ethical Conduct in the Care and Use of Animals (APA Committee on Animal Research and Ethics [CARE], 2012; http://www.apa.org/science/leadership/care/guidelines.aspx) state that psychologists conducting research with animals must be knowledgeable about the normal and species-specific behavior characteristics of their animal subjects and unusual behaviors that could forewarn of health problems.
- According to the task force on Ethical Practice in Organized Systems of Care, convened by the APA Committee for the Advancement of Professional Practice (CAPP), psychologists who are contracted providers for HMOs should only accept clients/patients whom they have the expertise to benefit (Acuff et al., 1999).
- The APA Guidelines for Education and Training at the Doctoral and Postdoctoral Levels in Consulting Psychology/Organizational Consulting Psychology (APA, 2007a) details three domains of competencies required for organizational consulting psychology: (1) individual (i.e., career and vocational planning, employee selection and promotion, employee job analysis, executive and employee coaching), (2) group (i.e., assessment and development of teams and functional and dysfunctional group behavior, work flow, technology, and stress management), and (3) organization/systemwide/intersystem (i.e., organizational assessment and diagnosis, corporate-wide job analysis, centralizing and decentralizing decision making, strategic planning).
- The American Statistical Association's (ASA) Ethical Guidelines for Statistical Practice (1999) warns that selecting one "significant" result from multiple analyses of the same data set poses a risk of incorrect conclusions and that failing to disclose the limits of conclusions drawn is highly misleading.
- According to the National Association of School Psychologists' ethical standards (NASP, 2010), school psychologists recognize conflicting loyalties that may emerge when their services involve multiple clients (i.e., students, teachers, administrators, and parents) and make known their priorities and commitments in advance to all parties to prevent misunderstandings (see also M. A. Fisher, 2014).

Digital Ethics: Competence in Basic Knowledge of Electronic Modalities

Psychologists utilizing the Internet, mobile phone, and other technologies for research, practice, consulting, and other activities need to obtain appropriate knowledge or training in the technical requirements necessary to ensure adequate provision of services, test administration, or data collection and analysis. This may require knowledge of the necessary screen size, speed of and bandwidth for Internet connections, storage capacity, and servers compatible with downloading programs, applications, or other materials. Basic competencies also include awareness of software options for conducting surveys and mobile applications for behavioral management and their related security protections.

> Practitioners and researchers working with protected health information (PHI) need to ensure that encryption is consistent with HIPAA requirements; for example, not all video conferencing services meet government encryption standards (see American Telemedicine Association, 2014; Colbow, 2013).

(b) Where scientific or professional knowledge in the discipline of psychology establishes that an understanding of factors associated with age, gender, gender identity, race, ethnicity, culture, national origin, religion, sexual orientation, disability, language, or socioeconomic status is essential for effective implementation of their services or research, psychologists have or obtain the training, experience, consultation, or supervision necessary to ensure the competence of their services, or they make appropriate referrals, except as provided in Standard 2.02, Providing Services in Emergencies.

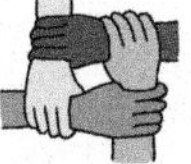

Understanding the ways in which individual differences relate to psychological phenomena is essential to ensure the competent implementation of services and research. Insensitivity to factors associated with age, gender, gender identity, race, ethnicity, culture, national origin, religion, sexual orientation, disability, language, or socioeconomic status can result in underutilization of services, misdiagnosis, iatrogenic treatments, impairments in leadership effectiveness and member cohesion in group therapy, and methodologically unsound research designs (APA, 2000, 2003, 2012a, 2012c; Ridley, Liddle, Hill, & Li, 2001; Trimble & Fisher, 2006).

Standard 2.01b requires that psychologists have or obtain special understanding and skills when the scientific and professional knowledge of the discipline establishes that an understanding of factors associated with these individual differences is essential to competent work. According to this standard, the competencies required to work with such populations are determined by the knowledge and skills identified by the scientific and professional knowledge base—not by personal differences or similarities between psychologists and those to whom they provide services or involve in research.

Under Standard 2.01b, psychologists have three sequentially related obligations: (1) familiarity with professional and scientific knowledge, (2) appropriate skills, and (3) knowledge of when to refrain and refer.

Familiarity With Professional and Scientific Knowledge

For each activity in which they engage, psychologists must be sufficiently familiar with current scientific and professional knowledge to determine whether an understanding of factors associated with the individual characteristics listed above is necessary for effective implementation of their services or research.

- Research and professional guidelines suggest that familiarity with the concept of cultural paranoia and culturally equivalent norms on certain scales of psychopathology is required for competent clinical assessment of African

American clients/patients with presenting symptoms of subclinical paranoia (APA, 1993, 2003; Combs, Penn, & Fenigstein, 2002).

- Professional guidelines require knowledge of the mental health risks of social stigmatization and individual differences in the developmental trajectories of lesbian, gay, bisexual, and transgender (LGBT) youths, as well as cohort and age differences when treating LGBT clients/patients (APA, 2012c).
- Psychologists providing treatment must be alert to how religious ideals and internalized religious norms may positively or negatively influence clients'/patients' reactions to life events such as the death of a loved one or their attitudes and behaviors regarding sexual relationships, child rearing, and self-evaluation (APA, 2007d).
- There is growing awareness that research, assessment, and treatments involving girls and women need to be informed by biological, psychological, social, and political influences that may uniquely affect the development and well-being of this population. The APA *Guidelines for Psychological Practice With Girls and Women* (APA, 2007b) provides a historical overview as well as guidance for identifying and addressing areas in which a special understanding of factors associated with women's issues is required for competent provision of mental health services.

Appropriate Skills

If current knowledge in the field indicates that an understanding of one or more of the factors cited in Standard 2.01b is essential to conduct activities competently, psychologists must have or obtain the training, experience, consultation, or supervision necessary. The type of knowledge and training required depends on the extent to which the individual difference factor is central or peripheral to the service required as well as the psychologist's prior training or experience.

- ✓ A psychologist providing bereavement counseling to a recently widowed 70-year-old woman noticed that the client was reporting difficulties shopping for groceries and finding it frustrating to be among friends. While these difficulties might be attributed to depression following the loss of her husband, given the client's age, the psychologist advised the client to get a full medical checkup and sought additional consultation with a geropsychologist on changes associated with and techniques for enhancing functional capacities related to age-related declines in vision, hearing, and activities of daily living (APA, 2012d).
- ✓ A rehabilitation psychologist who began to receive referrals for work with hearing-impaired clients sought training in sign language and other appropriate communication techniques (Hanson & Kerkoff, 2011).
- ✓ A psychologist with prescribing authority was treating a woman for depression who was also under the care of a medical doctor for diabetes. The psychologist made sure he was up-to-date on research on potential interactions between insulin and antidepressants (APA, 2011a).

☒ A counseling psychologist working at a college counseling center typically provided either behavioral or interpersonal psychotherapy for non-Hispanic white students who met diagnostic criteria for anxiety disorder. However, he limited the treatment plan to behavioral therapy for students of Chinese and Korean heritage based on his erroneous assumption that members of this cultural group were not comfortable with treatments that involved insight-oriented techniques (Wang & Kim, 2010).

Need to Know: Critical Self-Reflection and Personal and Professional Bias

Familiarity with professional and psychological knowledge may also require critical self-reflection and the courage and vigilance to continually confront biases, prejudices, and privileges held by oneself, one's profession, and one's society (Allen, Cherry, & Palmore, 2009; Dovidio & Gaertner, 2004; Smith, Constantine, Graham, & Dize, 2008; Spanierman, Poteat, Wang, & Oh, 2008; Sue et al., 2007; Vasquez, 2009). This includes (a) acquiring the skills to identify and resist simplistic and monolithic stereotypes of clients/patients, research participants, and students in terms of their race, ethnicity, gender, social class, sexual orientation, or other socially constructed categories and (b) openness to see how an individual's strengths or vulnerabilities are or are not related to cultural issues (APA, 2012f; C. B. Fisher, 2014; Fisher, Busch-Rossnagel, Jopp, & Brown, 2012; Fisher et al., 2002; Hayes & Erkis, 2000; Hoop, DiPasquale, Hernandez, & Roberts, 2008; J. Johnson, 2009; Stuart, 2004; S. Sue, 1999).

Knowing When to Refrain and Refer

Under Standard 2.01b, psychologists who have not had or cannot obtain the knowledge or experience required must refrain from engaging in such activities and make referrals when appropriate, except in emergencies when such services are immediately needed but unavailable (Standard 2.02, Providing Services in Emergencies; see also Standard 2.01d).

⊘ A psychologist trained only in adult assessment was asked to assess a child for learning difficulties. The psychologist referred the family to another psychologist with the specialized knowledge and experience necessary to conduct child assessments in general and developmental disabilities assessments in particular (APA, 2012a; Childs & Eyde, 2002).

☒ A counseling psychologist agreed to provide career services to a client with mild bilateral deafness. The psychologist had no education or training in

(Continued)

(Continued)

career skills and opportunities available to people who are hearing impaired, employment-relevant disability law, hearing loss–appropriate counseling techniques, the use of American Sign Language and other modes of communication, and the appropriate use of interpreters (Leigh, 2010).

Need to Know: Guidelines for Psychological Practice With Transgender and Gender-Nonconforming People (TGNC)

There is growing recognition that gender identity is a nonbinary construct that is defined as a person's inherent sense of being a female, a male, a blend of male–female, or an alternative gender (Bethea & McCollum, 2013). Transgender and gender-nonconforming (TGNC) people are those who have a gender identity that is not fully aligned with their sex assignment at birth (APA, 2015b). A person's identification as TGNC is not inherently pathological; it can be healthy and self-affirming. It can also be associated with dysphoria due to discordance between one's gender identity and one's body or distress associated with societal stigma and discrimination (Coleman et al., 2012). Gender identity is theoretically and clinically distinct from sexual orientation, defined as a person's sexual and/or emotional attraction to other people.

The guidelines for psychological practice with TGNC people adopted by the American Psychological Association (2015b) were developed to assist psychologists in the provision of culturally competent, developmentally appropriate, and trans-affirmative practice. The guidelines provide recommendations helpful to ensure compliance with Standard 2.01b. For example, when TGNC people seek assistance from psychologists in addressing gender-related concerns or other mental health issues, practitioners must have the competencies required (a) to distinguish between mental health problems that may or may not be related to that person's gender identity; (b) to identify psychologically relevant direct and indirect effects of hormonal and other medical treatments for physical gender transitioning; and (c) to recognize how stigma, prejudice, and violence can affect clients' health and well-being.

Psychologists working with youth must also understand the different developmental needs of gender-questioning and TGNC children and adolescents. Research indicates that not all youth will continue in a TGNC identity into adulthood (Steensma, McGuire, Kreukels, Beekman, & Cohen-Kettenis, 2013). Individual differences in developmental trajectories of children with gender identity concerns mean that psychologists must be familiar with current approaches to these children's care and have the necessary skills to work with parents in ways that provide optimal conditions for positive development (Tishelman et al., 2015). Psychologists working with clients of any age should never make assumptions about TGNC people's sexual orientation, desire for hormonal or medical treatments, or other aspects of their identity or transition plans (http://www.apa.org/topics/lgbt/transgender.pdf). (See also the discussion of conversion therapy involving children and adolescents in Chapter 6 under Standard 3.04, Avoiding Harm and in the Hot Topic "Ethical Issues for the Integration of Religion and Spirituality in Therapy" in Chapter 13.)

(c) Psychologists planning to provide services, teach, or conduct research involving populations, areas, techniques, or technologies new to them undertake relevant education, training, supervised experience, consultation, or study.

©iStockphoto.com/voinSveta

Standard 2.01c applies when psychologists wish to expand the scope of their practice, teaching, or research to populations, areas, techniques, or technologies for which they have not obtained the necessary qualifications established by the field.

- ⊘ Prior to offering psychological rehabilitation services, a clinical psychologist without previous training in this area obtained knowledge and supervised experience with individuals with sensory impairments; burns; spinal cord, brain, and orthopedic injuries; catastrophic injury and illness; and chronically disabling conditions (Patterson & Hanson, 1995; Scherer, 2010).
- ⊘ A psychologist trained solely in individual psychotherapy obtained appropriate advanced education and training prior to extending his practice to group and family therapy work (Stanton & Welsh, 2011; Wilcoxon, Remley, & Gladding, 2012).
- ⊘ To deliver the short-term treatment required under the practice guidelines of the HMO for which she worked, a psychologist acquired additional supervised experience in the delivery of time-limited services (Haas & Cummings, 1991; Parry, Roth, & Kerr, 2005).
- ⊘ A developmental psychologist who wished to test a theory of genetic and environmental influences on cognitive aging using an animal population obtained knowledge and supervised experience in animal models, animal care, and animal experimental techniques prior to conducting the research (APA CARE, 2012).
- ⊘ Prior to implementing an executive coaching program in a South Asian country, a consulting psychologist obtained knowledge about the culture's orientation toward collective versus independent goals, receptivity to authoritative versus collegial coaching approaches, and preferences for launching quickly into a task versus spending time getting to know the coach personally (Peterson, 2007).
- ⊘ A teaching psychologist who planned to offer an interactive Internet course consulted with a specialist to ensure the information would be presented accurately (e.g., Graham, 2001; Randsdell, 2002).

(d) When psychologists are asked to provide services to individuals for whom appropriate mental health services are not available and for which psychologists have not obtained the competence necessary, psychologists with closely related prior training or experience may provide such services in order to ensure that services are not denied if they make a reasonable effort to obtain the competence required by using relevant research, training, consultation, or study.

Standard 2.01d applies to situations in which a psychologist without the appropriate training or experience is the only professional available to provide necessary mental health services. Such situations often arise in rural settings or small ethnocultural communities where a single psychologist serves a diverse-needs population (Werth, Hastings, & Riding-Malon, 2010). The standard reflects the balance, articulated in Principle A: Beneficence and Nonmaleficence, between the obligation to do good (to provide needed services) and the responsibility to do no harm (to avoid providing poor services as an unqualified professional). The standard also reflects the importance of providing fair access to services (Principle D: Justice).

Standard 2.01d stipulates two conditions in which psychologists may provide services for which they do not have the required education or experience: (1) Psychologists must have prior training or experience closely related to the service needed, and (2) having agreed to provide the service, psychologists must make reasonable efforts to obtain the knowledge and skills necessary to conduct their work effectively.

CASE EXAMPLE

Services to Under-Served Populations

A psychologist with expertise in culturally sensitive assessment of childhood personality and educational disorders was the only Spanish-speaking mental health professional with regularly scheduled appointments with individuals in a Mexican–migrant worker community. A social worker serving the community asked the psychologist to evaluate a Spanish-speaking 80-year-old man for evidence of depression. The nearest mental health clinic was 500 miles away, and the elder was too feeble to travel. The psychologist's expertise in multicultural assessment of mental disorders in children was related though not equivalent to the knowledge and expertise necessary for a culturally sensitive geropsychological diagnosis. The psychologist agreed to conduct the evaluation. Prior to evaluating the elder, she consulted by phone with a geropsychologist in another state. She also informed the elder, the elder's family, and the social worker that because she did not have sufficient training or experience in treating depression in elderly persons, if treatment was necessary, it would have to be obtained from another provider.

(e) In those emerging areas in which generally recognized standards for preparatory training do not yet exist, psychologists nevertheless take reasonable steps to ensure the competence of their work and to protect clients/patients, students, supervisees, research participants, organizational clients, and others from harm.

Standard 2.01e applies when psychologists wish to develop or implement new practice, teaching, or research techniques for which there are no generally agreed upon scientific or professional training qualifications. The standard recognizes the value of innovative techniques as well as the added risks such innovations may pose for those with whom psychologists work.

Psychologists must take reasonable steps to ensure the competence and safety of their work in new areas. In using the term *competence,* the standard assumes that all work conducted by psychologists in their role as a psychologist draws upon established scientific or professional knowledge of the discipline (see Standard 2.04, Bases for Scientific and Professional Judgments). Adherence to this standard requires that psychologists have the foundational knowledge and skills in psychology necessary to construct or implement novel approaches and to evaluate their effectiveness.

©iStockphoto.com/voinSveta

- Psychologists planning to offer executive coaching services must demonstrate a knowledge and expertise in (a) techniques for fostering and measuring change within business, government, nonprofit, or educational organizations; (b) the nature of executive responsibility and leadership; (c) targeted goal setting within organizational cultures; (d) succession planning; and (e) relevant factors associated with executive challenges such as information technology and globalization (Brotman, Liberi, & Wasylyshyn, 1998; Diedrich, 2008; Kampa-Kokesch & Anderson, 2001).
- As states begin to grant psychologists prescriptive authority, psychologists proposing to practice in this area will need the education and training outlined in the evolving practice guidelines for this field (Fox et al., 2009). Psychologists who do not have prescription privileges but are knowledgeable about pharmacotherapy must continue to be cautious when discussing medications with clients/patients to ensure that they are not working outside evolving professional and legal boundaries of competence (Bennett et al., 2006; Sechrest & Coan, 2002).

Standard 2.01e also requires that psychologists working in emerging areas take reasonable steps to protect those with whom they work from harm, recognizing that novel approaches may require greater vigilance in consumer or research protections.

For example, the application of neurocognitive enhancement techniques to healthy individuals and those displaying no signs of neurocognitive degeneration or dysfunction is an emerging field. To date, there is little research documenting positive effects of neurocognitive pharmacological treatments, cognitive exercises, neuroimaging, neurosurgery, and noninvasive cerebral manipulation such as transcranial magnetic stimulation (Bush, 2006). Psychologists investigating these techniques and practitioners who wish to incorporate them into current modes of counseling or treatment must ensure they have the knowledge and skills to not only administer, assess, and monitor participant or patient reactions to these new methods but also remedy negative reactions if they arise (Standards 3.04, Avoiding Harm; 8.08, Debriefing). Psychologists must also inform prospective research participants and patients of the experimental nature of the techniques (see Standards 8.02b, Informed Consent to Research; 10.01b, Informed Consent to Therapy).

Digital Ethics: Competence in the Use of Telepsychology

Continuous advances in the use of electronic media present new opportunities and ethical challenges for psychologists. At present, there is a small but growing body of research suggesting equivalence of certain types of interactive telepsychological interventions (e.g., videoconferencing) to their in-person counterparts. However, traditional psychotherapy techniques based on oral and nonverbal cues may not transfer to audio, email, text message, or other forms of asynchronous communication, and there are no generally accepted theories or comprehensive models specific to telehealth psychological assessments or treatments (Backhaus et al., 2012; Colbow, 2013; Heinlen, Welfel, Richmond, & O'Donnell, 2003; Yuen, Goetter, Herbert, & Forman, 2012).

As with all new and emerging areas in which generally recognized standards for preparatory training do not yet exist, practicing psychologists using telepsychology must keep abreast of developing knowledge in the field and assume the responsibility of assessing and continuously evaluating whether they have sufficient knowledge or can obtain additional training or consultation necessary for competent practice (APA, 2013d; Standards 2.01e, Competence, 2.03, Maintaining Competence, 2.04 Bases for Scientific and Professional Judgments). Psychologists must also be attentive to harm that may be inflicted on clients/patients when the use of electronic media results in misdiagnosis, failure to identify suicidal or homicidal ideation, or inadvertent reinforcement of maladaptive behavior (e.g., social phobia). To ensure the competence of their work and to protect clients/patients from harm when using telehealth assessment or therapeutic services, psychologists should take the following recommended steps (APA, 2013d; Fried & Fisher, 2008; Maheu, 2001; Maheu, Pulier, Wilhelm, McMenamin, & Brown-Connolly, 2005; Shore & Lu, 2015):

- Stay abreast of advances in the field (Standard 2.03, Maintaining Competence).
- Identify professionals and health and social service agencies in the locality in which the client/patient lives who can be enlisted in crisis situations (Standard 3.04, Avoiding Harm).
- Provide clients with a clear written plan for what to do in an emergency (Standard 10.01, Informed Consent to Therapy).
- Document the rationale for selecting a specific telepsychology modality based on client/patient needs and current scientific and clinical knowledge of the field (Standard 2.04, Bases for Scientific and Professional Judgment).
- Consider termination and referral plans when telepsychology services are no longer needed, ineffective, or harmful (Standard 10.10, Terminating Therapy).

(f) When assuming forensic roles, psychologists are or become reasonably familiar with the judicial or administrative rules governing their roles.

According to the Specialty Guidelines for Forensic Psychology (APA, 2013e) psychologists assume forensic roles when they engage in activities intended to provide scientific, technical, or specialized knowledge of psychology to the legal system to assist in addressing legal, contractual, and administrative matters. Forensic roles include clinical forensic examiner, trial behavior consultant, psychologist working in a correctional system, researcher who provides expert testimony on the relevance of psychological data to a legal issue, practitioner who is called to appear before the court as a fact witness, and psychologist who otherwise consults with or testifies before judicial, legislative, or administrative agencies acting in an adjudicative capacity.

Need to Know: Expert and Fact Witnesses

Psychologists serving as *expert witnesses* are those who have, through education and experience, gained specialized knowledge in forensic psychology or other subjects relevant to the legal question at hand. The role of an expert witness is to educate the judge or jury on topics of which the average person is unlikely to have knowledge (Costanzo & Krauss, 2012). Sometimes the court calls on a psychologist who does not have specialized training in forensic psychology or the confluence of psychology and law to serve as a *fact witness,* whose role is to provide records or testify to knowledge of a patient's psychological functioning or treatment not originally obtained for legal purposes (Gottlieb & Coleman, 2012). For example, an independent practitioner seeing a client for anxiety-related disorders might be called as a fact witness in a workers' compensation case for mental distress involving the client. Under Standard 2.01f, even when psychologists have no advance knowledge that their work will be used in a legal or administrative setting, when called on to provide such a service, they are nonetheless responsible for becoming reasonably familiar with the rules governing their forensic role.

✓ A licensed practitioner was called to testify as a fact witness regarding the diagnosis, treatment, and treatment progress of a child he was seeing in group therapy. Prior to going to court, the psychologist obtained consultation on rules governing privileged communications for children and for patients in group therapy in the state in which the psychologist practiced (Glosoff, Herlihy, Herlihy, & Spence, 1997; Knapp & VandeCreek, 1997).

Familiarity With Law, Regulations, and Governing Authority

The provision of competent forensic services requires not only education and training in a psychologist's specific area of expertise but also knowledge of the judicial or administrative rules governing various forensic roles.

- Scientific psychologists serving as expert witnesses should be familiar with federal rules of evidence regarding case law and expert testimony (e.g., *Daubert v. Merrell Dow Pharmaceuticals, Inc.*, 1993; *Kumho Tire Co., Ltd. v. Carmichael*, 1999; see also the Hot Topic "The Use of Assessments in Expert Testimony: Implications of Case Law and the Federal Rules of Evidence" in Chapter 12).
- Psychologists offering trial consultation services to organizations may need to have an understanding of change in venue motions and sexual harassment or retaliation work policies and laws (Weiner & Bornstein, 2011).
- Psychologists conducting custody evaluations should have sufficient understanding of the hearsay rule and what the term *best interests of the child* means in legal proceedings. They should also understand the distinction between criminal and civil law. The purpose of criminal law is to determine a person's guilt or innocence as it relates to violation of law and to determine appropriate sanctions if the defendant is found guilty. On the other hand, the purpose of civil law is to determine the best interests of minors or others who are under guardianship (e.g., child custody disputes, adoption processes, capacity determinations), assign responsibility for claims of harm (e.g., workers' compensation, personal injury litigation), and provide legal remedies (Bush, Connell, & Denney, 2006).
- Psychologists administering psychological services in correctional facilities should be familiar with guidelines and regulations governing the minimum ratio of licensed mental health staff to adult and to juvenile inmates as well as regulations governing access to confidential information by nonpsychologist correctional staff (International Association for Correctional and Forensic Psychology, 2010).

Evolving Law and School Psychologists

School or educational psychologists who serve as expert witnesses in due process hearings for educational services need to be familiar with the legal foundations of special education law, such as *Brown v. Board of Education* (1954), and federal regulations, including Section 504 of the Rehabilitation Act of 1973 (1993), Education for All Handicapped Children Act of 1975, the Americans with Disabilities Act of 1990 (ADA), and the Individuals with Disabilities Education Improvement Act of 2004 (IDEA; Burns, Parker, & Jacob, 2013).

As district employees, school psychologists also have a legal duty to protect all students attending the school from reasonably foreseeable risk of harm, such as from student-on-student violence or harassment or student suicide (Marachi, Astor, & Benbenishty, 2007). When involved in school discipline decisions, they must also be familiar with the Gun-Free Schools Act (see No Child Left Behind Act, 2001), which requires every state that receives funding from the No Child Left Behind Act to have a law that expels any student who brings a firearm to school for no less than 1 year (Mayworm & Sharkey, 2014). The most common tort against school personnel is the claim of negligence in this duty. Jacob and Hartshorne (2007) identified four questions school psychologists may be called upon to address when testifying in a negligence suit: Was a wrong or damage done to the student's person, rights, reputation, or property? Did the school owe a duty in law to the student? Did the school breach that duty? Was there a proximate cause (causal) relationship between the injury and the breach of duty?

Distinguishing Forensic From Clinical Assessments

Knowing the difference between clinical and forensic evaluations is also important. The clinician's goal is to help the client/patient adjust positively to life circumstances (Bush et al., 2006). The purpose of a forensic evaluation, on the other hand, is to assist the "trier of facts" (a judge, jury, or administrative hearing officer) with determining a legal question. While forensic evaluators must respect the legal rights and welfare of defendants or litigants whom they assess, techniques aimed at promoting the testee's mental health or therapeutic alliance, for example, are not necessary and, in fact, may be inappropriate (Greenberg & Shuman, 1997). In addition, legal definitions of mental disorders may differ from those ordinarily applied for diagnosis and treatment. For example, psychologists conducting competency assessments should know that the term *insanity* has different meanings in different jurisdictions (Denney, 2012). Readers may also wish to refer to the Hot Topic in Chapter 4 on forensic assessment of intellectual capacity in death penalty cases.

According to the Specialty Guidelines for Forensic Psychology (APA, 2013e), psychologists who conduct psychological evaluations of those accused of a crime must know how to acquire and report details about the defendant's intent, motivation, planning, thought processes, and general mental state at the time of the crime. When examinees divulge information not previously known by the court that could aid prosecutorial investigation, psychologists should carefully consider the extent to which the information is germane to assisting the triers of fact in understanding the defendant's mental condition. Psychologists should also be aware of ongoing debate regarding whether expert testimony should answer the "ultimate issue" under court consideration (e.g., Was the defendant sane at the time of the offense?) and consider using terms such as *clinical opinion* rather than *finding* to help triers of fact distinguish between legal conclusions and those based in psychological science and practice (Brodsky, 2013).

Need to Know: Treatment of Alleged Child Victims

Children who are alleged victims of child abuse may be referred for psychological treatment prior to trial. In such contexts, practitioners must become reasonably familiar with empirical data on how treatment may influence the children's testimony by intruding into or altering their memory of an event, whether or not they have been victimized. Branaman and Gottlieb (2013) provided the following guidance for psychologists conducting pretrial therapy with alleged child victims:

(Continued)

(Continued)

- Carefully screen referrals to determine whether the child is actually exhibiting symptoms that require clinical care.
- Do not assume that the child's presenting symptoms are a consequence of the alleged abuse and avoid helping the patient "process through the trauma" when the child has not raised it as an issue.
- When therapeutic services are indicated, consider appropriate interventions that are symptom/solution focused and future oriented.
- Obtain skills necessary to avoid suggestive questioning or encouraging the child to recount alleged events when doing so is not clinically indicated.
- Be able to distinguish between your therapeutic role and that of a forensic interviewer or child advocate.
- Be aware that what the child tells you during therapy may be relayed to the court through the child's testimony or your testimony as a potential fact witness.

2.02 Providing Services in Emergencies

In emergencies, when psychologists provide services to individuals for whom other mental health services are not available and for which psychologists have not obtained the necessary training, psychologists may provide such services in order to ensure that services are not denied. The services are discontinued as soon as the emergency has ended or appropriate services are available.

Individual and public trauma following the Oklahoma City bombing; the September 11, 2001, attacks on the United States; the aftermath of Hurricane Katrina; and mass shootings such as at Sandy Hook Elementary School in Newtown, Connecticut, and the Inland Regional Center in San Bernardino, California, illustrate the important public role of psychological expertise during and after disasters. Standard 2.02 recognizes that when adequate mental health services are not available during emergencies, psychologists without training in therapeutic services or crisis intervention may still have knowledge and expertise that can benefit the public. The standard permits psychologists who do not have the necessary training to offer such services, but it requires that they limit services to the immediate time frame and to cease as soon as the emergency has passed or appropriate services become available. When a disaster erupts unexpectedly, psychologists wishing to offer their immediate services should have some knowledge of the efficacy of different intervention techniques to ensure that their services do not exacerbate psychological trauma.

✓ A family psychologist lived in a rural area that had just suffered a devastating tornado. Families were experiencing evacuation, loss of their homes, loss of a loved one, and other overwhelming changes in their normal role relationships and responsibilities, family rules and processes, values they deem important, and family goals that provide the motivation for family member engagement (Myer et al., 2014). The psychologist realized that his family therapy training had not adequately prepared him to address these unique family systems needs. As the only family therapist in the area, he offered emergency services and at the same time contacted experts in the field of emergency family health to help him implement specific skills required for family crisis intervention.

⊘ An Army psychologist was deployed for the first time to a country in which American soldiers were involved in active combat. The military health care setting she was assigned to was small, and she would be replacing the sole behavioral health practitioner. Although she had treated returning armed forces personnel in the United States, she had no experience treating patients who had just experienced a traumatic combat event requiring both immediate medical and behavioral health care. As soon as she knew the setting to which she was being deployed, she consulted with other military psychologists about her responsibilities while recognizing that such consultation was not a substitute for needed training. Once on site, so as not to deprive soldiers of emergency services, she provided treatment, exchanged emails with the prior provider to obtain additional information on effective treatment strategies, and continued to read training manuals and other materials to gain the competencies needed. (Adapted from Dobmeyer, 2013; see also Johnson et al., 2014).

Emergency Care and Suicidality

In rare instances, psychologists who do not have education or training related to suicidality assessment or intervention may come in contact with an individual who appears imminently suicidal and for whom no mental health or other health services are immediately available. Under Standard 2.02, psychologists without the necessary competencies would be permitted to try to reduce the immediate risk of suicide. However, the psychologist should call for emergency services or attempt to obtain appropriate services for the individual or refer the person to such services as soon as feasible. Unqualified psychologists should be wary of providing such services, recognizing the potentially harmful nature of uninformed interventions and the ethical inappropriateness of providing unqualified treatment if medical or other suicide crisis services are available (American Psychiatric Association, 2003).

⊘ A second-year clinical psychology doctoral student was leaving her social services externship site when she received an emergency call from a guard who told her a member of the custodial staff was threatening to commit suicide. The student had never treated a suicidal patient but knew she was the only mental health provider still in the building. She immediately called her supervisor, who gave her instructions on how to provide limited support to the individual while the supervisor called the nearby hospital emergency services to send a treatment team to the building.

Need to Know: Provision of Emergency Services to Forensic Examinees

During a forensic examination, an examinee may manifest psychological symptoms or behaviors that require short-term emergency services to prevent imminent harm to the examinee or others. In such cases, forensic practitioners can provide such services. Once such services have been provided, psychologists must inform the retaining attorney or the examinee's legal representative and determine whether they can continue to provide a forensically valid assessment of the examinee and the appropriate limitations on the information about the emergency that should be disclosed to the court (APA, 2013e; see also Standards 2.01f, Competence; 3.04, Avoiding Harm; 3.05, Multiple Relationships; 4.01, Maintaining Confidentiality; 9.06 Interpreting Assessment Results).

Emergencies and Public Health Ethics

The ethical principles and standards guiding the work of psychologists trained to provide services for individuals and their families are concerned with the moral obligations of providers to the health of the specific individuals they serve. However, disasters often challenge core assumptions about these obligations because treatment relationships have not been formalized and providers must make difficult decisions about whom to treat among survivors with different and competing needs. In these situations, fairness requires that prioritizing whom to treat must be decided on evidence-based differences in the mental health needs of individuals (e.g., those most vulnerable or at greatest risk) or of particular groups essential to promoting the health of others (e.g., first responders). (See Principle A, Beneficence and Nonmaleficence; Principle D, Justice; Standard 3.01, Unfair Discrimination; Thoburn, Bentley, Ahmad, & Jones, 2012). To avoid conflicts between responsibilities to the public health and individual clients/patients, the Institute of Medicine (IOM, 2012) recommends that, whenever possible, those assigned to such triage responsibilities (assignment of treatment based on urgency) should be different from those providing direct delivery of services (Principle B: Fidelity and Responsibility; Standard 3.05, Multiple Relationships).

2.03 Maintaining Competence

Psychologists undertake ongoing efforts to develop and maintain their competence.

The scientific and professional knowledge base of psychology is continually evolving, spawning new research methodologies, assessment procedures, and forms of service delivery. Information and techniques constituting the core curricula of psychologists' doctoral education and training often become outdated and are replaced by new information and more effective practices as decades pass. Lifelong learning is fundamental to ensure that teaching, research, and practice

provide a positive effect for those with whom psychologists work. Standard 2.03 requires that psychologists undertake ongoing efforts to ensure continued competence. This standard is consistent with mandatory requirements for continuing education of many psychology licensing boards (Wise et al., 2010). The foundational competencies developed through graduate education and training (e.g., reflective practice/self-assessment, scientific knowledge/methods, ethical/legal standards, individual/cultural diversity) provide psychologists with the basic knowledge and skills to maintain and foster postgraduate developmental progressions in functional competence in specific work domains, for example, research evaluation, intervention, assessment, and consulting (Rodolfa et al., 2005). The requirements of this standard can be met through independent study, continuing education courses, supervision, consultation, or formal postdoctoral study.

- School psychologists are faced with a continuously evolving knowledge base and laws relevant to effective teacher and school consultation. They must be aware of requirements for statewide reading and mathematics tests and state and local board of education criteria pertaining to the attainment of academic proficiency for all students, availability of public school choice, supplemental tutoring, and criteria for evaluating teacher proficiencies (Jacob & Hartshorne, 2007). Psychologists must also understand the requirements of and fiscal implications for schools of federal laws such as the No Child Left Behind Act (2001) and keep abreast of future changes to the act (Dillon, 2010).
- Industrial–organizational psychologists developing personnel screening and employment practices must stay abreast of continually changing equal employment legislation (e.g., Title VII of the Civil Rights Act of 1964, Americans with Disabilities Act, Uniformed Services Employment and Reemployment Rights Act of 1994, Age Discrimination in Employment Amendments of 1996), administrative laws (e.g., Equal Employment Opportunity Act of 1972, Family and Medical Leave Act of 1993, Pregnancy Discrimination Act of 1978), executive orders (e.g., Executive Order No. 11246, 1964–1965), and court decisions (e.g., *Griggs v. Duke Power,* 1971; *Wards Cove Packing Company v. Antonio,* 1989; see also Cornell University Law School, 2007; Lowman, 2006; McAllister, 1991; Sireci & Parker, 2006).
- Forensic psychologists are often asked to assess the validity of an examinee's symptoms and presentation to determine whether the examinee is attempting to manage impressions of his or her psychological status. Impression management is highly variable both between and within individual examinees, and as a consequence, accepted measures and techniques for assessing symptom validity are continuously evolving. Failing to detect malingering or failing to recognize symptoms as indicators of a valid mental health disorder results in harm to all stakeholders in the legal process. Forensic psychologists need to keep abreast of evolving research on the assessment of facetious disorders (Larrabee, 2007; see also sections on malingering in Chapter 12).
- Investigators and statistical consultants should remain current in dynamically evolving statistical methodology and avoid the use of antiquated statistical methods (ASA, 1999; Panter & Sterba, 2011).

Competencies for Collaborative Group Practices and Primary and Integrated Care Settings

With the passing of the Affordable Care Act, psychologists will need to acquire competencies in collaborative practice. Collaborative practice in health care occurs when multiple health workers from different professional backgrounds provide comprehensive services by working with patients and their families to deliver the highest quality of care. This can take place in small group practices or in primary care facilities and other integrated care organizational settings such as patient-centered medical homes (PCMH). The ability to deliver collaborative care requires psychologists to have a unique set of competencies, including (a) keeping up-to-date on the expectations and requirements of the systems of care in which they work, (b) remaining cognizant that psychologists have ethical and legal obligations as members of a distinct and autonomous profession, and (c) being prepared to clarify their distinct roles and services and how these relate to the roles and services of other health care professionals (APA, 2013c).

Working in a primary care context also requires the following (see also APA, 2013a, 2014; Johnson & Freeman, 2014; Nash et al., 2013):

- Knowledge of the psychological, behavioral, and social components of health and illness
- Knowledge of how families affect and are affected by a family member's health
- Ability to implement empirically supported preventive interventions for primary care and to develop collaborative treatment plans for patients with mental health and medical disorders
- Competencies in crisis management and the technique of brief interviewing for screening mental health problems in the undifferentiated medical populations seen in hospital exam rooms or emergency departments
- Awareness of quality improvement standards and the ability to effectively use information technology to track patient outcomes and provide a means for program evaluation

Consulting and Professional Competencies for Collaborative Care in Global Health

The World Health Organization's *Framework for Action on Interprofessional Education and Collaborative Practice* (WHO, 2010) recognizes education in interprofessional collaboration as important for meeting the urgent need to address worldwide crises in preventable infectious diseases and to provide coordinated responses to natural disasters and war. Psychologists working in international settings need to understand the large differences in health care and educational systems, water and food security, and exposure to violence that exist across countries and regions (Jacob, Vijayakumar, & Jayakaran, 2008). Competency to provide services requires understanding cultural beliefs and misconceptions about disease and determinants of health, as well as governance structures that impede or facilitate health services. Collaborative care in international settings also requires culturally competent communication skills that help health care providers, policy makers, and civil leaders understand one another and work together to promote the development and evaluation of health policies and community education.

2.04 Bases for Scientific and Professional Judgments

Psychologists' work is based on established scientific and professional knowledge of the discipline (see also Standards 2.01e, Boundaries of Competence, and 10.01b, Informed Consent to Therapy).

Standard 2.04 requires psychologists to select methods and provide professional opinions firmly grounded in the knowledge base of scientific and professional psychology. *Scientific knowledge* refers to information generated according to accepted principles of research practice. *Professional knowledge* refers to widely accepted and reliable clinical reports, case studies, or observations. Standard 2.04 is firmly rooted in psychology's historic recognition of the importance of the reciprocal relationship between science and practice (APA, 1947). The current APA Competency Benchmarks (APA, 2012f) consider knowledge of the scientific, theoretical, and contextual bases of assessment and intervention core competencies for training in professional psychology.

Psychologists engaged in innovative activities who do not draw on established knowledge of the field may fail to anticipate or detect aspects of their work that could lead to substantial misrepresentation or harm. The standard permits the use of novel approaches, recognizing that new theories, concepts, and techniques are critical to the continued development of the field. It does, however, prohibit psychologists from applying idiosyncratic theories and techniques that are not grounded in either accepted principles or the field's cumulative knowledge of psychological research or practice.

☒ Several families who believed that their children had been the victims of sexual abuse in the day care center they attended retained the services of a clinical psychologist to evaluate and testify in court that the children had been abused. During her years in practice, the psychologist had created for her own use a set of criteria for determining abuse based on her clinical observations and the writings of two leading practitioners who observed what they determined were universal syndromes of child sexual abuse. The psychologist's testimony played an important role in convicting the day care staff members. On appeal, however, the conviction was overturned based

(Continued)

(Continued)

on the appellate court's finding that the psychologist's evaluation methods were invalid, unreliable, and not probative of sexual abuse. For additional discussion of these issues, see Fisher (1995), Fisher and Whiting (1998), and Kuehnle and Sparta (2006).

☒ On the day of and immediately following the attacks on September 11, 2001, psychologists from across the country who were not trained in trauma treatment rushed to provide services to victims, rescuers, and their families. An immediate controversy arose regarding their application of the popular but unvalidated Critical Incident Stress Debriefing (CISD) technique. The CISD encourages individuals to discuss their emotional reactions to a traumatic event immediately following exposure; proponents claim that doing so reduces immediate distress, prevents later adverse psychological reactions, and helps screen for individuals who are at risk for developing more serious disorders (Everly, Flannery, & Mitchell, 2000). Critics claimed the debriefing treatment had no efficacy or was potentially harmful to victims of the terrorist attacks (van Emmerik, Kamphuis, Hulsbosch, & Emmelkamp, 2002). By the second day, there was a public call to stop untrained "trauma tourists" from using the technique based on concerns they might have actually compounded the effects of trauma on those they "treated" (Bongar et al., 2002).

Psychologists trained in more traditional techniques also have a responsibility to keep up with evolving knowledge of the field to know under which conditions and for which disorders treatments do and do not work and which have iatrogenic risks (Pope & Vasquez, 2007; see also Standard 2.03, Maintaining Competence).

Evidence-Based Practice

The APA Presidential Task Force report on evidence-based practice in psychology (EBPP), which was adopted as policy in 2005 (see APA, 2006), emphasized both the importance of scientific knowledge to treatment decisions and the importance of clinical judgment to determining the applicability of research findings to individual cases. The task force defined EBPP as the integration of the best available research with clinical expertise in the context of client/patient characteristics, culture and preferences, and relevance to the client's/patient's treatment and assessment needs. *Clinical expertise* was defined as competence attained by psychologists through education, training, and experience resulting in effective practice and the ability to identify the best research evidence and integrate it with clinical data (e.g., patient information obtained over the course of treatment or assessment; see also APA, 2002a).

Other professional groups have endorsed the integration of research and practice knowledge as an ethical obligation.

- The National Association of School Psychologists' Principles for Professional Ethics (NASP, 2010) requires that "school psychologists use assessment techniques, counseling and therapy procedures, consultation techniques, and other direct and indirect service methods that the profession considers to be responsible, research-based practice" (Standard II.3.2).

- The Specialty Guidelines for Forensic Psychology includes a provision that "forensic practitioners seek to provide opinions and testimony that are sufficiently based upon adequate scientific foundation, and reliable and valid principles and methods that have been applied appropriately to the facts of the case" (Guideline, 2.05, APA, 2013e).
- The *Journal of Clinical Psychology: In Session* recently published a series of articles describing the convergence of evidence-based practice (EBP) and multiculturalism with illustrations of EBP that have successfully addressed the clinical needs of cultural minority populations (Morales & Norcross, 2010).

Implicit in Standard 2.04 is the assumption that when patient characteristics and treatment context meet EBP criteria, psychologists implement the evidence-based treatments as designed, a practice known as "treatment integrity." This includes applying an evidence-based model to the assessment of psychological disorders to avoid incorrect diagnoses and subsequent treatment plans based on the idiosyncrasies of the clinicians and/or the setting in which the assessment is conducted (Barry, Golmaryami, Rivera-Hudson, & Frick, 2013; Standard 9.01, Bases for Assessments).

Digital Ethics: Navigating the Online Search for Evidence-Based Practices

The ability to use online searches to quickly identify evolving best practices may become an essential competency required by health insurance organizations (Standard 2.03, Maintaining Competence; Berke, Rozell, Hogan, Norcross, & Karpiak, 2011; Guyatt, Rennie, Meade, & Cook, 2008; Weinfeld & Finkelstein, 2005). New research on EBP for diverse disorders, populations, and treatment modalities is constantly emerging. Primary databases such as PubMed Clinical Queries (http://www.ncbi.nlm.nih.gov/pubmed/clinical/) and psycINFO (APA, 2010b) have begun to contain references to individual studies that clinicians must individually evaluate with respect to their validity and relevance to the current treatment question. Other EBP databases are designed to facilitate practitioner searches by including summaries of new empirical studies on clinical efficacy that have been evaluated for scientific validity and applicability (e.g., the National Registry of Evidence-Based Programs and Practices, http://www.nrepp.samhsa.gov; see also Hennessy & Green-Hennessy, 2011).

Falzon, Davidson, and Bruns (2010) have developed a formula to guide practitioner online searches for the EBP most applicable to a particular client/patient. Their PICO formula includes finding appropriate search terms for four components: (P) patient disorder, for example, depression with suicidal ideation; (I) type of intervention the clinician is considering, for example, dialectical behavior therapy (DBT); (C) the comparison intervention the clinician is considering, for

(Continued)

(Continued)

example, cognitive–behavioral therapy; and (O) the outcome measure of interest, for example, reduction in symptoms or need for hospitalization. After identifying the research, psychologists need to draw on their scientific and professional training to critically evaluate which studies best meet criteria for ecological validity, relevance, and utility for the individual clinical case.

In many instances, the EBPs reviewed may not provide a perfect match to all aspects of the clinical question. Appropriate application of the EBP thus requires clinical judgment to determine how best to integrate or adapt the EBP in ways that are best fitted to the psychologist's clinical expertise, the treatment context, and the patient's clinically relevant needs and characteristics (see also Standard 2.04, Bases for Scientific and Professional Judgments). Final steps in the process include monitoring and evaluating the effectiveness of the EBP-informed treatment for the specific client, making clinically informed modifications, and, if needed, conducting a new database search (McGivern & Walter, 2014).

Implications of the Affordable Care Act (ACA)

Evidence-based health care is a major tenet of accountability within the ACA. To meet criteria for services coverage, psychologists working in group practices and primary care patient-centered health systems must be able to describe and utilize evidence-based practices that enhance the cost-effective quality of care. Practitioners will also need to be able to identify evolving evidence-based strategies for measuring and monitoring client progress within team-based care, including empirically derived signal–alarm systems to identify patients at risk for treatment failure (Lambert, 2013). In addition, the ACA focus on prevention and the integration of behavioral health into primary care will require the ability to identify evidence-based psychosocial practices involving brief interventions supported by self-management strategies, effective liaisons with specialty mental health providers such as those of substance abuse and obesity-related services, developmental assessments, and involvement of family members in brief episodes of care (Nash et al., 2013; Rozensky, Celano, & Kaslow, 2013). For adolescents, the law mandates that insurers cover screening for depression, assessments for substance use, sexual health counseling, and HIV screening (Tynan & Woods, 2013).

In addition, research psychologists with expertise in quality improvement and patient outcome research will become increasingly in demand and will need to develop research designs capable of assessing comparative clinical effectiveness and quality management. Psychologists will also need to develop new methods for continuous quality improvement research that conforms to the actual flow of patient care in a primary care setting and does not interfere with ongoing clinical practice while, at the same time, maintaining fidelity of recruitment and research procedures (Kanzler, Goodie, Hunter, Glotfelter, & Bodart, 2013a).

2.05 Delegation of Work to Others

Psychologists who delegate work to employees, supervisees, research or teaching assistants, or who use the services of others, such as interpreters, must take reasonable steps to: (1) avoid delegating such work to persons who have a multiple relationship with those being served that would likely lead to exploitation or loss of objectivity; (2) authorize only those responsibilities that such persons can be expected to perform competently on the basis of their education, training, or experience, either independently or with the level of supervision being provided; and (3) see that such persons perform these services competently. (See also Standards 2.02, Providing Services in Emergencies; 3.05, Multiple Relationships; 4.01, Maintaining Confidentiality; 9.01, Bases for Assessments; 9.02, Use of Assessments; 9.03, Informed Consent in Assessments; and 9.07, Assessment by Unqualified Persons.)

In their obligation to protect the rights and welfare of those with whom they work, psychologists who delegate or use the services of others are responsible for ensuring that such work is performed competently. To be in compliance with Standard 2.05, psychologists should (a) evaluate whether employees, supervisees, assistants, or others whose services are used have the skills to implement the task independently or under appropriate supervision; (b) assign such individuals only those tasks for which they are qualified; and (c) monitor the activities to ensure competent implementation.

- Consulting and industrial–organizational psychologists who delegate employee assessments or organizational research responsibilities to others must ensure to the extent feasible that such individuals have adequate training in the testing or data collection skills necessary to implement the work proficiently.
- Psychologists in academia must take reasonable measures to ensure that research and teaching assistants have the knowledge and skills required to implement valid and ethical research procedures, teach or advise students, or grade exams.
- Psychologists in mental health settings who supervise psychologist and nonpsychologist staff (e.g., lay leaders for group work; see Glass, 1998) must take steps to determine that these individuals have the necessary training to perform or assist in therapeutic procedures (Stratton & Smith, 2006).
- School psychologists must read and approve before signing pupil reports based on assessments that are administered, scored, or prepared by graduate students, externs, or others under the psychologists' supervision.

Implications of HIPAA

Psychologists who are covered entities under HIPAA should be aware that the act requires covered entities to train, document, and appropriately sanction employees regarding federal policies and procedures involving Protected Health Information (PHI; see "A Word About HIPAA" in the preface of this book).

Use of Interpreters

Standard 2.05 specifically draws attention to the appropriate delegation of work to interpreters who assist psychologists in providing services for or conducting research involving individuals who use American Sign Language or who do not speak the same language as the psychologist. Psychologists must ensure that interpreters have adequate translation skills and sufficient understanding of the psychological nature and ethical responsibilities of the duties to be performed. Some clients/patients who are hearing impaired or do not speak English live, work, or socialize in close-knit communities in which those who serve as interpreters are known personally. In such settings, psychologists should avoid delegating work to such individuals when it will create a multiple relationship between the interpreter and the research participant or person receiving services that could reasonably be expected to lead to breaches in confidentiality, exploitation, or loss of objectivity.

☒ At the beginning of the fall academic year, a public school experienced an influx of new pupils who had recently emigrated from Russia and who did not speak English. In the rush to ensure adequate academic placement for the students, the school psychologist asked a member of the custodial staff who was fluent in Russian and English to serve as an interpreter for administration of tests to determine whether any of the pupils had learning disabilities.

⊘ A research psychologist received IRB approval to conduct a study concerning health knowledge and behaviors of illegal immigrants. All informed consent and interview scripts were translated into the participants' language. The psychologist realized that legal residents of the community trusted by prospective participants would be more effective participant recruiters than university staff. He placed an ad in the local papers and spent a week training newly hired community-based recruiters in methods to protect prospective participants from coercion, ensure confidentiality of information collected, and avoid exploitative or otherwise harmful multiple relationships.

Reasonable Steps

The phrase *take reasonable steps* recognizes that despite their best efforts, persons to whom work is delegated may fail to perform their duties appropriately. The phrase also recognizes that sometimes psychologists working in organizations, in the military and other public service positions, or at the bequest of the legal system may be assigned assistants, employees, or interpreters insufficiently qualified to perform their duties. Psychologists must at minimum discuss their concerns and ethical obligations with those responsible for such assignments, provide appropriate training when feasible, and closely supervise and monitor performance (see Standards 1.02, Conflicts Between Ethics and Law, Regulations, or Other Governing Legal Authority; 1.03, Conflicts Between Ethics and Organizational Demands).

- ⊘ A consulting psychologist was hired to conduct a job analysis to determine hiring needs for an organization. The company agreed to provide the psychologist with an administrative assistant to help schedule meetings and provide other clerical assistance. The consulting psychologist discovered that the assistant was discussing with other employees her misimpression of the goals and preliminary findings of the job analysis in a manner that compromised the validity of future assessments. The psychologist immediately brought this matter to the assistant's attention and began to have biweekly monitoring meetings with the assistant to ensure her understanding of her role responsibilities.
- ⊘ A prescribing psychologist worked in a hospital that employed nurse practitioners to conduct patient medical histories at intake. The psychologist noticed that while the nurses' reports contained detailed information regarding physical health, the histories were incomplete in terms of information relevant to mental health. The psychologist requested and received approval from the medical director to run a brief training session on mental health intake procedures for the nurses.

2.06 Personal Problems and Conflicts

(a) Psychologists refrain from initiating an activity when they know or should know that there is a substantial likelihood that their personal problems will prevent them from performing their work-related activities in a competent manner.

A growing body of research indicates that emotional, social, health-related, and other personal problems can interfere with psychologists' ability to use their skills effectively. Substance abuse problems, acute depression or other mental disorders, chronic or life-threatening diseases, and other stressful life events such as divorce or the death of a loved one are situations that sometimes prevent psychologists from performing their work in a competent manner (Johnson & Barnett, 2011; O'Connor, 2001; Sherman & Thelen, 1998). Work-related stressors, such as social isolation in private practice, burnout, and the vicarious traumatization encountered by some psychologists working with survivors of trauma, can lead to boundary violations and otherwise compromise effective job performance (Mahoney & Morris, 2012). Clients/patients, students, employers, and employees suffer when personal problems prevent psychologists from competently implementing their work, and the misconduct that is often a product of these circumstances harms public perceptions of psychology.

Standard 2.06a requires psychologists to refrain from beginning an activity when there is a substantial likelihood their personal problems may impair their ability to perform their work competently. The phrases *refrain from beginning* and *substantial likelihood* indicate that the intent of this standard is preemptive: It prohibits psychologists from taking on a professional or scientific role when their personal problems have the potential to impair their work. As signified by the phrase *or should know,* psychologists suffering from problems that would reasonably be expected by members of the profession to cause work-related impairment will not avoid a finding of violation of this standard by claiming they did not know that their problems could interfere with their work. Psychologists should develop the skills necessary to monitor their own emotional strengths and weaknesses, needs and resources, and abilities and limits (APA, 2012f). Signs that personal problems may be interfering with work-related activities may include intense emotional reactions to students, supervisees, research participants, colleagues, or clients/patients.

☑ A psychologist had just returned to independent practice following chemotherapy for a cancer that was now in remission. The psychologist believed that she had recovered from the fatigue and mental stress of the chemotherapy but recognized that such symptoms may persist. She set up a weekly consultation with a colleague to help monitor her work until she was confident that the symptoms had fully abated.

☒ An industrial–organizational psychologist responsible for preemployment screening for an organization had begun to drink heavily and found that he needed to have several beers before seeing candidates in the morning and several more drinks throughout the workday. In response to a complaint to the APA Ethics Committee filed by an applicant who was appalled by the psychologist's slurring of words during a screening, the psychologist claimed that his alcoholism had prevented him from acknowledging he had a problem.

Strategies for Preventing Work-Related Stress Involving High-Risk Clients/Patients

Kristen Webb (2011) addressed the ethical dilemma of providing consistent and reliable care to a patient with suicidal urges, self-harming behaviors, and significant abandonment issues with the need to ensure competent provision of services in formal sessions and via telephone contact. She scheduled brief (8-minute) regular telephone check-ins between sessions to assure the patient of her availability to assist with life-threatening urges, but she limited these phone calls to skills coaching. She adhered to firm boundaries for beginning and ending sessions. Webb carefully used self-disclosure to provide the patient with examples of how she had weathered storms in her life, consistently monitoring the effect of the disclosures on her patient and the therapeutic (vs. countertransferential) motivation for the disclosures, and she sought regular peer consultation. She was alert to feelings of professional discouragement, physical exhaustion, and stress related to fears of a poor outcome for her patient. She monitored her sleep and eating, created transitional activities between work and home, and made time to set aside her worries and counter, through self-nourishing exercise and socializing, the self-isolation that therapists can experience. Readers may also wish to refer to the Hot Topic in Chapter 3 on the ethics of self-care.

(b) When psychologists become aware of personal problems that may interfere with their performing work-related duties adequately, they take appropriate measures, such as obtaining professional consultation or assistance, and determine whether they should limit, suspend, or terminate their work-related duties. (See also Standard 10.10, Terminating Therapy.)

Standard 2.06b applies to situations in which psychologists who are already providing services, teaching, or conducting research become aware that their personal problems are interfering with their work. The standard calls for psychologists to take appropriate steps to remedy the problem and to determine whether such remedies are sufficient for them to continue work-related activities.

✓ A teaching psychologist who was undergoing outpatient treatment for a life-threatening medical disorder found it increasingly difficult to prepare lectures, grade papers, and mentor students effectively. The psychologist consulted with the chair of the department, who agreed to assign an experienced graduate teaching assistant to give the lectures. The psychologist also asked a colleague to serve as a consultant on the two dissertations he was currently mentoring.

Distinguishing between personal and professional impairment is not always easy, nor is there consensus among members of the profession on how to identify work-related impairment (Smith & Burton Moss, 2009; Williams, Pomerantz, Segrist, & Pettibone, 2010). Fear of losing highly valued abilities in the face of serious, chronic, or life-threatening disease or being judged by colleagues as incompetent can create denial and professional blind spots (Barnett, 2008). Health problems and personal distress become professional deficits when they make services ineffective or compromise functioning in ways that harm students, research participants, organizational clients, and patients (Munsey, 2006). Signs of impairment may include intense emotional reactions (e.g., anger or uncontrolled sexual attraction), disrespectful comments to clients/patients or students, lack of energy or interest in work, or using work to block out negative personal feelings to the detriment of those with whom one works (Pope & Vasquez, 2007; Smith & Burton Moss, 2009).

Need to Know: Seeking Personal Psychotherapy

Practicing psychologists, like other persons in need of treatment, may be deterred from seeking psychotherapy because of social stigma, fears of expressing emotion or self-disclosure, loss of self-esteem, time constraints because of heavy course loads, or financial concerns such as paying off educational loans (Barnett, Baker, Elman, & Schoener, 2007; Bearse et al., 2013). In addition, psychologists may have privacy concerns related to finding a suitable therapist outside one's own circle of professional contacts. They may also be wary of violations of privacy that may jeopardize future work and income potential if colleagues question their objectivity or competence. Contrary to these concerns, surveys indicate that approximately 85% of psychologists obtain treatment, do not report personal or professional stigma as a significant deterrent to seeking treatment, and experience positive outcomes (Bearse et al., 2013; Bike, Norcross, & Schatz, 2009; S. B. Phillips, 2011).

To comply with this standard, psychologists can turn to the increasing number of state licensing boards and state psychological associations that provide colleague assistance programs to help psychologists deal proactively with and remediate impairment (APA Committee on Colleague Assistance, 2006; Barnett & Hillard, 2001). If such steps are not adequate to ensure competence, Standard 2.06a requires that psychologists appropriately limit, suspend, or terminate work-related duties.

☑ A counseling psychologist returned to her position at a college counseling center after sick leave for physical injuries incurred during a car accident. Within a week at the counseling center, the psychologist realized the pain medication she was frequently taking during the day was interfering with her ability to focus on clients' problems. She contacted a psychologist assistance program in her state that helped her taper off the medication, provided ongoing supervision to help her self-monitor her ability to perform her tasks, and supported her in approaching the director of the counseling center to seek a reduction in her hours.

☒ A psychologist working in a correctional facility was attacked violently by a new prisoner during a psychological assessment interview. The psychologist did not seek psychological counseling for his reaction to the assault. A month later, the psychologist was conducting an intake of a prisoner who reminded him of his attacker. Although the psychological assessment did not provide evidence of extreme dangerousness, the psychologist's report indicated the prisoner was highly dangerous and should be assigned to the most restrictive environment (adapted from Weinberger & Sreenivasan, 2003).

Need to Know: Stressors During Graduate and Postdoctoral Training

Graduate students are vulnerable to stressful life experiences, physical and mental illness, and substance use problems. In addition, graduate schools and postdoctoral internships or research can create distress related to financial concerns, relocation, lack of social support, and academic achievement and deadlines (APA, Committee on Colleague Assistance, 2006; Tamura, 2012). Education and training programs can increase the competent conduct of practice and research by providing (a) materials on how personal problems can diminish professional competence; (b) strategies for assessing and monitoring when these problems may compromise effectiveness and harm those with whom one works; (c) opportunities to openly discuss these issues with faculty and supervisors; and (d) fair and effective approaches to remediation and, if necessary, termination, when a student exhibits signs of impairment (N. J. Kaslow, et al. 2007; Tamura, 2012; see also Hot Topic "The Ethical Component of Self-Care" in Chapter 3).

HOT TOPIC

Multicultural Ethical Competence

Ethical decision making for psychological research and practice in diverse cultural venues must be sensitive to cultural attitudes toward individual autonomy and communal responsibility; historical and contemporary discrimination within society and psychology as a discipline; sociopolitical factors influencing definitions of race and ethnicity; and variations in immigration history, acculturation, cultural/ethnic identity, language, and mixed race/ethnic heritage (Arredondo & Toporek, 2004; Fisher, 2014; Fisher et al., 2012; Fisher et al., 2002; Lyon & Cotler, 2007; Johnson, 2013; Ponterotto, Casas, Suzuki, & Alexander, 2001; Sue & Sue, 2003; Trimble & Fisher, 2006). "Multicultural psychology views human behavior as influenced by an individual's culture and the cultures surrounding and acting upon the individual" (Hall, 2014, p. 3) and increasingly considers class, sexual orientation and gender identity, disability, and other contexts. Multicultural responsibility requires "a fusion of personal and professional commitments to consider culture during ethical encounters" (Ridley et al., 2001, p. 176). Psychologists can use the ethical decision-making model introduced in Chapter 3 to identify key questions to consider as a means of acquiring the attitudes and knowledge essential to multicultural ethical competence.

Multicultural Ethical Commitment

Multicultural ethical commitment requires a strong desire to understand how culture is relevant to the identification and resolution of ethical problems. It demands a moral disposition and emotional responsiveness that moves psychologists to explore cultural differences and creatively apply the APA Ethics

(Continued)

(Continued)

Code to each cultural context. Cultivation of these competencies thus includes motivation to consider the influence of culture in psychologists' work conscientiously, prudently, and with caring discernment.

The desire to ensure that cultural sensitivity is integrated into ethical decision making requires a willingness to reflect on how one's own cultural values and cultural identity influence the way one conceives ethics in one's activities as a psychologist (Arredondo, 1999; Helms, 1993; Trimble, Trickett, Fisher, & Goodyear, 2012). Furthermore, multicultural ethical competence entails recognition of harms that psychology can exert on culturally diverse groups by invalidating their life experiences, defining their cultural values or differences as deviant, and imposing the values of dominant culture upon them (David, Okazaki, & Giroux, 2014; Fisher, 1999; Fisher et al., 2002; Fowers & Davidov, 2006; Prilleltensky, 1997; Trimble & Fisher, 2006; Trimble, Scharrón-del Rio, & Casillas, 2013; Vasquez, 2012).

In psychological research and practice, multicultural ethical commitment involves motivation to do the following:

- Critically examine moral premises in the discipline that may largely reflect Eurocentric conceptions of the good.
- Question "deficit" and "ethnic group comparative" approaches to understanding cultural differences.
- Address the reality and impact of racial discrimination in the lives of cultural minorities.
- Recognize that socially constructed racial/ethnic labels can strip participants of their personal identity by promoting responses to them only in terms of racial or ethnic categorizations.
- Avoid conceptually grouping members of ethnic minority groups into categories that may not reflect how individuals see themselves.
- Engage in self-examination about how institutional racism may have influenced each psychologist's own role, status, and motivation to develop a professional identity free from these influences.
- Develop the flexibility required to respond to rapid cultural diversification and fluid definitions of culture, ethnicity, and race.

Multicultural Ethical Awareness

Multicultural ethical commitment is just the first step toward multicultural ethical competence. Good intentions are insufficient if psychologists fail to acquire relevant knowledge about cultural differences and how they may affect the expression of and solutions to ethical problems. To work ethically with diverse populations, psychologists must remain up-to-date on advances in multicultural research, theory, and practice guidelines relevant to their work (Hall & Yee, 2014; Salter & Salter, 2012). These areas of understanding may include the following:

- The history of ethical abuses of cultural minorities in the United States and how past treatment may exacerbate disparities in mental health care, employment, criminal justice, and involvement in psychological research
- The impact on mental health of historical and contemporary discrimination in employment, education, housing, and other areas
- Cultural and contextual factors that may facilitate or interfere with psychological well-being or responsiveness to treatment
- Scientific, social, and political factors influencing the definitions of race, ethnicity, and culture and how these factors may serve as barriers to conducting psychological activities that protect individuals' rights and welfare
- Within-group as well as between-group differences that may be obscured by cultural stereotypes in society and within the discipline of psychology

- Knowledge and skills in constructing and implementing culturally valid and language-appropriate assessments, treatments, research procedures, teaching strategies, and consulting and organizational evaluation techniques
- Knowledge of relevant ethical standards in the APA Ethics Code and organizational guidelines relevant to multicultural ethical competence in research and practice
- Knowledge of antidiscrimination federal and state laws relevant to the contexts in which psychologists work

Goodness-of-Fit Ethics and Multicultural Ethical Decision Making

Multicultural ethical commitment and ethical awareness are essential but not sufficient to ensure the ethical resolution of multicultural challenges. Given the dynamic nature of individual, institutional, and sociopolitical concepts of race, culture, and ethnicity, ethical decision making across cultural contexts can be informed but may not be resolved by previous approaches to ethical problems. Many multicultural ethical challenges are unique to the culture, the salience of the culture for a particular individual in a particular context, other within-culture individual differences, the environment in which the psychological activity occurs, and the goals of that activity (Nicolaidis et al., 2010). In applying the steps for ethical decision making described in Chapter 3, multicultural ethical competence includes (a) creating a goodness of fit between the cultural context and the psychologist's work setting and goals and (b) engaging in a process of colearning that ensures this fit (Fisher, 1999, 2002a, 2014; Fisher et al., 2012; Fisher & Goodman, 2009; Fisher & Masty, 2006; Fisher & Ragsdale, 2006; Trimble, Trickett, Fisher, & Goodyear, 2012).

Applying goodness-of-fit ethics to multicultural contexts requires reflection on the following questions:

- What cultural circumstances might render individuals more susceptible to the benefits or risks of the intended psychological assessment, treatment, or research?
- Are cultural factors under- or overestimated in the assessment, treatment, organizational evaluation, or research plan?
- Do psychologists and members of cultural groups with whom they work have different conceptions of practice goals or research benefits?
- Are traditional approaches to informed consent and confidentiality protections compatible with the values of spirit, collectivity, and harmony characteristic of different ethnocultural populations?
- Are any aspects of the psychological work setting "misfitted" to the competencies, values, fears, and hopes of recipients of psychological services, examinees, employees, or research participants?
- How can the setting (including the aims and procedures to accomplish these aims) be modified to fit the requirements of culturally sensitive and responsibly conducted psychology?
- How can psychologists engage organizations and employees, clients/patients and practitioners, students and school personnel, research participants, and investigators in discussions that will help illuminate the cultural lens through which each views the psychologist's work?

Culture is a dynamic construct influenced by an ever-changing sociopolitical landscape. Ethical decision making that includes multicultural commitment and awareness can help psychologists correct cultural misimpressions and biases in their work. An openness to learning from and collaborating with stakeholders can help psychologists implement and monitor the cultural adequacy of ethical decisions and make appropriate adjustments when necessary. Multicultural ethical competence requires a process of lifelong learning that enables psychologists to make ethical decisions that reflect and respect the values of the discipline of psychology and the values of cultural communities.

Chapter Cases and Ethics Discussion Questions

Dr. Fein was treating a retired executive for obsessive-compulsive disorder who had made significant progress after four sessions. During the fifth session, the client began to describe daily rituals he used to protect himself from Jewish bankers and creditors who "wanted to steal his money." Dr. Fein applied empirically validated techniques to help the client reduce these rituals. However, the client's rants against Jews escalated during the next two sessions. Dr. Fein's parents were Nazi concentration camp survivors, and she was finding the anti-Semitic comments upsetting and distracting from her work with the client. Which standards on competence are most relevant to this case? What are the ethically appropriate steps for Dr. Fein to take to resolve this dilemma?

A human rights organization asked researchers at a US university to design an open-access interactive website to encourage nonviolent alternatives to political oppression in a Latin American country. The web-based intervention would include assessment of an individual's propensity for collective violence, an individually tailored remediation to help overcome "moral disengagement" and increase "peace attitudes," and a postintervention questionnaire to evaluate the program's success. What competencies would you require the investigators to apply to this study in order to ensure the research was scientifically and socially valid and the rights and welfare of all participants were protected? How would the Ethics Code General Principles and standards on competence help the researchers determine whether working on this project is ethically justified?

Dr. Dragic, a clinical neuropsychologist, operated a single-practitioner practice for the assessment of childhood disorders in a neighborhood with a large number of Serbian immigrant families. He began having to turn down clients because of a rapid and unanticipated increase in his caseload. To expand the number of clients he could serve, he contacted the chair of a clinical program at a nearby university and offered to hire and supervise graduate students who had at least 2 years of coursework in psychological assessment and had taken a course in neuropsychology. What ethical issues would Dr. Dragic and the department chair need to consider before agreeing on such an arrangement?

CHAPTER 6

Standards on Human Relations

3. Human Relations

3.01 Unfair Discrimination

In their work-related activities, psychologists do not engage in unfair discrimination based on age, gender, gender identity, race, ethnicity, culture, national origin, religion, sexual orientation, disability, socioeconomic status, or any basis proscribed by law.

Psychologists respect the dignity and worth of all people and appropriately consider the relevance of personal characteristics based on factors such as age, gender, gender identity, race, ethnicity, culture, national origin, religion, sexual orientation, disability, or socioeconomic status (Principle E: Respect for People's Rights and Dignity). Much of the work of psychologists entails making valid discriminating judgments that best serve the people and organizations they work with and fulfilling their ethical obligations as teachers, researchers, organizational consultants, and practitioners. Standard 3.01 of the APA Ethics Code does not prohibit such discriminations.

- ⊘ The graduate psychology faculty of a university used differences in standardized test scores, undergraduate grades, and professionally related experience as selection criteria for program admission.
- ⊘ A research psychologist sampled children identifying as non-Hispanic white to study the development of racial, ethnic, and national prejudice.

(Continued)

(Continued)

- ✓ An organizational psychologist working for a software company designed assessments for employee screening and promotion to distinguish individuals with the requisite information technology skills to perform tasks essential to the positions from individuals not possessing these skills.
- ✓ A school psychologist considers factors such as age, English language proficiency, and hearing or vision impairment when making educational placement recommendations.
- ✓ A family bereavement counselor working in an elder care unit of a hospital regularly considered the extent to which factors associated with the families' culture or religious values should be considered in the treatment plan.
- ✓ A psychologist conducting couples therapy with gay and lesbian partners worked with clients to explore the potential effects of homophobia, relational ambiguity, and family support on their relationship (Green & Mitchell, 2002).

Standard 3.01 does not require psychologists offering therapeutic assistance to accept as clients/patients all individuals who request mental health services. Discerning and prudent psychologists know the limitations of their competence and accept to treat only those whom they can reasonably expect to help based on their education, training, and experience (Striefel, 2007; Standard 2.01a, Competence). Psychologists may also refuse to accept clients/patients on the basis of individuals' lack of commitment to the therapeutic process, problems they have that fall outside the therapists' area of competence, or individuals' perceived inability or unwillingness to pay for services (Knapp & VandeCreek, 2003).

Psychologists must, however, exercise reasonable judgment and precautions to ensure that their work does not reflect personal or organizational biases or prejudices that can lead to injustice (Principle D: Justice). For example, the American Psychological Association's (APA's) *Resolution on Religious, Religion-Based, and/or Religion-Derived Prejudice* (APA, 2007d) condemns prejudice and discrimination against individuals or groups based on their religious or spiritual beliefs, practices, adherence, or background.

Standard 3.01 prohibits psychologists from making unfair discriminations based on the factors listed in the standard.

- ☒ The director of a graduate program in psychology rejected a candidate for program admission because the candidate indicated that he was a Muslim.
- ☒ A consulting psychologist agreed to a company's request to develop preemployment procedures that would screen out applicants from Spanish-speaking cultures based on the company's presumption that the majority of such candidates would be undocumented residents.

☒ A psychologist working in a Medicaid clinic decided not to include a cognitive component in a behavioral treatment based solely on the psychologist's belief that lower-income patients were incapable of responding to "talk therapies."

☒ One partner of a gay couple who had recently entered couple counseling called their psychologist when he learned that he had tested positive for the HIV virus. Although when working with heterosexual couples the psychologist strongly encouraged clients to inform their partners if they had a sexually transmitted disease, she did not believe such an approach was necessary in this situation based on her erroneous assumption that all gay men engaged in reckless and risky sexual behavior (see Palma & Iannelli, 2002).

Refusing or Referring Clients Based on Religious Beliefs

What actions should psychologists take to comply with Standard 3.01 when they have a moral or religious objection to client/patient beliefs and behaviors associated with personal characteristics listed in the standard? For example, the Specialty Guidelines for Forensic Psychology (APA, 2013e) recommends that when psychologists recognize that their beliefs or biases may affect the ability to practice in a competent and impartial manner, they take steps to correct or limit such effects, declining to participate or limiting their participation in a manner consistent with professional obligations to avoid harm, exploitation, and termination (see also Standards 3.04, Avoiding Harm; 3.08, Exploitative Relationships; 10.01, Terminating Therapy).

The delivery of competent services does not and should not require psychologists to share or endorse the personal values of their clients/patients. Rather, competent practice draws on training and experience that enables psychologists to bring about therapeutic change through scientific and professional knowledge of the discipline and therapeutic skills that facilitate their understanding of client values as a means of enabling client insight and behaviors that help promote their mental health and psychological well-being (Campbell, 2014). When practitioners encounter a situation in which their own values appear to conflict with the personal characteristics, values, religious beliefs, political attitudes, or behaviors of a client, a decision regarding treatment or referral can be facilitated by considering the following questions:

- Is there established scientific and professional knowledge documenting that psychologists with values that conflict with client values cannot competently apply effective evidence-based treatments (Standard 2.04, Bases for Scientific and Professional Judgments)?
- Are practitioners engaging in financial exploitation (e.g., bait and switch tactics) if they agree to see clients knowing that they will make a referral if uncomfortable topics arise during treatment (Standards 3.08, Exploitative Relationships; 6.04, Fees and Financial Arrangements)?

- Will explaining the reason for the referral prior to or during treatment harm the client/patient and/or exacerbate his or her mental health problems (Standard 3.04, Avoiding Harm)?

Need to Know: Can Religious Beliefs Exempt Students From Supervised Treatment of Specific Clients/Patients?

Julea Ward was a student in the counseling program at East Michigan University. During the course of her practicum, she received a referral to treat a young man who was experiencing depression. Upon learning that the man was gay, she told her supervisor that based on her strong religious convictions, she would not treat the man if issues regarding a homosexual relationship arose during counseling, since it would force her to affirm the client's same-sex relationship. She asked for advice as to whether she should begin to see the client or whether he should be referred to another student. After an informal and formal review, the university terminated Ms. Ward from the program, citing its policy that students must adhere to professional ethics codes in counseling that prohibit discrimination based on sexual orientation and other factors. Ms. Ward brought a lawsuit against the school for infringing upon her First Amendment right to free expression of religion. After several lawsuits, the university agreed to a settlement that included removing the expulsion from her record (*Ward v. Polite*, 2012).

In response to the issues raised in this case, the American Psychological Association's Education Directorate (2013) developed the following policies:

- Professional psychology training programs are accountable for ensuring that all trainees exhibit the ability to work effectively with clients/patients whose group membership, demographic characteristics, or worldviews create conflict with their own.
- Programs cannot permit some students to avoid obtaining core competencies needed for the practice of psychology because these competencies are determined by the profession to be essential for the benefit of the public.
- This policy should be explicitly presented in all publicly and internally available program documents, admissions materials and program curricula (Standards 7.01, Design of Education and Training Programs; 7.02, Descriptions of Education and Training Programs).
- At times, training programs may consider client/patient reassignment so trainees have time to develop their competence to work with client/patients who challenge their sincerely held beliefs, with the overriding consideration in such cases always being the welfare of the client/patient.
- Programs should ensure that trainees and their values and beliefs are treated with dignity and respect and that determinations of whether remediation or program dismissal is required are based on prudent, consistent, and fair adherence to established program and institutional policies (Standard 7.06, Assessing Student and Supervisee Performance).

For additional information, readers may refer to Campbell (2014) and Hancock (2014).

Discrimination Proscribed by Law

Standard 3.01 prohibits psychologists from discriminating among individuals on any basis proscribed by law. For example, industrial–organizational psychologists need to be aware of nondiscrimination laws relevant to race, religion, and disability that apply to companies for which they work (e.g., Americans with Disabilities Act (ADA), http://www.ada.gov; Title VII of the Civil Rights Act of 1964, http://www.eeoc.gov/laws/statutes/titlevii.cfm; Workforce Investment Act of 1998, http://www.doleta.gov/usworkforce/wia/wialaw.txt). For example, under ADA (1990), disability-relevant questions can only be asked of prospective employees after the employer has made a conditional offer. In some instances, ADA laws for small businesses, such as laws concerning wheelchair accessibility, also apply to psychologists in private practice. In addition, based on recent legal decisions, psychologists conducting personnel performance evaluations should avoid selecting tests developed to assess psychopathology (see *Karraker v. Rent-a-Center,* 2005; see also Standard 9.02, Use of Assessments). In addition, HIPAA prohibits covered entities from discriminating against an individual for filing a complaint, participating in a compliance review or hearing, or opposing an act or practice that is unlawful under the regulation (see also Standard 1.08, Unfair Discrimination Against Complainants and Respondents).

Digital Ethics: Use of Internet Searches for Evaluation of Student Applicants

Some educational and training programs have begun to use the Internet to search for information about student applicants. Several states ban universities from requiring applicants to disclose their social network passwords as a condition of enrollment, but these states do not prohibit searching or utilizing applicant information that can be obtained without passwords. Online searches used to supplement application materials may pose potential problems when they reveal protected information regarding pregnancy, marital status, disability, sexual orientation, or religion. Acquiring such information may unintentionally lead to violation of affirmative action laws that prohibit applicants being questioned about these identity or affiliation variables or lead to discrimination prohibited by Standard 3.01, Unfair Discrimination. (See Wester, Danforth, & Olle, 2013, for a comprehensive review.)

3.02 Sexual Harassment

Psychologists do not engage in sexual harassment. Sexual harassment is sexual solicitation, physical advances, or verbal or nonverbal conduct that is sexual in nature, that occurs in connection with the psychologist's activities or role as a psychologist, and that either (1) is unwelcome, is offensive, or creates a hostile workplace or educational environment, and the psychologist knows or is told this; or (2) is sufficiently severe or intense to be abusive to a reasonable person in the context. Sexual harassment can consist of a single intense or severe act or of multiple persistent or pervasive acts. (See also Standard 1.08, Unfair Discrimination Against Complainants and Respondents.)

It is always wise for psychologists to be familiar with and comply with applicable laws and institutional policies regarding sexual harassment. Laws on sexual harassment vary across jurisdictions, are often complex, and change over time. Standard 3.02 provides a clear definition of behaviors that are prohibited and considered sexual harassment under the Ethics Code. When this definition establishes a higher standard of conduct than required by law, psychologists must comply with Standard 3.02.

According to Standard 3.02, sexual harassment can be verbal or nonverbal solicitation, advances, or sexual conduct that occurs in connection with the psychologist's activities or role as a psychologist. The wording of the definition was carefully crafted to prohibit sexual harassment without encouraging complaints against psychologists whose poor judgments or behaviors do not rise to the level of harassment. Thus, to meet the standard's threshold for sexual harassment, either (1) behaviors must be either so severe or intense that a reasonable person would deem them abusive in that context or (2) regardless of intensity, the psychologist was aware or had been told that the behaviors were unwelcome or offensive or that they created a hostile workplace or educational environment.

For example, a senior faculty member who places an arm around a student's shoulder during a discussion or who tells an off-color sexual joke that offends a number of junior faculty may not be in violation of this standard if such behavior is uncharacteristic of the faculty member's usual conduct, if a reasonable person might interpret the behavior as inoffensive, and if there is reason to assume the psychologist neither is aware of nor has been told the behavior is offensive.

A hostile workplace or educational environment is one in which the sexual language or behaviors of the psychologist impair the ability of those who are the target of the sexual harassment to conduct their work or participate in classroom and educational experiences. The actions of the senior faculty member described above might be considered sexual harassment if the psychologist's behaviors reflected a consistent pattern of sexual conduct during class or office hours, if such behaviors had led students to withdraw from the psychologist's class, or if students or other faculty had repeatedly told the psychologist about the discomfort produced.

- ☒ During office hours, a professor often put her arm around male students and made suggestive comments about campus hookups.
- ☒ A professor often made jokes about female body parts in his Adolescent Development course, causing a number of female students to drop the class.
- ☒ A clinical psychologist working in a mental health clinic continued to give female staff members a kiss on the cheek even after he was told to refrain from such behaviors.

According to this standard, sexual harassment can also consist of a single intense or severe act that would be considered abusive to a reasonable person.

☒ During clinical supervision, a trainee had an emotional discussion with her female supervisor about how her own experiences recognizing her lesbian sexual orientation during adolescence were helping her counsel the gay and lesbian youths she was working with. At the end of the session, the supervisor kissed the trainee on the lips.

☒ A senior psychologist at a test company sexually fondled a junior colleague during an office party.

A violation of this standard applies to all psychologists irrespective of the status, sex, or sexual orientation of the psychologist or individual harassed.

3.03 Other Harassment

Psychologists do not knowingly engage in behavior that is harassing or demeaning to persons with whom they interact in their work based on factors such as those persons' age, gender, gender identity, race, ethnicity, culture, national origin, religion, sexual orientation, disability, language, or socioeconomic status.

According to Principle E: Respect for People's Rights and Dignity, psychologists should eliminate from their work the effect of bias and prejudice based on factors such as age, gender, gender identity, race, ethnicity, national origin, religion, sexual orientation, disability, language, and socioeconomic status. Standard 3.03 prohibits behaviors that draw on these categories to harass or demean individuals with whom psychologists work, such as colleagues, students, research participants, or employees. Behaviors in violation of this standard include ethnic slurs and negative generalizations based on gender, sexual orientation, disability, or socioeconomic status whose intention or outcome is lowering status or reputation.

The term *knowingly* reflects the fact that evolving societal sensitivity to language and behaviors demeaning to different groups may result in psychologists unknowingly acting in a pejorative manner. The term *knowingly* also reflects awareness that interpretations of behaviors that are harassing or demeaning can often be subjective. Thus, a violation of this standard rests on an objective evaluation that a psychologist would have or should have been aware that his or her behavior would be perceived as harassing or demeaning.

This standard does not prohibit psychologists from making critical comments about the work of students, colleagues, or others based on legitimate criteria. For example, professors can inform, and often have a duty to inform, students that their writing or clinical skills are below program standards or indicate when a student's classroom comment is incorrect or inappropriate. It is the responsibility of employers or chairs of academic departments to critically review, report on, and discuss both positive and negative evaluations of employees or faculty. Similarly, the standard does not prohibit psychologists conducting assessment or therapy from applying valid diagnostic classifications that a client/patient may find offensive.

3.04 Avoiding Harm

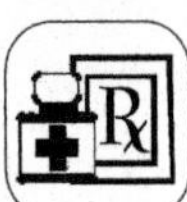

Psychologists take reasonable steps to avoid harming their clients/patients, students, supervisees, research participants, organizational clients, and others with whom they work, and to minimize harm where it is foreseeable and unavoidable.

As articulated in Principle A: Beneficence and Nonmaleficence, psychologists seek to safeguard the welfare of those with whom they work and avoid or minimize harm when conflicts occur among professional obligations. In the rightly practiced profession and science of psychology, harm is not always unethical or avoidable. Legitimate activities that may lead to harm include (a) giving low grades to students who perform poorly on exams, (b) providing a valid diagnosis that prevents a client/patient from receiving disability insurance, (c) conducting personnel reviews that lead to an individual's termination of employment, (d) conducting a custody evaluation in a case in which the judge determines one of the parents must relinquish custodial rights, or (e) disclosing confidential information to protect the physical welfare of a third party.

- ✓ Parents of a fourth-grade student wanted their child placed in a special education class. After administering a complete battery of tests, the school psychologist's report indicated that the child's responses did not meet established definitions for learning disabilities and therefore did not meet the district's criteria for such placement.
- ✓ A forensic psychologist was asked to evaluate the mental status of a criminal defendant who was asserting volitional insanity as a defense against liability in his trial for manslaughter. The psychologist conducted a thorough evaluation based on definitions of volitional insanity and irresistible impulse established by the profession of psychology and by law. While the psychologist's report noted that the inmate had some problems with impulse control and emotional instability, it also noted that these deficiencies did not meet the legal definition of volitional that would bar prosecution (see also Hot Topic "Human Rights and Psychologists' Involvement in Assessments Related to Death Penalty Cases" in Chapter 4).
- ☒ A psychologist with prescription privileges prescribed a Food and Drug Administration–approved neuroenhancer to help a young adult patient suffering from performance anxiety associated with his responsibilities as quarterback for his college varsity football team. The psychologist failed to discuss the importance of gradual reduction in dosage, and she was dismayed to learn that her patient had been hospitalized after he abruptly discontinued the medication when the football season ended (APA, 2011a; McCrickerd, 2010; I. Singh & Kelleher, 2010).

☒ Consistent with Standard 10.10a, Terminating Treatment, a psychologist treating a client/patient with a diagnosis of borderline disorder terminated therapy when she realized the client/patient had formed an iatrogenic attachment to her that was clearly interfering with any benefits that could be derived from the treatment. However, her failure to provide appropriate pretermination counseling and referrals contributed to the client's/patient's emergency hospitalization for suicidal risk (Standard 10.10c, Terminating Treatment).

☒ A psychologist assisted a community organization in establishing a hotline for women who were victims of interpersonal violence (IPV). Although he developed guidelines for reducing anxiety and providing information on community services for IPV victims, he did not include procedures for evaluating risk and obtaining emergency services for women callers who were in imminent danger of being attacked (see Denny, 2014).

Steps for Avoiding Harm

Recognizing that such harms are not always avoidable or inappropriate, Standard 3.04 requires psychologists to take reasonable steps to avoid harming those with whom they interact in their professional, educational, and scientific roles and to minimize harm where it is foreseeable and unavoidable.

These steps often include complying with other standards in the Ethics Code, such as the following:

- Clarifying course requirements and establishing a timely and specific process for providing feedback to students (Standard 7.06, Assessing Student and Supervisee Performance)
- Selecting and using valid and reliable assessment techniques appropriate to the nature of the problem and characteristics of the testee to avoid misdiagnosis and inappropriate services (Standards 9.01, Bases for Assessments; 9.02, Use of Assessments)
- When appropriate, providing information beforehand to employees and others who may be directly affected by a psychologist's services to an organization (Standard 3.11, Psychological Services Delivered To or Through Organizations)
- Acquiring adequate knowledge of relevant judicial or administrative rules prior to performing forensic roles to avoid violating the legal rights of individuals involved in litigation (Standard 2.01f, Boundaries of Competence)
- Taking steps to minimize harm when, during debriefing, a psychologist becomes aware of participant distress created by the research procedure (Standard 8.08c, Debriefing)
- Becoming familiar with local social service, medical, and legal resources for clients/patients and third parties who will be affected if a psychologist

is ethically or legally compelled to report child abuse, suicide risk, elder abuse, or intent to do physical harm to another individual (Standard 4.05b, Disclosures)

- Monitoring patient's physiological status when prescribing medications (with legal prescribing authority), particularly when there is a physical condition that might complicate the response to psychotropic medication or predispose a patient to experience an adverse reaction (APA, 2011a)

Digital Ethics: Avoiding Harm in Telepsychology Services

Telepsychology is an emerging area of practice that is only beginning to develop recognized standards for choice of modality, nature of treatment, and clients/patients most likely to benefit—and thus requires additional efforts to protect clients/patients from harm (Standards 2.01e, Competence; 3.04, Avoiding Harm). Therefore, the APA Telepsychology Taskforce (APA, 2013d) urges psychologists offering telepsychological services to conduct an initial review to determine the risks and benefits of the service for each client/patient. Factors to consider include the following:

- Are comparable in-person services available? Does the client/patient live in an underserved area without access to in-person treatment, or does the client's/patient's physical health preclude office visits?
- Are services delivered through telepsychology equivalent or preferable to available in-person services?
- What is the most clinically appropriate medium (video-conference, web-based psychoeducational material, mobile text messaging, telephone) for the client's/patient's treatment needs?
- Does the client's/patient's presenting problem suggest there may be an imminent or frequent need for emergency services (e.g., suicidality) or that the client/patient is subject to distractions (e.g., attentional problems) such that treatment effectiveness will be reduced?
- Will asynchronous (time-delayed communications such as email) increase client frustration or anxiety?
- Is there a language difference, special need, or cultural factor that will benefit or impede treatment effectiveness?
- Can the client/patient adequately protect the privacy and confidentiality of communications with the therapist, and/or will a breach of privacy affect client/patient safety in his or her home or other locale?
- Does the psychologist have an adequate backup plan in case of unforeseen technical difficulties?
- Does the psychologist have an adequate plan for crises that require immediate in-person attention, including arrangements with local professionals or client social support systems, and does the plan comply with local laws governing involuntary hospitalization?

☒ A psychologist conducted therapy over the Internet for clients/patients in a rural area 120 miles from her office. The psychologist had not developed a plan with each client/patient for handling mental health crises. During a live video Internet session, a client who had been struggling with bouts of depression showed the psychologist his gun and said he was going outside to "blow his head off." The psychologist did not have the contact information of any local hospital, relative, or friend to send prompt emergency assistance.

Is Use of Aversion Therapies Unethical?

Aversion therapy involves the repeated association of a maladaptive behavior or cognition with an aversive stimulus (e.g., electric shock, unpleasant images, nausea) to eliminate pleasant associations or introduce negative associations with the undesirable behavior. Aversion therapies have proved promising in treatments of drug cravings, alcoholism, and pica (Bordnick et al., 2004; Cellini & Parma, 2015; Ferreri, Tamm, & Wier, 2006; Hulse, 2013) and have been used with questionable effectiveness for pedophilia (Hall & Hall, 2007). It is beyond the purview of this volume to review literature evaluating the clinical efficacy of aversion therapies for different disorders. However, even with evidence of clinical efficacy, aversion therapies have and will continue to require ethical deliberation because they purposely subject clients/patients to physical and emotional discomfort and distress. In so doing, they raise the fundamental moral issue of balancing doing good against doing no harm (Principle A: Beneficence and Nonmaleficence).

Psychologists should consider the following questions before engaging in aversion therapy:

- Have all empirically and clinically validated alternative therapeutic approaches been attempted?
- Is there empirical evidence that the aversive therapeutic approach has demonstrated effectiveness with individuals who are similar to the client/patient in mental health disorder, age, physical health, and other relevant factors? (Standard 2.04, Bases for Scientific and Professional Judgments)
- To what extent is the behavior endangering the life or seriously compromising the well-being of the client/patient?
- For this particular patient, will the discomfort and distress of the aversive treatment outweigh its potential positive effects?
- To what extent is the urgency to use the aversive treatment defined by the needs of third parties rather than the client/patient? (Standards 3.05, Multiple Relationships; 3.07, Third-Party Requests for Services; 3.08, Exploitative Relationships)
- Am I competent to administer the aversive treatment? (Standards 2.01a, Boundaries of Competence; 2.05, Delegation of Work to Others)

- If aversive treatment is the only remaining option to best serve the needs of the client/patient, how can harm be minimized?
- Have I established appropriate monitoring procedures and termination criteria?

CASE EXAMPLE

An Ethical Approach to the Use of Aversion Therapies

Prescribing psychologists trained in addiction treatments opened a group practice to provide assessment and individual and group therapy for substance abuse and comorbid disorders. Occasionally, some clients who were long-term cocaine users could not overcome their cravings despite positive responses to therapy. In such cases, the team would offer the client a chemical aversion therapy with empirical evidence of treatment efficacy. The therapy was supervised by a member of the team who was a prescribing psychologist and who had acquired additional training in this technique (see also Standards 2.01, Competence; 2.05, Delegation of Work to Others).

In the same setting, prior to initiating the aversion therapy, clients/patients were required to undergo a physical examination by a physician to rule out those for whom the treatment posed a potential medical risk. The treatment consisted of drinking a saltwater solution containing a chemical that would induce nausea. Saltwater was used to avoid creating a negative association with water. As soon as the client began to feel nauseated, he or she was instructed to ingest a placebo form of crack cocaine using drug paraphernalia. A bucket was available for vomiting. Patients were monitored by a physician assistant and the prescribing psychologist during the process and recovery for any medical or iatrogenic psychological side effects (Standard 3.09, Cooperation With Other Professionals). Following the recommended minimum number of sessions, patients continued in individual psychotherapy, and positive and negative reactions to the aversion therapy continued to be monitored (see Bordnick et al., 2004).

Standard 3.04 and Violation of Other Standards

Often, violation of Standard 3.04 will occur in connection with the violation of other standards in the Code that detail the actions required to perform psychological activities in an ethically responsible manner. Following are some examples:

- Providing testimony on the poor parenting skills of an individual whom the psychologist has never personally examined that contributed to that individual's loss of child custody (Standard 9.01b, Bases for Assessments)
- Engaging in a sexual relationship with a current therapy client/patient that was a factor leading to the breakup of the client's/patient's marriage (Standard 10.05, Sexual Intimacies With Current Therapy Clients/Patients)
- Asking students to relate their personal experience in psychotherapy to past and current theories on mental health treatment when this requirement

was not stipulated in admissions or program materials, causing some students to drop out of the program (Standard 7.04, Student Disclosure of Personal Information)

- Deceiving a research participant about procedures that the investigator expected would cause some physical pain (Standard 8.07b, Deception in Research)
- Invalidating the life experience of clients from diverse cultural backgrounds by defining their cultural values or behaviors as deviant or pathological and denying them culturally appropriate care (Sue & Sue, 2003; Standard 2.01b, Boundaries of Competence)

Some contexts require more stringent protections against harm. For example, psychologists working within institutions that use seclusion or physical restraint techniques to treat violent episodes or other potentially injurious patient behaviors must ensure that these extreme methods are employed only upon evidence of their effectiveness, when other treatment alternatives have failed, and when the use of such techniques is in the best interest of the patient and *not* to administer punishment, to alleviate staff inconvenience or anxiety, or to reduce costs (Jerome, 1998).

☒ The director of psychological services for a children's state psychiatric inpatient ward approved the employment of time-out procedures to discipline patients who were disruptive during educational classes. A special room was set up for this purpose. The director did not, however, set guidelines for how the time-out procedure should be implemented. For example, he failed to set limits on the length of time a child could be kept in the room, to require staff monitoring, and to ensure the room was protected against fire hazard, and he did not develop policies that would permit patients to leave the room for appropriate reasons. The director was appalled to learn that staff had not monitored a 7-year-old who was kept in the room for over an hour and was discovered crying and self-soiled (see, e.g., *Dickens v. Johnson County Board of Education,* 1987; *Goss v. Lopez,* 1975; *Hayes v. Unified School District,* 1989; Yell, 1994; see also Standard 2.05, Delegation of Work to Others).

Psychotherapy and Counseling Harms

Psychologists should also be aware of psychotherapies or counseling techniques that may cause harm (Barlow, 2010). If psychological interventions are powerful enough to improve mental health, it follows that they can be equally effective in worsening it. In the normative practice of mental health treatment, the diversity of patient/client mental health needs and the fluid nature of differential diagnosis will mean that some therapeutic approaches will fail to help alleviate a mental health problem. In such circumstances, psychologists will turn to other techniques, seek consultation, or offer an appropriate referral. In other circumstances, negative symptoms are expected to increase and then subside during the natural course of evidence-based treatment (e.g., exposure therapy). When treating naturally deteriorating conditions (e.g., Alzheimer's disease), a worsening of symptoms does not necessarily indicate treatment harms (Dimidjian & Hollon, 2010). By contrast, harmful psychotherapies are defined as those that produce outcomes worse than what would have occurred without treatment (Dimidjian & Hollon, 2010; Lilienfeld, 2007). Such harmful effects are easiest to detect for mental health problems whose natural course is constant.

Need to Know: When HMOs Refuse to Extend Coverage

When health maintenance organizations refuse psychologists' request to extend coverage for clients/patients whose reimbursement quotas have been reached, psychologists may be in violation of Standard 3.04 if they (a) did not take reasonable steps at the outset of therapy to estimate and communicate to patients and their insurance company the number of sessions anticipated, (b) did not familiarize themselves with the insurers' policy, (c) recognized a need for continuing treatment but did not communicate with insurers in an adequate or timely fashion, or (d) were unprepared to handle client/patient response to termination of services.

Harms are more difficult to anticipate and identify for mental health problems, such as trauma, that vary in their temporal course of symptoms, the eliciting situations, the nature of the traumatic event, and other contextual and client/patient characteristics. Psychologists providing such treatments need to be alert to increasing risk of client retraumatization and consider whether informed consent adequately prepares clients for the opening up of wounds that may heighten distress levels or increase risk of retraumatization (Standard 10.01, Informed Consent to Therapy). Psychologists must also consider whether the experience of betrayal or resistance to disclosure based on the silence grooming that often accompanies traumatic abuse will interfere with the client's ability to communicate negative reactions to treatment (Courtois, 2015; Mailloux, Scholar, & Isidore, 2014). In all these circumstances, failure to terminate treatment when it becomes clear that continuation would be harmful is a violation of Standard 3.04 and Standard 10.10a, Terminating Therapy.

Need to Know: How to Detect Harm in Psychotherapy and Counseling

Psychologists should be aware of the evolving body of knowledge on potential contributors to the harmful effects of psychotherapy and keep in mind the following suggestions drawn from Beutler, Blatt, Alimohamed, Levy, and Angtuaco (2006); Castonguay, Boswell, Constantino, Goldfried, and Hill (2010); Lilienfeld (2007); and O'Donohue and Engle (2013):

- Obtain training in and keep up-to-date on the flexible use of interventions and treatment alternatives to avoid premature use of clinical interpretations, rigid theoretical frameworks, and singular treatment modalities.
- Be familiar with the degree to which each client/patient and treatment setting matches those reported for a specific EBP and look for multiple knowledge sources as support for different approaches. (Readers may also want to refer to the Digital Ethics section "Navigating the Online Search for Evidence-Based Practices" in Chapter 5.)
- Monitor changes that suggest client/patient deterioration or lack of improvement; continuously evaluate what works and what interferes with positive change.
- Attend to treatment-relevant characteristics such as culture, sexual orientation, religious beliefs, and disabilities and be aware of the possibility of over- or underdiagnosing the mental health needs of clients/patients with these characteristics.
- Carefully attend to a client's/patient's disclosures of frustration with treatment and use the information self-critically to evaluate the need to modify diagnosis, adjust treatment strategy, or strengthen relational factors that may be jeopardizing the therapeutic alliance.

Conversion Therapy Involving Sexual and Gender Minority (SGM) Children and Adolescents

In 2015, the Substance Abuse and Mental Health Services Administration (SAMHSA) and the APA issued a joint report based on a consensus panel of experts titled *Ending Conversion Therapy: Supporting and Affirming LGBTQ Youth* (http://store.samhsa.gov/product/SMA15-4928). The report concluded that conversion therapy perpetuates outdated gender roles and negative stereotypes that being a sexual or gender minority or identifying as LGBTQ is an abnormal aspect of human development. According to the report, conversion therapy puts young people at risk of serious harm with no demonstrable benefits. Appropriate therapeutic approaches to providing services to children and adolescents distressed by their sexual orientation or gender recommended by the consensus panel include the following:

- Provide children and parents with accurate information on the development of sexual orientation and gender identity and expression.
- Conduct a comprehensive evaluation and focus on identity development and exploration, allowing the child freedom of self-discovery within a context of acceptance and support.
- Identify and work to ameliorate sources of distress experienced by SGM youth and their families.
- Use client-centered and developmentally appropriate treatments to attain the best possible level of psychological functioning rather than any specific gender identity, gender expression, or sexual orientation.

- Consider when appropriate recommending school and community interventions to increase emotional support and reduce possibility of harms.

For additional discussion of ethical issues related to conversion therapy, see the Hot Topic "Ethical Issues for the Integration of Religion and Spirituality in Therapy" at the end of Chapter 13.

Research Risks

Under federal regulations governing the protection of human participants in research (45CFR46; DHHS, 2009) to approve a research protocol, institutional review boards (IRBs) must determine that risks to subjects are reasonable in relation to anticipated benefits, if any, to participants and the importance of the knowledge that may reasonably be expected to result. Harms can be (a) psychological (e.g., increased anxiety due to an experimental manipulation); (b) physical (e.g., increased symptomology due to participation in a treatment study); (c) legal (e.g., arrest or imprisonment based on a disclosure of illegal activities); (d) economic (e.g., higher insurance rates based on a diagnosis entered into health records); or (e) social (e.g., stigma or harm to reputation resulting from identification during recruitment for, participation in, or dissemination of research).

Consistent with the requirements of Standard 3.04, under 45CFR46 risks to participants must be minimized by using procedures that are consistent with sound research design, that do not unnecessarily expose participants to risk, and, whenever appropriate, that are already being used with the participants for diagnostic or treatment purposes.

Psychologists must also be familiar with the regulatory definition of "minimal risk" (DHHS, 2009, §46.102i): "procedures for which the probability and magnitude of harm or discomfort anticipated in the research are not greater in and of themselves than those ordinarily encountered in daily life or during the performance of routine physical or psychological examinations or tests". This definition is key to determining whether or not a research proposal must undergo a full board IRB review, a critical time-saving process. In addition, the minimal risk criteria strictly determine what type of research can be conducted involving children (Fisher, Kornetsky, & Prentice, 2007).

The ambiguity of language in the minimal risk definition has often given rise to IRB overestimations of risk in social behavioral research involving individuals who might suffer adverse social, economic, or legal effects if their identities were exposed (e.g., sexual minorities, illicit drug users, illegal immigrants, underage college students engaged in alcohol use; National Research Council, 2014). Psychologists planning to conduct research with such populations may minimize risk overestimations by taking appropriate steps to protect participant confidentiality (Standard, 4.01, Maintaining Confidentiality) and noting in their IRB protocols that under current regulations, research posing confidentiality risks can be considered minimal-risk research if reasonable and appropriate protections are implemented so that disclosure risks are no greater than minimal (http://www.hhs.gov/ohrp/policy/expedited98.html). (Additional recommendations for working with IRBs to avoid risk overestimation can be found in Fisher, Brunnquell, et al., 2013; Iltis et al., 2013; National Research Council, 2014).

Need to Know: Clinical Equipoise and Evaluating Risk in Randomized Clinical Trials

Important questions of treatment efficacy and effectiveness driving the conduct of randomized clinical trials (RCTs) for mental health treatments raise, by their very nature, the possibility that some participants will fail to respond to experimental treatment conditions or experience a decline in mental health during the trial. Such studies may include a potential for harm because the intervention is novel, the study population is deemed high risk (e.g., individuals with acute psychosis), the study targets risky behavior (e.g., suicidality), or the study targets disorders in which risky behaviors are features of the illnesses (e.g., intermittent explosive disorder). Under Principle A: Beneficence and Nonmaleficence, psychologists have an obligation not to needlessly expose research participants to harm and, when possible, promote their welfare. It is thus unethical to assign subjects to either a treatment or control condition if one of those conditions is known to be inferior.

To ethically justify the selection of different treatment or control conditions in an RCT, investigators must draw on established scientific or professional knowledge to demonstrate that the likelihood of benefit or risk is at the moment equal among the different conditions or there is a current or likely dispute among experts as to which of the conditions is superior. This is called "clinical equipoise" (Freedman, 1987; Weijer & Miller, 2004). Studies that meet the clinical equipoise criteria must still take steps to minimize risk under Standard 3.04. To do so, research psychologists should develop procedures to identify and address such possibilities. Such steps can include (a) scientifically and clinically informed inclusion and exclusion criteria for patient participation; (b) the establishment of a data safety–monitoring board to evaluate unanticipated risks that may emerge during a clinical trial; and (c) prior to the initiation of the research, the establishment of criteria based on anticipated risks for when a trial should be stopped to protect the welfare of participants. For additional information on monitoring anticipated and unanticipated adverse events, readers can refer to http://www.hhs.gov/ohrp/policy/advevntguid.html.

⊘ There is professional and scientific disagreement over the risks and benefits of prescribing methylphenidate (Ritalin) for treatment of attention-deficit/hyperactivity disorder (ADHD) in children less than 6 years of age. An interdisciplinary team of behavioral and prescribing psychologists sought to empirically test the advantages of adding psychopharmaceutical treatment to cognitive–behavioral therapy (CBT) for 3- to 5-year-old children previously diagnosed with ADHD. To avoid unnecessarily exposing children to the potential side effects of medication, the team decided that preschoolers would first participate in a multiweek parent training and behavioral treatment program and that only those children whose symptoms did not significantly improve with the behavioral intervention would continue to the medication clinical trial.

3.05 Multiple Relationships

(a) A multiple relationship occurs when a psychologist is in a professional role with a person and (1) at the same time is in another role with the same person, (2) at the same time is in a relationship with a person closely associated with or related to the person with whom the psychologist has the professional relationship, or (3) promises to enter into another relationship in the future with the person or a person closely associated with or related to the person. A psychologist refrains from entering into a multiple relationship if the multiple relationship could reasonably be expected to impair the psychologist's objectivity, competence, or effectiveness in performing his or her functions as a psychologist, or otherwise risks exploitation or harm to the person with whom the professional relationship exists.

Multiple relationships that would not reasonably be expected to cause impairment or risk exploitation or harm are not unethical.

Individual psychologists may perform a variety of roles. For example, during the course of a year, a psychologist might see clients/patients in private practice, teach at a university, provide consultation services to an organization, and conduct research. In some instances, these multiple roles, which may be concurrent or sequential, will involve the same person or persons who have a close relationship with one another.

Not All Multiple Relationships Are Unethical

Multiple relationships that would not reasonably be expected to cause impairment or risk exploitation or harm are not unethical. For example, it is not unethical for psychologists to serve as clinical supervisors or dissertation mentors for students enrolled in one of their graduate classes because supervision, mentoring, and teaching are all educational roles.

Standard 3.05 does not prohibit attendance at a client's/patient's, student's, employee's, or employer's family funeral, wedding, or graduation; the participation of a psychologist's child in an athletic team coached by a client/patient; gift giving or receiving with those with whom one has a professional role; or entering into a social relationship with a colleague as long as these relationships would not reasonably be expected to lead to role impairment, exploitation, or harm. Incidental encounters with clients/patients at religious services, school events, restaurants, health clubs, or similar places are also not unethical as long as psychologists react to these encounters in a professional manner. Nonetheless, psychologists should always consider whether the particular nature of a professional relationship might lead to a client's/patient's misperceptions regarding an encounter. If so, it is advisable to keep a record of such encounters and discuss them with the client/patient when clinically indicated (Standard 6.01, Documentation of Professional and Scientific Work and Maintenance of Records).

☑ A client with a fluctuating sense of reality coupled with strong romantic transference feelings for a treating psychologist misinterpreted two incidental encounters with his psychologist as planned romantic meetings. The client subsequently raised these incidents in a sexual misconduct complaint against the psychologist. The psychologist's recorded notes, made immediately following each encounter, were effective evidence against the invalid accusations.

Posttermination Nonsexual Relationships

The standard does not have an absolute prohibition against posttermination *non*sexual relationships with persons with whom psychologists have had a previous professional relationship. However, such relationships are prohibited if the posttermination relationship was promised during the course of the original relationship or if the individual was exploited or harmed by the intent to have the posttermination relationship. Psychologists should be aware that posttermination relationships can become problematic when personal knowledge acquired during the professional relationship becomes relevant to the new relationship (see Anderson & Kitchener, 1996; Sommers-Flanagan, 2012).

☒ A psychologist in independent practice abruptly terminated therapy with a patient who was an editor at a large publishing company so that the patient could review a book manuscript that the psychologist had submitted to the company.

Clients in Individual and Group Therapy

In most instances, treating clients/patients concurrently in individual and group therapy does not represent a multiple relationship because the practitioner is working in a therapeutic role in both contexts (Taylor & Gazda, 1991), and Standard 3.05 does not prohibit such practice. Psychologists providing individual and group therapy to the same clients/patients should consider instituting special protections against inadvertently revealing to a therapy group information shared by a client/patient in individual sessions (Standard 4.01, Maintaining Confidentiality). As in all types of professional practice, psychologists should avoid recommending an additional form of therapy based on the psychologist's financial interests rather than the client's/patient's mental health needs (Knauss & Knauss, 2012; Standards 3.8, Exploitative Relationships, 3.06, Conflict of Interest).

Need to Know: Ethical "Hot Spots" of Combined Therapy

Brabender and Fallon (2009) have identified ethical "hot spots" of combined therapy that should be addressed at the outset of plans to engage clients/patients in individual and group therapy. First, clients/patients should know that they have a choice in being offered an additional therapy beyond what they expected, and their concerns about costs in time and money should be respected and discussed (Standards 10.01, Informed Consent to Therapy; 10.03, Group Therapy). Second, psychologists should describe how private information disclosed in individual therapy will be protected from transfer during group sessions (Standard 4.02, Discussing the Limits of Confidentiality). Finally, psychologists should explain their policies on client/patient decisions to choose to terminate one of the treatment modalities (Standard 10.10a, Terminating Therapy).

Judging the Ethicality of Multiple Roles

Several authors have provided helpful decision-making models for judging whether a multiple relationship may place the psychologist in violation of Standard 3.04 (Brownlee, 1996; Gottlieb, 1993; Oberlander & Barnett, 2005; Younggren & Gottlieb, 2004). The majority looks at multiple relationships in terms of a continuum of risk. From these models, the ethical appropriateness of a multiple relationship becomes increasingly questionable with

- increased incompatibility in role functions and objectives;
- the greater power or prestige the psychologist has over the person with whom there is a multiple role;
- the greater the intimacy called for in the roles;
- the longer the role relationships are anticipated to last;
- the more vulnerable the client/patient, student, supervisee, or other subordinate is to harm; and
- the extent to which engaging in the multiple relationship meets the needs of the psychologist rather than the needs of the client/patient.

Entering Into Another Role

Psychologists may encounter situations in which the opportunity to enter a new relationship emerges with a person with whom they already have an established professional role. The following examples illustrate multiple relationships that, with rare exception, would be prohibited by Standard 3.05a because each situation could reasonably be expected to impair psychologists' ability to competently and objectively perform their roles or lead to exploitation or harm.

- ☒ A company hired a psychologist for consultation on how to prepare employees for a shift in management anticipated by the failing mental health of the chief executive officer (CEO). A few months later, the psychologist agreed to a request by the board of directors to counsel the CEO about retiring. The CEO did not want to retire and told the psychologist about the coercive tactics used by the board. The psychologist realized too late that this second role undermined both treatment and consultation effectiveness because the counseling role played by the psychologist would be viewed as either exploitative by the CEO or as disloyal by the board of directors.
- ☒ A school psychologist whose responsibilities in the school district included discussing with parents the results of their children's psychoeducational assessments regularly recommended to parents that they bring their children to his private practice for consultation and possible therapy.
- ☒ As part of their final class assignment, a psychologist required all students in her undergraduate psychology class to participate in a federally funded research study that she was conducting on college student drinking behaviors.
- ☒ A psychologist treating an inmate for anxiety disorder in a correctional facility agreed with a request by the prison administrator to serve on a panel determining the inmate's parole eligibility (Anno, 2001).
- ☒ A graduate student interning at an inpatient psychiatric hospital asked her patients if they would agree to participate in her dissertation research.
- ☒ An applied developmental psychologist conducting interview research on moral development and adolescent health risk behaviors often found herself giving advice on how to engage in safer sex behaviors to adolescent female participants who asked for her help during the interviews.
- ☒ A psychologist agreed to see a student in the psychologist's introductory psychology course for brief private counseling for test anxiety. At the end of the semester, to avoid jeopardizing the student's growing academic self-confidence, the psychologist refrained from giving the student a legitimate low grade for poor class performance. The psychologist should have anticipated that the multiple relationship would impair her objectivity and effectiveness as a teacher and create an unfair grading environment for the rest of the class.

Forensic Roles

Forensic psychologists may be called upon to fulfill a variety of assessment roles whose goals and responsibilities differ from those of treating psychologists. Whereas the responsibility of the treating psychologist is to help clients/patients achieve mental health, the responsibility of forensic psychologists serving as experts for the court, the defense, or the plaintiff is to provide objective information to assist the finder of facts in legal determinations. In most instances, psychologists who take on both roles concurrently or sequentially will be in violation of Standard 3.05a. For example, in the treatment context, the format, information sought, and psychologist–client/patient relationship are guided by the psychologist's professional evaluation of client/patient needs. Information obtained in a standardized or unstructured manner or in response to practitioner empathy and other elements of the therapeutic alliance is a legitimate means of meeting treatment goals. In determining whether court-ordered therapeutic services are forensic in nature, psychologists should consider the potential impact of the legal context on treatment and the potential for treatment to impact the psycholegal issues involved in the case (APA, 2013c, 2013e).

However, when mixed with the forensic role, the subjective nature of such inquiries and the selectivity of information obtained impair the psychologist's objectivity and thus ability to fulfill forensic responsibilities. Moreover, the conflicting objectives of the treating and forensic roles will be confusing and potentially intimidating to clients/patients, thereby undermining the psychologist's effectiveness in functioning under either role. Gottlieb and Coleman (2012) advised forensic psychologists to play only one role in legal matters and to notify the interested parties if a role change is contemplated.

☒ A forensic psychologist was hired by the court to conduct a psychological evaluation for a probation hearing of a man serving a jail sentence for spousal abuse. At the end of the evaluation, the psychologist suggested that if the inmate were released, he and his wife should consider seeing the psychologist for couples therapy.

Bush et al. (2006) suggested that one potential exception to multiple relationships in forensic contexts may be seen in psychologists who transition from the role of forensic evaluator to trial consultant. For example, in some contexts it may be ethically permissible if a psychologist originally retained by a defense attorney to evaluate a client also performs consultative services for the attorney regarding the testimony of other psychologists during a trial if (a) the psychologist initially provided only an oral report on his or her diagnostic impressions and (b) the psychologist would not be called on to provide court testimony. Psychologists should, however, approach such a multiple relationship with caution if, by ingratiating themselves with the attorney, they intentionally or unintentionally bias their evaluation or otherwise violate Standards 3.05a, Multiple Relationships, or 3.06, Conflict of Interest. (For additional discussion of the role of forensic experts, see the Hot Topics in Chapters 8 and 12 on psychologists providing testimony in courts.)

Personal–Professional Boundary Crossings Involving Clients/Patients, Students, Research Participants, and Subordinates

Boundaries serve to support the effectiveness of psychologists' work and create a safe place for clients/patients, students, employees, and other subordinates to benefit from psychologists' services (Burian & Slimp, 2000; Russell & Peterson, 1998). Boundaries protect against a blurring of personal and professional domains that could jeopardize psychologists' objectivity and the confidence of those with whom they work that psychologists will act in their best interests. Unethical multiple relationships often emerge after psychologists have engaged in a pattern that "progresses from apparently benign and perhaps well-intended boundary crossings to increasingly intrusive and harmful boundary violations and multiple relationships" (Oberlander & Barnett, 2005, p. 51). Boundary crossings can thus place psychologists on a slippery slope leading to ethical misconduct (Gutheil & Gabbard, 1993; Norris, Gutheil, & Strasburger, 2003; Sommers-Flanagan, 2012).

Clients/patients, students, research participants, and supervisees have less experience, knowledge, and power compared with psychologists providing assessment, treatment, teaching, mentoring, or supervision. Consequently, they are unlikely to recognize inappropriate boundary crossings or to express their concerns. It is the psychologist's responsibility to monitor and ensure appropriate boundaries between professional and personal communications and relationships (Gottlieb, Robinson, & Younggren, 2007).

Self-Disclosure

Self-disclosure, such as sharing aspects of personal history or current reactions to a situation with those they work with, is not unethical if psychologists limit these communications to meet the therapeutic, educational, or supervisory needs of those they serve.

- ⊘ A graduate student expressed to his dissertation mentor his feelings of inadequacy and frustration upon learning that a manuscript he had submitted for publication had been rejected. The mentor described how she often reacted similarly when first receiving such information but framed this disclosure within a "lesson" for the student on rising above the initial emotion to objectively reflect on the review and improve the chances of having a revised manuscript accepted.
- ⊘ A psychologist in private practice was providing CBT to help a client conquer feelings of inadequacy and panic attacks that were interfering with her desired career advancement. After several sessions, the psychologist

(Continued)

(Continued)

realized that the client's distorted belief regarding the ease with which other people and the psychologist, in particular, had attained their career goals was interfering with the effectiveness of the treatment. The psychologist shared with the client a brief personal story regarding how he had experienced and reacted to a career obstacle, limiting the disclosure to elements the client could use in framing her own career difficulties.

Boundary crossings can become boundary violations when psychologists share personal information with clients/patients, students, or employees to satisfy their own needs.

☒ A psychologist repeatedly confided to his graduate research assistant about the economic strains his marriage was placing on his personal and professional life. After several weeks, the graduate student began to pay for the psychologist's lunches when they were delivered to the office.

☒ A psychologist providing services at a college counseling center was having difficulties with her own college-aged son's drinking habits. She began to share her concerns about her son with her clients and sometimes asked their advice.

Practitioners should be especially wary of self-disclosure to clients/patients who have suffered child abuse or other forms of family victimization because dual relationships are frequently the norm in the context of such abuse. Such relational traps can include information about the therapist's upbringing, experience with trauma, and sexual orientation and functioning. Courtois (2015) recommended that psychotherapists predetermine their general stance and comfort with self-disclosure to avoid inappropriate disclosures in response to pressure from the client/patient, recognizing that information once disclosed cannot be taken back.

Research

Boundary crossings can also lead to bidirectional coercion, exploitation, or harm. For example, the intimacy between researchers and study participants inherent in ethnographic and participant observation research can create ambiguous or blurred personal–professional boundaries that can threaten the validity of data collected (Fisher, 2004, 2011). Study participants may feel bound by a personal relationship with an investigator to continue in a research project they find distressing, or investigators may feel pressured to yield to participant demands for involvement in illegal behaviors or for money or other resources above those allocated for participation in the research (Singer et al., 1999).

☒ A psychologist was conducting ethnographic research on the lives of female sex workers who were also raising young children. In an effort to establish a sense of trust with the sex workers, she spent many months in the five-block radius where they worked, sharing stories with them about her own parenting experiences. One day, when the police were conducting a drug raid in the area, a participant the psychologist had interviewed numerous times begged the psychologist to hold her marijuana before the police searched her, crying that she would lose her child if the drugs were discovered. The psychologist felt she had no choice but to agree to hide the drugs because she had shared personal worries about the safety of her own children with the participant (adapted from Fisher, 2011).

Nonsexual Physical Contact

Nonsexual physical contact with clients/patients, students, or others over whom the psychologist has professional authority can also lead to role misperceptions that interfere with the psychologist's professional functions. While Standard 3.05 does not prohibit psychologists from hugging, handholding, or putting an arm around those with whom they work in response to a special event (e.g., graduation, termination of therapy, promotion) or showing empathy for emotional crises (e.g., death in the family, recounting of an intense emotional event), such actions can be the first step toward an easing of boundaries that could lead to an unethical multiple relationship.

Whenever such circumstances arise, psychologists should evaluate, before they act, the appropriateness of the physical contact by asking the following questions:

- Is the initiation of physical contact consistent with the professional goals of the relationship?
- How might the contact serve to strengthen or jeopardize the future functioning of the psychologist's role?
- How will the contact be perceived by the recipient?
- Does the act serve the immediate needs of the psychologist rather than the immediate or long-term needs of the client/patient, student, or supervisee?
- Is the physical contact a substitute for more professionally appropriate behaviors?
- Is the physical contact part of a continuing pattern of behavior that may reflect the psychologist's personal problems or conflicts?

Digital Ethics: Professional Boundaries and Self-Disclosure Over the Internet

The Internet has complicated psychologists' control over access to personal information. Psychologists can control some information disclosed on the Internet through carefully crafted professional blogs, participation on professional or scientific listservs, and credentials or course curricula posted on individual or institutional websites. However, accidental self-disclosure (Zur, Williams, Lehavot, & Knapp, 2009) can occur when clients/patients, students, employees, or others (a) pay for legal online background checks that may include information on divorce or credit ratings, (b) conduct illegal searches of cell phone records, or (c) use search engines to find information that the psychologist may not be aware is posted online. Even when psychologists refuse "friending" requests, it is increasingly easy for individuals to find information on social networks such as Facebook through the millions of interconnected links and "mutual friends" who may have personal postings from and photos of the psychologist on their websites (Luo, 2009; Taylor, McMinn, Bufford, & Chang, 2010; Zur et al., 2009). Given the risks of accidental self-disclosure, psychologists should consider taking the following measures to limit access to personal information (Barnett, 2008; Lehavot, Barnett, & Powers, 2010; Nicholson, 2011):

- Set one's social network settings to restrict access to specifically authorized visitors only.
- Consider whether posted personal information, if accessed, would cause harm to those with whom one works; undermine therapeutic, teaching, consultation, or research effectiveness; or compromise the public's trust in the discipline.
- Periodically search one's name online using different combinations (e.g., Dr. Jones, Edward Jones, Jones family).
- Consult with experts on how to remove personal or inaccurate information from the Internet.
- When appropriate, discuss one's Internet policies during informed consent or the beginning of other professional relationships (see "Digital Ethics: Setting an Internet Search and Social Media Policy During Informed Consent" in Chapter 13).

Relationships With Others

Psychologists also encounter situations in which a person closely associated with someone with whom they have a professional role seeks to enter into a similar professional relationship. For example, the roommate of a current psychotherapy client/patient might ask the psychologist for an appointment to begin psychotherapy. The CEO of a company that hires a psychologist to conduct personnel evaluations might ask the psychologist to administer psychological tests to the CEO's child to determine whether the child has a learning disability. With few exceptions, entering into such relationships would risk a violation of Standard 3.05a because it could reasonably be expected that the psychologist's ability to make appropriate and objective judgments would be impaired, which in turn would jeopardize the effectiveness of services provided and result in harm.

Referrals From Clients

Receiving referrals from current or recent clients/patients should raise ethical red flags. In many instances, accepting into treatment a friend, relative, or others referred by a current client can create a real or perceived intrusion on the psychologist–patient relationship. For example, a current client/patient may question whether the psychologist has information about him or her gained from the person he or she referred or whether the psychologist is siding with one person or the other if there is a social conflict. Psychologists must also guard against exploiting clients/patients by explicitly or implicitly encouraging referrals to expand their practice (see also Standard 3.06, Conflict of Interest).

Some have suggested that treating psychologists should consider a referral from a current client/patient in the same way they would evaluate the therapeutic meaning of a "gift" (Shapiro & Ginzberg, 2003). In all circumstances, psychologists must evaluate the extent to which accepting a referral could impair their objectivity and conduct of their work or lead to exploitation or harm. One way of addressing this issue is to clearly state to current patients the psychologist's policy of not accepting patient referrals and, if a situation arises requiring an immediate need for treatment, to provide a professional referral to another psychologist (see also Standard 2.02, Providing Services in Emergencies).

When practicing psychologists receive referrals from former clients/patients, it is prudent to consider (a) whether the former client/patient may need the psychologist's services in the future, (b) whether information obtained about the new referral during the former client's/patient's therapy is likely to impair the psychologist's objectivity, and (c) the extent to which the new referral's beliefs about the former client's/patient's relationship with the psychologist are likely to interfere with treatment effectiveness.

Preexisting Personal Relationships

Psychologists may also encounter situations in which they are asked to take on a professional role with someone with whom they have had a preexisting personal relationship. Such multiple relationships are often unethical because the preexisting relationship would reasonably be expected to impair the psychologist's objectivity and effectiveness.

☒ A psychologist agrees to spend a few sessions helping his nephew overcome anxiety about going to school. As a result, the nephew's parents do not seek psychological services for their son even as his school anxiety continues to persist.

(Continued)

(Continued)

☒ At a colleague's request, a psychologist agreed to administer a battery of tests to assess whether the colleague had adult attention deficit disorder (ADD). After the psychologist informed his colleague that the test results suggested a form of ADD, the colleague began to suspect that the psychologist was talking about his problem to other colleagues.

Sexual Multiple Relationships

Sexual relationships with individuals with whom psychologists have a current professional relationship are always unethical. Because of the strong potential for harm involved in such multiple relationships, they are specifically addressed in several standards of the Ethics Code that will be covered in greater detail in Chapters 10 and 13 (Standards 7.07, Sexual Relationships With Students and Supervisees; 10.05, Sexual Intimacies With Current Therapy Clients/Patients; 10.06, Sexual Intimacies With Relatives or Significant Others of Current Therapy Clients/Patients; 10.07, Therapy With Former Sexual Partners; 10.08, Sexual Intimacies With Former Therapy Clients/Patients).

"Reasonably Expected"

It is important to note that the phrase "could reasonably be expected" indicates that violations of Standard 3.05a may be judged not only by whether actual impairment, harm, or exploitation has occurred but also by whether most psychologists engaged in similar activities in similar circumstances would determine that entering into such a multiple relationship would be expected to lead to such harms.

✓ A judge asked a psychologist who had conducted a custody evaluation to provide 6-month mandated family counseling for the couple involved, followed by a reevaluation for custody. The psychologist explained to the judge that providing family counseling to individuals whose parenting skills the psychologist would later have to evaluate could reasonably be expected to impair her ability to form an objective opinion independent of knowledge gained and the professional investment made in the counseling sessions. She also explained that such a multiple relationship could impair her effectiveness as a counselor if the parents refrained from honest engagement in the counseling sessions for fear that comments made would be used against them during the custody assessment. The judge agreed to assign the family to another psychologist for counseling.

Unavoidable Multiple Relationships

In some situations, it may not be possible or reasonable to avoid multiple relationships. Psychologists who live and work in rural communities, in small towns, on American Indian reservations, in small insulated religious or immigrant communities, or within unique language groups are often the only qualified professional available to provide specialty services for clients/patients whom they may encounter outside of the professional setting on a regular basis (e.g., store owners; teachers at their child's school; members of their church, synagogue, or mosque; Sanders, Swenson, & Schneller, 2011). When alternative psychological services are not available, providing such services is not in violation of Standard 3.05 if psychologists take reasonable steps to safeguard their objectivity and effectiveness and protect against the possibility of exploitation and harm (Werth et al., 2010).

CASE EXAMPLE

Navigating Multiple Relationships in Shared Communities

A rabbi in a small Orthodox Jewish community also served as the community's sole licensed clinical psychologist. The psychologist was careful to clearly articulate to his clients the separation of his role as a psychologist and his role as their rabbi. His work benefited from his ability to apply his understanding of the Orthodox faith and community culture to help clients/patients with some of the unique psychological issues raised. He had been treating a young woman in the community for depression when it became clear that a primary contributor to her distress was her deep questioning of her faith. The psychologist knew from his years in the community that abandoning Orthodox tenets would most likely result in the woman being ostracized by her family and community. As a rabbi, the psychologist had experience helping individuals grapple with doubts about their faith. However, despite the woman's requests, he was unwilling to engage in this rabbinical role as a part of the therapy, believing that helping the woman maintain her faith would be incompatible with his responsibility as a psychologist to help her examine the psychological facets of her conflicted feelings. The rabbi contacted the director of an Orthodox rabbinical school, who helped him identify an advanced student with experience in Jewish communal service who was willing to come to the community once a week to provide a seminar on Jewish studies and meet individually with congregants about issues of faith. The psychologist explained the role conflict to his patient. They agreed that she would continue to see the psychologist for psychotherapy and meet with the visiting rabbinical student to discuss specific issues of faith. Readers may also wish to refer to the Hot Topic in Chapter 13 on the role of religion and spirituality in psychotherapy.

Need to Know: Avoiding Harmful Multiple Relationships in Embedded Communities

Practitioners may also be embedded in communities defined by shared identities and common goals that transcend issues of geographic proximity and regularly find themselves at centers of social contact for these communities (Fried, 2015). For example, even in large cities, psychologists may be personally or professionally active in LGBT or Deaf communities as members, volunteers, or politically active advocates (Kessler & Waehler, 2005; Smith, 2014). To remove oneself from all such activities out of fear of encountering clients/patients deprives the psychologist of opportunities for personal and professional development and communities of the unique perspectives psychologists can provide. Fried (2015) recommended the following considerations to help clinicians avoid unethical multiple relationships with clients when there is a possibility that they may regularly encounter the client at embedded community activities:

- Obtain the appropriate training or consultative resources to take the professional steps required to ensure that your dual role as community member and therapist will not impair your judgment or objectivity and will not lead to client exploitation or harm. In some cases, this may mean strategically limiting but not necessarily eliminating your role in community activities.
- As early as possible, discuss with the client the nature and importance of the boundaries and affirm the professional nature of the relationship.
- When an encounter occurs, revisit with the client the previous discussion about the therapeutic importance of boundaries and work together on a plan for how to handle such encounters in a manner that empowers the client and reduces the possibility of confusion, hurt feelings, and misunderstandings. Such discussions should include how to address potential questions from the client's romantic partners, friends, or other companions.
- Process during sessions any feelings of discomfort or other concerns that the client may have experienced during an out-of-office encounter. When there will be regular outside contact (e.g., such as attendance at scheduled organization meetings), develop a plan for "check-ins" during sessions. Continue to monitor your own ability to maintain objectivity and the effectiveness of these strategies in ensuring the client's continued treatment progress.

Correctional and Military Psychologists

Psychologists working in correctional settings and those enlisted in the military often face unique multiple relationship challenges. In some prisons, correctional administrators believe that all employees should provide services as officers. As detailed by Weinberger and Sreenivasan (2003), psychologists in such settings may be asked to search for contraband, use a firearm, patrol to prevent escapes, coordinate inmate movement, and deal with crises unrelated to their role as a psychologist.

Any one of these roles has the potential to undermine the therapeutic relationship a psychologist establishes with individual inmates by blurring the roles of care provider and security officer. Such potentially harmful multiple relationships are also inconsistent with the Standards for Psychological Services in Jails, Prisons, Correctional Facilities, and Agencies (Althouse, 2000).

As required by Standard 1.02, Conflicts Between Ethics and Organizational Demands, prior to taking a position as a treating psychologist or whenever correctional psychologists are asked to engage in a role that will compromise their health provider responsibilities, they should clarify the nature of the conflict to the administrator, make known their commitment to the Ethics Code, and attempt to resolve the conflict by taking steps to ensure that they do not engage in multiple roles that will interfere with the provision of psychological services.

⊘ A psychologist working in a correctional facility had successfully established his primary role as that of mental health treatment provider with both prison officials and inmates. He was not required to search his patients for contraband or to perform any other security-related activities. As required of all facility staff, he received training in the use of firearms and techniques to disarm prisoners who had weapons. On one occasion, several newly admitted inmates suddenly began to attack some of the older prisoners with homemade knives. As one of the few correctional staff members present at the scene, the psychologist assisted the security staff in disarming the inmates. Although none of the attacking inmates were in treatment with him, he did discuss the incident with his current patients to address any concerns they might have about the therapeutic relationship.

Psychologists in the military face additional challenges (Kennedy & Johnson, 2009). Johnson, Bacho, Heim, and Ralph (2006) highlighted multiple role obligations that may create a conflict between responsibilities to individual military clients/patients and their military organization: (a) As commissioned officers, psychologists' primary obligation is to the military mission; (b) embedded psychologists must promote the fighting power and combat readiness of individual military personnel and the combat unit as a whole; (c) since many military psychologists are the sole mental health providers for their unit, there is less room for choice of alternative treatment providers; (d) there is less control and choice regarding shifts between therapeutic and administrative role relationships (e.g., seeing as a patient a member about whom the psychologist previously had to render an administrative decision); and (e) like rural communities, military communities are often small, with military psychologists having social relationships with individuals who may at some point become patients.

To minimize the potential harm that could emerge from such multiple relationships, Johnson et al. (2006) suggested that military psychologists

- strive for a neutral position in the community, avoiding high-profile social positions;
- assume that every member of the community is a potential client/patient and attempt to establish appropriate boundaries accordingly (e.g., limiting self-disclosures that would be expected in common social circumstances);
- provide informed consent immediately if a nontherapeutic role relationship transitions into a therapeutic one;
- be conservative in the information one "needs to know" in the therapeutic role to avoid, to the extent feasible, threats to confidentiality that may emerge when an administrative role is required;
- collaborate with clients/patients, when possible and appropriate, on how best to handle role transitions; and
- carefully document multiple role conflicts, how they were handled, and the rationale for such decisions.

✓ A military psychologist provided therapy to an enlisted officer who was ordered to enter treatment for difficulties in job-related performance. During treatment, the client and psychologist were assigned to a field exercise in which the client would be under the psychologist's command. To reassign the client to a different officer for the exercise, the psychologist would need to speak with a superior who was not a mental health worker. Recognizing that the client's involvement in therapy would have to be revealed in such a discussion, the psychologist explained the situation to the enlisted member and asked permission to discuss the situation with her superiors. The client refused to give permission. The psychologist was the only mental health professional on the base, so transferring the client to another provider was not an option. The psychologist therefore developed a specific plan with the client for how they would relate to each other during the field exercise and how they would discuss in therapy issues that arose. (This case is adapted from one of four military cases provided by Staal & King, 2000.)

(b) If a psychologist finds that, due to unforeseen factors, a potentially harmful multiple relationship has arisen, the psychologist takes reasonable steps to resolve it with due regard for the best interests of the affected person and maximal compliance with the Ethics Code.

There will be instances when psychologists discover that they are involved in a potentially harmful multiple relationship of which they had been unaware. Standard 3.05b requires that psychologists take reasonable steps to resolve the potential harms that might arise from such relationships, recognizing that the best interests of the affected person and maximal compliance with other standards in the Ethics Code may sometimes require psychologists to remain in the multiple roles.

- ✓ A psychologist responsible for conducting individual assessments of candidates for an executive-level position discovered that one of the candidates was a close friend's husband. Because information about this prior relationship was neither confidential nor harmful to the candidate, the psychologist explained the situation to company executives and worked with the organization to assign that particular promotion evaluation to another qualified professional.
- ✓ A psychologist working at a university counseling center discovered that a counseling client had enrolled in a large undergraduate class the psychologist was going to teach. The psychologist discussed the potential conflict with the client and attempted to help him enroll in a different class. However, the client was a senior and needed the class to complete his major requirements. In addition, there were no appropriate referrals for the student at the counseling center. Without revealing the student's identity, the psychologist discussed her options with the department chair. They concluded that because the class was very large, the psychologist could take the following steps to protect her objectivity and effectiveness as both a teacher and a counselor: (a) a graduate teaching assistant would be responsible for grading exams and for calculating the final course grade based on the average of scores on the exams, and (b) the psychologist would monitor the situation during counseling sessions and seek consultation if problems arose.
- ✓ A psychologist in independent practice became aware that his neighbor had begun dating one of the psychologist's psychotherapy patients. Although telling the patient about the psychologist's social relationship with her new significant other could cause distress, it was likely that the patient would find out about the relationship during conversations with the neighbor. The psychologist considered reducing his social exchanges with the neighbor, but this proved infeasible. After seeking consultation from a colleague, the psychologist decided that he could not ensure therapeutic objectivity or effectiveness if the situation continued. He decided to explain the situation to the patient, provide a referral, and assist the transition to a new therapist during pretermination counseling (see also Standard 10.10, Terminating Therapy).

(c) When psychologists are required by law, institutional policy, or extraordinary circumstances to serve in more than one role in judicial or administrative proceedings, at the outset they clarify role expectations and the extent of confidentiality and thereafter as changes occur. (See also Standards 3.04, Avoiding Harm; and 3.07, Third-Party Requests for Services.)

Standard 3.05c applies to instances when psychologists are required to serve in more than one role in judicial or administrative proceedings because of institutional policy or extraordinary circumstances. This standard does *not* permit psychologists to take on these multiple roles if such a situation can be avoided. When

such multiple roles cannot be avoided, Standard 3.05c requires, as soon as possible and thereafter as changes occur, that psychologists clarify to all parties involved the roles that the psychologist is expected to perform and the extent and limits of confidentiality that can be anticipated by taking on these multiple roles.

In most situations, psychologists are expected to avoid multiple relationships in forensically relevant situations or to resolve such relationships when they unexpectedly occur (Standards 3.05a and b). When such circumstances arise (e.g., performing a custody evaluation and then providing court-mandated family therapy for the couple involved), the conflict can often be resolved by explaining to a judge or institutional administrator the ethically problematic nature of the multiple relationship (Standards 1.02, Conflicts Between Ethics and Law, Regulations, and Other Governing Legal Authority; 1.03, Conflicts Between Ethics and Organizational Demands).

> ✓ A consulting psychologist developed a company's sexual harassment policy. After the policy was approved and implemented, the psychologist took on the position of counseling employees experiencing sexual harassment. One of the psychologist's clients then filed a sexual harassment suit against the company. The psychologist was called on by the defense to testify as an expert witness for the company's sexual harassment policy and by the plaintiff as a fact witness about the stress and anxiety observed during counseling sessions. The psychologist (a) immediately disclosed to the company and the employee the nature of the multiple relationship; (b) described to both the problems that testifying might raise, including the limits of maintaining the confidentiality of information acquired from either the consulting or counseling roles; and (c) ceased providing sexual harassment counseling services for employees. Neither party agreed to withdraw its request to the judge for the psychologist's testimony. The psychologist wrote a letter to the judge explaining the conflicting roles and asked to be recused from testifying (see Hellkamp & Lewis, 1995, for further discussion of this type of dilemma).

3.06 Conflict of Interest

Psychologists refrain from taking on a professional role when personal, scientific, professional, legal, financial, or other interests or relationships could reasonably be expected to (1) impair their objectivity, competence, or effectiveness in performing their functions as psychologists or (2) expose the person or organization with whom the professional relationship exists to harm or exploitation.

Psychologists strive to establish and benefit from relationships of trust with those with whom they work through the exercise of professional and scientific judgments based on their training and experience and established knowledge of the discipline (Principle A: Beneficence and Nonmaleficence and Principle B: Fidelity

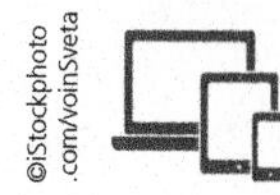

and Responsibility). Standard 3.06 prohibits psychologists from taking on a professional role when competing professional, personal, financial, legal, or other interests or relationships could reasonably be expected to impair their objectivity, competence, or ability to effectively perform this role. Psychologists, especially those with prescription privileges, should also be sensitive to the effect of gifts from pharmaceutical companies or others who might exert influence on professional decisions (Gold & Appelbaum, 2011). Examples of conflicts of interest sufficient to compromise the psychologist's judgments include the following:

- ☒ Irrespective of patients' treatment needs, to save money, a psychologist reduced the number of sessions for certain patients after he had exceeded his yearly compensation under a capitated contract with an HMO (see the Hot Topic in Chapter 9, "Managing the Ethics of Managed Care").
- ☒ A member of a faculty-hiring committee refused to recuse herself from voting when a friend applied for the position under the committee's consideration.
- ☒ A psychologist in private practice agreed to be paid $1,000 for each patient he referred for participation in a psychopharmaceutical treatment study.
- ☒ A research psychologist agreed to provide expert testimony on a contingent fee basis, thereby compromising her role as advocate for the scientific data.
- ☒ A psychologist who had just purchased biofeedback equipment for his practice began to increase his billing by overstating the effectiveness of biofeedback to his clients.
- ☒ A prescribing psychologist failed to disclose to patients her substantial financial investment in the company that manufactured the medication the psychologist frequently recommended.
- ☒ A psychologist used his professional website to recommend Internet mental health services in which he had an undisclosed financial interest.
- ☒ A school psychologist agreed to conduct a record review for the educational placement of the child of the president of a foundation that contributed heavily to the private school that employed the psychologist.

Conflicts of interest can extend to financial or other gains that accrue to psychologists indirectly through the effect of their decisions on the interests of their family members, as in these examples:

- ☒ An educational psychologist hired as a consultant in a school system encouraged the school system to purchase learning software from the company that employed her husband.
- ☒ An organizational psychologist was hired by a company to provide confidential support and referral services for employees with substance abuse problems. The psychologist would refer employees he counseled to a private mental health group practice in which his wife was a member.

Psychologists also have a fiduciary responsibility to avoid actions that would create public distrust in the integrity of psychological science and practice (Principle B: Fidelity and Responsibility). Accordingly, Standard 3.06 also prohibits taking on a role that would expose a person or organization with whom a psychologist already works to harm or exploitation.

☒ A research psychologist on the board of a private foundation encouraged the foundation to fund a colleague's proposal from which he would be paid as a statistical consultant.

☒ A psychologist accepted a position on the board of directors from a company for which she was currently conducting an independent evaluation of employee productivity.

☒ A psychologist took on a psychotherapy client who was a financial analyst at the small local brokerage company the psychologist used for his personal investments.

Psychologists in administrative positions have a responsibility to resist explicit or implicit pressure to bias decisions regarding the adequacy of research participant or patient protections to meet the needs of the institution's financial interests. Organizational and consulting psychologists should be wary of situations in which an employer may ask the psychologist to assist with managerial directives that may be ethically inappropriate and harmful to the well-being of employees (Lefkowitz, 2012).

☒ A psychologist serving on her university's IRB gave in to pressure to approve a study with ethically questionable procedures because it would bring a substantial amount of funding to the university.

✓ A school psychologist refused the district superintendent's request that she conduct training sessions for teachers at an overcrowded school that would result in the misapplication of behavioral principles to keep students docile and quiet.

✓ An organizational psychologist refused a request by the company CEO to conduct workshops for older employees designed to motivate them to take early retirement.

Conflicts of Interest in Forensic Practice

Psychologists seek to promote accuracy and truthfulness in their work (Principle C: Integrity). Forensic psychologists hired to provide expert testimony based on forensic assessment or research relevant to the legal decision need to be aware of potential conflicts of interest that may impair their objectivity or lead them to distort their testimony (APA, 2013e). For example, psychologists providing expert testimony should avoid providing such services on the basis of contingent fees (fees adjusted according to whether a case is won or lost) since this can exert pressure on psychologists to intentionally or unintentionally modify their reports or testimony in favor of the retaining party. However, if a psychologist is serving as a consultant to a legal team and will not be testifying in court, a contingency fee may not be unethical as long as it does not lead psychologists to distort facts in giving their advice (Heilbrun, 2001). Psychologists should also avoid charging higher fees for testimony since this may motivate writing a report that is more likely to lead to a request to testify (Heilbrun, 2001). Bush et al. (2006) suggested that psychologists set fixed rates (which may be required in some states) and bill at a consistent hourly rate for all activities.

Forensic psychologists hired by the defense team must also avoid explicit or subtle pressure to use more or less sensitive symptom validation measures to assess the mental status of the defendant. Psychologists should also not submit to pressure by a legal team to modify a submitted report. Amendments to the original report may be added to correct factual errors, and if a report is rewritten, the rationale for the changes should be given within the report (Bush et al., 2006; Martelli, Bush, & Sasler, 2003). Interested readers may also refer to the Hot Topic in Chapter 8, "Avoiding False and Deceptive Statements in Scientific and Clinical Expert Testimony."

Corporate Funding and Conflicts of Interest in Research, Teaching, and Practice

The APA Task Force on External Funding (http://www.apa.org/pubs/info/reports/external-funding.aspx) provides a detailed history of conflicts of interest in related fields and provides specific recommendations for psychology (see also Pachter, Fox, Zimbardo, & Antonuccio, 2007). Recommendations include the following:

- When research is industry sponsored, psychologists should ensure that they have input into study design, independent access to raw data, and a role in manuscript submission.
- Full public disclosure regarding financial conflicts of interest should be included in all public statements.
- Psychologists should be aware of and guard against potential biases inherent in accepting sponsor-provided inducements that might affect their selection of textbooks or assessment instruments.
- Practitioners should be alert to the influence on clients/patients of sponsor-provided materials (e.g., mugs, pens, notepads) that might suggest endorsement of the sponsor's products.

Many federal agencies, professional and scientific organizations, and academic and other institutions have conflict-of-interest policies of which psychologists should be aware.

- The National Institutes of Health (NIH) Office of Extramural Research requires every institution receiving Public Health Service (PHS) research grants to have written guidelines for the avoidance and institutional review of conflict of interest. These guidelines must reflect state and local laws and cover financial interests, gifts, gratuities and favors, nepotism, political participation, and bribery. In addition, employees accepting grants or contracts are expected to be knowledgeable of the granting and contracting organization's conflict-of-interest policy and to abide by it (http://grants.nih.gov/grants/policy/coi/). In addition, the PHS Regulations 42 CFR Part 50 (Subpart F) and 45 CFR Part 94 provide conflict-of-interest guidelines for individual investigators (http://www.hhs.gov/ohrp/archive/humansubjects/finreltn/fguid.pdf).

- The APA *Editor's Handbook: Operating Procedures and Policies for APA Publications* (APA, 2006, Policy 1.03) requires that journal reviewers and editors avoid either real or apparent conflicts of interest by declining to review submitted manuscripts from recent collaborators, students, or members of their institutions or work from which they might obtain financial gain. When such potential conflicts of interest arise or when editors or associate editors submit their own work to the journal they edit, the *Handbook* recommends that the editor (a) request a well-qualified individual to serve as ad hoc action editor, (b) set up a process that ensures the action editor's independence, and (c) identify the action editor in the publication of the article. APA also requires all authors to submit a Full Disclosure of Interests form that certifies whether the psychologist or his or her immediate family members have significant financial or product interests related to information provided in the manuscript or other sources of negative or positive bias.
- The APA Committee on Accreditation's Conflict of Interest Policy for Site Visitors includes prohibitions against even the appearance of a conflict of interest for committee members and faculty in the program being visited. Possible conflicts include former employment or enrollment in the program or a family connection or close friend or professional colleague in the program (http://www.apa.org/ed/accreditation/visits/conflict.aspx).
- The National Association of School Psychologists' *Professional Conduct Manual* requires psychologists to avoid conflicts of interest by recognizing the importance of ethical standards and the separation of roles and by taking full responsibility for protecting and informing the consumer of all potential concerns (NASP, 2010, V.A.1).
- According to the Specialty Guidelines for Forensic Psychology (APA, 2013e), psychologists should strive to avoid providing services to parties to a legal proceeding on the basis of a contingent fee (Guideline 5.02).

3.07 Third-Party Requests for Services

When psychologists agree to provide services to a person or entity at the request of a third party, psychologists attempt to clarify at the outset of the service the nature of the relationship with all individuals or organizations involved. This clarification includes the role of the psychologist (e.g., therapist, consultant, diagnostician,

or expert witness), an identification of who is the client, the probable uses of the services provided or the information obtained, and the fact that there may be limits to confidentiality. (See also Standards 3.05, Multiple Relationships, and 4.02, Discussing the Limits of Confidentiality.)

Psychologists are often asked to conduct an assessment, provide psychotherapy, or testify in court by third parties who themselves will not be directly involved in the evaluation, treatment, or testimony.

In all these cases, Standard 3.07 requires psychologists at the outset of services to explain to both the third party and those individuals who will receive psychological services the nature of the psychologist's relationship with all individuals or organizations involved. This includes providing information about the role of the psychologist (i.e., therapist, consultant, diagnostician, expert witness) and identifying whether the third party or the individual receiving the services is the client, who will receive information about the services, and probable uses of information gained or services provided.

- ⊘ A company asked a psychologist to conduct preemployment evaluations of potential employees. The psychologist informed each applicant evaluated that she was working for the company, that the company would receive the test results, and that the information would be used in hiring decisions.
- ⊘ A school district hired a psychologist to evaluate students for educational placement. The psychologist first clarified state and federal laws on parental rights regarding educational assessments, communicated this information to the school superintendent and the child's guardian(s), and explained the nature and use of the assessments and the confidentiality and reporting procedures the psychologist would use.
- ⊘ A legal guardian requested behavioral treatment for her 30-year-old developmentally disabled adult child because of difficulties he was experiencing at the sheltered workshop where he worked. At the outset of services, using language compatible with the client's/patient's intellectual level, the psychologist informed the client/patient that the guardian had requested the treatment, explained the purpose of the treatment, and indicated the extent to which the guardian would have access to confidential information and how such information might be used.
- ⊘ A defense attorney hired a psychologist to conduct an independent evaluation of a plaintiff who claimed that the attorney's client had caused her emotional harm. The plaintiff agreed to be evaluated. The psychologist first explained to the plaintiff that the defense attorney was the client and that all information would be shared with the attorney and possibly used by the attorney to refute the plaintiff's allegations in court. Once the evaluation commenced, the psychologist avoided using techniques that would encourage the plaintiff to respond to the psychologist as a psychotherapist (Hess, 1998).
- ⊘ A judge ordered a convicted sex offender to receive therapy as a condition of parole. The psychologist assigned to provide the therapy explained to the parolee that all information revealed during therapy would be provided to the court and might be used to rescind parole.

Legal Representatives Seeking to Retain a Forensic Psychologist

In many instances, forensic psychologists will be retained by the attorney representing the legal party's interests. In such instances, the attorney is the psychologist's client. During the initial consultation with a legal representative seeking the psychologist's forensic services, psychologists should consider providing the following information: (a) the fee structure for anticipated services; (b) previous or current obligations, activities, or relationships that might be perceived as conflicts of interest; (c) level and limitations of competence to provide forensic services requested; and (d) any other information that might reasonably be expected to influence the decision to contract with the psychologist (see APA, 2013e; Standard 6.04a, Fees and Financial Arrangements).

Implications of HIPAA

Psychologists planning to share information with third parties should also carefully consider whether such information is included under the HIPAA definition of Protected Health Information (PHI), whether HIPAA regulations require prior patient authorization for such release, or whether the authorization requirement can be waived by the legal prerogatives of the third party. Psychologists should then clarify beforehand to both the third party and recipient of services the HIPAA requirements for the release of PHI (see also "A Word About HIPAA" in the preface of this book).

3.08 Exploitative Relationships

Psychologists do not exploit persons over whom they have supervisory, evaluative, or other authority such as clients/patients, students, supervisees, research participants, and employees. (See also Standards 3.05, Multiple Relationships; 6.04, Fees and Financial Arrangements; 6.05, Barter With Clients/Patients; 7.07, Sexual Relationships With Students and Supervisees; 10.05, Sexual Intimacies With Current Therapy Clients/Patients; 10.06, Sexual Intimacies With Relatives or Significant Others of Current Therapy Clients/Patients; 10.07, Therapy With Former Sexual Partners; and 10.08, Sexual Intimacies With Former Therapy Clients/Patients.)

Standard 3.08 prohibits psychologists from taking unfair advantage of or manipulating for their own personal use or satisfaction students, supervisees, clients/patients, research participants, employees, or others over whom they have authority. The following are examples of actions that would violate this standard:

- Repeatedly requiring graduate assistants to work overtime without additional compensation
- Requiring employees to run a psychologist's personal errands
- Taking advantage of company billing loopholes to inflate rates for consulting services

- Encouraging expensive gifts from psychotherapy clients/patients
- Using bait-and-switch tactics to lure clients/patients into therapy with initially low rates that are hiked after a few sessions

Violations of Standard 3.08 often occur in connection with other violations of the Ethics Code. For example:

- Psychologists exploit the trust and vulnerability of individuals with whom they work when they have sexual relationships with current clients/patients or students (Standards 10.05, Sexual Intimacies With Current Therapy Clients/Patients; 7.07, Sexual Relationships With Students and Supervisees).
- Exploitation occurs when a psychologist accepts nonmonetary remuneration from clients/patients, the value of which is substantially higher than the psychological services rendered (Standard 6.05, Barter With Clients/Patients).
- Psychologists exploit patients with limited resources who they know will require long-term treatment plans when the psychologists provide services until the patients' money or insurance runs out and then refer them to low-cost or free alternative treatments.
- It is exploitative to charge clients/patients for psychological assessments to which the client/patient did not initially agree and that are unnecessary for the agreed-on goals of the psychological evaluation (Standard 6.04a, Fees and Financial Arrangements).
- School psychologists exploit their students when, in their private practice, they provide fee-for-service psychological testing to students who could receive these services free of charge from the psychologist in the school district in which they work (Standard 3.05a, Multiple Relationships; see also the Principles for Professional Ethics, National Association of School Psychologists, 2010, http://www.nasponline.org/assets/Documents/Standards%20and%20Certification/Standards/1_%20Ethical%20Principles.pdf).

Standard 3.08 does not prohibit psychologists from having a sliding-fee scale or different payment plans for different types or amount of services, as long as the fee practices are fairly and consistently applied (see also Standards 6.04, Fees and Financial Arrangements; 6.05, Barter with Clients/Patients).

Recruitment for Research Participation

Institutionalized populations are particularly susceptible to research exploitation. Prisoners and youth held for brief periods in detention centers, for example, are highly vulnerable because of their restricted autonomy and liberty, often compounded by their low socioeconomic status, poor education, and poor health (Gostin, 2007). Incarcerated persons have few expectations regarding privacy protections and may view research participation as a means of seeking favor with or avoiding punishment from prison guards or detention officials. Inpatients in psychiatric centers or nursing homes are also vulnerable to exploitive recruitment practices that touch upon their fears that a participation refusal will result in denial of other needed services. Investigators should ensure through adequate informed consent procedures and discussion with institutional staff that research participation is not coerced (Fisher, 2004; Fisher et al., 2002; Fisher & Vacanti-Shova, 2012; see also Standards 8.02, Informed Consent to Research, and 8.06, Offering Inducements for Research Participation).

3.09 Cooperation With Other Professionals

When indicated and professionally appropriate, psychologists cooperate with other professionals in order to serve their clients/patients effectively and appropriately. (See also Standard 4.05, Disclosures.)

Individuals who come to psychologists for assessment, counseling, or therapy are often either receiving or in need of collateral medical, legal, educational, or social services. Collaboration and consultation with, and referral to, other professionals are thus often necessary to serve the best interests of clients/patients. Standard 3.09 requires psychologists to cooperate with other professionals when it is appropriate and will help serve the client/patient most effectively.

- ✓ With permission and written authorization of the parent, a clinical child psychologist spoke with a child's teacher to help determine whether behaviors suggestive of attention deficit disorder exhibited at home and in the psychologist's office were consistent with the child's classroom behavior.
- ✓ With consent from the parent, a school psychologist contacted a social worker who was helping a student's family apply for public assistance to help determine the availability of collateral services (e.g., substance abuse counseling).
- ✓ A psychologist with prescribing privileges referred a patient to a physician for diagnosis of physical symptoms thought by the patient to be the result of a psychological disorder that were actually more suggestive of a medical condition.

In schools, hospitals, social service agencies, and other multidisciplinary settings, a psychologist may have joint responsibilities with other professionals for the assessment or treatment of those with whom they work. In such settings, psychologists should develop a clear agreement with the other professionals regarding overlapping and distinct role responsibilities and how confidential information should be handled in the best interests of the students or clients/patients. The nature of these collaborative arrangements should be shared with the recipients of the services or their legal guardians.

Implications of HIPAA

Psychologists who are covered entities under HIPAA should be familiar with situations in which regulations requiring patients' written authorization for release of PHI apply to communications with other professionals. They should also be aware of rules governing patients' rights to know when such disclosures have been made (e.g., Notice of Privacy Practices and Accounting of Disclosures of Protected Health Information described in "A Word About HIPAA" in the preface of this book).

Need to Know: Essential Skills for Interprofessional Models of Primary Care

In patient-centered medical homes (PCMHs) and other integrated primary care organizations, psychologists' roles extend beyond providing direct patient care to include making contributions to primary care operations. Thus, these psychologists must collaborate with patients, families, and a team of health care professionals from diverse disciplines. Psychologists in these settings need to understand the dynamics of team-based care so that they can contribute to improving team functioning through developing the skills to

- negotiate treatment plans that are mutually acceptable to patients, their families, and their health care team;
- develop behavioral management interventions that meet the treatment goals prescribed by medical and other health professionals;
- develop behavioral components of a collaborative care plan that may be implemented by other professionals;
- communicate in a clear, concise, and timely manner in ways that are meaningful to patients and colleagues when making or receiving referrals; and
- exhibit professional behavior and comportment consistent with the operations and culture of primary care practice while maintaining their professional identity as psychologists.

For additional information, see McDaniel, Belar, Schroeder, Hargrove, and Freeman (2002); Nash, Khatri, Cubic, and Baird (2013); and Rozensky, Celano, and Kaslow (2013).

3.10 Informed Consent

(a) When psychologists conduct research or provide assessment, therapy, counseling, or consulting services in person or via electronic transmission or other forms of communication, they obtain the informed consent of the individual or individuals using language that is reasonably understandable to that person or

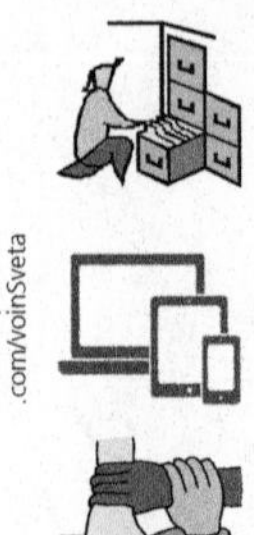

persons except when conducting such activities without consent is mandated by law or governmental regulation or as otherwise provided in this Ethics Code. (See also Standards 8.02, Informed Consent to Research; 9.03, Informed Consent in Assessments; and 10.01, Informed Consent to Therapy and description of the Notice of Privacy Practices described in "A Word About HIPAA" in the preface to this book.)

Informed consent is seen by many as the primary means of protecting the self-governing and privacy rights of those with whom psychologists work (Principle E: Respect for People's Rights and Dignity). Required elements of informed consent for specific areas of psychology are detailed in Standards 8.02, Informed Consent to Research; 9.03, Informed Consent in Assessments; and 10.01, Informed Consent to Therapy. The obligations described in Standard 3.10 apply to these other consent standards.

Language

In research, assessment, and therapy, psychologists must obtain informed consent using language reasonably understandable by the person asked to consent. For example, psychologists must use appropriate translations of consent information for individuals for whom English is not a preferred language or who use sign language or Braille. Psychologists should also adjust reading and language comprehension levels of consent procedures to an individual's developmental or educational level or reading or learning disability.

Culture

Individuals from recently immigrated or disadvantaged cultural communities may lack familiarity with assessment, treatment or research procedures, and terminology typically used in informed consent documents (Fisher, 2014). These individuals may also be unfamiliar with or distrust statements associated with voluntary choice and other client/patient or research participant rights described during informed consent. Standard 3.10 requires sensitivity to the cultural dimensions of individuals' understanding of and anticipated responses to consent information and the tailoring of informed consent language to such dimensions. This may also require psychologists to include educational components regarding the nature of and individual rights in agreeing to psychological services or research participation. For individuals not proficient in English, written informed consent information must be translated in a manner that considers cultural differences in health care or scientific concepts that present challenges in a word-for-word translation. When using interpreters to conduct informed consent procedures, psychologists must follow the requirements of Standard 2.05, Delegation of Work to Others, in ensuring the interpreters' competence, training, and supervision. Readers may also wish to refer to Hot Topic "Multicultural Ethical Competence" in Chapter 5.

> **Digital Ethics: Consent via Electronic Transmission**
>
> Standard 3.10a requires that informed consent be obtained when research, assessment, or therapy is conducted via electronic transmission such as the telephone or the Internet. Psychologists need to take special steps to identify the language and reading level of those from whom they obtain consent via electronic media. In addition, psychologists conducting work via email or other electronic communications should take precautions to ensure that the individual who gave consent is in fact the individual participating in the research or receiving the psychologist's services (i.e., use of a participant/client/patient password).

Exemptions

Some activities are exempt from the requirements of Standard 3.10. For example, psychologists conducting court-ordered assessments or evaluating military personnel may be prevented from obtaining consent by law or governmental regulation. In addition, several standards in the Ethics Code detail conditions under which informed consent may be waived (Standards 8.03, Informed Consent for Recording Voices and Images in Research; 8.05, Dispensing With Informed Consent for Research; 8.07, Deception in Research). HIPAA also permits certain exemptions from patient authorization requirements relevant to research and practice, which are discussed in later chapters on standards for research, assessment, and therapy (see also "A Word About HIPAA" in the preface of this book).

> (b) For persons who are legally incapable of giving informed consent, psychologists nevertheless (1) provide an appropriate explanation, (2) seek the individual's assent, (3) consider such persons' preferences and best interests, and (4) obtain appropriate permission from a legally authorized person, if such substitute consent is permitted or required by law. When consent by a legally authorized person is not permitted or required by law, psychologists take reasonable steps to protect the individual's rights and welfare.

Adults who have been declared legally incompetent and most children younger than 18 years of age do not have the legal right to provide independent consent to receive psychological services or participate in psychological research. In recognition of these individuals' rights as persons, Standard 3.10b requires that psychologists obtain their affirmative agreement to participate in psychological activities after providing them with an explanation of the nature and purpose of the activities and their right to decline or withdraw from participation. The phrase *consider such persons' preferences and best interests* indicates that although in most instances, psychologists respect a person's right to dissent from participation in psychological activities, this right can be superseded if failure to participate would deprive persons of psychological services necessary to protect or promote their welfare.

For individuals who are legally incapable of giving informed consent, psychologists must also obtain permission from a legally authorized person if such substitute consent is permitted or required by law. Psychologists working with children in the foster care system and in juvenile detention centers and those working with institutionalized adults with identified cognitive or mental disorders leading to decisional impairment must carefully determine who has legal responsibility for substitute decision making. Psychologists should be aware that in some instances, especially for children in foster care, legal guardianship may change over time.

Informed Consent in Research and Practice Involving Children and Adolescents

In law and ethics, a guardian's permission is required to protect children from consent vulnerabilities related to immature cognitive skills, lack of emotional preparedness and experience in clinical or research settings, and actual or perceived power differentials between children and adults (Fisher & Vacanti-Shova, 2012; Koocher & Henderson Daniel, 2012). Despite these limitations, the landmark "Convention on the Rights of the Child" (United Nations General Assembly, 1989) established international recognition that children should have a voice in decisions that affect their well-being. Out of respect for their developing autonomy, the APA Ethics Code and federal regulations governing research (DHHS, 2009) require the informed assent of children capable of providing assent. Psychologists working with children should be familiar with the growing body of empirical data on the development of children's understanding of the nature of medical and mental health treatment and research and with rights-related concepts such as confidentiality and voluntary assent or dissent (Bruzzese & Fisher, 2003; Condie & Koocher, 2008; Daniels & Jenkins, 2010; Field & Behrman, 2004; Fisher, 2002a; Gibson, Stasiulis, Gutfreund, McDonald, & Dade, 2011; Koelch et al., 2009; Miller, Drotar, & Kodish, 2004; Unguru, 2011).

Need to Know: Ethically Appropriate Child and Adolescent Assent Procedures

When creating the content and language of ethically appropriate assent procedures, psychologists should be guided by the following (Chenneville, Sibille, & Bendell-Estroff, 2010; Fisher & Vacanti-Shova, 2012; Masty & Fisher, 2008):

- Empirical literature on children's understanding of the nature and purpose of mental health treatment or research, confidentiality protections and limitations, and the voluntary nature of participation (Standard 2.01, Boundaries of Competence)
- Scientific and clinical knowledge of the relationship between specific pediatric mental health disorders and the cognitive and emotional capacity to assent (Standard 2.04, Bases for Scientific and Professional Judgments)

- Individual evaluation, when relevant, of the child's appreciation of his or her mental health status and treatment needs, understanding of the risks and benefits of assent or dissent, the information he or she may want or need to make an informed assent decision, and whether an assessment of assent capacity is required
- The child's experience with his or her own health care decision making and preference for the degree of involvement the child wishes to have in the treatment or research participation decision
- Never asking children to assent to or dissent from participation if their choice will not be respected, that is, in situations in which assessment or intervention is necessary to identify or alleviate a mental health problem (see also "Parental Permission and Child Assent to Pediatric Clinical Trials" in the section on Standard 8.02, Informed Consent to Research, Chapter 11).

Emancipated and Mature Minors

There are instances when a guardian's permission for treatment or research is not required or possible for children younger than 18 years of age. For example, *emancipated minor* is a legal status conferred on persons who have not yet attained the age of legal competency (as defined by state law) but are entitled to treatment as if they have such status by virtue of assuming adult responsibilities, such as self-support, marriage, or procreation. A *mature minor* is someone who has not reached adulthood (as defined by state law) but who, according to state law, may be treated as an adult for certain purposes (e.g., consenting to treatment for venereal disease, drug abuse, or emotional disorders). Psychologists working with children need to be familiar with the definition of emancipated and mature minors in the specific states in which they work. When a child is an emancipated or a mature minor, informed consent procedures should follow Standard 3.10a.

Best Interests of the Child

The requirement for a guardian's permission may be inappropriate if there is serious doubt as to whether the guardian's interests adequately reflect the child's interests (e.g., cases of child abuse or neglect, genetic testing of a healthy child to assist in understanding the disorder of a sibling) or the permission can reasonably be obtained (e.g., treatment or research involving runaways). In such cases, the appointment of a consent advocate can protect the child's rights and welfare by verifying the minor's understanding of assent procedures, supporting the child's preferences, ensuring participation is voluntary, and monitoring reactions to psychological procedures. Psychologists conducting therapy need to be familiar with their state's laws regarding provision of therapy to children and adolescents without parental consent (Fisher, Hatashita-Wong, & Isman, 1999; Koocher & Henderson Daniel, 2012). Psychologists conducting research need to be familiar with federal regulations regarding waiver of guardian permission (45 CFR 46.408c) and have such waivers approved by an IRB (Standard 8.01, Institutional

Approval; Fisher, Hoagwood, & Jensen, 1996; Fisher & Mustanski, 2014; Fisher & Vacanti-Shova, 2012; see also the discussion on waiver of guardian permission for research in Chapter 11).

Need to Know: Re-consent for Use of Stored Data When Minor Participants Reach Adulthood

Guardian permission for data storage, long-term use, and sharing of de-identified data from research involving children typically provides adequate permission for future use and analysis by the original investigator or secondary analysis by other investigators. However, emerging software and biomedical technologies may present re-identification risks unknown at the time of the original consent. A report addressing this problem issued by the Society for Research in Child Development (SRCD) Common Rule Task Force (Fisher, Brunnquell, et al., 2013) recommends that at the time of data collection, guardian permission and child assent forms indicate that all investigators who will have access to data in the future will be bound by both the best practices in data and confidentiality protections at the time of data collection and new protections as they emerge. Furthermore, investigators responsible for data storage and sharing should comply with this promise by continually updating data security protections.

The Task Force also recommends that parental permission obtained for identifiable information should be considered default permission for continued use of those data after the child has reached the age of majority as long as (a) appropriate security protections are in place and updated as may be required by evolving information technologies as well as federal standards and (b) the level of harm associated with informational risk has not increased with changes in societal attitudes, health coverage, or other norms or policies. Re-consent should be sought, however, for new data collection that will be linked to an archival data set with access to participant contact information permitted only if there is a signed letter of agreement between the institutions of all investigators involved stating that security and confidentiality rules will be followed (see also Standard 8.14, Sharing Research Data for Verification; Chapter 11, "Need to Know: Proposed Changes to Federal Regulations").

Guardian Authority Under HIPAA

HIPAA requires that if, under applicable law, a person has authority to act on behalf of an individual who is an adult or minor in making decisions related to health care, a covered entity must treat such a person (called a personal representative) as the individual. Exceptions are permitted if there is reason to believe that the patient has been abused or is endangered by the personal representative or that treating the individual as a personal representative would not be in the best interests of the client/patient. This requirement refers to court-appointed guardians or holders of relevant power of attorney of adults with impaired capacities, parents who are generally recognized as personal representatives of their minor children, and individuals designated as a representative by the patient. To comply with both Standard 3.10b and the HIPAA Notice of Privacy Practices (see "A Word About HIPAA" in the preface of this book), psychologists should provide the Notice of Privacy Practices to both the individual's legal guardian or personal representative and the client/patient.

(c) When psychological services are court ordered or otherwise mandated, psychologists inform the individual of the nature of the anticipated services, including whether the services are court ordered or mandated and any limits of confidentiality, before proceeding.

When informed consent is prohibited by law or other governing authority, psychologists must nonetheless respect an individual's right to know the nature of anticipated services, whether the services were court ordered or mandated by another governing authority, and the limits of confidentiality before proceeding.

Military Psychologists

When regulations permit, military psychologists should inform active-duty personnel of the psychologist's duty to report to appropriate military agencies information revealed during assessment or therapy that may be related to violations of the Uniform Code of Military Justice.

Court-Ordered Assessments

Psychologists conducting a court-ordered forensic assessment must inform the individual tested (a) why the assessment is being conducted, (b) that the findings may be entered into evidence in court, and (c) if known to the psychologist, the extent to which the individual and his or her attorney will have access to the information. The psychologist should not assume the role of legal adviser but can advise the individual to speak with his or her attorney when a testee asks about potential legal consequences of noncooperation.

Need to Know: Working With Involuntary Clients

Psychologists entering a treatment relationship with involuntary clients who indicate they are reluctant or feel coerced into treatment need to be wary of personal reactions to patient opposition and of applying therapeutic strategies effective for voluntary clients that may contribute to treatment failure. Brodsky and Titcomb (2013) presented the following advice for avoiding treatment pitfalls:

(Continued)

(Continued)

- Clarify the reason for the referral, do not assume that all defendants or offenders require psychotherapy, and remain open to the possibility that an initial goal of therapy may be to move clients toward a consideration of psychotherapy and openness to change or to life skills enhancement (Principle E: Respect for People's Rights and Dignity).
- Involuntary clients mandated for court-ordered treatment may view the psychotherapist with a mixture of distrust and fear of the considerable control that the therapist has over prison privileges, release, or parole decisions. Psychologists need to delineate the limits of confidentiality during informed consent and ensure a clear separation of therapeutic from evaluative and organizational roles (Standards 3.05, Multiple Relationships; 3.10b, Informed Consent; 4.02, Discussing the Limits of Confidentiality).
- When the client considers mandated treatment an aversive experience, the motivation to terminate treatment by reaching therapeutic goals may be a realistic incentive for client engagement. In such instances, therapists may apply techniques such as motivational interviewing that honor the client's resistance in ways that potentially increase client trust and self-awareness. At the same time, psychologists should never utilize coercive techniques and should guard against colluding with clients to report false evidence of actual behavioral or other change (Principle B: Fidelity and Responsibility; Standards 3.06, Conflict of Interest; 3.08, Exploitation).

(d) Psychologists appropriately document written or oral consent, permission, and assent. (See also Standards 8.02, Informed Consent to Research; 9.03, Informed Consent in Assessments; and 10.01, Informed Consent to Therapy.)

Standard 3.10d requires psychologists conducting research or providing health or forensic services to document that they have obtained consent or assent from an individual or permission from a legal guardian or substitute decision maker. In most instances, individuals will sign a consent, an assent, or a permission form. Sometimes, oral consent is appropriate, such as when obtaining a young child's assent, when working with illiterate populations, when there is concern that confidentiality may be at risk (e.g., illegal immigrants whose consent documents may be confiscated by local authorities; see Brabeck, Lykes, Sibley, & Kene, 2015), or when a signature would risk identification in anonymous surveys. In these situations, documentation can be provided by a note in the psychologist's records or, in the case of anonymous, web-based or mail surveys, by the participants' checking a box to indicate that they have read the consent information and agree to participate.

Implications of HIPAA

Appropriate documentation can also be related to legal requirements. For example, HIPAA requires that all valid client/patient authorizations for the use and disclosure of PHI be signed and dated by the individual or the individual's personal representative.

3.11 Psychological Services Delivered to or Through Organizations

(a) Psychologists delivering services to or through organizations provide information beforehand to clients and when appropriate those directly affected by the services about (1) the nature and objectives of the services, (2) the intended recipients, (3) which of the individuals are clients, (4) the relationship the psychologist will have with each person and the organization, (5) the probable uses of services provided and information obtained, (6) who will have access to the information, and (7) limits of confidentiality. As soon as feasible, they provide information about the results and conclusions of such services to appropriate persons.

The informed consent procedures described in Standard 3.10, Informed Consent, are often not appropriate or sufficient for consulting, program evaluation, job effectiveness, or other psychological services delivered to or through organizations. In such contexts, psychologists have dual responsibility to both the organization that has requested their services and the individuals who will be affected by the services provided. For example, psychologists may be hired by police departments to assess the emotional stability of applicants or by insurance agencies to assess the eligibility of employees to collect workers' compensation for brain injuries (see Candilis & Neal, 2014). Standard 3.11 requires that organizational clients, employees, staff, or others who may be involved in the psychologists' activities be provided information about (a) the nature, objectives, and intended recipients of the services; (b) which individuals are clients and the relationship the psychologist will have with those involved; (c) the probable uses of and who will have access to information gained; and (d) the limits of confidentiality. Psychologists must provide results and conclusions of the services to appropriate persons as early as is feasible.

✓ An industrial–organizational psychologist was hired to conduct mandatory cultural sensitivity training for all middle managers working for a large shipping company that had been the defendant in a racial discrimination case. Prior to beginning the training sessions, the psychologist distributed a document to all managers that explained (a) the purpose of the program, which was to help improve relationships between managers and employees; (b) the nature of the training, which would entail reading materials, attending three half-day group sessions, and filling out brief cultural knowledge questionnaires before and after each training session; (c) the scope of confidentiality, such that although the psychologist was required to share the attendance list with upper management, the delivery of the results and conclusions would be presented to the company's board of directors in a manner that protected confidentiality.

(Continued)

(Continued)

- ✓ A psychologist was hired by a school district to observe teacher management of student behavior during lunch and recess to help the district determine how many teachers were required for such activities and whether additional staff training was needed for these responsibilities. The psychologist held a meeting for all teaching staff who would be involved in the observations. At the meeting, the psychologist explained why the school district was conducting the evaluation, how long it would last, the ways in which notes and summaries of observations would be written to protect the identities of individual teachers, that a detailed summary of findings would be presented to the school superintendent, and that, with the district's permission, teachers would receive a summary report.
- ✓ A health psychologist was hired by a primary care medical home (PCMH) to conduct an internal quality improvement (QI) study on the PCMH's mobile health (mHealth) outpatient treatment program for adolescent substance users. The psychologist would review patient records to ascertain the effectiveness of the program and interview mental health and social services staff to identify current facilitators and barriers to implementation. Prior to each interview with staff, the psychologist explained (a) the purpose of the QI, which was to help the PCMH decide whether it should maintain or modify the mHealth program; (b) the rationale for the record review, which was to determine the effectiveness of the intervention, and for the staff interviews, which was to identify facilitators and barriers to program effectiveness; (c) the nature of staff interviews, which would entail a 45-minute meeting by each individual with the psychologist; and (d) the scope of confidentiality, such that the information gained from the interviews reported to PCMH interviews would not include any staff names or identifiers.

(b) If psychologists will be precluded by law or by organizational roles from providing such information to particular individuals or groups, they so inform those individuals or groups at the outset of the service.

Standard 3.11b pertains to situations in which psychological services not requiring informed consent are mandated by law or governmental regulations and the law or regulations restrict those affected by the services from receiving any aspect of the information listed in Standard 3.11a. This standard helps forensic psychologists who are conducting court-mandated assessments to ethically exercise their dual responsibilities to examinees and to courts or other legal bodies (Principles B: Fidelity and Responsibility; C: Integrity; D: Respect for People's Rights and Dignity).

- ⊘ A psychologist providing court-ordered therapy to a convicted pedophile submitted a report to the court regarding the therapy client's attendance and responsiveness to treatment. The therapist was prohibited from releasing the report to the client. At the beginning of therapy, the psychologist had informed the client that such a report would be written and that the client would not have access to the report through the psychologist.
- ⊘ A company stipulated that the results of a personality inventory conducted as part of an employee application and screening process would not be available to applicants. Psychologists informed applicants about these restrictions prior to administering the tests.
- ⊘ An inmate of a correctional institution was required to see the staff psychologist after repeatedly engaging in disruptive and violent behaviors that were jeopardizing the safety of the staff and other prisoners. The psychologist explained to the inmate that in this situation she was acting on the request of prison officials to help the inmate control his behaviors. She also informed the inmate that she would be submitting formal reports on the sessions that might be used by prison officials to determine whether the inmate would be assigned to a more restrictive facility.

3.12 Interruption of Psychological Services

Unless otherwise covered by contract, psychologists make reasonable efforts to plan for facilitating services in the event that psychological services are interrupted by factors such as the psychologist's illness, death, unavailability, relocation, or retirement or by the client's/patient's relocation or financial limitations. (See also Standard 6.02c, Maintenance, Dissemination, and Disposal of Confidential Records of Professional and Scientific Work.)

Planned and unplanned interruptions of psychological services often occur. For example, a psychologist can leave a job at a mental health care facility for a new position, take parental or family leave, interrupt services for a planned medical procedure, or retire from private practice. Clients/patients may move out of state or have a limited number of sessions covered by insurance.

When interruption of services can be anticipated, Standard 3.12 requires psychologists to make reasonable efforts to ensure that needed services are continued. Such efforts can include (a) discussing the interruption of services with the clients/patients and responding to their concerns, (b) conducting pretermination counseling, (c) referring the client/patient to another mental health practitioner, and, if feasible and clinically appropriate, (d) working with the professional who will be responsible for the client's/patient's case (see also Standard 10.10, Terminating Therapy).

✓ A psychologist providing Internet-mediated psychological services to clients in a distant rural community included in her informed consent information the address of a website she created providing continuously updated information on the names, credentials, and contact information of local and electronically accessible backup professionals available to assist clients if the psychologist was not immediately available during an emergency.

Standard 3.12 also requires psychologists to prepare for unplanned interruptions such as sudden illness or death. In most cases, it would suffice to have a trusted professional colleague prepared to contact clients/patients if such a situation arose. Pope and Vasquez (2007) recommended that psychologists create a professional will, including directives on the person designated to assume primary responsibility, backup personnel, coordinated planning, office security and access, easy to locate schedule, avenues of communication, client records and contact information, client notification, colleague notification, professional liability coverage, attorney for professional issues, and billing records and procedures.

The phrase *reasonable efforts* reflects awareness that some events are unpredictable and even the best-laid plans may not be adequate when services are interrupted. The *unless otherwise covered by contract* recognizes that there may be some instances when psychologists are prohibited by contract with a commercial or health care organization from following through on plans to facilitate services.

HOT TOPIC

Goodness-of-Fit Ethics for Informed Consent to Research and Treatment Involving Adults With Impaired Decisional Capacity

An outgrowth of the person-centered care movement has been growing recognition that adults with cognitive disorders have rights, including the right to make decisions related to their own health care, independent living, financial management, and participation in research (McKeown, Clarke, Ingleton, & Repper, 2010). The process of obtaining informed consent presents unique ethical challenges for mental health treatment and research involving adults with schizophrenia, developmental disabilities, Alzheimer's disease, and other disorders characterized by fluctuating, declining, or long-term impairments in decisional capacity (Morris & Heinssen, 2013). The heterogeneity of cognitive strengths and deficits within each of these diagnostic groups means that judgments about each individual's decisional capacity cannot be based solely on his or her diagnosis (Kaup, Dunn, Saks, Jeste, & Palmer, 2011; Moye, Marson, & Edelstein, 2013; Pierce, 2010). Obtaining informed consent from these populations raises a fundamental ethical question: How can psychologists balance their ethical obligation to respect the dignity and autonomy of persons with mental disorders to make their own decisions with the obligation to ensure that ill-informed or incompetent choices do not jeopardize their welfare or leave them open to exploitation (Fisher, 1999; Fisher, Cea, Davidson, & Fried, 2006)?

Legal Status and Diagnostic Labels

Some adults with serious mental disorders have been declared legally incompetent to consent. Removal of a person's legal status as a consenting adult does not, however, deprive him or her of the moral right to be involved in treatment or research participation decisions. For these adults, APA Ethics Code Standard 3.10b requires that psychologists obtain the appropriate permission from a legally authorized person and provide an appropriate explanation to the prospective client/patient or research participant, consider such person's preferences and best interests, and seek the individual's assent.

There may be adults, such as those with Alzheimer's disease, those in acute stages of schizophrenia, or those with developmental disabilities, who do not have a legal guardian but whose ability to fully understand consent-relevant information is impaired (APA, 2012d). For example, clinical geropsychologists frequently work with older persons with progressive dementia who live in nursing homes and assisted-living and residential care facilities where substitute decision making is typically handled informally by family members or others. In addition to obtaining consent from the individual, psychologists can seek additional patient protections by encouraging a shared decision-making process with or seeking additional permission from these informal caretakers (Fisher, 1999, 2002b, 2003c; Fisher et al., 2006; Peisah, Sorinmade, Mitchell, & Hertogh, 2013).

The increasing age of the global population and the prevalence of age-related dementia raise ethical issues regarding advanced directives for treatment and research. Patient wishes and preferences may change considerably as their dementia worsens, not simply because their reasoning may be impaired but because the perceptions of risks and benefits may differ when people experience impaired states that could not be anticipated before they were impaired. Thus, a change in preference should not be assumed to be a sign of deteriorated problem solving (President's Bioethics Commission, 2014).

Fitting Consent to Individual Strengths and Vulnerabilities

The implementation of ethically appropriate consent procedures is more complex for the many situations in which individuals diagnosed with neurological or other mental health disorders retain the legal status of a consenting adult, though their capacity for making informed, rational, and voluntary decisions may be compromised. Each person with a serious mental disorder is unique. Sole reliance on a diagnostic label to determine a client's/patient's capacity to make treatment or research participation decisions risks depriving persons with mental disorders of equal opportunities for autonomous choice.

From an ethical perspective, assessing capacity is a necessary but insufficient basis for determining whether an individual should be granted or deprived of the right to autonomously consent to treatment, assessment, or research. In her Goodness-of-Fit Ethics (GFE) for informed consent, Fisher argued that the burden of consent capacity must be shared by psychologists and the individuals from whom consent is sought (Fisher, 2002a, 2002b, 2003c). According to GFE, just and respectful informed consent processes require psychologists not only to identify the consent strengths and vulnerabilities of the specific individuals or groups with whom they will work but also to take

(Continued)

(Continued)

responsibility to create consent procedures that can minimize vulnerabilities, enhance consent strengths, and provide consent supports when feasible (Fisher, 2005b; Fisher & Masty, 2006; Fisher & Ragsdale, 2006; Fisher & Vacanti-Shova, 2012).

Assessing Consent Capacity

Informed consent may be seen as part of a part of the broader spectrum of an individual's decisional capacity related to treatment, research, and everyday decision making. Assessing an individual's ability to provide consent involves four criteria reflecting the individual's ability to (1) *understand* the nature of the treatment, assessment, or research to which they are asked to consent; (2) *appreciate* the relationship of their own mental health condition to the reason for the treatment or research and how their involvement will affect them personally; (3) *reason* through the information provided, weigh the risks and benefits, and make a rational decision to consent or dissent; (4) *express a voluntary choice* that is not hampered by an inability to communicate or by coercion from family members or professional staff (Appelbaum & Grisso, 2001; Beebe & Smith, 2010; Dunn, Nowrangi, Palmer, Jeste, & Saks, 2006; Grisso & Appelbaum, 1998; Volicer & Ganzine, 2003).

Understanding

Understanding reflects comprehension of factual information about the nature, risks, and benefits of treatment or research. When understanding is hampered by problems of attention or retention, psychologists can incorporate consent enhancement techniques into their procedures such as by employing pictorial representations of treatment or research procedures, presenting information in brief segments, or using repetition. Person–consent context fit also requires identifying which information is and is not critical to helping an individual make an informed choice. For example, when seeking consent for a behavioral intervention for aggressive disorders in a residence for adults with developmental disabilities, it may be important for clients to understand the specific types of behaviors targeted (e.g., hitting other residents), the reward system that will be used (e.g., points toward movies or other special activities), and who will be responsible for monitoring the behavior, for example, residential staff (Cea & Fisher, 2003; Fisher et al., 2006). Although individuals should be informed about the confidentiality and privacy of their records, from a goodness-of-fit perspective, psychologists should consider whether it is important to limit the right to make autonomous decisions to only those individuals who understand details of residential policies regarding the protection of residents' health records, especially if the confidentiality protections do not differ from those that are a natural and ongoing part of the residential experience.

Appreciation

Appreciation refers to the capacity to comprehend the personal consequences of consenting to or dissenting from treatment or research. For example, an adult with a dual diagnosis may understand that treatment will require limiting aggressive behavior but not appreciate the difficulties he or she may have in adhering to the behavioral rules. An individual suffering from schizophrenia may understand that clinical research is testing treatment effectiveness but may not appreciate that he or she has a disorder that requires treatment.

A sliding-scale approach based on the seriousness of personal consequences of the consent decision can be helpful in evaluating the ethical weight that should be given to the client's/patient's or prospective research participant's capacity for appreciation. For example, understanding may be sufficient for consent decisions to standard or experimental interventions that present minimal risk and are supplemental to current treatment programs. On the other hand, appreciation may be essential when the treatment or experimental intervention may expose the individual to the risk of serious side effects or offer an opportunity to receive needed services not otherwise available.

Reasoning

Reasoning reflects the ability to weigh the risks and benefits of consent or dissent. For example, an adult with schizophrenia with paranoid features may understand the nature of a treatment and appreciate its potential for reducing his anxiety but may reason that the risks outweigh the potential benefits because the psychologist offering the treatment is part of a government conspiracy to undermine his freedom. There is also preliminary evidence that severe empathic deficits may confound reasoning about research participation even when other cognitive skills are preserved (Supady, Voelkel, Witzel, Gubka, & Northoff, 2011). At the same time, psychologists should be cautious about the legal consequences of erroneously assuming that paper-and-pencil assessments of reasoning associated with decisional capacity are sufficient to evaluate "performative capacity," defined as the ability of individuals to perform particular tasks (Appelbaum, 2009).

From a goodness-of-fit perspective, asking individuals with questionable reasoning capacity to select a family member, friend, or other trusted person to be present during an informed consent discussion can be empowering and avoid the risk of triggering a legal competency review solely for the purposes of a single mental health treatment or research participation decision (Fisher, 2002a; Fisher et al., 2006; Roeher Institute, 1996).

Choice

Evidencing a choice reflects the ability to actively indicate consent or dissent. For example, some adults suffering from catatonia or Parkinson's dementia may be unable to communicate a choice verbally or nonverbally. While these individuals may understand some of the consent information presented and may have a participation preference, their inability to communicate agreement or dissent necessitates stringent safeguards against harmful or exploitative consent procedures.

In such settings, creating a goodness of fit between person and consent context often requires the respectful inclusion of a consent surrogate who has familiarity with the patient's preference history. The proxy can help ensure that the consent decision reflects, to the extent feasible, the patient's attitudes, hopes, and concerns. Once proxy consent has been obtained, respect for personhood and protection of individual welfare requires psychologists to be alert to patient expressions of anxiety, fatigue, or distress that indicate an individual's dissent or desire to withdraw from participation.

Consent and Empowerment

People with long-standing, declining, or transient disorders related to decisional capacities may be accustomed to other people making decisions for them and may not understand or have experience applying the concept of autonomy. In institutional contexts, individuals with mental disorders

(Continued)

(Continued)

may fear disapproval from doctors or residence supervisors or feel that they must be compliant in deference to the authority of the requesting psychologist. Some may have little experience in exercising their rights or, if they are living in a community residence, may be fearful of discontinuation of other services. Baeroe (2010) has described current approaches to competency evaluations and surrogate consent in health care settings as arbitrary and inconsistently applied. She questioned whether the capacity decision of a single practitioner and the health care decision of a single guardian are sufficient means of respecting patient autonomy, particularly for individuals with borderline decision-making capacity. While recognizing the potential strain on institutional resources, she recommended a "collective deliberation" for hospitalized patients with ambiguous capacity that would include the patient, his or her guardian, health care workers with specific knowledge about the patient, and patient advocates.

To empower and respect the autonomy of patients or prospective research participants, psychologists can study the nature of consent misconception among diagnostic groups and use this knowledge to develop brief interventions to enhance consent capacity (Cea & Fisher, 2003; Fisher et al., 2006; Kaup et al., 2011; Kazuko & Shimanouchi, 2014; Mittal et al., 2007). Modifying the consent setting to reduce the perception of power inequities, providing opportunities to practice decision making, demonstrating that other services will not be compromised, and drawing on the support of trusted family members and peers can strengthen the goodness of fit between person and consent setting and ensure that informed consent is obtained within a context of justice and care.

Chapter Cases and Ethics Discussion Questions

A graduate student working as a research assistant in a psychology professor's lab lost her apartment when her parents learned that she was involved in a lesbian relationship and as a result stopped all financial support. The professor, concerned about the student's psychological and physical welfare, considered inviting her to live with his family until she could find alternative living arrangements. How could the professor determine whether such an invitation would be an ethical or unethical multiple relationship (Standard 3.05)? How might appreciation of differences in personal versus professional values, discussed in Chapter 2, be relevant to this case?

Although several studies have demonstrated the efficacy of psychotherapy as a treatment for non-suicidal self-injury (NSSI), some patients with rare neurological disorders do not respond well to these behavioral treatments. A prescribing psychologist proposes a randomized clinical trial to evaluate the efficacy and safety of a new pharmacotherapy for this group of patients compared to an empirically validated behavioral treatment that has variable success rates with this population. Patients in both groups would be treated by trained mental health therapists and screened regularly for symptomology. Drawing on ethical Standards covered in this chapter, discuss (a) whether this study meets the criteria for clinical equipoise and (b) whether the principal investigator, the individual therapists, or a third party should have ultimate authority for determining whether a participant should be withdrawn from the study based on lack of improvement or increased symptomology.

John is a 40-year-old man with intellectual and developmental disabilities (IDD) who has lived in a community residence for the past 20 years. His legal competency has never been challenged, and although he does not have a legal guardian, staff often consult with his elderly parents about issues related to his welfare. For the past 10 years he has sustained a job at a sheltered workshop and, with assistance from the community residence staff, he is able to manage his small income. Over the past 12 months, he has been involved in physical fights with other consumers at his residence. John has refused to participate in the behavioral treatment available at the residence, and his aggressive behavior is increasingly seen as placing staff and other consumers living in the residence in danger. If he cannot control his behavior, he may have to be moved to a more restrictive institution, resulting in the loss of his job and a departure from the only nonfamily home he has ever known (adapted from Fisher, 2002a, 2002b; Fisher et al., 2006). What steps might Dr. Rosenquist take to create a goodness of fit between John's abilities and attitudes that might lead to John's consent to treatment and increase the likelihood of treatment success? If despite goodness-of-fit efforts John continues to refuse treatment, in consultation with John's parents would it be ethically justified to begin behavioral treatment found effective for this population? Draw on APA Ethical Principles in your discussion of these questions. (Readers may also wish to refer to the APA Ethical Principles and Standards 3.05b, Informed Consent, and 10.01, Informed Consent to Therapy.)

CHAPTER 7

Standards on Privacy and Confidentiality

4. Privacy and Confidentiality

4.01 Maintaining Confidentiality

Psychologists have a primary obligation and take reasonable precautions to protect confidential information obtained through or stored in any medium, recognizing that the extent and limits of confidentiality may be regulated by law or established by institutional rules or professional or scientific relationship. (See also Standard 2.05, Delegation of Work to Others.)

Psychologists respect the privacy and dignity of persons by protecting confidential information obtained from those with whom they work (Principle E: Respect for People's Rights and Dignity). Standard 4.01 of the APA Ethics Code (APA, 2002b) is broadly written and requires all psychologists to take reasonable precautions to maintain confidentiality. The nature of precautions required will differ according to the psychologist's role, the purpose of the psychological activity, the legal status of the person with whom the psychologist is working, federal regulations, state and local laws, and institutional and organizational policies. The term *reasonable precautions* recognizes both the responsibility to be familiar with appropriate methods of protecting confidentiality and the possibility that confidentiality may be broken despite a psychologist's best efforts. The following are general recommendations for maintaining confidentiality across a variety of psychological activities.

Use of the Internet and Other Electronic Media

When providing services, conducting distance learning, or collecting research data over the Internet, psychologists must become knowledgeable about or obtain technical assistance in employing appropriate methods for protecting confidential records concerning clients/patients, organizations, research participants, or students.

- When files are stored via a common server or backed up on a university system or hub server, discuss and develop security measures with appropriate personnel.
- Use encrypted data transmission, password-protected data storage, and firewall techniques.
- When confidential information is emailed, faxed, or otherwise electronically transmitted to scientists, professionals, or organizations, take reasonable steps to ensure that recipients of the information have an adequate confidentiality policy (see also discussion of HIPAA later in this chapter).
- Psychologists using the Internet for clinical supervision should instruct trainees on appropriate procedures to protect client/patient confidentiality.
- Avoid leaving telephone messages for clients/patients on answering machines. When such a message is unavoidable, take precautions to ensure the message does not reveal to others that the client/patient is in treatment or any other confidential information.

Digital Ethics: Cybersecurity Is a Two-Way Street

Cybersecurity at only one end of a network of communication is insufficient. Psychologists should work with organizations, clients/patients, students, and others regarding how to install appropriate security protections. This may include discussion of shared encryption methods and adequate password protection for communications conducted on mobile computing devices, such as smartphones and other digital devices (for a detailed review of security concerns and practices, see Schwartz & Lonborg, 2011).

Audio, Video, or Digital Recordings of Voices or Images

Protecting confidentiality when recording the voice or images of clients/patients, research participants, employees, or others may require technical advice or assistance.

- Store recordings in safe locations or use passwords to protect computer access.
- Distort voice recordings or mask faces in visual images to protect confidentiality.
- Destroy recordings when they are no longer needed, as long as their destruction does not conflict with other ethical obligations to maintain scientific, organizational, or professional records.

⊘ An educational psychologist sought consent and parental permission to use teacher and student images in a web-based instructional video for science education. To address parental concerns that students might be identified by Internet predators, she used "masking" effects on video shots of students' faces and sound editing to remove any reference to names. When there were too many faces to conceal through masking, she extracted a digital photograph from a scene in which only activities and not identities were visible and then used editing software to extract appropriate audio to supplement the photograph (see Schuck & Kearney, 2006).

Research

Psychologists must follow the procedures below to ensure confidentiality:

- Use participant codes on all data collection materials and data entered for analysis.
- Maintain records linking participant codes to personal identifiers in a secure file and destroy such records once they are no longer needed.
- Limit access to personally identifiable information and supervise research personnel in routine confidentiality precautions.
- Separate consent forms from coded materials to avoid participant identification.
- When publishing or otherwise disseminating research findings, consider special confidentiality protections when unnamed but small, unique samples can be identified through descriptions of demographic variables (e.g., persons with rare diseases from distinct communities).
- Apply for a Certificate of Confidentiality (CoC) under 301(d) of the Public Health Service Act of 1946 (https://history.nih.gov/research/downloads/PL79-725.pdf). The CoC provides investigators with immunity from a subpoena requiring disclosure of identifiable information when there is a possibility that data collected are of a sensitive nature and, if released, could result in stigmatization, discrimination, or legal action, possibly jeopardizing an individual's financial standing, employment, or reputation (see Chapter 11, Standard 8.02, Informed Consent to Research, for a discussion of the CoC limitations).
- Ensure that recruitment and research procedures do not inadvertently reveal confidential information. For example, when studying addictions, mental disorders, sexually transmitted diseases, or other potentially stigmatizing conditions, approaching target populations for recruitment may result in public identification of the condition.
- Ensure that participant inclusion criteria to study school-based prevention programs for students at risk for behavioral, academic, or other problems do not inadvertently create teacher bias or socially stigmatize students (Polanin & Vera, 2013).

Research Conducted in Unique or Cross-Cultural Communities

Increasing sophistication of data analysis programs is increasing the ability to identify individuals from a handful of data points even when the data has been de-identified. Psychologists disseminating research results or sharing data with others should take steps to protect participant populations from these informational risks. Examples of populations specifically vulnerable to informational risk include individuals with rare genetic markers or health disorders, those from small or unique cultural communities, and those engaging in illegal behaviors in easily identifiable locales. (See also Standards 4.02, Discussing the Limits of Confidentiality, and 8.14, Sharing Research Data for Verification; Chapter 11 Hot Topic "Informational Risk and Disclosure of Genetic Information for Research Participants.")

☒ A health psychologist conducted a qualitative study on health disparities among illegal immigrants in a small Southwestern city. Her demographic data included gender, age, type of housing, and type of employment. In addition, her informed consent included permission to access the participants' emergency room health records at the local hospital. She presented the results of the study at professional workshops and at public meetings in the town, hoping to inform changes in government policy that would reduce health disparities in this population. Although she kept her records confidential, it was not difficult for immigration officials to identify participants by linking their demographic information to the hospital records, and several participants were visited by immigration department officials following the psychologist's public presentations (see Brabeck et al., 2015)

Psychologists conducting research in small, unique cultural populations in the United States and internationally should also become familiar with cultural and contextual factors that may influence participant confidentiality preferences and concerns.

⊘ A psychologist conducting cross-cultural research in the Amazon arranged to have individual interviews conducted in a private area of the village to protect participant confidentiality. To the psychologist's surprise, the villagers objected to these arrangements as strange and uncomfortable because they did not ordinarily conduct social or business interactions in private settings. In addition, those who did express interest in participation brought their family members to the interview. With permission from his IRB, he modified the procedures so that interviews were conducted in a corner of

(Continued)

(Continued)

a public space within the village, and family members were permitted to be present at the invitation of the participants. Informed consent clarified to villagers the type of information to be discussed, how the discussion with each individual would be kept confidential from all who were not present during the interview, and steps the psychologist would take to ensure that individual participants could not be identified by others when the study results were disseminated (adapted from Monshi & Zieglmayer, 2004).

Assessment and Psychotherapy Records

The following procedures assist in maintaining confidentiality:

- Store therapy notes or client/patient records in locked file cabinets or in password-protected computer files.
- When working with an HMO or within an institution, personally confirm that client/patient permission for sharing confidential information has been obtained appropriately through third-party contractual or institutional release forms.
- Protect the identity of clients/patients or other persons not covered by an HMO when the HMO conducts a utilization review that includes inspection of noncovered clients'/patients' records.
- Obtain appropriate written permission and/or signed HIPAA-compliant authorization before releasing confidential information to third parties (see below).

Implications of HIPAA for Practice and Research

Practitioners and scientists whose work includes creating, using, disclosing, collecting, storing, or analyzing PHI should become familiar with requirements of the HIPAA Privacy Rule summarized below (see also "A Word About HIPAA" in the preface of this book).

Notice of Privacy Practices

Prior to beginning treatment or treatment-relevant assessments or randomized clinical trials in which health care is provided, HIPAA-covered entities must provide patients with a Notice of Privacy Practices that describes the psychologist's policies for use and disclosure of PHI, the clients'/patients' rights regarding their PHI under HIPAA, and the provider's obligations under the Privacy Rule. In most instances, the notice will be given to prospective clients/patients at the same time as informed consent is obtained since the notice provides information relevant to the scope and limits of confidentiality. As of 2013, HIPAA also requires that the Notice inform clients/patients that they (a) have the right to restrict certain disclosures of protected health information (PHI) to a health plan if they pay out-of-pocket in full for health services; (b) have the right to be notified if there is a breach of unsecured PHI; (c) have a right to opt out of fund-raising communications; (d) must sign an authorization before release of PHI for use or disclosures not described in the Notice, including sale of PHI to others, receipt of marketing materials related to their PHI (e.g., treating psychologists sending their patients information about new services they are offering), or disclosure of psychotherapy notes.

Privacy Officer

Under HIPAA, "covered entities" must designate a "privacy officer" to oversee and ensure that HIPAA-compliant privacy procedures are developed and implemented. This requirement is "scalable," in that meeting the requirement will differ depending on whether a psychologist is in solo practice, directs a group practice, or administers a large institutional program. Covered entities must implement security procedures that prevent unauthorized access to health records. They must also take steps to ensure that employees, business associates, individual contractors, consultants, collection agencies, third-party payors, and researchers with whom PHI is shared comply with HIPAA regulations. Psychologists transferring PHI files to or from HMOs or other companies are required to take steps to ensure that confidential records are transmitted in secure ways, for example, by means of a secured fax machine. Requirements for HIPAA compliance also vary with each state's privacy laws.

Small Group Practices

HIPAA distinguishes between large and small health care practices, recognizing that for the latter, it is impractical to expect that employees will not handle PHI. The following is a partial list of requirements when staff members have access to such records (see Rada, 2003):

- All staff must be formally trained in HIPAA regulations, including state laws relevant to faxing information that includes PHI and the group's sanction policy for violators.
- Staff must sign an employee confidentiality form, which is placed in their personnel record along with a record of their training.
- Emails and fax coversheets used to communicate PHI must indicate that the information is confidential.
- The fax policy must be posted beside the fax machine.
- All vendors used by the practice for accounting, legal, actuarial, billing, or other services must sign a business associate contract with the practice.
- In addition to a privacy officer responsible for the development and implementation of the policies and procedures, each group practice must have an office manager who (a) oversees HIPAA authorizations, completion and maintenance of required records, and new staff training; (b) receives privacy

complaints and mitigates harmful effects of privacy disclosures; and (c) applies sanctions when appropriate. In small clinics or practices, one person may perform both these roles.

Research Creating, Using, or Disclosing PHI

Psychologists who are health care providers or who employ health care providers to conduct research involving assessments or diagnoses that will be entered into a participants' permanent health record or used for treatment decisions involving research participants should consider themselves or their research team covered entities under HIPAA. Investigators who are not themselves health care providers but who conduct intervention evaluation research or quality improvement research for a health care facility or any other organization that is a covered entity must also ensure that their procedures are HIPAA compliant. Additional details are provided in Chapter 11 in the sections on Standards 8.02, Informed Consent to Research, and 8.05, Dispensing With Informed Consent for Research.

Implications of FERPA for Psychologists Working in Schools

The Family Educational Rights and Privacy Act of 1974 (FERPA) is a federal law that protects the privacy of student education records in all schools that receive funds under an applicable program of the US Department of Education (http://www2.ed.gov/policy/gen/guid/fpco/ferpa/index.html). FERPA gives certain rights to parents that get transferred to the student at age 18 or after leaving high school. A student's educational record may not be released without written permission from the parent or the eligible student. Parents and eligible students have the right to inspect and review the student's education records, to request the school correct records they believe are inadequate or misleading, to have a formal hearing if the record is not amended, and to place a statement in the record about the contested information.

FERPA does allow disclosure of records without written consent (a) in cases of health and safety emergencies; (b) to comply with a judicial order or with state or local authorities within the juvenile justice system; (c) to school officials with legitimate educational interest; (d) to accrediting agencies, specified officials, or organizations in connection with auditing or certain studies on behalf of the school; (e) to schools to which the student is transferring; or (f) to parties in connection with the student's financial aid. HIPAA regulations do not apply to records that fall under FERPA regulations. FERPA, unlike HIPAA, does not make distinctions between student health and academic records. School psychologists need to be familiar with state and district policies, which may be more protective of student health privacy (e.g., HIV/AIDS). Readers may wish to refer to "Need to Know: Avoiding Conversion of Treatment Records to Educational Records" in the Chapter 9 section on Standard 6.01, Documentation of Professional and Scientific Work and Maintenance of Records.

4.02 Discussing the Limits of Confidentiality

(a) Psychologists discuss with persons (including, to the extent feasible, persons who are legally incapable of giving informed consent and their legal representatives) and organizations with whom they establish a scientific or professional relationship (1) the relevant limits of confidentiality and (2) the foreseeable uses of the information generated through their psychological activities. (See also Standard 3.10, Informed Consent.)

Legal, institutional, or professional obligations frequently place limits on the extent to which private information acquired during psychological activities can be kept confidential. Psychologists are often legally required to (a) report suspected child abuse or neglect to child protection agencies; (b) contact family members or other professionals to protect an individual from imminent self-harm; (c) warn a potential victim of a client's/patient's intent to harm him or her; (d) contact a law enforcement agency when they have foreknowledge of certain crimes; (e) assist in lawful military investigations; (f) provide companies, police departments, or military agencies psychological information to determine suitability for employment, promotion, or assignments; (g) provide treatment or assessment information in criminal or civil cases; or (h) provide information to third-party payors when mental health treatment is covered by a health plan.

Disclosure of such information can have serious material consequences for clients/patients, research participants, organizational clients, and others with whom psychologists work. Promising confidentiality without revealing its known limitations is a misrepresentation of fact that may violate a person's privacy and liberty (Bersoff, 1976). Release of confidential information poses risks to individuals and their families when disclosures lead to investigation by child protective services, arrest, conviction, institutionalization, loss of health or disability insurance, loss of child custody, or social stigmatization. Disclosures of confidential information can also lead to financial or legal risk for organizations.

Under Standard 4.02a, psychologists must discuss with persons and organizations with whom they work reporting obligations and other limits on the confidentiality of information that can be reasonably anticipated. This includes informing those with whom one works about (a) state-mandated reporting requirements related to suspicion of child maltreatment and elder abuse and foreknowledge of specific types of crimes and (b) the psychologist's own professionally derived standards for disclosing information (see Standard 4.05b, Disclosures).

Children and Persons Legally Incapable of Consent

This requirement extends to persons who are legally incapable of giving informed consent and their legal representatives (see Standard 3.10b, Informed Consent; "A Word About HIPAA" in the preface of this book). Practicing psychologists should inform children and, when appropriate, adult clients/patients and their legal guardians about the nature of information that will be shared with guardians and with others based on law, institutional or organizational regulations, or the psychologist's policies regarding disclosure of information related to self-harm or harm to others (Fisher, 2002a; Fisher & Oransky, 2008; Zeranski & Halgin, 2011; see also the Hot Topic "Confidentiality and Involvement of Parents in Mental Health Services for Children and Adolescents" at the end of this chapter). For example, as detailed in sections below, legal guardians have access to health records under HIPAA and receive "explanations of benefits" from health insurers under the Affordable Care Act (ACA). School psychologists may need to inform students, guardians, and school personnel about laws governing the release of school records—for example, FERPA, which establishes the right of parents to obtain copies of their children's school records. Research psychologists should inform legal guardians and, to the extent possible, the prospective participants themselves about any limitations in confidentiality. Such limitations might include reporting requirements, if investigators are state-mandated child abuse or elder abuse reporters, or protective policies, if the investigators have elected to disclose to guardians or professionals information about participants with suicidal ideation or other serious health-compromising behaviors (Fisher 2002b, 2003a, 2003c; Fisher & Goodman, 2009; Fisher & Vacanti-Shova, 2012).

Third-Party Payors

When services will be covered by third-party payors, psychologists need to inform clients/patients about information that will be shared with the third party, including treatment plans, session notes, and diagnoses. Some contractual agreements with health maintenance organizations (HMOs) permit utilization reviews that provide HMO access to information about clients/patients not covered under the policy. Clients/patients must be informed of such limits on confidentiality if records cannot be adequately de-identified. Psychologists receiving payment through credit cards should inform persons about the possible use of this information by credit card companies, which may sell their client lists to organizations specializing in self-help or other related products.

Military

In the military, there is no psychologist–client confidentiality in the traditional sense. Military psychologists are required to release information on command to assist in the lawful conduct of investigations or to determine suitability of persons for service or assignments. During informed consent, military clients/patients must be informed about the disclosure policies that may affect them (see Hoyt, 2013, for a detailed summary of Department of Defense [DoD] and US Army regulations regarding limited confidentiality for behavioral health assessment and treatment). One of the most noteworthy gains in confidentiality and respect for the rights of the individual was the implementation of DoD Directive 6490.1 (U.S. DoD, 1997a) and DoD Instruction 6490.4 (U.S. DoD, 1997b). Thanks to the efforts of military psychologists, active-duty service members sent for commander-directed mental health evaluations now have (a) the right to know why they were referred for the evaluation and who will be conducting that evaluation; (b) an opportunity for a second opinion following receipt of a summary of the findings; and (c) a right to speak with legal counsel, a chaplain, and a member of Congress regarding their situation (see Orme & Doerman, 2001). Johnson, Grasso, and Maslowski (2010) pointed out that actual "conflicts" between the APA Ethics Code and military law (Standard 1.02, Conflicts Between Ethics and Law, Regulations, or Other Governing Legal Authority) can be avoided by skilled clinicians who work within the chain of command. For example, when ordered to provide a client's/patient's record under the DoD need-to-know statute, a psychologist could work with the requesting officer to determine the specific information of interest (e.g., Is this member fit to deploy?) so that the client's/patient's privacy could be protected with a general response that does not include specific details of mental health history and current specific problems (Johnson et al., 2010).

Implications of HIPAA

Psychologists creating, transferring, analyzing, or storing PHI via electronic transmission or working with a managed care company, bill collection agency, or other organization that does so are required to provide individuals with a Notice of Privacy Practices that details the uses and disclosures of PHI and the individuals' privacy rights under relevant federal or state law. Notice of Privacy Practices and informed consent forms used by psychologists working in small group practices need to clarify the extent to which confidential information will be shared with other practicing professionals in the group on a regular basis and how confidentiality protections will be protected (see "A Word About HIPAA" in the preface of this book).

Implications of the Affordable Care Act (ACA)

One provision of the Affordable Care Act is extension of dependent coverage for young adults aged up to 26 years on their parent's private insurance plan. This change, meant to increase insurance coverage for young adults, can exacerbate the risk of confidentiality breaches since by law, insurance companies must send an "explanation of benefits" (EOB) to the policy holder, which in these cases will be the parents (Frerich, Garcia, Long, Lechner, Lust, & Eisenberg, 2012; Sedlander, Brindis, Bausch, & Tebb, 2015). Under Standard 2.02, as early as feasible, psychologists treating young adults should inquire about the nature of their insurance coverage and, when appropriate, discuss the limits on confidentiality if the client/patient is covered under a parent's policy (see also Standard 10.01, Informed Consent to Therapy). Psychologists can further protect the confidentiality of young adults by appropriately limiting the information included in health records (Standards 2.04, Minimizing Intrusions on Privacy; 6.01, Documentation of Professional and Scientific Work and Maintenance of Records).

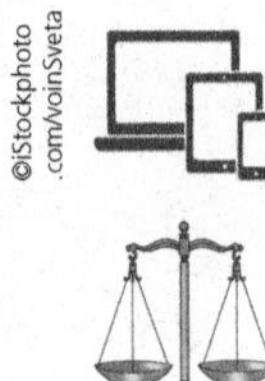

(b) Unless it is not feasible or is contraindicated, the discussion of confidentiality occurs at the outset of the relationship and thereafter as new circumstances may warrant.

Clients/patients, research participants, organizations, and others are entitled to know the limits of confidentiality and its potential consequences before deciding whether or how to engage in a scientific or professional relationship with a psychologist. Standard 4.02b requires that psychologists discuss the known extent and limits of confidentiality at the outset of the relationship. The phrase *unless it is not feasible or is contraindicated* permits psychologists to delay discussion of confidentiality in cases in which the treatment needs of a new client/patient, such as acute trauma, must take priority. It also permits delays when the limits of confidentiality need to be further explored. For example, a therapist may need to call a client's/patient's health plan to determine its utilization review policies. In such situations, confidentiality is discussed as soon as the crisis has subsided or all information has been obtained.

In some instances, the scientific or professional relationship may change over time, requiring renewed discussion of confidentiality. For example, in longitudinal studies involving children extending over several years, both participants and their guardians may need to be reminded of confidentiality policies, especially if a change in such policies is warranted as the child matures into adolescence or adulthood.

A psychologist whose client/patient asks him or her to testify as a fact witness on the client's/patient's behalf should carefully explain to the client/patient how this changes the nature of confidentiality and the implications of waiving client–therapist privilege.

Digital Ethics: Should Psychologists Search the Internet for Information on Clients/Patients, Students, Employees, and Others With Whom They Work?

The informational opportunities offered by new technologies raise ethical questions regarding confidentiality and informed consent when psychologists' search cyberspace for information about those with whom they work. Kaslow, Patterson, and Gottlieb (2011) suggested that intentional Internet searches conducted without the knowledge of those with whom psychologists work may violate an individual's expected zone of privacy, erode trust in the professional relationship, shift the psychologist's role to that of an investigator, and impede the developing autonomy of clients/patients, students, or employees (Principle A: Beneficence and Nonmaleficence; Principle B: Fidelity and Responsibility; Principle C: Integrity; Principle E: Respect for People's Rights and Dignity). These authors suggested the following:

- Psychologists' Internet search policies should be made clear at the outset of any professional relationship, and communication should be similarly direct when the psychologist obtains information through such a search.

- Before conducting an Internet search, psychologists should consider whether it would violate fundamental assumptions of privacy, integrity, and trust held by clients, students, prospective employees, and others with whom they work.
- Intentionally searching for information over the Internet without the knowledge of clients, students, and others should only be undertaken when absolutely necessary (e.g., when there is a concern about potentially violent behavior or self-harm).
- Psychologists should also keep in mind that information on the Internet is not always accurate, and they should guard against unverified assumptions.

(c) Psychologists who offer services, products, or information via electronic transmission inform clients/patients of the risks to privacy and limits of confidentiality.

Psychological services or transmission of records conducted over the Internet and other electronic media are vulnerable to breaches in confidentiality that may be beyond the psychologist's individual control. Under Standard 4.02c, clients/patients must be made aware of the risks to privacy and limitations of protections that the psychologist can institute to guard against violations of consumer confidentiality when information is transmitted electronically (see Standard 4.01, Maintaining Confidentiality).

- Psychologists conducting therapy or assessments via email or through secure chat rooms should inform clients/patients about the possibility of strangers hacking into secure sites or, when applicable, the extent to which institutional staff have access to secure sites on a hub server.
- Sometimes, clients/patients may send unsolicited sensitive communications to a therapist's personal email account. Once psychologists become aware that such an email has been sent, they should inform such clients about the risk that others may read these emails and discourage clients/patients from future email communications if such communications are clinically contraindicated.
- Clients/patients who discuss sensitive information with psychologists over a cell phone should be warned about the limits of confidentiality when this medium is used.
- Psychologists transmitting health records to managed care companies or other health providers need to alert clients/patients to potential breaches that may occur when health information is passed through multiple systems, including utilization reviewers, case managers, bookkeepers, and accountants (such information may be included in the HIPAA Notice of Privacy Practices discussed earlier in this chapter).
- Psychologists providing services on a website should include a visible and easy to understand privacy statement whenever a consumer's personal information is requested. In addition to information regarding site privacy protections (e.g., firewalls), the privacy statement should advise consumers of how

personal information will be used (e.g., sold to other sites, used to contact the consumer at a later date) and whether they can opt out of these uses.

4.03 Recording

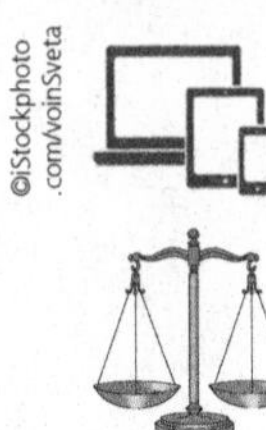

Before recording the voices or images of individuals to whom they provide services, psychologists obtain permission from all such persons or their legal representatives. (See also Standards 8.03, Informed Consent for Recording Voices and Images in Research; 8.05, Dispensing With Informed Consent for Research; and 8.07, Deception in Research.)

Psychologists who use audio, visual, or digital recordings of voices or images to provide services to individuals must obtain permission from all such persons or their legal representatives before recording begins. Although exceptions exist for informed consent to recording voices and images in research (see Standards 8.03, 8.05, and 8.07), under Standard 4.03, no such exceptions are permissible for service providers. The following are examples of violations of this standard:

- ☒ A court-appointed forensic psychologist conducting a competency evaluation of a prisoner audiotaped the assessment without informing the prisoner or the prisoner's attorney.
- ☒ A clinical psychologist conducting behavior therapy with a 6-year-old diagnosed with attention deficit disorder decided to videotape the therapy sessions to better analyze the child's behavioral responses to different situations. The psychologist did not obtain permission from the child's parents to videotape the session.

4.04 Minimizing Intrusions on Privacy

(a) Psychologists include in written and oral reports and consultations only information germane to the purpose for which the communication is made.

Clients/patients, research participants, and organizational clients often share or unintentionally reveal private information to psychologists that is not germane to the purpose of the psychological activities. Under Standard 4.04, psychologists are prohibited from including such information in their reports or consultations. For example, adhering to this standard, forensic practitioners will avoid offering information that does not bear directly upon the legal purpose of an examination or consultation and will carefully consider whether an examinee's membership in a particular racial/ethnic, sexual orientation, or other group is relevant to the question at hand (APA, 2013e; Otto, DeMier, & Boccaccini, 2014). Examples of potential violations of this standard include the following:

- ☒ A woman referred for a neuropsychological evaluation to assess the cause of a speech disorder immediately following a head injury was accompanied to the psychologist's office by an individual she introduced as her wife. The psychologist's report referred to the client as a lesbian, even though sexual orientation was not a relevant factor in the diagnosis.
- ☒ During a break in an assessment battery for a competency determination of an incarcerated young man, the forensic psychologist heard the man brag about the crime to another inmate. During the competency hearing, the psychologist's expert testimony included mention of the casual admission to the crime.
- ☒ A school psychologist who evaluated children with learning disabilities for academic placement typically met with parents to obtain a developmental history and information about the child's study habits at home. During one of these discussions, a parent mentioned that her husband had lost his job a few months ago. The psychologist's report included mention of the father's unemployment, although it was not a factor in the report's conclusions regarding the child's learning status and schooling needs.

Implications of HIPAA (Standard 4.04a)

Standard 4.04a is consistent with HIPAA regulations regarding the "minimum necessary." When disclosing or requesting PHI, a covered entity must make reasonable efforts to limit the information to the *minimum necessary* to accomplish the intended purpose of the use, disclosure, or request. This requirement does not apply to disclosures to another health care provider for treatment or to the individual client/patient, disclosures required by law, or disclosures for other purposes under the HIPAA regulation.

(b) Psychologists discuss confidential information obtained in their work only for appropriate scientific or professional purposes and only with persons clearly concerned with such matters.

With rare exceptions (see Standards 4.05, Disclosures; 4.07, Use of Confidential Information for Didactic or Other Purposes), psychologists should never discuss confidential information obtained in their work without the permission of research participants, clients/patients, organizational clients, or others who have been promised confidentiality. In some instances, consent is implicit or refers to a category of individuals, such as when research participants and patients/clients consent to have confidential information shared with members of a research team or treatment staff.

In other instances, clients/patients with psychological impairments may not have a legally appointed guardian but do have a family caregiver actively involved in their treatment with whom confidential information can be shared. Standard 4.04b requires in such situations that psychologists discuss confidential information only with persons who are clearly concerned with the matter and limit disclosures only to information that is pertinent to the scientific or professional issue at hand. The intent of the standard is to permit discussions with others necessary to competently conduct psychological activities, to prohibit unnecessary discussion of confidential information, and to avoid the use of such information as gossip among professionals.

- ✓ A school psychologist evaluated a fourth-grade student for placement in a special education class. With permission and signed permission from the child's parents, the psychologist discussed the need for such a placement with the school principal. However, the psychologist refused to discuss the child's diagnosis when questioned by several concerned teachers in the faculty dining room.
- ✓ A clinical gerontologist developed behavioral treatment plans for Alzheimer's patients at a long-term care facility. Although staff psychologists implemented the behavioral plans, it was often necessary to coordinate the patients' psychological services with staff and family members. The psychologist provided nursing staff and family members with only the information they needed to ensure the consistency of the plan and carefully refrained from sharing with anyone who was not the patient's legal representative information about the patient's diagnosis or other personal information.

Implications of HIPAA (Standard 4.04b)

Under the HIPAA Privacy Rule, psychologists working in independent practice, group practices, or systems of health care are permitted to share PHI internally. The nature of information shared is not restricted when disclosure is with other health professionals for the purposes of providing treatment. However, psychologists must disclose nontreatment personnel, such as staff responsible for scheduling appointments or billing, only the minimum amount of information necessary for them to perform their duties.

4.05 Disclosures

(a) Psychologists may disclose confidential information with the appropriate consent of the organizational client, the individual client/patient, or another legally authorized person on behalf of the client/patient unless prohibited by law.

Standard 4.05a permits but does not require psychologists to disclose confidential information if appropriate consent has been obtained from the organizational client, the individual client/patient, or another legally authorized person. Psychologists should have persons or organizations provide a signed release, provide a signed authorization if HIPAA is applicable, or otherwise document the permission or request to have confidential information disclosed. Documentation should specifically identify the persons or organizations to whom confidential information

may be released, should be time limited, and should, where applicable, be HIPAA compliant. Psychologists should not ask individual or organizational clients to sign blanket releases for the disclosure of confidential information over an indeterminate period of time. Before releasing confidential information at the request of a hospital, organization, agency, or HMO, psychologists should confirm that the institution or organization obtained appropriate consent or authorization for the disclosure (see also the Hot Topic "Managing the Ethics of Managed Care" in Chapter 9).

Implications of HIPAA

Standard 4.05a requires psychologists to be mindful of laws that prohibit disclosure. HIPAA requires that covered entities obtain written valid authorization from the individual or his or her personal representative prior to releasing PHI (see "A Word About HIPAA" in the preface of this book for a list of authorization criteria). In addition, when appropriate release and authorizations are obtained, psychologists should remember to share only the minimum amount of information necessary for billing agencies and non–health provider internal staff to perform their roles (see Standard 4.04, Minimizing Intrusions on Privacy).

Declining Requests

Under Standard 4.05a, psychologists may decline an appropriately obtained request to release confidential information if the psychologist believes that disclosure will cause harm. However, psychologists should be aware that certain federal and statutory laws limit providers' rights to withhold such information. Under the HIPAA Privacy Rule, covered entities have an obligation to agree to a patient's reasonable requests for release of PHI and can deny a request only if it is reasonably likely to endanger the life or physical safety of the individual or another person or is likely to cause equally substantial harm. In addition, under HIPAA clients/patients have the right to have the denial reviewed by another designated licensed health care professional. Readers should refer to Chapter 12 for how decisions regarding disclosure of information relate to Standards 9.04, Release of Test Data, and 9.11, Maintaining Test Security.

Research

Under HIPAA, an individual's access to PHI created or obtained in the course of treatment research may be suspended temporarily for as long as the research is in progress, provided the individual has agreed to the denial of access when consenting to the research and has been promised right of access upon completion of the research (Standard 8.02, Informed Consent to Research).

Psychotherapy (Process) Notes

Under HIPAA, patients do *not* have the right to access psychotherapy notes, and a client/patient must provide a separate signed authorization specific to the release

of psychotherapy notes when a covered entity agrees to their release (see "A Word About HIPAA" in the preface to this book). HIPAA defines *psychotherapy notes* (also known as *process notes*) as notes recorded in any medium by a mental health professional documenting or analyzing the contents of conversation during a private counseling session or a group, joint, or family counseling session and that are separated from the rest of the individual's medical record. To ensure that psychotherapy notes are distinguishable from PHI, psychologists should refrain from including in the process notes the summary of the theme of the psychotherapy session, medication prescription or monitoring, and any other information necessary for treatment or billing (Hecker & Edwards, 2014).

PHI Compiled for Legal or Administrative Action

Certain forensic records are also protected under HIPAA. Patients do not have the right of access to information compiled in reasonable anticipation of, or for use in, a civil, criminal, or administrative action or procedure. For information on other exceptions, see discussions of Standards 6.03, Withholding Records for Nonpayment, and 9.04, Release of Test Data.

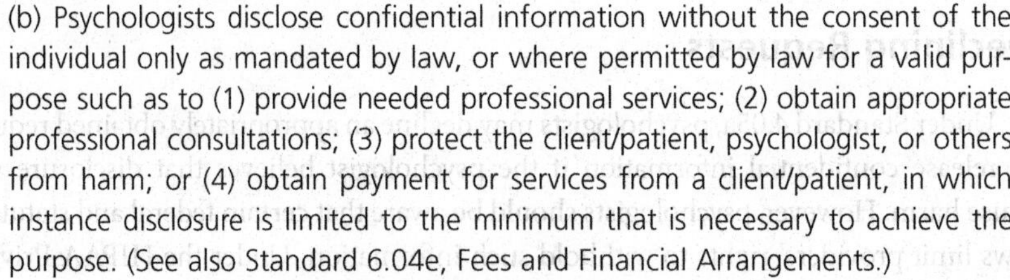

(b) Psychologists disclose confidential information without the consent of the individual only as mandated by law, or where permitted by law for a valid purpose such as to (1) provide needed professional services; (2) obtain appropriate professional consultations; (3) protect the client/patient, psychologist, or others from harm; or (4) obtain payment for services from a client/patient, in which instance disclosure is limited to the minimum that is necessary to achieve the purpose. (See also Standard 6.04e, Fees and Financial Arrangements.)

Standard 4.05b describes those situations in which it is ethically permissible to disclose identifiable confidential information without the consent of an individual or organization. The standard is permissive rather than mandatory, leaving the decision to disclose confidential information without consent under the above-listed categories to the psychologist's discretion. At the same time, the standard prohibits disclosure of confidential information without consent for any purpose other than those listed.

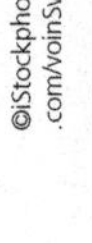

Clients/patients, research participants, organizational clients, and others with whom a psychologist works must be informed as early as feasible in the professional or scientific relationship about the potential for such disclosures when it is reasonable for the psychologist to anticipate that disclosures may be necessary (see Standard 4.02, Discussing the Limits of Confidentiality).

Disclosures Mandated by Law

The standard permits psychologists to disclose confidential information without consent when the disclosure is mandated by law.

- Following the Child Abuse Prevention and Treatment Act of 1976, all 50 states enacted statutes mandating mental health professionals and, in some states, requiring researchers to report suspected child abuse or neglect as members of the general citizenry. In addition, some states specifically require mandated reporters to alert child protection agencies when they learn about child abuse from a client/patient who is no longer a minor if other children are or may be at risk of being abused by the perpetrator of the abuse. Most statutes protect mandatory reporters from liability claims, including those for breach of confidentiality (http://www.childwelfare.gov/pubPDFs/immunity.pdf).

- The majority of states include psychologists as mandated reporters of elder abuse, variously defined as deliberate acts that can cause physical, emotional, or psychological harm and nonintentional acts of neglect and self-neglect (Zeranski & Halgin, 2011).
- Some states have mandatory reporting laws for domestic abuse or situations in which a practitioner has foreknowledge that a crime will be committed.
- Therapists are legally required at times to disclose confidential information by a court order, even when they have informed the judge that the disclosure is inconsistent with their ethical obligations to protect confidentiality (Standard 1.02, Conflicts Between Ethics and Law, Regulations, or Other Governing Legal Authority).

Need to Know: Are Therapists Required to Report Abuse Already Under Investigation?

There will be instances in which nonforensic practitioners treating a child for anxiety or other disorders may learn from the child or a guardian of a current child protection services (CPS) investigation into an accusation of child abuse. In such instances, psychologists should clarify their reporting obligations to the client/patient and/or guardian, follow their state-mandated child abuse reporting duties, and include in the report to the registry that they have been informed by the client/patient or guardian that this disclosure is under investigation. If, in addition, a psychologist wishes to be kept informed about an ongoing CPS investigation, he or she should obtain a release from the child's legal guardian. Psychologists should also report any new indications of abuse that may emerge during the course of treatment since an ongoing investigation is no guarantee that a child's welfare will be protected. Finally, under such conditions practitioners should assume that they may be called upon as a fact witness and, if clinically appropriate, avoid probing the abuse specifically so as not to contaminate the investigation (APA, 2013b; Branaman & Gottlieb, 2013).

"Duty-to-Protect" Laws

Clients who indicate violent tendencies or threaten to harm another person pose special challenges for psychologists, who may have a fiduciary or legal obligation to protect others from imminent harm. A number of states have adopted "duty-to-protect" (also known as "duty-to-warn") laws following the landmark court case *Tarasoff v. Regents of the University of California* (1976). In that case, a psychologist at a university health center recognized that Prosenjit Poddar, a client with a pathological attachment to his ex-girlfriend, Tatiana Tarasoff, was a danger to her after he made some threats. The psychologist and his supervisor notified campus police that the client was dangerous and should be committed, but after interviewing him, the police released him. Poddar did not return for therapy and murdered Tatiana 2 months later. Her parents brought a successful suit against the university, arguing that the therapist had a duty to warn Tarasoff.

Duty-to-protect laws typically require certain classes of health care providers to inform a third party of the prospect of being harmed by a client/patient if the provider has (a) a "special relationship" with the prospective assailant (i.e., a client–therapist relationship), (b) the ability to predict that violence will occur (e.g., the client/patient has made a credible threat against a third party), and (c) the ability to identify the potential victim (i.e., the client/patient has named the potential victim). Some court decisions have broadened the third requirement to a more generalized duty to protect third parties from foreseeable harm in the absence of an identifiable victim. These cases typically involve the release from hospitalization or the failure to commit for psychiatric treatment clients/patients whose danger to nonidentified others is foreseeable (Quattrocchi & Schopp, 2005).

State laws differ widely in psychologists' Tarasoff-like obligations, psychologists' immunity from liability as long as the duty is discharged in good faith, and, in the case of minors, when psychologists can communicate concerns to parents (Kangas & Calvert, 2014; Younggren, 2011). Some states have sharply contrasting laws. For example, in 1999 the Texas Supreme Court determined that a mental health professional only has an obligation to the patient and not to a nonpatient third party (*Thapar v. Zezulka*, 1999). Psychologists are advised to keep up-to-date on evolving law in this area in the state(s) in which they work. In addition, psychologists conducting psychotherapy should develop a priori competencies in assessing an individual's potential for violence and document in their records all decisions about dangerous clients regarding treatment, confidentiality, and reporting (VandeCreek, 2013; Standards 2.01, Competence; 3.04, Avoiding Harm; 6.01, Documentation of Professional and Scientific Work and Maintenance of Records).

Research

Psychologists should remain up-to-date on controversies as to whether duty-to-protect laws apply to research or to situations involving a professional's knowledge of intentional or reckless transmission of HIV or other sexually transmitted diseases to partners or other identified victims (Appelbaum & Rosenbaum, 1989; Chenneville, 2000; Fisher, 2011; Fisher, Oransky, et al., 2009; http://www.cdc.gov/hiv/policies/law/states/exposure.html). In addition, psychologists providing services or conducting research over the Internet need to be familiar with state laws governing mandatory reporting in jurisdictions where recipients of Internet services or Internet-administered research instruments reside.

Need to Know: Assessing Duty-to-Warn Obligations

In all situations suggesting potential harm to a third party, psychologists should carefully consider whether the threat to harm actually meets the Tarasoff requirements described above and consider the following questions suggested by Younggren (2011). Is there an identifiable victim? Is the threat immediate? Is there an established scientific or clinical basis for judging the probability of violence for the specific case (Standard 2.04, Bases for Scientific and Professional Judgment)? Can the risk be reduced (Standard 3.04, Avoiding Harm)? Does the psychologist have the risk management competencies required? If not, what steps should be taken to ensure that the situation is handled competently (Standard 2.01, Boundaries of Competence)?

School Violence

In response to the rise in public awareness of school violence, statutory and case laws are increasingly recognizing the need to balance the interest of the state (school) in fulfilling its duty to protect the rights of individual children and to maintain order and ensure pupil safety. In many states, school personnel are required or permitted to detain and question students suspected of planning acts of violence. If a student poses a threat to a minor child, school psychologists may notify the threatened student's parents, supervise the potentially violent child in the school setting, take reasonable steps to encourage out-of-school supervision, and ensure that the student does not have access to weapons.

Systematic assessments of foreseeable school violence may include (a) a student's past violent, menacing, or stalking acts and the precipitants to those acts; (b) recent events that might instigate violent behavior; (c) cognitive and physical capability of following through on violent intentions (e.g., availability of weapons); and (d) protective factors in place within and outside the school to prevent violence (Jacob & Hartshorne, 2007; Reddy et al., 2001; see also the National Association of School Psychologist's position statement on violence prevention (NASP, 2015).

Privileged Communications, Subpoenas, and Court Orders

In treatment and assessment contexts, the ethical responsibility to maintain or disclose confidential information belongs to the psychologist, but in legal settings, this information is classified as "privileged communications," and the decision to maintain or disclose such information rests with the client/patient or his or her legal guardian. There are exceptions. Therapeutic communications are often not privileged when clients/patients decide to make their mental health part of litigation or when the court has ordered psychological examinations, civil commitment hearings, or custody cases.

Practicing psychologists need to be knowledgeable about how to ethically and legally respond to subpoenas or compelled testimony for client records or test data (APA Committee on Legal Issues, 2006). A subpoena is issued by an attorney instructing the psychologist to provide documents or appear for oral testimony. Psychologists are required to respond to a subpoena, but when the subpoena asks for "privileged communications," psychologists cannot release confidential information without a signed client/patient release or authorization. If no release is forthcoming, psychologists should advise the requesting party that they are waiting for further instruction from the presiding judge (Bennett et al., 2006). A court order to provide documents or oral testimony is issued by a presiding judge, who has the power to waive client/patient privilege and legally require that mental health records be released. A court order does not preclude psychologists from communicating to the judge their confidentiality obligations under the Ethics Code and requesting limitations on the information released (see Standard 1.02, Conflicts Between Ethics and Law, Regulations, or Other Governing Legal Authority). If such requests are denied, Standard 4.05b permits psychologists to disclose records requested.

Disclosures Permitted by Law

Standard 4.05b also permits psychologists to disclose confidential information without consent if the disclosure is permitted by law *and* the disclosure is for a valid purpose. Valid purposes include those initiated to provide needed professional services; obtain appropriate professional consultation; protect the client/patient, psychologist, or others from harm; or obtain payment for services.

- It is ethically appropriate to disclose personally identifiable confidential information to another professional or family member if such notification is required to hospitalize or otherwise protect clients/patients, research participants, students, or others who have indicated credible suicidal intent or whom psychologists believe to be engaged in activities that are likely to result in imminent and substantial harm.
- Irrespective of whether the jurisdiction in which a psychologist works has a duty-to-protect law, Standard 4.05b permits psychologists to disclose confidential information obtained from clients/patients or research participants to protect others from harm.
- Psychologists are permitted to report to appropriate law enforcement agencies credible threats to their welfare or to the welfare of their family or colleagues made by clients/patients, students, research participants, or others with whom they work.
- When a client/patient or organizational client fails to pay for a psychologist's services, the psychologist may disclose information to a bill collection agency to obtain payment. The information must be limited to the individual's or organization's name, contact information, amount of payments still outstanding, number of sessions or billable hours for which payment is due, and other factual information necessary to collect outstanding funds. Psychologists

should not disclose to bill collection agencies a client's/patient's diagnosis, the nature of treatment, or other personal information. Nor should they disclose the purpose or nature of their work for a company or organization (see also Standard 6.04e, Fees and Financial Arrangements).

- In most states, school psychologists do not have a legal obligation to report student substance abuse or criminal acts committed by students or their parents that do not involve child abuse. However, disclosure of such information to parents or others in authority is permissible under Standard 4.05b and, in most cases, legally permissible (Jacob & Hartshorne, 2007).
- School psychologists are mandated by their state laws to report suspected child abuse to the appropriate authorities; the responsibility to confirm or disconfirm the suspected abuse is the responsibility of the child protection service, not school personnel (Jacob, Decker, & Hartshorne, 2011).
- Military psychologists may disclose to officers and employees in the DoD sensitive patient health information of military personnel without a client's/patient's signature for release when the record is needed in the performance of their duties, such as referring military personnel for evaluation (Hoyt, 2013; Johnson et al., 2010).

Suicidal Intent

Under Standard 4.05b, psychologists are permitted to disclose confidential information to protect clients/patients from self-harm. Client/patient suicidality is a stressful experience for practitioners and a frequent cause of malpractice suits (Bennett et al., 2006). Good ethical practice in response to indications of suicidal intent requires (a) competence to recognize, manage, and treat suicidality (Standard 2.01, Boundaries of Competence); (b) identification of community resources for client/patient emergencies outside the treatment setting; (c) development of consultative relationships with other professionals (e.g., prescribing psychologists or psychiatrists) to assist in case management (Standard 3.09, Cooperation With Other Professionals); and (d) understanding of legal principles and institutional policies regarding voluntary or involuntary commitment (Helms & Prinstein, 2014; Jobes, 2012).

Need to Know: Suicide Helpline Assessment and Disclosure Policies

The National Suicide Prevention Lifeline (NSPL) has developed suicide risk assessment standards as well as an imminent risk policy that can guide psychologists involved in direct interactions with callers, development of hotline guidelines, or supervision of hotline staff (http://www.suicidepreventionlifeline.org/crisiscenters/bestpractices.aspx). The suicide risk assessment focuses on four core principles: (1) suicidal desire, (2) capability, (3) suicidal intent, and (4) buffers. Following an assessment identifying a caller at imminent risk, the NSPL policy requires hotline staffers to use the following:

(Continued)

(Continued)

- *Active engagement,* making reasonable efforts to collaborate with callers to better secure their safety
- *Active rescue,* taking all action necessary to secure caller safety and initiate emergency response, without the caller's consent if the caller is unwilling or unable to take action on their own behalf
- *Collaboration* with other community services to better ensure the continuous care and safety of hotline callers

Implications of HIPAA for Law Enforcement, Public Safety, and Public Policy

Standard 4.05b is consistent with the HIPAA Privacy Rule that permits disclosure of PHI without authorization (a) when required by law; (b) for public health activities, such as for preventing or controlling disease, injury, or disability; (c) for individuals whom the covered entity reasonably believes to be victims of abuse, neglect, or domestic violence; (d) for health oversight activities, such as audits, criminal investigations, or licensure or disciplinary actions; (e) for judicial or administrative hearings; and (f) for activities deemed necessary by appropriate military command to ensure the proper execution of the military mission.

In some instances, HIPAA regulations may be more permissive of disclosure without client/patient consent than either state law or the Ethics Code. For example, HIPAA permits disclosure of information without consent for law enforcement purposes such as reporting wounds or other physical injuries, when issued a court-ordered subpoena, when the information sought is relevant and material to a legitimate law enforcement inquiry, or to protect the nation's public health (Department of Health and Human Services, 2013). HIPAA also permits medical and mental health practitioners to report incidences of disease/disorder for public health surveillance purposes. Psychologists can comply with HIPAA and continue to protect client/patient confidentiality by de-identifying data before it is disclosed (Emam & Moher, 2013).

Disclosure of Client/Patient Possession of Firearms

As detailed by Kangas and Calvert (2014), in recent years there has been an increasing push under federal law to reduce gun violence by limiting the purchase and possession of firearms on the basis of mental health. For example, proposed reforms by the Obama administration have included encouraging mental health practitioners to increase their reporting of clients/patients to local law enforcement for inclusion in the National Instant Criminal Background Check System (NICS, 2006; The Office of the President of the United States, 2013). Before considering whether client/patient information should be reported to a NICS or other firearm database, psychologists should be familiar with their state law on firearm reporting specifically and "duty-to-protect" laws generally. For example, in New York State, mental health professionals are required to report clients/patients for removal of a firearm if they are judged likely to harm themselves or others; however, the state allows for a reasonable professional judgment and provides legal immunity for decisions to report or not report made reasonably and in good faith (Kangas & Calvert, 2014).

In making firearm disclosure or background check decisions, psychologists should also be aware of the probabilistic nature of data on prediction of violence, the potential for stigmatization of individuals with mental illness, and ethnic/racial disparities in law enforcement that may be exacerbated by overestimations of mental illness or potential for violence (Institute of Medicine, 2006; Standards 2.04, Bases for Scientific and Professional Judgments; 3.04, Avoiding Harm; 9.01, Bases for Assessment).

Need to Know: Disclosure in Response to Nonsuicidal Self-Injury in Adolescents and Young Adults

Nonsuicidal self-injury (NSSI) has become a public health problem for mental health practitioners working with clinical and nonclinical samples of adolescents and young adults in school and college settings (Klonsky, 2011). NSSI is defined as deliberate harm to the body in order to reduce psychological stress without suicidal intent (Muehlenkamp & Gutierrez, 2004; Walsh, 2008). Irrespective of the client's/patient's degree of psychopathology, decisions regarding whether to disclose self-injurious behaviors to school officials, medical practitioners, or family members require the competencies necessary to (a) understand the relationship of NSSI to suicidality; (b) assess the specific behaviors within the context of the client's/patient's current mental health status, environmental (e.g., academic), cultural and interpersonal (e.g., family) stressors, and peer influences; and (c) have a developed plan for disclosure in place to ensure the client's/patient's safety and promote future treatment effectiveness (Walsh, 2008). Additional factors to be considered include the following (see Andover, Primack, Gibb, & Pepper, 2010; Cervantes, Goldbach, Varela, & Santisteban, 2014; Lieberman, Toste, & Heath, 2008; Nock, Joiner, Gordon, Lloyd-Richardson, & Prinstein, 2006; Walsh, 2008):

- For each case of self-injury (e.g., cutting on extremities), clearly distinguish NSSI from suicidal behavior (e.g., cutting of arms or legs vs. the carotid artery or disclosure of plan to use lethal methods). While NSSI is distinct from suicidal intent, the behaviors may co-occur, and a percentage of NSSI patients have a history of suicidality.
- Become familiar with the ways in which gender and culture influence age of onset, precipitating factors (e.g., menses, acculturative stress), degree of medical injury, and NSSI methods.

(Continued)

(Continued)

- When self-injury involves atypical areas of the body such as face, eyes, or genitals that have been associated with psychotic decompensation, be able to distinguish this self-harm from body piercing that may be peer rather than pathology related.
- Recognize when self-injury requires medical attention and become knowledgeable about local emergency medical services so that protective interventions can be immediately initiated.
- Even when self-injury is common, has a low risk of lethality, and does not require medical attention, psychologists working in schools should consider whether the self-injury can be best addressed through a referral to outpatient treatment; in most instances, parents should be informed.
- When disclosing self-injuring behavior to parents, while it is helpful to distinguish between self-harm and suicidality, it is also important to make them aware of the possibility of future suicidal behaviors.
- Psychologists working in schools should be aware of the possibility of contagion, identify members of the at-risk peer group, and assess each student individually.

4.06 Consultations

©iStockphoto.com/voinSveta

When consulting with colleagues, (1) psychologists do not disclose confidential information that reasonably could lead to the identification of a client/patient, research participant, or other person or organization with whom they have a confidential relationship unless they have obtained the prior consent of the person or organization or the disclosure cannot be avoided, and (2) they disclose information only to the extent necessary to achieve the purposes of the consultation. (See also Standard 4.01, Maintaining Confidentiality.)

Consultation with colleagues is an important means of ensuring and maintaining the competence of one's work and the ethical conduct of psychology. Standard 4.06 permits discussion of confidential information with colleagues without prior consent as long as the identity of the client/patient, research participant, organizational client, or other person with whom they have a confidential relationship can be adequately protected. In some instances, the obligation to provide the highest quality service or to address an ethical problem may require consultation that reveals a person's or organization's identity without prior consent. Standard 4.06 permits such actions only if the disclosure cannot be avoided and the psychologist only discloses information that is necessary to achieve the purposes of the consultation. The following is an example of how a psychologist might comply with this standard:

⊘ A psychologist was hired by a bank to conduct crisis counseling for employees who had witnessed a recent armed robbery. During the course of counseling, the psychologist came across information suggesting that one of the employees had helped plan the robbery. The psychologist consulted with a colleague and an attorney to help determine whether the psychologist was ethically or legally required to report this information to the company or law enforcement. Because the bank robbery had been highly publicized, the psychologist was unable to disguise the bank's identity. However, during each consultation, the psychologist took specific steps to avoid mentioning the gender, job title, or any other details about the employee in question that could lead to personal identification.

Digital Ethics: Consultation Over the Internet

The Internet is a continuously evolving medium in which psychologists may consult with colleagues via email, professional chat rooms, or listservs to (a) provide clients/patients with the best standard of care, (b) obtain referral or placement recommendations, (c) develop evaluation plans for organizations, (d) advise students on career-planning or academic problems, and (e) address unexpected research participant challenges. Psychologists seeking or offering advice over the Internet must abide by the same ethical standards currently used in in-person or other traditional forms of consultations. To do so, psychologists should consider the following before receiving or providing consultation over the Internet (Behnke, 2007):

- Both consultants and consultees utilizing email or listservs should explicitly acknowledge that they are engaged in the professional activity of consultation (Principle B: Fidelity and Responsibility).
- Psychologists giving advice over the Internet should only do so within the boundaries of their professional competence and state the nature and limitations of their expertise (Standard 2.01, Boundaries of Competence).
- Psychologists requesting advice over the Internet should consider the qualifications of those offering recommendations (Standard 2.04, Bases for Scientific and Professional Judgments).
- Email communications between professionals for client/patient treatment are part of the client's/patient's record and should be appropriately documented and maintained (Standard 6.01, Documentation of Professional and Scientific Work and Maintenance of Records). Whether listserv communications also fall under this category will depend on the educative versus consultative nature of the correspondence and whether the correspondence influenced treatment decisions.
- Psychologists utilizing email to obtain professional consultation from a specific identified professional must make reasonable efforts to ensure

(Continued)

(Continued)

that the consultant has sufficient email security protections, obtain appropriate consent or permission if the disclosure of identifying information is unavoidable, and disclose the minimal amount of information necessary for the consultation (Standards 3.11, Psychological Services Delivered To or Through Organizations; 4.02. Discussing the Limits of Confidentiality; 4.04, Minimizing Intrusions on Privacy; 4.06, Consultations).

- Since neither the confidentiality practices of members nor the Internet security of listservs can be verified, psychologists seeking advice through these sites do not disclose confidential information that could reasonably lead to identification of a person or organization (Standards 3.11, Psychological Services Delivered To or Through Organizations; 4.01, Maintaining Confidentiality).
- Since client/patient, organizational, or other information provided on listservs for consultation purposes is often incomplete or out of context, psychologists responding will not have an adequate basis for their assessment of the problem and should acknowledge these limitations when providing recommendations (Standard 9.01, Bases for Assessments).
- Comments on listservs are public statements, and psychologists are prohibited from making statements that are knowingly false, deceptive, or fraudulent (Standard 5.01, Avoidance of False or Deceptive Statements).

4.07 Use of Confidential Information for Didactic or Other Purposes

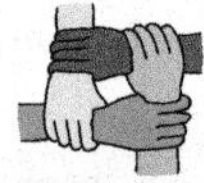

Psychologists do not disclose in their writings, lectures, or other public media, confidential, personally identifiable information concerning their clients/patients, students, research participants, organizational clients, or other recipients of their services that they obtained during the course of their work, unless (1) they take reasonable steps to disguise the person or organization, (2) the person or organization has consented in writing, or (3) there is legal authorization for doing so.

Professionals, students, and the public benefit when psychologists use case material and other examples from their scientific or professional work to illustrate knowledge, concepts, challenges, and techniques in psychology. Psychologists must guard against harms that can occur when such materials contain confidential, personally identifiable information disseminated without the permission of the client/patient, student, research participant, organizational client, or other service recipient. Material relevant to this standard must be both confidential (the information was shared with the psychologist under expectations that it would not be released to others) and personally identifiable (the identity of the specific person or organization described could be recognized by others).

Informed Consent to Publication or Presentation of Identifying Material

Psychologists are permitted to reveal confidential information if the person or organization has consented in writing or there is legal authorization for doing so, such as if the material is authorized for release at a public hearing. When making such requests, psychologists should consider whether the request reflects a conflict of interest that can impair their effectiveness, lead to client/patient exploitation, damage the reputation of an organizational client, contribute to stigmatization, or otherwise harm the individual or organization (Standard 3.06, Conflict of Interest). Further, asking a client's/patient's permission to use his or her personal experiences in a public forum can have significant effects on the therapeutic process. For example, Sieck (2012) recommended considering the following questions when determining whether informed consent to clinical writing is ethically appropriate: Does the client have sufficient ego strength to engage in a thorough clinical-writing informed consent process? Are you concerned that the clinical-writing consent process will reinforce dysfunctional client behaviors? Is there insufficient time to devote to the clinical-writing informed consent process and its potential aftermath? If a client/patient refuses to consent to the psychologist's request, it would be unethical to proceed with a disguised case (Principle B: Fidelity and Responsibility, and Principle C: Integrity).

Disguising Information

Consent to utilize organizational or client/patient need not be sought for presentation of material for didactic or other professional purposes if the psychologist takes reasonable steps to adequately disguise the identity of the person or organization. When disguising information, simply using a pseudonym is insufficient when other aspects of the case contain details that make the individual or organization easily identifiable. Psychologists may wish to consider HIPAA's policy on de-identifying private health information, which requires the exclusion of names, birthdates, and locations smaller than a state. Altered names and places should be distinct from the real ones (e.g., do not use the client's/patient's initials in creating a pseudonym). Psychologists should also consider changing the season or year of an event or modifying details of family composition and other social networks that are not essential to the didactic goal. Disguising information should not change characteristics critical to the phenomenon being portrayed (VandenBos, 2001). For example, gender or ethnicity should not be changed if they play an important role in the services or research analyses described. Psychologists should keep in mind that in many cases, the unique nature of each client's/patient's personal history and interpersonal relationships cannot be easily de-identified, and presenting a composite case or refraining from public presentations of the case may be the only ethical alternatives (Duffy, 2010).

The term *reasonable steps* in Standard 4.07 recognizes that sometimes, despite acceptable efforts to disguise information, an individual or organization might be recognized by others.

> ✓ A psychologist gave a public lecture on dream analysis that included a case example in which the occupation, family constellation, city of residence, and other patient characteristics were disguised. However, a friend of the patient in the audience was able to identify the patient because the patient had told the dream to her friend.

Privacy can also be violated when psychologists describe individuals living in small or distinct populations who can be readily identified by others in the community in which they live.

> ☒ A psychologist published ethnographic data on spiritual concerns, job stressors, and psychological distress facing gay and lesbian teachers working in religious schools. In the published report, the psychologist described the school where data were collected as a prestigious Catholic school affiliated with his university. The school was readily recognized by individuals who lived in the community, and many were able to correctly identify respondents from the specific narratives described in the report.

HOT TOPIC

Confidentiality and Involvement of Parents in Mental Health Services for Children and Adolescents

Involvement of parents is often a key factor in engaging children and adolescents in psychotherapy (Dailor & Jacob, 2011; Oetzel & Scherer, 2003; Weisz & Hawley, 2002). At the same time, establishing the boundaries of client/patient confidentiality is critical to establishing a trusting relationship among psychologist, child client/patient, and parents (Principle B: Fidelity and Responsibility; Standard 4.01, Maintaining Confidentiality). While federal and state laws grant minors limited access to mental health services without guardian consent, they often permit (and sometimes require) parents to be involved in their child's treatment plan, provide parental access to treatment records, send all insurance billing related to a legal minor's health care directly to parents (e.g., the ACA-mandated explanation of benefits sent to policy owners, who are usually parents), and permit disclosure of information to protect the child or others from harm (English & Kenney, 2003; Frerich et al., 2012; Sedlander et al., 2015; Weithorn, 2006).

In making confidentiality and disclosure decisions, psychologists should be aware that parents' perceptions of confidentiality may differ from those of their children (Byczkowski, Kollar, & Britto, 2010). Psychologists must also consider practical issues such as the parent's withdrawing the child from therapy due to lack of access to information or children's misuse of confidentiality as a weapon in their conflict with parents. Psychologists working with children and adolescents thus need to anticipate and consistently reevaluate how they will balance confidentiality considerations with parental involvement in the child's best interests.

Establishing Confidentiality Limits at the Outset of Therapy

The nature of information that will be shared with parents should begin with a consideration of the child's cognitive and emotional maturity, the child's understanding of mental health and mental health problems, the nature and severity of the presenting problem, treatment goals, and age-appropriate expectations regarding the role parents can play in facilitating treatment (Cohen & Cicchetti, 2006; Mendenhall, Frauenholtz, & Conrad-Hiebner, 2014; Morris & Mather, 2007). For example, younger children's cognitive limitations and dependence on significant adults suggest that maintenance of strict confidentiality procedures may hinder treatment by failing to reflect the actual contexts in which children grow and develop. By contrast, increasing protection of private thoughts and feelings may facilitate treatment by demonstrating respect for older children's developing autonomy, comprehension of the nature and purpose of therapy, and ability to take a self-reflective perspective on their own thoughts and feelings (Hennan, Dornbusch, Herron, & Herting, 1997).

The Consent Conference

Engaging parents and children in discussion about the nature and rationale for confidentiality and disclosure policies is the first step to creating a trusting relationship. This can be accomplished during the consent conference when psychologists

- explain their ethical and legal responsibilities, describe the benefits of confidentiality or information sharing relevant to the child's developmental status and treatment plan, and provide age-appropriate examples of the type of information that will and will not be confidential;
- obtain feedback from and address client's/patient's and parent's concerns; and
- tailor a confidentiality policy to the cultural and familial context in which information sharing is viewed by parent and child.

Parental Requests for Information

There will be times when parents request information the psychologist had not previously considered appropriate for disclosure. The first response should be to determine whether the parents' request relates to an issue that does not require confidentiality consideration. While parental demands should never supersede ethical, legal, and professional responsibilities to protect client/patient confidentiality, they should always be given the following respectful considerations (Fisher et al., 1999; Mitchell, Disque, & Robertson, 2002; Taylor & Adelman, 1989):

- Employ empathic listening skills and convey respect for parental concerns.
- Assume, unless there is information to the contrary, that parents' queries reflect a genuine concern about their child's welfare.
- Avoid turning parental requests for information into a power struggle among psychologist, parent, and client/patient.
- Guard against taking on the role of therapist or counselor to the parent (Standard 3.05, Multiple Relationships).

(Continued)

(Continued)

- Help the parent reframe confidentiality in terms of (a) the child's developing autonomy, (b) encouraging the child to share information with parents by choice rather than requirement, and (c) maintaining therapeutic trust.
- If appropriate, suggest that the parent ask the child about the desired information or, with the parent's knowledge, explore with the child the clinically indicated ways in which information might be shared.

Disclosing Confidential Information in Response to Client/Patient Risk Behavior

Psychologists working with children and adolescents often become aware of behaviors hidden from parents that place the child at some physical, psychological, or legal risk. Sexual activity, alcohol and drug use, gang involvement, truancy, and vandalism or theft are some of the "secret" activities that require consideration for the protection of others or whether confidentiality or disclosure is in the best therapeutic interests of the child (Standard 4.05, Disclosures).

For example, disclosures can lead to physical protections for a child who is beginning to show signs of an eating disorder or involvement in gang behavior through increased parental monitoring of behaviors in and outside the home. Alternatively, sharing such information with parents may damage the therapeutic alliance or place the child at greater risk if parental reactions can be predicted to be physically violent or emotionally abusive. For example, the consequences of disclosing to parents high-risk sexual activity of lesbian, gay, bisexual, transgendered, and questioning youth (LGBTQ) who have not discussed their sexual orientation with their parents are more complex and potentially more hazardous than would occur when disclosing information regarding a minor's heterosexual activities (D'Amico & Julien, 2012; Ginsberg et al., 2002; Lemoire & Chen, 2005).

Psychologists must also consider how entering into a secrecy pact with a minor client can adversely affect the therapeutic alliance and be wary when assuming that minor clients expect and desire confidentiality when they reveal during therapy that they are engaging in high-risk behaviors (Fisher, 2003a).

Steps to consider in deciding whether and how to disclose confidential information when clients/patients are engaging in high-risk behaviors include the following.

Step 1: Assess and Clinically Address Risk Behaviors

- Confirm that the child is actually engaging in the risk behavior and whether it is an isolated incident or a continuing pattern.
- Evaluate the danger of the behavior to the client/patient or others.
- Assess developmental, psychological, and situational factors that might impair the child's ability to terminate or reduce behaviors.
- Conduct intervention strategies to help the client/patient terminate or reduce risk levels of behavior.
- Monitor whether the client/patient has terminated or limited the behavior.

Step 2: Consider Options If the Client/Patient Is Unable or Unwilling to Terminate or Reduce Behaviors

- Know federal and state laws on reporting requirements regarding prior or planned self-harming, illegal, or violent client/patient behavior.

- Weigh legal, therapeutic, social, and health consequences of confidentiality and disclosure for the client/patient.
- Anticipate, to the extent possible, parents' ability to appropriately respond to disclosure.
- Consult with other professionals regarding alternatives to disclosure (Standard 3.09, Cooperation With Other Professionals).

Step 3: Prepare Client/Patient for Disclosure

- Frame the current need to disclose information in terms of the limits of confidentiality discussed during informed consent and the psychologist's responsibility to protect the welfare of the client/patient and others.
- Respond to the child's feelings and concerns while focusing discussion on the process of disclosure and not on ways to avoid it.
- Evaluate the client's/patient's willingness and ability to disclose information to parents.
- When appropriate, go over the steps that will be taken to share the information with parents and involve the client/patient as much as possible.

Step 4: Disclosing Information to Parents

- Involve the client/patient as much as clinically appropriate in the disclosure discussion.
- Focus on the positive actions parents can take to help their child and, whenever feasible, place the child's actions within the context of continued treatment progress.
- Discuss additional treatment options such as joint parent–child or more frequent goal-setting sessions.
- Identify appropriate referral sources for parents to help them address their child's behaviors following disclosure.
- Empathize with and respond to the parent's feelings and concerns and refer the parent to individual counseling if it appears necessary.
- Schedule one or more follow-up meetings with parents and clients/patients to monitor their reactions to the disclosure and the steps taken to reduce the risk behaviors and provide additional recommendations if necessary.
- If the risk increases or remains at dangerous levels, consider other therapeutic, community, and legal options.

Chapter Cases and Ethics Discussion Questions

A research psychologist has obtained a grant to examine factors influencing whether children are perpetrators or victims of school violence. A total of 300 junior high school students whose parents have given permission and who have assented to participate will fill out surveys that include questions such as "Have you been bullied by one or several students?" "Have students stolen or extorted money from you at school?" "Do you know students in your school who have access to a firearm?" "Have you started a physical fight with another student" "Have you taken lunch money from other students?" and "Do you have access to a firearm?" The psychologist also has permission to link the survey responses to student academic and disciplinary records; thus, data cannot be collected anonymously. Drawing on Ethics Code standards on confidentiality, discuss both the most appropriate confidentiality protections and potential disclosure responsibilities that need to be considered, how they should be implemented for this study, and how they should be described in guardian permission and child assent forms.

A state university counseling center seeks to develop an online counseling service for students in large rural areas of the state who are enrolled in the university's undergraduate distance learning program. Discuss the confidentiality policies that would need to be considered by the information technology staff developing the program and the confidentiality policies that would need to be implemented by counselors providing the web-based services.

A general practitioner at a primary care medical center (PCMC) asks his colleague, Dr. Mustanski, a geriatric psychologist, to see a patient, Ms. Nordel, whom he suspects may be a victim of elder abuse. The patient is 85 years old, has seriously impaired vision and limited mobility, and has been treated for the second time for burns on her arms, which Ms. Nordel claims are the result of cooking accidents. During the initial interview, Dr. Mustanski learns that Ms. Nordel lives in her daughter's home and that she often argues with her daughter, whom she describes as having a problem with alcohol and a "very bad temper." When asked if she would like to bring her daughter in for a session to help make the kitchen and home more suited to her physical needs, the patient becomes very anxious and begs the doctor not to contact her daughter or mention to anyone that her daughter has a drinking problem. As the session goes on, the patient vaguely indicates that her burns may have been the result of an argument with her daughter. Discuss how Dr. Mustanski should handle confidentiality and disclosure issues in this situation with attention to the interprofessional context in which she works.

CHAPTER 8

Standards on Advertising and Other Public Statements

5. Advertising and Other Public Statements

5.01 Avoidance of False or Deceptive Statements

(a) Public statements include but are not limited to paid or unpaid advertising, product endorsements, grant applications, licensing applications, other credentialing applications, brochures, printed matter, directory listings, personal résumés or curricula vitae, or comments for use in media such as print or electronic transmission, statements in legal proceedings, lectures and public oral presentations, and published materials. Psychologists do not knowingly make public statements that are false, deceptive, or fraudulent concerning their research, practice, or other work activities or those of persons or organizations with which they are affiliated.

Psychologists aspire to promote accuracy, honesty, and truthfulness in the science, teaching, and practice of psychology and do not engage in subterfuge or intentional misrepresentation of fact (Principle C: Integrity). Standard 5.01a of the APA Ethics Code (APA, 2010b) prohibits false, deceptive, or fraudulent public statements regarding work activities or the activities of persons or organizations with which psychologists are affiliated.

The terms *avoidance* and *knowingly* exclude as violations statements that psychologists would reasonably be expected to believe are true but that they may later learn are false.

- ✓ A psychologist in a group practice distributed brochures with a listing of the group members' credentials, only to discover that one member had submitted false credentials. She ceased distribution and ordered a corrected brochure.
- ✓ A research psychologist gave a public lecture, a series of media interviews, and congressional testimony during which he publicly concluded that current empirical evidence supported a particular policy initiative. Six months later, the release of results from a large federally funded study challenged those conclusions. Based on this new information, the psychologist decided to modify her recommendations in future reports.
- ✓ A clinical psychologist, whose professional website included links to online listings of national and local mental health informational services, vetted the accuracy of the information on each listed website before the initial listing and periodically thereafter.
- ✓ A forensic psychologist providing expert testimony on the risks of social media addiction clearly stated the limitations of scientific and clinical knowledge in this emerging field (see also Standard 2.04, Bases for Scientific and Professional Judgments).

Definition of Public Statements

This standard begins with a definition of public statements. This definition applies to the use of the term *public statement* or *statement* in all standards under Section 5, Advertising and Other Public Statements. The definition refers only to statements made in the public domain. It does not apply to statements made during private professional or personal conversations with clients/patients, organizational clients, attorneys, students, colleagues, or others with whom psychologists have a professional or personal relationship.

The following are the types of statements included in this definition along with examples of false or deceptive statements that would be in violation of this standard:

- ☒ *Paid or unpaid product endorsements.* A toy company paid a school psychologist for her endorsement stating the proven effectiveness of a tape-recorded language lesson for infants that would improve reading comprehension in elementary school. There was no empirical evidence supporting this claim.
- ☒ *Self-marketing.* A neuropsychologist conducted a series of laboratory studies in which participants were asked to undertake a minor theft in the lab and then deny stealing while their brain patterns were analyzed using functional magnetic resonance imaging (fMRI). She bought advertising space in a monthly professional magazine, offering her paid services to police investigators who wished to use a "scientifically proven method" to detect deception in criminal interrogations (see Farah, Hutchinson, Phelps, & Wagner, 2014; Presidential Commission for the Study of Bioethical Issues, 2014).

☒ *Licensing, grant applications, and other credentialing applications.* In the "Preliminary Studies" section of a federal grant application, an experimental psychologist listed as completed a pilot study that was still in the data collection phase.

☒ *Directory listings, personal résumés, or curricula vitae.* A psychologist with a PhD in social psychology and no specialized clinical or other practice-oriented postdoctoral training listed himself in the city directory under health care providers.

☒ *Business cards.* A clinical neuropsychologist set up a practice in which she prescribed psychotropic medications through her license as a nurse practitioner. Her business cards only included her degree and title as a neuropsychologist but listed both her psychology and nursing state licensure numbers.

☒ *Comments for use in print, electronic, or other media.* In a television interview, a psychology professor who had filed an academic freedom suit against his university claimed that the university refused to allow any faculty to teach courses that included discussion of human sexuality when, in fact, the university catalog listed several such courses.

☒ *Statements in legal proceedings, lectures, public oral presentations, and published materials.* An industrial–organizational psychologist was hired as an expert witness by an attorney for a large retailing firm accused of discriminatory hiring practices. She testified that data on the firm's hiring of women and ethnic minority applicants were not significantly different from national data on employment practices in similar companies, despite the fact that she had not examined any of the firm's actual employment data. (See the Hot Topic at the end of this chapter, "Avoiding False and Deceptive Statements in Scientific and Clinical Expert Testimony.")

☒ *Commenting on the work of other experts at trial.* A forensic psychologist testified that an expert hired by the opposing attorney did not correctly score the defendant's responses on the Lie scale of the MMPI-2-RF, even though the psychologist had not reviewed the expert's assessment report (see APA 2013e; Otto, DeMier, & Boccaccini, 2014).

(b) Psychologists do not make false, deceptive, or fraudulent statements concerning (1) their training, experience, or competence; (2) their academic degrees; (3) their credentials; (4) their institutional or association affiliations; (5) their services; (6) the scientific or clinical basis for, or results or degree of success of, their services; (7) their fees; or (8) their publications or research findings.

©iStockphoto .com/voinSveta

In contrast to Standard 5.01a, 5.01b does not include the term *knowingly* because it is assumed that psychologists would have sufficient information about the facts listed to avoid false, deceptive, or fraudulent statements.

The following are examples of violations of the eight types of statements listed under Standard 5.01b.

- ☒ *Training, experience, or competence.* On a professional liability insurance application, a psychologist stated that she had obtained substance abuse certification from the APA College of Professional Psychology when in fact she had only attended a workshop on substance abuse treatment at an APA meeting.
- ☒ *Degree.* A health psychologist applying to the American Board of Professional Psychology (ABPP) for diplomat status in behavioral psychology falsely claimed he had received his doctorate in clinical psychology.
- ☒ *Credentials.* On her business cards, a clinical psychologist with formal postdoctoral training in neuropsychology listed herself as a "licensed clinical neuropsychologist" when her state only issued licenses in psychology (see Meharg & Bush, 2010).
- ☒ *Institutional or association affiliations.* A psychologist in independent practice who rented office space from a university created a stationery letterhead that suggested he was affiliated with the institution.
- ☒ *Services.* A psychology group practice website listed family therapy as one of the services offered, even though the only psychologist offering this service had left the group more than a year ago.
- ☒ *Scientific or clinical basis for, or results or degree of success of, their services.* A behavioral psychologist running a weight loss program for obese adolescents stated in the program brochure that "99% of clients maintain their weight loss after they leave the program." The statement did not include the fact that for most of these clients, the maintenance of weight loss lasted for less than 3 weeks.
- ☒ *Brochures and printed matter.* A consulting psychologist distributed brochures to personnel departments of banks in major cities stating that he had developed a foolproof psychological technique for preemployment integrity screening to weed out applicants who were prone to dishonesty. The claim was based on undocumented consultations conducted by the psychologist over several years.
- ☒ *Fees.* A child clinical psychologist presented a talk on childhood disorders at a parents' association meeting. After the talk, she handed out printed information about her practice that stated that she offered all clients a sliding scale of fees beginning at $40 a session. The handout did not mention that the $40 rate was only for clients specifically referred by the HMO with which the psychologist had a contract.
- ☒ *Publications or research findings.* A school psychologist on the faculty of a large university received a grant from an educational services company. The purpose of the funded project was to compare student academic achievement in city-administered public schools with those run by the educational services company. Data from schools in the eight cities studied indicated significant differences in favor of the city-run schools in two cities, significant differences in favor of the company-run schools in two cities, and no significant differences in the other four school districts. The psychologist published only data from the two cities in which a positive effect of company-contracted schools was found and suggested in the conclusion of the article that these results could be generalized to other cities (see also Standard 3.06, Conflict of Interest).

Comparative statements regarding the desirability of one type of service over another are not prohibited *if* there is substantial evidence to support the claim (Shead & Dobson, 2004; Standard 2.04, Bases for Scientific and Professional Judgments).

Deceptive Web-Based Services

Potentially deceptive web-based advertisements and claims regarding Internet-based mental health services risk violating Standard 5.01b. Some have argued that direct-to-consumer advertising for health care services should be more restricted than for other services (e.g., car repair) because most potential clients/patients are not in a good position to evaluate their mental health, to assess the quality of care they receive, or to evaluate the legitimacy of claims made in the advertisement (Schenker, Arnold, & London, 2014). Substantial gaps in ethical compliance on websites advertising mental health services can include (a) failure to inform consumers that the psychologist's license to provide mental health services online might be restricted by state law; (b) unsupported statements disparaging face-to-face therapies in comparison to online services; (c) descriptions of psychoeducational web-based services that could lead consumers to believe that they would receive individualized counseling, assessment, or therapeutic services; and (d) failure to clarify the boundaries of the psychologist's competence to provide services across a broad spectrum of psychological disorders (Heinlen et al., 2003).

☒ A psychologist developed a web-based service for parents of children with behavioral problems at "www.parent-therapy-online.com." Parents could pay $25 to email a specific question about how to help their child that would be answered within 24 hours by one of eight psychologists identified on the website as "child experts who will provide therapeutic advice personalized to each request." In actuality, the "personal" email responses provided prewritten general statements about behavioral child management techniques. In small print at the bottom of the web page appeared the following statement: "The information provided on this website is for educational purposes and does not constitute treatment."

Website advertising can place psychologists in violation of other Ethics Code standards (Koocher & Keith-Spiegel, 2008; Nagy, 2011; Nicholson, 2011). Below are examples of such violations:

☒ A neuropsychologist posted quasi-psychological screening tools with questionable validity and items drawn from standardized tests to "help" potential clients evaluate whether they needed his services (Standards 9.02a and b, Use of Assessments; 9.11, Maintaining Test Security).

☒ A school psychologist's professional website included information sheets on different disorders and treatments related to learning disabilities without appropriate citation (Standard 8.11, Plagiarism). The violation was exacerbated when her website was listed by search engines as providing expert information for consumers on childhood learning disorders.

☒ A psychologist was hired by one of the fathers of an 8-year-old boy to conduct a custody assessment. Before she had an opportunity to complete her report, the boy's other father threatened to write a negative review on the psychologist's professional website. The psychologist assured the father who had made the threat that her report would be neutral in its recommendation (2.06, Conflict of Interest).

Psychologists may wonder when it is ethically acceptable to include personal information about themselves on a professional website. For example, should a psychologist offering art therapy services include information about public recognition she may have received as an artist? Knapp, VandeCreek, Handelsman, and Gottlieb (2013) recommended that self-disclosure in web-based advertisements should focus on the needs of the client and avoid exploitation. According to the authors, it is ethically appropriate to include a psychologist's secondary occupation or personal experience when it is directly relevant to his or her ability to provide professional services (as in the art therapy example above) and *inappropriate* if it constitutes soliciting "customers" for a side business (as in the example below).

☒ A psychologist developed a professional website to advertise his music therapy practice for children. The website also included a link to a site where the psychologist advertised his services as a piano teacher (3.05, Multiple Relationship).

(c) Psychologists claim degrees as credentials for their health services only if those degrees (1) were earned from a regionally accredited educational institution or (2) were the basis for psychology licensure by the state in which they practice.

Standard 5.01c applies only to psychologists who are claiming degrees or credentials as evidence of their competence to provide health services. Unlike Standard

5.01b, this standard is not directed at whether a psychologist actually obtained the degree but whether the degree can be claimed as a basis for offering therapy or diagnostic or other types of health services.

Psychologists may refer to only two types of degrees as evidence of education and training in the field of psychology that qualify them as a health service provider. The first type is a degree in psychology (e.g., PhD, EdD, or PsyD) earned from a regionally accredited educational institution (e.g., the Commission on Higher Education of the Middle States Association of Colleges and Schools). The second type of degree is from a program in a nonaccredited institution whose curriculum and training experiences have been approved by the state in which the psychologist practices as qualifying him or her for eligibility for licensure in psychology.

A psychologist who claims a degree as a credential for health services that does not meet the above criteria would be in violation of this standard:

☒ An individual licensed as a social worker in his state acquired a PhD in counseling psychology from a nonaccredited university. He was unable to obtain licensure in psychology because the state in which he practices did not recognize his doctoral training as a basis for licensure in psychology. His business cards and professional letterhead included a PhD after his name, the title "Counseling Psychologist," and his social work licensure ID number. The letterhead did not indicate that his license was in social work and not psychology.

☒ On her curriculum vitae, a psychologist claimed that she had received her PhD from an accredited university when her degree was from an unaccredited school to which she had transferred after attending the accredited university.

5.02 Statements by Others

(a) Psychologists who engage others to create or place public statements that promote their professional practice, products, or activities retain professional responsibility for such statements.

Psychologists retain professional responsibility for false, deceptive, or fraudulent public statements by others whom they have engaged to promote their work or products. Failure to prevent or to correct such misstatements is a violation of Standard 5.02.

⊘ A psychologist viewed the website of the company that was publishing a book she had just completed. She was surprised and pleased to see the company had started advertising the book as "forthcoming." She then

(Continued)

(Continued)

noticed that she was wrongly listed on the website as professor of psychology at a university where she had taught as an adjunct several years ago. She called her editor at the company to notify him of the error and to ask him to take steps to correct the website. She followed up with a letter to him reiterating this request and copied the chair of the psychology department at the university mentioned.

☒ A psychologist developed a program that enabled other psychologists to score a popular psychological test on their computers. The psychologist had not yet completed complementary software that would provide narrative interpretations of the scores. The marketing staff at the distribution company he contracted with to sell his product advised him that the scoring software would sell better if it was advertised as providing both scoring and interpretation. They argued that even though this was not currently true, because he was already working on the new program, eventually those who bought the original software would be able to use the complementary software for narrative interpretations. The psychologist agreed to the misleading advertisement.

(b) Psychologists do not compensate employees of press, radio, television, or other communication media in return for publicity in a news item. (See also Standard 1.01, Misuse of Psychologists' Work.)

Standard 5.02b underscores psychologists' obligations to avoid actions that might encourage others to make false or fraudulent statements about their work. This standard prohibits psychologists from paying or otherwise compensating members of the media in return for news coverage of their work. The use of the term *compensate* rather than *pay* means that psychologists who give nonmonetary gifts or pay for expensive dinners for journalists or others in the media in return for publicity in a news item may be considered in violation of this standard.

(c) A paid advertisement relating to psychologists' activities must be identified or clearly recognizable as such.

Standard 5.02c permits psychologists to run paid advertisements describing their services, publications, products, or other aspects of their work, as long as it is stated or otherwise clear to consumers that they are paid advertisements. The standard applies to advertisements on the Internet, in print, or in other media. "Canned columns" are an example of a paid advertisement that often is presented in a way that can be deceptive to consumers. Canned columns written and paid for by psychologists are typically presented in news or advice column format intended to mislead readers into believing that the psychologist has been invited or hired by the magazine or other media outlet to write the column because of his or her expertise. The "column" usually includes a description of the psychologist's services, the psychologist's picture, and contact information. Canned columns that do not include a clear statement that the column is a "paid advertisement" are in violation of this standard. In some instances, psychologists do not write the column themselves but purchase it from a writer who sells columns to psychologists nationwide. In such instances, the column must state that the psychologist is providing but has not written the column (see also Standard 5.01a, Avoidance of False or Deceptive Statements).

5.03 Descriptions of Workshops and Non-Degree-Granting Educational Programs

To the degree to which they exercise control, psychologists responsible for announcements, catalogs, brochures, or advertisements describing workshops, seminars, or other non-degree-granting educational programs ensure that they accurately describe the audience for which the program is intended, the educational objectives, the presenters, and the fees involved.

©iStockphoto.com/VoinSveta

Standard 5.03 applies to workshops, seminars, and non-degree-granting educational programs that are not part of the established degree-granting education and training programs covered under Standard 7.02, Descriptions of Education and Training Programs. Psychologists who offer non-degree-granting programs are responsible for ensuring the accuracy of announcements, catalogs, brochures, or advertisements appearing in print, the Internet, or other media. Announcements must clearly specify the intended audience, educational objectives, presenters, and fees. The phrase *to the degree to which they exercise control* is included in the standard in acknowledgment that despite a psychologist's best efforts to control and monitor the process, errors or misrepresentations by others may occur during the production and distribution of materials. Psychologists should take reasonable steps to correct these errors.

☒ Registration for a 1-day workshop on projective assessment techniques given by a well-known psychologist was advertised in several psychology journals and newsletters. Individuals paid in advance to reserve a seat in the course. Registration money could be partially refunded up to 2 days prior to the workshop. Several registrants who arrived to take the workshop were surprised to learn that although they were permitted to attend, they would not be given a certificate of completion because they were not licensed psychologists. The registrants complained that the advertisement had not mentioned that a license was required to receive the certificate and asked for their money back. Stating the cancellation policy, the psychologist refused to return the fees.

(Continued)

(Continued)

- ☒ A psychologist offered a seminar on child abuse identification and reporting that was advertised as fulfilling the state licensing board requirement for child abuse reporting training. Attendees who later submitted their seminar completion certificate to the state board were told that the curriculum did not satisfy the state's educational requirement.
- ☒ A group of psychologists offered an 8-week certificate program on drug addiction counseling. Advertisements for the seminar listed the fee as $1,000. During the last week of the program, attendees were told that those who wished to obtain an official certificate documenting their participation must pay an additional $100.

Industry-Sponsored Workshops

The pharmaceutical industry has become a primary sponsor of continuing medical education because sponsors have found that it is a tool for influencing audiences to use their products (Pachter et al., 2007). Psychologists conducting industry-sponsored continuing education programs must ensure that the teaching materials are not biased toward the marketing interests of the sponsor (see also Standard 3.06, Conflict of Interest).

5.04 Media Presentations

When psychologists provide public advice or comment via print, Internet, or other electronic transmission, they take precautions to ensure that statements (1) are based on their professional knowledge, training, or experience in accord with appropriate psychological literature and practice; (2) are otherwise consistent with this Ethics Code; and (3) do not indicate that a professional relationship has been established with the recipient. (See also Standard 2.04, Bases for Scientific and Professional Judgments.)

Standard 5.04 applies to psychologists who issue public advice or comment via print, Internet, television, radio, or other media. Such activities can include an occasional news media interview, a regular column in a print or Internet publication, a recurring spot on television or radio talk shows, or advice giving on one's own professional blog. The standard does not apply to comments made to individuals with whom psychologists have an established professional relationship, such as an Internet communication or videoconferencing with a client/patient, student, colleague, or organizational client.

Competence and Bases for Judgments

Research and professional psychologists working through the media make important contributions to the accuracy of reporting and societal awareness of scientific and professional knowledge relevant to issues of public concern. This can include explaining (a) current research findings on human cognition, behavior genetics, emotion, personality, and behavior; (b) contributions of forensic psychology to legal decisions broadly or with respect to cases capturing media attention; (c) factors underlying organizational, military, political, religious, and other group attitudes and behaviors; or (d) the nature of and effective approaches to widely experienced psychological challenges (e.g., parent–adolescent conflict, stressors associated with caring for disabled children or elderly parents); and (e) the nature and treatment of psychological problems or mental health disorders (e.g., learning disabilities, schizophrenia, bipolar disorder).

Standard 5.04 prohibits psychologists from giving public advice or comment on the radio, in print media, on television, on the Internet, or via other forms of communication on topics and issues that are outside the boundaries of their competence based on their education, training, supervised experience, or other accepted means of acquiring professional or scientific expertise (see Standard 2.01a, Boundaries of Competence). The standard also prohibits psychologists from giving public comment or advice that significantly deviates from or is otherwise inconsistent with established psychological literature and practice (see Standard 2.04, Bases for Scientific and Professional Judgments). This standard thus reflects the importance of establishing public trust in the discipline through adherence to professional standards of conduct (Principle B: Fidelity and Responsibility).

☒ A comparative psychologist who had spent her career specializing in language in primates appeared on several talk shows providing public advice on how parents could identify and correct child language disorders.

☒ In a television interview, a counseling psychologist advised college students to follow his 10-step cure for test anxiety. The steps included drinking green tea, taking vitamin supplements, studying in groups, and other recommendations not in accord with recent research or established counseling techniques for test anxiety.

Otherwise Consistent With the Ethics Code

Public comment or advice through the media or the Internet must be in compliance with all relevant standards of the Ethics Code.

☒ After speaking with a listener for 3 minutes on a live radio talk show, a psychologist stated over the air that the listener showed definite signs of obsessive–compulsive disorder. Before going to a commercial break, the psychologist asked the listener to stay on the line "for a referral to a health

(Continued)

(Continued)

care professional who can help you with this serious disorder" (violation of Standard 9.01a and b, Bases for Assessments).

☒ A developmental psychologist created a blog on which he provided critiques and recommendations for age-appropriate children's products. The blog did not include a statement informing readers that the psychologist was on the board of directors of a company whose toys he regularly reviewed favorably (violation of Standard 3.06, Conflict of Interest).

☒ In response to a reporter's request for background on a highly publicized murder, a psychologist described details of items on psychological tests typically administered in these cases (violation of Standard 9.11, Maintaining Test Security).

☒ In a televised interview, a forensic psychologist who had not been involved in a child abuse case nonetheless gave an opinion about the psychological characteristics of the parents involved (Standard 9.01b, Bases for Assessments).

Do Not Indicate a Professional Relationship Has Been Established

Psychologists providing public advice in response to questions over the radio, on television, on the Internet, or in published advice columns should clarify the educative versus therapeutic nature of their answers, avoid language that implies personal knowledge about the person asking the question, and take steps to avoid repeat communications with the person that may encourage the mistaken impression that a professional relationship has been established.

⊘ A group of psychologists established a psychology advice email service. The group's website included each participating psychologist's credentials and picture. The website described the service as one that provided advice for people suffering from "social anxiety." Individuals were charged by credit card for an answer to each email question they submitted. The site specifically stated that the service was not therapy. However, the psychologists' answers were written in a very individualized and personalized manner rather than in broad educative statements, and individuals were encouraged to identify the psychologist whom they would like to answer their question. There was no limit to the number of questions that could be submitted, and some clients submitted daily questions to the same psychologist over several weeks or even months. (See Shapiro & Schulman, 1996, for an excellent discussion of such a case and related issues.)

Need to Know: Working With the Media

Below are some general points to consider when working with the media (for these and other excellent recommendations, see Friedland & Kaslow, 2013; McGarrah, Alvord, Martin, & Haldeman, 2009):

- When asked to comment on psychological factors influencing the behavior of a person in the news, make general comments only and explicitly state that you have not personally evaluated this person.
- Be wary of potential client/patient exploitation and harm as well as unanticipated violations of confidentiality when reporters ask you to recommend clients who might be part of the interview or when clients grant a reporter the right to speak with you about their case.
- When illustrating a point with a case example on blogs, talk shows, or interviews, avoid risks to client/patient confidentiality and potential harm by presenting explicitly labeled hypothetical cases.
- Before an interview or broadcast, know its length and the nature of the medium (e.g., live or pretaped), carefully plan what you will say to limit the possibility of distortion, and be aware that whether or not they provide you with an opportunity to fact-check their report in advance, members of the media have final control over the information disseminated (Standard 1.01, Misuse of Psychologists' Work).

5.05 Testimonials

Psychologists do not solicit testimonials from current therapy clients/patients or other persons who because of their particular circumstances are vulnerable to undue influence.

Psychologists are prohibited from asking individuals who are vulnerable to undue influence to provide commercial statements testifying to the benefits of the psychologist's services. Standard 5.05 specifically prohibits solicitation of testimonials from clients/patients currently in therapy with the psychologist. Clients/patients are particularly vulnerable to exploitation by a psychologist who seeks their public testimonials because of power inequities between the therapist and client/patient, the psychological problems that brought clients/patients to therapy, the sharing of personal thoughts and feelings in therapy, and dependence on the psychologist for treatment.

☒ A psychologist used testimonials from current clients on a website advertising his Internet-based counseling services.

Parents of children with learning disabilities, who depend on a school psychologist's yearly evaluation to qualify for special education services for their children, might, because of their particular circumstances, be considered vulnerable to undue influence to offer testimonials for the psychologist. Family members in therapy with a psychologist for court-ordered treatment might also be considered vulnerable to threat or exploitation if approached to give a testimonial.

The standard does not prohibit unsolicited testimonials or the solicitation of testimonials from former clients/patients who are not vulnerable. However, psychologists should be cautious about approaching former therapy clients/patients who may be vulnerable to undue influence based on their mental status, the duration and intensity of the therapy, the circumstances of termination, the amount of time that has passed since termination, or comments that the psychologist might have made during therapy inviting the possibility of a posttermination testimonial.

5.06 In-Person Solicitation

Psychologists do not engage, directly or through agents, in uninvited in-person solicitation of business from actual or potential therapy clients/patients or other persons who, because of their particular circumstances, are vulnerable to undue influence. However, this prohibition does not preclude (1) attempting to implement appropriate collateral contacts for the purpose of benefiting an already engaged therapy client/patient or (2) providing disaster or community outreach services.

Standard 5.06 prohibits psychologists from soliciting business from individuals who, because of their particular circumstance, are vulnerable to undue influence. The standard addresses business solicitation behaviors often characterized as "ambulance chasing." Individuals who are current or potential therapy clients/patients are specifically identified as vulnerable in this standard. Others who may be vulnerable to undue influence are individuals whose loved one has just committed suicide or a person who is abusing drugs or alcohol. Psychologists are prohibited from approaching these individuals either directly or through another person to solicit business if the psychologist has not been invited by the individual or a legally authorized representative to do so.

Need to Know: HIPAA Marketing Prohibitions

Under the HIPAA Omnibus Rule (2013), clients/patients must sign an authorization to permit their protected health information (PHI) to be used for marketing purposes or sold to third parties. This means that psychologists or members of their treatment team cannot send communications to a list of clients/patients about new services that they or their organization may be offering unless the client/patient has signed a prior agreement form to receive marketing materials.

Although not explicitly prohibited in the language of Standard 5.06, psychologists should be wary of issuing public statements, brochures, and web-based or other descriptions of services that are intended to exploit populations vulnerable to undue influence by generating fear and anxiety (Shead & Dobson, 2004).

☒ A clinical child psychologist sought to generate clients by speaking to breast cancer survivor support groups about "serious psychological disorders of childhood" that "often" emerge in children as a reaction to maternal illness.

Permitted Behaviors

The standard does not prohibit psychologists from establishing a professional relationship with persons in therapy with another professional or who are otherwise vulnerable to undue influence if the person approaches the psychologist for services (see also Standard 10.04, Providing Therapy to Those Served by Others).

Collateral Treatment

The standard does not preclude psychologists from approaching a family member or significant other to invite them to participate in collateral treatment to benefit a client/patient with whom a psychologist has a professional relationship.

⊘ A psychologist treating an adult woman for bulimia, with the patient's permission, invited her husband to participate in family therapy sessions where the focus was on the woman's health. Whether the husband was currently in therapy with another professional was not an issue because the reason he had been approached was to participate in therapy where the wife was the identified patient (see also Standard 10.02a, Therapy Involving Couples or Families).

Disaster and Community Outreach

The standard also explicitly permits psychologists to approach individuals to provide disaster or community outreach services. Psychologists may offer emergency services to individuals who are distraught or otherwise vulnerable as a result of a natural or other type of disaster. However, compliance with this standard will depend on other related ethical issues, including (a) the extent to which individuals are capable of giving informed consent to treatment while dealing with immediate trauma and loss (Standards 3.04, Informed Consent; 10.01, Informed Consent to Therapy); (b) whether psychologists have the competencies to provide services under disaster conditions and, if not, whether they are the best suited professional available to aid individuals during the emergency (Standards 2.02, Providing Services in Emergencies; 3.04, Avoiding Harm); and (c) whether the intent to provide services is based on actual community needs or on the psychologist's own professional or personal needs (Standards 3.06, Conflict of Interest; 3.08, Exploitive Relationships; see also Schwartz, Hunt, Redwood-Campbell, & de Laat, 2014).

Within the fields of mental health and geriatric health services, it is generally recognized that older adults may not spontaneously self-refer for mental health services. A variety of outreach activities have been used in public and private services for older adults that involve approaching persons who are not thinking of seeking psychological interventions, educating them about the benefits of mental health intervention, and encouraging them to seek such help. Such outreach is permissible under Standard 5.06.

HOT TOPIC

Avoiding False and Deceptive Statements in Scientific and Clinical Expert Testimony

When research and professional psychologists provide oral testimony or prepare written reports for legal proceedings conducted in the public domain, they are engaging in public statements as defined under Standard 5.01a, Avoidance of False or Deceptive Statements, of the APA Ethics Code. As articulated in Principle C: Integrity, psychologists seek to promote accuracy, honesty, and truthfulness in the science and practice of psychology. When forensically relevant statements or reports misrepresent facts through commission or omission, psychologists can be in violation of Standard 5.01a. False, deceptive, or fraudulent statements most often emerge in legal contexts when psychologists lose their objectivity as a consequence of misunderstanding the psychologist's role, conflicts of interest, or susceptibility to attorney influences. This Hot Topic identifies and suggests preventive actions to avoid these ethical pitfalls.

Navigating Relationships With Attorneys

Engagement in the legal system thrusts psychologists into dynamic relationships with attorneys whose role obligations will sometimes converge but often conflict with the ethical responsibilities of psychologists.

Understanding Distinctive Roles

The rules embedded within constitutional, civil, and criminal law ensure that justice is served by protecting the rights of each party in a dispute to control what information will be placed into evidence and debate its legal merits. The primary responsibility of attorneys is therefore to advocate on behalf of their client and ensure that the party they represent has presented the best case possible before the court.

By contrast, in the legal context, the primary responsibility of psychologists serving as expert witnesses is to provide the triers of fact (e.g., the judge, jury, administrative hearing officer) with the information they need to make determinations about the legal question at hand. The primary responsibility of psychologists providing opinions to the court is therefore to advocate for the facts and not for the legal position advanced by either of the disputing parties (Brodsky & Gutheil, 2016; Melton, 1990). The objectivity necessary to advocate for the facts can be compromised when psychologists' legal opinions are influenced by pressure from the retaining attorney.

Establishing Boundaries

Prior to trial, the retaining attorney may pressure the psychologist to provide an opinion that goes beyond or is unsupported by the scientific or clinical data. Anticipating this possibility provides the psychologist with the opportunity to establish boundaries between the expert's objective role and the attorney's advocacy role (Bush et al., 2006; Woody, 2009).

Initial conversations with the retaining attorney should clarify the boundaries of competence within which the psychologist will testify (Standard 2.01f, Boundaries of Competence). Psychologists should also clarify their obligation to offer an honest opinion based on available facts (Principle C: Integrity). Shuman and Greenberg (2003) recommended that the initial conversation be followed up with a retaining letter from the attorney documenting the issues on which the psychologist will be asked to testify.

Avoiding Bias in the Collection and Interpretation of Forensic Data

In the legal context, biased expert testimony can cause significant harm to the legal system and its stakeholders if it misleads the triers of fact into unfounded legal determinations (Principle A: Beneficence and Nonmaleficence; Standard 3.04, Avoiding Harm).

Inferential and Confirmation Bias

Data collection and interpretation biases can result in misdiagnosis, selective data collection, inaccurate and misleading expert reports, and fraudulent or deceptive statements in court (Bull, 2015; Deidan & Bush, 2002).

The following behaviors should be avoided:

- Seeking out information to confirm the litigant's argument or the psychologist's own theoretical or personal view (Bush et al., 2006; Neoh & Mellor, 2009; Shuman & Greenberg, 2003; Stern, 2001)
- Overreliance on diagnoses with which the psychologist is most familiar
- Over- or underattribution of behaviors to situational versus stable personal characteristics
- Preconceptions or initial impressions resistant to challenge by conflicting data
- Reliance on reconstructive memory to fill in gaps in evidence or failure to adequately record facts that arise during evidence collection (Deidan & Bush, 2002; Otto & Martindale, 2007)

(Continued)

(Continued)

Strategies to reduce the potential for such biases include the following:

- Generating alternative hypotheses (Bush et al., 2006)
- Using comprehensive batteries for forensic assessments
- Carefully recording all facts uncovered during pretrial data collection
- Examining which facts support and challenge initial impressions or preconceptions (Deidan & Bush, 2002)
- Guarding against assumptions that the attorney has provided all relevant facts and asking for pleadings and legal memorandums and competing perspectives of stakeholders in the legal case at hand (Saks & Lanyon, 2007; Shuman & Greenberg, 2003)

Resisting Requests to Alter Reports

Irrespective of the format in which the expert's opinion will be provided, psychologists are ethically required to maintain accurate records of their work for the period of time in which the documentation may be needed to ensure the accuracy of their testimony (Standard 6.01, Documentation of Professional and Scientific Work and Maintenance of Records).

In their advocacy role, retaining attorneys may ask psychologists to modify their report in ways that bias information or opinion in favor of their client. Compliance with Standard 5.01a, Avoidance of False or Deceptive Statements, requires that psychologists deny such requests. If an attorney's suggestion represents a valid factual correction, the correction should either be presented in an amendment to the original document or be included in a clearly identified revision of the report with a written rationale for the modification (Bush et al., 2006).

Acknowledging the Limitations of Data or Conclusions

Psychologists should always anchor their scientific opinions to available empirical data and their clinical opinions to collected data. False or deceptive statements emerge in forensic testimony or reports when psychologists fail to adequately indicate limits to the certainty with which clinical data or research findings can diagnose or predict conclusions drawn about individuals (Standards 5.01a, Avoidance of False or Deceptive Statements; 9.06, Interpreting Assessment Results).

Misuse of Psychologists' Work

Attorneys will often attempt to control the nature of oral testimony to omit facts that would hurt their case or inaccurately represent the psychologist's statements to support their client's case. To take reasonable steps to correct the misrepresentation of their work, psychologists who provide expert testimony must be familiar with the judicial rules governing their ability to correct misstatements regarding their testimony (Standards 1.01, Misuse of Psychologists' Work; 2.01f, Boundaries of Competence).

For example, attorneys often attempt to limit an expert's comments to yes or no responses. Psychologists should be aware that some jurisdictions provide expert witnesses greater leeway than other witnesses in requesting the court's permission to qualify their statements when they believe attorney questioning has created confusion or misrepresentation of their opinion. Another strategy for limiting attorneys' ability to misrepresent their findings is for psychologists to avoid declarative oral or written statements that do not reflect the balancing of facts that contributed to their opinion.

Limiting Attorney Attempts to Impeach Testimony

Opposing attorneys will often attempt to impeach the credibility of an expert witness. In addition to the recommendations discussed above, forensic psychologists should be prepared to counter accusations of conflict of interest and inadequate qualifications and to competently address hypothetical and difficult questions during cross-examination (Eisner, 2010).

Maintaining Objectivity and Avoiding Bias: The Importance of Self-Evaluation

In their reports, responses to discovery requests, or testimony, forensic psychologists do not misrepresent, by omission or commission, their evidence or participate in partisan attempts to subvert the presentation of evidence contrary to their own opinion or the legal position of the retaining party. Prior to agreeing to serve as an expert witness, psychologists are encouraged to engage in the following forms of self-inquiry regarding possible biases that might lead to false or deceptive testimony (Bush et al., 2006; Fisher, 1995; Gutheil & Simon, 2004; Saks & Lanyon, 2007):

Conflicts of Interest

- Will financial interests influence my willingness to go beyond my expertise or the facts to give opinions supporting the attorney's case?
- Am I tempted to sell my testimony for monetary gain?
- Am I fearful an objective opinion will deter the attorney from hiring me in the future?
- Am I being sought because of a reputation for providing opinions consistently favoring the retaining party?

Personal and Professional Bias

- Have I already determined the nature of the testimony I will provide based on the attorney's initial description of the case?
- Am I unduly influenced by sympathy for the plaintiff or defendant?
- Does the case touch upon a personal issue?
- Will I use my testimony to advocate for a cause I believe in?
- Will moral, religious, political, or other biases intrude upon my ability to present all sides of the issue?

Multiple Relationships

- Do I have a special relationship with the attorney or the attorney's client that would impair my objectivity?
- Do I know the attorney or litigant socially?
- If these relationships are present, to what degree will I feel pressure to change my opinion if it is in conflict with the litigant's legal argument?

Chapter Cases and Ethics Discussion Questions

Dr. Challen, a psychologist working at a university counseling center, wanted to develop his own fee-based web resource page that would provide advice to college students on how to overcome test anxiety. The advice would be prepackaged "tips" based on students' responses to a survey he created for the website. To attract a large national representation of students to the website, he planned to use Facebook advertising targeted to individuals whose Facebook profiles indicated they were in college and who "liked" existing Facebook pages on test anxiety. Discuss the ethical issues that Dr. Challen would need to address in describing his web-based service and his advertising plan.

Dr. Abrantes, a developmental psychologist specializing in sexual and gender minority (SGM) youth health, agreed to appear on a panel for a Sunday morning cable news program. She was informed that the topic was on the design and evaluation of college faculty- and staff-training programs developed to increase SGM-sensitive and affirming campus environments, an area she felt competent discussing. Minutes before the program began, one of her former undergraduate students was also seated at the panel table. Dr. Abrantes was surprised when the moderator began the discussion by asking the student to describe her unfavorable experiences as an SGM student at Dr. Abrantes's university. The moderator then turned to Dr. Abrantes for comment. Discuss the nature of the ethical quandary that Dr. Abrantes finds herself in and how she might best respond to the moderator's question and additional questions she might be asked during the half-hour program.

Dr. Kovacs, a licensed forensic psychologist, agreed to conduct a forensic assessment of a defendant accused of being an accomplice in a robbery. The hiring attorney told Dr. Kovacs that the defendant had a medical history of bipolar disorder and that, during the robbery, she had been in a manic state due to her inability to afford psychotropic medication prescribed by a clinic doctor. The initial assessment did not yield any current indications of mania or depression. The defendant told Dr. Kovacs that she was currently taking lithium and that, during the week the robbery took place, she did not sleep much, spent money excessively, and believed she was about to become rich. Questions about her medical and social history did not provide a clear picture of behavioral or mood patterns typical of bipolar or other affective disorders. Despite multiple requests, the attorney had not provided Dr. Kovacs with the defendant's prior medical records but was pressuring the psychologist for his forensic report, noting that Dr. Kovacs had received an initial payment for administering the forensic interview and that the hearing at which Dr. Kovacs was expected to testify was scheduled for the next week. Discuss the ethical challenges Dr. Kovacs is facing and steps he should take to ethically resolve this dilemma.

CHAPTER 9

Standards on Record Keeping and Fees

6. Record Keeping and Fees

6.01 Documentation of Professional and Scientific Work and Maintenance of Records

> Psychologists create, and to the extent the records are under their control, maintain, disseminate, store, retain, and dispose of records and data relating to their professional and scientific work in order to (1) facilitate provision of services later by them or by other professionals, (2) allow for replication of research design and analyses, (3) meet institutional requirements, (4) ensure accuracy of billing and payments, and (5) ensure compliance with law. (See also Standard 4.01, Maintaining Confidentiality.)

In appropriately documenting and maintaining records, psychologists benefit those with whom they work (Principle A: Beneficence and Nonmaleficence) and fulfill their responsibilities to the society and the specific organizations and communities in which they work (Principle B: Fidelity and Responsibility). Responsible creation and maintenance of assessment and treatment records benefit clients/patients by ensuring continuity of services provided by the individual psychologist and other qualified professionals. Scientific records provide the necessary information required for replication of research and for peer, sponsor, and IRB evaluation of methodological modifications that may be required. Appropriate record keeping by industrial–organizational and consulting psychologists assists organizations in maintaining and improving work performance and in ensuring compliance with relevant regulations and law. Record keeping also benefits psychologists by providing documentation of appropriate planning, implementation, evaluation, and modifications of services or research. Good record keeping also includes documentation of ethical, scientific, or practice decision making that can assist in effectively responding to ethics complaints.

Under Standard 6.01 of the APA Ethics Code (APA, 2010b), psychologists must create, maintain, disseminate, store, retain, and dispose of records and data in a manner that enables the records to be used effectively and appropriately by the psychologist or others and to benefit those with whom the psychologist works. Steps necessary to comply with this standard will vary with the purpose of the psychological activity and applicable state and federal regulations and institutional policies. The standard applies to written reports, computer files, audio- and videotapes, and reports in any other media in which information can be created and stored. Creating or maintaining records that are disorganized, are illegible to others, or have not been appropriately updated would be a violation of this standard. The phrase *to the extent the records are under their control* recognizes that psychologists may have limited or no control over records once they are appropriately released to third parties or when they are the property of an organization, company, institution, or government agency for which a psychologist works or consults (see also Standards 1.01, Misuse of Psychologists' Work; 1.03, Conflicts Between Ethics and Organizational Demands; 3.06, Conflict of Interest).

Records for Mental Health Services

According to the Record Keeping Guidelines developed by the APA Committee on Professional Practice and Standards, Board of Professional Affairs (APA, 2007c), the level of detail and adequacy of content included in records is determined by the information necessary to

> (a) provide good care, (b) assist collaborating professionals in delivery of care, (c) ensure continuity of services in the case of a psychologist's injury, disability, or death or with a change of provider; (d) provide for relevant supervision or training; (e) provide documentation required for reimbursement or required administratively under contracts or laws; (f) effectively document any decision making, especially in high-risk situations; and (g) allow the psychologist to effectively answer a legal or regulatory complaint. (p. 995)

The drafters of the guidelines recognized that across the diverse settings in which psychologists work, the content of records will depend upon legal requirements (rules of evidence) and regulatory factors (ACA, FERPA, HIPAA); work settings (schools, independent practice, interprofessional health organizations, disaster relief); requirements of third parties (Medicare, Medicaid, managed care organizations), and the nature of the services provided (assessment, psychotherapy; for additional discussion, see Call, Pfefferbaum, Jenuwine, & Flynn, 2012;

Drogin, Connell, Foote, & Sturm, 2010). The guidelines thus specify the basic components that psychologists should always consider including in records of psychological services:

- Information for the client's ongoing file
- Identifying data and contact information
- Fees and billing arrangements
- Guardianship status, if appropriate
- Informed consent/assent and any waivers of confidentiality
- Mandated reporting, if relevant
- Diagnosis or basis for request for services
- Treatment plan (updated as appropriate)

The guidelines also recommend the type of information that should be recorded for each substantive contact with clients as follows:

- Date of service and session duration
- Type of service (e.g., consultation, assessment, treatment)
- Nature of professional intervention (e.g., modality)
- Nature of professional contact (e.g., in-person, email, phone)
- Current assessment (formal or informal) of client/patient status

Need to Know: Unexpected Contacts With Clients/Patients

It may be necessary to record additional information depending on the circumstances and client needs. For example, under HIPAA, protected health information (PHI) includes patient contact information, even if it does not include clinical information. Thus, it is wise for practicing psychologists to note in their records unexpected contacts with clients/patients outside of the office or by phone or Internet. As described in greater detail in the section of Chapter 6 on Standard 3.05, Multiple Relationships, such records are often helpful in understanding clients'/patients' misperceptions about the therapeutic relationship or responding to ethics complaints based on misperceptions. Emergency interventions, including contacts with other professionals, family members, partners, or others to ensure adequate services or protect client/patient welfare, should also be included.

Multiple Client Records

Psychologists providing couples, family, or group therapy must be alert to issues that may arise when keeping multiple client records. For example, following marital dissolution, it may be unclear who should have access to records created during couples or family therapy. Points for consideration for multiple client records highlighted by the Record Keeping Guidelines (APA, 2007c) include (a) whether the identified client is the couple/family unit or each individual, (b) legal requirements and implications for creating separate or a single joint record, and (c) agreement of all concerned on the record keeping policy during informed consent (see also Standards 3.10, Informed Consent; 4.01, Maintaining Confidentiality; 4.02, Discussing the Limits of Confidentiality; 10.01, Informed Consent to Therapy; 10.02, Therapy Involving Couples or Families; 10.03, Group Therapy). Relatedly, when other individuals are involved to provide collateral support for an identified patient, these individuals are not the "client/patient," and the psychologist does not maintain separate health records for them. Rather, information provided by the collateral that is relevant to the primary client's/patient's treatment is entered in the client's/patient's record (Knauss & Knauss, 2012; Younggren, 2009).

☒ A psychologist working as a behavioral health clinician in an integrated primary care setting was responsible for providing clinical care to patients diagnosed with terminal diseases. This often involved discussions with patients and families about end-of-life decision making. When one of her patients was too ill to make his appointment at the health center, the psychologist visited the patient in his home to see if he and his young children were OK. In his home she sat on the floor playing with his children while she chatted with the patient. She did not document the visit in the patient's records (adapted from Rosenberg & Speice, 2013; see also Standards 3.05, Multiple Relationships; 10.02, Therapy Involving Couples and Families).

Length of Record Retention

The number of years for retention of records varies with respect to state law, federal regulations, and institutional requirements. The APA Record Keeping Guidelines (APA, 2007c) recommend that, in the absence of specific legal requirements for record retention, complete records are maintained at minimum until 7 years after the last date of service delivery for an adult or until 3 years after a minor reaches the age of majority, whichever is later.

HIPAA. HIPAA regulations require that policies and procedures used to comply with the Privacy Rule are documented and retained for 6 years from the date of creation or the last date in which it was in effect, whichever is later (45 CFR 164.530[j][2]). If state law establishes longer periods of record retention than HIPAA, psychologists who are covered entities must follow the state law (see "A Word About HIPAA" in the preface to this book).

Digital Ethics: HIPAA Regulations on Email and Texting With Clients/Patients and Other Professionals

The HIPAA Security Rule requires covered entities (i.e., practitioners in independent practice and health organizations) and their business associates to implement appropriate physical, administrative, and technical safeguards to ensure the confidentiality, integrity, and availability of all electronic protected health information (ePHI) they create, receive, maintain, or transmit (45 CFR 164.306[a]). As of 2013, the regulations are more explicit regarding email and texting between health professionals and clients and among covered-entity staff. To adhere to these requirements, psychologists should store in patients' records all clinically relevant email and text messages, including the full text of a patient's query and a psychologist's reply.

In general, if a psychologist or the client/patient is sending clinically relevant communications via email or text messaging, in most cases those communications will be considered part of the treatment record, and copies of those communications must be maintained. In addition, psychologists in private practice and those working in health organizations who use mobile devices for text messaging must stay up-to-date on the constantly changing security procedures and applications needed to ensure their devices are HIPAA compliant (Greene, 2012; HealthIT.gov, 2014).

Psychotherapy Notes

Psychotherapy notes (also known as process or personal notes) are considered a work product privilege and are immune from subpoena (Mental Health and Developmental Disabilities Confidentiality Act of 1979, ¶ 802, § 2[4]). Accordingly, psychotherapy notes can be disposed of at any time, unless state law provides otherwise.

HIPAA. HIPAA creates a separate category for "psychotherapy notes," defined as

> notes recorded (in any medium) by a health care provider who is a mental health professional documenting or analyzing the contents of conversation during a private counseling session or a group, joint, or family counseling session and that are separated from the rest of the individual's medical record. (45 CFR 164.501)

Patients do not have a right of access to psychotherapy notes. Psychologists may choose to provide patient access or agree to release psychotherapy notes to others with the appropriate authorization of the patient. Psychotherapy notes are exempted from HIPAA general provisions for sharing PHI for the treatment, payment, or health care operations of another entity. For example, health plan providers and other HIPAA-covered entities may *not* condition the provision of treatment, payment, enrollment in the health plan, or eligibility for benefits on a patient's authorization for a psychologist release of psychotherapy notes. For psychotherapy notes to meet HIPAA exemption criteria, psychologists *must* store the notes in a file separated from the client's/patient's other health records.

Billing and Fees

The Record Keeping Guidelines (APA, 2007c) highlight a few areas relevant to Standard 6.01 that call for special attention from psychologists in independent or group practices. First, records should include documentation of a fee and billing agreement between the psychologist and client/patient, including when applicable agreements regarding third-party payment for services (e.g., the client's/patient's health insurance, billing of services to a family member). When appropriate, acknowledgment of client/patient receipt of the psychologist's standard written fee policy should be included in the record (see Standard 6.04, Fees and Financial Arrangements, for additional detail on fee and billing information). Second, as detailed later in this chapter under Standard 6.05, Barter With Clients/Patients, barter agreements and transactions can be ethically complex and thus require careful documentation to ensure that compensation is fair to both the client/patient and the psychologist. Third, psychologists need to document and justify any adjustment in the balance owed for services, especially when third parties are involved (see Standard 6.06, Accuracy in Reports to Payors and Funding Sources). Fourth, any fee collection efforts should also be recorded (see Standard 6.04e, Fees and Financial Arrangements). Psychologists providing health care–related services also need to be aware of the HHS Standards for Electronic Transactions requiring standard formatting of electronic patient records for health care claims and other purposes (see https://www.cms.gov/Regulations-and-Guidance/HIPAA-Administrative-Simplification/TransactionCodeSetsStands/TransactionsandCodeSetsRegulations.html). Increasing involvement of psychologists in interprofessional organizations will require an understanding of how these ethical responsibilities will be realized when record keeping and billing procedures transition from individual practitioner to team-based health charts and reimbursement procedures.

Digital Ethics: Electronic Health Records (EHR) in Interprofessional Organizations

Hospitals, accountable care organizations (ACOs), and primary care medical homes (PCMHs) are increasingly using electronic health records (EHRs) to increase efficiency, treatment quality, and cost control. This type of streamlining can improve interprofessional communication and decision making, but as detailed by Bernat (2013), the following ethical pitfalls must be avoided:

- Copying and pasting the notes of others (e.g., patient medical or family history) without proper attribution or otherwise relying on secondhand information that can perpetuate errors of fact or incompleteness

- Eliminating or obscuring externs or interns as the original source of data when notes require countersignatures from higher-level clinicians or supervisors
- Failing to edit EHR predesigned note templates that allow for reproduction of standard intake data but may not reflect unique aspects of a patient's given history
- Relying on time-saving binary yes/no "symptom grids" that automatically convert into predrafted sentences and paragraphs, producing a pseudo-history that does not recount the patient's actual symptoms
- Failing to read prepopulated laboratory and imaging data that are automatically downloaded into the EHR, resulting in a lack of interprofessional communication to the detriment of the client

Additional Implications of HIPAA

Access of Individuals to PHI. Clients/patients have the right to inspect and obtain a copy of their PHI records used by the psychologist to make diagnostic, treatment, and billing decisions (45 CFR 164.524). For exceptions to this rule, see discussions in Chapter 12 on Standards 9.04, Release of Test Data, and 9.11, Test Security. Where HIPAA regulations apply, psychologists' records must be created and stored in a manner that facilitates compliance with this and other aspects of the Privacy Rule and Security Rule. For group practices, records must also include the name of the privacy officer.

Right to Amend. Clients/patients have the right to request that their PHI be amended if they believe that the information provided is incorrect (45 CFR 164.526). If a psychologist believes that the amendment is justified, the amendment should be attached to the record; the psychologist should never alter the original record.

Right to an Accounting. Clients/patients have a "right to an accounting" of disclosures of PHI that entails a list of individuals or organizations to whom PHI has been disclosed in the past 6 years. Content of the accounting must include the date of the disclosure, the name of the entity or person who received the PHI and the address if known, a brief description of the PHI disclosed, and the purpose of its disclosure (45 CFR 164.528). Failure to keep an accurate record of such disclosures would be in violation of Standard 6.01.

Record Keeping in Organizational Settings

The Record Keeping Guidelines (APA, 2007c) recognize that organizational settings may present unique challenges for record keeping. First, organizations have their own record keeping requirements that differ from those outlined previously. These requirements are influenced by organization mission and local, state, and federal laws. These requirements may or may not be clearly defined within the organization itself. The guidelines recommend that psychologists consult with organizational representatives and colleagues and the relevant law to identify differences in record keeping requirements. In the event there is a conflict between the Ethics Code and organizational record keeping policies, psychologists should follow the recommendations under Standard 1.03, Conflict Between Ethics and Organizational Demands.

Second, record ownership is often defined by the psychologist's legal relationship with the organization. For example, in consultative relationships record ownership is typically maintained by the psychologist, whereas in staff relationships the organization has ownership, and the physical records may not be able to travel with the psychologist upon departure or be shared with others without organizational permission (see also Standard 6.02b, Maintenance, Dissemination, and Disposal of Confidential Records of Professional and Scientific Work). The guidelines recommend that psychologists clarify the issue of ownership at the beginning of their professional relationship with an organization.

Third, in organizational settings multiple staff members may have access and contribute to the record, and their disciplinary standards for record creation, maintenance, and confidentiality may differ from those of the discipline of psychology or may be undefined. The guidelines encourage psychologists to participate in the development and refinement of multidisciplinary organizational policies involving record keeping.

Need to Know: Evolving Codes for Biopsychosocial Services

The newly established accountable care organizations (ACOs) and primary care medical homes (PCMHs) represent a transition away from individual provider care to comprehensive, team-based coordinated systems of care. Psychologists who participate in ACOs and PCMHs will have to gain the necessary skills to appropriately create electronic health records that are part of a multidisciplinary team patient information-sharing system, rather than a separate mental health care chart (D'Amour & Oandasan, 2005). To comply with Standard 6.01, psychologists working within these interprofessional systems will need to become familiar with new and evolving health and behavior codes for biopsychosocial psychological services and, in some cases, abandon current *DSM* psychiatric classifications for other systems seeking global uniformity in diagnoses, such as the World Health Organization's International Classification of Diseases (ICD; http://www.who.int/classifications/icd/en/).

Educational Records

Psychologists working in schools need to be familiar with the Family Educational Rights and Privacy Act (FERPA; 20 U.S.C. § 1232–34 CFR Part 99; http://www.ed.gov/offices/OM/fpco/ferpa/index.html) to ensure compliance with Standard 6.01.

Under FERPA, parents and students older than age 18 or attending college have the right to (a) inspect and review the student's education records maintained by the school, (b) request that a school correct records that they believe to be inaccurate or misleading, (c) call for a formal hearing if the school does not amend the record, and (d) place a statement with the record setting forth the parent's or student's views if the school still does not decide to amend the report. Records are not considered part of a student's education record and therefore are not subject to parental or student inspection or amendment if they are (a) kept in the sole possession of the school psychologist, (b) used only as a personal memory aid, and (c) not accessible to or revealed to any other person except a temporary substitute for the maker of the record. In addition, under IDEA (Pub. L. No. 108–446, § 682[c]), schools must develop policies for the storage, retrieval, and disposal of educational records, and parents of students must be provided a statement of these policies.

Need to Know: Avoiding Conversion of Treatment Records to Educational Records

School-employed and community-based psychologists need to be aware of the need to maintain the separation of mental health records from educational records to avoid unintended violations of youth privacy. Once mental health records are included in a student's educational file, the HIPAA privacy protections no longer apply. Rather, FERPA law becomes applicable, and all information in the now "educational record" can be inspected by school officials, instructors, or campus security without consent and without accounting for the disclosure. To ensure that mental health treatment records are appropriately maintained, Doll, Strein, Jacob, and Prasse (2011) and Wise, King, Miller, and Pearce (2011) highlighted the following:

- FERPA does not apply to students' psychological treatment records unless they are converted into educational records through inclusion in the educational record or verbal or written disclosure to other school personnel. To protect student privacy rights, school psychologists and college counseling center treatment personnel should (a) clearly differentiate psychological from educational records through labeling and maintaining separate files and (b) not discuss student treatment with other school or university personnel and ensure that school staff do not have access to psychological records.
- When parents request that an outside assessment or treatment record be sent to their child's school, community-based psychologists should explain the implications of FERPA for confidentiality limitations and proactively review written documents with parents prior to sending the documents to the school. When these records are sent only to the school-employed psychologist, after review and when appropriate, the psychologist should consider returning the materials rather than letting them become part of the educational record.

(Continued)

(Continued)

- College counseling center staff need to be aware of their institution's billing arrangements for mental health counseling, and during informed consent, students should be made aware when billing records are considered part of the educational record and other limits on confidentiality imposed by FERPA.

Forensic Records

Psychologists conducting forensically relevant activities need to be familiar with laws governing the creation, maintenance, and disposal of records to ensure their records allow for reasonable judicial scrutiny and adequate discovery by all parties. In the legal arena, letters, consultations, notes, test data, recordings, testing protocols, and research protocols are governed by the rules of evidence in the court's jurisdiction (APA, 2013e; see also Standard 2.01f, Boundaries of Competence). For example, with the exception of relevant client/patient privilege, the entirety of the psychologist's records created or used in a case is subject to discovery. In addition, in deposition and court testimony, psychologists are often asked when certain facts became known and, if so, by whom and in what context. Sufficiently detailed records are essential when there is an extended period between relevant interviews or data collection and hearing of a case (Martindale, 2004). Forensic practitioners should also consider maintaining records until notified that all appeals in the matter have been exhausted or transferring unique components of the record to the retaining party prior to disposal (APA, 2013e).

Documentation of Scientific Work and Maintenance of Records

Psychologists conducting research must create and maintain records in a manner that allows for replication of the research design by the psychologist or others. This includes an adequate description of recruitment procedures, documentation of informed consent, relevant demographic characteristics of participants, data collection procedures, materials or equipment, and data analysis strategies. Raw data should be stored in a form accessible to analysis or reanalysis by the psychologist or other competent professionals who seek to verify substantive claims (see Standard 8.14, Sharing Research Data for Verification).

The number of years of retention of raw data for investigators will vary with state law, federal regulations, and institutional policies. Federal regulations (Office of Management and Budget Circular A-110) and PHS Grants Policy (NIH Grants Policy Statement, revised October 2011) require that data generated through federal support be maintained by institutions for at least 3 years following the completion of the project and the filing of the final progress and financial reports. The number of years may be longer if a patent is involved. Specific record keeping requirements for IRBs include maintenance of copies of the scientific proposal, the informed consent document, summaries of the project, financial reports, and reports of injuries or other serious adverse events. Authors of articles published in APA journals must have their raw data available for at least 5 years after the date of publication (APA, 2010e).

Under Standard 6.01, principal investigators on federally funded grants must also create and maintain accurate records of costs associated with the research, including participant compensation, research assistant salaries, investigators' percent effort working on the grant, equipment, travel, and other supplies necessary to conduct the research. For federally funded projects, IRBs are subject to federal grants compliance and oversight. For each grant, the IRB must account for cost allocations/cost transfers, time and effort reporting, allowable grant charges, and unobligated balances (see http://grants.nih.gov/grants/compliance/compliance.htm).

6.02 Maintenance, Dissemination, and Disposal of Confidential Records of Professional and Scientific Work

(a) Psychologists maintain confidentiality in creating, storing, accessing, transferring, and disposing of records under their control, whether these are written, automated, or in any other medium. (See also Standards 4.01, Maintaining Confidentiality, and 6.01, Documentation of Professional and Scientific Work and Maintenance of Records.)

©iStockphoto.com/VoinSveta

Standard 6.02 requires that psychologists protect the confidentiality of professional or scientific information in all phases of record creation, maintenance, dissemination, and disposal. The standard refers to confidential records or data in the form of written and printed materials, faxes, automated scoring reports, audio and video recordings, Internet websites, or emails or stored on company computer networks or flash drives. Steps that can be taken to protect confidentiality include (a) keeping records in a secure place, (b) limiting access to staff or team members who must use the record to competently perform their duties, (c) de-identifying records using code numbers or other methods, and (d) disposing of tapes and other identifiable records when they are no longer needed and their disposal is consistent with law.

Psychologists should be careful not to assume that their staff or employees of an institution or company with which they work are familiar with confidentiality requirements or appropriate confidentiality procedures. To the extent it is under their control, they must take steps to ensure that confidential records are kept secure from staff who do not have approved access. Consider the following example of a violation of Standard 6.02a.

☒ A consulting psychologist was contracted to evaluate whether on-site day care centers set up at the company's offices in 10 states were fostering a positive organizational climate. The psychologist conducted taped interviews with

(Continued)

(Continued)

employees to find out whether the day care centers had minimized their need to take days off from work for child care and their satisfaction with the plan. Each month, she traveled to a company's office in a different city to conduct the interviews. As she left, she usually asked one of the office secretaries to box up the tapes and ship them to the company's main headquarters.

Implications of HIPAA

HIPAA compliance is required whenever PHI is transmitted in electronic form for health care claims, health plan premium payments, referral certification and authorization, injury reports, health care payment and remittance advice, and transfer of records to other professionals. HIPAA regulations require that client/patient authorization to transfer records of PHI to third parties should be different from and visually and organizationally separate from other permission forms, include a statement that the client/patient may revoke authorization in writing, and be signed and dated (45 CFR 164.508).

When transmitting PHI to other covered entities or others, psychologists must ensure its security in transit and protect it from unauthorized access, alteration, deletion, and transmission (HIPAA Security Standards 45 CFR 160). Covered entities are also expected to keep office doors locked when no one is inside, store patient records in such a way that guests are unlikely to see PHI, and ensure for group practices that terminated employees cease to have access to files.

Digital Ethics: Deleting Electronic Protected Health Information (PHI)

New and unanticipated challenges to record keeping and security may arise as the wider health care community transitions from practitioner control of paper files to electronic health records (EHR) systems. For example, merely deleting or moving an electronic record containing PHI to the Trash folder does not count as secure deletion because the information can still be recovered through a variety of means. Ideally, data should be securely destroyed by clearing or purging the device, "scrubbing" the files using software designed for that purpose, and contacting provider services to ensure copies of the files have also been deleted (American Telemedicine Association, 2014; Burnette & Padmanabhan, 2014; see also http://www.hhs.gov/ocr/privacy/hipaa/enforcement/examples/disposalfaqs.pdf).

In addition, the HIPAA rule requires psychologists and other covered entities to give notice to clients/patients and HHS if they discover that "unsecured" (e.g., not properly encrypted according to HHS standards) PHI has been "breached" (e.g., stolen or improperly accessed). When applicable, psychologists should identify limitations on efforts to protect confidentiality of databases and systems of records and inform clients/patients, organizational clients, research participants, or others with whom they work about such limitations (see also Standard 4.02c, Discussing the Limits of Confidentiality).

☒ Complying with HIPAA breach notification provisions, a psychologist notified HHS that his laptop with hundreds of unencrypted patient files on it had been stolen. The psychologist's failure to attempt to comply with data safety standards under the Security Rule triggered aggressive reinforcement, and his failure to inform his clients about potential limitations in confidentiality led to a complaint to his state licensing board (adapted from http://store.apapractice.org/files/HIPAA_Final_Rule_July_2013.pdf).

(b) If confidential information concerning recipients of psychological services is entered into databases or systems of records available to persons whose access has not been consented to by the recipient, psychologists use coding or other techniques to avoid the inclusion of personal identifiers.

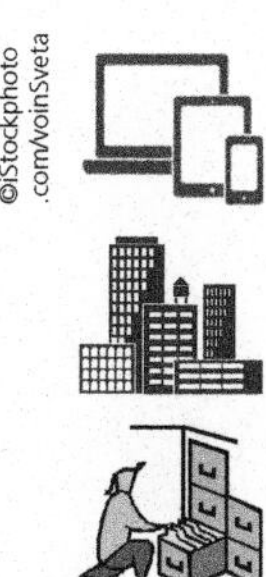

Standard 6.02b draws attention to the need to take specific steps to protect confidential records when these records are stored in record systems or databases available to persons whose access has not been consented to by the recipient. To comply with this standard, practitioner and research psychologists storing data on institutional networks can use protected passwords, de-identify information, and discuss with institutional staff responsible for network maintenance and monitoring appropriate procedures for confidentiality protections. Psychologists working in group practices should be aware of and comply with HIPAA security rules governing office and other infrastructure PHI protections, including access to offices, files, and secure transmission procedures (see the section "Implications of HIPAA" under Standard 6.02a above).

Digital Ethics: Record Keeping in the Cloud

Health care providers are increasingly storing PHI on remote servers known generally as "cloud services." Some cloud storage providers offer mirroring services that ensure both that records will remain archived if inadvertently lost on a local device *and* that records can also be immediately deleted from the cloud when a user intentionally deletes records locally. However, other cloud-based service providers may maintain user accounts even after the user has requested they be deactivated. Devereaux and Gottlieb (2012) have offered the following recommendations for ethically utilizing cloud services for maintenance and disposal of confidential information:

(Continued)

(Continued)

- Contact the provider to determine the robustness of firewalls and other security features, how breaches if they occurred were handled in the past, how records are deleted upon termination, and what other privacy protection practices are in place (such as whether data are immediately encrypted when uploaded from a local computer).
- Consider using a two-tiered identification system to de-identify records in which a key file listing identification numbers for clients/patients, organizational clients, or research participants is stored separately from records detailing confidential information with only the numbered identifier.
- Develop informed consent documents that include information on the use of and extent and limits of confidentiality protections of cloud storage.
- Consult with professional liability insurance or institutional legal counsel to understand coverage for possible liability in the event of an electronic breach.

Psychologists Working With or in Organizations

For psychologists working in or consulting to organizations, record keeping procedures may be governed by the legal relationship established between the psychologist and the organization. In some instances, the physical records belong to the organization and cannot be secured solely by the psychologist or leave the organization's premises. In other instances (e.g., individual consulting services), the records may belong to the psychologist. In either situation, to the extent feasible, the psychologists are responsible for the appropriate documentation and maintenance of the records and must clarify to organizations their obligations under the Ethics Code if a conflict arises (see Standard 1.03, Conflicts Between Ethics and Organizational Demands).

Digital Ethics: HIPAA and Internet-Based Document Sharing

In 2015, the Office of Civil Rights found workforce members at St. Elizabeth's Medical Center (SEMC) in violation of HIPAA. The complaint arose because workforce members were using an Internet-based document-sharing application to store documents containing electronic protected health information (ePHI) of at least 498 individuals without having analyzed the risks associated with such a practice. Additionally, OCR's investigation determined that SEMC failed to identify and respond to the known security incident in a timely manner, mitigate the harmful effects of the security incident, and document the security incident and its outcome (http://www.hhs.gov/ocr/privacy/hipaa/enforcement/examples/SEMC/ra.pdf).

(c) Psychologists make plans in advance to facilitate the appropriate transfer and to protect the confidentiality of records and data in the event of psychologists' withdrawal from positions or practice. (See also Standards 3.12, Interruption of Psychological Services, and 10.09, Interruption of Therapy.)

The obligation to maintain the confidentiality of professional or scientific records includes advance planning for the secure transfer of such records in case of planned or unplanned withdrawals from a position or practice because of job termination, promotion, a new position, parental or family leave, retirement, illness, or death. Information may be transferred in person, by mail or by fax, through the Internet, or through private company networks. Psychologists planning in advance for the transfer of PHI need to be aware of the HHS Standards for Electronic Transactions requiring standard formatting of electronic patient records for health care claims and other purposes.

Failure to take appropriate steps to protect the confidentiality of a records or data transfer would be a violation of Standard 6.02c. The following are three examples of such violations:

- ☒ A research psychologist who had conducted a 20-year large-scale longitudinal study retired from her faculty position. She agreed to allow the university to keep her data set for archival research by graduate students and other faculty. Among the records that she donated to the university was the coding file linking subject numbers to the names and contact information of participants.
- ☒ After a 2-year postdoctoral fellowship in neuropsychology at a university hospital, a psychologist prepared to leave for a new position in a different state. The day before he left, he met the new postdoctoral fellow assigned to his office space. The psychologist apologized to the new fellow about leaving his patient records in the unlocked office file cabinets. He told her that the records were important to ensure continuity of care for patients that he had assessed but that the hospital administrators had not gotten back to him about where the records should be moved. He asked the new fellow to keep them in her office or to have one of the maintenance crew move the files to a temporary place in the basement.
- ☒ A psychologist in independent practice was told by the HMO with which he had a contract that it would not extend benefits for one of the psychologist's clients unless the psychologist provided the HMO with his psychotherapy notes. Knowing that his client needed and wanted to continue therapy, the psychologist reluctantly complied without getting written authorization from the client to release the notes. A week later, he attended a professional workshop on HIPAA regulations and learned that not only is a signed client/patient authorization required to release psychotherapy notes but also managed care companies are prohibited from conditioning treatment benefits on access to psychotherapy notes.

Psychologists planning to transfer forensically relevant records should be familiar with laws in their state governing the extent to which licensed psychologists' privacy protections extend to their staff. Correctional psychologists need to be familiar with their organization's policies regarding the transport of mental health records for prisoners undergoing routine and emergency facility transfers (International Association for Correctional and Forensic Psychology, 2010).

6.03 Withholding Records for Nonpayment

Psychologists may not withhold records under their control that are requested and needed for a client's/patient's emergency treatment solely because payment has not been received.

Psychologists, like other professionals, have the right to be paid for their services. However, the ideal of nonmaleficence, to do no harm, articulated in Principle A: Beneficence and Nonmaleficence, is a core value of the discipline that obligates psychologists to provide informational assistance, if not doing so would jeopardize the welfare of a current or former client/patient. Standard 6.03 prohibits psychologists from withholding records needed for a client's/patient's emergency treatment solely because payment for services has not been received. The term *solely* allows the psychologist to withhold such records if disclosure is prohibited by law or, in the psychologist's judgment, release of records would cause substantial harm to the client/patient or others.

The standard does not apply to nontreatment situations, such as when parents who have not paid for a completed psychological assessment of their child request the records for an application for special educational services. Similarly, the standard does not apply to treatments that are not an emergency, such as when a therapy client/patient who has not paid for services asks a psychologist to send treatment records to a new therapist.

Emergency Treatment

The standard refers only to the provision of records for treatment and only when emergency treatment is needed. For example, a client's/patient's therapy or assessment records may be needed immediately to help other health professionals provide appropriate emergency treatment for a client/patient in an acute state of mental disorder, such as a schizophrenic episode or a depression accompanied by suicidal ideation. Records may also be required to help health professionals quickly determine whether an incapacitating cognitive or language disorder is the result of an injury or a medical problem or is a symptom of a previous mental disorder. Under the Ethics Code, psychologists are not required to obtain the client's/patient's consent to release information if it is requested for emergency treatment (see Standard 4.05b, Disclosures). Similarly, the HIPAA Privacy Rule permits disclosure of PHI without patient authorization to avert a serious threat to health or safety (45 CFR 164.512[j]).

Control and Requests

For the standard to apply, two other criteria must be met. The records must be under the psychologist's control. For example, Standard 6.03 would not apply if the health care system that a psychologist works for is legally responsible for the records and the institution refuses to release the records because of nonpayment. The records must also be requested, meaning that psychologists do not have to provide such records if they simply learn that a client/patient is receiving emergency treatment.

Regulatory and Legal Caveats

The HIPAA Privacy Rule establishing the rights of clients/patients to receive their PHI records does not distinguish between emergency and nonemergency requests, nor does it consider failure to pay for services, other than copying fees, as a legitimate reason to refuse a patient request to release records. Thus, although ethically permissible under Standard 6.03, withholding records for nonpayment under nonemergency conditions may not be legally permissible. Psychologists should also carefully review their contracts with HMOs to establish whether providers retain the right to withhold client/patient treatment records if the HMO has delayed or refused to reimburse for services.

6.04 Fees and Financial Arrangements

(a) As early as is feasible in a professional or scientific relationship, psychologists and recipients of psychological services reach an agreement specifying compensation and billing arrangements.

An individual's or organization's decision to enter into a professional or scientific relationship with a psychologist will depend in part on the costs and billing arrangements for the services. Failure to specify and agree on compensation and billing arrangements can lead to mistrust or financial exploitation (Principle B: Fidelity and Responsibility). According to Standard 6.04a, psychologists providing counseling, therapy, assessment, consultation, forensic, scientific, or other services must reach an agreement about compensation and billing with the service recipient as early as is feasible in the professional or scientific relationship.

Specifying Compensation

In specifying compensation, psychologists must include a description of all reasonably anticipated costs so that organizations, attorneys, or clients can make an informed hiring decision. For organizational or research services, this might include charges for telephone or other electronically mediated conversations; client, employee, or participant interviews; library or computer research; statistical analysis; travel;

postage; or duplication. Psychologists arranging compensation for assessment services should provide information about fees for test administration, scoring, interpretation, and report writing. Forensic evaluators may bill for time spent reviewing case materials for deposition or court testimony, briefing the retaining attorney on findings (Barnett & Walfish, 2011). Financial agreements for therapy should include, where appropriate, discussion of (a) payment schedules, fees for therapy sessions, telephone or other electronically mediated sessions, sessions with family members or significant others, charges for consultation with other professionals and appointment cancellations, acknowledgment of third-party payor preauthorization requirements, and copayment agreements and (b) whether costs may be covered by health insurance, as well as time or cost limitations regarding third-party payors.

☒ A research psychologist agreed to provide expert testimony on developmental differences in the effect of divorce and step-parenting on child and adolescent development. The psychologist reached agreement with the attorney stipulating a flat fee for reviewing the case material and writing a background paper relevant to her testimony. After receiving compensation for this work, the psychologist sent the attorney a bill for duplication, computer supplies, and telephone and book purchase costs with a note saying that she would not be available to testify unless these costs were reimbursed immediately.

Digital Ethics: Fees for Telehealth Services

Telehealth services are increasingly being regarded as a means to provide wider access to services and to decrease health care costs in the 21st century. When determining the fee structure for telehealth or electronically mediated correspondence as an adjunct to face-to-face sessions (e.g., mobile phone therapeutic applications as behavioral reminders), psychologists should calculate fees based on fair pricing for these services (Colbow, 2013; Dombo, Kays, & Weller, 2014; Standard 3.08, Exploitative Relationships). One strategy for assessing fair pricing is to refer to Medicare fee schedules, which are increasingly including reimbursement for services under new telehealth codes.

Billing Arrangements

Standard 6.04a requires psychologists to reach an agreement about billing arrangements as early as is feasible in the professional relationship. Psychologists must notify and reach an agreement regarding when bills will be rendered and payments expected, for example, weekly or monthly. Billing arrangements may also include agreement on a series of scheduled prepayments or compensation for different phases of the psychologist's services. For organizational consulting and forensic evaluation, psychologists are encouraged to develop a written financial agreement clarifying all payment agreements before services are rendered (Barnett & Walfish, 2011). For forensic practitioners, this will include clarifying the nature of the relationship and the psychologist's role (e.g., trial consultant, forensic examiner, treatment provider, expert witness; APA, 2013e).

- ⊘ An organizational psychologist hired by a hospital to conduct a quality improvement study set up a payment schedule tied to completion of data collection, completion of the first draft of the report, and completion of the final draft.
- ⊘ A forensic psychologist included in the initial contract with the retaining attorney her fees for costs associated with contacting and interviewing collateral sources, the storage and reproduction of records, and explanation of results to the retaining party and others the attorney might explicitly designate (APA, 2013e).

To avoid billing disputes that may later arise between couples or family members, psychologists conducting couples therapy or child custody assessments may wish to consider reaching an agreement in advance regarding which member of the couple or which parent will assume responsibility for payments.

Timing

The use of the phrase *as early as is feasible* permits psychologists to delay finalizing a financial arrangement to obtain additional information. For therapy, this may refer to the need for additional information about the client's/patient's service needs or health care benefits. In addition, discussion of fees in the first session may be clinically contraindicated if a new client/patient is experiencing a crisis needing immediate therapeutic attention. In such situations, agreement on compensation and billing must be finalized as soon as all information is available or the crisis has subsided (see also Standard 10.01a, Informed Consent to Therapy).

- ⊘ A series of consultations with different company executives was required before a psychologist could develop a comprehensive plan for and pricing of services required.
- ⊘ A psychologist was aware that a new patient's HMO frequently failed to provide timely feedback about the extent and limits of patient health care benefits. During the initial consultation with the patient, the psychologist mentioned the possibility of this occurring and discussed delaying additional sessions until the extent of coverage could be clarified.
- ⊘ At his first session with a psychologist for treatment for alcoholism, the client was obviously intoxicated, evidencing speech impairment and a lack of coherence in his remarks. The psychologist addressed clinical issues with the client relevant to the immediate situation and made an appointment with him to discuss fees and other issues regarding therapy at a time when he would be sober.

Contingent Fees

A contingent fee is typically defined as a fee to be paid only in the event of a future occurrence. Psychologists should avoid contingent fees that have the potential to impair objectivity and unduly influence their methods, activities, or reports (see Standard 3.06, Conflict of Interest). In forensic contexts, psychologists should avoid accepting contingent fees when the services delivered involve offering evidence to a court or administrative body or affirmations or representations intended to be helpful to a court or to be relied upon by third parties. Other promises of future payment that might be considered contingent fees are those that are promised depending on the outcome of the legal matter at hand, such as future proceeds or settlement benefits (APA, 2013e).

(b) Psychologists' fee practices are consistent with law.

This standard specifically requires psychologists' activities to be consistent with relevant laws. To comply with Standard 6.04b, psychologists must be familiar with and develop fee practices compatible with local, state, and federal laws governing fee practices, including legal contracts with HMOs or other third-party insurers. Health care fraud or the submission of false claims opens the psychologist to legal censure and actions, which can result in costly fines or imprisonment. Fraud includes falsifying costs of services, intentionally overdiagnosing mental health disorders, or omitting information that might lead to denial of benefits. The following are examples of fee practices violating this standard:

- ☒ An HMO agreed to pay a psychologist 80% of his standard $100 hourly fee. The psychologist typically waived the $20 copayment for patients insured by this HMO. The HMO eventually accused the psychologist of insurance fraud, noting that in reality, her standard hourly fee for its insured patients had become $80.
- ☒ A single mother who had a minimum-wage job sought treatment for depression. She informed the psychologist that because of her limited funds, she had purchased health insurance for her 3-year-old daughter but not for herself. The psychologist reasoned that her mental health would affect her child's well-being and told her he would be willing to bill the insurance company under the daughter's policy.
- ☒ A client's health insurer did not cover mental health services for emotional problems associated with bereavement over the death of a spouse. The psychologist gave the client a diagnosis of major depressive disorder when she submitted the insurance form to gain coverage for sessions.
- ☒ The Medicaid system in the state in which a psychologist worked required professionals to have a preliminary meeting with a child to provide an initial diagnostic report, which would then be used to request approval for a full battery of psychological testing. The psychologist routinely wrote the preliminary report without interviewing children to limit the loss of school time and to shorten the approval period.

☒ A psychologist charged a first-time fee when a client asked for a list of individuals to whom the psychologist had released the client's PHI over the past 2 years. The psychologist was unaware that under HIPAA, each year clients/patients have the right to receive one free accounting of all disclosures of PHI information made within the previous 6 years.

Digital Ethics: Submitting Claims for Telehealth Services

To date, approximately 80% of Medicare and Medicaid policies and less than a third of states have enacted regulation requiring insurance companies to pay for telehealth services (APA, 2013e; Dombo et al., 2014). Some licensing laws restrict reimbursement to certain areas (e.g., rural and other underserved settings) while others exclude services provided through email, audio-only telephone, or facsimile. When submitting claims, psychologists need to clearly identify the services as using electronic media with specific codes provided by the insurers. Psychologists should also check with federal or state insurance regulators to determine potential differentials in reimbursement for in-person versus telehealth services (see Baker & Bufka, 2011, for a detailed review of legal, regulatory, reimbursement, and ethical issues in telehealth).

Implications of the Affordable Care Act (ACA) for Psychologists in Primary Care Settings

Psychologists' increasing involvement in primary care organizations require practitioners to stay up-to-date on ethical and legal aspects of billing codes and reimbursement policies in integrated care settings. For example, compliance with Standard 6.04a in patient-centered medical homes and other primary care organizations will require an understanding of salaried versus fee-for-service models of primary care as well as differences in billing codes and insurance coverage for psychologists' services differentially defined as *mental health* or *medical care.* Psychologists must also be knowledgeable about reimbursable services available for underinsured and uninsured citizens and undocumented immigrants (McDaniel et al., 2002; Nordal, 2012; Nutting et al., 2011; Rozensky et al., 2013).

Medicare and Physician Quality Reporting Systems (PQRS)

Psychologists in independent and group practices who are enrolled as Medicare providers will need to be familiar with reporting requirements of the Physician Quality Reporting System (PQRS) to ensure the accuracy of billing through adequate documentation meeting PQRS requirements. As of January 2015, HHS mandates that for 50% of Medicare patients seen by eligible professionals, including psychologists, documentation must be submitted on the quality (type of services provided) and value (treatment outcomes) of the service. This mandate includes both financial bonuses for reporting and financial penalties for failure to participate. To ensure compliance with law, psychologists need to be familiar with continuously updated codes for identifying mental health services provided and additional G-codes to indicate whether or not PQRS-designated treatment actions were taken. Several registry services have been approved to help professionals navigate the somewhat cumbersome PQRS reporting system. In March 2015, the APA Practice Organization (APAPO) launched such a registry for psychologists in individual and group practices (http://apapo.pqrspro.com). As with any other insurance-billing procedures, psychologists should ensure that they choose only registries that are also compliant with HIPAA regulations for protecting PHI.

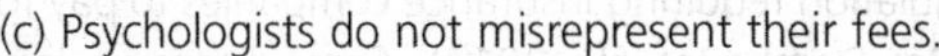

(c) Psychologists do not misrepresent their fees.

This standard requires that psychologists provide clients/patients, organizational clients, and others who will be charged for services an accurate statement of the costs of the services that will be offered. For example, under Standard 6.04c, psychologists are prohibited from the following:

- Listing in advertisements, brochures, websites, or other public representations fees lower than those the psychologist actually charges (see also Standards 5.01a, Avoidance of False or Deceptive Statements; 5.02, Statements by Others)
- Adding unnecessary tests to an assessment battery to raise the cost of services after reaching an agreement about fees with the client/patient
- Failing to disclose expectable costs of secretarial assistance or time devoted to telephone conversations, library reference work, or travel during fee negotiations for consulting or forensic work
- Using bait-and-switch tactics, such as offering low rates to lure a client/patient into therapy only to raise the rates after a few sessions
- Inflating reports of hourly fees for noninsured patients to obtain a higher rate for covered services when submitting a provider application to an HMO

(d) If limitations to services can be anticipated because of limitations in financing, this is discussed with the recipient of services as early as is feasible. (See also Standards 10.09, Interruption of Therapy, and 10.10, Terminating Therapy.)

In some instances, financial limitations on providing services may be anticipated at the beginning or during the course of a professional or scientific relationship. This most frequently occurs when HMOs readily provide health care professionals with their policies on the type of mental health services and number of sessions that are covered by a client's/patient's health plan. When, in a psychologist's professional judgment, clients/patients will require more therapy than their health plan covers, the psychologist must discuss this as early as is feasible in the professional relationship. Such discussion enables clients/patients to decide whether they want to begin the treatment under the HMO's limitations and provides the psychologist the opportunity to inform clients/patients about other financial arrangements that can be made to ensure continued care. Alternative financial arrangements can include reduced fees, deferred payment, limited sessions, or referral to lower cost services.

☒ A psychologist in independent practice had an initial consultation with a patient who appeared to be suffering from obsessive–compulsive disorder. The psychologist was aware that short-term treatments for this disorder have not proved to be effective. However, the patient's HMO would approve only 10 sessions. The psychologist told the patient that she was confident that she could convince the HMO to extend payments after 10 sessions and recommended they begin treatment. After 10 sessions, the HMO refused approval for additional sessions, and the patient could not afford additional treatment on his own.

Standard 6.04d also applies to instances when, during the course of a contractual agreement, organizational, consulting, forensic, or research psychologists become aware that the actual costs of a project will exceed the agreed-on costs. As soon as this becomes apparent, psychologists must discuss the limitations with the parties with whom they are contracted.

⊘ A consulting psychologist was aware that the hospital that had hired him to conduct a quality assurance study had a limited budget. His original proposal for the study was well within this budget. As the study was getting started, the hospital became involved in a lawsuit that required in-depth evaluation of practices that were only of marginal interest in the original quality assurance study. The psychologist quickly estimated the additional costs of examining these practices in depth and set up a meeting to discuss the limitations of the original proposal and its budget with respect to the hospital's sudden needs.

Digital Ethics: Third-Party Reimbursement for Telehealth Services

Psychologists are increasingly turning to wireless devices, web-based video communications, and other forms of electronic media as useful tools for scheduling and delivering mental health care services. Third-party payors differ in the type of electronic media–delivered services they will reimburse (Baker & Bufka, 2011). Consequently, psychologists considering the use of telehealth tools with specific clients/patients should determine the type and the extent to which the client's/patient's health care insurer will cover services and discuss any limitations in reimbursements with the client/patient as soon as feasible.

(e) If the recipient of services does not pay for services as agreed, and if psychologists intend to use collection agencies or legal measures to collect the fees, psychologists first inform the person that such measures will be taken and provide that person an opportunity to make prompt payment. (See also Standards 4.05, Disclosures; 6.03, Withholding Records for Nonpayment; and 10.01, Informed Consent to Therapy.)

Psychologists are permitted to use collection agencies or other legal measures to obtain compensation when the recipient of services has not made agreed-on payments. Before using such services, under Standard 6.04e, psychologists must inform the client/patient or other service recipient that such measures will be taken and provide that person an opportunity to make prompt payment. The definition of *prompt payment* should be reasonable but need not extend beyond a month depending on how long payments have been delinquent. As a rule of thumb, most businesses turn unpaid bills over to a collection agency after 60 to 90 days.

⊘ During informed consent, a psychologist always informed clients/patients that his fee policy was to be paid in full for services on a bimonthly basis, that bill collection procedures would be initiated when clients/patients reached an accumulated debt of the cost of six sessions, and that a letter alerting patients about billing concerns would be mailed to them if billing accumulated at 4 weeks to give them time to pay the bill.

Standard 6.04e applies to psychologists providing therapy, assessment, consultation, forensic, and other services when the service recipient is an individual, couple, or family. The standard does not apply when psychologists choose to use a collection agency or legal measures to collect unpaid fees from attorneys, companies, organizations, or institutions.

Implications of HIPAA

Several HIPAA regulations are relevant to Standard 6.04e. First, HIPAA permits covered entities to use and disclose PHI to carry out treatment, payment, or health care operations without specific authorization from the patient (45 CFR 164.506). Although specific requirements regarding consent were removed from the final HIPAA Privacy Rule, clients/patients must be aware of the covered entity's disclosure policies. Thus, covered entities who want the option of using collection agencies for nonpayment for health services must include this information in a Notice of Privacy Practices given to the client/patient at the onset of services, and the notice must be a separate document from the consent materials (45 CFR 164.520). Psychologists should also include this information in their informed consent procedures (see Standards 4.02, Discussing the Limits of Confidentiality; 9.03, Informed Consent in Assessments; 10.01, Informed Consent to Therapy). During informed consent, clients/patients should also be informed that under the most recent changes in the HIPAA rules, when individuals pay for health services by cash, they can instruct their provider not to share information about their treatment with their health plan (http://www.hhs.gov/news/press/2013pres/01/20130117b.html).

Collection agencies hired by a psychologist may be considered a "business associate" under HIPAA (45 CFR 160.103). A business associate is an entity who acts on behalf of a covered entity but not as an employee of the covered entity. An arrangement with a business associate must ensure that the business associate, on behalf of the covered entity, agrees to safeguard the use and disclosure of PHI in ways that are HIPAA compliant (45 CFR 164.504[e]).

What to Disclose to Collection Agencies

HIPAA's "minimum necessary" standard (45 CFR 164.502[b]), as well as Standard 4.01, Maintaining Confidentiality, in the APA Ethics Code can be interpreted as requiring psychologists to limit the information provided to collection agencies to the minimum necessary to accomplish the intended purpose. Information to such agencies should be limited to (a) the client's/patient's name; (b) the dollar amount of the fee that is overdue; (c) the date of services for which the unpaid fee was billed; and (d) the client's/patient's address, telephone number, and other relevant contact information. Psychologists should never reveal a client's/patient's diagnosis or reason for seeking services. In most instances, psychologists do not need to mention the type of services provided (e.g., therapy) and can simply inform the collection agency that the overdue bill is for "services provided." ☒

☒ A patient who had terminated therapy with a psychologist had failed to pay for sessions during the last 2 months of treatment. After sending the former patient several notices requesting payment and the psychologist's intention to use a collection agency if payment was not received, the psychologist turned the matter over to a collection agency. During the course of treatment, the psychologist had observed signs of explosive anger in the patient. Concerned that individuals at the collection agency might place themselves in danger if they angered the patient, the psychologist informed the head of the collection agency of the diagnostic reasons for these concerns.

6.05 Barter With Clients/Patients

Barter is the acceptance of goods, services, or other nonmonetary remuneration from clients/patients in return for psychological services. Psychologists may barter only if (1) it is not clinically contraindicated, and (2) the resulting arrangement is not exploitative. (See also Standards 3.05, Multiple Relationships, and 6.04, Fees and Financial Arrangements.)

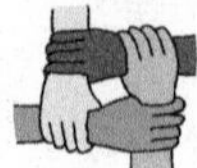

This standard applies when psychologists accept from clients/patients nonmonetary remuneration for services. The issue of bartering often emerges in response to a client's/patient's financial limitations or lack of affordable health insurance. Providing services in return for bartered goods is ethically permissible in situations when to not do so would deprive clients/patients of needed services or run counter to a community's economic or cultural practices. Although barter is not a per se violation of the Ethics Code, psychologists need to be cautious about accepting bartered goods or services from clients/patients in lieu of monetary payments because such arrangements have an inherent potential for client/patient harm, exploitation, and unethical multiple relationships (Standard 3.05a, Multiple Relationships). For example, it is often difficult to determine the extent to which a bartered good is equivalent in price to the dollar amount of a psychologist's fee, running the risk that clients/patients will be exploited or the psychologist underpaid. Bartering clerical or other (e.g., house painting, babysitting) services for psychological services risks creating potentially harmful multiple relationships resulting from interactions with the client/patient outside a professional role or loss of professional objectivity in reaction to the quality of the client/patient bartered services.

Standard 6.05 specifically prohibits barter with clients/patients when it is clinically contraindicated or exploitative. The following are an example of a potential violation of this standard and an example of ethically permissible barter.

☒ A psychologist in independent practice in a wealthy suburban community saw clients in an office attached to her home. One of her clients, a landscaper, noticed that her driveway and landscaping in front of her home were in serious disrepair. He suggested that instead of paying fees for 2 months, he would landscape her home. Although the cost of the landscaping would be greater than the psychologist's fees during this period, the psychologist agreed. The client was unable to complete the job in the 2-month period, leading to increased tension during the therapy sessions.

⊘ A school psychologist worked 2 days a week at an isolated Alaskan Native fishing community providing parent and teacher consultations and behavior therapy for children diagnosed with ADHD and other learning problems. During the year, an oil spill created serious economic consequences for the village. It was estimated that it would take 2 months for normal fishing to resume. The tribal leader, on behalf of the parents and school, asked the psychologist if she would be willing to take free room, board, office space, and travel to the village donated by the tribe equivalent to her fees during this period. The psychologist agreed and set up a time-limited remuneration contract specifying the equivalent monetary value of the services. The psychologist reasoned that barter in this case would be ethically permissible because the barter did not directly affect her therapeutic relationships with the children, parents, or teachers with whom she consulted and the exchange was a fair rate that was not exploitative. In addition, the psychologist's agreement to barter demonstrated her recognition of and respect for the value and importance the tribe attributed to her services.

6.06 Accuracy in Reports to Payors and Funding Sources

In their reports to payors for services or sources of research funding, psychologists take reasonable steps to ensure the accurate reporting of the nature of the service provided or research conducted, the fees, charges, or payments, and where applicable, the identity of the provider, the findings, and the diagnosis. (See also Standards 4.01, Maintaining Confidentiality; 4.04, Minimizing Intrusions on Privacy; and 4.05, Disclosures.)

This standard requires accuracy in reports to payors and funding sources and reflects the values of honesty and truthfulness articulated in Principle C: Integrity. The standard applies when psychologists bill insurance companies for client/patient therapy or assessments, charge companies for consulting fees or forensic clients for services, or document grant-related research expenses. The phrase *take reasonable steps* recognizes that in some instances, psychologists may have limited control over financial reports sent to third-party payors (e.g., psychologists working in group practices or in health delivery systems) or to funding sources (e.g., research psychologists working in academic institutions through which reports to external funders must be made).

Research and Industrial–Organizational and Forensic Services

Psychologists receiving research support from their institution, private foundations, or federal programs must provide accurate reports of charges for and the research-related purpose of equipment and supplies; travel; and payments to research participants, investigators, and research assistants. Psychologists billing companies or forensic clients for services should provide an accurate accounting of the number of hours worked on the particular project, the nature of and work product produced during those hours, and any other legitimate expenses (e.g., additional staff, travel, and duplication or postage costs) associated with the work contracted for.

Therapy

Accurate Diagnosis

Psychologists conducting therapy must provide an accurate diagnosis to third-party payors. Psychologists who provided an incorrect diagnosis to obtain reimbursement from a client's/patient's health plan would be in violation of this standard. In addition, such practices would represent insurance fraud and violation of Standard 6.04b, Fees and Financial Arrangements.

Billing for Missed Appointments

Some psychologists have a policy of charging for sessions missed when a client/patient cancels a therapy appointment. Health insurers will not reimburse these charges because no mental health services were provided. In their report to third-party payors, psychologists must clearly identify sessions for which charges are for a client/patient cancellation. Psychologists must also make any missed-appointment policies clear to clients/patients at the outset of the professional relationship (Standards 6.04a, Fees and Financial Arrangements; 10.01, Informed Consent to Therapy).

Accurate Representation of Billing Practices

Some HMOs calculate reimbursement for provider services as a percentage of the psychologist's fee scale. Psychologists must provide these organizations with an accurate representation of their billing practices for all clients/patients for the period requested by the HMO, including use of a sliding-fee scale if relevant. In some instances, licensed psychologists may supervise therapy or assessments conducted by unlicensed trainees or employees. When reimbursement for such therapy or assessment is sought from third-party payors, the licensed psychologist must clearly identify the actual provider of the services. Readers may wish to refer to Hot Topic "Managing the Ethics of Managed Care" at the end of this chapter.

6.07 Referrals and Fees

When psychologists pay, receive payment from, or divide fees with another professional, other than in an employer–employee relationship, the payment to each is based on the services provided (clinical, consultative, administrative, or other) and is not based on the referral itself. (See also Standard 3.09, Cooperation With Other Professionals.)

Psychologists often have pay arrangements with other mental health professionals. These may include renting out office space, referring new clients/patients to another psychologist when one's own schedule is filled, assigning a client to a member of a group practice, or contracted payment for collateral services provided to a client/patient. Standard 6.07 is intended to protect the welfare of clients/patients and the integrity of the profession by ensuring that payments between practitioners are based on professional services rendered and are in the best interest of the client/patient.

Referrals

One reason psychologists are sued is for improper referral (Bennett et al., 2006). Standard 6.07 is meant to ensure that client/patient referrals among professionals are based on the expertise of the professional to whom the referral is being made, as well as the appropriateness of the service for the client/patient, and not on the basis of the referral itself. Standard 6.07 prohibits psychologists from charging other professionals for client/patient referrals or, conversely, from paying another professional for a referral. Such payments place psychologists in a potential conflict of interest if the referral is based on the financial remuneration rather than on the match between a psychologist's expertise and the needs of the client/patient (see Standard 3.06, Conflict of Interest).

The standard does not prohibit psychologists who are members of a psychotherapy referral service from paying a percentage of a referred client's/patient's fee to support the administrative costs of the service, including the intake interview, as long as (a) the service follows a policy of making referrals only to those members who have expertise appropriate to a client's/patient's treatment needs and (b) the costs of the administrative and professional services are spread over the membership so that no individual psychologist is treated as a preferred referral solely because of his or her financial contribution to the service. However, psychologists need to be familiar with their state regulations regarding kickbacks and fee splitting to ensure these activities are consistent with law.

☒ A group of psychologists started a mental health referral service. Referrals were selected from a computerized list of psychologists' fees and available office hours. The group charged participating psychologists a first-time fee for each referral and a fee for each subsequent session based on the patient's monthly bill. This method of reimbursement violated Standard 6.07 and state laws prohibiting kickbacks and fee splitting for both the referral service and the participating psychologists.

Need to Know: Fees and Group Practice

Unlike the mental health service referral practices described above, it is ethically acceptable for a group practice to charge its employees a percentage of their client's/patient's fee. This is because the employer (the group practice) is not referring but assigning a client/patient to an employee, who in turn has a fiduciary responsibility to provide acceptable services on the employer's behalf (Woody, 2011).

Prohibition Against Fee Splitting

Standard 6.07 is also meant to ensure that fees charged to clients/patients reflect the services provided. A psychologist may divide fees with another professional only if both have contributed to the service.

⊘ A clinical geropsychologist regularly consulted with a neurologist when conducting cognitive assessments of patients with Parkinson's disease and other neurological disorders. The patient fee included the amount of money

(Continued)

(Continued)

the psychologist paid the neurologist for the consultation. These billing arrangements were described to the patient or his or her legal guardian in advance, and the psychologist accurately described the arrangement in billing statements to patients and third-party payors (see Standards 6.06, Accuracy in Reports to Payors and Funding Sources; 9.03, Informed Consent in Assessments; 10.01, Informed Consent to Therapy).

Other Permissible Payments

The standard does not prohibit psychologists from (a) charging another psychologist for office space, (b) paying professionals who are employees a percentage of a client/patient fee, (c) paying an institution for referrals, or (d) having membership in an HMO (Canter et al., 1994).

HOT TOPIC

Managing the Ethics of Managed Care

The primary function of HMOs and other forms of managed health care, such as managed care organizations (MCOs), preferred provider organizations, Medicare, and Medicaid, is to control health care costs while maintaining high-quality care. HMOs seek to accomplish this by (a) identifying which health conditions will qualify for benefits, (b) determining the manner and frequency in which services will be provided, (c) monitoring their delivery, and (d) regulating distribution of monetary reimbursement. This is accomplished through forming contractual relationships among insurers, providers, and clients/patients.

Ideally, managed mental health should enhance accountability, treatment effectiveness, and quality assurance. However, even when conducted properly, managed care plans raise a unique set of ethical challenges for psychologists. This Hot Topic highlights ethical pitfalls related to fees and financial arrangements under managed care.

Payment for Services

Practicing psychologists have different payment relationships with HMOs and other third-party insurers. Some psychologists contract directly with an HMO and receive referrals from that company. Others bill the insurer directly or bill the client/patient directly while providing the information necessary for the clients/patients to receive reimbursement from the insurer. Irrespective of payment arrangements, psychologists are responsible for fact-finding about and communicating to clients/patients the nature of their HMO or other third-party coverage.

As soon as feasible, psychologists should inform clients/patients about the following (Acuff et al., 1999; Standards 6.04, Fees and Financial Arrangements; 9.03, Informed Consent in Assessments; and 10.01, Informed Consent to Therapy):

- The insurer's provisions related to the number of authorized sessions
- The method and timing of utilization review
- The nature of the information required by the insurer to authorize services
- The amount of reimbursement provided
- The patient's share of any expenses (copayment or deduction)
- The services that are covered or excluded
- The responsibility for payment if the insurer determines that a particular service is not covered under the patient's plan

When a delay in the insurer's determination of coverage and length of care presents a problem for establishing a therapeutic relationship, psychologists should consider and discuss with clients/patients delaying future sessions until benefits are determined.

Perverse Incentives

Clients/patients should receive the same quality of care no matter what type of insurance they may have (Principle D: Justice; Shipman, Hooten, & Roa, 2011). Capitation is a specific cost containment model adopted by a number of HMOs and government-sponsored health plans that sets outpatient mental health benefits at a certain fixed price per client/patient. Capitation guarantees a provider a fixed (capitated) amount of dollars for each patient, irrespective of disorder or number of sessions. It is intended to incentivize practitioners to provide the most cost-effective treatment by providing briefer sessions for clients/patients with less severe disorders, thus allowing for more sessions for individuals with severe disorders. In some states, this model has been shown to reduce mental health care costs by lowering utilization of high-cost inpatient services (Bloom et al., 2011).

While capitation offers psychologists greater flexibility in determining treatment modality and frequency of sessions, it also establishes a financial incentive to keep sessions for all clients/patients to a minimum to maximize profits (Berenson & Rich, 2010). Capitation thus runs the risk of becoming a "perverse incentive" (Haas & Cummings, 1991) that places psychologists in a conflict of interest between patient care and their financial gain (see Standard 3.06, Conflict of Interest). Acuff et al. (1999) recommended that to avoid unintentionally downgrading services for financial gain under capitation, psychologists develop an internal monitoring system for their practice to compare the length of care for patients in the capitated plans with that of patients receiving fee-for-service or other forms of coverage.

Diagnosing for Dollars

The American Psychiatric Association's (2013) *Diagnostic and Statistical Manual of Mental Disorders* (DSM-V) is the most widely used system for classifying mental health disorders in the United States. Health insurers use the *DSM* classifications to determine criteria for coverage, length of treatment, and treatment outcomes. They often deny insurance reimbursement for certain *DSM* classifications that are common among clients/patients served by psychologists, including adjustment disorders, diagnostic codes that are exclusive to *DSM* Axis II (Personality Disorders), and *DSM* V codes (Relational Problems and Other Conditions That May Be a Focus of Clinical Attention; Braun & Cox, 2005).

Patients with diagnoses not covered by their insurer may not be able to pay for out-of-pocket costs. In response, some psychologists may be tempted to "upcode" (overdiagnose) a disorder or

(Continued)

(Continued)

exaggerate or exclude relevant client symptoms to establish a diagnosis that meets an insurer's benefits criteria. Upcoding also occurs when a psychologist conducting couples or family counseling services not covered by a health plan provides a false diagnosis for one spouse to obtain individual benefits to cover the joint counseling. Wylie (1995) labeled these practices "diagnosing for dollars," and Rappo (2002) noted that this term adequately describes diagnoses aimed at managing health costs rather than managing care.

Legal and Ethical Implications

Upcoding and other false diagnoses are illegal and unethical. Overdiagnosing a client/patient to receive health care benefits is insurance fraud and thus a violation of Standard 6.04, Fees and Financial Arrangements. It is also inconsistent with Principle C: Integrity, under which psychologists do not engage in fraud, subterfuge, or intentional misrepresentation of fact. Moreover, it violates Standard 3.06, Conflict of Interest, by allowing personal financial interests to interfere with psychologists' objectivity.

Psychologists suspected of upcoding can be investigated and prosecuted under the False Claims Amendments Act of 1986 (U.S. Code 31, Chapter 37, Subchapter III), which permits clients/patients to bring cases against practitioners on behalf of the government for which a practitioner's claim of ignorance is an insufficient defense (see Braun & Cox, 2005). Psychologists found guilty of insurance fraud will most likely lose their state license to practice, be required to pay substantial monetary penalties, and, in the case of criminal charges based on defrauding Medicare or Medicaid, may spend time in prison.

Distributive Justice

Some psychologists defend overdiagnosis as an ethical choice that places the best interests of the client over the "unjust" criteria used by health care management organizations to distribute health care. This defense rests on the fallacious assumption that health care resources are unlimited. While it is beyond the scope of this book to address political and economic influences on the availability and costs of health care, health resources are finite. Therefore, when psychologists upcode a client's/patient's diagnosis to receive reimbursement for services, they are further limiting the resources available for individuals who actually have more serious disorders and, in the long run, potentially contributing to a rise in insurance costs to cover the number of clients/patients who are meeting diagnostic criteria (Principle D: Justice).

Client/Patient Harm

Upcoding a diagnosis to gain health care benefits can lead to multiple foreseeable harms (Principle A: Beneficence and Nonmaleficence; Standard 3.04, Avoiding Harm). First, the exaggerated diagnosis becomes a permanent part of the client's/patient's health record and potentially could be categorized as a "preexisting condition" that would form the basis of insurance denial or increased costs for the client/patient in the future. Second, a false diagnosis can lead to inappropriate treatment decisions by the HMO or future care providers that are iatrogenic for the client/patient and outside the psychologist's control. Overdiagnoses can also create social stigma and negatively affect clients'/patients' assessment of their psychological well-being and their responsiveness to therapy or contribute to a harmful self-fulfilling prophecy.

Colluding With Clients/Patients in Upcoding

Some psychologists erroneously believe that they should involve clients in decisions regarding which diagnosis to submit to their health care insurer. Such actions compromise the psychologist–client/patient relationship. First, it represents an abdication of the psychologist's fiduciary responsibility to arrive at a diagnosis and treatment plan that accurately reflects the client's/patient's psychological problems (Principle B: Fidelity and Responsibility). It can thus set the stage for clients/patients to lose faith in or mistrust the psychologist's intent and ability to provide the best standard of care. Second, it communicates to the client/patient that the psychologist believes that deception, false claims, and lies are acceptable forms of achieving goals—a message inconsistent with the aims of therapy (Principle C: Integrity).

Chapter Cases and Ethics Discussion Questions

Amala, a 24-year-old graduate student, comes to Dr. Orenstein for treatment for gender dysphoria. During the initial interview, Amala indicated that while her birth certificate indicated she was male, she had always known she was female and finally had saved up enough of her own money to begin a medical transition. She made the appointment with Dr. Orenstein because her physician requires a mental health evaluation before he will approve the medical treatment. Amala is enrolled in her parents' health insurance plan and cannot afford to pay out of pocket for psychotherapy. She is afraid that because under the ACA her parents will receive an "explanation of benefits" regarding coverage for her psychotherapy, they will learn about her gender identity and take her off their insurance policy. Identify the ethical and legal issues Dr. Orenstein needs to consider with respect to record keeping and potential confidentiality breaches associated with Amala's insurance coverage and describe how Dr. Orenstein should integrate these concerns into the informed consent process.

Dr. Balcan, a clinical psychologist with a specialization in addiction, is on the staff of a hospital that provides inpatient and outpatient care. She has been providing psychotherapy to Jerome, who was hospitalized following an alcohol-induced psychotic episode. Jerome's health insurance will cover only 5 days of inpatient care for this type of disorder. The first half of Jerome's stay was focused on detoxification and withdrawal symptoms. Although Jerome's functioning has significantly improved, as the 5th day approaches, Dr. Balcan is concerned that the episode may reflect an underlying bipolar disorder that may need further inpatient observation. The psychiatrist who directs the department tells her a request for an inpatient insurance coverage extension would be fruitless unless the new diagnosis could be immediately substantiated and tells her to prepare Jerome for outpatient services. Discuss the ethical issues that Dr. Balcan needs to consider and how she should resolve this dilemma.

A research psychologist is conducting a multisite study on the effectiveness of adding daily text messages to standard cognitive–behavioral therapy for the treatment of adolescent eating disorders. Participants are current patients at five different eating disorder clinics in the United States. Following appropriate informed consent and HIPAA authorization, the investigators will have access to participants' prior treatment records, and all study-derived assessments and treatment plans will be included in patient's health records. In addition, all data from the five sites will be stored on a cloud-based system to facilitate analysis. Discuss the ethical issues that must be considered and practices implemented to ensure appropriate documentation and maintenance of participant records, protection of confidentiality (Standards 6.01 and 6.02), and assurance of participant access to their records (see also discussion in Chapter 11 on "Implications of HIPAA" under Standard 8.02, Informed Consent to Research).

CHAPTER 10

Standards on Education and Training

7. Education and Training

7.01 Design of Education and Training Programs

Psychologists responsible for education and training programs take reasonable steps to ensure that the programs are designed to provide the appropriate knowledge and proper experiences, and to meet the requirements for licensure, certification, or other goals for which claims are made by the program. (See also Standard 5.03, Descriptions of Workshops and Non-Degree-Granting Educational Programs.)

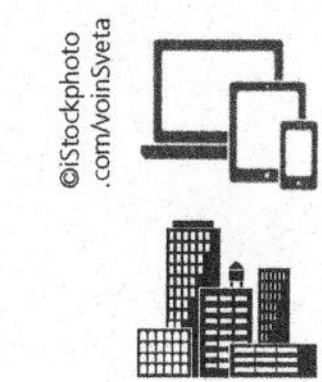

Psychologists responsible for education and training programs have an obligation to establish relationships of loyalty and trust with their institutions, students, and members of society who rely on academic institutions to provide the knowledge, skills, and career opportunities claimed by the specific degree program (Principle B: Fidelity and Responsibility). This requires knowledge of system change and competencies in academic program management and leadership skills (APA, 2012f; Standard 2.03, Maintaining Competence). Psychologists responsible for administering academic programs must ensure that course requirements meet recognized standards in the relevant field and that students have sufficient practicum, externship, and research experiences to meet the career outcome goals articulated by the program (Wise & Cellucci, 2014).

- Department chairs and other faculty responsible for undergraduate curricula development need to ensure that course requirements expose undergraduates majoring and minoring in psychology and students taking survey courses to the knowledge and skills considered fundamental to the discipline.
- Chairs or directors of doctoral programs claiming to produce graduates competent to conduct psychological research need to ensure that students receive education and training in research ethics and the theoretical, methodological, and statistical skills required to competently conduct psychological science in the specific fields emphasized by the program (APA, 2011b; Fisher, Fried, & Feldman, 2009).
- Psychologists responsible for professional degree programs need to ensure that course requirements and field experiences meet those required by potential employers, relevant state or professional organizations for program accreditation, internship placements where relevant, and applicable individual licensure and credentialing bodies.
- Psychologists administering internship programs must ensure that supervisory and training experiences meet the standards of the specific areas of psychological practice claimed, appropriate state and professional accreditation criteria, and state licensing board requirements (APA, 2015e).

Need to Know: Competency Benchmarks in Professional Psychology

The American Psychological Association's *Competency Benchmarks for Professional Psychology* (APA, 2011b) delineates core competencies that students should develop during training. Essential competencies are nested in six clusters: professionalism, relational, application, science, education, and systems. Programs are encouraged to choose the core competencies within each cluster that match their program goals. Behavioral anchors for each core competency are described at three developmental levels: readiness for practicum, readiness for internship, and readiness for entry to practice. The APA also provides a detailed guidebook (APA, 2012f) on how programs can adapt a rating system for their current training goals; the guide includes suggestions for sharing competence evaluations with students and creating remediation plans for students who do not reach required levels of competence. For additional discussion, see the Hot Topic at the end of this chapter, "Ethical Supervision of Trainees in Professional Psychology Programs."

The term *reasonable steps* reflects recognition that despite a program administrator's best efforts, there may be periods during which curriculum adjustments must be made in reaction to changes in faculty composition, departmental reorganizations, institutional demands, modifications in accreditation or licensure regulations, or evolving disciplinary standards.

Digital Ethics: Online Distance Education

Discussion of teaching ethics for online psychology curricula and distance learning programs has not kept pace with the rapid evolution and availability of online education. Distance learning using information technology raises complex questions regarding the adequacy of psychology programs to meet education and training requirements for a diverse student body from across the United States and in different countries. Psychologists administering online distance education might consider the following questions (Anderson & Simpson, 2007; Brey, 2006):

- Can the use of information technology ensure that the appropriate knowledge can be transmitted to students and that student acquisition of such knowledge can be appropriately evaluated?
- To what extent does the program meet accreditation, certification, licensure, or other requirements across different localities? Is the program description clear regarding the states or countries in which it meets such requirements (see also Standard 7.02, Descriptions of Education and Training Programs)?
- Does the use of web-based or Internet-mediated technology in higher education foster or undermine student diversity?
- Are the program admissions criteria and educational materials appropriate for the diversity of students who will apply for and be admitted into the program?
- Can experiential requirements be adequately provided, supervised, monitored, and evaluated at a distance through informational technology?
- Can the ethical values of the discipline be successfully transmitted and student ethical behavior adequately monitored through electronic media?
- Are faculty adequately trained in the use of online distance learning?

Interprofessional Training for Practice and Research in Primary Care

Doctoral programs in psychology will increasingly need to equip students with the skills necessary for professional practice, quality improvement and outcomes research, and team management and consulting in the integrated patient care systems of the future. Systems such as patient-centered medical homes (PCMH) and accountable care organizations (ACO) will need psychologists trained in applying patient-centered, accountability-focused, evidence-based, and team-based approaches to enhancing access to quality (Belar, 2014; DeLeon, Sells, Cassidy, Waters, & Kasper, 2015; see also the section on the Patient Protection and Affordable Care Act (ACA) in Chapter 1). Program administrators need to be aware of evolving APA accreditation requirements for externships and internships that provide trainees with opportunities to acquire direct experience and supervision in interprofessional systems of care and when appropriate documentation of specialization as a basic credential for a practicing psychologist once licensed (Standard 7.01, Design of Education and Training Programs). Compliance with Standard 7.01 will also require curricula that foster competencies in the following:

- Implementation of ACA and related health policy goals and infrastructure
- Application of team science to outcome research within integrated health organizations
- Selection and integration of evidence-based practices within an interprofessional care model
- Appropriate integrated care patient electronic record keeping and billing
- Skills facilitating consultation with medical providers on behavioral management techniques to improve patient adherence to health care regimens

Readers might also refer to Standards 2.04, Bases for Scientific and Professional Judgments; 3.09, Cooperation with Other Professionals; 6.01 Documentation of Professional and Scientific Work and Maintenance of Records as well as Nash et al. (2013) and Rozensky (2014a, 2014b).

7.02 Descriptions of Education and Training Programs

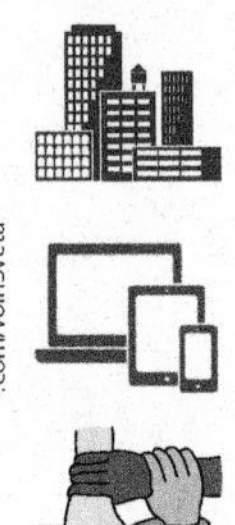

Psychologists responsible for education and training programs take reasonable steps to ensure that there is a current and accurate description of the program content (including participation in required course- or program-related counseling, psychotherapy, experiential groups, consulting projects, or community service), training goals and objectives, stipends and benefits, and requirements that must be met for satisfactory completion of the program. This information must be made readily available to all interested parties.

Department and program chairs and psychologists responsible for internship training programs must also ensure that prospective and current students have an accurate description of the nature of the academic and training programs to which they may apply or have been admitted. This standard of the APA Ethics Code (APA, 2010c) requires psychologists responsible for these programs to keep program descriptions up-to-date regarding (a) required coursework and field experiences; (b) educational and career objectives supported by the program; (c) current faculty or supervisory staff; (d) currently offered courses; and (e) the dollar amount of available student stipends and benefits, the process of applying for these, and the obligations incurred by students, interns, or postdoctoral fellows who receive stipends or benefits.

Standard 7.02 specifically obligates teaching psychologists to ensure that prospective and current students, externs, or interns are aware of program requirements to participate in personal psychotherapy or counseling, experiential groups, or any other courses or activities that require them to reveal personal thoughts or feelings.

Many program descriptions now appear on university or institutional websites. Psychologists need to ensure to the extent possible that these websites are appropriately updated. The term *reasonable steps* recognizes that efforts to ensure up-to-date information may be constrained by publication schedules for course catalogs, webmasters not directly under the auspices of the department or program, and other institutional functions over which psychologists may have limited control.

☒ A psychology graduate department described itself as offering an industrial–organizational track that included paid summer placements at companies in the city in which the university is located. The required curriculum included only one class in industrial–organizational psychology taught by an adjunct professor. Other required courses for the industrial–organizational track consisted of traditional intelligence and personality test administration classes, test construction classes, and statistics courses offered by faculty in the department's clinical and psychometric programs. For the past 2 years, the department had been able to place only one or two students in paid summer internships.

Need to Know: Language-Matching Training Experiences

The increasing language diversity of client/patient populations in the United States sometimes leads to matching bilingual graduate students with externship and internship populations for which their language skills are considered an advantage. Limiting bilingual trainees to work experiences with non-English-speaking clients or to one cultural–language group may deprive students of the broad educational training opportunities promised by the graduate or training program (Fields, 2010; see also Standard 3.08, Exploitative Relationships). Such assignments may also implicitly lead to misconceptions by bilingual and other students in the program that language competence is equivalent to multicultural treatment competence (Schwartz, Rodríguez, Santiago-Rivera, Arredondo, & Field, 2010). Faculty advisers and supervisors should actively assess bilingual students' training needs as well as their comfort and desire to work with same-language populations to ensure these students are afforded the same quality of education, respect, and autonomy that other trainees enjoy (Schwartz et al., 2010). English-only-speaking supervisors who rely on a trainee's language translations of sessions should also be aware that they may be providing feedback on clients that they cannot actually work with themselves (Standard 2.01b, Boundaries of Competence), and in some states, this lack of "proper" supervision might mean that the trainee is perceived to be practicing "independently" without a license (Schwartz et al., 2010).

7.03 Accuracy in Teaching

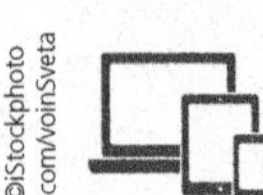
©iStockphoto.com/voinSveta

(a) Psychologists take reasonable steps to ensure that course syllabi are accurate regarding the subject matter to be covered, bases for evaluating progress, and the nature of course experiences. This standard does not preclude an instructor from modifying course content or requirements when the instructor considers it pedagogically necessary or desirable, so long as students are made aware of these modifications in a manner that enables them to fulfill course requirements. (See also Standard 5.01, Avoidance of False or Deceptive Statements.)

Standard 7.03a requires that teaching psychologists provide students with accurate and timely information regarding course content; required and recommended readings; exams, required papers, or other forms of evaluation; and extra-classroom experiences if required. Psychologists who provide their syllabi via the Internet or who require students to use web-based references need to keep these websites accurate and appropriately updated.

Modifying Course Content or Requirements

This standard also recognizes that syllabi may sometimes include an unintentional error, required readings may become unavailable, changes in institutional scheduling may create conflicts in dates set for exams, and many times, psychologists have valid pedagogical reasons for changing course content or requirements at the beginning or middle of a semester. For example, a professor may find that assigned readings are too difficult or not sufficiently advanced for the academic level of students in the class. In such instances, it would be appropriate for professors to modify course reading requirements as long as materials are available to students and they are given sufficient time to obtain and read the materials. Similarly, in response to constraints imposed by publishers, bookstores, other professors, or the institution, psychologists may rightly need to modify required texts or exam schedules.

Modifications to course content or requirements do not violate this standard as long as students are made aware of such modifications in a clear and timely manner that enables them to fulfill course requirements without undue hardship. However, a professor who has neither discussed nor specified how students will be evaluated until the last week of class or one who fails to update an old syllabus that does not reflect the current content of the course would be in violation of this standard.

⊘ In his first year of teaching, an assistant professor prepared a syllabus for an undergraduate developmental psychology course that drew largely on required readings from books by well-known developmental theorists. He carefully planned weekly quizzes, a midterm exam, and a term paper requiring a critique of several journal articles. Students performed very poorly on the first two quizzes and did not seem to be involved in class discussions. The professor learned that for reasons unknown to the department chair, the dean's office had assigned this class as a "non-major" section. The students were therefore not as prepared as had been anticipated because, unlike psychology majors, most had not taken an introductory psychology course. The psychologist decided to modify the curriculum to ensure that students received a basic foundation in developmental psychology. He rush-ordered a basic developmental psychology text, extended the date of the midterm, and changed the topic of the term paper to a review of sections of the originally assigned books. He distributed a revised syllabus detailing the changes and gave the students the option of using the first two quizzes as extra credit.

(b) When engaged in teaching or training, psychologists present psychological information accurately. (See also Standard 2.03, Maintaining Competence.)

Standards prescribing the nature of information that teachers should provide raise legitimate concerns about academic freedom. At the same time, in many ways, teaching is a "process of persuasion" where instructors are in the unique socially sanctioned and desired role of systematically influencing the knowledge base and belief systems of students (Friedrich & Douglass, 1998). Standard 7.03b reflects the pedagogical obligation of psychologists to share with students their scholarly judgment and expertise along with the right of students to receive an accurate representation of the subject matter that enables them to evaluate where a professor's views fit within the larger discipline.

The narrowness or breadth of information required to fulfill this standard will depend on the nature of the course. For example, a psychologist who presented readings and lectures only on psychodynamic theories of personality would be presenting accurate information in a course by that name but inaccurate information if teaching a general survey course on theories of personality. A professor who has been teaching the same material for 20 years when such material is considered obsolete in terms of the discipline's recognized standards would be providing students inaccurate information about the current state of the subject matter.

7.04 Student Disclosure of Personal Information

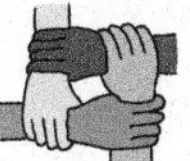

Psychologists do not require students or supervisees to disclose personal information in course- or program-related activities, either orally or in writing, regarding sexual history, history of abuse and neglect, psychological treatment, and relationships with parents, peers, and spouses or significant others except if (1) the program or training facility has clearly identified this requirement in its admissions and program materials or (2) the information is necessary to evaluate or obtain assistance for students whose personal problems could reasonably be judged to be preventing them from performing their training- or professionally related activities in a competent manner or posing a threat to the students or others.

This standard requires psychologists to respect the privacy rights of students and supervisees. In many instances, information about students' or supervisees' sexual history; their personal experience of abuse or neglect; whether they have or are currently receiving psychotherapy; and their relationships with relatives, friends, or significant others is outside the legitimate boundaries of academic or supervisory program inquiry.

With two exceptions, Standard 7.04 prohibits psychologists from requiring students or supervisees to disclose such information.

Clear Identification of Requirements

Teaching and supervisory psychologists may require disclosure of information about sexual experiences, history of abuse, psychological treatment, or relationships with significant others only if the admissions and program materials have clearly identified that students or supervisees will be expected to reveal such information if admitted to the program. The requirement for advance notification includes programs that explore countertransference reactions during supervisory sessions if questions about such reactions will tap into any of the categories listed above. Clear and advance notification about the types of disclosures that programs require will allow potential students to elect not to apply to a program if they find such a requirement intrusive or otherwise discomforting.

Interference With Academic Performance or Self-Harm or Other Harm

The standard also recognizes that there are times when students' personal problems may interfere with their ability to competently perform professionally related activities or pose a threat of self-harm or harm to others. In such instances, psychologists are permitted to require students or supervisees to disclose the personal information necessary to help evaluate the nature of the problem, to obtain assistance for the student or supervisee, or to protect others' welfare.

✓ A psychologist supervising a third-year clinical student's work at the university counseling center was growing increasingly concerned about the sexual nature of verbal exchanges the student reported having with one of her undergraduate clients. The psychologist also suspected from one of the student's comments that she had been meeting with the client outside of the counseling sessions. Concerned that the student might be in violation of Standards 3.05, Multiple Relationships, or 10.05, Sexual Intimacies With Current Therapy Clients/Patients, the supervisor asked the student whether she had been seeing the client socially. When she responded yes, the psychologist probed further to find out if she was having a romantic relationship with the client.

☒ A student came to see a professor during office hours to discuss his poor grade on the midterm exam in a graduate course on human sexuality. The professor asked the student if he might be doing poorly in the course because of anxieties about his own sexuality.

Need to Know: Supervision of Trainees With Disabilities

The field of rehabilitation psychology is increasing the discipline's familiarity with reasonable accommodations and training requirements for students with disabilities (Americans with Disabilities Act [ADA], 1990; Falender, Collins, & Shafranske, 2009). The nascent status of the field leaves unexplored potentially prejudicial beliefs held by supervisors that may unintentionally lead to inequities and inadequacies in the training experiences of graduate students with disabilities enrolled in psychology practitioner programs. For example, there is no empirical support for the assumption that a trainee with disabilities cannot perform the essential functions of a psychologist or that this individual is at a disadvantage in establishing a therapeutic alliance with clients/patients (Taube & Olkin, 2011).

Supervision competencies in the area of disability require familiarity with the ADA, models of ableness, and influence of multiple minority statuses and group histories of oppression on the perspectives of individuals with disabilities. Supervisors will also need to acquire the skills to neither over- nor under-attend to a supervisee's disability, support necessary adaptations to clinical tools, and create a safe environment for supervisees to discuss issues relevant to their disability that may emerge in their clinical or supervisory settings (Cornish & Monson, 2014).

Digital Ethics: Disclosure of Student Personal Information Through Social Media

Teaching psychologists may use Facebook, Twitter, blogs, chat rooms, and other forms of social media to engage students in discussions regarding academic material or university events. However, students may sometimes use these sites to share or link to information about themselves or other students that describes sexual behaviors, family relationships, or other personal information. Faculty access to such information may be inconsistent with the goal of Standard 7.04, which is to protect students from disclosing personal information that may unfairly influence evaluation of their academic performance (Standard 7.06b, Assessing Student and Supervisee Performance). Psychologists who utilize electronic media for instructional purposes should clarify in advance restrictions on the type of information that can be posted on these sites. Instructors should also

(Continued)

(Continued)

educate students on their responsibilities and strategies to avoid privacy violations that may emerge when academic sites are linked to other sources of personal information. Furthermore, faculty should develop procedures for removing such information if it appears. If a situation arises and faculty are concerned that becoming aware of such information may bias their evaluation of student performance, they should seek consultation while at the same time protecting the student's identity (Standards 4.04b, Minimizing Intrusions on Privacy; 4.06, Consultations).

7.05 Mandatory Individual or Group Therapy

(a) When individual or group therapy is a program or course requirement, psychologists responsible for that program allow students in undergraduate and graduate programs the option of selecting such therapy from practitioners unaffiliated with the program. (See also Standard 7.02, Descriptions of Education and Training Programs.)

Standard 7.05a addresses the privacy rights of psychology students enrolled in programs that require individual or group psychotherapy. During the commenting period for the revision of the current APA Ethics Code, a number of graduate students raised concerns about revealing personal information (a) in the presence of other students in required group therapy or experiential courses and (b) to therapists in required individual psychotherapy if the therapist was closely affiliated with their graduate program. In response to these concerns, this standard requires programs that have such requirements to allow students to select a therapist unaffiliated with the program.

Standard 7.05a does not prevent programs from instituting a screening and approval process for practitioners outside the program whom students may see for required psychotherapy. It is sound policy for programs to ensure that required individual or group therapy is conducted by a qualified mental health professional. In addition, in some programs, the therapeutic experience may be seen as one facet of training about a particular form of psychotherapy, and the program is entitled to require students to select a private therapist who conducts treatment consistent with the program's training goals.

Need to Know: Ethical Criteria for Mandatory Personal Psychotherapy (MPP)

The training goal of program-mandated personal psychotherapy (MPP) is to maximize therapeutic efficacy through self-awareness that heightens appreciation of the therapeutic relationship and client/patient vulnerability and minimizes the possibility of harming clients or acting in ways that are not in their best interests (Norcross, 2005). However, due to the diversity of theoretical frameworks for clinical care and the paucity of empirical data to support its efficacy in comparison to other training models, the value of MPP remains contested. One issue is whether imposing psychotherapy on well-functioning trainees who display no pathological behavior and feel no need for treatment is consistent with the ethical practice of psychotherapy, including respect for client/patient autonomy and obligation to terminate treatment when the client/patient does not need health services (Ivey, 2014; Principle E: Respect for People's Rights and Dignity; Standards 3.10, Informed Consent; 10.01, Informed Consent to Therapy; 10.10, Terminating Therapy). Below are useful guidelines for programs requiring MPP (see Ivey, 2014, for an excellent summary):

- The requirement must be justified by the nature and training objectives of the program (Standard 7.01, Design of Education and Training Programs).
- The MPP requirement as well as the risks and benefits and planned safeguards should be clear in application materials (Standard 7.02, Descriptions of Education and Training Programs).
- There should be no multiple relationships between therapists and trainee–clients, and trainees should have some choice in selecting a psychotherapist (Standards 3.05, Multiple Relationships; 7.05, Mandatory Individual or Group Therapy).
- Students should be provided with financially feasible alternatives to ensure affordable treatment without undue hardship (Principle D: Justice).

Postdoctoral Training

This standard does not apply to postdoctoral programs, such as postgraduate psychoanalytic programs, that require a training analysis with a member of the faculty. These advanced programs, unlike graduate programs, are optional for individuals who seek specialized training beyond a doctoral degree in psychology, and a decision not to enroll in such programs because of therapy requirements does not restrict opportunities to pursue a career in professional psychology.

(b) Faculty who are or are likely to be responsible for evaluating students' academic performance do not themselves provide that therapy. (See also Standard 3.05, Multiple Relationships.)

This standard is designed to protect the integrity and fairness of evaluations of student academic performance. Whereas Standard 7.05a protects a student's right to keep personal information private from program-affiliated practitioners, Standard 7.05b protects the student from grading or performance evaluation biases that might arise if a faculty member who serves as the student's psychotherapist is also involved in judging his or her academic performance. This standard pertains not only to faculty who might teach a course in which a student who is in therapy with them might enroll but also to faculty who may be involved in decisions regarding passing or failing of comprehensive exams, advancement from master's-level to doctoral-level status, training supervision, and dissertation committees. As indicated by the cross-reference to Standard 3.05, Multiple Relationships, serving in the dual roles of therapist and academic evaluator can impair the therapist's objectivity when knowledge gained from one role is applied to the other, or it can undermine treatment effectiveness when students are afraid to reveal personal information that might negatively affect their academic evaluations.

☒ A clinical psychology program that required first-year graduate students to receive 1 year of individual psychotherapy had a referral list of 20 "approved" independent practitioners in the area that students could select as their therapist. The program often drew on these same practitioners as adjunct professors to teach required courses when regular faculty were on sabbatical.

7.06 Assessing Student and Supervisee Performance

(a) In academic and supervisory relationships, psychologists establish a timely and specific process for providing feedback to students and supervisees. Information regarding the process is provided to the student at the beginning of supervision.

Psychologists establish academic and supervisory relationships of trust with students and supervisees based on fair processes of evaluation that provide students and supervisees with the opportunity to learn from positive and negative feedback of their work (Principle B: Fidelity and Responsibility). As in other domains of psychological activities, supervisors need to be familiar with the knowledge base for models of enhancing and monitoring the professional functioning of supervisees (APA, 2012f; Standards 2.01, Competence; 2.03, Maintaining Competence). Under Standard 7.06a, psychologists must inform students and supervisees (a) when and how often they will be evaluated, (b) the basis for evaluation (e.g., performance in exams, attendance, implementation of various phases of research, summaries of client/patient sessions, and administration and interpretation of psychological assessments), and (c) the timing and manner in which feedback will be provided.

☒ A psychology professor teaching a graduate course in statistics used a midterm and final exam to evaluate students. The professor delayed returning the midterm, telling the students they should not worry because most of them would do very well. When she returned the graded midterms during the last week of class, most students were shocked to discover they had received Cs and Ds on the exam. Many felt the delay caused them to miss opportunities to learn what aspects of course material they had misunderstood and to prepare adequately for the final.

Providing specific information about student evaluation at the beginning of the process is especially important for the supervision of clinical work, psychological assessment, or research because these supervisory activities are often less uniformly structured than classroom teaching.

☒ A student in a PhD program in school psychology had a second-year externship in a residential school for students with severe emotional disorders. The school psychologist serving as her on-site supervisor relied on "countertransference" techniques to train his externs. Each time the student asked her supervisor for specific information on how her work with student clients would be evaluated, the supervisor would shift the discussion to how the extern's personal reactions to her clients were causing her anxiety about the evaluation of her performance. The extern felt increasingly frustrated and anxious about the lack of specific feedback. At the end of the year, the supervisor gave her a poor evaluation, stating that the student's anxieties had interfered with her ability to take direction.

☒ A research psychologist who agreed to mentor a graduate student's doctoral research consistently postponed or missed meetings with the student, resulting in the student missing the departmental deadline for dissertation proposals. The mentor gave the student an incomplete for the semester, and the student had to pay additional tuition to propose the following semester.

Group Supervision

Group supervisees can benefit from the multiple input, support, and shared experiences of their peer colleagues while also learning how to provide effective feedback and gain initial competencies required for their own future skills as supervisors. Psychologists engaged in group supervision must develop competencies in creating a safe environment for group discussion and disagreement and for clarifying the roles of supervisor and supervisees. At the beginning of the supervision, they need to clarify the purpose of group supervision and how responsibilities and supervisee evaluation differ from those under individual supervision. For example, most students will be unfamiliar with the unique learning experiences and responsibilities of group supervisees, which include providing feedback to one another, both formally and informally, at specified periods in a respectful manner; preparing case presentations and questions on group materials prior to each meeting; refraining from discussing material about an absent supervisee; and maintaining the confidentiality of group discussions, including information pertaining to other group members, their clients, and specific training sites (see Smith, Cornish & Riva, 2014, for additional details).

Military Supervision

Johnson and Kennedy (2010) eloquently described the unique responsibilities of military psychologists supervising trainees in American combat theaters and the need to provide timely and constructive feedback under intense and fast-paced conditions. Military supervisors are often torn between a duty to help trainees meet their active duty responsibilities and concerns that some trainees may not be adequately prepared during the initially agreed-upon time frame. According to the authors, military supervisors need enhanced competencies to address the unique nature of trainee stress produced by almost continuous exposure to life-threatening combat conditions and deceased and severely injured and traumatized service members (Standard 2.01, Boundaries of Competence). They recommended that for each trainee soon to be deployed, supervisors develop "the best mix of training and supervision in psychotherapy, battlefield triage, combat-related psychopathology, treatments for trauma-related disorders, neuropsychology, and ethical decision making" (p. 300) and make sure the trainee is clear about the training components and expectations of the supervised experience, including the physical dangers and stresses of performing their roles in combat situations.

Digital Ethics: Use of Technology for Supervision

Increasingly, state licensure boards are permitting email, teleconferencing, or other forms of online supervision on their own or as adjuncts to face-to-face supervision to satisfy training requirements. As noted by Dombo et al. (2014), whether or not the use of these modalities fulfills obligations to trainees depends upon how accessible the supervisor is to the trainee, the timeliness of the supervision, the supervisor's experience with using these technologies, and the trainee's comfort level. Supervisors should also keep in mind that through their online supervision, they are modeling ethical practice and decision making regarding the use of social media and other technologies (Falender, Shafranske, & Falicov, 2014). Issues to consider include the following:

- Is the supervisor licensed to practice in the state in which the trainee is conducting treatment?
- Does the supervisor have sufficient familiarity with the clients and treatment context in which the trainee is working?
- Does the modality inhibit rapport building, engagement, and sensitivity to verbal or nonverbal cues essential to effective supervisor–trainee communication?

- Has the supervisor considered the appropriate and inappropriate use of the Internet to search for information regarding the trainee's ability to perform professionally related activities?

(b) Psychologists evaluate students and supervisees on the basis of their actual performance on relevant and established program requirements.

Fairness and justice require that academic and supervisory evaluations should never be based on student personal characteristics that have not been observed to affect their performance or that are outside the established bounds of program requirements.

☒ A psychologist learned from a member of the clinic staff that one of her supervisees had expressed harsh, racially prejudiced attitudes at a staff party. Over the course of the supervisory period, there was no evidence that the supervisee treated clients in a racially biased manner. However, in the final written evaluation, the psychologist reported that the supervisee appeared to have difficulty working with clients from other racial backgrounds.

☒ During a health psychology class discussion, an undergraduate student made disparaging remarks about individuals with mental disorders. Although the student had met all course requirements and his grade point average entitled him to a grade of B, the psychologist gave him a C+ because she felt his class comments indicated he had not really digested the material. However, the course outline did not indicate class participation would be included in the final grade.

Additional discussion regarding psychologists' ethical responsibilities during supervision can be found in the Hot Topic "Ethical Supervision of Trainees" at the end of this chapter.

7.07 Sexual Relationships With Students and Supervisees

Psychologists do not engage in sexual relationships with students or supervisees who are in their department, agency, or training center or over whom psychologists have or are likely to have evaluative authority. (See also Standard 3.05, Multiple Relationships.)

Having sexual relationships with students or supervisees is specifically prohibited by Standard 7.07. The student–professor/supervisor role is inherently asymmetrical in terms of power. Teachers and supervisors have the power to affect

student careers through grading, research and professional opportunities, letters of recommendation, scholarships and stipends, and reputation among other faculty or staff. Using this power to coerce or otherwise unduly influence a student to enter a sexual relationship is exploitative (Standard 3.08, Exploitative Relationships). The prohibition against sex with students and supervisees applies not only to those over whom the psychologist has evaluative or direct authority but also to anyone who is a student or supervisee in the psychologist's department, agency, or training center or over whom the psychologist might be likely to have evaluative authority in the program or supervised setting.

Sexual relationships with students and supervisees are a specific example of an unethical multiple relationship (Standard 3.05, Multiple Relationships). When psychologists enter into a sexual relationship with a student or supervisee, their ability to judge the student's/supervisee's academic, professional, or scientific performance objectively is impaired. In addition, when other students learn about such relationships, their knowledge can jeopardize the psychologist's ability to maintain an impression of professional impartiality. Furthermore, the behavior provides students with a model of unethical conduct that jeopardizes the psychologist's effectiveness as a teacher or supervisor. Such relationships also risk compromising psychologists' ability to exert appropriate authority or make objective evaluations regarding the student/supervisee and others with whom they work if the sexual partner can manipulate the psychologist through threats of exposure or complaints of misconduct.

In many psychology programs, graduate students serve as teaching or research assistants charged with evaluating undergraduate or graduate students' academic performance or supervising their research projects. Standard 7.07 applies to sexual relationships between graduate assistants and students when assistants are either student members of the American Psychology Association or their department has adopted the APA Ethics Code in its policies and procedures.

HOT TOPIC

Ethical Supervision of Trainees in Professional Psychology Programs

Supervision is a primary means by which students in professional psychology programs acquire and develop skills needed to provide effective and ethical mental health services (Shallcross, Johnson, & Lincoln, 2010). Competent and ethical supervision provides a foundation for the attitudes, skills, and commitment supervisees will need to know what is right and the motivation for self-evaluation and lifelong learning necessary to do what is right throughout their careers (see Chapter 3). The American Psychological Association (APA, 2011b), the Health Service Psychology Education Collaborative (2013), and proposed Standards for Accreditation for Health Service Providers (APA, 2015e) now include supervision as an essential competency for psychologists at the highest levels of the profession. Thus, psychology graduate students need to have training in supervisory competencies through classroom lectures and readings as well as learning through modeling the practices of their own supervisors.

Supervisors have a fiduciary obligation to their supervisees, the clients/patients under the supervisees' care, and the public (Principle B: Fidelity and Responsibility). They must (a) nurture the supervisees' professional skills and attitudes, (b) ensure that supervisees' clients/patients are provided appropriate mental health treatment, and (c) serve as gatekeepers who take appropriate actions to prevent supervisees not able to demonstrate the needed professional competence from entering the profession and practicing independently (Principle A: Beneficence and Nonmaleficence; Barnett & Molzon, 2014). Supervision should be marked by mutual respect, with supervisor and supervisee both contributing to the process of establishing goals and role responsibilities (Principle E: Respect for People's Rights and Dignity; Pettifor, McCarron, Schoepp, Stark, & Stewart, 2011). The goal of this Hot Topic is to describe the competencies needed to provide effective and ethical supervision, desired outcomes on which to fairly evaluate supervisee performance, and how trainees can contribute to their supervisory experience.

Competencies for Effective Supervision

Efforts to provide faculty with the skills necessary for competent supervision have not kept pace with psychology's growing commitment to a culture of competence in training and supervision (Standard 2.01, Boundaries of Competence; APA, 2011b). Competencies for effective supervision include professional knowledge and expertise and the interpersonal skills necessary to create a trusting supervisory alliance (Falender et al., 2004). A competence-based approach to supervision also requires techniques for successfully monitoring, assessing, and providing feedback to trainees and an emphasis on self-reflection and self-assessment on the part of supervisor and trainee (Kaslow, Falender, & Grus, 2012).

Professional Knowledge and Expertise

Supervisors must have the necessary clinical knowledge and expertise to identify client mental health needs within a diversity-sensitive context, guide supervisees in client-appropriate treatment techniques, and recognize when clients are not responding to supervisee interventions (Accurso, Taylor, & Garland, 2011). They must also be familiar with academic credit or credentialing supervision requirements, on-site institutional policies, and relevant laws as well as appropriate risk management strategies. Adequate preparation includes the following (see Baird, 2014; Barnett & Molzon, 2014; Moffett, Becker & Patton, 2014; Wise & Cellucci, 2014):

- Helping supervisees understand their obligations under HIPAA or FERPA policies and obtain the skills necessary to protect client/patient confidentiality when using different treatment modalities (e.g., group therapy, telehealth) and within interprofessional settings (Standards 3.09, Cooperation With Other Professionals; 6.01, Maintenance, Dissemination, and Dissemination of Confidential Records of Professional and Scientific Work; and 6.02, Maintenance, Dissemination, and Disposal of Confidential Records of Professional and Scientific Work).
- Discussing supervisees' legal and ethical obligations to determine whether disclosure of confidential information is necessary to protect clients/patients or third parties from harm and the importance of documenting the rationale and steps taken in deciding whether or not disclosure was required (Standards 4.01, Maintaining Confidentiality; 4.02, Discussing the Limits of Confidentiality).

(Continued)

(Continued)

- Being alert to potential boundary violations that may arise between supervisees and their clients/patients as well as within the supervisory relationship itself and the steps necessary to avoid exploitation, harm, and diminished objectivity (Standard 3.05, Multiple Relationships).
- Becoming aware of supervisees' personal problems or biases that may interfere with their ability to provide effective treatment and establishing a trusting relationship in which these problems or biases can be adequately addressed (Standard 2.06, Personal Problems and Conflicts).
- Preparing students for orderly and appropriate resolution of client responsibility when the training rotation ends (Standards 10.09, Interruption of Therapy; 10.10, Terminating Therapy).

Interpersonal Competencies

The supervisory context should encourage open discussion of treatment challenges and attempt to try new strategies by providing constructive feedback in a manner that minimizes trainee anxiety and decreased feelings of self-efficacy (Barnett et al., 2007; Daniels & Larson, 2001). At the same time, supervisors cannot shy away from providing negative feedback when it is necessary to ensure that clients are receiving adequate care; supervisors' evaluations of supervisee clinical acumen must be objective and in accord with the standards of the profession.

Diversity Competencies

There is increasing recognition that competent supervision requires sensitivity to the attitudes, values, and sociopolitical experiences of supervisees from diverse racial/ethnic, cultural, sexual minority, disability, social class, immigrant, and other groups, including when multiple identities intersect (Falender, Shafranske, & Falicov, 2014). The dynamic and continuously evolving nature of group identity and experiences requires supervisors to acquire the skills to engage in a collaborative process in which the effect of differing supervisor–supervisee worldviews is respectfully discussed (including targeted self-disclosure when appropriate), and the important role of diversity factors should be clearly introduced and reinforced throughout the supervision (Pettifor, Sinclair, & Falender, 2014). Competent diversity supervision also includes (a) recognizing factors of power, privilege, and personal bias that may be barriers to a trainee's full participation in the supervisory relationship; (b) being alert to the fact that trainees may be wary of honest engagement in the supervisory process based on previous training experiences that were diversity insensitive; (c) acquiring the skills to help trainees overcome past dignitary harms as well as the consequences of the supervisor's own actions that may result from diversity misunderstandings; (d) being mindful that through their supervision, they are modeling the ethical practice of diversity sensitivity for supervisees to apply to clinical work and future positions as supervisors (Falender et al., 2014; Fouad & Chavez-Korell, 2014).

Structuring the Supervisory Process

Structuring the supervisory process requires the ability to tailor training to the supervisee's level of competence, identify appropriate outcome measures for evaluation, and present clear standards for assessment. Both supervisors and supervisees need to be familiar with the APA core benchmark components (APA, 2011b) that their program has designated as appropriate for its training goals (see discussion under Standard 7.01, Design of Education and Training Programs).

Identifying Supervisee's Competencies

The goals and desired outcomes of a training experience need to be tailored to the supervisee's current competencies in relation to client needs and institutional requirements. To meet obligations to trainees and the trainees' clients, supervisors need to evaluate each supervisee's developing competence and the clinical responsibilities with which he or she can be entrusted (Falender & Shafranske, 2007; Standard 2.05, Delegation of Work to Others).

Identifying Appropriate Training Outcomes

Evaluations must be based on the supervisee's actual performance on relevant and established requirements (Standard 7.06, Assessing Student and Supervisee Performance). Falender and Shafranske (2007) identified the following general abilities by which the trainee's professional growth can be evaluated:

- Apply clinical knowledge and skills in a consistent fashion and incorporate new knowledge into existing competencies.
- Deal with increased confusions and varied situational aspects that shape clinical work.
- Respond to constructive feedback.
- Carry out recommendations to ensure adequate client care.
- Use problem-solving and clinical reasoning skills appropriate to specific clinical tasks and ethical challenges.
- Master technical and facilitative variables appropriate to the student's stage of training.

The APA also provides a "Competency Remediation Plan" template to assist supervisors and supervisees in planning and evaluating progress (http://www.apa.org/ed/graduate/competency.aspx). The plan begins with an identification of competency weaknesses, when the problem(s) was brought to the trainee's attention, steps already taken by the supervisor to address the problem(s), and steps already taken by the trainee to rectify the problem(s). This is followed by a written plan identifying the essential competency domain and problem behaviors, expectations for acceptable performance, trainee's and supervisee's responsibilities, a time frame for acceptable performance, assessment methods, and consequences for unsuccessful remediation.

Feedback and Evaluation

Standard 7.06 also requires that supervisors establish a timely and specific process for providing feedback to supervisees and explain the process to trainees at the beginning of supervision. This includes delineating setting-specific competencies the supervisee must attain for successful completion of the supervised interval (Falender & Shafranske, 2007).

Meaningful evaluations, scheduled at predetermined intervals, provide trainees with adequate time to improve their skills and the supervisor with opportunity to evaluate the trainee's responsiveness to

(Continued)

(Continued)

constructive feedback. When supervisees are unresponsive, fail to demonstrate needed competence, or exhibit impaired professional competence as a result of personal problems, these issues should be addressed in supervision, and the trainee should be provided reasonable opportunities for remediation or intervention. When necessary, the supervisor must act to prevent inappropriate actions resulting in poor-quality client care, violation of ethical standards, or harm to the institution through the supervisee's violation of policy or law. When appropriate, supervisors should inform their institution or the students' academic program and provide a written report documenting the reasons for their concerns (see Gizara & Forest, 2004).

Off-Site Supervision

Externships and internships in professional psychology programs are often off-site and supervised by nonfaculty members. Supervisors at practicum, externship, and internship sites need to provide supervisees with copies of the relevant institutional and agency policies and procedural manuals, including mandatory and discretionary reporting policies and steps to be taken in case of an emergency.

When applying for training at these sites, students should obtain the following information:

- Has the graduate program and externship training site entered into a formal relationship that includes articulation of specific training goals and standards, open communication between program faculty and on-site supervisors, and a system of formalized feedback from students regarding the quality of the training experience?
- Whom in their graduate program or externship or internship site can students go to if they have a problem with an off-site supervisor? Is there a formal complaint process?
- If a supervisor is providing inadequate training, will the department or training site assist the student in obtaining the necessary clinical experience and supervision?

Responsibilities of Supervisees

Self-reflection, ethical commitment, and the motivation to improve one's clinical knowledge and skills are fundamental to having a successful supervisory relationship. To help supervisors establish appropriate training experiences and evaluation criteria, supervisees should do the following:

- Be honest and open when asked to discuss their current level of clinical competence and training goals.
- Ask questions at the beginning of supervision to ensure that they clearly understand the goals of and evaluation process for the supervision and the criteria on which they will be assessed.
- Ask for all relevant information describing practicum, externship, or internship site institutional policies and legal responsibilities (e.g., HIPAA, FERPA, or ACA requirements; child abuse–reporting duties; policies regarding record creation, storage, and sharing of information with other professionals at the site).
- Come prepared with case material, questions, and other relevant materials for supervisory feedback and discussion.
- Be open to constructive feedback and integrate such feedback into subsequent clinical encounters.

- Be frank about and ask for guidance in addressing concerns regarding professional anxieties, personal biases, or lack of diversity training that may be a barrier to providing effective clinical services.
- Ask for guidance in cultivating patterns of self-care into their professional growth and development.
- Let their graduate program supervisor know if they are having difficulties in obtaining sufficient client/patient assignments or adequate on-site supervision at their practicum or externship site.
- Continue throughout the training experience to ask for additional or more focused training in a specific area of clinical or ethical concern, including asking the supervisor about APA Ethics Code requirements and how they relate to current treatment issues.

Chapter Cases and Ethics Discussion Questions

Dr. Kekoa is mentoring the dissertation of a psychology student who emails him that she has collected half of her dissertation data. She comes to his office to report that the preliminary analyses support her research hypotheses. He reviews the data and realizes that, in fact, the results are in the opposite direction of her hypotheses. He corrects her confusion about the type of statistical results that would support her thesis. Two months later, the student returns with her completed data collection, and this time the analysis indicates that all the data collected since their last conversation support the hypotheses. Dr. Kekoa is concerned that the student may be fabricating or biasing the data. Drawing on the ethical decision model in Chapter 3, how might Dr. Kekoa best approach this dilemma?

Dr. Braithwaite, a psychologist at a popular externship site, is conducting clinical supervision with Derek, a clinical graduate student with legal blindness. This is the first time Dr. Braithwaite has supervised a student with an apparent disability. She wants to ensure that Derek's clinical externship is a positive experience for him and his potential clients. She is unsure whether she should disclose Derek's disability to his potential clients before their first session so that clients who would be uncomfortable have the opportunity to request another therapist. Drawing on the Ethics Code Principles and relevant standards (i.e., Standards 2.01, Boundaries of Competence; 3.01, Unfair Discrimination; 3.04, Avoiding Harm; 7.06 Assessing Student and Supervisee Performance), discuss whether client preferences for practitioner attributes in general (e.g., race/ethnicity, gender, age, religion) and disability specifically should be considered in assigning trainees to clients (see also Taube & Olkin, 2011).

Dr. Yazzie conducts group supervision of graduate students who have placements in the counseling centers of a large multisite university. Students are required to make individual presentations and provide feedback on the presentations of other students on an online blog set up specifically for the purposes of the group supervision with the appropriate firewalls and other privacy protections. Supervisees often insert links to relevant materials in their shared reports and feedback. Dr. Yazzie notices that one of his supervisees, Jasmine, appears uncomfortable in group when other students discuss clinical issues involving client victims of abuse and often excuses herself to use the restroom. He reviews her online submissions and notices that they often emphasize the inadequacy of services for victims of abuse rather than specific clinical approaches and include a link to her personal blog @RecoveryTogether. Dr. Yazzie does not know whether he should read the blog links that Jasmine has provided to get a better sense of the student's professional development and personal reaction to abuse-related clinical issues. Discuss the best approach to this ethical dilemma drawing on Standards 7.04, Student Disclosure of Personal Information; 7.06, Assessing Student and Supervisee Performance, the sections on "Digital Ethics"; and the Hot Topic on supervision in this chapter.

CHAPTER 11

Standards on Research and Publication

8. Research and Publication

8.01 Institutional Approval

When institutional approval is required, psychologists provide accurate information about their research proposals and obtain approval prior to conducting the research. They conduct the research in accordance with the approved research protocol.

The Nuremberg Code (1949), the first international document establishing participant rights in research, was created in response to the notorious involvement of German Nazi doctors in medical research on concentration camp prisoners without the prisoners' consent. In the United States, however, regulations protecting the rights of human research participants did not emerge until the late 1970s, following the 1972 public disclosure of the government-sponsored Tuskegee Syphilis Study. In this 30-year study, 399 African American rural men were left untreated for diagnosed syphilis even after effective antibiotics became available (Jones, 1993). Over time, the US Code of Federal Regulations Title 45, Part 46, Protection of Human Subjects (DHHS, 2009) has undergone a number of additions and now includes a general section on research protections (Subpart A, known as the Common Rule) and subsections specifically detailing special protections for pregnant women, fetuses, and neonates (Subpart B), prisoners (Subpart C), and children (Subpart D).

Under these regulations, IRBs are charged with ensuring that investigators protect the rights and welfare of research participants. Specific IRB requirements reflect three general moral principles proposed in the landmark Belmont Report written by the National Commission for the Protection of Human Subjects of Biomedical and Behavioral Research (NIH, 1979): beneficence, justice, and respect.

These principles are also incorporated into the APA Ethics Code (see Principle A: Beneficence and Nonmaleficence, Principle D: Justice, and Principle E: Respect for People's Rights and Dignity). The ideals reflected in the principle of beneficence require IRBs to ensure that research is designed to maximize benefits for science, humanity, and research participants and to avoid or minimize risk or harm. Applied to the research context, the moral principle of justice means that IRBs must ensure that investigators equitably select participants and that the potential benefits and burdens of research participation are fairly distributed among persons and diverse groups. The moral principle of respect for personhood requires IRBs to ensure that informed consent and confidentiality procedures protect the autonomy and privacy rights of participants.

Need to Know: Proposed Changes to Federal Regulations

On July 26, 2011, the Office of Human Research Protections (OHRP) published a call for comments on a proposal for changes to the major section of federal regulations (45 CFR 46) governing how IRBs operate to protect human subjects in research. This section is called the "Common Rule," and there have been no modifications since it was originally adopted in 1981. On October 8, 2015, OHRP published a revised draft in response to comments received and called for additional comments (Federal Register, 2015). The purpose of the proposed changes is to reduce the burden on investigators and IRBs and to enhance protections for research participants by better calibrating IRB reviews to the level of research risk. Proposed changes include the following:

- A new category of low-risk interventions that would be "excluded" from IRB review as determined by the investigator
- Expansion of the categories of research determined by an IRB to be "exempt" from Common Rule requirements
- Clarification of "minimal risk" studies eligible for expedited review
- Reduction of IRB burden by eliminating the requirement for continued review in the data analysis and clinical follow-up stages of research
- A streamlining of the informed consent process to increase clarity and reduce extraneous information and posting consent forms on a government website to increase transparency
- Permit "broad consent" for the storage or maintenance of biospecimens and identifiable private information for secondary research use
- A mandate that multisite research studies must rely on a single IRB
- Redefinition of *human subjects* to include biospecimens and increased protection for collection and storage of identifiable genetic data
- Expansion of the scope of the rule to cover all clinical trials conducted at any US institution receiving federal funding for nonexempt human subjects research, regardless of funding sources

The changes, if adopted, will expand the type of minimal-risk social science research studies that can be excluded or exempted from IRB review (National Research Council, 2014). Readers can stay up-to-date on the proposed change process through the OHRP website at http://www.hhs.gov/ohrp/index.html.

Four Requirements of Standard 8.01

Standard 8.01 of the APA Ethics Code (APA, 2010b) has four basic requirements. First, psychologists must know whether and from whom institutional approval is required. All institutions receiving federal funding for biomedical or behavioral research are required to establish IRBs to protect the rights and safety of research participants. Institutions must also follow federal, state, and local laws requiring the review and regulation of research involving animal subjects. In addition, many social welfare agencies, health care facilities, schools, correctional facilities, businesses, and other public and private organizations have their own internal review requirements for research.

The remaining three requirements within the standard are that applications for institutional review must be accurate, approval must be obtained before the research is conducted, and research procedures must follow the approved protocol. Failure to meet any of these conditions violates this standard. It is not unusual for methods to be modified during different phases of research. Any changes in participant informed consent language or procedures, compensation, confidentiality protections, or methods that increase human or animal participant risk or safety should be resubmitted for institutional approval prior to implementation. Psychologists should consult the appropriate IRB about the need to provide an informative memo or to resubmit proposals for minor changes unrelated to participant protections or welfare.

Implications of HIPAA

Investigators conducting program evaluation or archival research involving protected health information (PHI) as defined under HIPAA should be aware that institutions, health plans, or providers who have obtained the information in many instances must have a waiver from either an IRB or a "privacy board" before they may provide such information to an investigator without specific written patient authorization. (For additional information on when a researcher is affected by HIPAA regulations, see "A Word About HIPAA" in the preface to this book.)

Need to Know: Submitting Successful IRB Proposals

The diversity of expertise and wide latitude in decision making given to individual IRBs under federal regulations can be intimidating to psychologists new to the process. As a first step, psychologists should familiarize themselves with federal regulations and the Office for Human Research Protection's "Frequently Asked Questions" site (http://www.hhs.gov/ohrp/policy/faq/index.html). *The Research Protocol Ethics Assessment Tool* (RePEAT; Roberts, 1999) provides a useful checklist that can be adapted to evaluate a protocol's scientific merit, its

(Continued)

(Continued)

risks and benefits, the scientific and clinical expertise needed to adequately protect participants, the characteristics of participants that may affect informed consent capacity, the appropriateness of incentives, and the adequacy of confidentiality protections. Additional ways to make the IRB submission process less daunting and increase the probability of successful review include the following:

- Provide a scientific justification for the research. A common error in IRB submissions is omitting an explanation of the scientific justification for the study based on the erroneous assumption that IRBs are not responsible for evaluating scientific merit. Although IRBs should never take on the role of a scientific peer review panel, they are obligated to consider scientific validity in order to evaluate the potential ratio of research benefits to participant risks.
- Monetary or other compensation is not a research benefit. When describing research benefits, be aware that the Office for Human Research Protections (http://www.hhs.gov/ohrp/policy/faq/index.html) has interpreted federal regulations as prohibiting investigators from describing participant compensation as a benefit when obtaining informed consent (see Standard 8.06, Offering Inducements for Research Participation).
- Justify requests for expedited review. Under "expedited" review procedures, protocol evaluation may be carried out by the IRB chairperson or designee in lieu of full board review if the research involves no more than "minimal risk" or consists of only minor changes to previously approved research (45 CFR 46.102i, 46.110). Psychologists should be familiar with the federal definition of minimal risk and provide IRBs with documentation supporting the minimal risk designation for their research design and population (http://www.hhs.gov/ohrp/humansubjects/guidance/45cfr46.html). Helpful guidance with examples of research meeting "*minimal risk* requirements" includes the following: Part (C) of the "Categories of Research That May Be Reviewed by the Institutional Review Board (IRB) Through Expedited Review" (63 FR 60364–60367, November 9, 1998); Proposed Revisions to the Common Rule for the Protection of Human Subjects in the Behavioral and Social Sciences (NRC, 2014); and the DHHS Secretary's Advisory Committee on Human Research Protections (http://www.hhs.gov/ohrp/sachrp/; Fisher et al., 2007).
- Be familiar with institutional policies that may or may not require review of student-conducted psychology laboratory course experiments.
- Stay current with changes in federal regulations that may increase categories of low-risk research excluded or exempted from IRB review and associated changes in investigator requirements for implementing appropriate and reasonable safeguards (see Need to Know: Proposed Changes to Federal Regulations earlier in this chapter).

8.02 Informed Consent to Research

(a) When obtaining informed consent as required in Standard 3.10, Informed Consent, psychologists inform participants about (1) the purpose of the research, expected duration, and procedures; (2) their right to decline to participate and to withdraw from the research once participation has begun; (3) the foreseeable consequences of declining or withdrawing; (4) reasonably foreseeable factors that may be expected to influence their willingness to participate such as potential risks, discomfort, or adverse effects; (5) any prospective research benefits; (6) limits of confidentiality; (7) incentives for participation; and (8) whom to contact for questions about the research and research participants' rights. They provide opportunity for the prospective participants to ask questions and receive answers. (See also Standards 8.03, Informed Consent for Recording Voices and Images in Research; 8.05, Dispensing With Informed Consent for Research; and 8.07, Deception in Research.)

Ensuring Consent Is Informed, Rational, and Voluntary

Within the context of research, informed consent requirements reflect Principle E: Respect for People's Rights and Dignity by ensuring that individuals' decision to participate is informed, voluntary, and rational. To comply with this standard, psychologists must obtain and document written or oral consent in the manner set forth in Standard 3.10, Informed Consent. The informed component of consent requires that individuals are provided all the pertinent information needed to make a reasoned choice about whether they wish to participate in a study. This includes providing information in a language and at a language level understood by prospective participants and, where applicable, their legally authorized representative. When obtaining guardian permission and participant assent for research involving populations that do not speak English or for whom English is a second language, psychologists should be alert to the possibility that prospective participants and their legal guardians may have different language preferences and proficiencies (APA, 2003; Council of National Psychological Associations for the Advancement of Ethnic Minority Interests, 2000; Fisher et al., 2002). Psychologists employing research assistants to translate consent forms or obtain informed consent from non-English-speaking participants are responsible for ensuring that employees are sufficiently trained to adequately protect participants' rights (Standard 2.05, Delegation of Work to Others).

✓ A psychologist sought to conduct a study on perceived racial/ethnic discrimination among graduate students at a university with a large number of students who had emigrated from Vietnam. While courses at the university were given in English, the psychologist knew that there was great diversity in English proficiency among the Vietnamese students. She created consent forms written in English on one side and Vietnamese on the other side. The psychologist met frequently with the language expert hired for the Vietnamese translation to ensure that the expert understood the elements of informed consent that needed to be communicated to prospective participants.

Describing the Nature of Participation

Prospective participants and, when appropriate, their legal guardians must be given information and the opportunity to ask questions about the purpose, duration, procedures, foreseeable risks, potential benefits, and compensation involved in participation. The information obtained must be sufficient to make an informed decision.

Need to Know: When Does Informed Consent Begin and End?

According to the recent Department of Health and Human Services *Draft Guidance on Informed Consent Information Sheet* (DHHS, 2014; http://www.fda.gov/downloads/RegulatoryInformation/Guidances/UCM405006.pdf) for research regulated by the FDA (e.g., the testing of new psychopharmaceutical agents), informed consent begins at recruitment and includes advertising used to recruit for a clinical trial. In addition, informed consent must be considered an ongoing process that does not end with the signing of a document. Thus, beginning with recruitment and throughout the study, investigators need to ensure that prospective participants are provided appropriate information to make decisions to learn more about the study, to agree to initial participation, and to determine whether they wish to continue or withdraw.

Compensation

Prospective participants must also be informed about the conditions under which they will qualify for partial or full compensation for participation or continuation of experimental interventions if they withdraw from the study (see Standard 8.06, Offering Inducements for Research Participation).

⊘ A health psychologist was conducting a study on the impact of nutritional knowledge and food resources on eating habits in economically marginalized communities. The study required participants to maintain weekly food diaries as well as meet for weekly interviews over a 5-week period. During informed consent, the researcher carefully explained that participants would receive $20 dollars for each of the 5 weekly diaries submitted and $20 for each weekly interview they attended. The investigator emphasized that payment for the diaries and interviews would be considered separately (i.e., if they did not keep a diary for the week but attended an interview, they would be paid $20 for the interview) and if they missed a week, they could continue in the study. This information was repeated each time participants came in for their interviews.

The Right to Decline or Withdraw Participation

Consent procedures must directly inform participants that they will not be penalized for declining or withdrawing from participation, especially when the prospective participant has reason to believe that dissent may result in adverse consequences (see Standards 8.02b, Informed Consent to Research, and 8.04, Client/Patient, Student, and Subordinate Research Participants). Institutional populations are particularly vulnerable to involuntary participation in research. Prisoners and youth held for brief periods in detention centers, for example, are highly vulnerable because of their restricted autonomy and liberty, often compounded by their low socioeconomic status, poor education, and poor health (Gostin, 2007). Incarcerated persons have few expectations regarding privacy protections and may view research participation as a means of seeking favor with or avoiding punishment from prison or detention guards or officials (see also Standard 3.08, Exploitative Relationships; DHHS, 2009, Subpart C).

Confidentiality

Disclosure of confidential information can result in criminal or civil liability or financial or social damage to participants. Informed consent procedures must provide a clear explanation of the extent and limits of confidentiality, including (a) whether investigators must comply with reporting requirements such as mandated child abuse and elder abuse reporting or duty-to-warn laws; (b) the investigator's confidentiality and disclosure policy for responses, indicating that a participant or another person is in immediate danger or otherwise at a high level of risk; and (c) whether the method of data collection itself may limit the extent of confidentiality protections, as may be the case when research is conducted via the Internet (see discussions of confidentiality in research in Chapter 7 under Standards 4.01, Maintaining Confidentiality; 4.02, Discussing the Limits of Confidentiality; and 4.05, Disclosures). Readers may also wish to refer to the Hot Topic "Informational Risk and Disclosure of Genetic Information to Research Participants" at the end of this chapter.

Digital Ethics: Confidentiality and Informed Consent for Facebook-Based Research

Facebook is increasingly used as a powerful platform for social science research. It allows for selective recruiting through targeted advertising to individuals and the mining of vast stores of data about both individuals who agree to participate in research and those in their social network. Although informed consent may not be required for research involving Facebook profile and other information approved by the user for public posting, it is required for studies that utilize the Facebook platform for the collection of survey, focus group, or other forms of data collected specifically for research purposes.

(Continued)

(Continued)

Informed consent for research involving the collection of nonpublic Facebook data should include clear details on the nature of information that will be extracted, who will have access to the data, *and* how participants can best use Facebook privacy options to limit investigator access to non-research-related data and to preclude members of their social network from being aware of their participation in a study and accessing any data that may be produced. The Facebook pages of users who consent to participation will contain comments and pictures of Facebook friends and others who are not participants. Kosinski, Matz, Gosling, Popov, and Stillwell (2015) suggested that such nonparticipant data could be used without consent if third party identifiers are not collected and if collected in the aggregate with the purpose of extracting knowledge about consenting participants, such as their popularity or social activity (Standards 4.02, Discussing the Limits of Confidentiality; 8.05, Dispensing With Informed Consent).

☒ A psychologist began conducting a survey study over the Internet on marital conflict. She posted an explanation of the study on a university website. Those who wished to participate were asked to copy and then paste the questions and answers into an email response to the psychologist. The website claimed that participant responses were anonymous and thus there were no risks to confidentiality. However, this was not true since the responses were embedded in the email and therefore linked to respondents' identifying email addresses. The psychologist did not realize her error until she discovered that her research assistants had identified a faculty member as one of the respondents as they were coding the data.

The Certificate of Confidentiality

Investigators working with vulnerable populations can apply to the Department of Health and Human Services (DHHS) to obtain a Certificate of Confidentiality (CoC) (http://www.hhs.gov/ohrp/policy/certconf.html). The CoC protects investigators from being forced or compelled by law enforcement or subpoena to disclose personally identifiable research information that could place participants in legal jeopardy or damage their financial standing, employability, insurability, or reputation (http://grants.nih.gov/grants/policy/coc/faqs.htm#367). Investigators who use a CoC must include this information in their informed consent using DHHS-approved language describing the extent of protection and the fact that the CoC does not cover subpoenas related to legal investigations of child abuse. The CoC does not prohibit investigators from voluntarily disclosing confidential information. If investigators who have acquired a CoC intend to make certain voluntary disclosures to protect the research participant or others from harm (see Standard 4.05, Disclosures), the consent form should detail the types of information that will be disclosed.

☒ The consent form used by a psychologist conducting a year long community-based study on membership in urban gangs included a statement that a Certificate of Confidentiality had been obtained that protected the psychologist from being compelled by law enforcement to reveal information regarding illegal drug activities of participants. The consent form did not specify that the psychologist would voluntarily disclose confidential information to protect participants or others from harm. During the course of the study, the psychologist informed local police when he learned during an interview that several participants were planning to set fire to a school playground over the weekend. While some participants were grateful the fire was prevented, they all felt that the psychologist had violated the informed consent agreement and refused to continue participation in the study.

Need to Know: Legal Challenges to the Certificate of Confidentiality

Although the CoC is presumed to offer strong privacy protections, case law has been variable on the extent of protection offered (*State of North Carolina v. Bradley*, 2006; Wolf et al., 2012), and future cases may rest on whether a defendant's constitutional rights are privileged over statutory protections offered by the CoC, especially within the context of government's increasingly broad legal powers to obtain confidential information since 9/11 (Beskow, Dame, & Costello, 2008). Investigators should be aware that refusal of court orders may result in fines or a finding of contempt for research institutions or investigators (see Standards 1.02, Conflicts Between Ethics and Law, Regulations, and Other Governing Legal Authority; 4.05, Disclosures). In addition to acquiring a CoC, psychologists collecting sensitive data for populations who are at higher risk for court or government requests for information should consider additional data protections, including de-identification or destruction of data as soon as scientifically feasible and in accord with record-keeping responsibilities, and describing such protections during informed consent (Standards 4.01, Maintaining Confidentiality; 4.02, Discussing the Limits of Confidentiality; 6.02, Maintenance, Dissemination, and Disposal of Confidential Records of Professional and Scientific Work).

Adults With Questionable Capacity to Consent

The rational component of informed consent requires that prospective participants be able to understand the information presented. Psychologists often conduct research involving adult populations with questionable consent capacity. The rational decision-making capacity of active drug users, for example, will vary with their state of intoxication or withdrawal (Fisher, 2004; Jeste & Saks, 2006). The consent capacity of adults with schizophrenia and related disorders is often transient depending on whether they are in an acute stage, remission, or responding positively or negatively to medication. Elder adults or individuals with Alzheimer's may also have fluctuating or decreasing ability to understand consent information. General requirements for informed consent detailed in Standard 3.10b, Informed Consent, require that psychologists provide appropriate explanations and obtain assent for research participation from persons legally incapable of informed consent and, when required or permissible, obtain appropriate permission from a legally authorized person. When consent capacity of a participant population is known to be questionable, psychologists should use available assessment techniques to determine the ability of prospective participants to understand the nature of and their rights in research and when possible implement procedures to enhance their understanding (see, e.g., APA, 2012d; Appelbaum & Grisso, 2001; Carpenter et al., 2000; Fisher, 2010; Fisher et al., 2006). Readers may also want to consult the Hot Topic "Goodness-of-Fit Ethics for Informed Consent to Research and Treatment Involving Adults With Impaired Decisional Capacity" in Chapter 6).

Need to Know: NIH Points to Consider for Research Involving Adults With Cognitive Impairments

At present, no specific federal regulations govern research involving adults with schizophrenia, developmental disabilities, dementia, or other disorders characterized by permanent or transient cognitive impairments. However, the NIH has developed an interim list of points to consider (http://grants2.nih.gov/grants/policy/questionablecapacity.htm). To facilitate IRB review, psychologists should show evidence that their consent procedures

- are consistent with legal, psychological, and ethical criteria for determining consent capacity;
- are sensitive to differing and fluctuating levels of capacity;
- are tailored to the specific research context;
- are timed to avoid periods of heightened vulnerability;
- include information, when relevant, on when and from whom surrogate consent will be sought; and
- are repeated when studies are longitudinal or when cognitive status has changed.

✓ A psychologist was conducting a study on language skills involving adults with moderate intellectual and developmental disabilities (IDDs) living in community group residences. Some of the prospective participants had a parent or sibling who was their legal guardian. The psychologist obtained signed permission from all legal guardians followed by the signed assent of individuals who wished to participate. Other prospective participants had maintained the legal right to consent to decisions affecting their lives, but such decisions were often made in collaboration with residence staff and family. The psychologist obtained signed consent from all adults with IDD who had the legal right to consent. Letters describing the study also were sent in advance to the family members on whom these individuals relied for support in decision making. In all situations, the psychologist did not attempt to obtain consent from a prospective participant until after a resident staff member had confirmed that the individual wanted to be approached.

Parental Permission and Child Assent to Pediatric Clinical Trials

Designing appropriate parental permission and child assent procedures is an ongoing challenge for psychologists conducting clinical trials for children's mental health disorders. Consent procedures require sensitivity to family stress associated with the child's cognitive and emotional maturity and treatment needs, the parent–child relationship, and potential parent–child disputes regarding participation (Joffe et al., 2006). Under US federal regulations, the assent requirement may be waived when the child's age, maturity, psychological state, or health status indicates an inability to provide informed or rational assent or when the research offers a benefit to the health of the child that cannot be obtained through treatment outside the context of research (DHHS, 2009, 45 CFR 46.408). In the latter condition, guardian permission overrides child dissent to participate. Consequently, children should never be asked to assent or dissent to participation if their choice will not be respected. In such situations, when it is in the child's best interest, he or she may have his or her opinions sought and considered but be made aware that the parents will make the final decision (Masty & Fisher, 2008).

The decision to obtain child assent for pediatric clinical trials requires careful reflection on the goodness of fit between the research design and children's assent capacity as well as a balancing of respect for the child's developing autonomy and parents' duty and responsibility to make decisions in their child's best interest (Fisher, 2005a, 2015; Fisher & Masty, 2006; Masty & Fisher, 2008).

When deciding whether it is ethically appropriate to obtain child assent in pediatric clinical trials, psychologists should consider the following:

- To what extent does the complexity of the research design fit the child's current experience and cognitive capacity to understand information essential to a participation decision? Can the language level and content of the assent be sufficiently modified to enhance this understanding?
- What is the child's current understanding and appreciation of his or her mental health status and treatment needs, and how would this affect his or her reaction to information provided during assent?

- Which aspects of the research setting (e.g., a hospital) or nature of the research (e.g., use of a placebo or treatment as usual control group) may create participant stress or affect the child's or parent's understanding of the voluntary nature of participation and the distinction between research and treatment?
- What is the family's history of shared decision making for the child's health-related matters, and how might this affect the child's emotional readiness and willingness to make a participation decision?
- How might the child's behavioral problems that brought the family to the research yield different parent and child reactions to information about the study, especially when the disorder to be treated has been associated with family conflict?
- Does the research offer a benefit to the health of the child that cannot be obtained through treatment outside the context of research?

Digital Ethics: Documentation of Informed Consent for Internet Research

The absence of direct, in-person contact for Internet research raises concerns regarding verification of identity (e.g., ensuring participants are of legal age), ensuring comprehension, and obtaining appropriate documentation when needed. According to the DHHS Secretary's Advisory Committee on Human Research Protections (SACHRP, 2013), adequate identity verification may often be handled by the host provider (or may not be necessary if research poses minimal risk), comprehension can be addressed by quizzes embedded in consent information, and documentation of consent can be obtained through a check box indicating agreement with consent information or through electronic signatures when necessary (e.g., when research poses greater than minimal risk). In some cases, the posted recruitment information can include a link for potential participants to permit a member of the research team to contact them by phone to conduct screening and informed consent. As with in-person minimal risk research, documentation of and other elements of informed consent (e.g., guardian permission) can be waived (Standard 8.05, Dispensing With Informed Consent). For all Internet-based research, the consent process should include explanations of how data are maintained, ranging from individually identifiable to aggregate forms, and what linking or re-identification measures are possible (Standard 4.02, Discussing the Limits of Confidentiality).

Research Involving US Tribal Nations or International Research

Research Involving US American Indian and Alaskan Native Tribes

When conducting research involving American Indian and Alaskan Native communities, tribal law and traditions sometimes require investigators to obtain permission from tribal leaders (Lakes et al., 2012; Mohatt & Thomas, 2006; Noe et al., 2006; Pearson, Parker, Fisher, & Moreno, 2014) or the village council before researchers can approach individual tribal or community members. Obtaining tribal leaders' permission to recruit individuals for research participation should not be confused with or compromise individual consent. After gaining tribal permission, investigators should approach each individual member and implement consent procedures that ensure that agreement to participate is informed, rational, and voluntary.

International Research

In some developing nations, an investigator may be required to obtain permission from a woman's husband, father, or other male relative before she can be approached for research participation. In such situations, similar protections must be put in place to ensure that the woman's consent is informed and voluntary (NBAC, 2001; Pratt & Loff, 2011). Research should never be conducted in communities where the political structure or power imbalances based on gender compromise the voluntary requirement of consent by placing pressure on individuals to participate or when such procedures will justify or defend the violation of human rights (Standards 1.02, Conflicts Between Ethics and Law, Regulations, or Other Governing Legal Authority; 3.08, Exploitative Relationships).

In international mental health research, the investigator and participant community may differ in their concepts of physical, informational, and decisional privacy (Goldman & Choy, 2001). In some communities with living arrangements and cultural values emphasizing community openness and family interdependence, participants may question the motives of an investigator who attempts to protect privacy by conducting research interviews in a secluded area and in the absence of family members (Monshi & Zieglmayer, 2004). In cross-cultural research, therefore, it is important to determine how the participant population defines and values privacy, design confidentiality procedures to reflect these values, and clarify during informed consent how confidentiality safeguards have been selected to respect community values and fulfill investigators' ethical responsibilities.

Community Consultation

Community consultation is an essential step in identifying and avoiding potential ethical pitfalls of informed consent when the research population will be selected on the basis of health, social, economic, legal, or other vulnerabilities. *Community* can refer to individuals of a common geographic area, economic status, ethnic group, or religion (Weijer & Emanuel, 2000). However, within these larger definitions of communities are subgroups who share similar mental health disorders or are confronting similar barriers to employment, education, housing, or quality health care. When these subgroups are the focus of research, their interests may not be congruent with those of the larger community (Dickert & Sugarman, 2005; Fisher et al., 2002; Macklin, 1999). Principle D: Justice requires that the design of informed consent information adequately reflect the research risks and benefits of participants who are marginalized within their communities. Seeking community consultation and establishing community advisory boards (CABs) thus requires an understanding of the social structures and relationships that define the particular community and identification of persons who can best represent participants' research-relevant concerns (E. E. Anderson et al., 2012; DuBois et al., 2011; Fisher et al., 2002).

☒ Researchers interested in testing an afterschool assertiveness training program for fifth- and sixth-grade victims of school bullying convened a CAB composed of school administrators, school counselors, and teachers. The CAB did not have a parent member. The CAB strongly supported the goals of the research and suggested that to reach as many children as possible, parental permission and assent forms be distributed to all fifth and sixth graders. Less than 5% of permission forms were returned. The investigators later learned that their recruitment strategy had failed because parents of the children were afraid that since all students knew the purpose of the afterschool program, participation would increase stigmatization and bullying by those not in the program.

Informed Consent for Qualitative Research

The open-ended nature of ethnographic, phenomenological, and participant observation studies can make it difficult to anticipate the exact nature of information that may be gained through participant–investigator interactions. The focus on discovering emergent themes in qualitative research means that investigators do not always know beforehand privacy and confidentiality issues that may emerge during the course of research (Fisher, 2004; Sanjari, Bahramnezhad, Fomani, Shoghi, & Chiraghi, 2014). Investigators should alert the prospective participant to this possibility during informed consent, monitor verbal or behavioral information during the course of the study, and remind the participant about confidentiality protections and limitations when unexpected subjects arise (Standard 4.02, Discussing the Limits of Confidentiality). If a new direction of inquiry emerges that might be in conflict with a participant's confidentiality expectations, this should be identified and the participant given the opportunity to reconsent. In observational field studies involving drug use or other illegal behaviors, an agreement can be reached during informed consent about which activities will and will not be asked or witnessed (Singer et al., 2000).

Implications of HIPAA

Data generated by a research study that is placed in a participant's health records or otherwise used or disclosed for treatment or payment for health services are considered PHI under HIPAA. Researchers on the staff of a covered entity (e.g., a medical center) must comply with HIPAA regulations. Researchers who are using or creating PHI but are not on the staff of a covered entity are considered *business associates* and must provide the covered entity a written assurance that they will comply with HIPAA standards. HIPAA often does not apply to health-related data generated solely for research purposes if these data will not be shared with participants or third parties, will not be included in participants' health records, and will not be collected on behalf of a covered entity.

Authorization and Revocation of the Use of PHI for Research Purposes

HIPAA permits covered entities to transmit PHI to researchers if (a) a patient or his or her legal guardian signs an authorization to release information that is project specific (*not* a general authorization for use of PHI for future unspecified research); (b) an IRB or privacy board approves in writing a waiver of the requirement for such authorization and the investigator provides the covered entity with written assurances that HIPAA-compliant procedures are in place to protect confidentiality; or (c) the records are de-identified, as specifically defined by HIPAA regulations.

Additional HIPAA regulations specific to research include the following:

- Authorization for the creation, use, or disclosure of PHI for research purposes is combined with informed consent information and other types of written permission for the same research.
- If the PHI already has been collected during the study and used on the basis of the original authorization, participants do *not* have the right to revoke the use of their PHI from further data analysis, although no additional information may be used or disclosed following revocation.
- Intervention research is one of the few conditions in which HIPAA permits the offer of treatment to be conditioned upon authorization for PHI to be used for study purposes.

Health Records Research

HIPAA is also relevant for research psychologists conducting record review or archival research on PHI collected by social services agencies, hospitals, or other health care or service provider institutions. With some exceptions, covered entities can allow investigators access to PHI only if the covered entity obtains authorization by the client/patient or a legally authorized representative to release PHI for the specific research purpose and to the specific investigator or investigative team. Whenever a covered entity releases PHI to an investigator, the covered entity is required to disclose only the "minimum necessary" to reasonably achieve the purpose of the disclosure (see also Standard 4.04, Minimizing Intrusions on Privacy).

Implications of Protection of Pupil Rights Amendment for US Department of Education–Funded Research

The Protection of Pupil Rights Amendment (PPRA) of 2004 (http://www2.ed.gov/policy/gen/guid/fpco/ppra/index.html) seeks to ensure that certain instructional materials used in connection with the US Department of Education–funded survey, analysis, or evaluation of students are available for inspection by parents and that written parental permission is obtained before minor students participate in such research. The types of materials to which PPRA applies include the following:

- Political affiliations
- Mental and psychological problems potentially embarrassing to the student and his or her family
- Sexual behaviors and attitudes
- Illegal, antisocial, self-incriminating, and demeaning behaviors
- Critical appraisals of other individuals with whom respondents have close family relationships
- Legally recognized privileged or analogous relationships, such as those of lawyers, physicians, and ministers
- Income (other than that required by law to determine eligibility for participation in a program or for receiving financial assistance under such programs)

(b) Psychologists conducting intervention research involving the use of experimental treatments clarify to participants at the outset of the research (1) the experimental nature of the treatment; (2) the services that will or will not be available to the control group(s) if appropriate; (3) the means by which assignment to treatment and control groups will be made; (4) available treatment alternatives if an individual does not wish to participate in the research or wishes to withdraw once a study has begun; and (5) compensation for or monetary costs of participating including, if appropriate, whether reimbursement from the participant or a third-party payor will be sought. (See also Standard 8.02a, Informed Consent to Research.)

This standard governs research on behavioral, psychosocial, biomedical, psychopharmacological, or other interventions involving individuals, families, groups, or communities.

Explanation About Control Groups and Methods of Assignment to Treatment Conditions

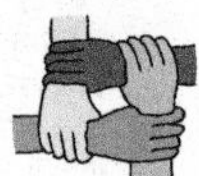

The principles of good scientific design often require investigators to (a) assign some participants to control group conditions as a point of comparison for the experimental treatment (between-group designs) or (b) vary the treatment and control conditions for individual participants (within-group designs). Control conditions may consist of participants receiving different levels of the investigational intervention, a treatment of documented effectiveness, currently available services

(treatment as usual), a placebo, or no treatment. Provisions 2 and 3 of Standard 8.02b require that informed consent adequately describe the nature, potential risks, and probable benefits of control group assignment, as well as how assignment to experimental group and control group conditions will be made. When appropriate, the nature of random assignment should be explained in language that can be understood by individuals unfamiliar with the scientific method. Informed consent for studies using single- or double-blind procedures should describe the extent to which participants and members of the treatment and research teams will know which group the participant has been assigned to and steps that will be taken to determine if and how the blind will be broken.

CASE EXAMPLE

Consent to Random Assignment

A new medication approved for obsessive–compulsive disorder was associated with uncomfortable side effects that led some patients to discontinue the treatment. To reduce the severity of these side effects, prescribing psychologists designed a study to evaluate the efficacy of different dosing levels. The within-subjects design required that participants who would ordinarily meet criteria for taking the medication would be given 2 weeks of each of four experimental conditions (placebo and three different dosages of the medication). In addition, all participants would receive weekly medical examinations, behavioral assessments, and mental health counseling. The informed consent explained how the order of these conditions would be randomly assigned for each participant and that neither the participant nor the mental health providers who saw the participants weekly would know which treatment condition the participant was receiving during any 2-week period. The consent form further explained that the mental health staff would be carefully monitoring participants' mental health status and, if there was evidence of significant deterioration in mental health status, the "blind" for that participant would be broken, the participant withdrawn from the study, and appropriate treatment provided.

Addressing the "Therapeutic Misconception"

Appelbaum, Roth, and Lidz (1982) coined the term *therapeutic misconception* to describe two common but incorrect beliefs held by participants regarding intervention research that randomly assigns participants to experimental treatment and control groups: (1) that their individualized needs will be taken into account in condition assignment and (b) that there is a high probability that they will benefit from research participation (see also Appelbaum, Lidz, & Grisso, 2004). These misconceptions may be due to poorly implemented informed consent, underestimation of risks or dispositional optimism on the part of a participant, and different cognitive "mind-sets" for planned actions, and they may be compounded by therapeutic mistrust in underserved or marginalized populations (Fisher, Oransky, et al., 2009; Jansen, 2014).

Standard 8.02b requires that psychologists address such potential misconceptions during informed consent. The first provision, clarifying the experimental nature of the treatment, requires that informed consent procedures address the general misconception that "experimental" treatment means "better" treatment with known direct benefits for participants. The primary goal of intervention research is to provide generalizable information on whether a particular type of intervention is successful. Depending on the stage of research, an untested experimental treatment may place participants at greater risk than a no-treatment or treatment-as-usual condition. Most important, psychologists must take reasonable steps to communicate to prospective participants that the purpose of conducting treatment research is to determine whether a treatment works or how it works in comparison to another treatment (Fried & Fisher, 2008).

This standard does not prevent psychologists from describing direct benefits that may be derived from participation, such as (a) access to new experimental treatments not yet available for general use, (b) receipt of the experimental treatment if it proves effective during or following the conclusion of the study, (c) comprehensive psychological assessment and monitoring, (d) treatment referrals, or (e) upon participant-signed authorization, the forwarding of a summary of the participant's response to the treatment conditions to a qualified mental health professional.

⊘ A team of developmental psychologists designed an innovative prevention study to determine whether integrating readings on alcohol use and abuse into 11th-grade English and biology classes would more effectively reduce use of alcohol than the 2-week section on substance abuse currently taught in the 10th-grade health course. The district superintendent gave the investigators permission to randomly assign the 10 district schools to either the new or existing curriculum condition. Students in both conditions whose parents gave signed permission and who assented would be surveyed through 12th grade to compare the short- and long-term effectiveness of the programs on student alcohol attitudes and use. Prior to initiating the study, discussions with parent groups indicated concern that students in the control schools would be deprived of an effective intervention. On the basis of this information, the investigators worked with parent groups to ensure that the language of the parental permission and assent forms clarified that the study was being conducted because at this time it was unknown whether one curriculum-based approach would be more effective than the other in reducing high school drinking. In addition, the psychologists agreed to offer a yearly talk about adolescent drinking to each school's parent organization and provide a report on the results of the study to both school administrators and parents (see also Standard 8.08, Debriefing).

⊘ Prescribing psychologists at a medical school received IRB approval to assess the treatment efficacy of a medication for children with dual diagnoses of developmental disabilities and aggressive behavioral disorder. The medication was approved by FDA for treatment with developmentally disabled adults but had not been tested with children. Only children who had failed to respond to currently prescribed pediatric medications were to be recruited. To avoid inadvertently implying to these parents that the effectiveness of the drug for adults meant it was a powerfully effective drug for their children, the consent form (a) described differences between child and adult physiological reactions to medication and (b) clarified that the study was being conducted because there was as yet no empirical evidence indicating that the medication would be more effective than currently used medications for children with this dual diagnosis (adapted from Fisher, Hoagwood, & Jensen, 1996).

Therapeutic Misconception in Translational and Community-Engaged Research

In 2006, NIH instituted a new emphasis on research focused on the translation of evidence-based practices (EBPs) into practical applications that improve human health. Engagement of community members as partners in different stages of the study has increasingly become an essential component of community-based translational research protocols. Friedman Ross et al. (2010) have offered intriguing insight into the potential for therapeutic misconception in community-engaged research. They pointed out that community support for a translational research project is often based on the perceived benefits of increased access of community members to health services they assume will be beneficial, irrespective of whether the practical efficacy of the program is still being debated. While optimism regarding the potential benefits of participation in a treatment study is not the same as an unjustified belief that the investigators know the treatment to be effective, it is imperative that community consultation and individual informed consent for such studies clarify the degree to which the extent of benefits is still unknown.

The Right to Refuse Participation Without Penalty

Provision 4 of Standard 8.02b addresses the need to ensure that research participation is voluntary. Individuals who apply for or who already receive nonexperimental services at the study site may fear that failure to participate will result in deterioration or removal of existing services (see also Standard 8.04, Client/Patient, Student, and Subordinate Research Participants). Informed consent procedures must assure participants currently receiving services that dissent will not disrupt their ongoing treatment and inform individuals new to the treatment facility of available alternative services. This standard does not require psychologists to describe or provide treatment alternatives when they are not otherwise available.

Costs and Compensation

Treatments provided in intervention research may be provided at no cost to the participant through federal or private funding of the research, charged to the participant, or billed through a participant's health plan. Understanding the financial costs and the extent to which third-party payors will be aware of diagnoses and services received during a research study is essential for informed decision making. In some cases, participants may be provided monetary compensation for participation. Provision 5 requires that prospective participants are given sufficient information about the nature of such financial arrangements to make an informed decision about participation (see also Standards 6.04, Fees and Financial Arrangements; 8.06, Offering Inducements for Research Participation).

8.03 Informed Consent for Recording Voices and Images in Research

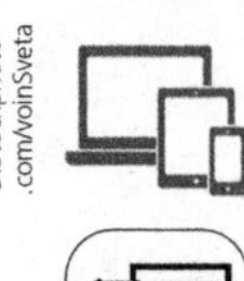

Psychologists obtain informed consent from research participants prior to recording their voices or images for data collection unless (1) the research consists solely of naturalistic observations in public places, and it is not anticipated that the recording will be used in a manner that could cause personal identification or harm, or (2) the research design includes deception, and consent for the use of the recording is obtained during debriefing. (See also Standard 8.07, Deception in Research.)

New recording technologies are providing researchers with powerful ways of collecting, storing, archiving, and disseminating data for current and future studies, professional presentations, training, and teaching (Derry et al., 2010). Psychologists must obtain informed consent to electronically record research participation before beginning data collection. Stored auditory and visual records pose a greater risk of personal identification over time than do other data formats, and therefore, consent procedures must allow individuals to evaluate the personal consequences of such risks prior to research participation. Restricting data access to the research team best protects personal identification. In some instances (e.g., recordings used for training purposes or presentation at professional meetings), participants can be informed about confidentiality protections such as image scrambling, transcripts, voice distortion, or other identity-masking techniques (see also Standards 4.02, Discussing the Limits of Confidentiality; 4.07, Use of Confidential Information for Didactic or Other Purposes). This option is becoming less feasible with the increase in multisite and multinational research, requirements for data sharing by NIH (although video data may be exempt), the creation of digital archives for future research, teleconferencing, and online training and teaching modules. In other instances, these identity protection measures may compromise the validity of future social science data analyses that require attention, for example, to facial or vocal expressions. If identifiable data are to be shared with other investigators, informed consent must provide participants with information regarding who will have access to and the nature of the questions addressed by the data.

The inclusion of the phrase *prior to recording their voices or images for data collection* allows investigators to record the consent procedure itself for documentation or other legitimate purposes as long as participant permission is obtained in advance and recording ceases if the individual refuses participation.

CASE EXAMPLE

Recording Informed Consent

A research team was conducting a study on neurological functioning in HIV-positive adults living in homeless shelters or other types of marginalized housing. The researchers planned to screen for sobriety prior to obtaining informed consent, and as part of street recruitment, individuals were informed that participation required them to be sober when they arrived at the testing site. The investigators realized that some consent-relevant cognitive impairments might be detected only by neurological tests administered as part of the study. With approval from the IRB, the investigators decided to tape-record the informed consent procedures so that they could incorporate the neurological test results in an analysis of participants' consent understanding with the goal of developing ways of improving the consent process for this population. At the beginning of the consent conference, investigators explained to each prospective participant that they were going to describe the study so the individual could decide whether he or she wanted to participate and ask the participants questions to make sure they understood the consent information. They then asked for permission to tape-record responses to the consent procedure, underscoring that participants who refused to have the consent conference recorded would still be eligible for participation in the study. Only the consent conferences of individuals who gave permission were recorded.

Exceptions

Investigators may record the voices and images of persons without their consent if (a) observations occur in a public setting in which one would have no reasonable expectation of privacy, for example, a public park, a hotel lobby, or a street corner; (b) procedures do not disturb or manipulate the natural surroundings; and (c) protections are in place to guard against personal identification and harm, especially when the behaviors observed (e.g., vandalism) place participants at legal or social risk. Investigators conducting deception research that meets the requirements of Standard 8.07, Deception in Research, can receive approval from their IRB to waive the requirement to obtain consent for recording prior to data collection, but they must seek permission to use recordings for data analysis from participants during debriefing. Recordings must be destroyed if the participant declines permission.

Need to Know: Consent to Digital Archives

When voices and images are archived for future use, the original investigator may not know who will access the data or the purpose of future studies. Derry et al. (2010) suggested a two-stage process for archived recorded data in which participants have the option of (a) consenting to only the "collection" of data and confidentiality protections for the current study or (b) also consenting to the "use" of the data for

(Continued)

(Continued)

archival and emergent research purposes. Depending on the nature of the data, the "use" consent protocol can encompass a narrow or broad range of researchable topics, and the use limits must be accessible and adhered to by future investigators.

The storage of biological materials in data banks raises similar issues for informed consent. Readers may wish to refer to the newly proposed category of "broad consent" listed under Need to Know: Proposed Changes to Federal Regulations and the Hot Topic "Informational Risk and Disclosure of Genetic Information to Research Participants" at the end of this chapter.

8.04 Client/Patient, Student, and Subordinate Research Participants

(a) When psychologists conduct research with clients/patients, students, or subordinates as participants, psychologists take steps to protect the prospective participants from adverse consequences of declining or withdrawing from participation.

Clients/patients, students, employees, prisoners, or other institutionalized persons may not feel free to decline or withdraw participation in a study conducted by a psychologist serving as their treatment provider, professor, supervisor, employer, or member of the institutional staff. Standard 8.04a requires psychologists to take specific steps to ensure that (a) refusal to participate does not result in a reduction in the amount or quality of services, lowered grades, poor job performance evaluations, or loss of institutional privileges and (b) prospective participants are aware of these protections during recruitment and throughout the course of research (see 8.02, Informed Consent to Research). When power differentials inherent in an existing professional relationship are apparent (e.g., when the investigator is also the student's professor or a participant's service provider), psychologists should refrain from conducting the informed consent process and any research procedures involving direct contact with the individual (see also Standard 3.05, Multiple Relationships). In some settings, it may be desirable to appoint a participant advocate to (a) explain to prospective participants the purpose of the study, the role of the investigator, and protections against adverse consequences of nonparticipation; (b) determine if vulnerable persons wish to be approached by the research team to give informed consent; and (c) monitor the continued voluntariness of participation.

✓ A graduate student member of the APA received permission to collect data for her doctoral dissertation at her internship site. The methodology included individual interviews with patients at the veterans hospital where she interned. The graduate student restricted her recruitment to hospital patients who were not in the section in which she worked. In addition, she hired and trained a research assistant to recruit participants and obtain informed consent.

Conducting Quality Improvement or Comparative Effectiveness Research in Health Care Settings

The Affordable Care Act (ACA) has increased the need for quality improvement (QI) studies designed to continuously assess the quality, outcomes, and costs of health care in patient-centered medical homes (PCMHs) and other integrated care organizations. To accomplish this aim, the regulations set up the Patient-Centered Outcomes Research Institute (PCORI; http://www.pcori.org). Research activities may include "comparative effectiveness" studies that evaluate different "standards of care," defined as interventions normally used in health care settings and for which there are insufficient empirical data to determine relative effectiveness (DHHS, 2014). IRB review of such studies may or may not be required, and psychologists should check with their IRB and evolving federal regulations to determine whether their specific study is excluded or exempt from review (see the feature earlier in this chapter "Need to Know: Proposed Changes to Federal Regulations").

Consistent with Standard 8.04a, psychologists conducting these studies will need to consider the impact on practitioners and patients of introducing such protocols into normal delivery of health services. For example, using random assignment to assess potentially different health outcomes of commonly used services within the primary care setting may or may not be seen as depriving practitioners and patients of their right to choose between such services (IOM, 2015). In addition, the more detailed informed consent information required for such research may communicate possible risks and benefits of participating that are not normally discussed during clinical care, which in turn may deter patients from participating in the research or discourage them from receiving standard services (DHHS, 2014). Further, the use of an extensive and repeated battery of assessment instruments required for adequate evaluation of services may place a burden on practitioners and patients, disrupting the natural flow of clinical care in a manner not reflective of usual practices (Goodie, Kanzler, Hunter, Glotfelter, & Bodart, 2013).

To avoid such ethical pitfalls, during the design stage psychologists should seek input from staff representatives and patient advocates who will be affected by the research activities and use this input to select assessment instruments and procedures that minimally intrude on the flow of patient care within the unit and do not compromise the ethical responsibilities of care providers (Goodie et al., 2013). Similarly, in designing informed consent, researchers should work closely with clinicians to understand the everyday nature of and rationale for the content and process of informed consent for the health care services to be studied. They should also consult with appropriate institutional staff to ensure that consent for research participation neither deprives patients of the critical medical information they would normally receive nor overstates the risks and potential benefits of these services. Finally, in quality improvement studies, the validity of the data obtained will often depend upon the participation of all relevant staff and thus may be a requirement of their employment. Psychologists should be knowledgeable about the legal obligations of service providers in the institution in which quality improvement research will be conducted to determine when it is ethically appropriate to dispense with informed consent for their participation (see also Standard 8.05, Dispensing With Informed Consent).

> (b) When research participation is a course requirement or an opportunity for extra credit, the prospective participant is given the choice of equitable alternative activities.

In many colleges and universities, psychology instructors require or give extra course credit for undergraduate student participation in research. The pedagogical rationale for required research participation is to provide direct experience with the process of research. Yet the requirement can be coercive to students who do not want to be involved in experimental procedures. In addition, psychology faculty and graduate students conducting research at the university benefit from a yearly "subject pool" of prospective participants, creating the potential for student exploitation (Standards 3.06, Conflict of Interest, and 3.08, Exploitative Relationships). Standard 8.04b addresses these concerns by requiring that psychologists offer students pedagogical alternatives equivalent in time and effort to research participation, such as watching a video on a research topic, summarizing an article on research techniques, or assisting with the conduct of an experiment. Psychologists conducting such studies or approving them for extra credit should also ensure that the experience is educational both in terms of a comprehensive description of the rationale for and methodology employed and in modeling appropriate informed consent and other human participant protections (Standards 8.02, Informed Consent to Research; 8.08, Debriefing). The extent to which recruiting introductory psychology students for participation in deception research meets Standard 2.07, Deception in Research should be carefully considered (Fisher & Fyrberg, 1994).

☒ A psychology department instituted a 2-hour research participation requirement for all students enrolled in introductory psychology classes. Students who did not wish to participate in the research had to set up a meeting to explain their objection to the instructor and write a 10-page paper on a research topic approved by the professor. In anonymous course evaluations, many students said they had participated in the required research because they were afraid they would get a bad grade in the course if the professor knew they did not want to participate in the subject pool or because they believed it would take more than 2 hours to complete a 10-page paper.

✓ A psychology department offered introductory students who did not wish to participate in the course research participation requirement the alternative to view a video on research methods.

8.05 Dispensing With Informed Consent for Research

Psychologists may dispense with informed consent only (1) where research would not reasonably be assumed to create distress or harm and involves (a) the study of normal educational practices, curricula, or classroom management methods conducted in educational settings; (b) only anonymous questionnaires, naturalistic observations, or archival research for which disclosure of responses would not place participants at risk of criminal or civil liability or damage their financial standing, employability, or reputation, and confidentiality is protected; or (c) the study of factors related to job or organization effectiveness conducted in organizational settings for which there is no risk to participants' employability, and confidentiality is protected or (2) where otherwise permitted by law or federal or institutional regulations.

This standard restricts dispensing with informed consent for research to three well-defined conditions—all of which are predicated on the condition that the research will not create distress or harm. Criteria (a) and (b) of the standard are consistent with the criteria for research that is exempt from IRB review under federal regulations 45 CFR 46.101 (b)(1). Psychologists should remember that the determination of whether a study meets the criteria for dispensing with informed consent or exempt status is the responsibility of the IRB and not the individual investigator, although this obligation may fall to investigators conducting research meeting criteria for the proposed new "excluded" research category (see the feature earlier in this chapter Need to Know: Proposed Changes to Federal Regulations). This is particularly true for the still controversial status of quality improvement/quality assurance research (Miller & Emanuel, 2008). Therefore, when working in an institution with an IRB, investigators designing research that meets the criteria of Standard 8.05 must still obtain appropriate institutional approval for such waivers (Standard 8.01, Institutional Approval).

Research Conducted in Schools

Ethical justification for waiving the informed consent requirement for specific types of research conducted in educational settings is predicated on the right and responsibility of educational institutions to evaluate their own programs, practices, and policies to improve services as long as the research procedures themselves do not create distress or harm. Studies of normal educational practices that do not require informed consent include comparisons of different instructional methods for academic topics (e.g., reading, math) and classroom management techniques or evaluation of educational placements.

In elementary and secondary school settings, dispensing with informed consent is a waiver of guardian permission for research involving persons who are legally incapable of consent. Irrespective of whether the type of research conducted meets the criteria for waiving parental permission under this standard, psychologists should consider state and federal laws and parental expectations regarding parental involvement in children's participation in normal educational practices before deciding whether to dispense with parental permission or student assent. Psychologists conducting program evaluation in the schools should also be familiar with FERPA and other federal regulations that may require parental access to their child's school records irrespective of whether parental permission for the evaluation was required or obtained.

Permission to dispense with informed consent for research in educational settings does not apply to studies designed to describe or test hypotheses regarding the relationship between student personality traits or mental health disorders and school performance (e.g., gender differences in internal and external disorders and their relationship to scores on a math achievement test). The assessment of such personal characteristics is not a part of normal educational practice and could constitute an invasion of privacy. In addition, some investigator-initiated school-based programs, such as drug prevention programs, may or may not be considered a normal educational practice or part of the school curricula across different school districts. Investigators conducting school-based studies not considered normal educational practice must either follow the consent requirements outlined in Standards 3.10, Informed Consent, and 8.02a, Informed Consent to Research, or obtain a waiver of parental permission from their IRB in compliance with Part 2 of this standard.

☒ A developmental psychologist received permission from a local school district to design and test a conflict resolution program for fifth and sixth graders. The school permitted her to offer the program during regularly scheduled health classes. Half of the classes served as controls. The success of the program was evaluated by comparing baseline and postprogram responses of children to questions about their conflicts with peers, siblings, and parents. Without consulting with her IRB, the psychologist told the school superintendent that the research was exempt from IRB review and that parental permission would not be required for this type of research.

Anonymous Survey Research

When anonymous surveys will be conducted in person, research is conducted through the mail or on the Internet and adequate protections are put in place to ensure that participants' responses are anonymous (e.g., no names will appear on the survey, postmarks will not reveal participants' home addresses, web-based responses cannot be linked to identifying information), informed consent information must be provided at the beginning of the survey in the same detail as required by Standards 3.10, Informed Consent, and 8.02, Informed Consent to Research. However, documentation of consent (e.g., name and signature confirming agreement) is not required because (a) completing the survey, mailing it to the investigator, or submitting it via the Internet is considered evidence of voluntary consent and (b) requiring identifying documentation would compromise participant anonymity.

✓ An anonymous survey on attitudes toward caretaking of ill elderly household members included (a) a brief questionnaire asking for general demographic information such as gender, age, and ethnicity of household members and (b) health-related information such as whether there was an ill elderly person living in the household, which family member did or would take care of an elder family member if he or she was ill, how the respondents rated the adequacy of their health insurance plan for elder care, and several questions tapping who the respondent thought should be most responsible for elder care (e.g., spouses, adult children, private nursing homes, or government-run hospitals). The survey was mailed to 10,000 randomly selected households in a large metropolitan area where respondents could not reasonably be expected to be identified by their answers or ZIP code. No names were on the survey, and the mailed packet included a self-addressed stamped envelope. The IRB agreed that signed informed consent was not required but that the investigators should include a statement explaining the nature, purpose, anonymity and other identity protections, and their contact information and a box that participants could check indicating they had read the information.

Naturalistic and Archival Research

Informed consent is not required for investigations using naturalistic observations or archival research when (a) confidentiality is protected; (b) disclosure of responses would not place participants at legal, financial, or social risk; and (c) the research methods would not reasonably be expected to cause distress or harm. The phrase *for which disclosure of responses would not place participants at risk* refers to both the certitude that participants could never be identified and the nature of the data collected. Thus, unless anonymity can be ensured, psychologists should avoid dispensing with informed consent when the personal information collected could cause participants distress or involve criminal activity, substance abuse, or other activities that, if known, would place the participant at risk.

Naturalistic Observation on the Internet

Studies of individual responses in chat rooms, blogs, and on listservs may be considered naturalistic observation if the users have no reasonable expectation of privacy, the investigator is a passive observer who does not manipulate the discussion to test or elicit particular responses, data are appropriately de-identified, and publication of results will not cause distress or harm to those whose responses were used as data. Under Standard 8.05, psychologists may dispense with informed consent when these criteria are met. However, in the constantly changing modalities of online expression and social conceptions of net privacy, meeting these criteria often depends on the topic of online discussion, the expectations for group membership and perceived level of privacy, and the vulnerability of the population to identification or harm. For example, the Internet provides individuals and family members confronting serious illness the opportunity to interact with others who share their health challenges. While individuals are aware that they are posting personal information on a publicly accessible website, they may not be aware that their online illness narratives may be used and disseminated by researchers (Heilferty, 2011).

Digital Ethics: Determining Public Versus Private Information

There are multiple forms of Internet research that examine information already available on or via the Internet without direct interaction with human participants; such information includes use patterns of social media sites or participation in public chat rooms. Determination of the public versus private nature of Internet postings will affect whether consent is or is not required (Standards 8.02, Informed Consent to Research; 8.05, Dispensing With Informed Consent).

- Naturalistic observation of forms of virtual representation, including avatars, bots, and other Internet personae that cannot be linked to personal identifiers, does not require informed consent as *long as the investigator did not interact with or attempt to manipulate the web-based comments, behaviors, or decisions of those being observed.*
- The use for research purposes of intentional posts on public Internet sites does not need informed consent *unless existing law or privacy policies associated with terms of service of the entity receiving or hosting the information explicitly preclude use of data for research or other related purposes.*
- There is a lack of consensus on whether an individual's reasonable expectation of privacy, whether correct or incorrect, should preclude accessing specific available Internet information about that person without consent. For example, if a password is required to join a chat room to discuss mental health or other socially sensitive topics, can an investigator assume the information is public if the investigator also obtains password entry to the venue? A conservative ethical approach to this question is to follow the published privacy/confidentiality policy at the site, which can be assumed to reflect the shared privacy priorities of the members (e.g., privacy practices paralleling "anonymous" meeting standards of Alcoholics Anonymous). (See also the DHHS Secretary's Advisory Committee on Human Research Protections [SACHRP], 2013.)

When informed consent is not obtained, publication of material may also raise questions regarding ownership of data, website/blog propriety, copyright, representativeness and validity of material, and participant exploitation (Standards 3.04, Avoiding Harm, and 3.08, Exploitative Relationships; Heilferty, 2011). Investigators planning observational studies on the Internet should consider either obtaining informed consent or developing effective protections against participant identification and harm when (a) quotes will be used verbatim; (b) group membership requires registration, user names, or passwords; (c) the observed group is small and unique with high probability of identification (e.g., a chat room for individuals with a rare genetic disorder); or (d) the level of intimate details provided precludes anonymity (Eysenbach & Till, 2001; Serfaty, 2004).

Unique or Small Communities

Investigators should also consider whether the uniqueness of the population studied (e.g., individuals from small and geographically restricted ethnocultural communities; persons with rare genetic, medical, or psychological disorders) increases the probability that anonymous, naturalistic, or archival procedures may not be sufficient to safeguard identification of participants or their immediate community (Fisher et al., 2002). In such conditions, consent would be required (Fisher & Vacanti-Shova, 2012).

☒ A health psychologist decided to conduct a naturalistic observation of the interactions among health care providers and patients in the emergency room of a small hospital in an isolated Appalachian town. He would sit in the back of the room on Saturday nights when the emergency room was most crowded. He dressed in such a way as to ensure that he would not be recognized from week to week. The psychologist took detailed notes on how specific doctors responded to the patients. He published an article highly critical of some of the interactions he had observed. Although the psychologist used pseudonyms for the hospital and the doctors, the unique location of the hospital, the medical events reported, and the detailed descriptions of the treatment staff made them readily identifiable. Following the publication, several members of the treatment staff were sued for malpractice.

Psychobiographical Research

Psychobiographical research, a narrative method of applying psychological theory to the study of an individual living or deceased, has a long history in psychology beginning with Freud's psychoanalytic profiles and continued by scholars in personality psychology (Barenbaum & Winter, 2013). When information is gained solely from publically available documents, the study would fall under the Standard 8.05 criteria for dispensing with informed consent. Although such research may not require IRB review (see the feature earlier in this chapter "Need to Know: Proposed Changes to Federal Regulations), the decision to obtain informed consent from living subjects or surviving family members or friends (if the subject is deceased) should be calibrated to the temporal frame of events that will be the focus of the psychobiography and the potential to cause harm (Ponterotto, 2014; Standards 3.04, Avoiding Harm; 3.10, Informed Consent; 4.02, Discussing the Limits of Confidentiality).

Studies of Job or Organization Effectiveness

Subpart 1c recognizes the right and responsibility of organizations to draw on the research expertise of psychologists to investigate factors related to job or organization effectiveness as long as (a) research participation does not pose a direct risk to an individual's current employment status, (b) confidentiality is adequately protected, and (c) the research procedures themselves would not be expected to create distress or harm. This standard is meant to apply to dispensing with informed consent to research directly linked to a specific organization's needs and not to studies designed to test general hypotheses regarding organizational effectiveness.

The phrase *not reasonably be assumed to create distress or harm* highlights the fact that in most circumstances, it would be ethically inappropriate to dispense with informed consent for organizational effectiveness studies using measures of psychopathology or biological data because assessment of mental health or physiological responses without consent can violate an individual's right to privacy of information not directly related to job performance and be experienced as personally intrusive and distressful.

✓ An industrial–organizational psychologist collected criterion-related validation data on a test designed to help a company select future sales personnel by administering the test to all current sales employees. The company told its employees that they were expected to participate in the validation, and informed consent was not obtained. Nonetheless, the psychologist informed the employees that their test performance would be kept confidential and would not affect their employment status. To match the test data on measures of job performance (sales volume and supervisor performance ratings), the psychologist needed to collect identifying information on the test form. The psychologist maintained several levels of security on the test materials and associated database. As soon as the predictor test and performance criterion data were matched, all identifying information was stripped from both the hard-copy test materials and electronic database. No personally identifiable information collected for purposes of the validation was released to anyone in the organization, and there were no consequences for those incumbents who performed poorly on the experimental test.

Dispensing With Guardian Permission

Standard 3.10b, Informed Consent, and federal regulation 45 CFR 46.408b require guardian permission for research involving children, with exceptions for research involving no more than minimal risk detailed in 45 CFR 46.402a and 46.408c. Requests to IRBs to waive guardian permission should refer to these standards and, when relevant, describe the rationale for the exceptions. Rationales include (a) state laws defining emancipated and mature minor status; (b) justification of the minimal risk status of the research; (c) why guardian consent would not be in the child's best interest or is unavailable; and (d) how an independent participant advocate will be appointed to verify youths' understanding of procedures, support their participation preferences, and assess their reactions to planned procedures. Research psychologists conducting longitudinal studies with minors should also consider reconsent procedures appropriate to youths' developing consent maturity.

> ⊘ For a minimal-risk ethnographic study of HIV risk attitudes and behaviors among gay youth, investigators received approval from their IRB to waive guardian permission for 16- to 17-year-olds to avoid selection biases present in recruiting only youth whose parents were both aware of and comfortable with their sexual orientation and protect youth who might be subjected to punitive guardian responses if their sexual orientation was revealed (Fisher & Mustanski, 2014). The investigators worked with staff from an advocacy center for LGBT youth to ensure that the informed consent procedures were understood and viewed as voluntary by youth recruited for participation. See Fisher, Arbeit, Dumont, Macapagal, & Mustanski (in press) for youth perspectives on ethical issues involving self-consent for HIV biomedical prevention research.

Prohibition Against "Passive" Consent

Under federal regulations, passive consent procedures (sending guardians forms asking for a response only if they do *not* wish their child to participate in the research) are not an ethical substitute for guardian permission. Psychologists who do not obtain the active affirmative permission of guardians violate this standard except when the research meets the conditions for Standard 8.05, Dispensing With Informed Consent for Research, or when an IRB waives the requirement for guardian permission under federal regulation 45 CFR 46.116d and 46.408c.

Where Otherwise Permitted by Law or Federal or Institutional Regulations

Part 2 of this standard permits psychologists to dispense with informed consent for reasons not included in Part 1 where consent waiver is permitted by law or federal or institutional regulations. In such instances, researchers bear the burden of demonstrating that such conditions are met.

HIPAA Requirements for Use of PHI for Research Without Client/Patient Authorization

Under HIPAA, PHI may be used for research purposes without client/patient authorization if the covered entity who is being asked to disclose the PHI receives written documentation that waiver of patient authorization has been approved by an IRB in conformance with federal guidelines, and if

- the use or disclosure of PHI involves no more than minimal risk to the individuals;
- the alteration or waiver will not adversely affect the privacy rights and the welfare of the individuals;
- the research could not practicably be conducted without the alteration or waiver;
- the research could not practicably be conducted without access to and use of the PHI;
- the privacy risks to individuals whose PHI is to be used or disclosed are reasonable in relation to the anticipated benefits, if any, to the individuals and the importance of the knowledge that may reasonably be expected to result from the research;
- there is an adequate plan to protect the identifiers from improper use and disclosure;
- there is an adequate plan to destroy the identifiers at the earliest opportunity consistent with conduct of the research, unless there is a health or research justification for retaining the identifiers or such retention is otherwise required by law; and
- there are adequate written assurances that the PHI will not be reused or disclosed to any other person or entity, except as required by law, for authorized oversight of the research project or for other research for which the use or disclosure of PHI would be permitted by the subpart.

Covered entities may also waive the requirement for client/patient authorization for the use and disclosure of their PHI for research under the following conditions:

- Information is de-identified by the covered entity. If de-identified information is later re-identified by the covered entity, a client/patient authorization is required.
- The researcher is reviewing the PHI for the sole purpose of preparing a research protocol or for similar purposes preparatory to research, the information is necessary for the research purposes, and the PHI is not removed from the covered entity's premises.
- Research is on decedents' information, and the researcher provides the covered entity with representation that the use or disclosure sought is solely for research on the PHI of the decedents, the death is documented, and the PHI is necessary for the research.
- Disclosure is restricted to a limited data set (as specifically defined by HIPAA), and the investigator enters into a "data use agreement" with the covered entity.
- The investigator signs a business associate contract with a covered entity to use PHI to conduct data analysis or quality assurance or other activities on behalf of the covered entity and to comply with all HIPAA regulations.
- The research is to support public health policies and practices.

8.06 Offering Inducements for Research Participation

(a) Psychologists make reasonable efforts to avoid offering excessive or inappropriate financial or other inducements for research participation when such inducements are likely to coerce participation.

Individuals participate in research for a variety of reasons, including the opportunity to gain knowledge about themselves through surveys that encourage self-reflection, to obtain the potential health benefits of participating in a randomized clinical trial, the desire to contribute to the public good, and curiosity about the scientific process. In many cases, researchers also provide modest expressions of gratitude such as snacks or gift certificates or reimbursement for travel. However, modest tokens of appreciation are often not sufficient to attract individuals to participate in a research study. Standard 8.06 recognizes that some compensation is often necessary to ensure a sufficiently large and representative sample and that it is possible for investigators to distinguish between "due" and "undue" inducements (Macklin, 1981; VanderWalde & Kurzban, 2011). In many instances, financial compensation for research participation is not in itself coercive (Wertheimer & Miller, 2008), and as Grady (2005) has noted, "money for research participation is an offer of opportunity and not a threat" (p. 1783).

Some institutions adopt a standard compensation rate for all research participation. Others have defined noncoercive financial inducements as the amount of money a normal, healthy volunteer would lose in work and travel time or as fair market value for the work involved. The APA Ethics Code Standard 8.06 and federal regulations require investigators to minimize the possibility that incentives or compensation for research participation are coercive. However, neither regulations nor professional standards provide a metric for determining what form of research compensation is or is not coercive. This often leads investigators and their IRBs to arrive at disparate and idiosyncratic conclusions about the amount of monetary or health-related services that are noncoercive, especially when the research population is economically disadvantaged, lacks health insurance, or has addictions to drugs or alcohol. When payments are too low, they may deprive economically disadvantaged groups the opportunity to benefit from research knowledge (T. Phillips, 2011). Relatedly, psychologists should be wary of the argument that people of less economic means should be paid less than other participants to prevent "coercion" of a "vulnerable" group. Such economic "discrimination" goes against the principle of fairness and justice, which entitles all persons to equal compensation for equal levels of participation in research (Principle D: Justice; Fisher, 1999, 2004). Consulting with members of the population who will be recruited for research participation about different types of research compensation can help investigators and their IRBs determine the extent to which cash or nonmonetary compensation is fair or coercive (Fisher, 2003b; Oransky, Fisher, Mahadevan, & Singer, 2009).

Need to Know: When Are Research Inducements Coercive?

Ezekiel Emanuel (2005) has provided a useful decision-making tool for determining undue inducements that includes the following four elements, *all* of which must be satisfied for research compensation to be considered coercive:

1. The prospective participant perceives the inducement as valuable or desirable.
2. The inducement is so large or excessive that it is irresistible in the context of the participation request.
3. The offer leads prospective participants to exercise poor judgment during recruitment or informed consent, making decisions that a reasonable person would not otherwise make.
4. The individual's poor judgment leads to a sufficiently high probability that the participation decision will result in a harmful experience that "seriously contravenes his or her interests." (p. 9)

- ⊘ A developmental psychologist was studying the relationship of asthma, discrimination distress, and health knowledge and attitudes among African American students in a large urban school district. Students who participated would spend an hour in focus group discussion and 30 minutes responding to focus group questions. Prestudy interviews with parents, teachers, and students indicated that compensation of $15 would be considered fair and noncoercive for the time students would give to the study. However, representatives from two schools in crime-ridden neighborhoods expressed concern that cash payments would place students in danger as they left the study. The psychologist and representatives agreed that offering a popular school sweatshirt worth $15 instead of cash would be equitable and safety-sensitive compensation for research participation in those schools.
- ⊘ Community psychologists wanted to study the effectiveness of a needle exchange program for injecting drug users. While the investigators' preliminary community interviews suggested that $30 was a fair and noncoercive compensation for research participation, the psychologists were concerned that cash payments might be used by participants to purchase illegal drugs, encourage them to maintain their drug habits, or distort the evaluation of drug use dangers. The researchers obtained IRB approval to compensate participants with $30 coupons to a local food market. The investigators were surprised to learn that many participants did not usually purchase food at that market, were selling their coupons for less cash than they were worth, and perceived the investigators' efforts as paternalistic and disrespectful of participant judgment and autonomy. The psychologists began to collect data on the participants' reactions to the coupons, which they then presented to the IRB as justification to switch to cash payments. The IRB's community representative strongly supported the investigators' request, which received IRB approval (see Oransky et al., 2009).

(b) When offering professional services as an inducement for research participation, psychologists clarify the nature of the services, as well as the risks, obligations, and limitations. (See also Standard 6.05, Barter With Clients/Patients.)

Providing psychological services as compensation for research participation is ethical when participants are fully aware of (a) the nature and risks of services (e.g., the type of treatment, the type of provider, risks to confidentiality), (b) the personal and financial obligations and time commitment involved in receiving the services, and (3) limitations of the type and in the length of services provided (see also Standards 6.04, Fees and Financial Arrangements; 6.05, Barter With Clients/Patients; 10.01, Informed Consent to Therapy). Linking involvement in nontherapeutic research with treatment that immediately follows may encourage participants with mental health problems to engage or continue in treatment. However, psychologists should take special steps to ensure that offering such services does not compromise the voluntary nature of research participation of individuals who do not have access to adequate health care and social services (Fisher, 2004; Oransky et al., 2009).

⊘ A team of health psychologists conducted a study to determine whether financial incentives would increase 18-year-old female adolescents' participation in a community-run human papillomavirus (HPV) vaccination program in a middle-class neighborhood. Following community consultation on age-appropriate compensation for the required three visits ($25/visit), youth who had been unresponsive to initial outreach were offered the financial incentive. In addition to evaluating whether the financial incentive increased uptake of the previous nonresponders, the investigators also assessed whether the financial compensation negatively affected youth's ability to make an informed medical choice and whether participation decisions were related to relative economic deprivation. The findings indicated compensation increased uptake and did not affect decisional quality and that response to the compensation was not affected by economic status (adapted from Mantzari, Vogt, & Marteau, 2015).

8.07 Deception in Research

(a) Psychologists do not conduct a study involving deception unless they have determined that the use of deceptive techniques is justified by the study's significant prospective scientific, educational, or applied value and that effective nondeceptive alternative procedures are not feasible.

Throughout the history of psychological science, deception studies have fostered the most pronounced debates about the ethical conduct of social science research (Baumrind, 1964; Benjamin & Simpson, 2009; Milgram, 1963). Deceptive techniques intentionally withhold information or misinform participants about the purpose of the study, the experimental procedures or equipment, or the roles of research team members (Sieber, 1982; McCambridge, Kypri, Bendtsen, & Porter, 2013). Under Principle C: Integrity, deception should be avoided unless it is necessary to maximize benefits and minimize harms. Deception research may produce benefits unavailable through alternative methods by keeping participants naive about the purpose and procedures of a study, thereby increasing methodological realism and spontaneous response to experimental manipulation (Fisher & Vacanti-Shova, 2012). However, these advantages may not be actualized if participants are predisposed to be suspicious of psychology experiments or are actively engaged in hypotheses regarding an experiment's true purpose (Fisher & Fyrberg, 1994).

The "Consent Paradox"

By its very nature, informed consent for participation in a deception study creates a moral paradox by compromising an individual's ability to make a fully informed decision about research participation (Fisher, 2005a; Principle E: Respect for People's Rights and Dignity). The ethical imperative for informed consent to research participation arose following the revelation during the Nuremberg trials of Nazi medical science atrocities. The Nuremberg Code (1949) and more recently the World Medical Association (2008) codified the international community's distrust in scientists' motivation to make decisions that serve the best interests of participants; informed consent of the participant, rather than morally responsible decisions by scientists, came to be seen as the primary means of protecting participant autonomy and welfare.

Informed consent to a deception study reflects the moral ambiguity continuing to surround respect for participant autonomy inherent in professional ethics codes and federal regulations. During the consent process, investigators conducting deception research intentionally give participants false information about the purpose and nature of the study. Individuals providing an affirmative response to participate are therefore erroneously led to believe that they have autonomy to decide the type of experimental procedures to which they are willing to be exposed when, in fact, they do not have such autonomy and thus have no decisional control over these experiences or the potential discomfort that may arise at the end of the study when they are debriefed about the deception (Standards 8.07c, Deception in Research; 8.08, Debriefing). Fisher (2005a) has coined the term *consent paradox* to describe this ethical conundrum. It is for these reasons that Standard 8.07 requires that deception research meet more stringent criteria for implementation than is required of nondeceptive studies.

Scientific and Social Justification

Under Standard 8.07a, deception studies are ethically justified only if psychologists demonstrate that (a) prospective benefits to science or society significantly outweigh violating participants' right to determine whether they want to be involved in the type of experimental procedures for which they are recruited and

(b) nondeceptive alternative procedures do not offer sufficient scientific controls to test the hypothesis under investigation. Some alternative methodologies that can be considered include naturalistic observation, field or game simulations, role-playing, or experimental methods. Failure to use scientifically valid nondeceptive alternative methods simply because of inconvenience or financial cost may be a violation of this standard under some circumstances.

> (b) Psychologists do not deceive prospective participants about research that is reasonably expected to cause physical pain or severe emotional distress.

Even if deceptive techniques have significant scientific, educational, or social value and effective nondeceptive alternatives are not feasible, thus meeting the criteria of Standard 8.07a, Standard 8.07b prohibits withholding or misleading prospective participants about procedures causing physical pain or severe emotional distress. The prohibitions in this standard are absolute and do not depend on the duration of physical pain or whether severe emotional harm can be alleviated during debriefing procedures.

☒ Following the September 11, 2001, attacks on the United States, a social psychologist at a university in New York City decided to study ways in which three types of warning systems would positively or negatively affect crowd behavior in response to a perceived terrorist attack. The psychologist had confederates enter nine classrooms and use one of three types of warning systems instructing students in evacuation procedures for a "suspected bomb that might be planted in the building by a terrorist group." Many students started crying or screaming, some called their parents on cell phones to say goodbye, and two students fainted during the exercise.

> (c) Psychologists explain any deception that is an integral feature of the design and conduct of an experiment to participants as early as is feasible, preferably at the conclusion of their participation, but no later than at the conclusion of the data collection, and permit participants to withdraw their data. (See also Standard 8.08, Debriefing.)

When deception is used, individuals must be informed about a study's deceptive aspects as soon as possible, preferably at the end of their participation. This type of debriefing procedure is often called dehoaxing. In some instances, participants may find revelations about the deception and true purpose of the study to be educative; in other cases, there may be transient or longer-term discomfort or distress arising from perceptions of invasion of privacy or loss of self-esteem and negative reactions to being observed or induced to commit what the participant may perceive as embarrassing or reprehensible acts (Baumrind, 1985; Fisher & Fyrberg, 1994). Oczak and Niedźwieńska (2007) have suggested that debriefing include an extended educational procedure that enables participants to gain insight into the methodological reasons for, to recognize, and to deal effectively with deceptive procedures as a positive educational debriefing experience.

The design of dehoaxing procedures must be sensitive to individual differences in participant reactions (see Standard 8.08, Debriefing). There may be situations in which explaining the deception can compromise the methodological validity of the research involving future participants, for example, if research is conducted in a small university where students are likely to speak with one another about their experiences. In such circumstances, dehoaxing may be delayed until data collection is completed. Psychologists must also take reasonable steps to alleviate psychological harm resulting from dehoaxing and may withhold information about deceptive procedures to protect the participant from harm (see Standard 8.08b and c, Debriefing).

Data Withdrawal

Psychologists must permit participants to withdraw their data after learning about the deception. Although the standard stops short of requiring psychologists to ask participants if they want to withdraw their data, dehoaxing procedures should not preclude participants from making such a request. Giving individuals an opportunity to withdraw data should not be interpreted as implying their "deferred" consent to the deception—informed consent can only be obtained prospectively (Office for Protection From Research Risks, 1993). Pascual-Leone, Singh, and Scoboria (2010) provided a helpful checklist for new researchers to facilitate the development and review of ethically designed deception studies.

8.08 Debriefing

(a) Psychologists provide a prompt opportunity for participants to obtain appropriate information about the nature, results, and conclusions of the research, and they take reasonable steps to correct any misconceptions that participants may have of which the psychologists are aware.

To protect methodological validity, informed consent procedures often do not include the hypothesis or other information about the research that would not be expected to affect willingness to participate but might bias participant responses. Debriefing procedures provide participants the opportunity to be informed about such undisclosed information and to ask questions about the research. Standard 8.08a requires that psychologists take reasonable steps to correct any misconceptions about the research of which they are aware. The use of the terms *reasonable* and *aware* in this standard reflect the fact that despite the best efforts of a psychologist, some participants may continue to hold misimpressions about the research or may not share these misperceptions with the investigator. As part of debriefing, psychologists should make a summary of the results of the research available to participants. Because data analysis and interpretation of results typically occur after data collection is completed, psychologists can make summaries available through mailings to participants, newsletters to the site at which the research occurred, websites or social media pages describing study progress or results, or other mechanisms that do not incur unreasonable expense.

Psychologists conducting descriptive studies are not required to provide participants information on their individual results and should never do so unless the data collected have demonstrated clinical value and utility (for further discussion, see the Hot Topic "Informational Risk and Disclosure of Genetic Information to Research Participants" at the end of this chapter).

Digital Ethics: Debriefing for Online Studies

The use of debriefing for online studies may be complicated by the fact that participants can choose to quit responding to web-based surveys or interviews at any time during the study. To address this challenge, investigators can create a "Quit the study" link that pops up when a participant closes a study window and directs participants to debriefing text (Wang & Kitsis, 2013).

Community-Engaged Research (CEnR)

The continued growth of community-engaged research (CEnR; also described as community-based participatory research CBPR) broadens the application of Standard 8.08 to not only research participants but also community partners in the research process. Involving community partners in the dissemination of research results can be helpful in developing participant- and community-sensitive language to describe the study purposes and results. CEnR can also assist researchers who are involved in longitudinal or other long-term aspects of a study in fulfilling their obligations under 8.08 by utilizing existing community networks to hold research follow-up meetings or distribute flyers or engage in outreach procedures (e.g., via local media or websites) to reach participants months or years after they may have initially participated (McShane, Davey, Rouse, Usher, & Sullivan, 2014).

Implications of HIPAA

When individuals participate in a treatment study, debriefing can include discussion and a written summary describing the participant's responsiveness to experimental or control conditions. There may be an opportunity for the participant to provide a signed HIPAA authorization for a summary to be sent to his or her own health care provider including the nature of the treatment conditions, observed behavioral changes in reaction to the different experimental conditions, and any recommendations for treatment that emerged. The research team member who provides this type of debriefing should be skilled in mental health counseling (Standards 2.01, Boundaries of Competence; 2.05, Delegation of Work to Others). Investigators must follow HIPAA regulations for creation and maintenance of records and authorization to share information with other professionals if assessment results or summaries of treatment efficacy collected as part of a research study are to be entered into a participant's health records.

(b) If scientific or humane values justify delaying or withholding this information, psychologists take reasonable measures to reduce the risk of harm.

There may be humane justification for withholding information about the nature, results, and conclusions of research. For example, individuals participating in deception research may experience loss of self-esteem or other negative psychological reactions if told that they committed a social or moral breach of which they were not aware or that they did not know others had observed. In other situations, child participants may not have the recursive thinking skills to understand the rationale behind the research and feel confused upon debriefing or, in the case of deception research, may feel embarrassed or betrayed. In such circumstances, the study should be explained to the children's guardians.

✓ Investigators working with inpatient boys diagnosed with conduct disorder designed an analog task that could distinguish between the children's use of instrumental and hostile aggression. The task was a computer game in which the boys played against an unseen "boy" (in actuality, formatted responses programmed by the investigators) in an adjacent room. According to the rules of the game, opponents could block each other's game (instrumental aggression) or send a noxious, but not harmful, noise through the computer headsets (hostile aggression). The investigators believed that these deceptive conditions were safer for the participants than alternative methodologies that manipulated or observed aggression in actual competitive situations. Parents thought the research was important but voiced concern that if the boys were told about the deception, they would lose trust in the staff at the facility. The investigators agreed. To minimize any distress that might emerge during the computer game, the boys could not see their scores during the game, and when the game was over, all boys were told that they had won (adapted from Fisher et al., 1996).

(c) When psychologists become aware that research procedures have harmed a participant, they take reasonable steps to minimize the harm.

Consistent with Principle A: Beneficence and Nonmaleficence, psychologists must try to alleviate psychological distress or harm that they are aware has arisen from research participation. Psychologists may not always be able to anticipate participant stress reactions in response to debriefing. In such cases, psychologists might alleviate distress by explaining participant responses within the context of normative behavior if appropriate. In other situations, such as research involving genetic screening for predisposition for a serious medical or mental health disorder, psychologists may anticipate postexperimental stress if the debriefing includes information concerning personal health vulnerabilities and should be prepared to provide referrals for appropriate counseling services (see the Hot Topic "Informational Risk and Disclosure of Genetic Information to Research Participants" at the end of this chapter).

✓ In a study to examine psychosocial factors contributing to the spread of the HIV/AIDS virus among persons who use injection drugs (PWIDs), participants (a) answered questions about their drug use, needle sharing, sexual history, and sexual practices; (b) responded to standardized psychological assessments; and (c) had their blood tested for the HIV virus, hepatitis C, and other sexually transmitted diseases. The results of these blood tests were provided to participants during debriefing. The investigators developed two types of debriefing procedures. Aware that telling PWIDs that they had tested negative for sexually transmitted diseases might lead them to falsely assume that they were "AIDS safe," debriefing for these participants included counseling on continued risk of infection and risk reduction practices. Debriefing for participants who had tested positive for any of the diseases included counseling on availability of current treatments, risk reduction practices, and referrals to appropriate health care providers.

8.09 Humane Care and Use of Animals in Research

In 1981, police raided the Institute of Behavioral Research in Silver Spring, Maryland, in response to a complaint from an animal rights group advocate about unacceptable living conditions for macaque monkeys. The monkeys were part of a research program conducted by Edward Taub, a psychologist interested in using an animal model to explore whether stroke victims and others who had lost sensation in their limbs could relearn how to use these limbs. The study involved cutting the afferent ganglia that supplied sensation to the brain from the monkeys' arms to determine whether the brain could reorganize itself to use the limbs that the animal could not feel (Matfield, 2002). The incident and court case that followed (in which Taub was acquitted) rekindled a historical debate on the use of animals in research, especially studies involving invasive procedures (Akins & Panicker, 2012; Dewsbury, 1990; Perry & Dess, 2012).

The goal of animal research can be to understand and improve the lives of the species studied. More frequently, however, the use of animals in psychological research is aimed at increased understanding of the human condition. This raises ethically complex questions, especially when methods will cause animals discomfort or pain. Society has yet to reach consensus on whether nonhuman animals have the right not to be harmed by virtue of the fact that they have inherent moral value and should be accorded the same protections as human animals, whether humans as moral agents have an obligation to treat all life with dignity, or what role animals' relative lack of self-awareness and limited cognitive capacities to anticipate pain and distress or consequences make them more or less vulnerable to research participation (Perry & Dess, 2012).

The use of nonhuman animals in research enables a control and manipulation of environmental, biological, and genetic factors that leads to scientific discoveries producing tangible benefits for humans and animals not possible otherwise. However, research involving nonhuman animals is only ethically justified when there is a clear scientific purpose supported by empirical data or theory established in the discipline, there is evidence that the species chosen is best suited to answer the research questions, and there are no scientifically valid non-animal research alternatives (APA, 2012b). Psychologists conducting research involving animal subjects have a moral obligation to protect the animal subjects' welfare, use the least number of animals necessary to answer the research question, and assume, unless there is evidence to the contrary, that procedures that are likely to produce pain in humans may also do so in other animals (APA, 2012b). When the scientific question involves inducing pain or serious discomfort, the magnitude of harm ethically permitted should be proportional to the magnitude of potential benefits to humans or nonhumans that will be derived. Drawing on Principle A: Beneficence and Nonmaleficence, the benefits of animal research never justify inhumane treatment. The inclusion of the phrase *humane care* in the title chosen for Standard 8.09 reflects the fact that Standard 8.09a–g represents conditions that must be met to ensure that care and use of animals in research is humane.

> (a) Psychologists acquire, care for, use, and dispose of animals in compliance with current federal, state, and local laws and regulations, and with professional standards.

The federal government, through the Health Research Extension Act of 1985 (Public Law 99–158), regulates the humane care and protection of animals used in research. The NIH, through the Office of Laboratory Animal Welfare, administers programs and provides guidance to institutions that must comply with the policy. Among the regulations is the requirement that all institutions covered by the act have an Institutional Animal Care and Use Committee (IACUC) to approve and monitor the ethical acquisition, care, use, and disposal of animals in research. IACUC approval and efforts to minimize harm are required for both laboratory studies and research conducted in natural habitats that carries a risk of materially altering the behavior of nonhuman animals or their ecosystems.

The US Department of Agriculture requires the planned and unscheduled inspections of animal research facilities twice a year to ensure that animal housing and research procedures are safe, sanitary, and appropriate for the particular environmental and nutritional needs of the species. In addition, animals not bred in the psychologist's laboratory must be acquired lawfully and with appropriate permits. State and local governments also have regulations regarding housing standards, veterinary care and inspection, research procedures, and disposal.

Animal research practices must also be in compliance with the Guidelines for Ethical Conduct in the Care and Use of Nonhuman Animals in Research (APA, 2012b). Other organizations, such as the American Association for Laboratory

Animal Science, the American Association for the Accreditation of Laboratory Animal Care, and the National Association for Biomedical Research, have comprehensive rules for the conduct of animal research. Psychologists conducting research with animals must adhere to all relevant regulations and guidelines. The APA requires members working outside the United States to follow all applicable laws and regulations of the country in which the research is conducted.

> (b) Psychologists trained in research methods and experienced in the care of laboratory animals supervise all procedures involving animals and are responsible for ensuring appropriate consideration of their comfort, health, and humane treatment.

This standard requires that psychologists conducting animal research have appropriate training and carefully supervise all personnel involved in the acquisition and care of, research procedures used with, and disposal of animal subjects. Competencies include education, training, or experience with relevant animal research models; behavioral and surgical techniques; and knowledge of species-specific behavioral, social, and medical requirements. Psychologists conducting animal field research should have sufficient knowledge of the ecosystems that they will observe to minimize harm to the natural behaviors and environment of the animal population under investigation and other plant and animal life.

> (c) Psychologists ensure that all individuals under their supervision who are using animals have received instruction in research methods and in the care, maintenance, and handling of the species being used, to the extent appropriate to their role. (See also Standard 2.05, Delegation of Work to Others.)

Psychologists must ensure that all personnel involved in the housing and care of, experimental methods used with, or disposal of animal research subjects are competent to fulfill these duties in a way that ensures the animals are treated humanely and appropriately (see also Standard 2.05, Delegation of Work to Others). A wide range of animal species are used in research, and each species has its own unique housing, nutrition, medical, and psychological needs. Psychologists must make sure that individuals to whom animal care is delegated are sufficiently knowledgeable about the species and the duties they must perform through prior education, training by the psychologist, or close supervision.

☒ A psychologist who conducted research on aggressive behavior in male rats hired a research assistant to clean each animal's housing. Rather than provide direct supervision, the psychologist told the assistant to begin work and to feel free to ask the psychologist any questions that arose. To facilitate cleaning, the assistant decided to take three of the animals out of their separate housings and place them in a larger empty glass enclosure. The animals immediately began to fight with each other, incurring several injuries.

(d) Psychologists make reasonable efforts to minimize the discomfort, infection, illness, and pain of animal subjects.

Species-appropriate housing, sanitary conditions, feeding, regular veterinary checkups, and development and monitoring of safety conditions during active experimentation should be implemented to protect the health and welfare of animal research subjects. Psychologists and their staff should be alert and competent to detect signs of illness or injury in animal subjects and be able to obtain the immediate and appropriate treatment. When alternative experimental procedures are available, psychologists should select the one that will produce the minimum amount of animal discomfort. The APA Guidelines for Ethical Conduct in the Care and Use of Nonhuman Animals in Research (http://www.apa.org/science/leadership/care/guidelines.aspx) also recommends that, whenever possible, psychologists try to provide care and housing that can enrich the psychological well-being of the animal subject.

> ✓ A psychologist studying cognition in pigeons presented various landmarks and observed the pigeons' use of these cues. During initial testing, the psychologist unexpectedly found that some arrangements caused confusion, resulting in minor injuries when several pigeons flew into the landmarks. The psychologist modified these arrangements to protect the animals' safety.

(e) Psychologists use a procedure subjecting animals to pain, stress, or privation only when an alternative procedure is unavailable and the goal is justified by its prospective scientific, educational, or applied value.

Exposing animals to experimentally induced pain or suffering is not ethically justified unless the psychologist can demonstrate that the knowledge produced from experimentation has the clear potential to substantially contribute to science, to teaching about animal behavior or research techniques, or to benefit other animals or humans. Animals should never be subjected to pain, physical or psychological stress, or food deprivation if alternative procedures have equal pedagogical value or can adequately test the research question. When aversive procedures cannot be avoided, psychologists must select the minimal level of pain, stress, or privation necessary to achieve the goals of the research. IACUC or appropriate committee approval is also required if psychologists wish to use animals for teaching purposes. As with research, consideration should be given to using non-animal alternatives (e.g., videos, simulations, online materials; Baker & Serdikoff, 2013) and the minimum number of animals necessary to meet pedagogical criteria. Procedures for inducing pain or discomfort that may be justified by potential benefits of the research may not be justified for educational purposes.

☒ An introductory psychology laboratory instructor decided to demonstrate to the class how the phenomenon of learned helplessness is experimentally tested. Although educational videos on the procedure were available, the demonstration included placing laboratory rats in a cage with an electrified grid and preventing them from escaping when a painful shock was distributed through the grid.

(f) Psychologists perform surgical procedures under appropriate anesthesia and follow techniques to avoid infection and minimize pain during and after surgery.

Research requiring surgery must be conducted by appropriately trained psychologists or other competent personnel using methods that minimize risks of infection and pain. Unless there is a legitimate scientific or medical reason to do otherwise, animals must be anesthetized throughout the surgical procedure. Psychologists are responsible for monitoring postoperative care of research animals using appropriate medications to minimize discomfort and avoid infection. Exposing animals to multiple surgeries as a matter of convenience or to minimize cost is unethical.

⊘ Researchers designed a study with rhesus monkeys to test the reinforcing effects of three commonly abused drugs. To enable the animals to reinforce their behavior with the drugs, a catheter was implanted in a jugular vein. The procedure was conducted under effective anesthesia and aseptic conditions. Monkeys were treated postoperatively with antibiotics for 10 days and with an analgesic for 3 days. Testing was not begun until it was determined that the monkey was in good postoperative health. The investigators also determined that using a within-subjects design could minimize the number of monkeys needed to adequately test the reinforcing properties of the drugs. After the experiment, the catheters were removed under the same careful anesthesia and aseptic conditions, and each monkey was given appropriate postoperative care.

(g) When it is appropriate that an animal's life be terminated, psychologists proceed rapidly, with an effort to minimize pain and in accordance with accepted procedures.

Humane or scientific considerations may necessitate terminating the life of animal research subjects when experimental procedures create chronic pain or discomfort that cannot be alleviated through medication or other remedies. Participation sometimes renders an animal unsuitable for future research, and returning it to the wild or giving it a home outside the laboratory is not safe or possible. Other times, autopsies are necessary to validate the efficacy of the surgical technique or to understand physiological processes and structures related to the psychological phenomenon under investigation. When termination is necessary, psychologists must use procedures that are humane, immediate, and appropriate for the species. According to the APA Guidelines for Ethical Conduct in the Care and Use of Animals, termination procedures should be in accordance with procedures of the latest version of the American Veterinary Medical Association Panel on Euthanasia (2007), and disposal of euthanized animals should be consistent with law.

8.10 Reporting Research Results

(a) Psychologists do not fabricate data. (See also Standard 5.01a, Avoidance of False or Deceptive Statements.)

Principle C: Integrity underscores the centrality of accuracy, honesty, and truthfulness in the conduct of science. Fraud in research is one of the most serious forms of scientific misconduct because it disrupts the scientific process, dilutes community confidence in the integrity of science, and can lead to misinformed interventions and policies. Psychologists do not falsify, make up, alter, or distort the responses of human participants or animal subjects or the results of data analysis. This standard is not limited to published reports and applies as well to the fabrication of data in journal entries or intentional manipulation of the data collection process itself that would lead to a false report. See Standard 5.01, Avoidance of False or Deceptive Statements, for additional prohibitions against publishing or presenting research findings psychologists know are false.

Ethical issues in data analysis may also lead to a violation of Standard 8.10. Researchers may sometimes disagree on methods to conduct data analysis. However, in some cases the decision to utilize a specific statistical method to support a hypothesis when other established methods have not been successful may be an ethically questionable research practice (see Panter & Sterba, 2011); Principle B: Fidelity and Responsibility; Standard 2.04, Bases for Scientific and Professional Judgments). Wasserman (2013) has summarized the major pitfalls for ethical misconduct in data analysis, including lack of adequate training, carelessness, intentional dishonesty, inadequate supervision of research assistants, and personal conflicts that prevent a researcher from carrying out the work (Standards 2.01, Competence; 2.05, Delegation of Work to Others; 2.06, Personal Problems and Conflicts).

☒ After conducting planned statistical analyses of the data, a psychologist realized that if the data from just 4 of the 30 participants were eliminated, the statistical analyses would yield significance. The characteristics of these four participants met all the original inclusion criteria for the study, and there was no deviation in the administration of testing procedures for these individuals. Reasoning that there must be some undetected characteristic responsible for these participants' outlier responses, the psychologist decided to eliminate their data from the analysis. Because there were no criteria other than their responses on which to exclude them, the psychologist decided not to report their elimination in a manuscript submitted for publication.

(b) If psychologists discover significant errors in their published data, they take reasonable steps to correct such errors in a correction, retraction, erratum, or other appropriate publication means.

The research design, measurement tools, and analytic strategies selected by an investigator may lead to erroneous conclusions based on honest differences in interpretation, chance responding, or extraneous influences that are revealed only when new techniques are used to examine the hypothesis tested. Erroneous conclusions about natural phenomena based on methodologically sound research designs are themselves a natural part of the scientific process and are not unethical. A cornerstone of scientific progress is the process of self-correction in which the validity of results obtained in a single experiment can be confirmed or refuted following replication by others within the scientific community. Accurate reporting of research is essential to this process because it enables others to critique, replicate, dispute, and expand on the methods and interpretations reported.

The purpose of this standard is to safeguard the self-correction process by requiring that psychologists take steps to correct errors in published reports that compromise the readers' ability to replicate the research design or interpret the results because the methodology, data, or statistical analysis was incorrectly described. Informing the journal editor or publisher about the error and requesting a published correction can comply with this standard. The use of the term *reasonable steps* recognizes that investigators have limited control over editors or publishers who refuse to publish corrections.

⊘ Following the publication of an article, a psychologist realized that the *F* values and probability levels in one of the tables had been wrongly transcribed. The psychologist wrote to the editor of the journal requesting that an addendum be published briefly describing the error and informing readers that they could obtain the corrected table from the author. The psychologist also placed an addendum page in all reprints distributed to other investigators.

Need to Know: Program Evaluation, Policy Studies, and Accountability

The increasing societal push toward accountability in education, health care, and social policy is involving research psychologists in the evaluation of programs and policies that can have high stakes for service providers, service recipients, and policy makers. This is especially true when funding and program continuation or discontinuation decisions are made based on the aggregate performance of a sample or an entire population. For example, state adoption of drug rehabilitation versus incarceration programs for repeat offenders may be judged in

(Continued)

(Continued)

part by the results of assessments selected to determine changes in substance use dependence, cost-effectiveness of health services for related diseases (e.g., HIV acquisition/transmission), provider competencies, or recidivism. Funding for school districts may rely on the selection of appropriate tests for reading, math, and other academically relevant tests and longitudinal assessments of graduation rates and postschool employment. Below are ethical considerations for investigators involved in program evaluation, policy study, or accountability systems (AERA, APA, & NCME, 2014):

- Psychologists should select outcome measures based on their validity, reliability, and fairness for each purpose for which they are used and provide evidence of the relevance of the measures to the goals of the program, policy, or system under study and the suitability of the measures for the populations involved (e.g., regular or special education teachers; licensed practitioners or trainees).
- When change or gain scores are used, psychologists need to carefully consider and report the validity and limitations of procedures for constructing the scores, the rationale for the time periods between measurements, steps taken to reduce the influence of practice effects, and effects of participant attrition over time on interpretation of results.
- Most educational and diagnostic assessment instruments are designed to evaluate individual performance or health and have not been validated as indicators of aggregate outcomes. In addition to assessing and stating the limitations of such measures for program, policy, and accountability evaluations, investigators should consider performance indicators other than tests such as (a) patient/client, student, teacher, and provider selection criteria; (b) the nature of and variations in services provided; (c) the setting; (d) additional available resources; (e) relevant demographic characteristics; and (f) the degree of motivation of the those being evaluated.

8.11 Plagiarism

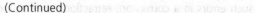

Psychologists do not present portions of another's work or data as their own, even if the other work or data source is cited occasionally.

Plagiarism is the representation of another person's ideas or words without appropriate credit. Plagiarism is inconsistent with Principle C: Integrity, since it deceives readers into believing that the words and ideas of others are original to the author. A common misconception is that plagiarism is limited to word-for-word replication or paraphrasing of another's written work without appropriate citation. Whereas this form of plagiarism is clearly prohibited, violation of this standard also occurs when a psychologist knowingly presents throughout a publication or formal report another's ideas as his or her own, citing the work from which it was drawn in a manner intended to obscure the original author's contribution. (See Standard 5.01, Avoidance of False or Deceptive Statements, for situations in which a psychologist may be in violation of the Ethics Code for appropriating the work of others outside the research or publication context.)

☒ In a manuscript submitted for publication, a psychologist used the organization, heading formats, and arguments presented by authors in an article published in an obscure journal. The psychologist cited the original article once in the opening paragraph of the manuscript. Two paragraphs duplicated word-for-word sentences in the original article, and many of the original article's paragraphs were paraphrased. The psychologist added five new references that appeared after the original plagiarized article was published.

8.12 Publication Credit

(a) Psychologists take responsibility and credit, including authorship credit, only for work they have actually performed or to which they have substantially contributed. (See also Standard 8.12b, Publication Credit.)

This standard prohibits psychologists from taking credit for research they did not directly perform or for which they did not make a substantial intellectual contribution. Substantial intellectual contributions include formulating the hypothesis, developing the experimental design, selecting the analytic procedures, interpreting the data, writing the first draft of the article, or providing important intellectual revisions to the manuscript content (APA, 2001). According to this standard, any psychologist listed as an author must take responsibility for the content of the publication. This means that all coauthors must review the final draft of a manuscript before it is submitted for publication. In recent years, many scientific journals have required that all authors of a submitted manuscript sign a statement confirming that they contributed to the research and reviewed the written content of the paper.

☒ A junior faculty member asked a nationally recognized senior research psychologist to collaborate on an article based on data that the junior faculty member had collected. The junior member thought that including the accomplished researcher as an author would improve the chances of the manuscript being accepted for publication. The senior psychologist agreed to have his name included and told the junior faculty member that after hearing a description of the writing plan, he would not have to read the manuscript before it was submitted for publication.

☒ A research psychologist agreed to conduct a study funded by a pharmaceutical firm to test the comparative efficacy of two psychoactive drugs. The psychologist sent the collected data to the sponsor for statistical analyses. After the data were analyzed, the sponsor offered to ghostwrite the article. The psychologist agreed and submitted it to a journal as sole author (see also Standard 3.06, Conflict of Interest; Pachter et al., 2007).

(b) Principal authorship and other publication credits accurately reflect the relative scientific or professional contributions of the individuals involved, regardless of their relative status. Mere possession of an institutional position, such as department chair, does not justify authorship credit. Minor contributions to the research or to the writing for publications are acknowledged appropriately, such as in footnotes or in an introductory statement.

Principal authorship must reflect the extent to which each individual contributed to the origination of the research problem, research design, interpretation of results, and drafting of the manuscript. In addition to underscoring the importance of the relative contribution as the determining factor for authorship credit, the wording of this standard is intended to protect students and junior faculty or research associates from exploitation by professors, supervisors, or senior administrators who might demand principal authorship based simply on the status of their position (McCarthy, 2012). The standard also requires that minor contributions not constituting authorship be acknowledged. Minor contributions include supportive functions such as designing or building the apparatus, suggesting or advising about the statistical analysis, collecting or entering the data, modifying or structuring a computer program, and recruiting participants or obtaining animals (APA, 2001).

⊘ A psychologist was the director of a large research center where postdoctoral students were encouraged to apply for young investigator awards listing the director as mentor. The psychologist always commented on drafts of manuscripts that the highly competent postdoctoral students submitted for publication but had a policy of being included as an author only if she directly contributed to the design, implementation, analysis, data interpretation, or writing.

(c) Except under exceptional circumstances, a student is listed as principal author on any multiple-authored article that is substantially based on the student's doctoral dissertation. Faculty advisors discuss publication credit with students as early as feasible and throughout the research and publication process as appropriate. (See also Standard 8.12b, Publication Credit.)

This standard recognizes that doctoral work is expected to represent an independent and original contribution devised and conducted largely by the student. Consequently, doctoral students should receive principal authorship on publications substantially based on their dissertation. The rare exception to this standard might occur when a student's doctoral dissertation is published in monograph form as part of a collection of studies by other researchers that cumulatively substantiates a phenomenon or supports or refutes a hypothesis.

Whether students merit principal authorship on master's-level or other predoctoral research will depend on their specific contributions to the research. When a student makes the primary contribution to a study, Standard 8.12b requires that she or he should be listed as the first author. Some students conducting master's and undergraduate honors research theses choose to work within an apprenticeship model distinctly different from the independent work model of the dissertation (Fine & Kurdek, 1993; Fisher & Younggren, 1997). For students who are only beginning to acquire the theoretical, methodological, statistical, and writing skills necessary to make a primary scientific contribution, the apprenticeship model provides the opportunity to learn these skills through collaboration on a faculty-originated project. In such cases, authorship should be determined by the relative contributions of student and faculty member to the project.

Standard 8.12c affords additional student protections by requiring that faculty advisers discuss publication credit with students as early as is feasible to provide students an opportunity to evaluate their skills and select the best mentoring experience (apprenticeship vs. independent scholar model) to meet their training needs and expectations for publication credit. Recognizing that research collaboration is a dynamic process in which relative contribution can change over time, research mentors should discuss with students any such changes they observe or anticipate that would affect publication credit at the point at which they emerge. For all student–faculty research collaborations, assignment of principal authorship must follow the rule of relative scientific contribution established in Standard 8.12b.

8.13 Duplicate Publication of Data

Psychologists do not publish, as original data, data that have been previously published. This does not preclude republishing data when they are accompanied by proper acknowledgment.

Scientific knowledge is based on cumulative evidence of the reliability of observations and relationships among variables tested over time and in different experimental contexts. When psychologists present the same data in different publications without proper acknowledgment, they jeopardize the evolution of scientific knowledge by giving the erroneous impression that replication of results has occurred (see Principle B: Fidelity and Responsibility and Principle C: Integrity). Duplicate publication of data without appropriate citation can jeopardize the validity of meta-analyses that shed light on a problem through a statistical synthesis of the data from a set of independent but comparable studies examining the problem. Publishing original data in more than one source without proper attribution also misrepresents the amount of experimental work the author has actually conducted and, in some instances, may result in violation of copyright law. Standard 8.13 does not prohibit psychologists from publishing the same data in different journals for the purpose of reaching different audiences, as long as proper citations of the original publication source are provided and psychologists have confirmed that such publication does not violate the original publisher's copyright.

The extent to which posting a manuscript on a psychologist's or his or her employer's website in manuscript form submitted, accepted, or published by a journal will depend on the journal's policy for such posting and whether the relationship of the posted document to prepublished or published materials is clearly posted along with the manuscript. For example, APA Publications frequently updates its Internet posting policies at http://www.apa.org/pubs/authors/posting.aspx. The most recent policy (APA, 2015a) is as follows:

- Authors can post unpublished papers on a website prior to submission as long as the papers are clearly labeled as unpublished.
- Editors must be advised of the website posting when the manuscript is submitted for review.
- Manuscripts of accepted articles can be posted in word-processing form, provided they carry an APA copyright notice and link to the journal home page, as well as include the following statement: "This article may not exactly replicate the final version published in the APA journal. It is not the copy of record."
- The manuscript cannot be archived with any non-APA repositories.
- The APA-published version must not appear in a scanned or otherwise copyrighted form.

Publishing multiple or piecemeal reports of different aspects of a single research project may be unethical without a reasonable theoretical, methodological, or practical justification for doing so. In such cases, investigators should inform the editor of the publication where the manuscript was submitted about their plans for publishing different parts of the study. Usually, Standard 8.13 does not preclude publication of full-length reports of materials published as conference abstracts or manuscripts with limited circulation (e.g., US dissertations or internal agency reports; see APA, 2015a). Exceptions occur when conference proceedings are published as full-length presentations in a volume that has an International Standard Book Number (ISBN).

The NIH Public Access Policy

The NIH Public Access Policy, implementing Division G, Title II, Section 218 of Public Law 110-161 (Consolidated Appropriations Act, 2008), was developed to ensure that published results based on NIH-funded research are available to the public (http://publicaccess.nih.gov/index.htm). It requires that as of April 7, 2008, investigators submit the accepted version of a peer-reviewed manuscript arising from NIH funds to PubMed Central (http://www.ncbi.nlm.nih.gov/pmc/). To comply with the policy, investigators must do the following:

- Make sure that any copyright transfer allows the final peer-reviewed manuscripts to be submitted to NIH in accordance with the policy. Journals that have agreed to do this automatically are listed at http://publicaccess.nih.gov/submit_process_journals.htm. For those journals not listed, the author must inform the journal that the final peer-reviewed manuscript is subject to the Public Access Policy when submitting it for publication.
- Submit the final draft of the accepted peer-reviewed manuscript to NIH.
- When citing their NIH-funded papers in NIH applications, proposals, or progress reports, include the PubMed Central reference number for each article (effective May 25, 2008).

8.14 Sharing Research Data for Verification

(a) After research results are published, psychologists do not withhold the data on which their conclusions are based from other competent professionals who seek to verify the substantive claims through reanalysis and who intend to use such data only for that purpose, provided that the confidentiality of the participants can be protected and unless legal rights concerning proprietary data preclude their release. This does not preclude psychologists from requiring that such individuals or groups be responsible for costs associated with the provision of such information.

The self-correcting nature of science requires investigators to share research data for the purpose of replication and reanalysis. Such openness protects the integrity of science through independent validation of data coding, analysis, and interpretation and reflects awareness of researchers' responsibilities to the scientific community and the public (Principle B: Fidelity and Responsibility). Sharing data also promotes data aggregation for the purposes of hypothesis testing and programmatic decision making and allows individuals with limited resources or access to specific populations to investigate scientific questions (APA Data Sharing Working Group, 2015).

Psychologists should follow appropriate guidelines for retention of data (see also Standard 6.01, Documentation of Professional and Scientific Work and Maintenance of Records). For example, authors of articles published in APA journals are required to have their raw data available for at least 5 years after the date of publication (APA, 2001).

The term *competent professionals* as used in this standard limits the obligation to provide data to individuals competent in the research methods and data-analytic techniques necessary to substantiate claims through reanalysis. Psychologists are not required to share data with individuals for purposes of developing and testing new theories or other goals beyond reanalysis and verification of data. The standard recognizes that there may be legitimate ethical, legal, and financial barriers to data sharing. In some instances, it may be impossible to de-identify data to adequately protect the confidentiality rights of those who participated in the research (Standard 4.01, Maintaining Confidentiality). In other instances, a third party who is not a psychologist may own the proprietary rights to the data. To avoid subjecting investigators to financial hardship or harassment, the standard permits psychologists to require that costs of the exchange be borne by the requesting party.

Need to Know: Procedures for Sharing and Using "Big Data"

New technologies continue to increase the capacity to re-identify previously de-identified data, resulting in a greater emphasis on restricted-use data and the ability to update privacy protections in response to changing information risk circumstances (NRC, 2014). Psychologists creating data sets that will be stored in repositories and shared with other competent professionals or those utilizing data from large-scale national surveys or genetic databases need to remain constantly updated on evolving policies for data sharing adopted by government agencies, academic and research institutions, and scientific societies (see the feature earlier in this chapter "Need to Know: Proposed Changes to Federal Regulations").

The APA Data Sharing Working Group (2015) recommended that institutions include in their evaluations and promotion of researchers knowledge of appropriate value and use of shared data. The APA Working Group also recommended the following:

- Sharing of data should conform to prior agreement with involved parties, including participants' consent and, in the case of community-based participatory research, agreements concerning community ownership.
- Investigators need to set levels of access to their data appropriate to the potential for re-identification. This includes consideration of information harms that may arise for sharing of de-identified survey data that include information about illegal or stigmatized behaviors (e.g., drug use, sex work), qualitative data (e.g., transcripts of interviews or focus groups that include discussion of identifiable locals or persons), geographical data (e.g., GPS) that track participants' activity, or video or audio data.
- How long researchers are entitled to wait to share data they have produced should be commensurate with the nature of data collection and the time required for the research team to conduct its own analysis.
- The principal investigator is responsible for ensuring that data are prepared in a form that is usable by others (e.g., sufficient demographic information) and appropriately stored for accessibility in a data repository.
- Secondary data users are responsible for protecting the identities of participants in accordance with prior agreements.

(b) Psychologists who request data from other psychologists to verify the substantive claims through reanalysis may use shared data only for the declared purpose. Requesting psychologists obtain prior written agreement for all other uses of the data.

This standard protects the intellectual property rights of the owner of the data by prohibiting the requesting psychologist from piggybacking on the work of another by using the data for any purpose other than reanalysis or to verify substantive claims. The data cannot be used to test related or peripheral hypotheses or to develop new research or analytic techniques unless the psychologist obtains prior written agreement.

☒ On the basis of a written request, a psychologist received data from another psychologist to verify through inspection of the data and reanalysis the interpretation of findings stated in a recent publication. After receiving the data, the psychologist realized that there were several additional hypotheses that could be tested with the data set. The psychologist quickly developed an analytic plan and gathered a team of graduate students to implement the plan in time to submit the analysis of new hypotheses for presentation at an upcoming professional meeting.

8.15 Reviewers

Psychologists who review material submitted for presentation, publication, grant, or research proposal review respect the confidentiality of and the proprietary rights in such information of those who submitted it.

Research psychologists have an obligation to establish relationships of trust and are aware of their responsibilities to other investigators and the scientific community (Principle B: Fidelity and Responsibility). Psychologists are prohibited from using privileged and proprietary information obtained through confidential review of research materials, including the review of grant applications and papers submitted for publication or presentation at professional meetings. This standard protects the intellectual property rights of individuals who describe their theories, research designs, and data in unpublished materials from use by others who obtain this information during the peer review process. If for reasons of expertise or training reviewers wish to have a colleague or graduate student review the material, they must first obtain prior permission of the grants program officer, journal editor, or meeting chair. Reviewed materials should be returned or destroyed following completion of the review. Psychologists should also guard against potential conflicts of interest when they are reviewing articles that support, conflict, or compete with their own published or current research endeavors (see Standard 3.06, Conflict of Interest; Greenwald, 2009).

☒ A research psychologist on an NIH special emphasis panel was primary reviewer on an R01 grant application addressing a conceptual problem that the psychologist had been tackling in her own lab. The psychologist wrote a critical review of the proposal and argued strongly for a score in the unfundable range. Several months later, the principal investigator of the R01 application was distressed to learn that the psychologist had begun a series of studies almost identical to those in the rejected proposal (see also Standard 3.06, Conflict of Interest).

HOT TOPIC

Informational Risk and Disclosure of Genetic Information to Research Participants

The Human Genome Project and rapid technological advances in genomics have begun to enrich psychological science's contributions to understanding the role of genetic factors in normative cognitive and emotional functioning and in the etiology, onset, and escalation of bipolar disorder, schizophrenia, and other mental health disorders (Kremen et al., 2011; Singh et al., 2011; Tarbox & Pogue-Geile, 2011; Zavos, Gregory, & Eley, 2012). Advanced genomic technology has also illuminated distinct and intersecting influences of genetics and psychosocial and environmental stressors on a range of psychosocial behaviors (e.g., parenting style, political orientation, gender values), the unique and interacting roles of genetic and environmental factors in academic achievement and responsivity to educational interventions, and psychopathology (e.g., conduct disorder, adult antisocial behavior, binge eating; Beach et al., 2012; Belsky & Pluess, 2009; Haworth & Plomin, 2012; Kandler, Bleidorn, & Riemann, 2012; Meier, Slutske, Heath, & Martin, 2011; Musci et al., 2013; Racine, Burt, Iacono, McGue, & Klump, 2011; Wang et al., 2014). Psychosocial research on the intervention responsivity of children with specific genetic susceptibilities for behavioral problems has just begun to attract psychological scientists (Brody, Chen, Beach, Philibert, & Kogan, 2009). However, advances in the integration of genomic science into psychological research have also illuminated significant limitations in the translation of research findings to the prediction, identification, or treatment of psychological disorders.

Attention to the risks and benefits of disclosing personal genetic information to research participants has not kept pace with the techniques, data, and limitations produced in this rapidly evolving field. At this early stage of the science, the ethical challenges for research involving the study of genetic variants are "informational" in nature (Beskow & Burke, 2009), affecting the extent and limits of personal data that should be disclosed to participants (Standard 8.08, Debriefing) and providing information on those limitations during informed consent (Standard 8.02, Informed Consent to Research). This Hot Topic identifies key questions to consider in determining the ethical justification for disclosing personal genetic information of research participants (for additional information, see the NIH Genomic Data Sharing (GDS) Policy effective January 25, 2015, at http://gds.nih.gov/03policy2.html).

The Probabilistic Nature of Gene–Environment Influences on Behavior

Most psychological disorders do not emerge from single gene–environment interactions. Rather, research suggests that mental health risks and outcomes involve the interplay of multiple genetic and nongenetic factors, that different gene variants can influence similar psychological disorders, and that even when specific gene–environment effects on behavior have been identified, the actual emergence of the behavior is only probabilistic (Plomin & Davis, 2009; Schlomer, Cleveland, Vandenbergh, Fosco, & Feinberg, 2015). At this early stage of the science, the relatively small sample size of available study populations at genetic risk for specific mental health disorders, variability in the life contexts interacting with genetic factors, the variability of prevention and intervention strategies, and lack of replication limit the generalizability and individual relevance of research results (Henderson, 2008). Moreover, while the identification of gene markers can help elucidate the factors placing certain individuals at increased risk for disorder development, many studies will lack clinical or personal relevance to individual study participants (Fisher & McCarthy, 2013). Disclosure of personal data from research results linking genetic factors to the development of psychological disorders can thus lead to the over- or underestimation of mental health risk for individual participants.

Informational Risk

Personal genetic information influences our own identity and the identities we are assigned by others (Ossorio & Duster, 2005; Svendsen & Koch, 2006). Sharing individual research results with participants can demonstrate respect for their right to determine the utility of personal information and to acquire health information that can help them make life plans (Principle E: Respect for People's Rights and Dignity). However, investigators also have a responsibility to promote accuracy and truthfulness in science and accept appropriate responsibility for acknowledging limitations of research results that have yet to meet criteria for validity and reliability (Principle B: Fidelity and Responsibility, Principle C: Integrity). While scientists recognize that single genetic variants have limited predictive power, individuals often adopt a genetic essentialism that perceives genetic markers to be more deterministic than other risk factors in their potential to predict future disorders (Dar-Nimrod & Heine, 2011; Kendler, 2005). Thus, decisions to share research-derived personal genetic information with participants require a consideration of informational benefits and harms that may result (Principle A: Beneficence and Nonmaleficence).

Informational risk is often related to the initial phase of a new line of research exploring genetic correlates of mental health. During this phase, data are not collected with the aim of generating health information relevant to prediction of individual risk but with testing hypotheses about gene–environment–behavior relationships targeted to the understanding of probabilistic differences among groups sharing similar characteristics (Bioethics Advisory Committee, 2005). Providing participants with personal genetic information within the context of data on yet to be replicated group differences may lead to over- or underestimation of personal risk, which in turn may negatively influence future health decisions.

Investigators may find other ethical challenges associated with informational risk. Although psychologists may implement appropriate confidentiality protections for genetic data (Standards 4.01,

(Continued)

(Continued)

Maintaining Confidentiality; 6.02 Maintenance, Dissemination, and Disposal of Confidential Records of Professional and Scientific Work), providing participants with personal genetic information with empirically unreliable implications for health may be a form of "inflicted insight" that carries its own burdens of disclosure. For example, healthy adults informed that they possess a gene marker that may or may not be predictive of a mental health disorder may struggle with whether this incurs an obligation to report this vulnerability to family members, future employers, or health insurance companies (Fisher & McCarthy, 2013). Preliminary clinical trials for established mental disorders that explore the association of gene variants with treatment outcomes can also influence future employment and health insurance options if genetic data collected solely for research purposes are included in participants' health records (see "A Word About HIPAA" in the preface of this book).

Scientific Validity

The weaker the scientific foundation for a hypothesized relationship between genetic factors and psychosocial or behavioral risk, the weaker the ethical argument for disclosure (Fisher, 2006). Given the diversity and complexity of gene–environment prevention studies, a singular approach to disclosure of personal genetic information to participants is inadequate protection against informational harm (Standard 2.04, Bases for Scientific and Professional Judgments). Several investigators have suggested that ethical decisions regarding whether to report personal genetic information to research participants must be based on the accuracy, reliability, and replicability of laboratory-based genetic testing and its relationship to measures of mental health (Fisher & McCarthy, 2013; Grandjean & Sorsa, 1996; O'Connell, Boat, & Warner, 2009; Ravitsky & Wilfond, 2006). Based on this work, psychologists should consider the following questions when determining disclosure policies:

- Is there a body of empirical evidence clearly demonstrating an association between a genetic marker and a specific mental health risk for individuals with other relevant personal and environmental characteristics in common with the participant?
- Is there a low probability of false positives?
- What proportion of risk is attributed to heritability versus environmental factors?
- Is the magnitude of the gene–disorder association sufficiently large and disorder sufficiently severe to justify informational risks associated with under- or overestimation of risk?

Severity of Disorder and Treatment Options

The extent to which participants have a right to personal data collected solely for research purposes will vary depending on the direct relevance of the information to their current or future health (Principle E: Respect for People's Rights and Dignity). The more serious the disorder, the stronger is the ethical argument for disclosure (Fisher & McCarthy, 2013). When making ethical decisions to share personal genetic information with participants, psychologists must weigh the degree of scientific certainty regarding gene–environment–behavior associations against the informational value of disclosure (Grandjean & Sorsa, 1996; Ravitsky & Wilfond, 2006). The World Health Organization (WHO, 2003) addressed this problem for information gained from genetic databases, setting criteria for individual disclosure based on whether (a) the data can be instrumental in identifying a clear clinical benefit to identifiable individuals and (b) disclosure to relevant individuals will avert or minimize harm to those individuals. These perspectives inform the evaluation of the personal and clinical utility of providing participants with individual research results within the framework of scientific validity:

- Is there sufficient quality and quantity of empirical evidence of the association between the genetic characteristic and manifestation of the disorder?
- Is there a low probability of false-positive genetic test results?
- Does the disorder present a major risk to participants' future health?
- Will accessible, safe, and effective preventive interventions or treatments be available to participants following the disclosure of individual results?
- If not, to what extent may knowledge of one's personal genotype positively or negatively affect a participant's well-being and influence future health decisions?

Ethically Appropriate Disclosure Procedures

When the balance between scientific validity and personal utility meets the criteria for individual disclosure, investigators must also demonstrate the capacity to communicate results to participants in a clinically competent manner (Knoppers, Joly, Simard, & Durocher, 2006; Standard 2.01, Boundaries of Competence). This can include working with genetic counselors to assist in appropriate disclosure and referral procedures (WHO, 2003).

An additional disclosure consideration is the participant's preference for or against disclosure (Fisher & McCarthy, 2013; Murphy et al., 2008). Under current federal regulations and international guidelines, participants have a right to decide whether or not to be informed about the results of genetic testing, especially in cases in which early treatment is not available (DHHS, 2009; United Nations Educational, Scientific and Cultural Organization, 1997). If criteria for individual disclosure are met, psychologists should consider the following:

- How can the benefits and limitations of disclosure be adequately communicated during informed consent? The more complex the gene–risk association, the greater the ethical responsibility to provide genetic literacy education to participants during the consent process so that they can make an informed choice about their preference for disclosure (Fisher & McCarthy, 2013; readers might also wish to refer to the general principles of goodness-of-fit ethics for informed consent described in the Hot Topic of Chapter 6).
- Does the investigator or members of his or her research team possess the necessary knowledge and skills for communicating genetic test results to participants (Standard 2.01, Boundaries of Competence)?
- If a genetic counselor is employed to carry out disclosure of test results, has the investigator developed an appropriate monitoring procedure for ensuring the competency of the counselor's work (Standard 2.05, Delegation of Work to Others)?
- Has the investigator identified appropriate referral sources for preventive intervention or treatment to which participants can be referred following disclosure (Standard 3.04, Avoiding Harm)?

Security of De-Identified Information in Genetic Data in Repositories

Long-term data storage and data analytic technologies have and will continue to undergo rapid advances. These advances contribute to new ways of analyzing previously unidentified genetic

(Continued)

(Continued)

markers and linking such markers to social–behavioral data years after a data collection has been completed. At the same time, rapidly emerging technologies mean that original de-identification data security protections may become obsolete (de Montjoye, Radaelli, Singh, & Pentland, 2015). To ensure that participants are aware of confidentiality risks, some have suggested that reconsent for data housed in biobanks should be required every 10 years and a secondary analysis of genomic data collected from children should require reconsent once they reach the age of maturity (Fisher, Brunnquell, et al., 2013; see also the feature earlier in this chapter "Need to Know: Proposed Changes to Federal Regulations").

Social Responsibility

The current expansion of genetics as a major explanatory framework for mental health disorders and treatment responsivity has the potential to increase society's genetic literacy and improve public health. At the same time, misunderstanding and misuse of genetic research results can perpetrate social inequities by ignoring more powerful and enduring social and political inequities that sustain mental health disparities among marginalized populations (Fisher et al., 2012). When a genetic influence on risk is reported, a new "geneticized" disease may be created in the public's mind (Lippman, 1991), irrespective of the probabilistic and multifactorial nature of gene influences on mental health. Public responses to population-based genetics research can also stigmatize an entire community as being predisposed to specific diseases, simultaneously affecting members' public and personal identities, especially in research involving racial/ethnic minorities (Fisher & McCarthy, 2013). Psychologists' ethical awareness of the potential informational goods and harms of genetic research and heightened sensitivity to the social and political realities in which participants live will yield scientific data that minimizes informational risk, optimizes participant informed choice, and advances public health.

Chapter Cases and Ethics Discussion Questions

The Centers for Disease Control has identified young men who have sex with men (YMSM) as a population at high risk for HIV and encourages physicians to consider prescribing for this population pre-exposure prophylaxis (PrEP), a pill taken daily, which has been found to be an effective prevention against HIV infection. To date, however, there has been no research involving YMSM under the age of 18 who may find it difficult to take the pill everyday due to normative developmental factors related to adherence and structural barriers facing this population, including stigma and discrimination. One barrier to research participation is youths' concern that requiring guardian permission will "out" them to family, resulting in punishment and rejection. A psychologist submits a protocol for studying whether text messages can help increase adherence to PrEP among YMSM between 15 and 17 years of age. She asks her IRB to waive the requirement for guardian permission. Discuss whether the psychologist's request meets ethical standards for waiving guardian permission and the steps that she would need to take to ensure that the youths' self-consent was informed, rational, and voluntary.

In 2014, investigators from several academic research institutions collaborated with Facebook to test whether reducing the number of positive or negative messages people saw made them less likely to post positive or negative content themselves (Kramer, Guillory, & Hancock, 2014). The experiment was carried out by manipulating the algorithm by which Facebook sweeps posts into members' news feeds. Participants were not informed they were a part of this research. Investigators involved in the study defended the absence of informed consent for a study designed to influence emotions, arguing that the manipulation was consistent with Facebook's Data Use Policy, to which all users must agree at the time they join Facebook (Goel, 2014). However, the Facebook policy only mentions "research" in general terms (e.g., "We may use the information we receive about you . . . for internal operations, including troubleshooting, data analysis, testing, research and service improvement" (Waldman, 2014). The investigators also argued that they were using "archival" data collected by a business entity, despite the fact that they were involved in the initial study design. According to the APA Ethics Code, was the psychologists' involvement in this study ethical or unethical?

Drawing on the limited success of a research study in Switzerland, a psychologist with expertise in drug addiction proposes to conduct a randomized clinical trial to assess whether a heroin prescription under supervised conditions is more effective than the standard harm reduction behavioral treatment for treating opiate addiction among persons in the United States who inject drugs and who are homeless or have minimal housing. To motivate participants to return for regular treatments, the investigator proposes to offer $30 for each visit. In reviewing the case, some IRB members argue that receiving medical care that would not otherwise be available to this population is sufficient motivator for participation. Drawing on the sections in this chapter under Standards 8.06a and 8.06b, discuss whether either monetary payment or provision of services is a fair or coercive incentive for this population or whether an ethically preferable alternative compensation or inducement exists.

CHAPTER 12

Standards on Assessment

9. Assessment

9.01 Bases for Assessments

(a) Psychologists base the opinions contained in their recommendations, reports, and diagnostic or evaluative statements, including forensic testimony, on information and techniques sufficient to substantiate their findings. (See also Standard 2.04, Bases for Scientific and Professional Judgments.)

Psychological assessment serves the public good by providing information to guide decisions affecting the well-being of individuals, families, groups, organizations, and institutions. Psychologists who base their conclusions about information and techniques on the scientific and professional knowledge of the discipline are uniquely qualified to interpret the results of psychological assessments in ways that merit the public trust. However, the public and the profession are harmed when psychologists provide opinions unsubstantiated by information obtained or drawn from data gathered through improper assessment techniques (Principle A: Beneficence and Nonmaleficence; Principle B: Fidelity and Responsibility). Standard 9.01a of the APA Ethics Code (APA, 2010b) prohibits psychologists from providing written or oral opinions that cannot be sufficiently substantiated by the information obtained or the techniques employed.

The standard is broadly worded to apply to all written and oral professional opinions, irrespective of information recipient, setting, or type of assessment.

Need to Know: Assessment in Child Protection Matters

Forensic examiners retained in response to an accusation of child abuse and neglect need to obtain competencies relevant to the intersecting interests of the child, the parents, and the state, including laws on parental termination and the role of kinship and policies favoring child placement with extended family members in favor of foster care (Standard 2.01f, Competence; APA, 2013b). The primary purpose of the assessment is to help government agencies and courts determine whether a child's health and welfare may have been and/or may be harmed. Consequently, in addition to the broader parent–child "fit" considerations typical of custody evaluations, psychologists need to select assessment techniques sufficient to address the particular vulnerabilities and risks of maltreatment associated with specific child characteristics (e.g., children with developmental disabilities or other medical needs) and the need for and likelihood of success of clinical interventions for problems associated with abuse, maltreatment, or neglect. This may include familiarity with techniques for assessing the role of specific cultural patterns of parenting, impact of familial separation, and foster and kinship-based alternative care. In interpreting results, psychologists must also refrain from assuming a child advocacy role and gather information impartially based on reliable methods established in the field (Standard 2.04, Bases for Scientific and Professional Judgments).

Information Recipient

The standard prohibits unfounded professional opinions offered to, among others, (a) individual clients/patients or their representatives; (b) other professionals; (c) third-party payors; (d) administrative and professional staff at schools, hospitals, and other institutions; (e) businesses, agencies, and other organizations; (f) the courts; (g) the military or other governing legal authorities; and (h) callers to talk radio programs or those interacting with psychologists via the Internet or through other media.

Setting

Standard 9.01a applies to (a) diagnostic opinions offered orally in the office of a private practitioner; (b) written reports provided to clients/patients, other practitioners, or third-party payors through the mail, the Internet, or other forms of electronic transmission; (c) testimony provided in the courts; and (d) opinions about an individual's mental health offered over the Internet, radio, television, or other electronic media.

Types of Assessment

The standard pertains to all unfounded opinions claiming to be based on any form of evaluation, including but not limited to (a) standardized psychological, educational, or neuropsychological tests; (b) diagnostic information gained through clinical interviews; (c) collateral data obtained through discussions with family members, teachers, employee supervisors, or other informants; (d) observational techniques; or (e) brief discussion or correspondence with an individual via radio, television, telephone, or the Internet.

Violations of this standard are often related to failure to comply with other standards, including Standards 2.04, Bases for Scientific and Professional Judgments; 9.01b, Bases for Assessments; and 9.02b, Use of Assessments. For example, psychologists should not use test scores as sole indicators for diagnostic or special program placement but instead use multiple sources of information and, when appropriate, provide alternative explanations for test performance (AERA, APA, & NCME, 2014). The following are examples of opinions based on insufficient information or techniques that would be considered violations under this standard:

- ☒ Testifying on the validity of a child abuse allegation based on the results of an idiosyncratic, improperly constructed parent checklist of child behaviors
- ☒ Diagnosing an adult with impaired decisional capacity as developmentally disabled without taking a developmental history
- ☒ Providing preemployment recommendations on the basis of a personality test with no proven relationship to job performance
- ☒ Submitting a diagnosis of neurological impairment to a health insurance company based solely on information derived during therapy sessions
- ☒ Informing parents that their preschooler is autistic on the basis of a single observational session
- ☒ Recommending a child for special education placement solely on the basis of scores on a standardized intelligence test
- ☒ Offering a diagnosis of PTSD based on a 5-minute discussion with a listener who calls in to a radio program hosted by the psychologist
- ☒ Offering a diagnosis of bipolar disorder based on an individual's comments on the psychologist's blog
- ☒ Submitting for health insurance reimbursement a diagnosis of dementia in an elderly patient complaining of memory lapses, without conducting a neuropsychological assessment

Psychologists who knowingly provide unsubstantiated opinions in forensic, school, or insurance reports fail to live up to the ideals of Principle C: Integrity and may also find themselves in violation of Standard 5.01, Avoidance of False or Deceptive Statements (see Hot Topic "Avoiding False and Deceptive Statements in Scientific and Clinical Expert Testimony," Chapter 8). However, psychologists should also be alert to personal and professional biases that may affect their choice and interpretation of instruments. For example, in a survey of forensic experts testifying in cases of child sexual abuse allegations, Everson and Sandoval (2011) found that evaluator disagreements could be explained, in part, by individual differences in three forensic decision-making attitudes: (1) emphasis on sensitivity, (2) emphasis on specificity, and (3) skepticism toward child reports of abuse.

Digital Ethics: Use of Mobile Phones for Treatment Adherence Monitoring

For some mental health disorders such as anorexia nervosa, borderline personality disorder, and substance dependency, downloadable mobile phone applications (mHealth) for client/patient self-monitoring can be a valuable adjunct to in-person psychotherapy, as they can reduce vulnerabilities of memory and help clients/patients reflect critically on their thoughts and behaviors (Aardoom Dingemans, Spinhoven, & Van Furth, 2013; Ambwani, Cardi, & Treasure, 2014; Dimeff, Rizvi, Contreras, Skutch, & Carroll, 2011; Dombo et al., 2014). When deciding whether mHealth is clinically indicated for a specific client/patient, psychologists should consider (a) whether the client/patient can effectively use the technology without supervision, based on diagnostic assessment as well as conducting an in-office assessment of the client's/patient's ability to utilize the technology, and (b) the likelihood that clients/patients will become overdependent on the mobile technology in ways that jeopardize their ability to implement behavior management skills independent of the technology (Ambwani et al., 2014; Standards 2.04, Bases for Scientific and Professional Judgments, and 3.04, Avoiding Harm). To ensure appropriate confidentiality protections, psychologists should (a) assess risks to confidentiality that may be inherent in the client's/patient's home, work, and other treatment management–related environments; (b) utilize behavior management mobile applications and/or Internet sites with adequate security protections; and (c) provide clients/patients with instruction on how to protect their privacy and confidentiality (Standards 4.01, Maintaining Confidentiality; 4.02, Discussing the Limits of Confidentiality).

(b) Except as noted in 9.01c, psychologists provide opinions of the psychological characteristics of individuals only after they have conducted an examination of the individuals adequate to support their statements or conclusions. When, despite reasonable efforts, such an examination is not practical, psychologists document the efforts they made and the result of those efforts, clarify the probable impact of their limited information on the reliability and validity of their opinions, and appropriately limit the nature and extent of their conclusions or recommendations. (See also Standards 2.01, Boundaries of Competence, and 9.06, Interpreting Assessment Results.)

Standard 9.01b specifically addresses the importance of in-person evaluations of individuals about whom psychologists will offer a professional opinion. Under this standard, with few exceptions, psychologists must conduct individual examinations sufficient to obtain personal verification of information on which to base their professional opinions and refrain from providing opinions about the psychological characteristics of an individual if they themselves have not conducted an examination of the individual adequate to support their statements or conclusions. As video conferencing and other electronically mediated sources of video communication become increasingly common, appropriately conducted assessments via these media may meet the requirements of this standard if the psychologist has had the appropriate preparatory training and the validity of the video methods of assessment has been scientifically and clinically established for use with members of the population tested (Standards 2.01e, Boundaries of Competence; 2.04, Bases for Scientific and Professional Judgment; 9.02, Use of Assessments).

☒ A psychologist testified about a parent's psychological fitness for visitation rights, drawing his opinion solely from comments made by the child and divorced spouse in the absence of an individual examination of the parent.

☒ A psychologist contracted by an insurance company to evaluate an individual's mental health as part of a current disability claim provided an opinion based solely on job performance evaluations written by the insured's immediate supervisors and diagnostic information collected by another psychologist prior to the incident cited in the claim.

☒ A psychologist working in a correctional facility who was asked to recommend whether a prison guard's mental status was a risk to prisoner protections did not personally examine the guard but instead gave an opinion based on reports by facility administrators, staff, and prisoners.

Standard 9.01b also recognizes that in some cases, a personal examination may not be possible. For example, an individual involved in a child custody suit, a disability claim, or performance evaluation may refuse or, because of relocation or other reasons, be unavailable for a personal examination. The standard requires that psychologists make "reasonable efforts" to conduct a personal examination. Efforts that would not be considered reasonable in the prevailing professional judgment of psychologists engaged in similar activities would be considered a violation of this standard. Consider the following two examples of potential violations:

☒ A psychologist was contracted by a prison to evaluate the job potential of guards hired for a probationary period. Without conducting an individual interview, the psychologist wrote a report concluding that emotional instability of one job candidate made him ineligible for full-time employment. The psychologist justified the lack of a personal examination on the fact that several coworkers had claimed the guard was too dangerous to interview.

☒ A psychologist hired by the attorney of a husband engaged in a custody suit provided court testimony on the wife's parenting inadequacies without having interviewed her personally. The psychologist claimed that the wife had not responded to the psychologist's letter requesting the interview. On cross-examination, it was revealed that the letter written by the psychologist included the following language seemingly designed to discourage agreement to be examined: "I have reason to believe from interviews with your spouse and an examination of your children that you are responsible for the children's current mental health problems and would like to conduct an examination to confirm or dispute these assumptions."

When, despite reasonable efforts, a personal interview is not feasible, under Standard 9.01b psychologists in their written or oral opinions must document and explain the results of their efforts, clarify the probable impact that the failure to personally examine an individual may have on the reliability and validity of their opinions, and appropriately limit their conclusions or recommendations to information they can personally verify. Psychologists may report relevant consistencies or inconsistencies of information found in documents they were asked to review (see Standard 9.01c below). However, they should avoid offering opinions regarding the personal credibility or truthfulness of individuals they have not examined or when basic facts contested have not been resolved through assessments (APA, 2013b).

⊘ A court-appointed psychologist attempted to contact the biological parent of a child currently in foster care to make recommendations regarding parental visitation. The parent was no longer at the last known residence and had not left a forwarding address. In testimony, the psychologist described the current mental health status of the child, the child's statements regarding the biological parent, and the observed relationship between the child and foster parents. In referring to the biological parent, the psychologist informed the court of efforts to contact the parent, described how failure to interview the parent limited any conclusions that could be drawn regarding the parent's psychological characteristics and parenting competence, and clarified that recommendations regarding visitation were based on the child's attitudes, mental health, and foster care arrangements.

(c) When psychologists conduct a record review or provide consultation or supervision and an individual examination is not warranted or necessary for the opinion, psychologists explain this and the sources of information on which they based their conclusions and recommendations.

This standard applies to those assessment-related activities for which an individual examination is not warranted or necessary for the psychological opinion.

Such activities include record or file reviews where psychologists are called on to review preexisting records and reports to assist or evaluate decisions made by schools, courts, health insurance companies, organizations, or other psychologists they supervise or with whom they consult. Record reviews can be performed to (a) determine whether a previously conducted assessment was appropriate or sufficient; (b) evaluate the appropriateness of treatment, placement, employment, or continuation of benefits based on the previously gathered information and reports; (c) adjudicate a disability or professional liability claim based on existing records; or (d) resolve conflicts over the applicability of records to interpretations of federal and state laws in administrative law or due process hearings (Bartol & Bartol, 2014; Hadjistavropoulos & Bieling, 2001).

Reviewers provide a monitoring function for the court or a function of forensic quality control so the court will not be misled by *expert testimony* of evaluators that is based on flawed data collection and/or analysis (Austin, Kirkpatrick, & Flens, 2011). According to Standard 9.01c, psychologists who provide such services must clarify to the appropriate parties the source of the information on which the opinion is based and why an individual interview conducted by the psychologist is not necessary for the opinion.

Simply complying with this standard may not be sufficient for psychologists who are in supervisory roles that carry legal responsibility for the conduct of assessments by unlicensed supervisees or employees. In many of those instances, psychologists may be directly responsible for ensuring that individuals are qualified to conduct the assessments and do so competently (see Standard 2.05, Delegation of Work to Others).

Review of Data From Surreptitious Investigative Recording

There are instances when forensic psychologists may be asked to evaluate past mental states from audio or video recordings of a defendant's behavior at the time of the alleged offense or surreptitious recordings of a plaintiff's behavior in a personal injury, insurance disability, or divorce case (Denney & Wynkoop, 2000). Before agreeing to review such recordings, psychologists should make sure that the surveillance information was obtained legally at the time it was recorded, that the party requesting the psychologist's evaluation has the legal right to share such information, and that inadmissibility of such information will not compromise the psychologist's findings. Psychologists should also take reasonable steps to ascertain that they have been provided with all legally available recordings and other available information relevant to the forensic opinion. The psychologist's oral testimony or written report should clarify the source of the information and why an individual examination is not warranted or necessary for the type of evaluation requested.

9.02 Use of Assessments

(a) Psychologists administer, adapt, score, interpret, or use assessment techniques, interviews, tests, or instruments in a manner and for purposes that are appropriate in light of the research on or evidence of the usefulness and proper application of the techniques.

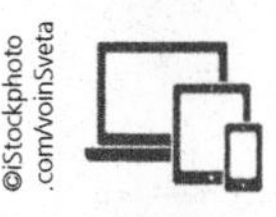
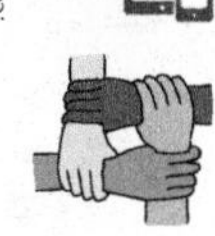

The appropriate use of psychological assessments can benefit individuals, families, organizations, and society by providing information on which educational placements, mental health treatments, health insurance coverage, employee selection, job placement, workers' compensation, program development, legal decisions, and government policies can be based. The inappropriate use of assessments can lead to harmful diagnostic, educational, institutional, legal, and social policy decisions based on inaccurate and misleading information.

Standard 9.02a is concerned with the proper selection, interpretation, scoring, and administration of assessments. It refers to the full range of assessment techniques used by psychologists, including interviews and standardized tests administered in person, through the Internet, or through other media. According to this standard, ethical justification for the use of assessments is determined by research on or evidence supporting the purpose for which the test is administered, the method of administration, and interpretation of scores (AERA, APA, & NCME, 2014). To comply with the standard, psychologists should be familiar with and be able to evaluate the data and other information provided in test manuals detailing (a) the theoretical and empirical support for test use for specific purposes and populations, (b) the test's psychometric validity, (c) administration procedures, and (d) how test scores are to be calculated and interpreted. Psychologists should also keep themselves apprised of ongoing research or evidence of a test's usefulness or obsolescence over time (see also Standards 2.03, Maintaining Competence; 2.04, Bases for Scientific and Professional Judgments; 9.08b, Obsolete Tests and Outdated Test Results). The standard also requires that psychologists adhere to standardized test administration protocols to ensure that test scores reflect the construct(s) being assessed and avoid undue influence of idiosyncrasies in the testing process (AERA, APA, & NCME, 2014).

Digital Ethics: Internet-Mediated Assessments

Psychologists administering assessments via the Internet need to remain up-to-date on research demonstrating the assessments' validity or lack thereof for use in this medium (Montalto, 2014; Standard 2.03, Maintaining Competence). Verification of the examinee's age, gender, and honesty of disclosures is important to the assessment's validity and reliability (Alleman, 2002). Some assessments developed for in-person administration require verbal, auditory, or kinesthetic clues for accurate diagnosis (Barak & English, 2002). When assessments have not been validated for use via the Internet, psychologists should make every effort to conduct an in-person evaluation. When this is not possible, psychologists should select instruments that research or other evidence indicates are

(Continued)

(Continued)

most appropriate for this medium, implement when possible information-gathering techniques that can best approximate in-person settings (e.g., video and auditory interactive technology), and acknowledge limitations of the assessment in interpretations of the data (Standard 9.06, Interpreting Assessment Results). Technology-based testing is also related to concerns regarding standardized administration and construct validation. Psychologists need to be aware of limitations in administration and interpretation for examinees who may not have access to or are unfamiliar with the use of new technologies or will be using older computers or devices with slower processing speed (AERA, APA, & NCME, 2014; Standard 3.01, Unfair Discrimination).

Violations of Standard 9.02a occur when psychologists use assessments in a manner or for a purpose that is not supported by evidence in the field (see also this chapter's Hot Topic "The Use of Assessments in Expert Testimony: Implications of Case Law and the Federal Rules of Evidence").

- ☒ A psychologist contracted to conduct employment testing for an organization administered a series of personality inventories with little or no validity evidence supporting the link between scores on the inventories and actual job performance.
- ☒ A counseling psychologist working with an isolated rural community administered a series of tests over the Internet without previously establishing whether the Internet-mediated scores measured the same construct as scores from the paper-and-pencil version (Buchanan, 2002).
- ☒ A school psychologist working under pressure to meet the school system's quotas for weekly testing gave the same battery of tests to all students irrespective of their grade level or presenting problem.
- ☒ A neuropsychologist conducted a forensic examination of a prisoner in a room occupied by other prisoners, thereby compromising the validity of score interpretation based on norms established under standardized distraction-free testing environments.

Modifications for Individuals With Disabilities

Test administration for individuals with disabilities may require modifications and adaptations in testing administration to minimize the effect of test taker characteristics incidental to the purpose of the assessment. Standard 9.02a permits departure from a standard administration protocol if the method of test adaptation can be justified by research or other evidence. For example, converting a written test to Braille for an individual who is legally blind, physically assisting a client with cerebral palsy to circle items on a written test, or providing breaks for an individual with a disability associated with frequent fatigue is acceptable if the particular disability is not associated with the construct to be measured by the test and there are professional or scientific reasons to assume that such modifications will not affect the validity of the test (AERA, APA, & NCME, 2014). However, such accommodations are not appropriate if the disability is directly related to the abilities or characteristics that the test is designed to measure. Any modifications to testing and potential limitations in interpretation must be documented. Federal regulations relevant to the assessment of individuals with disabilities include IDEA (http://idea.ed.gov), Section 504 of the Rehabilitation Act of 1973, revised 2006 (http://www.hhs.gov/civil-rights/for-individuals/disability/index.html), and ADA (http://www.ada.gov).

Need to Know: Assessment of Dementia

The APA Guidelines for the Evaluation of Dementia and Age-Related Cognitive Change (APA, 2012d) stress the importance of using age-normed standardized psychological and neurological tests, being aware of the limitations of brief mental status examinations, and estimating premorbid abilities. The Guidelines also describe the following key elements that should be obtained to ensure accurate diagnosis of conditions associated with cognitive decline (p. 5):

- The onset and course of changes in cognitive functioning
- Preexisting disabilities
- Educational and cultural background that could affect testing variability
- General medical and psychiatric history
- Past neurological history, including prior head injuries or other central nervous system insults (strokes, tumors, infections, etc.)
- Current psychiatric symptoms and significant life stressors
- Current prescription and over-the-counter medication use
- Current and past use and abuse of alcohol and drugs
- Family history of dementia

Presence of Third Parties to Assessments

Standard 9.02a requires that psychologists administer tests in a manner consistent with procedures and testing contexts used in the development and validation of the instruments. Many psychological assessment instruments and procedures are validated under administration conditions limited to the presence of the psychologist and testee. In rare instances, psychologists may judge it necessary to include third parties to control the behavior of difficult examinees (e.g., parents of young children, hospital staff for psychiatric patients with a recent history of violence). In such situations, psychologists should select assessment instruments that are least likely to lend themselves to distortion based on the presence of a third party and include in their interpretations of test results the implications of such violations of standardized testing conditions.

Psychologists providing expert forensic consultations in relation to a criminal case, tort litigation, insurance benefits, or workers' compensation claims may find that the assessment validity of tests is compromised when third parties are present as mandated by state law, institutional policy, or a judge's ruling. For example, in neuropsychological assessments related to workers' compensation cases, the presence of the plaintiff's legal counsel, family members, or company representatives may distort the testing process or render test scores and interpretations invalid if the third party influences the test taker's motivation or behavior or the psychologist–testee rapport (American Academy of Clinical Neuropsychology, 2001). The use of data from such assessments may be unfair to individuals if it leads to invalid test administration or misleading interpretations of the testee's responses (Principle D: Justice and Standards 1.01, Misuse of Psychologists' Work; 1.02, Conflicts Between Ethics and Law, Regulations, or Other Governing Legal Authority; and 9.06, Interpreting Assessment Results). When there is no legal flexibility to deny third-party presence during an assessment, psychologists should select those tests and procedures found to be least susceptible to distortion under such conditions and ensure that their written reports highlight the unique circumstances of the assessment and the limitations in interpretation.

Trainees and Interpreters as Third Parties

Third parties may observe evaluations for training purposes or serve as interpreters when translation is necessary to ensure accuracy and fairness of assessments (Standard 9.02c, Use of Assessments). In such instances, psychologists must select procedures that research or other evidence has demonstrated can be applied appropriately under these circumstances, ensure that trainees and interpreters are trained adequately to minimize threats to the proper test administration, and include in their reports any limitations on conclusions due to the presence of the third parties (Standards 2.05, Delegation of Work to Others; 9.06, Interpreting Assessment Results).

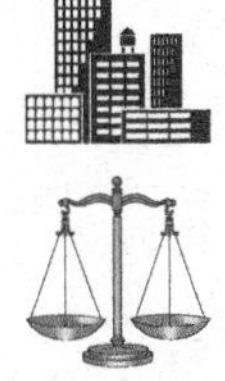

(b) Psychologists use assessment instruments whose validity and reliability have been established for use with members of the population tested. When such validity or reliability has not been established, psychologists describe the strengths and limitations of test results and interpretation.

The central idea of fairness in psychological and educational testing is to identify and remove construct-irrelevant barriers to maximal performance and allow for comparable and valid interpretation of test scores for all examinees (AERA, APA, & NCME, 2014). The proper use of tests can further principles of fairness and justice by ensuring that all persons benefit from equal quality of assessment measures, procedures, and interpretation (Principle D: Justice; Standard 3.01, Unfair Discrimination). Fair applicability of test results rests on assumptions that the validity and reliability of a test are equivalent for different populations tested. *Validity* refers to the extent to which empirical evidence and psychological theory support the interpretation of test data, that is, whether the test measures the psychological construct it purports to measure. *Reliability* refers to the consistency of test scores when a test is repeated for an individual or for a given population (see AERA, APA, & NCME, 2014).

A test that is a valid and reliable measure of a psychological construct in one population may not adequately measure the same construct in members of a different population, especially if members of the population of interest were represented inadequately in the normative sample or if test validity has not been established specifically for that group. Standard 9.02b requires psychologists to select assessment instruments whose validity and reliability have been established for use with members of the population tested. This standard applies to psychological assessment of any population, including clients/patients, students, job candidates, legal defendants, and research participants.

To comply with this standard, psychologists, when selecting a test, must be familiar with the specific populations included in the standardization sample and the test's validity and reliability estimates. At minimum, psychologists should determine the applicability of a test to an individual of a given age group, ethnicity/culture, language, and gender and, where applicable, disability or other population characteristic when scientific or professional evidence suggests that test scores may not be psychometrically, functionally, or theoretically comparable to scores for the reference groups on which the test was normed (Landwher & Llorente, 2012).

Psychologists should also be familiar with relevant federal laws on the selection and administration of nondiscriminatory assessment and evaluation procedures (e.g., IDEA, 34 CFR 300.30[c][1][i]).

- ☒ A school psychologist was asked to evaluate a bilingual child whose family had recently moved to New York from Puerto Rico. The psychologist used the English version of a well-known intelligence test without considering whether the standardized Spanish version of the test was or was not more appropriate for the child.
- ☒ A psychologist working in a nursing home always used the Beck Depression Inventory (Beck, Steer, & Brown, 1996) to assess patient depression without considering the appropriateness of other measures specifically standardized on elderly populations or populations with chronic illnesses.
- ☒ A consulting psychologist was hired to evaluate the job performance of a factory supervisor who had a visual disability. The psychologist limited her assessment to oral administration of tests that were validated on individuals without vision impairment and neglected to assess unique ways in which the supervisor might successfully compensate for his disability.

The dynamic and evolving nature of this country's cultural, political, and economic landscape creates situations in which population-valid and reliable tests of a psychological construct may not be available for the individual or group tested. Psychologists asked to evaluate individuals from such groups should select tests validated on other populations with caution because they may produce results that do not adequately assess the qualities or competencies intended to be measured (AERA, APA, & NCME, 2014). Recommendations based on these assessments in turn may lead to unfair denial of educational or employment opportunities, health coverage, legal rights, or necessary services (Principle D: Justice). According to Standard 9.02b, psychologists who use tests without established norms for the individual or population assessed must describe in their reports the strengths of using the specific test results as well as the limitations the use of such tests places on psychologists' interpretations and recommendations.

Psychologists conducting evaluations with members of racial/ethnic minority or immigrant groups must be particularly sensitive to the lack of cultural consideration inherent in the most popularly used mental health diagnostic and classification tools: the *Diagnostic and Statistical Manual of Mental Disorders* (*DSM-5*) and the *International Classification of Diseases* (*ICD-11*). To avoid errors that may be associated with applying these tools, Johnson (2013) recommended that psychologists (a) apply culturally competent skills to understand attitudes toward mental health that may affect the client's general response to testing; (b) establish an initial trusting relationship with clients; (c) consider including a measure of acculturation; (d) become familiar with cultural conditions that can impact the sharing of personal history information and the presentation of symptoms; and (e), when appropriate, draw on the appendices in the *DSM-5* and *ICD-11* to proactively use culture as a factor in the diagnostic process.

✓ A forensic psychologist was asked to evaluate the competence to stand trial of a prisoner who had recently immigrated to the United States from Botswana. The prisoner's English was poor, but there were no tests for competence standardized for individuals from the prisoner's cultural or language group. The psychologist selected the best culturally sensitive techniques and assessments available and in written conclusions to the court explained the limitations of the tests used.

Selection of "Culture-Free" Tests

School psychologists and neuropsychologists conducting assessments of intellectual, educational, and cognitive abilities may attempt to be culturally sensitive by "stacking" their test batteries with nonverbal visuoperceptual and motor tests when assessing patients who speak languages in which more traditional language-based tests are not available. The use of such tests requires ethical caution since nonverbal tests of cognitive ability can be just as culturally biased as verbal tests (Wong, Strickland, Fletcher-Janzen, Ardila, & Reynolds, 2000).

☒ A neuropsychologist was hired by an insurance company to assess a recent Nigerian immigrant who claimed he had suffered brain damage from falling on the premises of a store insured by the company. Because the man had

> such limited English skills and no test was available in his primary language, the neuropsychologist decided that the most culturally sensitive approach would be to assess the man's cognitive capacity with an assessment battery composed entirely of visuospatial, perceptual, and motor tasks. The psychologist's report did not describe the limitations of test results based on the absence of language-based assessments of reasoning and other cognitive abilities, nor did the report acknowledge the absence of preinjury cognitive tests necessary to determine whether behavioral and cognitive functioning had declined after the fall (adapted from Wong, 2000).

(c) Psychologists use assessment methods that are appropriate to an individual's language preference and competence, unless the use of an alternative language is relevant to the assessment issues.

Language differences are part of the cultural diversity, rich immigration history, and individual differences in hearing and other linguistically relevant disabilities that make up the demographic mosaic of the United States. The validity and applicability of assessment data can be severely compromised when testing is conducted in a language the testee is relatively unfamiliar with or uncomfortable using. Under Standard 9.02c, psychologists should select tests in the language that is most relevant and appropriate to the test purpose (AERA, APA, & NCME, 2014).

Whereas the inappropriateness of English-only-based psychological testing is obvious when testees speak little or no English, the hazards of English-only testing for bilingual persons or oral-language-only assessment of persons with hearing disabilities who can read lips and communicate in sign language are often overlooked. The linguistic competencies of individuals who are bilingual often vary with the mode of communication (e.g., oral vs. written language), language function (e.g., social, educational, or job related), and topical domain (e.g., science, mathematics, interpersonal relationships, self-evaluations). In addition, individuals' language preferences do not always reflect their language competence. Individuals may be embarrassed to reveal that their English, hearing, or oral language is poor; believe non-English or nonhearing testing will negatively affect their evaluations; or misjudge their language proficiency. The following steps are recommended to help psychologists comply with Standard 9.02c (see also AERA, APA, & NCME, 2014):

- Psychologists can use language tests that assess multiple language domains to determine language dominance and proficiency relevant to different modes of assessment (e.g., written, oral) and topics (e.g., academic, interpersonal).
- Whenever possible, psychologists should use test translations that have been developed according to accepted methods of test construction (see Standard 9.05, Test Construction).
- When a test is translated or adapted, test developers and test users must describe the adequacy of theory, evidence, and methods used to establish the

validity of test score interpretations for intended use (see Standard 2.04, Bases for Scientific and Professional Judgments).

- Additional testing or observation may be necessary to determine whether what appears to be eccentric behavior (e.g., short phrases or reticence in response to test questions) reflects differences in cultural communication styles or an individual characteristic.
- To the extent feasible, psychologists must ensure the language competence of the test administrator (see also Standards 2.05, Delegation of Work to Others; 9.03c, Informed Consent in Assessments).
- When interpreting assessment results, test norms for native speakers of English should not be used for individuals for whom English is a second language or should be understood in part as reflecting a level of English proficiency.

When English or Other Language Proficiency Is Essential

There are instances when proficiency in English or another language is essential to the goal of the assessment. For example, the ability to communicate with English-speaking employees may be a necessary qualification for a successful applicant for a personnel position. Evaluating a student's English proficiency may be necessary to determine appropriate educational placement. The ability to read and speak English may be important to certain service positions responsible for protecting public health, safety, and welfare. Inclusion of the phrase *unless the use of an alternative language is relevant to the assessment issues* indicates that Standard 9.02c permits psychologists to use tests in a language in which the testee may not be proficient, if effective job performance, school placement, or another goal of assessment requires the ability to communicate in that language.

9.03 Informed Consent in Assessments

(a) Psychologists obtain informed consent for assessments, evaluations, or diagnostic services, as described in Standard 3.10, Informed Consent, except when (1) testing is mandated by law or governmental regulations; (2) informed consent is implied because testing is conducted as a routine educational, institutional, or organizational activity (e.g., when participants voluntarily agree to assessment when applying for a job); or (3) one purpose of the testing is to evaluate decisional capacity. Informed consent includes an explanation of the nature and purpose of the assessment, fees, involvement of third parties, and limits of confidentiality and sufficient opportunity for the client/patient to ask questions and receive answers.

To comply with this standard, psychologists must obtain and document, with few exceptions, written or oral consent in the manner set forth in Standard 3.10, Informed Consent. Psychologists must provide individuals who will be assessed and, when appropriate, their legal representative a clear explanation of the nature

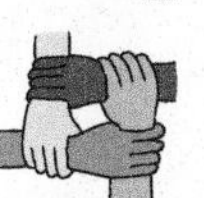

and purpose of the assessment, fees, involvement of third parties, and limits of confidentiality. Psychologists should also be attuned to consent vulnerabilities related to transient disorders, such as depression (Ghormley, Basso, Candlis, & Combs, 2011) and develop appropriate measures to ensure consent comprehension.

Core Elements of Informed Consent in Assessment

Nature of the Assessment

The *nature* of an assessment refers to (a) the general category of the assessment (e.g., personality, psychopathology, competency, parenting skills, neuropsychological abilities and deficits, employment skills, developmental disabilities), (b) procedures and testing format (e.g., oral interviews, written self-report checklists, behavioral observation, skills assessment), and (c) duration of the assessment (e.g., hours or multiple assessments).

Purpose of the Assessment

The *purpose* of the assessment refers to its potential use, for example, in employment decisions, school placement, custody decisions, disability benefits, treatment decisions, and plans for or evaluation of rehabilitation of criminal offenders.

Fees

Discussion of *fees* must include the cost of the assessment and payment schedule and should be consistent with requirements of Standard 6.04, Fees and Financial Arrangements. When applicable and to the extent feasible, psychologists must also discuss with relevant parties the extent to which their services will be covered by the individual's health plan, school district, employer, or others (see Standard 6.04a and 6.04d, Fees and Financial Arrangements).

Third Parties

Involvement of *third parties* refers to other individuals (e.g., legal guardians), HMOs, employers, organizations, or legal or other governing authorities that have requested the assessment and to whom the results of the assessments will be provided. Psychologists should be familiar with ethical standards, state law, and federal regulations relevant to the appropriate role of third parties and the release and documentation of release of such information to others (see Standard 4.05, Disclosures). Psychologists asked to evaluate a child by one parent should clarify custody issues to determine whether another parent must give permission.

Confidentiality

Informed consent to assessments must provide a clear explanation of the extent and limits of *confidentiality,* including (a) when the psychologist must comply with reporting requirements such as mandated child abuse reporting or duty-to-warn laws and (b) in the case of assessments involving minors, guardian access to records (see discussion of parental access involving HIPAA, FERPA, and other regulations in Standards 3.10, Informed Consent; 4.01, Maintaining Confidentiality; and 4.02, Discussing the Limits of Confidentiality). Psychologists who administer assessments over the Internet must inform clients/patients, research participants, or others about the procedures that will be used to protect confidentiality and the threats to confidentiality unique to this form of electronic transmission of information (see also Standard 4.02c, Discussing the Limits of Confidentiality).

Implications of HIPAA for Confidentiality-Relevant Information

The HIPAA regulation most relevant to informed consent in assessments is the Notice of Privacy Practices. At the beginning of the professional relationship, covered entities must provide clients/patients a written document detailing routine uses and disclosures of PHI and the individual's rights and the covered entities' legal duties with respect to PHI. Psychologists conducting assessments should also be familiar with HIPAA-compliant authorization forms for use and release of PHI and HIPAA requirements for Accounting of Disclosures. These regulations are described in greater detail in the section "A Word About HIPAA" in the preface of this book and in discussions of Standard 3.10, Informed Consent, in Chapter 6; Standards 4.01, Maintaining Confidentiality, and 4.05, Disclosures, in Chapter 7; Standard 6.01, Documentation of Professional and Scientific Work and Maintenance of Records, in Chapter 9; and Standard 9.04, Release of Test Data, in this chapter.

Dispensing With Informed Consent

Under Standard 9.03a, informed consent may be waived when consent is implied because testing is conducted as (a) a routine educational activity, such as end-of-term reading or math achievement testing in elementary and high schools; (b) regular institutional activities, such as student and teaching evaluations in academic institutions or consumer satisfaction questionnaires in hospitals or social service agencies; or (c) organizational activity, such as when individuals voluntarily agree to preemployment testing when applying for a job.

Standard 9.03a also permits psychologists to dispense with informed consent in assessment when testing is mandated by law or other governing legal authority or when one purpose of testing is to determine the capacity of the individual to give consent. For example, during an initial consultation, neuropsychologists may also need to determine whether a client/patient with suspected dementia or brain injury has the capacity to independently consent to a full cognitive and neuropsychological assessment. Forensic psychologists conducting civil capacity assessments of older adults must select appropriate assessment techniques for determining whether clients/patients meet the legal standards of diminished capacity, testamentary capacity, and other abilities relevant to decisional capacity as defined by law

(Moye, Marson, & Edelstein, 2013). Ethical steps that must be taken in these contexts are discussed next under Standard 9.03b.

> (b) Psychologists inform persons with questionable capacity to consent or for whom testing is mandated by law or governmental regulations about the nature and purpose of the proposed assessment services, using language that is reasonably understandable to the person being assessed.

Under Standards 3.10b, Informed Consent, and 9.03a, Informed Consent in Assessments, informed consent in assessment is not required when an individual has been determined to be legally incapable of giving informed consent, when testing is mandated by law or other governing legal authority, or when one purpose of testing is to determine consent capacity. These waivers reflect the fact that the term *consent* refers to a person's legal status to make autonomous decisions based on age, mental capacity, or the legal decision under consideration. Consistent with the moral value of respect for the dignity and worth of all persons articulated in Principle E: Respect for People's Rights and Dignity, under Standard 9.03c, psychologists must provide all individuals, irrespective of their legal status, appropriate explanations of the nature and purpose of the proposed assessment. Readers may also refer to the Hot Topic in Chapter 6, "Goodness-of-Fit Ethics for Informed Consent Involving Adults With Impaired Decisional Capacity."

Standard 9.03a often applies in situations where assessment is requested by parents of children younger than age 18 years or family members of adults with suspected cognitive impairments. In some contexts, the affirmative agreement of the testee is not required. In these situations, the psychologist must provide information in a language and at a language level that is reasonably understandable to the child or adult being assessed. When both the permission of the guardian and the assent of the child or cognitively impaired adult are sought, psychologists working with populations for whom English is not a first language should be alert to situations in which prospective clients/patients and their legal guardians may have different language preferences and proficiencies.

Need to Know: Informed Consent for Forensic Assessments Requested by an Examinee's Attorney

When testing is requested by an examinee's attorney, informed consent should help the examinee understand the difference between forensic and other psychological services. To accomplish this Younggren, Bennett, and Harris (https://www.trustinsurance.com/resources/download-documents/) recommended that forensic informed consent contracts include the following:

- The evaluation is not being conducted for the purposes of counseling or treatment. The results may or may not be personally helpful to you

(Continued)

(Continued)

but will provide your attorney with information on how you function psychologically.

- Your participation in the assessment is voluntary, and you have the right to stop the evaluation at any time. However, there may be legal consequences to stopping that should be discussed with your attorney.
- If you consent to the assessment, the report will be sent to the retaining party (e.g., the examinee's attorney), who will have complete authority over the results.
- When the evaluation is completed, with permission from your attorney, I may be able to meet with you to explain the results.
- Although the forensic report is normally protected by attorney–client privilege, if used for legal proceedings, the report may be admissible into evidence, and the extent of other confidentiality protections will be determined by the rules of that legal system.

Mandated Assessments

The term *informed consent* is applied when individuals are legally permitted to make their own decisions about undergoing a psychological assessment and whether and to whom the results of testing are disclosed. The term does not apply when testing is mandated through a court order or other governing authority. Psychologists conducting forensic, military, or other assessments that have been legally mandated should provide the examinee with a *notification of purpose* that explains the nature and purpose of the testing, who has requested the testing, and who will receive copies of the report. If the examinee is unwilling to proceed following a thorough explanation, the forensic practitioner may attempt to conduct the examination, postpone the examination, advise the examinee to contact his or her attorney, or notify the retaining attorney of the examinee's unwillingness to proceed (APA, 2013a).

Defendants who are entering a plea of insanity may not be able to act on their Fifth Amendment right to silence and avoidance of self-incrimination. To avoid compromising the admissibility of a comprehensive forensic evaluation, Bush et al. (2006) suggested that psychologists first assess competency, then sanity, and separate the reports given to the court to provide the court the opportunity to first determine the competence question.

Informed Consent for the Assessment of Malingering

Malingering refers to the intentional production of false symptoms to attain an identifiable external benefit (Butcher, Hass, Greene, & Nelson, 2015; Iverson, 2006; National Academy of Neuropsychology Policy and Planning Committee, 2000). Tests of symptom validity, exaggeration, and malingering have become integral components of neuropsychological evaluations for traumatic brain injury and other suspected neurological disorders. Some have argued that assessment of malingering is the number one priority of forensic assessment, preceding any professional conclusions in forensic evaluations (Brodsky & Galloway, 2003; Kocsis, 2011). Malingering can be manifested through intentional under- or overperformance during psychological assessment. Accurate assessment of malingering is ethically important because errors in diagnosis can impede justice when undetected in forensic procedures or obscure adequate treatment for psychopathology (Principle A: Beneficence and Nonmaleficence; Kocsis, 2011).

Some have questioned whether describing the purposes of tests for malingering during informed consent compromises the validity of the assessment or whether failing to include such information during informed consent violates testees' autonomy rights (Principle E: Respect for People's Rights and Dignity; Standard 9.03, Informed Consent in Assessments). Current standards of practice support communicating to testees prior to and during informed consent or notification of purpose that measures will be used to assess the examinee's honesty and efforts to do well, without describing the particularities of the tests that will be used to measure exaggeration or other elements of malingering (Carone, Bush, & Iverson, 2013). Individuals undergoing evaluation for Social Security Disability benefits or compensation for work-, sport-, or military-related injuries may be wary of practitioners and feel the need to prove that they are neurologically compromised. In such contexts, psychologists should take extra steps to develop rapport and a trusting relationship and to craft language and procedures that ensure testees understand that honesty and effort are required; in some cases, this may involve reading the informed consent material to clients/patients (Carone et al., 2013; Chafetz, 2010). Carone et al. (2013) also provided guidance for how to include the results of effort, exaggeration, and other tests during feedback sessions with clients/patients (Standard 9.10, Explaining Assessment Results).

Research on Coached Malingering

A practical concern in the forensic assessment of defendants or plaintiffs is whether existing tests of malingering can detect over- or underexaggeration of symptoms when the examinee has been coached by individuals familiar with the tests (Butcher et al., 2015; Jelicic, Cuenen, Peters, & Merckelbach, 2011). When researchers attempt to study the extent to which commonly used tests are vulnerable to coached faking, there is a risk that the information provided to research participants or disseminated through publication will be used to improve the success of coached malingerers (Berry, Lamb, Wetter, Baier, & Widiger, 1994). Ben-Porath (1994) suggested that to protect against these risks, investigators can (a) coach research participants on items similar but not identical to those on the test under investigation, (b) provide only a brief synopsis of coaching instructions in published articles, and (c) release information on verbatim instructions only to those bound by the APA Ethics Code to protect the integrity of tests (see also Standard 9.11, Maintaining Test Security).

(c) Psychologists using the services of an interpreter obtain informed consent from the client/patient to use that interpreter, ensure that confidentiality of test results and test security are maintained, and include in their recommendations, reports, and diagnostic or evaluative statements, including forensic testimony, discussion of any limitations on the data obtained. (See also Standards 2.05, Delegation of Work to Others; 4.01, Maintaining Confidentiality; 9.01, Bases for Assessments; 9.06, Interpreting Assessment Results; and 9.07, Assessment by Unqualified Persons.)

Compliance with the consent requirements outlined in Standard 3.10 obligates psychologists to provide information in a language and at a language level that is reasonably understandable to the client/patient and, where applicable, his or her legally authorized representative. Psychologists may use the services of an interpreter when they do not possess the skills to obtain consent in the language in which the client/patient is proficient.

When delegating informed consent responsibilities to an interpreter, psychologists must ensure not only that the interpreter is competent in the consent-relevant language (see Standard 2.05, Delegation of Work to Others) but that the interpreter also understands and complies with procedures necessary to protect the confidentiality of test results and test security. An interpreter who revealed the identity of a client/patient or the nature of specific test items used during the assessment would place the psychologist who hired the interpreter in potential violation of this standard. Because test validity and reliability may be vulnerable to errors in interpretation, Standard 9.03c also requires that the involvement of the interpreter and any related limitations on the data obtained be clearly indicated and discussed in any assessment-based report, recommendation, diagnostic or evaluative statement, or forensic testimony.

9.04 Release of Test Data

(a) The term *test data* refers to raw and scaled scores, client/patient responses to test questions or stimuli, and psychologists' notes and recordings concerning client/patient statements and behavior during an examination. Those portions of test materials that include client/patient responses are included in the definition of test data. Pursuant to a client/patient release, psychologists provide test data to the client/patient or other persons identified in the release. Psychologists may refrain from releasing test data to protect a client/patient or others from substantial harm or misuse or misrepresentation of the data or the test, recognizing that in many instances release of confidential information under these circumstances is regulated by law. (See also Standard 9.11, Maintaining Test Security.)

Definition of Test Data

In Standard 9.04a, the term *test data* refers to the client's/patient's actual responses to test items, the raw or scaled scores such responses receive, and a psychologist's written notes or recordings of the client's/patient's specific responses or behaviors during the testing. The term *notes* in this standard is limited to the assessment context and does not include psychotherapy (or process) notes documenting or analyzing the contents of conversation during a private counseling session.

Test Data and Test Materials

Recognizing that availability of test questions and scoring criteria may compromise the validity of a test for future use with a client/patient or other individuals exposed to the information, Standard 9.04a distinguishes *test data,* which under most circumstances must be provided upon a client/patient release, from *test materials,* which under most circumstances should not (see Standard 9.11, Maintaining Test Security). The definition of *test data* does *not* include test manuals, protocols for administering or scoring responses, or test items *unless* these materials include the client's/patient's responses or scores or the psychologist's contemporaneous notes on the client's/patient's testing responses or behaviors. If testing protocols allow, it is good practice for psychologists to record client/patient responses on a form separated from the test items themselves to ensure that upon client/patient request, only the test data and not the test material itself need be released.

The Affirmative Duty to Provide Test Data to Clients/Patients and Others Identified in a Client's/Patient's Release

Release to Clients/Patients

Under Standard 9.04a, psychologists have an affirmative duty to provide test data as defined above to the client/patient or other persons identified in a client/patient release. The obligation set forth by Standard 9.04a to respect clients'/patients' right to their test data is consistent with legal trends toward greater patient autonomy and the self-determination rights of clients/patients as set forth in Principle E: Respect for People's Rights and Dignity. Although not explicitly stated in the standard, it is always good practice for psychologists to have a signed release or authorization from the client/patient even if the data are to be given directly to the client/patient. This standard does not preclude psychologists from discussing with a client/patient the potential for misuse of the information by individuals unqualified to interpret it.

Digital Ethics: Client/Patient Requests for Electronic Records

The 2013 HIPAA Omnibus Rule permits patients to receive a copy of their health record in an electronic form. Covered entities are permitted to charge for the costs of supplies if the client/patient requires data to be provided on a USB flash drive, compact disc, or other electronic media and for the costs of having to hire technically trained staff to recover PHI (see Standard 6.04, Fees and Financial Arrangements).

Release to Others

A fundamental tension exists between the desire of psychologists to respect clients'/patients' right to determine who will have access to their assessment results and the desire to ensure that the data are not reviewed by unqualified individuals who might misinterpret or misuse the data or violate contractual agreements designed to protect a test publisher's proprietary interests (Principle A: Beneficence and Nonmaleficence; Principle D: Justice; Principle E: Respect for People's Rights and Dignity). The language of Standard 9.04 reflects this tension by providing exceptions to the release of test data under conditions in which the release might lead to substantial harm or misuse of the test.

There are several reasons why the standard supports release of test data to clients/patients and those whom they authorize to receive the data. First, whether a person designated by the client/patient is qualified to use test data is determined by the context of the proposed use. For example, restricting release of test data to individuals with advanced degrees or licensure in professional psychology would preclude other qualified health care professionals from using the information. Broadening but limiting the definition of *qualified person* to health professionals might jeopardize appropriate judicial scrutiny of psychological tests and a client's/patient's right to the discovery process to challenge their use in court. Second, even if a consensus around the definition of a "qualified" person could be achieved, requiring a psychologist to confirm the education, training, degrees, or certifications of other professionals would pose a burden that might not be feasible to meet. Third, as described below, with few exceptions, HIPAA regulations require that covered entities provide clients/patients and their personal representatives access to PHI.

Withholding Test Data

Standard 9.04a permits psychologists to withhold test data to protect the client/patient or another individual from substantial harm. The standard also permits withholding test data to protect misuse or misrepresentation of the data or the test. Before refusing to release test data under this clause, psychologists should carefully consider the proviso in the standard *that such decisions may be regulated by law.* For example, when refusing a client's/patient's request to release test data based on the psychologist's judgment that the data will be misused, psychologists should document in each specific case their rationale for assuming that the data will be misused and refrain from behaviors that may be in violation of other standards (e.g., Standard 6.03, Withholding Records for Nonpayment).

Need to Know: Access to Forensic Records

According to the Specialty Guidelines for Forensic Psychology (APA, 2013e), forensic psychologists should provide attorneys and others who retain their services access to and explanation of all information in their records relevant to the legal matter at hand, consistent with relevant law and applicable professional standards, institutional rules, and regulations. Forensic examinees are *not* provided access to their assessment data or records unless the retaining party provides written consent for their release (see Standard 9.03b, Informed Consent in Assessment).

Implications of HIPAA

Requiring psychologists to release test data to the client/patient or others pursuant to a client/patient release reflects a sea change in the legal landscape from paternalistic to autonomy-based rules governing access to health records. In particular, HIPAA establishes the right of access of individuals to inspect and receive copies of medical and billing records maintained and used by the provider for decisions about the client/patient. This requirement does not include psychotherapy notes or information compiled in reasonable anticipation of or use in civil, criminal, or administrative actions or proceedings. In addition, psychologists who are covered entities under HIPAA must provide such access to a client's/patient's personal representative.

HIPAA limits the ability of covered entities to use professional judgment to determine the appropriateness of releasing test data to clients/patients and their personal representatives. For example, the right of clients/patients to obtain their own test data under HIPAA regulations means in practice that they can pass it on to other individuals of their choice.

Harm

Under HIPAA, psychologists who are covered entities can deny client/patient access to test data if granting access is reasonably likely to endanger the life or physical safety of the individual or another person or, in some cases, likely to cause equally substantial harm (Principle A: Beneficence and Nonmaleficence). In addition, psychologists must allow clients/patients the right to have the denial reviewed by a designated licensed health care professional. HIPAA regulations thus limit psychologists' ability to independently exercise their professional judgment as to what constitutes substantial harm to clients/patients.

Misuse or Misrepresentation of the Test

Release of "test data" that include client/patient responses recorded on the test protocol itself can raise issues of copyright protection and fair use by test development companies (Principle B: Fidelity and Responsibility). If testing protocols allow, psychologists may wish to record client/patient responses on a form separated from the test items themselves to comply with contractual agreements with test developers and to maintain test security (Standard 9.11, Maintaining Test Security). When test data cannot be separated from test materials that are protected by copyright law, psychologists' decision to withhold release of test data would be consistent with HIPAA regulations and Standard 9.04a.

☒ To protect against the misuse of test data in possible instances when they would be released to clients/patients or another identified person, a psychologist used an idiosyncratic code to record testees' responses. When a client/patient requested the test data be released to another licensed practitioner, it was clear that the test data were undecipherable to others, and the psychologist refused to provide the code. The psychologist was in violation of Standard 9.04a and HIPAA regulations, because in this particular case there was no reason to assume misuse of test data. The psychologist's failure to appropriately create and store records also violated Standard 6.01, Documentation of Professional and Scientific Work and Maintenance of Records.

Withholding Data in Anticipation of Their Use for Legal Purposes

There are instances, however, when HIPAA constraints are not at issue. For example, HIPAA does not require release of PHI to clients in situations in which information is compiled in reasonable anticipation of, or for use in, civil, criminal, or administrative actions or proceedings. In other instances, such as certain educational evaluations, test data may not come under the PHI classification, and thus the HIPAA Privacy Rule would not apply (see Standard 4.01, Maintaining Confidentiality).

Organizations, Courts, and Government Agencies

The use of the term *client/patient* in this standard refers to the individual testee and not to an organizational client. This standard does not require industrial–organizational or consulting psychologists to release test data to either an organizational client or an employee when testing is conducted to evaluate job candidacy or employee or organization effectiveness and does not assess factors directly related to medical or mental health conditions or services. Psychologists working in these contexts would not be required to provide the test data to the employees themselves under this standard because the organization, not the employee, is the client (see also Standards 3.07, Third-Party Requests for Services; 3.11, Psychological Services Delivered To or Through Organizations; 9.03, Informed Consent in Assessments). Similarly, forensic psychologists, military psychologists, and others working under governing legal authority are permitted by the Ethics Code to withhold release of test data from a testee when the client is an attorney, the court, or other governing legal authority. Finally, all psychologists are permitted by the Ethics Code to withhold release of test data when required by law (Standard 1.02, Conflicts Between Ethics and Law, Regulations, or Other Governing Legal Authority).

(b) In the absence of a client/patient release, psychologists provide test data only as required by law or court order.

Standard 9.04b recognizes the clients'/patients' right to expect that in the absence of their release or authorization, psychologists will protect the confidentiality of test data. The standard does permit psychologists to disclose test data without the consent of the client/patient in response to a court order (including subpoenas that are court ordered) or in other situations required by law (e.g., an order from an administrative tribunal). In such instances, psychologists are wise to seek legal counsel to determine their legal responsibility to respond to the request (see also Standard 4.05b, Disclosures). Psychologists may also ask the court or other legal authority for a protective order to prevent the inappropriate disclosure of confidential information or suggest that the information be submitted to another psychologist for qualified review (see also Standard 1.02, Conflicts Between Ethics and Law, Regulations, and Other Governing Legal Authority).

Implications of HIPAA

Standard 9.04b provides stricter protection of confidential test data than does HIPAA. Under the HIPAA Privacy Rule, PHI may be disclosed in response to a subpoena, discovery request, or other lawful process that is not accompanied by an order of a court or administrative tribunal, if the covered entity receives satisfactory assurance from the party seeking the information either that reasonable efforts have been made to ensure that the client/patient has been notified of the request or reasonable efforts have been made to secure a qualified protective order. Psychologists who disclosed information in such an instance would be in violation of 9.04b. The greater protection provided by 9.04b is consistent with most states' more stringent psychotherapist–patient privilege communication statutes.

9.05 Test Construction

Psychologists who develop tests and other assessment techniques use appropriate psychometric procedures and current scientific or professional knowledge for test design, standardization, validation, reduction or elimination of bias, and recommendations for use.

Test development is the foundation of good psychological assessment. Psychologists who construct assessment techniques must be familiar with and apply psychometric methods for establishing the validity and reliability of tests, developing standardized administration instructions, selecting items that reduce or eliminate bias, and drawing on current scientific or professional knowledge for recommendations about the use of test results (see also Standard 2.01, Boundaries of Competence; Turchik, Karpenko, Hammers, & McNamara, 2007). Test developers and publishers who claim their test can be used with examinees from specific subgroups must provide the necessary documentation to support appropriate score interpretation for

examinees from these groups and make explicit any cautions against foreseeable misuse of test results (AERA, APA, & NCME, 2014; see Principle D: Justice and Standards 2.04, Bases for Scientific and Professional Judgments; 3.01, Unfair Discrimination; 9.09, Test Scoring and Interpretation Services).

Standard 9.05 applies to all test development activities, not just those implemented in professional testing services or research settings. Psychologists who develop tests or other assessment techniques to serve private practice clients/patients, organizational clients, or the courts can violate this standard if they fail to use proper psychometric methods for test construction.

Psychometric Procedures

To be in compliance with Standard 9.05, psychologists must be familiar with and competent to implement appropriate psychometric procedures to establish the usefulness of the test (Standard 2.01, Boundaries of Competence). The following are brief definitions of psychometric procedures presented in greater detail in the *Standards for Educational and Psychological Testing* (AERA, APA, & NCME, 2014).

Validity, Reliability, and Standardization

Validity is the degree to which theory and empirical evidence support specific interpretations of test scores. Methods for establishing test validity include content, concurrent, construct, and predictive validity as well as evidence-based response processes, the internal structure of a test, and the consequences of testing. *Reliability* is the degree to which test scores for a group of test takers are consistent over repeated administrations of a test or for items within a test. Methods for establishing test reliability include internal consistency coefficients, analysis of the standard error of measure, test–retest, split-half, or alternative form comparisons. *Standardization* refers to the establishment of scoring norms based on the test performance of a representative sample of individuals from populations for which the test is intended.

Validity and reliability must be assessed appropriately for each total score, subscore, or combination of scores that will be interpreted. Where relevant, descriptions of the test to users, school personnel, organizational clients, and the courts should include a description of the psychometric procedures used during test development.

☒ An industrial–organizational psychologist was hired by a firm to develop a selection system for promotion of line workers to supervisors. The psychologists used appropriate sampling and validation procedures to construct a 20-item measure. When he presented the final measure to the firm's board of trustees, the board president expressed concern that items on attitudes toward the firm were not included. The psychologist agreed to add a few of these to the test without further validation (see Lowman, 2006, Case 3).

☒ Over the years, a school psychologist had observed that students who had been removed from their homes because of child abuse or neglect frequently gave a set of common and unique narrative responses to items on the Wechsler Intelligence Scale for Children Comprehension subtest (WISC; Wechsler, 1991). Cognizant of school psychologists' legal duty to report suspected child abuse, she constructed a test composed of 10 narrative statements that she believed were typical of abused and neglected children. She developed a scoring system where 0 to 1 indicated that the child was probably not abused or neglected, 2 to 3 suggested that the child should be further observed, and 4 to 10 supported a suspicion of child abuse or neglect that should be reported to child protective services. She began to use the scale to decide whether to make a report of child abuse. When she became district supervisor of psychological and social services, she required all school psychologists and social workers to administer the scale to children with whom they worked despite the lack of evidence of its reliability or validity.

Reduction or Elimination of Test Bias

Test bias may refer to systematic errors in test scoring. The term is associated more frequently with test fairness and refers to assessment norms applied to persons from different populations that fail to establish measurement equivalence: the degree to which reliability and validity coefficients associated with a measure are similar across populations. Depending on the purpose and nature of testing, failure to determine item, functional, scalar, or predictive measurement equivalence when developing a test can lead to over- or underdiagnosis, faulty personnel recommendations, inappropriate educational placements, and misinformation to the courts (Principle D: Justice; Standard 3.01, Unfair Discrimination).

Threats to fair and valid interpretations of test scores also arise from construct-irrelevant content that differentially favors the experiences of individuals from some subgroups over others or a combination of test content and context that promotes differential engagement, motivation, or discomfort. Group-specific variance in test item response biases (e.g., social desirability), familiarity with test response formats (e.g., multiple-choice), and differences in the opportunity to learn (i.e., the extent to which examinees have been exposed to the content or skills targeted by the test) can also contribute to test bias. (See *Standards for Educational and Psychological Testing* for a detailed explanation of these concepts and steps to reduce test bias [AERA, APA, & NCME, 2014].)

☒ An industrial–organizational psychologist developed a prescreening employment test for a large personnel department. After demonstrating high levels of interitem and test–retest reliability, the scale was touted as a culture-free

(Continued)

(Continued)

measure of employment preparedness. However, the psychologist did not examine whether the factor structure, predictive validity of the test for job performance, or other psychometric factors were equivalent across members of major ethnic/cultural groups in the city who applied for positions in the company.

Recommendations for Use

In their recommendations for use, test developers must provide adequate guidance to allow users to administer tests in a standardized fashion and score and interpret responses according to established criteria. Psychologists who develop tests or assessment techniques must provide explanations of the meaning and intended interpretation of reported scores by users, school personnel, organizational clients, the courts, and others as appropriate. For example, a test manual might explain how score interpretation can be facilitated through norm- or criterion-referenced scoring, scaling, or cut scores.

☒ A psychologist working for a test company was responsible for developing a test for premorbid speech and language predictors of childhood-onset schizophrenia. Child inpatients who had already been diagnosed with schizophrenia were the only population available for test development. The test yielded good test–retest reliability and was validated on correlations with practitioner diagnoses of childhood schizophrenia. In writing the test manual, the psychologist described the test as useful for identifying children at risk for the disorder. The manual did not indicate that test norms were applicable only to inpatients who had already manifested the disorder.

Psychologists' validity reports should accurately reflect the soundness of the test validation research supporting the use of an assessment procedure. Psychologists should include in their reports methodological or statistical weaknesses that would limit the usefulness of the test.

☒ A psychologist was hired by a company to develop a work climate questionnaire to help in its restructuring plans. In her lengthy validity report to the company, the psychologist buried information that indicated problems with sample representativeness and low validity coefficients, and she failed to include this information in the executive summary (see Lowman, 2006, Case 8; Principle C: Integrity).

Test Revisions

Once tests have been developed, test developers are responsible for monitoring conditions that might warrant test revision, modifications in recommendations for test interpretation, or limitations on or withdrawal of test use. According to the *Standards for Educational and Psychological Testing,* tests should be amended or revised when new research data, significant changes in the domain represented, or newly recommended conditions of test use may lower the validity of test score interpretations, and any substantial modifications to the test must be included in the test documentation. (AERA, APA, & NCME, 2014). The scope of test revision will depend on the conditions warranting change and may include revisions in test stimuli, administration procedures, scales or units of measure, norms or psychometric features, or applications (Butcher, 2000). Bersoff et al. (2012) emphasized psychologists' responsibility to keep up-to-date on society-wide improvements or shifts in test performance, known as the Flynn effect (Flynn, 1984).

☒ A test company sold a popular test to help determine cognitive decline in newly admitted nursing home patients. The test had been used for more than 15 years. During the past 5 years, the psychologist directing the geropsychological test department of the company had been getting complaints that patients were being underdiagnosed. The psychologist reasoned that the test norms established 15 years ago might not be applicable to a better-educated cohort of elderly persons. However, the company's current 5-year plan focused on the development of new depression inventories and had no budget for revisions of current tests. The psychologist decided not to rock the boat and to wait for the next 5-year plan to recommend a revision of the test (see also Standard 1.03, Conflicts Between Ethics and Organizational Demands).

9.06 Interpreting Assessment Results

When interpreting assessment results, including automated interpretations, psychologists take into account the purpose of the assessment as well as the various test factors, test-taking abilities, and other characteristics of the person being assessed, such as situational, personal, linguistic, and cultural differences, that might affect psychologists' judgments or reduce the accuracy of their interpretations. They indicate any significant limitations of their interpretations. (See also Standards 2.01b and c, Boundaries of Competence, and 3.01, Unfair Discrimination.)

Accurate interpretations of assessment results are critical to ensure that appropriate decisions are made regarding an individual's diagnosis, treatment plan, legal status, educational placement, or employment and promotion opportunities. It is ethically imperative that when providing interpretations, psychologists take into

account the purpose of the test and testee characteristics and indicate any significant limitations of their interpretations.

The Purpose of the Test

As required by Standard 9.06, the *purpose* of the assessment must be considered carefully in the interpretation of test scores. At the same time, psychologists must resist allowing test interpretations to be biased by pressure from school personnel, parents, employers, attorneys, managed care companies, or others with a vested interest in a particular interpretation (Standard 3.06, Conflict of Interest).

When offering recommendations, drawing conclusions, or making predictions from test scores, psychologists should refer to test manuals prepared by the test developer as well as relevant research to understand the extent to which tests, in isolation or within the context of other tests, are directly related to the purpose of testing.

☒ A neuropsychologist was hired by an insurance claims company to evaluate whether an individual insured by the company had sustained neurological damage following a car accident or whether the individual was feigning symptoms. Following administration of a battery of tests, the psychologist determined that the individual's test scores were at the lower boundaries of normal functioning. Although the psychologist made no effort to obtain information regarding the patient's neurological functioning before the accident, he concluded in his report that there was no evidence to support an injury claim.

☒ A psychologist conducting employment assessment for law enforcement personnel interpreted candidates' scores using norms from a broad range of reference groups rather than police-normative data (Gallo & Halgin, 2011).

Test Factors and Examinee Characteristics

With the exception of perhaps some employment-related screenings, interpretations should never be based solely on test scores. Standard 9.06 requires psychologists to consider factors associated with the testing context, the examinee's test-taking abilities, and other characteristics that may affect or inappropriately bias interpretations. When relevant, psychologists should take into account observations of test-taking styles, fatigue, perceptual and motor impairments, illness, limited fluency in the language of the test, or lack of cultural familiarity with test items that would introduce construct-irrelevant variability into a test score (AERA, APA, & NCME, 2014).

In addition to familiarity with the test itself, psychologists should have the specialized knowledge necessary to formulate professional judgments about the meaning of test scores as they relate to the individual examinee (see Standard 2.01b and 2.01c, Boundaries of Competence).

Test takers' scores should not be interpreted in isolation from other information about the characteristics of the person being assessed. Such information may be gained from interviews; additional testing; or collateral information from teachers, employers, supervisors, parents, or school or employment records. Such information may lead to alternative explanations for examinees' test performance.

☒ An inpatient at a psychiatric hospital had a Monday appointment with a psychologist to help determine whether he was well enough to go home for the weekend. When he arrived for the appointment, he was obviously distressed and told the psychologist that the patient he shared his room with had threatened to kill him. The psychologist confirmed this story with one of the orderlies. Rather than reschedule the appointment, the psychologist decided to conduct the required standardized assessment and clinical interview. In his report, the psychologist noted that the patient had high scores on the Minnesota Multiphasic Personality Inventory (MMPI; Butcher, Dahlstrom, Graham, Tellegen, & Kaemmer, 2002), indicating paranoid tendencies and high levels of stress that might be interpreted as a lack of readiness to go home. The psychologist's report did not address how the events surrounding the roommate's threats might have influenced MMPI scores and responses to interview questions.

⊘ An industrial–organizational psychologist was responsible for administering and interpreting standardized group tests for employee promotion. During one testing session, two employees got into a shouting match that threatened but did not become a physical fight. In his reporting of the test results to managers, the psychologist mentioned there had been a disturbance that could have had a significant detrimental effect on testees' performance and recommended that those who requested should be permitted to retake the tests.

Need to Know: Sexual and Gender Minority (SGM) Parents and Determination of Child Custody

Psychologists conducting child custody assessments involving lesbian, gay, bisexual, transgender, or gender-nonconforming parents need to keep updated on evolving law and empirical data on parenting relevant to this area (Standard 2.03, Maintaining Competence). For example, contrary to public debates surrounding the relative parenting competencies of heterosexual and SGM parents, research indicates no differences in parenting practices or child outcomes related to children's psychological adjustment, sexual identity, or peer harassment (Cheng & Powell, 2015; Patterson, 2006). In a comprehensive summary of this issue, Haney-Caron and Heilbrun (2014) recommended several considerations for custody assessments. First, custody evaluations procedures should ensure that no assumptions are made that sexual orientation or gender identity favorably or unfavorably

(Continued)

(Continued)

impacts parenting effectiveness (Standard 3.01, Unfair Discrimination). Second, given the potential for social bias and judicial preconceptions regarding SGM parenting, psychologists should consider providing the court with empirical and other sources of information to address any misconceptions held by the judge. This is particularly relevant in states that rely on a "nexus" or "adverse impact" test that courts have used to conclude that a child of a sexual- or gender-minority parent will be exposed to social stigma, an "immoral" lifestyle, or "become" gay. Third, in jurisdictions in which the rights of SGM parents are significantly limited, psychologists' reports should consider the impact of separation from or loss of a caretaking relationship with a person who may not be a child's legal parent.

Limitations

Under Standard 9.06, psychologists must indicate any significant limitations of their interpretations. In general, interpretive remarks that are not supported by validity and reliability information should be presented as hypotheses. When test batteries are used, interpretations of patterns of relationships among different test scores should be based on identifiable evidence. If none is available, this fact must be stated in the report. Interpretations of test results often include recommendations for placement, treatment, employment, or legal status based on validity evidence and professional experience. Psychologists should refrain from implying that empirical relationships exist between test results and recommendations when they do not, as well as distinguish between recommendations based on empirical evidence and those based on professional judgment.

Automated Interpretations

Computer-generated interpretations are based on accumulated empirical data and expert judgment but cannot take into account the special characteristics of the examinee. Automated reports are not a substitute for the clinical judgment of a psychologist who has worked directly with the examinee or for the integration of other information, including other test results, behavioral observation, or interviews (AERA, APA, & NCME, 2014). Psychologists should use interpretations provided by automated and other types of services with caution and indicate their relevant limitations.

9.07 Assessment by Unqualified Persons

Psychologists do not promote the use of psychological assessment techniques by unqualified persons, except when such use is conducted for training purposes with appropriate supervision. (See also Standard 2.05, Delegation of Work to Others.)

Psychologists' professional and scientific responsibilities to society and those with whom they work (Principle B: Fidelity and Responsibility) include helping ensure that the administration, scoring, interpretation, and use of psychological tests are conducted only by those who are competent to do so by virtue of their education, training, or experience. Standard 9.07 prohibits psychologists from promoting the use of psychological assessment techniques by unqualified persons. For example, psychologists should not employ persons who have not received formal graduate-level training in psychological assessments to administer, score, or interpret psychological tests that will be used to determine an individual's educational placement, psychological characteristics for employment or promotion, competence to stand trial, parenting skills relevant to child custody, mental health status or diagnosis, or treatment plan.

☒ A group practice of consulting psychologists was hired to conduct psychological assessments of applicants for promotion to management positions in a large national company. After a month, the managing psychologists realized they had not negotiated a contractual fee large enough to employ the number of advanced-degree psychologists required to conduct all of the assessments. To stay within budget, they set up an internship program for business school seniors and trained them to administer the tests.

Psychological Assessments Conducted by Trainees

Standard 9.07 does not prohibit psychologists from supervising trainees in the administration, scoring, and interpretation of tests. However, (a) the trainees must be qualified on the basis of their enrollment in a graduate or postdoctoral psychology program or externship or internship and (b) supervision must be appropriate to their level of training. For example, psychologists teaching a first-year graduate-level personality assessment course that requires students to submit scored protocols of individuals they have independently assessed must ensure that (a) the course adequately prepares students for initial testing situations and (b) students inform persons tested or their legal guardians that the testing is for training purposes only and not for individual assessment.

When students registered in advanced practica, externships, or internships have had a sequence of courses in an assessment program, faculty and site supervisors must nonetheless provide a level of supervision appropriate to the trainees' previous education and experience and see that trainees administer, score, and interpret tests competently (see also Standard 2.05, Delegation of Work to Others).

⊘ A psychologist served as an on-site supervisor for externships of third-year school psychology graduate students in a large school district. All students had taken a series of advanced courses in educational assessment. In

(Continued)

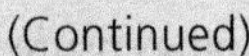

(Continued)

addition to reviewing their transcripts, during the first weeks of the externship, the psychologist observed each student administer tests and carefully reviewed and provided feedback on their scoring and interpretation of the standard battery of tests they were expected to use. She held weekly supervision meetings with the students and continued to review their reports throughout the year.

☒ Members of a group practice composed of educational, school, and clinical psychologists specializing in learning disabilities and school-related disorders were finding it difficult to keep up with the hours required to provide individualized treatment, family therapy, and psychological assessment. To meet their needs and keep costs down, they decided to hire and train recent college graduates who had majored in psychology or education to independently administer some of the assessments.

9.08 Obsolete Tests and Outdated Test Results

(a) Psychologists do not base their assessment or intervention decisions or recommendations on data or test results that are outdated for the current purpose.

Standard 9.08a prohibits psychologists from making evaluative, intervention, or treatment decisions or recommendations based on outdated data or test results, unless such information is specifically relevant to the diagnostic or placement decision. The standard applies to psychologists who administer, score, and interpret the test as well as to psychologists who use test results for intervention decisions or recommendations. Whether test data or results are outdated for the current purpose may be determined by whether the test from which scores were derived is itself obsolete (see Standard 9.08b, below).

Standard 9.08a is addressed to the use of test scores that may have been derived from currently used tests but are obsolete for the purposes of the evaluation. Previous scores derived from an up-to-date version of a test may be obsolete if individuals might be expected to score differently or require a different test based on (a) the amount of time between the previous administration and the current need for assessment, (b) maturational and other developmental changes, (c) educational advancement, (d) job training or employment experiences, (e) change in health status, (f) new symptomatology, (g) change in work or family status, or (h) an accident or traumatic experience.

In some instances, it may be appropriate to use outdated test scores as a basis of comparison with new test results to evaluate the long-term effectiveness of an educational program or intervention or to help identify cognitive decline or a sudden change in mental health or adaptive functioning relevant to treatment, placement in an appropriate educational or health care environment, disability claims, competency hearings, or custody suits. When outdated data or results are used, psychologists' reports and recommendations should include explanations for their use and their limitations (see Standard 9.06, Interpreting Assessment Results).

☑ A neuropsychologist was asked to evaluate cognitive and personality factors that might be responsible for a sudden change in adaptive functioning of an 80-year-old nursing home resident. The resident had been given a battery of intelligence and personality tests 5 years previously upon admission to the nursing home. Advances in geropsychology in the past 5 years had resulted in more developmentally appropriate and sensitive assessment instruments for this age group. The psychologist conducted a new evaluation using the more valid instruments. In her summary, she compared the results of the assessment with the results of the earlier evaluation, accompanied by a discussion of the limitations of comparing current performance with the older test results.

Psychologists should resist pressures to use obsolete test results from schools, health care delivery systems, or other agencies or organizations that seek to cut expenses by using outdated test results for employment, promotion, educational placement, or services (see Standard 1.03, Conflicts Between Ethics and Organizational Demands).

(b) Psychologists do not base such decisions or recommendations on tests and measures that are obsolete and not useful for the current purpose.

Test developers often construct new versions of a test to reflect significant (a) advances in the theoretical constructs underlying the psychological characteristic assessed; (b) transformations in cultural, educational, linguistic, or societal influences that challenge the extent to which current test items validly reflect content domains; or (c) changes in the demographic characteristics of the population to be tested affecting the interpretations that can be drawn from standardized scores. Standard 9.08b prohibits psychologists from using outdated versions of tests for assessment or intervention decisions when interpretations drawn from the test are of questionable validity or otherwise not useful for the purpose of testing.

The expense of purchasing the most up-to-date version of a test is not an ethical justification for using obsolete tests when the validity of interpretations drawn from such tests is compromised. Psychologists working with schools, businesses, government agencies, courts, HMOs, and health care delivery systems that resist purchasing updated tests because of costs or ease of record keeping should clarify the nature of the problem; urge organizational reconsideration; and, if such recommendations are not heeded, strive to the extent feasible to limit harms that will arise from misapplication of the test results, ensuring that their actions do not justify or defend violating testees' human rights (see Standards 1.02, Conflicts Between Ethics and Law, Regulations, or Other Governing Legal Authority; 1.03, Conflicts Between Ethics and Organizational Demands).

The standard does permit psychologists to use obsolete versions of a test when there is a valid purpose for doing so. In most cases, the purpose will be to compare past and current test performance. When use of an obsolete test is appropriate to the purpose of assessment, psychologists should clarify to schools, courts, or others that will use the test results which version of the test was used, why that version was selected, and the test norms used to interpret the results.

✓ A psychologist asked to evaluate an employee's claim that an industrial accident was responsible for a current disabling psychological disorder learned that the employee had been administered a battery of cognitive and personality tests several years earlier during preemployment screening. The psychologist decided it would be useful and appropriate to compare the complainant's current performance with his performance on test scores obtained prior to the accident. One of the previous scores was derived from an older version of a test that had been updated and revised recently. The psychologist decided to administer the older version of the test to better determine whether functioning had been affected by the accident. The psychologist's report included a rationale for the use of the older version of the test.

Need to Know: When to Use Obsolete Tests

The Ethics Code does not prescribe a specific time period in which psychologists should adopt a new version of a test. Such decisions depend on which version is best suited for an examinee within the context of the specific purpose of testing. Psychologists should be cautious about adopting a test publisher's recommendations for when they should purchase and transition to a revision, since such recommendations do not have legal standing and test developers have a financial stake in encouraging the purchase of new versions (Bush, 2010). Bush (2010) recommended that psychologists should be guided by whether independent research on the new or revised measure supports its use for a particular purpose or patient population; use of the prior version of the test may be preferable, and the rationale for selecting a specific edition should be included in the written assessment report.

9.09 Test Scoring and Interpretation Services

(a) Psychologists who offer assessment or scoring services to other professionals accurately describe the purpose, norms, validity, reliability, and applications of the procedures and any special qualifications applicable to their use.

Standard 9.09 applies to psychologists who develop or sell computerized, automated, web-linked, or other test-scoring and interpretation services to other professionals. Psychologists offering these services must provide in manuals, instructions, brochures, and advertisements accurate statements about the purpose, basis, and method of scoring; validity and reliability of scores derived from the service; professional contexts in which the scores can be applied; and any special user qualifications necessary to competently use the service.

When test interpretations, in addition to scores, will be provided to users of the services, psychologists providing the services must document the sources, theoretical rationale, and psychometric evidence for the validity and reliability of the particular interpretation method employed. Psychologists providing scoring services must include a summary of the evidence supporting the interpretations that includes the nature, rationale, and formulas for cutoff scores or configural scoring rules (rules for scoring test items or subtests that depend on a pattern of responses). If a discussion of the algorithms or other rules for scoring would jeopardize proprietary interests, copyrights, or other intellectual property rights issues, owners of the intellectual property are nevertheless responsible for documenting in some way evidence in support of the validity of score interpretations (AERA, APA, & NCME, 2014).

Descriptions of the application of test-scoring and interpretation procedures must include a discussion of their limitations. For example, computer-generated or automated systems may not be able to take into account specific features of the examinee that are relevant to test interpretation such as medical history, gender, age, ethnicity, employment history, education, or competence in the language of the test; motor problems that might interfere with test taking; current life stressors; or special conditions of the testing environment.

> (b) Psychologists select scoring and interpretation services (including automated services) on the basis of evidence of the validity of the program and procedures as well as on other appropriate considerations. (See also Standard 2.01b and c, Boundaries of Competence.)

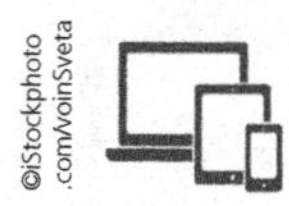

Standard 9.09b applies to psychologists who use computerized, automated, web-linked, or other test scoring and interpretation services developed by other professionals or test vendors. Psychologists should select only test scoring and interpretation services that provide evidence of the validity of the program and procedures for the types of evaluation or treatment decisions that are to be informed by the assessment and that are appropriate for the individual case under consideration. Psychologists should not use scoring and interpretation services if the psychometric information provided by the test-scoring or interpretation services is inadequate or fails to support the applicability of the scoring and interpretation methods to the goals of the particular assessment.

Implications of HIPAA

When the test data to be scored and interpreted by the service come under the HIPAA definition of PHI, the Notice of Privacy Practices must list the name of the service or the psychologist must obtain a valid authorization from the client/patient to transmit the information to the service (see more detailed discussion on core requirements for valid HIPAA authorizations under Standard 4.05a,

Disclosures). Psychologists must also ensure that the service receives, stores, transmits, and discloses client/patient information in a manner that is HIPAA compliant. In most instances, psychologists will enter into a business associate agreement with the testing service. As part of the HIPAA-required business associate contract, the service must provide assurances to the psychologist that information will be safeguarded appropriately. If a psychologist discovers that the service has violated HIPAA regulations in some way, the psychologist must correct the error or terminate the business associate contract.

(c) Psychologists retain responsibility for the appropriate application, interpretation, and use of assessment instruments, whether they score and interpret such tests themselves or use automated or other services.

Irrespective of whether psychologists use a service or score and interpret test data themselves, the psychologist is ultimately responsible for the appropriate selection, administration, scoring, interpretation, and use of the test. Under Standard 9.09c, psychologists must acknowledge this responsibility and take appropriate steps to ensure that tests were properly scored and interpreted.

To be in compliance with this Standard, psychologists must avoid simplified interpretations of test scores that can lead to misdiagnosis, inadequate or iatrogenic treatment plans, or unfair or invalid personnel decisions or that can mislead the trier of fact in judicial and government hearings. Psychologists must also possess the following competencies (AERA, APA, & NCME, 2014; Standard 2.01, Boundaries of Competence):

- Sufficient familiarity with scoring and interpretation techniques to adequately perform these tasks themselves, detect errors in test scores provided by a service, and critically evaluate canned interpretations.
- Training and experience necessary to identify the limitations of test service interpretations and know when collateral test scores and other relevant information are necessary to adequately interpret and apply test results. Such information might include an examinee's health status, culture, gender, age, employment history, educational experiences, language competencies, physical disabilities, symptoms of or empirical evidence supporting an assumption of comorbid disorders, current life stressors, and special conditions of the testing environment.

Digital Ethics: Security and Interpretation of Online Testing

The use of online preemployment testing is becoming increasingly popular because of its convenience and lower cost as well as an expansion of the pool of national and international applicants that can be screened. Organizational and consulting psychologists utilizing these systems need to be aware of the serious security risks associated with this new technology. As detailed by Foster (2010), these tests are often offered without security to enable easy administration and worldwide reach. This poses a threat to test interpretation, since there is usually no way to authenticate who actually took the test and test theft and cheating are easily accomplished.

9.10 Explaining Assessment Results

Regardless of whether the scoring and interpretation are done by psychologists, by employees or assistants, or by automated or other outside services, psychologists take reasonable steps to ensure that explanations of results are given to the individual or designated representative unless the nature of the relationship precludes provision of an explanation of results (such as in some organizational consulting, preemployment or security screenings, and forensic evaluations), and this fact has been clearly explained to the person being assessed in advance.

Psychologists who administer, supervise, or otherwise are responsible for test administration are also responsible for ensuring that the individuals tested, their guardians, or personal representative receive an explanation of the assessment results. The purpose of an explanation is to enable a client/patient to understand the meaning of a test score or test score interpretation as it relates to its purpose, implications, and potential consequences. An appropriate explanation "should describe in simple language what the test covers, what scores mean, the precision of the scores, common misinterpretations of the test scores, and how scores will be used" (AERA, APA, & NCME, 2014, p. 119). Whenever possible and clinically appropriate, psychologists assessing children and adolescents should provide feedback to the child as well as his or her guardian; the feedback should be appropriate to the child's developmental level.

Employees and Trainees

According to Standard 9.10, the responsibility for appropriate test explanation lies with the psychologist. It takes into account whether he or she personally scored or interpreted the test, assigned the scoring or interpretation to an employee or assistant, or used an outside service (Standard 2.05, Delegation of Work to Others). The standard does not require psychologists to provide the explanation but to take reasonable steps to ensure that one is given. The term *reasonable steps* is used to acknowledge situations in which the examinee may not wish to or is unable to meet for an explanation of results or an employee has misinformed the psychologist about an explanation taking place. If, however, a psychologist is aware that appropriate staff is unavailable or unable to provide the explanation, the psychologist should do so personally.

☒ A psychologist supervised several interns at an outpatient unit of a veterans hospital. The interns were responsible for administering a battery of psychological tests to new patients. Weekly supervision meetings with the interns included discussion of test selection, administration, scoring, and interpretation. The psychologist paid only cursory attention to instructing the supervisees on how to explain test results to patients. The clinic director received several complaints that interns' explanations of test results were confusing and distressing to patients (see also Standard 2.05, Delegation of Work to Others).

Use of Automated Scoring Services

A psychologist who asks a scoring service to send a computerized interpretation to a client/patient should take reasonable steps to ensure that the computerized interpretation provides an explanation adequate for conveying test performance information to examinees. As discussed under Standard 9.09b, psychologists who are covered entities under HIPAA and use scoring services must include this information in the Notice of Privacy Practices or obtain a specific client/patient authorization to use such services and ensure that the service transmits information and protects client/patient privacy in a HIPAA-compliant manner.

✓ A psychologist decided to use a popular scoring service for some frequently administered tests after examination of the company's materials indicated that the scoring system was reliable and valid. An added benefit of the service was that it would send test interpretations directly to the client. For the first set of test data the psychologist sent to the service, she asked the service to send her the test interpretation that is usually mailed directly to the client. The psychologist reviewed the interpretive materials and believed that the information was too sparse to adequately inform clients and might create confusion. She therefore decided to continue using the service for scoring but did not permit the service to send explanations directly to the client.

Exceptions

Standard 9.10 permits exceptions to this requirement when an explanation of the results is precluded by the psychologist–examinee relationship, such as when an organization or legal counsel has retained the psychologist's services or assessment has been ordered by a judicial referral. For example, it is usually inappropriate for psychologists to provide an explanation of test results directly to the examinee when testing is court ordered, when it involves employment testing, or when it involves eligibility for security clearances for government work. Rather, reports are released to the court or retaining party and cannot be released to examinees and their family members, doctors, lawyers, or other representatives without the permission of the retaining party or the court (Bush et al., 2006; National Academy of Neuropsychology Policy and Planning Committee, 2003). In such situations, prior to administering assessments, psychologists are required to inform examinees that the psychologist will not be providing them with an explanation of the test results. If legally permissible, the psychologist should provide the reason why an explanation will not be given (see Standards 3.10c, Informed Consent; 3.11, Psychological Services Delivered To or Through Organizations; 9.03, Informed Consent in Assessments).

9.11 Maintaining Test Security

The term *test materials* refers to manuals, instruments, protocols, and test questions or stimuli and does not include test data as defined in Standard 9.04, Release of Test Data. Psychologists make reasonable efforts to maintain the integrity and security of test materials and other assessment techniques consistent with law and contractual obligations, and in a manner that permits adherence to this Ethics Code.

©iStockphoto.com/voinSveta

An assumption of test validity is that individuals take the test under prescribed standardized conditions. For many tests, a critical aspect of standardization is that testees are equally unfamiliar with the test items. When some testees have access to test items prior to the administration of the test, the test norms and thus interpretations based on scaled scores may not be psychometrically defensible. Duplicating test materials or making video or audio recordings of an assessment session that subsequently enters the public domain also threatens the ongoing validity of tests. Individuals who have had uncontrolled access to test content can manipulate or coach others to manipulate test results that harm the public by enabling individuals to malinger or to obtain positions for which they are unqualified. Many tests consist of a static number of items that are costly to develop, take years to construct, and are not easily replaced. Thus, release of test materials can compromise the validity and usefulness of a test and jeopardize the intellectual property rights of test authors and publishers.

Definition of Test Materials and Test Security

Under Standard 9.11, *test materials* are manuals, instruments, protocols, and test questions or stimuli that do not come under the definition of *test data,* as defined in Standard 9.04a, Release of Test Data. Under Standard 9.11, psychologists have a duty to make reasonable efforts to protect the integrity and security of test materials and other assessment techniques. With few exceptions, test materials that do not include client/patient responses should never be released to clients/patients or others unqualified to use the instruments. Unless specifically recommended by the test developer, self-administered tests should not be given to clients/patients to take home. Additional security precautions need to be taken for tests administered through the Internet. Psychologists should consult test developers and, if necessary, seek legal consultation before distributing copyrighted tests over the Internet (Bersoff et al., 2012).

This standard does not prohibit psychologists from discussing individual test items with clients/patients if doing so assists in explaining test results (Standard 9.10, Explaining Assessment Results). Psychologists may also send test materials to other qualified health professionals bound by their ethical guidelines to protect the security of the instruments, taking appropriate steps not to violate copyright laws.

☒ A patient of a psychologist in independent practice was discussing her anxiety about an upcoming psychological evaluation for a job promotion that required security clearance. To reduce the patient's anxiety, the psychologist took out from his files several of the standardized tests that are usually administered for such purposes and went over them with the patient.

Laws Governing Release of Records

Implications of HIPAA

Although HIPAA recognizes the obligation of covered entities to protect test materials that come under copyright law, as a matter of practice, psychologists should keep test materials separated from a client's/patient's mental health records so the materials do not risk being included as a HIPAA-defined "designated record set," which may not be withheld pursuant to client/patient release under federal law. Test materials do not have to be included in the patient's record if *test data,* as defined by Standard 9.04, Release of Test Data, are not recorded on the test material itself. *Separated* does not necessarily mean that the test data and test material must be kept in a separate file cabinet, but it does require that they be separated by a folder or binding unit so they are not confused or commingled with the test data records. Psychologists should seek legal advice before making such a determination and be mindful that removing clients'/patients' responses from the test protocol after they have been recorded on the material can constitute unlawful alteration of the patient's record.

Implications of FERPA

School psychologists may also find that laws governing the release of school records supersede the requirements of Standard 9.11. FERPA establishes the right of parents to obtain copies of their children's school records where failure to provide the copies would effectively prevent a parent or eligible student from exercising his or her right to inspect and review the education records (20 U.S.C. § 1232G[a][1][A]; 34 CFR § 99.11b; http://www.ed.gov/offices/OM/fpco/ferpa/index.html). Schools are not required to provide copies of the records unless, because of distance or other considerations, it is impossible for the parent or student to review the records. Psychologists working in schools may also release test materials to attorneys or other nonprofessionals in response to a court order. In these situations, psychologists can request that the court issue a protective order requiring that test items not be duplicated or made available to the public as part of the court record and returned to the psychologist at the end of the proceedings.

Copyright Protection Laws

Release of "test data" that include client/patient responses recorded on the test protocol itself can raise issues of copyright protection and fair use by test development companies. If testing protocols allow, psychologists may wish to record client/patient responses on a form separated from the test items themselves to comply with contractual agreements with test developers and to maintain test security (Standard 9.11, Maintaining Test Security).

When test data consisting of PHI cannot be separated from test materials that are protected by copyright law, psychologists' decision to withhold the release of test data would be consistent with HIPAA regulations and Standard 9.04a. In school contexts, reproduction of a test without permission may also be a violation of copyright law, although providing a single copy of a used protocol to parents under FERPA regulations may fall under the "fair use doctrine" provisions of copyright law (Jacob & Hartshorne, 2007; *Newport-Mesa Unified School District v. State of California Department of Education,* 2005).

The increase in use of listservs, social media, and websites authored by psychologists has given rise to an increase in threats to test security. Psychologists need to monitor their online communications to ensure that they do not divulge sensitive information about the content or interpretation of frequently used psychological tests (Schultz & Loving, 2012).

HOT TOPIC

The Use of Assessments in Expert Testimony: Implications of Case Law and the Federal Rules of Evidence

In 1988, testimony by mental health professionals accepted as experts by the court played a key role in the conviction of Kelly Michaels on 115 counts of sexual offenses involving 20 nursery school children. The "experts" claimed that the responses of children to assessment questions fit the profiles of abuse "documented" by Roland Summit (1983) and Suzanne Sgroi (1982). However, these profiles, drawn from clinical work with sexually abused children, were largely theoretical and had never been subjected to tests of validity or reliability in or out of a forensic context (Fisher, 1995). Five years after Ms. Michaels's conviction, the Appellate Division ruled

(Continued)

(Continued)

that the data on which the experts' testimonies were based were unreliable, invalid, and not probative of sexual abuse and therefore could not be used as evidence of guilt (*State of New Jersey v. Margaret Kelly Michaels*, 1993).

The Kelly Michaels case served as a wake-up call for psychologists on the ethical and legal consequences of providing expert testimony based on assessment instruments and procedures that have not gained general acceptance within the field and do not have established relevance to the legal question at hand (Everson & Faller, 2012; Faller & Everson, 2012; Klee & Friedman, 2001; Olafson, 2012; Standards 2.04, Bases for Scientific and Professional Judgments, and 9.01, Bases for Assessments). This Hot Topic highlights ethical and legal challenges in selecting forensically valid assessment instruments for expert testimony.

Relevant Case and Federal Law

Mental health professionals are not alone in receiving increased scrutiny of expert opinion in criminal and civil cases. In recent years, there has been an increase in federal and case law requiring judges to determine evidentiary admissibility of expert testimony based on the general acceptance of methods and procedures within the expert's field (Heilbrun & LaDuke, 2015; Klee & Friedman, 2001; Sales & Shuman, 2007).

The "General Acceptance" Standard

The "general acceptance" standard for admissibility of expert testimony was first established by the Supreme Court in *Frye v. United States* (1923). In *Daubert v. Merrell Dow Pharmaceuticals, Inc.* (1993), the standard was expanded to require specific relevance to the legal question at hand and demonstrated scientific reliability and validity. In *General Electric Co. v. Joiner* (1997), the Court held that judges should exclude from evidence expert testimony when the data (and the methodology used to substantiate the data) are insufficiently linked to the legal question at hand (Grove & Barden, 1999). The "general acceptance" standard was explicitly extended to practitioners in *Kumho Tire Co., Ltd. v. Carmichael* (1999).

As of 2004, the Federal Rules of Evidence (70 FED. R. EVID. 702) require judges to permit expert testimony only if it is derived from reliable principles and methods in the expert's field and these principles and methods have been applied reliably to the facts of the case.

In light of case and federal law, appropriate selection of psychological assessment methods for forensic use should be determined by the legal question at hand, the psychometric properties of the instruments and procedures, and admissibility standards established by the court (Bush et al., 2006; Standards 2.01f, Boundaries of Competence; 9.01a, Bases for Assessments; and 9.02, Use of Assessments).

Challenges of the "General Acceptance" Standard to Selection and Use of Assessments in Forensic Contexts

The integration of *Daubert, Kumho,* and *Joiner* into courts' standards for admissibility of expert testimony has led to ethical and legal debate regarding whether assessments used in clinical settings should be included in forensic opinions if they have not been validated for application to issues before the court. For example, diagnostic categories derived from the *Diagnostic and Statistical Manual of Mental Disorders (DSM-5*, American Psychiatric Association, 2013), while useful in increasing the reliability of practitioners' agreement on a patient's diagnosis, may not be acceptable under the *Daubert–Kumho–Joiner* evidentiary criteria because they are derived from a process of consensus among a small group of professionals that sometimes draws upon available research but does not require scientific data to validate the existence or etiology of the disorder (Grove & Barden, 1999; Heilbrun, Grisso, & Goldstein, 2009).

Similar arguments have been made against the use of tests such as the Rorschach Comprehensive System as data for expert testimony regarding psychopathology, based on the fact, among others, that its validity and reliability in and outside of forensic settings continue to be the subject of intense scientific debate (Grove, Barden, Garb, & Lilienfeld, 2002; Ritzler, Erard, & Pettigrew, 2002). Others have challenged whether assessments for neurological injury claims meet the *Daubert–Kumho–Joiner* standard for evidentiary admissibility in the absence of premorbid baselines or empirically established ecological validity of the tests to predict functioning in everyday life (Stern, 2001).

Kaufman (2011) has identified four recurring challenges to the admissibility of neuropsychological evidence: (1) battery selection (fixed vs. flexible), (2) symptom validity measures, (3) causation opinions, and (4) nonpsychologists exerting neuropsychological opinions.

The Limits of Psychological Assessments for Child Custody Disputes

In recent years, courts have begun using the ambiguous standard "best interests of the child" as a means of resolving custody decisions (APA, 2010d; Elrod & Spector, 2004). Currently, there are no reliable legal criteria or any validated mental health or behavioral criteria on which a psychologist can provide an expert opinion on "best interests" (Krauss & Sales, 2000). Forensic psychologists hired to evaluate the mental health of one or more family members can provide expert opinion on the interpretation of data based on assessment instruments found to be reliable and valid indicators of children's or parents' emotional and cognitive status and their interpersonal interactions with one another (O'Donohue, Beitz, & Tolle, 2009). However, unless there is established scientific evidence that these instruments can reliably determine whether joint custody or the number of visitations permitted for a noncustodial parent would be in the best interests of the child, expert opinion that implies a direct empirical link between the data collected to specific recommendations regarding custody decisions before the court may be inadmissible under the *Daubert–Kumho–Joiner* standard and in violation of Standard 9.01a, Bases for Assessments (Ellis, 2012; Heilbrun & LaDuke, 2015; Otto & Martindale, 2007).

Forensic Assessment Relevant to Violent or Abusive Crimes

In criminal cases, forensic psychologists are often called upon to provide expert testimony based on a defendant's response to assessment instruments designed to measure inclinations toward violence or psychopathologies associated with abusive or other criminal behaviors (Nedopil, 2002; Tolman & Rotzien, 2007). Psychometric techniques for evaluating the validity of such assessment instruments most often depend on probability evidence and comparisons of within- and between-group responses to determine a test's reliability and validity. By contrast, the ultimate decision before the court in such cases is categorical: A defendant is either guilty or innocent. The opinions of psychologists testifying as expert witnesses must therefore reflect the limitations of the methods in which data were obtained (Vitacco, Gonsalves, Tomony, Smith, & Lishner, 2012). The clinical forensic evaluator can testify as to the degree to which a defendant's test scores reach criteria for

(Continued)

(Continued)

psychological characteristics associated with different criminal behaviors but cannot form an opinion as to whether those scores indicate the defendant's behavioral guilt or innocence in the legal case at hand (Fisher, 1995; Krauss & Lieberman, 2007).

Ultimate-Issue Testimony

The law is inconsistent on whether experts can testify to the ultimate legal issue (the question of law that is before the court). In some jurisdictions doing so is prohibited, while in others it is required. There is also continuing debate as to whether such testimony harms the legal process by invading the province of the judge or jury. For example, Grisso (2003) cautioned forensic psychologists to be aware that "an expert opinion that answers the ultimate legal question is not an 'expert' opinion, but a personal value judgment" (p. 477). If required to answer the ultimate legal issue, take steps to minimize any potentially adverse impact by explicitly recognizing in the forensic report and in testimony the court's responsibility for the legal decision and that the ultimate opinion expressed is a clinical opinion of the evaluator (Heilbrun & LaDuke, 2015).

Ethical and Legal Considerations in the Selection and Use of Assessment Instruments for Expert Testimony

Psychologists providing expert testimony based on psychological assessments with established relevance to the legal question at hand assist the courts in making fair determinations by illuminating data on the legal issue. However, neither justice nor the legal rights of plaintiffs or defendants are well served when psychologists declaring "expert" status present forensic opinions based on assessment instruments and techniques insufficient to substantiate their findings (Principle B: Fidelity and Responsibility and Principle D: Justice; Standards 2.04, Bases for Scientific and Professional Judgments, and 9.01, Bases for Assessments). The following are points that psychologists should consider when expert testimony will be based on psychological assessment:

- Select assessment instruments and procedures with established psychometric validity and reliability for the legal question at hand (Standards 9.01a, Bases for Assessments; 9.02a, Use of Assessments).
- Ensure that established principles of test interpretation have been applied reliably to the facts of the case (Standard 9.06, Interpreting Assessment Results).
- Prepare testimony that reflects awareness of and meets legal criteria for the admissibility of expert testimony based on the reliability of the scientific foundation on which an opinion is based and the established validity and reliability in providing data relevant to the legal question for which their opinion is sought (Bush et al., 2006; *Daubert–Kumho–Joiner*; Standards 2.01f, Boundaries of Competence, and 2.04, Bases for Scientific and Professional Judgments).
- Take full responsibility for ensuring testimony is not flawed by the use of unorthodox assessment procedures and provide the court with the reasoning that led from the data to the expert opinion (Grisso, 2003; Heilbrun, 2001).
- Acknowledge limitations in the applicability of the test data to the legal issue (Standard 9.06, Interpreting Assessment Results).
- Avoid omission of relevant data or overemphasis on minor facts to support an opinion (Bush et al., 2006).
- Avoid offering testimony beyond the data collected.

Chapter Cases and Ethics Discussion Questions

Dr. Romanoff, a neuropsychologist in a small interprofessional group practice has been asked by the practice's pediatrician to evaluate Tommy, a second grader who is displaying behavioral problems at home and at school. Tommy's parents have joint custody and alternate their child care responsibilities on a weekly basis. Dr. Romanoff conducted a standard battery of assessments that included neuropsychological testing; standardized instruments completed by Tommy, his parents, and teachers; and a family-based clinical interview. The majority of standardized assessments support a diagnosis of attention-deficit/hyperactivity disorder (ADHD). However, the family interviews indicate that behavioral problems largely emerge during weeks when Tommy stays at the home of his mother and her female romantic partner. Dr. Romanoff is aware that in the future, her report may be used in court if Tommy's father chooses to challenge the custody arrangements and is unsure whether her report should mention the gender of Tommy's mother's romantic partner. She is also concerned that if she includes a diagnosis of ADHD, the pediatrician will automatically prescribe medications without exploring the family factors that may also account for the symptoms. Discuss the ethical issues that Dr. Romanoff needs to consider as she is completing the assessment, writing the report, and interpreting the results.

Dr. Tagashi is a school psychologist who works in a district with very few resources. His responsibilities include developing an individualized educational plan (IEP) for students whose assessments indicate special needs. The district does not have the resources to provide most students with special needs the most up-to-date evidence-based practices (EBPs) for educational programs. Dr. Tagashi does not know whether he should recommend EBP programs when developing the IEPs or programs that reflect the resource limitations of the district. Discuss the ethical principles and Section 9 Assessment standards that Dr. Tagashi should consider in resolving his dilemma. How might a consideration of the virtues discussed in Chapter 3 also help guide ethical decision making?

Dr. Sharah, a clinical psychologist specializing in geriatric care, has a private practice that receives referrals from an integrated care facility. Under the Affordable Care Act (ACA) as a contracted mental health provider for the facility, she has access to every referred patient's electronic health record (EHR) and is required to enter her weekly session reports into the shared EHR as well. The facility has just referred Andre, a 67-year-old retiree who has been diagnosed by the staff psychiatrist with moderate (middle-stage) Alzheimer's disease. Andre, who lives with his daughter and her family, has been having increased episodes of anger and refusing to bathe. The EHR already includes a family medical and social history, but it appears incomplete. It is not clear from the record which practitioner (neurologist, psychiatrist, or primary care physician) collected the history or its timing. Dr. Sharah is concerned that if she doesn't conduct her own family and social history, she may miss some information that may be helpful to her treatment plan. At the same time, she is aware that Andre's insurer is reluctant to approve duplicative assessments. She is also concerned that subjecting Andre to another medical and social history interview will be frustrating for him and delay needed behavioral and family treatment. Drawing on the APA ethical principles and assessment standards, discuss how Dr. Sharah should resolve this dilemma. (Readers may wish to refer to the feature "Digital Ethics: Electronic Health Records (EHR) in Interprofessional Organizations" in Chapter 9).

CHAPTER 13

Standards on Therapy

10. Therapy

10.01 Informed Consent to Therapy

(a) When obtaining informed consent to therapy as required in Standard 3.10, Informed Consent, psychologists inform clients/patients as early as is feasible in the therapeutic relationship about the nature and anticipated course of therapy, fees, involvement of third parties, and limits of confidentiality and provide sufficient opportunity for the client/patient to ask questions and receive answers. (See also Standards 4.02, Discussing the Limits of Confidentiality, and 6.04, Fees and Financial Arrangements.)

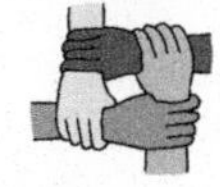

©iStockphoto.com/voinSveta

To comply with this standard of the APA Ethics Code (APA, 2002b), psychologists must obtain and document written or oral consent in the manner set forth in Standard 3.10, Informed Consent. They must also provide prospective therapy clients/patients and, when appropriate, their legal guardians a clear explanation of the nature and anticipated course of therapy, fees, involvement of third parties, and the limits of confidentiality. This information must be presented in a language reasonably understandable to the client/patient, and the consent process must provide sufficient opportunity for questions and answers.

As Early as Feasible

Standard 10.01 explicitly uses the phrase *as early as is feasible* to indicate that in some cases, obtaining informed consent during the first therapy session may not be possible or clinically appropriate. Psychologists may need to wait for feedback from a client's/patient's HMO before consent discussions regarding fees can be completed. Informed consent during the first session may be clinically contraindicated if a new client/patient is suicidal or experiencing some other crisis needing immediate therapeutic attention. In such situations, consent is obtained as soon as all information is available or the crisis has subsided (see also Standard 6.04a, Fees and Financial Arrangements).

✓ At the beginning of the first session, it became apparent that a new client was having difficulty communicating in a coherent fashion. With probing, the psychologist learned that the client had a history of schizophrenia and had recently gone off his medications because of its intolerable side effects. The psychologist postponed discussion relevant to informed consent and spent the rest of the session working with the client to determine the best course of action to deal with the immediate situation.

Nature of the Therapy

The *nature* of the therapy refers to information about the therapeutic process that would reasonably be expected to affect clients'/patients' decisions to enter into therapy with the psychologist. Informed consent should include discussion of the duration of each session (e.g., 50 minutes), appointment schedule (e.g., weekly), and the general objectives of treatment (e.g., crisis management, symptom reduction). Depending on the treatment modality, the consent process might inform clients/patients that therapy entails participating in biofeedback sessions, relaxation exercises, behavioral contracts, homework assignments, discussion of dreams and developmental history, collateral treatments, or other aspects of the therapeutic process relevant to an informed consent decision. Psychologists should not assume that all clients/patients are familiar with the nature of psychotherapy.

✓ A new patient who had recently immigrated to the United States from West Africa told a psychologist that his general practitioner had recommended that he see the psychologist because of headaches that had not responded to traditional medications. The psychologist explained her cognitive therapy approach to working with such problems, standard confidentiality procedures, and issues relevant to the patient's health plan and then turned to a discussion of issues relevant to the patient's presenting problem. Toward the end of the session, the psychologist asked the patient if he had any additional questions. The patient asked the psychologist if she was ready to give him a prescription for a medication that would cure his headaches. The psychologist then carefully explained in great detail the nature of cognitive therapy and the difference between such therapy and psychopharmacological approaches.

Anticipated Course of the Therapy

The *anticipated course* of therapy refers to the number of sessions expected, given the psychologist's current knowledge of the client's/patient's presenting problem and, when applicable, the company, institutional, or health plan policies that may affect the number of sessions. Depending on the treatment modality, consent discussions would also include expectable modifications such as the evolving nature of systematic desensitization or exposure therapy, the uncovering of as yet unidentified treatment issues, or, if the practitioner is a prescribing psychologist, adjustments in dosage levels of psychopharmacological medications.

Need to Know: Informed Consent With Suicidal Patients

For certain disorders and treatment contexts, informed consent will include discussion of empirically documented risks inherent in psychotherapy. Following a review of the literature, Rudd, Joiner, et al. (2009) concluded that given the available data on increased suicide risk during treatment involving multiple attempters, there is a need to include potential risks of death or suicide in the informed consent process. As a comparison, they noted the FDA black box warning label for antidepressant use with adolescents (Rudd, Cordero, & Bryan, 2009). According to the authors, frank discussions about suicide risk during informed consent offer the following benefits: (a) assisting clients/patients and their families to understand the true nature of suicide risk during the treatment process and to recognize shared responsibility to reduce its likelihood, (b) helping to clarify the importance of treatment compliance and crisis management to treatment effectiveness, (c) providing an opportunity to emphasize the need for effective self-management during outpatient care, (d) helping the psychologist to identify and target for treatment skill deficits that might limit the patient's willingness or ability to access emergency services, and (e) facilitating a frank exchange about the responsibilities of provider and client/patient.

In many instances, informed consent to therapy will be an ongoing process determined, for example, by the extent to which the nature of a client's/patient's treatment needs are immediately diagnosed or gradually identified over a series of sessions, cognitive and social maturation in child clients/patients, or functional declines in clients/patients with progressive disorders. Providing clients/patients with an honest evaluation of the anticipated and unanticipated factors that may determine the course of therapy demonstrates respect for their right to self-determination and can promote trust in the therapeutic alliance (Pomerantz, 2005; Principle C: Integrity; Principle E: Respect for People's Rights and Dignity).

☒ A psychologist saw a new client whose presenting problems appeared to be related to a debilitating social phobia. The client was to pay privately for treatment because her health plan did not cover psychotherapy. The client asked the psychologist how long she might have to be in therapy before she saw some relief from her symptoms. The psychologist responded, "We'll just see how it goes."

✓ A psychologist saw a new patient who appeared to be suffering from a mild form of agoraphobia. The psychologist explained his cognitive–behavioral approach to this type of problem and the average number of sessions after which patients often feel some relief from their symptoms. The psychologist stressed that each individual responds differently and that together they would reassess the patient's progress after a specific number of sessions.

Fees

Discussion of *fees* must include the cost of the therapy, the types of reimbursement accepted (e.g., checks, credit card payments, direct payment from insurance companies), the payment schedule (e.g., weekly, monthly), when fees are reevaluated (e.g., annual raise in rates), and policies regarding late payments and missed appointments.

When appropriate and as soon as such information can be verified, psychologists should also discuss with clients/patients the percentage of therapy costs reimbursed under the client's/patient's health plan and limitations on the number of sessions that can be anticipated because of limitations in insurance or other sources of client/patient financing (see also Standard 6.04, Fees and Financial Arrangements). Psychologists directly contracted with HMOs may have capitated or other types of business agreements that provide financial incentives to limit the number of treatment sessions. When permitted by law and contractual agreement, psychologists should inform clients/patients about such arrangements (Acuff et al., 1999; Barnett & Walfish, 2012) see also Standard 3.06, Conflict of Interest, and the Hot Topic in Chapter 9, "Managing the Ethics of Managed Care").

☒ On the initial visit, a psychologist told a client her fee for each session and mentioned that she was an approved provider for some HMOs. At the end of the first month in treatment, when the client asked the psychologist to fill out an insurance form, the client was shocked to learn that the psychologist was not an approved provider for his particular HMO plan, that she had not called the HMO to inquire about her eligibility for reimbursement, and that she had not informed him during the first session of the possibility that she was not an approved provider.

Involvement of Third Parties

The term *third parties,* as used in this standard, refers to legal guardians, health insurance companies, employers, organizations, and legal or other governing authorities that may be involved in the therapy. Psychologists should inform clients/patients if such parties have requested or ordered mental health treatment, are paying for the therapy, and are entitled to receive diagnostic information or details of the therapy based on law or contractual agreement—and to whom information may be provided—contingent on the client's/patient's appropriate written release or authorization (see section below on implications of HIPAA). Psychologists asked to evaluate a child by one parent should clarify, when appropriate, custody issues to determine if the other parent must also give permission.

⊘ A psychologist was assigned to see a couple for court-ordered therapy following a finding of child abuse and neglect resulting in the removal of the children from their home. The psychologist informed the couple that the treatment was mandatory, that it was paid for by a court-affiliated child protective services agency, and that the psychologist would be providing to the court a summary of the couple's compliance with and progress in therapy.

Confidentiality

Informed consent to therapy must provide a clear explanation of the extent and limits of *confidentiality,* including (a) when the psychologist must comply with reporting requirements, such as mandated child abuse reporting or duty-to-warn laws, and (b) guardian access to records in the case of therapy involving minors or individuals with impaired consent capacities. Psychologists who provide therapy over the Internet must inform clients/patients about the procedures that will be used to protect confidentiality and the threats to confidentiality unique to this form of electronic transmission of information (see also Standard 4.02c, Discussing the Limits of Confidentiality). Clients/patients enrolled in health plans must be informed about the extent to which treatment plans, diagnosis, or other sensitive information must be disclosed to case managers for precertification or continuing authorization for treatment (Acuff et al., 1999; Fisher & Oransky, 2008). When appropriate, psychologists providing treatment in forensic settings should inform clients/patients of the possibility that the psychologist may be obligated to disclose statements made in therapy in court testimony.

⊘ A psychologist had an initial appointment with an adolescent and his parents to discuss the 14-year-old's entry into individual psychotherapy for depression. The psychologist discussed with both the prospective patient

(Continued)

(Continued)

and his parents what information concerning the adolescent's treatment would and would not be shared with the parents, including her confidentiality and disclosure policies regarding adolescent risk behaviors such as sexual activity and use of illegal drugs. She also informed them about her legal obligations to report suspected child abuse or neglect and her own policy regarding disclosure of information pertaining to client/patient imminent self-harm or harm to others. In addition, she described the parents' right to access the adolescent's health records under HIPAA (see also the Hot Topic "Confidentiality and Involvement of Parents in Mental Health Services for Children and Adolescents" in Chapter 7).

Digital Ethics: Discussion of Confidentiality Risks in Telepsychology

The APA Telepsychology Task Force (APA, 2013d) identified the critical need to ensure clients'/patients' full understanding of the increased risks to security and confidentiality when using telecommunication technologies. During informed consent, psychologists should explain the steps they have taken to protect client/patient confidentiality and the web-based security risks that might still exist within a professional health care setting or private or group practice (Standard 4.02, Discussing the Limits of Confidentiality). They should also use the consent conference to help clients/patients evaluate the remote environment in which they will receive and send electronically mediated services (e.g., home computer, mobile phone) to determine what steps clients/patients can take to address technical issues and protect the privacy of their information and safety. In addition, the informed consent discussion provides an opportunity to discuss how to avoid interruptions and distractions during sessions, establish a setting conducive to effective delivery of services, and arrange for contacting emergency personnel or other supports.

☒ A psychologist began therapy with a client over the Internet. The psychologist failed to inform the client of the need for a password to protect the home computer from which the client would be interacting with the psychologist. The client's spouse opened the files in which therapeutic communications had been saved and printed them out to use against the client in petitioning for divorce.

Implications of HIPAA

Psychologists who are *covered entities* under HIPAA must inform clients/patients about their rights regarding the uses and disclosures of their PHI. This includes providing clients/patients with a Notice of Privacy Practices that explains the uses and disclosures of PHI that may be made by the covered entity, as well as the individual's rights and covered entity's legal duties with respect to PHI (see the discussions regarding HIPAA under Standard 3.01, Informed Consent, and in "A Word About HIPAA" in the preface of this book for definitions and discussion of these terms). Remember, the designation "covered entity" is not specific to an individual client/patient but to the psychologist's practice. Thus, even if a psychologist is not electronically transmitting health information about a particular client/patient, HIPAA is triggered if the psychologist or business associate (including clients'/patients' health insurer) has conducted any such transactions for others who are the psychologist's clients/patients. Readers may also wish to review HIPAA regulations governing the protection of psychotherapy notes discussed in Chapter 12.

Digital Ethics: Setting an Internet Search and Social Media Policy During Informed Consent

As discussed in Chapter 6, the continued growth, popularity, and accessibility of personal information online raises issues regarding appropriate privacy protections and personal/professional boundary setting in psychotherapy (Standards 3.05, Multiple Relationships; 4.01, Maintaining Confidentiality; 4.02, Discussing the Limits of Confidentiality). Situations may arise when it is ethically responsible to search online for client/patient information, for example, for an emergency contact or, in rare instances, to corroborate client/patient clinically relevant statements (Lehavot et al., 2010). As Internet searches become even more ubiquitous in personal and professional life, discussing the psychologist's policy for such web-based searches during informed consent may become another important contributor to the therapeutic alliance. The psychologist's restrictions on interaction with the client/patient through social networks or other online outlets should also be a part of the consent process. During informed consent, psychologists should also clarify policies against "friending" and "fanning" by clients/patients if the psychologist has a professional Facebook page, security concerns for clients/patients who might choose to follow a psychologist's professional Twitter posts or blog, policies on client/patient testimonials, and restriction of email for appointment purposes only.

Informed Consent Involving Children and Adolescent Clients/Patients

Psychologists providing therapy and counseling to children and adolescents face unique informed consent challenges tied to (a) state and federal laws governing the rights of minors to autonomous health care decisions; (b) laws related to the rights and obligations of minors' legal guardians; and (c) developmental changes in children's ability to understand their rights, the nature of their disorder, and the purpose of treatment (Standard 3.10b, Informed Consent). When working with children and adolescents, psychologists must constantly balance ethical obligations to protect client/patient welfare with respect for the client's/patient's development of autonomy and privacy (Principle A: Beneficence and Nonmaleficence; Principle E: Respect for People's Rights and Dignity).

When Guardian Consent Is Required by Law

According to Standard 3.10b, Informed Consent, for persons who are legally ineligible to provide informed consent, psychologists must obtain guardian permission, provide the client/patient with an appropriate explanation, seek the client's/patient's assent, and consider such person's preferences and best interests. This standard respects the developing autonomy needs and rights of minor children by requiring that they receive developmentally appropriate information regarding the reason for and nature of the treatment and, with some exceptions, are given the right to refuse treatment.

Exceptions to the requirement for child assent arise when children are too young or too impaired at the time treatment is initiated to appreciate their disorder or understand the nature of therapy, especially when treatment is necessary for their well-being. When children's mental health needs indicate that their dissent will not determine whether they will receive treatment, psychologists should provide them with an appropriate explanation but not seek their assent (Fedewa, Prout, & Prout, 2015; Fisher & Masty, 2006; Masty & Fisher, 2008).

When Guardian Consent Is Not Permitted or Required by Law

Parents are given significant responsibilities and rights to consent to health care treatments for their children who are below 18 years of age (*Parham v. J. R.*, 1979; Weithorn, 2006; *Wisconsin v. Yoder*, 1972). Psychologists should be familiar with relevant state and federal laws before they consider treating a minor client/patient without guardian permission (for a review of state laws, see English & Kenney, 2003). Psychologists providing counseling services in schools should also be aware of district rules and state and federal laws restricting services to children without parental consent (Fedewa et al., 2015; Jacob & Hartshorne, 2007). As outlined in Chapter 6, Standard 3.10b, Informed Consent, exceptions to requirements for parental permission to treatment include state laws defining (a) *emancipated minors*, (b) *mature minors*, and (c) minors for whom there is evidence that their guardians' decisions may not be in their best interests.

According to Standard 3.10b, Informed Consent, when consent by a legally authorized person is not permitted or required by law, psychologists must take reasonable steps to protect the child's rights and welfare. A first step in complying with this standard is to be familiar with research on developmental differences in children's understanding of consent information and clinical methods to evaluate the consent capacity of individual clients/patients. For example, research on children's ability to consent to medical treatment and clinical research suggests that between the ages of 12 and 14, many children understand treatment-relevant consent information as well as adults, although their relative lack of experience with independent health care decision making and power differentials with adult authorities may place them at a consent disadvantage (Alderson, Sutcliffe, & Curtis, 2006; Bluebond-Langner, DiCicco, & Belasco, 2005; Broome, Kodish, Geller, & Siminoff, 2003; Bruzzese & Fisher, 2003; Field & Behrman, 2004; Gormley-Fleming & Campbell, 2011; Hein et al., 2015; Masty & Fisher, 2008).

The next step is to tailor the consent information to the child's level of understanding of both the nature of treatment and their rights under law and ethics. This may include educating clients/patients about treatment terminology, the nature of treatment, and their right to refuse or withdraw from treatment. Finally, as detailed in the Hot Topic in Chapter 7, even when adolescents have the legal right to consent to their own treatment, parents may have legal access to their child's psychotherapy records. For example, in many instances, if parents are responsible for paying their child's health care costs directly or through insurers, they will have access to the records irrespective of whether a child has been designated a mature or emancipated minor. Psychologists working with adolescents in the absence of parental consent need to be familiar with state and federal laws governing parental access to records and include this information during informed consent (see "A Word About HIPAA" in the preface of this book).

Digital Ethics: Child Assent and Parental Permission for Online Therapies

As discussed throughout this book, the Internet has increased the availability of psychological services as well as the ethical issues that must be addressed. Since minors constitute a substantial portion of Internet users (Kaiser Family Foundation, 2001), psychologists need to have a method for verifying client/patient age and obtaining guardian permission if required by state law. Since state laws vary in these requirements, psychologists also need to verify the state in which the minor resides. When feasible, some practitioners choose to have an initial face-to-face meeting with clients/patients before initiating web-based treatments. When this is not feasible, an initial videoconference, phone call, or exchange of identifying documents may be useful. Compliance with law and ethics protecting minors' participation in treatment requires documenting the validity of parental permission when it is required. An initial in-person visit if feasible, a web-based video consent conference, or telephone discussion with the client's/patient's legal guardian can ensure that appropriate permission has been obtained, provide an opportunity to discuss with guardians specific confidentiality and disclosure policies, and initiate a collaborative relationship that will be beneficial to the child's treatment. Psychologists also need to verify to the best of their ability that the individual they are corresponding with is the same person from whom consent was obtained. Some psychologists have used personalized code names that clients/patients include in their exchanges to address this potential problem.

(b) When obtaining informed consent for treatment for which generally recognized techniques and procedures have not been established, psychologists inform their clients/patients of the developing nature of the treatment, the potential risks involved, alternative treatments that may be available, and the voluntary nature of their participation. (See also Standards 2.01e, Boundaries of Competence, and 3.10, Informed Consent.)

Most techniques that are now accepted practice in the profession of psychology emerged from treatment needs unmet by existing therapies. Standard 10.01b recognizes that innovation in mental health services is critical if a profession is to continue to adequately serve a diverse and dynamic public. The standard also recognizes that during the development and refinement of new therapeutic techniques, the risks and benefits to clients/patients are unknown. Consequently, respect for a client's/patient's right to informed, rational, and voluntary consent requires that when the treatment needs of a client/patient call for innovative techniques, during informed consent, psychologists have the obligation to explain the relatively new and untried nature of the therapy. Furthermore, they must clearly describe alternative established treatments and clarify the client's/patient's right to dissent in favor of more established treatments, whether they are offered by the psychologist obtaining the consent or other mental health professionals.

Telepsychology

Telepsychology has been described as a new modality for helping people resolve life and relationship issues using the power and convenience of telecommunication technologies to allow synchronous (simultaneous) and asynchronous (time-delayed) communication between client/patient and therapist (APA, 2013d; Godine & Barnett, 2013; Grohol, 2001; Maheu & Gordon, 2000). As detailed in the APA *Guidelines for the Practice of Telepsychology* (APA, 2013d), such technologies may augment in-person care (e.g., mobile phone behavioral management reminders, online psychoeducational materials) or be used as stand-alone services (e.g., therapy over video conferencing). A primary advantage of telepsychology is that through remote communication, it can provide clients/patients access to qualified mental health professionals regardless of geographical proximity.

To date, telepsychology does not represent a new theoretical approach to psychotherapy in the same vein as cognitive, psychodynamic, behavioral, or other theoretically driven approaches to treatment. Rather, it represents a new modality or process by which these forms of therapy can be provided. While great strides have been made, electronically mediated therapies (e.g., email, chat rooms, videoconferencing) have yet to emerge as "established" treatments in many contexts in which they are conducted (Pietrzak, Pullman, Campbell, & Cotea, 2010). This is due in part to continuously changing technology, use of different web-based modes of treatment, variability in which treatment techniques are viewed as compatible with web-based approaches, the range of disorders treated, and difficulty in obtaining empirical data on the demographics and other characteristics of individuals using web-based therapies (Cooper & Cody, 2015; Heinlen et al., 2003). For these reasons, psychologists providing web-based services should carefully consider the extent to which their services are considered "established" within the profession and whether their informed consent procedures need to comply with Standard 10.01b.

> ⊘ A psychologist working in a large, underserved rural community found that a number of his clients could not afford to make the 100-mile trip to his office on a weekly basis. After attending an intensive workshop on email therapy and developing a network of colleagues to consult with on behavioral telehealth techniques, the psychologist decided to use this form of therapy. He adopted the procedure of having an initial in-person meeting with each client who might be appropriate for email therapy. During the informed consent provided at this session, he explained the following: (a) Email therapy is a new and still-developing form of therapy; (b) although there was reason to believe this form of therapy would serve the client's mental health needs, the extent of such benefits was still largely unknown; (c) current risks associated with email therapy include confidentiality concerns and lack of immediacy; (d) there are traditional treatments available for the client's presenting problem; and (e) if the client preferred to receive a more traditional therapy, the psychologist would try to work out a schedule that could accommodate the client's travel difficulties.

Digital Ethics: State Laws Regulating Use of Telehealth Services

According to the most recent survey of state licensing laws, only a few states currently regulate the use of telehealth-related services by licensed psychologists (American Psychological Association Practice Organization, 2013; Webb & Orwig, 2015). Psychologists seeking to practice telehealth services need to be up-to-date on whether the state in which they are licensed (a) has specific statutes or regulations pertaining to telepsychology; (b) includes telepsychology in the statutory definition of psychological practice; or (c) includes psychologists as providers under a general telemedicine act. Psychologists providing telehealth services to clients residing in or visiting a state in which the practitioner is not licensed need to be similarly vigilant in understanding whether telepsychology is included in the state's temporary/guest provision act. States that have begun to regulate electronically communicated health care services require certain information to be disclosed during informed consent, largely focused on risks inherent in providing services via the Internet or other electronic media, including how records are stored and protected and communication alternatives in the event of technology failure (Baker & Bufka, 2011).

The Ongoing Nature of Consent

Informed consent should be conceptualized as a continuing process in which the clinically determined need to shift to treatment strategies distinctly different from those that were originally agreed upon during informed consent are discussed with the client/patient at appropriate points during the course of psychotherapy. If, after several sessions, a client's/patient's treatment needs call for a shift to innovative techniques that have not been widely used or accepted by practitioners in the field, psychologists should follow the requirements of Standard 10.01b. The following case illustrates a potential violation of this standard.

☒ A psychologist had just returned from a professional meeting in which she heard several other practitioners discuss a new technique for anxiety disorders that involved viewing video clips of people reacting to natural or human-made catastrophes. She decided to try this untested technique with one of her patients who had not been responding to traditional interpersonal approaches to anxiety. At the next session, rather than discussing with the patient the option of trying this new type of approach, she told the patient that as part of his ongoing treatment, they would look at a video together. The patient experienced an anxiety attack following exposure to the video and apologized to the therapist for failing to improve after so many sessions.

Need to Know: Expanded Informed Consent for Psychologists With Prescriptive Authority

Guideline 12 of the APA Practice Guidelines regarding Psychologists' Involvement in Pharmacological Issues (APA, 2011a, pp. 844–845) encourages psychologists with prescriptive authority to use an expanded informed consent process to incorporate additional issues specific to prescribing, including the following:

- The agent to be used
- Symptoms it is intended to address
- Potential adverse side effects, potential contraindications if the patient is taking other medications, and risks associated with sudden unilateral discontinuation
- Rationale for treatment relative to other treatments, including other medications, and, when appropriate, why psychotherapy and psychopharmacology are used together
- The estimated duration and cost of treatment, including any indicated physical or laboratory examinations and therapeutic monitoring of drug levels
- The potential reasons for reducing dosage or discontinuing medication

(c) When the therapist is a trainee and the legal responsibility for the treatment provided resides with the supervisor, the client/patient, as part of the informed consent procedure, is informed that the therapist is in training and is being supervised and is given the name of the supervisor.

Standard 10.01c applies to therapy conducted and supervised as part of practice, internships, or other training experiences in which the legal responsibility for treatment resides with the supervisor. In these contexts, clients/patients must be informed that the therapist is a trainee and that the therapy is supervised and be given the name and contact information of the supervisor. Both the trainee and the supervisor would be in potential violation of this standard if the supervisee failed to include this information during informed consent. This standard does not apply to therapy conducted by licensed psychologists obtaining postdoctoral training and supervision because, in such contexts, the legal responsibility most often resides with the psychologist (Barnett & Molzon, 2014).

☒ A student interning at a veterans hospital was concerned that her ability to help patients would be compromised if she told them that she was a trainee. When she discussed this with her supervisor, the supervisor told her the decision was up to her.

10.02 Therapy Involving Couples or Families

(a) When psychologists agree to provide services to several persons who have a relationship (such as spouses, significant others, or parents and children), they take reasonable steps to clarify at the outset (1) which of the individuals are clients/patients and (2) the relationship the psychologist will have with each person. This clarification includes the psychologist's role and the probable uses of the services provided or the information obtained. (See also Standard 4.02, Discussing the Limits of Confidentiality.)

Steps required to inform prospective clients/patients in couples or family therapy about the nature of treatment go beyond those described in Standards 3.10, Informed Consent, and 10.01, Informed Consent to Therapy. In some couples or family treatment modalities, the client/patient is the multiperson unit, and the primary obligation of the psychologist is to the parties as a whole. Under Standard 10.02, psychologists must identify and explain which members of the couple or family are the primary client/patient. They should also discuss issues related to termination, including whether treatment will continue if a member of the couple or family decides to discontinue (Knauss & Knauss, 2012). In other family or couple therapy modalities, the primary client/patient is a single individual, with family members involved only to provide collateral support for the client's/patient's treatment. While the psychologist does not have the same legal obligations to these individuals because they are not clients/patients (Younggren, 2009), they should be told how the information will be used and the therapist's confidentiality policy, including mandated reporting requirements.

✓ A divorced couple with joint custody of their children began family therapy to help their 10-year-old son, who had been having problems in school and with adjusting to living in two different homes. The father indicated that he was just attending sessions to support his son's therapy. The psychologist explained to the father, mother, and child that she offered family therapy in which all members are clients and their feelings and behaviors are equally explored during the treatment sessions. She also told them that if there were some indication that the son needed individual therapy, she would recommend an appropriate practitioner specializing in childhood disorders (see also Standard 2.01, Boundaries of Competence).

During informed consent, psychologists also need to ensure that all family members understand the nature of psychotherapy and are voluntarily agreeing to participate. If a family member joins the process at a later time, the informed consent process should be repeated (Knauss & Knauss, 2012).

✓ A 40-year-old woman sought family therapy for herself and her elderly mother. At the initial session, the psychologist learned that the daughter had given up her job to care for her mother and was frustrated by her mother's refusal to do simple chores around the house and their constant arguments. During the informed consent process, the mother appeared anxious. When the psychologist asked her whether she had any questions, she burst into tears and said she found it humiliating to speak to a stranger about family problems. The psychologist explained his role and his obligation to keep whatever he learned in therapy confidential. As the consent discussion continued, the mother became increasingly more agitated about sharing her personal thoughts and feelings. The psychologist concluded that her participation in the therapy would not be voluntary. He discussed his observations with the mother and daughter and recommended they consider seeing a pastoral counselor affiliated with their church as an alternative that might be more acceptable to the mother. He also let them know that he would be available if the mother changed her mind.

Clarifying the Psychologist's Role and Goals of Therapy

In addition to identifying who is the client/patient, discussions at the outset of couples or family therapy must clarify (a) the psychologist's responsibilities in balancing the interests of different individuals, (b) whether the psychologist will conduct individual or conjoint sessions, and (c) how often the psychologist will meet with each party (Principle B: Fidelity and Responsibility). The modifier *reasonable* indicates that a violation of this standard is limited to instances when psychologists do not take steps to clarify information in a manner that would be considered appropriate in the prevailing judgment of other similarly engaged psychologists. Clients'/patients' failure to understand the full implications of this information is not in itself sufficient evidence of violation.

> ✓ An elderly couple entered therapy to help them address feelings and conflicts arising from the husband's terminal illness. Upon initial assessment of their situation, the psychologist determined that the wife's and husband's emotional reactions to the illness should be explored in individual sessions before it would be helpful for the couple to meet with the therapist together. The therapist outlined a treatment plan that included scheduling of individual and joint sessions.

In many instances, the goals of treatment may be different for the individuals involved. For example, one member of a couple may see therapy as a means of strengthening the relationship, whereas the other sees it as a means of ending the relationship. Conflicting perspectives on the goals of therapy may also reflect conflicting value systems, for example, different beliefs about the importance of religion or different emphases on the well-being of the family as a whole versus the well-being of individual family members, and individuals may believe the psychologist shares and will promote their values (Lebow, 2014). Psychologists must take reasonable steps to correct such misimpressions.

> ✓ An interfaith couple began premarital counseling to help resolve conflicts regarding issues such as which clergy should perform their wedding ceremony and the religious upbringing of their children. In the first 10 minutes of the initial session, it became clear that one member of the couple believed the purpose of counseling was to convince his fiancée to agree to have the wedding ceremony performed and their children raised in his faith. During the process of informed consent and in subsequent sessions, the psychologist continued to clarify that involvement in premarital counseling could not predict the direction the couple's relationship would take.

Confidentiality

Psychologists working with couples and families must take reasonable steps to clarify how confidential information will be handled. Will the psychologist keep information received from one party secret from the other? Or will all information be shared (see Margolin, 1982; Snyder & Doss, 2005)? Psychologists must also clearly articulate their legal obligations and policies regarding confidentiality and disclosure of information about child abuse, domestic abuse, HIV status, high-risk behaviors of adolescent clients/patients, and other instances of potential harm.

☒ A gay couple had been in couples counseling for several sessions. One member of the couple called the psychologist and revealed that, without the knowledge of his significant other, he had begun seeing his former wife in what was progressing toward a renewal of their sexual relationship. The client asked the psychologist to keep the information secret. Although the psychologist had communicated a general confidentiality policy to the couple at the outset of therapy, she had not specifically discussed with them her policy regarding secrets between her and one member of the couple. She now felt in a terrible bind. If she refused to keep the information secret, she would violate the presumption of confidentiality held by the client who had called. If she respected the request for secrecy, she might be violating the other client's trust and expectation of openness.

Digital Ethics: Telepsychology Involving Family Members

For clients/patients living in underserved rural areas, comprehensive treatment of mental health disorders such as anorexia nervosa and schizophrenia requiring inpatient medical care is often only available in urban centers, which are not easily accessible to family members who may be critical to treatment effectiveness. In these settings, psychologists are increasingly using Internet-mediated services to involve families in the treatment plan. In addition to clarifying which individual is the client/patient, psychologists need to provide remote family members with all essential information regarding who will have access to electronically mediated sessions and information, the security protections in place (and their limitations when appropriate) at the psychologist's site, and how family members can protect their own privacy and security on their personal electronic media.

(b) If it becomes apparent that psychologists may be called on to perform potentially conflicting roles (such as family therapist and then witness for one party in divorce proceedings), psychologists take reasonable steps to clarify and modify, or withdraw from, roles appropriately. (See also Standard 3.05c, Multiple Relationships.)

It is not unusual for individuals who have sought couples or family therapy to become involved in litigation involving divorce, child custody, child abuse allegations, petitions for child or family services, or mental competency hearings. In such situations, psychologists may be asked by one party to testify on his or her behalf or receive a court order to serve as a fact witness for the legal matter at issue. When such situations arise, under Standard 10.02b, psychologists must first take steps to clarify to clients/patients the nature of the two roles and the potential effect on each party involved in the therapy. To comply with this standard, psychologists will need to be aware of and communicate to their patients/clients the extent to which state law defines as public or private the information revealed in couples or family therapy and whether one or all parties must agree to disclosure of information in court.

As with other forms of multiple relationships, sometimes the request to serve in a dual capacity risks impairing performance of one or both professional roles. In such cases, psychologists are required to take reasonable steps to modify or withdraw from one of the roles to ensure that services continue to be objective and effective and to avoid exploitation or harm to parties involved (Standard 3.05b and 3.05c, Multiple Relationships).

> ⊘ A psychologist providing therapy for a family with a terminally ill child received a court order to serve as a fact witness for a case against the couple alleging child neglect. The psychologist informed the parents of the court's request and took steps to clarify to them the nature of this role. The psychologist was concerned that testifying in court would harm the therapeutic relationship achieved with this family and informed the judge in writing of these concerns. The judge refused to comply with the psychologist's request not to testify. The psychologist discussed the situation further with the family, and they mutually agreed to a referral to another therapist (see also Standard 1.02, Conflicts Between Ethics and Law, Regulations, and Other Governing Legal Authority).

10.03 Group Therapy

When psychologists provide services to several persons in a group setting, they describe at the outset the roles and responsibilities of all parties and the limits of confidentiality.

In addition to responsibilities described in Standards 3.10, Informed Consent, and 10.01, Informed Consent to Therapy, psychologists conducting group therapy must describe at the outset of treatment the unique roles and responsibilities of both therapist and clients/patients in multiperson therapies. Such information may include discussion of (a) differences between the exclusivity of the therapist's attention in individual therapy and the attention to group dynamics in multiperson treatments; (b) group member responsibilities, including turn taking and prohibitions against group members socializing outside sessions; and (c) policies regarding such client/patient responsibilities as acceptance of diverse opinions, abusive language, coercive or aggressive behaviors, or member scapegoating. As in couple and family therapy, informed consent regarding termination policies is critical (e.g., disruptive group members; Knauss & Knauss, 2012). Group members need to know they have the right to voluntarily withdraw from the group as well as the consequences of member dropouts for the continuation of the group as a whole.

Digital Ethics: Setting Internet Use Policies for Group Therapy

When describing group member responsibilities, psychologists should develop guidelines for members' use of social media such as Facebook, Twitter, and Instagram and mobile phone technology. For example, Dombo, Kays, and Weller (2014) described an incident in which during a session, one group member pulled out his phone and stated, "I'm going to tweet that!" He then snapped and posted a picture of the therapist and another group member before the therapist could intervene. Psychologists should also discuss appropriate use of social media platforms to "friend" or discover background information about other group members.

Confidentiality

A frequently misunderstood aspect of group therapy concerns the limits of confidentiality. Although psychologists are professionally obligated to maintain the confidentiality of most statements made during group therapy sessions, decisions by members of a therapy group to disclose confidential information are neither bound by professional codes nor subject to legal liability. At the outset of group therapy, and each time a new member enters an ongoing group, psychologists must take reasonable steps to clarify that they can request, but not guarantee, that all group members maintain the confidentiality of statements made during sessions. Psychologists should also be familiar with and inform group members about state laws protecting or denying client/patient privilege (the right to limit the psychologist's disclosures to courts) for information shared during group therapy. When group therapy is conducted in response to court-ordered counseling, psychologists must also clarify to group members the parties in the justice system who will receive information learned during group therapy and how such information may be used.

Clients/Patients in Concurrent Single and Group Therapy

Psychologists who see clients/patients concurrently in individual and group therapy must take special precautions to ensure that they do not inadvertently reveal during a group session confidential information gained about a client/patient during an individual session. Psychologists must also clarify in advance to such clients differences between the goals, processes, and therapist–client relationships in single versus group therapy. When recommending that a client/patient seen in individual therapy also participate in group therapy conducted by the psychologist, steps should be taken to ensure that clients/patients understand that such a decision is voluntary and that reluctance to participate in the group will not compromise the current therapeutic relationship. This does not prohibit psychologists from having a policy of only accepting individuals as clients/patients if they participate in group therapy if (a) such multimodal treatment is clinically indicated and (b) clients/patients are informed of this requirement prior to or at the outset of therapy. For additional discussion, see Standards 3.05, Multiple Relationships, and 3.06, Conflict of Interest.

10.04 Providing Therapy to Those Served by Others

In deciding whether to offer or provide services to those already receiving mental health services elsewhere, psychologists carefully consider the treatment issues and the potential client's/ patient's welfare. Psychologists discuss these issues with the client/patient or another legally authorized person on behalf of the client/patient in order to minimize the risk of confusion and conflict, consult with the other service providers when appropriate, and proceed with caution and sensitivity to the therapeutic issues.

There may be instances when psychologists professionally encounter an individual already receiving mental health services from another professional who might benefit from or is requesting additional therapy with the psychologist. Standard 10.04 recognizes the rights of clients/patients to seek additional services and the potential benefits of collateral therapy, as well as the potential harm that can result from client/patient involvement in concurrent therapies.

Under this standard, careful consideration of the client's/patient's welfare and treatment needs determines the ethical appropriateness of providing therapy to those served by others. In some instances, clients/patients may benefit from consultation with a psychologist when they are uncertain about the effectiveness of their current therapy or uncomfortable with what they perceive as their current provider's boundary violations. In other instances, the expertise of the psychologist may provide needed collateral treatment, for example, when a client/patient who is under the care of a psychiatrist for psychopharmacological treatment of depression would also benefit from psychosocial or behavioral treatment. On the other hand, provision of concurrent services may be harmful if clients/patients consciously or unconsciously seek to use a second therapist as a means of triangulating issues arising in their current therapy, if they begin to receive conflicting therapeutic messages from the two service providers, or if the psychologist's choice to see the patient is governed by the psychologist's own financial interests rather than client/patient welfare (see also Standards 3.04, Avoiding Harm; 3.06, Conflict of Interest; 3.08, Exploitative Relationships; 5.06, In-Person Solicitation).

> ⊘ A psychologist had an initial consultation with an individual who was currently in treatment with another provider. During the consultation, the patient frequently asked questions about the appropriateness of certain therapeutic styles. The psychologist asked the patient why he sought the consultation. The patient stated that he liked his current therapist but thought he would benefit from two different perspectives on his problems. During further discussions, there was no evidence that the patient's current treatment was inadequate or that the psychologist could provide collateral therapy that would be helpful. The psychologist explained this to the patient and told him that under such circumstances, it would not be appropriate for her to see him as a regular patient.

In addition to careful consideration of the treatment issues and client/patient harm, under Standard 10.04, psychologists should take steps to minimize the risk that providing therapy to an individual already receiving mental health services will lead to confusion and conflicts that could jeopardize client/patient welfare. Such steps include discussing with the client/patient or his or her legally authorized representative the potential consequences of entering into a second therapeutic relationship and obtaining authorization from the client/patient to consult with the other service provider about the appropriateness and effectiveness of conjoint services.

> ⊘ An individual met with a psychologist to discuss joining one of the psychologist's therapy groups. The client was currently in individual psychotherapy with another practitioner and informed the psychologist that her current therapist had suggested that concurrent participation in group therapy might be helpful in addressing some of the social anxiety issues they had been discussing in treatment. The psychologist explained the differences in goals and modalities of group and single therapy and received written authorization from the client to discuss the treatment recommendation with her current therapist. After a conversation with the current therapist, the psychologist agreed that the client could be further helped through participation in group therapy.

Because conflicts and issues associated with providing therapy to those served by others may continue to emerge over the course of treatment, Standard 10.04 also requires that psychologists who decide to offer such services continue to monitor and proceed cautiously and sensitively in response to therapeutic issues that may arise.

10.05 Sexual Intimacies With Current Therapy Clients/Patients

Psychologists do not engage in sexual intimacies with current therapy clients/patients.

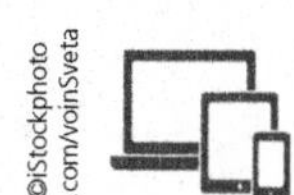

Sexual intimacies of any kind with a current therapy client/patient are harmful and prohibited by Standard 10.05. The term *sexual intimacies* is broadly interpreted and includes fondling, intercourse, kissing, masturbation in front of a client, telephone sex, touching of genitals, erotic hugging, verbal invitations to engage in sexual relationships, or communications (in person or via electronic transmission) intended to erotically arouse the patient. The ethical obligation to avoid sexual intimacies with clients/patients lies solely with the therapist, not with the client/patient. Any sexual intimacy between psychologists and clients/patients represents a violation of this standard regardless of whether clients/patients initiated sexual contact or voluntarily or involuntarily responded to therapists' overtures.

Sexual intimacies with current clients/patients exploit the explicit power differential and influence that psychologists have over those they treat in therapy and the vulnerabilities that led clients/patients to treatment in the first place. Sexual intimacies further harm clients/patients by impairing the provider's ability to objectively evaluate treatment issues and the client's/patient's ability to trust and respond to the psychologist in his or her professional role. In many cases, therapist–client sex exacerbates the client's/patient's symptoms or leads to more serious mental disorders (Pope, 2013).

Nonsexual physical contact with clients/patients such as handshakes or nonerotic hugging is not a violation of Standard 10.05. However, the nonerotic intentions of a therapist, such as meetings outside the therapist's office, are often misperceived as sexualized by clients/patients. Blurring of boundaries and self-disclosures can be misperceived as minimizing the client's mental health problems, and they may shift the identity of the therapist between hero and victim in a way that generates a false sense of equivalent responsibilities between the psychologist and client (Lamb & Catanzaro, 1998; McNulty, Ogden, & Warren, 2013). In addition, research indicates that for some psychologists, such seemingly minor blurring of boundaries as self-disclosures are often precursors of sexual misconduct, (Pope, Keith-Spiegel, & Tabachnick, 2006; see also the section on unforeseen potentially harmful multiple relationships in Chapter 6 under Standard 3.05a and 3.05b, Multiple Relationships).

10.06 Sexual Intimacies With Relatives or Significant Others of Current Therapy Clients/Patients

Psychologists do not engage in sexual intimacies with individuals they know to be close relatives, guardians, or significant others of current clients/patients. Psychologists do not terminate therapy to circumvent this standard.

Engaging in sexual intimacies with another person who is related to or in a significant relationship with a current client/patient is prohibited. Sexual intimacies with such persons harm the client/patient by impairing the psychologist's treatment objectivity, blurring the therapist–client roles and relationships, and risking exploitation of the client/patient to attain or maintain a sexual relationship with a third party. This standard applies to a client's/patient's parents, siblings, children, legal guardians, and significant others. It may also apply to other relatives if they are emotionally or otherwise close to the client/patient. The phrase *they know to be* applies to the rare instance when psychologists are unaware that someone they are seeing romantically is a close relative, guardian, or significant other of a current client/patient. Standard 10.06 also prohibits psychologists from terminating therapy to circumvent the prohibition.

☒ A psychologist began dating the mother of a child who was currently in therapy with the psychologist.

☒ A psychologist terminated marriage therapy with a couple with the intent to begin a sexual relationship with one of the spouses.

10.07 Therapy With Former Sexual Partners

Psychologists do not accept as therapy clients/patients persons with whom they have engaged in sexual intimacies.

Under Standard 10.07, psychologists are prohibited from providing therapy to former sexual partners. Conducting therapy with individuals with whom psychologists have had a previous sexual relationship risks compromising the effectiveness of professional services. The knowledge gained about the individual from former sexual relationships and romantic and sexualized feelings that may reemerge during therapy can impair the psychologist's ability to objectively evaluate the client's/patient's treatment needs and response to treatment. In addition, intimate and personal knowledge about the psychologist that the client/patient gained during the former relationship can create role confusion and interfere with the client's/patient's ability to benefit from the psychologist's professional communications.

☒ A psychologist received a call from a man with whom she'd had a sexual relationship during college. The man asked if he could see her professionally to discuss some serious problems that had recently arisen in his life. The psychologist told him that she did not think it was a good idea for her to see him professionally because they had been in a previous personal relationship. The man started crying and told the psychologist that he had just moved to the town in which the psychologist practiced and she was the only person he could trust with his problems. The psychologist agreed to see him for just one session.

10.08 Sexual Intimacies With Former Therapy Clients/Patients

(a) Psychologists do not engage in sexual intimacies with former clients/patients for at least two years after cessation or termination of therapy.

Standard 10.08a prohibits psychologists from engaging in sexual intimacies for at least 2 years after the therapy has ended. Posttherapy sexual relationships can be harmful to clients/patients in many ways, including (a) depriving former clients/patients of future services with a practitioner who is familiar with their mental history and with whom they had a good therapeutic rapport, (b) threatening client/patient privilege when the blurring of personal and professional boundaries allows a court to require the psychologist to testify about the former client/patient in his or her personal role, (c) compromising the credibility of previous professional reports written by the psychologist about the client/patient and jeopardizing the credibility of court testimony that may be needed regarding the client's/patient's past mental status, and (d) client/patient exploitation and psychological deterioration.

Two-Year Moratorium

Under Standard 10.08a, any sexual intimacies with a former client/patient within 2 years following the last professional contact are an ethical violation. The standard has a 2-year moratorium period rather than a permanent prohibition against sex with former clients/patients because most complaints involving sexual intimacies with former clients/patients received by the APA Ethics Committee and licensing boards pertain to relationships that began during the first year following the cessation of therapy, and complaints about relationships that began 2 years posttherapy are infrequent. However, as discussed below under Standard 10.08b, such behavior is not unconditionally acceptable after 2 years.

☒ A year after therapy ended, a traumatic event in a former patient's life created a need for additional treatment. The patient had begun a sexual relationship with his psychologist a few months following termination of treatment and thus could not reenter therapy with the psychologist. The former patient, fearful that another psychologist would be critical of his relationship with his former therapist, chose not to seek needed treatment.

☒ A year after therapy terminated, a client entered into a sexual extramarital relationship with her former therapist and continued to discuss her mental health problems in this nonprofessional relationship. During this period, her husband sued her for divorce, naming the therapist as his wife's extramarital partner. The former client wanted to exert her privilege to keep her mental status and thus her involvement in therapy confidential. Due to the blurring of personal and professional boundaries, the judge issued a court order to call the psychologist as a witness.

☒ A psychologist began a sexual relationship with a former patient soon after therapy was terminated. Several months later, the former patient was injured on the job, and his attorney advised him to pursue a disability insurance claim for mental distress created by the accident. The patient needed the psychologist to testify regarding his mental status prior to the injury. However, the psychologist–client sexual relationship compromised the psychologist's ability to provide or appear to provide objective information to the court.

☒ A client with a history of child sexual abuse had transferred to the psychologist the feelings of both powerlessness and eroticism that she felt for her childhood abuser. The psychologist took advantage of these feelings and told the client that she could overcome the mental health consequences of this early trauma by terminating therapy and becoming his lover. The patient agreed to end therapy. A few weeks into the posttherapy sexual relationship with the psychologist, her depression escalated and she attempted suicide.

(b) Psychologists do not engage in sexual intimacies with former clients/patients even after a two-year interval except in the most unusual circumstances. Psychologists who engage in such activity after the two years following cessation or termination of therapy and of having no sexual contact with the former client/patient bear the burden of demonstrating that there has been no exploitation, in light of all relevant factors, including (1) the amount of time that has passed since therapy terminated; (2) the nature, duration, and intensity of the therapy; (3) the circumstances of termination; (4) the client's/patient's personal history; (5) the client's/patient's current mental status; (6) the likelihood of adverse impact on the client/patient; and (7) any statements or actions made by the therapist during the course of therapy suggesting or inviting the possibility of a

posttermination sexual or romantic relationship with the client/patient. (See also Standard 3.05, Multiple Relationships.)

Standard 10.08a prohibits psychologists from engaging in a sexual relationship with a former client/patient for at least 2 years following the termination of therapy. However, sexual intimacies with former clients/patients even 2 years following the cessation of therapy can result in exploitation and harm. If an ethics complaint is made against the psychologist regarding a 2-year posttermination sexual relationship, Standard 10.08b places the ethical burden on the psychologist to demonstrate that the sexual relationship is not exploitative. The standard describes seven relevant factors that could be applied to determine such exploitation. These seven factors are listed along with examples of how they might be applied to a finding of violation of this standard for a psychologist who engaged in sexual relationships with a former client/patient after the 2-year period:

1. *The amount of time that has passed since therapy terminated.* Following the termination of therapy, the psychologist frequently met a former client/patient for lunch. A sexual relationship was initiated immediately following the 24-month period.
2. *The nature, duration, and intensity of the therapy.* The client/patient was seen by the psychologist three times a week for several years in intensive psychodynamic psychotherapy.
3. *The circumstances of termination.* The client/patient abruptly stopped coming to therapy after expressing strong erotic fantasies for the psychologist.
4. *The client's/patient's personal history.* During the therapy, the client/patient had been diagnosed with bipolar disorder marked by periods of mania involving promiscuous and high-risk sexual activity.
5. *The client's/patient's current mental status.* When the posttermination sexual relationship with the psychologist began, the patient was being treated by another psychologist for major depression.
6. *The likelihood of adverse impact on the client/patient.* Based on a family history of sexual abuse, borderline diagnosis, and current major depression, it was reasonable to assume that a client/patient would be extremely vulnerable to reexperiencing some of the early trauma if engaged in a sexual relationship with his or her former therapist, whom he or she perceived as a powerful parent figure.
7. *Any statements or actions made by the therapist during the course of therapy suggesting or inviting the possibility of a posttermination sexual or romantic relationship with the client/patient.* The psychologist had a habit of hugging the client/patient at the end of each therapy session.

10.09 Interruption of Therapy

When entering into employment or contractual relationships, psychologists make reasonable efforts to provide for orderly and appropriate resolution of responsibility for client/patient care in the event that the employment or contractual relationship ends, with paramount consideration given to the welfare of the client/patient. (See also Standard 3.12, Interruption of Psychological Services.)

This standard applies to ethical obligations of psychologists at the time they enter into employment or contractual agreements with other providers, group practices, managed care providers, institutions, or agencies. Employment or contractual agreements can end when psychologists have a time-limited contract or employment period, when they elect to leave for professional or personal reasons, or when the employer or company terminates their position or contract. Under Standard 10.09, psychologists must make reasonable efforts to ensure at the outset that the employment agreement or contract provides for an orderly and appropriate resolution of responsibility in the event that the employment or contractual arrangement ends (Principle B: Fidelity and Responsibility).

Psychologists can comply with Standard 10.09 by determining through pre-employment discussions whether the organization, group practice, or other entity in which a work arrangement is being considered has policies designed to ensure continuity of care when a practitioner can no longer provide services. If no such policies exist, psychologists can help develop such policies or include in their employment or contractual agreements permission to resolve treatment responsibility appropriately in the event their employment or contract ends (see Standard 1.03, Conflicts Between Ethics and Organizational Demands). Steps the psychologist can recommend be taken to protect client/patient welfare when treatment can no longer be provided by the psychologist include providing pretermination counseling and referrals, supervising appropriate transfer and storage of client/patient records, assisting in the transition of the client/patient to a new treatment provider if clinically indicated, or continuing treatment with the client/patient in a different venue. The phrase *make reasonable efforts* recognizes that in some situations, despite a psychologist's efforts, employers, organizations, group practices, or other providers will refuse to promise or follow through on promises to protect client/patient welfare through an orderly and appropriate resolution of care when there is a change in staff.

✓ A school psychologist was hired on a 9-month (October through June) contract to provide counseling services for grade school students who had lost parents in the September 11, 2001, attack on the World Trade

Center. It was reasonable to assume that some children might need continued care during the summer. The school psychologist raised this issue when asked to take the position. The school superintendent responded that such services were not available through the schools during the summer. The psychologist worked with the superintendent to develop an agreement with a social services agency to provide treatment for students who needed continued care over the summer. The superintendent agreed to set up a system that facilitated the appropriate transfer of student records to the social service agency, and the psychologist laid out a plan for identifying children who would need summer services and for informing their guardians about the availability of such services.

Standard 10.09 does not prohibit psychologists from signing a noncompete clause barring the psychologist from continuing to see specific clients/patients after the employment or contractual agreement has ended as long as other provisions for protecting client/patient welfare are in place.

10.10 Terminating Therapy

(a) Psychologists terminate therapy when it becomes reasonably clear that the client/patient no longer needs the service, is not likely to benefit, or is being harmed by continued service.

Psychologists are committed to improving the condition of individuals with whom they work and to do no harm (Preamble; Principle A: Beneficence and Nonmaleficence). In some instances, continued therapy with a client/patient may be nonbeneficial or harmful. Standard 10.10a requires psychologists to terminate therapy under three conditions in which therapy may either fail to benefit clients/patients or could be harmful if continued. Although the need to continue or terminate a therapeutic relationship requires professional judgment based on knowledge of the specific treatment context, the phrase *reasonably clear* in this standard indicates that it is ethically inappropriate for a psychologist to continue therapy under conditions in which most psychologists engaged in similar activities in similar circumstances would judge it unnecessary, nonbeneficial, or harmful.

Services Are No Longer Needed

Psychologists who continue to see clients/patients professionally after they no longer need mental health services are in violation of this standard. The need for continued services depends on the nature of the client's/patient's disorder and the goals of treatment as identified during the initial informed consent and throughout the therapeutic process. Psychologists who continue to treat clients/patients when the problems associated with entering treatment have been adequately addressed violate this standard. The standard does not prohibit psychologists and clients/patients from reevaluating treatment needs and continuing in a therapeutic relationship to address additional mental health needs. However, failure to reevaluate the need for continued therapy after treatment goals are met would violate the standard. Psychologists who continue to see clients/patients solely to fulfill the psychologists' own training requirements or for financial gain violate this standard and also risk violating Standards 3.06, Conflict of Interest, and 3.08, Exploitative Relationships. Psychologists who continue to bill a third-party payor for mental health services when the services are no longer required place themselves at risk for accusations of insurance fraud and are in potential violation of Standards 6.04b, Fees and Financial Arrangements, and 6.06, Accuracy in Reports to Payors and Funding Sources.

☒ A licensed psychologist in independent practice had sought additional training at a prestigious postgraduate psychotherapy institute. The institute required a certain number of hours of supervision with clients with specific disorders to obtain a certificate of completion. The psychologist needed to complete 8 more hours of supervision for treatment of anxiety disorders before he could qualify for the certificate. The client who met the diagnostic criteria for supervision had been doing very well in treatment. She had resolved most of the problems at work and at home that had brought her to therapy and viewed terminating treatment with eagerness and a sense of pride. She asked the therapist whether they could have one final session to complete the therapy. The psychologist told her that although she had been doing well, there were a few unresolved issues that would take about eight more sessions to address adequately. The client reluctantly agreed.

The Client/Patient Is Not Likely to Benefit

Psychologists must also terminate therapy when the client/patient is not likely to benefit from the treatment. This criterion applies when, during the course of therapy, it becomes reasonably clear that the client/patient is not responding to treatment, a newly uncovered aspect of the client's/patient's disorder is not amenable to the type of treatment modality in which the psychologist has been trained (see also Standard 2.01a, Boundaries of Competence), or a client/patient is unwilling or unable to comply with treatment (e.g., when a client/patient continuously refuses to follow the terms of a behavioral contract).

⊘ A psychologist was providing psychoanalytic therapy to a patient with narcissistic personality disorder. The treatment appeared to be going well until the patient began to discuss in detail a traumatic rape experience that had occurred when she was a young adult. In the weeks that followed, the patient kept putting herself in dangerous situations that appeared to be reenactments of the earlier event. She was engaging in sexual relationships with men she barely knew, having unprotected sex, and frequenting dangerous areas of the city. In therapy during the next 5 weeks, the psychologist continued to explore with the patient her feelings and behaviors associated with the initial trauma. Instead of abating the risky behavior, each session appeared to lead to more extreme behaviors. The psychologist was concerned that the patient might again be raped, assaulted, or contract HIV and consulted with several colleagues regarding continuation of services. On the basis of these consultations, he concluded that continuing the therapy would be harmful to this patient and that she might benefit from a different therapeutic approach. He discussed this with the patient over several sessions and referred her to a group practice specializing in treatments for rape trauma.

The Client/Patient Is Being Harmed by Continued Service

Psychologists are prohibited from continuing therapy if it is reasonably clear that the client/patient is being harmed by the treatment (Principle A: Beneficence and Nonmaleficence, Standard 3.04, Avoiding Harm). For example, in some instances clients/patients may unexpectedly react to a specific treatment modality with major depression, a psychotic episode, or an exacerbation of impulsive or addictive behaviors that do not respond to continued efforts by the psychologist. The phrase *reasonably clear* indicates that the criteria for determining whether a client/patient is being harmed by continued services are determined by what would be the prevailing judgment of psychologists engaged in similar activities in similar circumstances, given the knowledge the psychologist had or should have had at the time. Psychologists who find that a client's/patient's mental health is deteriorating may find it helpful therefore to consult with colleagues regarding whether services should be continued. When it is appropriate to terminate, patients should be referred to alternative treatments that may be more effective.

✓ A counseling psychologist had been seeing a client for career counseling who was recently fired from a management position that he had held for 10 years. The client was angry and believed that the termination was undeserved. After three sessions, the psychologist determined that there was a clinically paranoid feature to the client's distress and that more intensive psychotherapy was needed before career counseling could be beneficial. The psychologist discussed her concerns with the client and referred him to another practitioner who worked with more seriously disturbed clients. The psychologist also informed the client that her services would be available to him when he was ready to resume career counseling.

Need to Know: Abandonment Considerations

Although neither the APA Ethics Code nor case law defines termination of mental health services as "abandonment," and the terms *termination* and *abandonment* are often confused by the public and psychologists alike. Termination based on reasonable professional judgment and proper pretermination counseling is not abandonment. Abandonment occurs when a client/patient in imminent need of treatment is harmed by termination of services in the absence of a clinically and ethically appropriate process (Younggren, Fisher, Foote, & Hjelt, 2011; Younggren & Gottlieb, 2008; Standard 3.04, Avoiding Harm). Conducting appropriate terminations requires keeping up-to-date with the empirical and professional literature and consulting colleagues when necessary (Standards 2.03, Maintaining Competence; 2.04, Bases for Scientific and Professional Judgment). Davis and Younggren (2009) suggested the following additional steps to foster appropriate and client–therapist collaborative terminations:

- Develop plans for termination at the outset of psychotherapy and include a discussion of factors influencing the length of treatment during informed consent.
- Continuously evaluate client/patient progress.
- Review ethical and legal duties.
- Develop a well-conceptualized rationale for termination based on clinical, relational, and situational factors and consult with the client/patient on these factors when clinically feasible.
- Construct a timeline for termination and be responsive to client/patient responses.
- Create a record documenting key components of the termination rationale and process.

Clinicians should also proceed cautiously when considering persistence in contacting a client/patient who abruptly drops out of treatment. To avoid the necessity for potentially intrusive follow-up letters or other contacts, psychologists should consider inclusion during informed consent of the psychologist's policies for client/patient nonattendance (Davis & Younggren, 2009).

Digital Ethics: Terminating Telepsychology Services

The American Psychological Association's *Guidelines for the Practice of Telepsychology* (APA, 2013d) urges psychologists providing therapy through telecommunication services to monitor and assess regularly the progress of clients/patients to determine whether the provision of telepsychology services continues to be appropriate and beneficial. When psychologists become aware of a significant negative change in the therapeutic interaction or the client's/patient's functioning, they should take steps to adjust the treatment plan and reassess the appropriateness of delivering services through remote services. When it becomes reasonably clear that continuing to provide telepsychology services is no longer beneficial or presents a risk to the client's/patient's emotional or physical well-being, the Guidelines encourage psychologists to discuss these concerns with the client/patient and appropriately terminate remote services with adequate notice, care for client/patient well-being, and referral to any needed alternative services.

(b) Psychologists may terminate therapy when threatened or otherwise endangered by the client/patient or another person with whom the client/patient has a relationship.

Standard 10.10b permits psychologists to terminate therapy abruptly if they are threatened or endangered by a client/patient or another person with whom the client/patient has a relationship, such as a family member, significant other, friend, employer, or employee. Such situations can include verbal or physical threats or any other evidence that the psychologist is endangered (see Carr, Goranson, & Drummond, 2014, for guidance on reducing risk and managing stalking behavior by patients). In such situations, neither advance notification of termination nor pretermination counseling as described in Standard 10.10c is required. Psychologists may also request a protective order against clients/patients or others whom they suspect will threaten or harm them. Prohibitions against revealing confidential information do not apply when psychologists must call on authorities or others to protect them from threats or harm (see Standard 4.05b, Disclosures).

(c) Except where precluded by the actions of clients/patients or third-party payors, prior to termination psychologists provide pretermination counseling and suggest alternative service providers as appropriate.

Termination based on reasonable professional judgment and proper pretermination counseling is ethically appropriate. In addition to the situations described in Standard 10.10a and 10.10b above, ethically permissible and professionally appropriate reasons to end a therapeutic relationship include the following: (a) an organized system of health or managed care company rejects a psychologist's recommendations for additional therapy sessions; (b) an unforeseen potentially harmful multiple relationship arises (Standards 3.05b, Multiple Relationships; 10.02b, Therapy Involving Couples or Families); (c) a client/patient repeatedly refuses to pay for services (Standard 6.04e, Fees and Financial Arrangements); (d) a psychologist becomes ill or finds therapy with a particular client/patient stressful in a manner that risks compromising professional services (Standard 2.06b, Personal Problems and Conflicts); (e) during the course of therapy, unexpected treatment needs arise that are outside the psychologist's area of expertise (Standard 2.01, Boundaries of Competence); or (f) the psychologist is relocating or retiring.

Under Standard 10.10c, psychologists must provide pretermination counseling prior to ending a therapeutic relationship. Pretermination counseling includes (a) providing clients/patients sufficient advance notice of termination (when possible), (b) discussing with the client/patient the reasons for the termination, (c) encouraging the client/patient to ask questions regarding termination, and (d) providing referrals to alternate service providers when appropriate. Psychologists need to plan for pretermination counseling for group as well as individual therapies (Davis & Younggren, 2009; Mangione, Forti, & Iacuzzi, 2007). Psychologists are not in violation of this standard if pretermination counseling is precluded by client/patient or third-party payor actions. For example, parents may abruptly end their child's therapy, making further contact with the child inappropriate or unfeasible, or health plans may prohibit or place restrictions on provider referrals. When clients/patients who have paid for services abruptly cease coming to sessions, psychologists should carefully balance their concern with client/patient well-being with the client's/patient's right to privacy and exert caution in pursuing them through email, letters, phone calls, or other forms of contact (see Standards 3.06, Conflict of Interest; 3.08, Exploitation).

- ⊘ A psychotherapy patient changed to a health plan that she later realized would not reimburse her current psychologist's services. She told the psychologist that she would not be able to come to any more sessions because she could not afford to pay for therapy out of pocket and thus would be continuing services with a provider covered by her new health plan. The psychologist discussed the patient's concerns about leaving therapy. The patient appeared ready to terminate the relationship. The psychologist told her that he was not familiar with any of her new health plan's approved providers but, with her written authorization, would be willing to speak with her new therapist if the need arose.
- ⊘ A psychologist in independent practice accepted a job offer from a treatment center in another state. The psychologist agreed to start the new position in 4 weeks. At their next sessions, the psychologist told each of her clients that she would be relocating at the end of the month and that they would have time to discuss over the next few weeks their feelings about terminating therapy and their plans for the future. At each of the remaining sessions, she encouraged clients to discuss any concerns they might have about the termination. The psychologist provided appropriate referrals to those who wished to continue in therapy with another professional. She told the other clients how to contact her if they wished a referral in the future. One client had serious difficulty adjusting to the termination. The psychologist offered to have phone sessions with this client until a suitable referral could be found.
- ⊘ A patient who recently lost his job had not paid his last two monthly bills for psychotherapy. The psychologist had discussed the issue of nonpayment with the patient several times during the past month. Neither a reduced fee nor payment plan was economically feasible for the patient.

The psychologist told the patient that she would not be able to continue to see him pro bono indefinitely and that they would have two more sessions to discuss any questions he might have and his plans for the future. She also provided the patient with a list of several free clinics in the area that offered therapy.

☒ During the fourth session, a client who had begun cognitive–behavioral therapy for a mild case of anxiety disorder expressed frustration with the progress of treatment. Several days later, she left a phone message for the psychologist letting him know she had decided to seek services elsewhere. The psychologist sent the client an email suggesting that her mental health might be jeopardized by the abrupt termination and strongly urging her to attend the next session to obtain closure.

HOT TOPIC

Ethical Issues for the Integration of Religion and Spirituality in Therapy

The past decade has witnessed increased attention to the importance of understanding and respecting client/patient spirituality and religiosity to psychological assessment and treatment, as well as recognition that religious and spiritual factors remain underexamined in research and practice (APA, 2007d). Advances in addressing the clinical relevance of faith in the lives of clients/patients have raised new ethical dilemmas rooted in theoretical models of personality historically isolated from client/patient faith beliefs, the paucity of research on the clinical benefits or harms of injecting faith concepts into treatment practices, group differences in religious practices and values, and individual differences in the salience of religion to mental health (Rose, Westefeld, & Ansley, 2008; Shafranske & Sperry, 2005; Tan, 2003).

The Secular–Theistic Therapy Continuum

Integration of religion/spirituality in therapy can be characterized on a secular–theistic continuum (Fisher, 2009). Toward the secular end of the continuum are "religiously sensitive therapies" that blend traditional treatment approaches with sensitivity to the relationship of diverse religious/spiritual beliefs and behaviors to mental health. Midway on the continuum are "religiously accommodative therapies" that do not promote faith beliefs but, when clinically relevant, use religious/spiritual language and interventions consistent with clients'/patients' faith values to foster mental health. Toward the other end of the continuum are "theistic therapies" that draw on psychologists' own religious beliefs and use sacred texts and techniques (prayer, forgiveness, and meditation) to promote spiritual health.

The sections that follow highlight ethical challenges that emerge along all points of the secular–theistic therapy continuum.

(Continued)

(Continued)

Competence

All psychologists should have the training and experience necessary to identify when a mental health problem is related to or grounded in religious beliefs (Standards 2.01b, Boundaries of Competence, and 2.03, Maintaining Competence; see also Plante, 2014; Raiya & Pargament, 2010; Vieten et al., 2013). Personal faith and religious experience are neither sufficient nor necessary for competence (Gonsiorek, Richards, Pargament, & McMinn, 2009). There is no substitute for familiarity with the foundational empirical and professional mental health knowledge base and treatment techniques. While personal familiarity with a client's/patient's religious affiliation can be informative, religious/spiritual therapeutic competencies for mental health treatment include

- an understanding of how religion presents itself in mental health and psychopathology;
- the ability to identify internal and external spiritual and religious resources that may support psychological well-being and recovery from psychological disorders;
- techniques to inquire about spiritual and/or religious practices, beliefs, and experience as part of standard client history;
- self-awareness of religious bias that may impair therapeutic effectiveness, including awareness that being a member of a faith tradition is not evidence of expertise in the integration of religion/spirituality into mental health treatment;
- techniques to assess and treat clinically relevant religious/spiritual beliefs and emotional reactions; and
- knowledge of data on mental health effectiveness of religious imagery, prayer, or other religious techniques.

Collaboration With Clergy

Collaborations with clergy can help inform psychologists about the origins of the client's beliefs, demonstrate respect for the client's religion, and avoid trespassing into theological domains by increasing the probability that a client's incorrect religious interpretations will be addressed appropriately within his or her faith community (W. B. Johnson, Redley, & Nielson, 2000; Plante, 2014; Richards & Bergin, 2005; Standard 3.09, Cooperation With Other Professionals). For example, Hathaway (2013) described the case of a 15-year-old Catholic boy whose obsessive–compulsive disorder included a variety of religious practices to ward off reoccurring "blasphemous thoughts about cursing God" (p. 24). The boy's therapist asked permission to have a Catholic priest he had worked with professionally to participate in some sessions. The priest was able to successfully challenge the boy's beliefs about the spiritual necessity of the compulsive behaviors. The priest's continued participation assisted in the eventual success of the treatment.

When cooperation with clergy will be clinically helpful to a client/patient, psychologists should

- obtain written permission/authorization from the client/patient to speak with a specific identified member of the clergy,
- share only information needed for both to be of optimal assistance to the client/patient (Standard 4.04, Minimizing Intrusions on Privacy),
- discuss with the clergy where roles might overlap (e.g., family counseling, sexual issues), and
- determine ways in which the client/patient can get the best assistance.

Avoiding Secular–Theistic Bias

Psychologists must ensure that their professional and personal biases do not interfere with the provision of appropriate and effective mental health services for persons of diverse religious beliefs (Principle D: Justice and Principle E: Respect for People's Rights and Dignity; Standards 2.06, Personal Problems and Conflicts, and 3.01, Unfair Discrimination).

Disputation or Unquestioned Acceptance of Client/Patient Faith Beliefs

Trivializing or disputing religious values and beliefs can undermine the goals of therapy by threatening those aspects of life that some clients/patients hold sacred, that provide supportive family and community connections, and that form an integral part of their identity (Pargament, Murray-Swank, Magyar, & Ano, 2005; Standard 3.04, Avoiding Harm). Similarly, some religious coping styles can be deleterious to client/patient mental health (Sood, Fisher, & Sulmasy, 2006), and uncritical acceptance of theistic beliefs, when they indicate misunderstandings or distortions of religious teachings and values, can undercut treatment goals by reinforcing maladaptive ways of thinking or by ignoring signs of psychopathology. In addition, psychologists should not assume that religious or spiritual beliefs are static and be prepared to help clients/patients identify changes reflecting spiritual maturity positively tied to treatment goals (Knapp, Lemoncelli, & VandeCreek, 2010). To identify whether clients'/patients' religious beliefs are having a deleterious effect on their mental health, psychologists should explore whether their beliefs (a) create or exacerbate clinical distress, (b) provide a way to avoid reality and responsibility, (c) lead to self-destructive behavior, or (d) create false expectations of God (W. B. Johnson et al., 2000). When appropriate, psychologists should consider consulting with clergy to determine whether a clients'/patients' religious beliefs are distortions or misconceptions of religious doctrine.

Imposing Religious Values

Using the therapist's authority to indoctrinate clients/patients to the psychologists' religious beliefs violates their value autonomy and exploits their vulnerability to coercion (Principle E: Respect for People's Rights and Dignity; Standard 3.08, Exploitative Relationships). When clients/patients are grappling with decisions in areas in which religious and secular moral perspectives may conflict (e.g., divorce, sexual orientation, abortion, acceptance of transfusions, end-of-life decisions), therapy needs to distinguish between those religious values that have positive or destructive influences on each individual client's/patient's mental health—not the religious or secular values of the psychologist. Professional license to practice psychology demands that psychologists provide competent professional services and does not give them license to preach (Plante, 2014). Psychologists should guard against discussing religious doctrine when it is irrelevant to the clients'/patients' mental health needs (Richards & Bergin, 2005).

Confusing Religious Values With Psychological Diagnoses

The revised Guidelines for Psychological Practice With Lesbian, Gay, and Bisexual Clients (APA, 2012c) encourages psychologists to consider the influences of religion and spirituality on the lives of lesbian, gay, and bisexual clients specifically and transgender, gender-nonconforming, and

(Continued)

(Continued)

questioning clients in general. The linking of religious values and psychotherapies involving LGBT clients/patients has drawn a considerable amount of public attention. Spiritually sensitive, accommodative, and theistic therapies have a lot to offer LGBT clients/patients (Lease, Horne, & Noffsinger-Frazier, 2005). LGBT persons vary in their religious backgrounds and the extent to which faith affects their psychological well-being.

Ethical problems arise, however, when psychologists confuse a client's/patient's conflicted feelings about sexual orientation and religious values with psychological diagnoses (Page, Lindahl, & Malik, 2013). For example, psychologists must be sensitive to the fact that rejection by one's religious institution does not mean LGBTQ clients are not deeply religious or spiritual or seeking to be so. Competencies in addressing religion and spirituality among LGBTQ clients include training in therapeutic techniques to effectively address the following (see also Entengoff & Daiute, 2014; Magaldi-Dopman & Park-Taylor, 2010; Matthews & Salazar, 2012; Sherry, Adelman, & Whilde, 2010):

- Religious beliefs that may lead to higher levels of shame, guilt, and internalized homophobia
- Emotions associated with loss, grief, anger, reconciliation, or change in religious or spiritual identity
- Skills clients may need to separate spirituality from religion and to explore diversity of opinion within their faith community
- The liabilities and benefits of coming out to family members and others who endorse religious biases against LGBTQ individuals

Conversion Therapy

Ethical challenges around the application of conversion therapies to alter sexual orientation have stimulated considerable professional dialogue. All major professional mental health organizations have affirmed that variations in sexual orientation and gender identity are normative and not pathological (APA, 2009, 2015c; http://www.apa.org/pi/lgbt/resources/just-the-facts.aspx). In addition, empirical data indicate that conversion therapies or other efforts to change sexual orientation or gender identity are ineffective, harmful, and not appropriate for the delivery of mental health services (SAMHSA, 2015).

Based on the evidence, psychologists who offer such therapies to LGBT clients/patients are violating Standard 2.04, Bases for Scientific and Professional Judgments. Moreover, when psychologists offer "cures" for homosexuality, they falsely imply that there is established knowledge in the profession that LGBT sexual orientation is a mental disorder. This, in turn, may deprive clients/patients of exploring internalized reactions to a hostile society and risks perpetuating societal prejudices and stereotypes (Cramer, Golom, LoPresto, & Kirkley, 2008; Haldeman, 1994, 2004; Simons, Leibowitz, & Hidalgo, 2014; Vance, Ehrensaft, & Rosenthal, 2014; Principle A: Beneficence and Nonmaleficence; Principle B: Fidelity and Responsibility; Principle D: Justice; Standard 3.04, Avoiding Harm). In addition, when psychologists base their diagnosis and treatment on religious doctrines that view homosexual behavior as a "sin," they can be in violation of Standard 9.01, Bases for Assessments, and may be practicing outside the boundaries of their profession. (See also discussion of conversion therapy involving children and adolescents in Chapter 6 under Standard 3.04, Avoiding Harm).

Multiple Relationships

Multiple relationship challenges arise when clergy who have doctoral degrees in psychology provide mental health services to congregants or nonclergy psychologists treat members of their faith communities (Standard 3.05, Multiple Relationships).

Clergy–Psychologists

Clergy–psychologists providing therapy for members of their faith over whom they may have ecclesiastical authority should take steps to ensure they and their clients/patients are both aware of and respect the boundaries between their roles as a psychologist and as a religious leader. Distinguishing role functions becomes particularly important in addressing issues of confidentiality. Psychologists and clergy have different legal and professional obligations when it comes to mandated reporting of abuse and ethically permitted disclosures of information to protect clients/patients and others from harm (Standard 4.05, Disclosures).

Therapists at all points along the secular–theistic continuum who share the faith beliefs of clients/patients or work with fellow congregants must take steps to ensure that clients do not misperceive them as having religious or ecclesiastical authority and understand that the psychologists do not act on behalf of the church or its leaders (Gubi, 2001; Richards & Potts, 1995). This may be especially challenging for nonclergy religious psychologists working in faith-based environments (Sanders, Swenson, & Schneller, 2011). Psychologists also need to take steps to ensure that their knowledge of their joint faith community does not interfere with their objectivity and that clients/patients feel safe disclosing and exploring concerns about religion or behaviors that might ostracize them from this community.

Fee-for-Service Quandaries

While psychologists can discuss spiritual issues in therapy, when services are provided as a licensed psychologist eligible for third-party payments, the primary focus must be psychological (Plante, 2007). A focus on religious/spiritual rather than therapeutic goals may risk inappropriately charging third-party payors for non–mental health services not covered by insurance policies (Tan, 2003; see also Principle C: Integrity, and Standard 6.04, Fees and Financial Arrangements). Clergy and nonclergy psychologists practicing theistic therapies may find it difficult to clearly differentiate in reports to third-party payors those goals and therapeutic techniques that are accepted mental health practices and those that are spiritually based. In most instances, clergy–psychologists should encourage their congregants to seek mental health services from other providers in the community and refrain from encouraging their congregants to see them for fee-for-service therapy (Standard 3.06, Conflict of Interest). When clergy or nonclergy psychologists provide spiritual counseling free of charge in religious settings, they should clarify they are counseling in their ecclesiastical role and that content will be specific to pastoral issues (Richards & Bergin, 2005).

Informed Consent

The role of religion/spirituality in clients'/patients' worldviews may determine their willingness to participate in therapies along the secular–theistic continuum. Some may find the interjection of

(Continued)

(Continued)

religion into therapy discomforting or coercive, while others may find the absence of religion from therapy alienating.

When scientific or professional knowledge indicates that discussion of religion may be essential for effective treatment (Standards 2.01b, Boundaries of Competence; 2.04, Bases for Scientific and Professional Judgments), informed consent discussions can help the client/patient and psychologist identify and limit for treatment those religious beliefs and practices that facilitate or interfere with treatment goals (Rosenfeld, 2011; Shumway & Waldo, 2012). In some contexts, it may be ethically appropriate to discuss the risks involved in exploration of the client's religious beliefs, including loss of current coping mechanisms, stress produced by self-questioning of religious beliefs, and diminished capacity to seek support from one's religious community (Rosenfeld, 2011). The goal of such discussions is to enhance the therapeutic alliance and treatment context through client–therapist mutual understanding and respect.

When treatments diverge from established psychological practice, clients/patients have a right to consider this information in their consent decisions. Consequently, informed consent for theistic therapies should explain the religious doctrine and values upon which the treatment is based, the religious methods that will be employed (e.g., prayers, reading of scripture, forgiveness), and the relative emphasis on spiritual versus mental health goals. In addition, since theistic therapies are relatively new and currently lack empirical evidence or disciplinary consensus regarding their use (Plante & Sherman, 2001; Richards & Bergin, 2005), psychologists practicing these therapies should consider whether informed consent requirements for "treatments for which generally recognized techniques and procedures have not been established," described in Standard 10.01b, apply.

Conclusion

There is a welcome increase in research examining the positive and negative influences of religious beliefs and practices on mental health and the clinical outcomes of treatment approaches along the secular–theistic therapy continuum. Ethical commitment to do what is right for each client/patient and well-informed approaches to treatment will reduce, but not eliminate, ethical challenges, which will continue to emerge as scientific and professional knowledge advances. Psychologists conducting psychotherapy with individuals of diverse religious backgrounds and values will need to keep abreast of new knowledge and emerging ethical guidelines, continuously monitor the consequences of spirituality and religiously sensitive treatment decisions on client/patient well-being, and have the flexibility and sensitivity to religious contexts, role responsibilities, and client/patient expectations required for effective ethical decision making.

Chapter Cases and Ethics Discussion Questions

Amos, a devout Mormon whose company has just transferred him from Salt Lake City to New York City, identified Dr. Gail Main as a potential therapist by cross-listing psychologists with members of the Mormon Church in the city. In their initial interview, he describes his anxiety working with openly gay employees. He states that he has never known anyone personally who is gay and because the Church forbids "homosexual acts," he is afraid to go the men's room or be alone in an elevator with these employees because he is afraid they will make sexual advances toward him and try to "turn him gay." He tells Dr. Main that he chose her as a therapist because as a fellow Mormon, she will help him protect himself from "sinning." Discuss the steps Dr. Main should take to fulfill her ethical responsibility to provide Amos with the best treatment in a manner that clarifies the professional nature of her therapeutic services, is sensitive to Amos's religious values, and avoids blurring her own religious values with her professional standards.

Dr. Mizaki, a clinical psychologist working in a psychiatric facility, was preparing his patient, Donna, for discharge from the hospital. Donna had been diagnosed with schizophrenia. Donna lives in a rural area 500 miles from the hospital, and there are no mental health professionals in the area. The only way to provide Donna with outpatient services is through telepsychology. Dr. Mizaki wants to initiate a new telehealth procedure that has been developed by a colleague at the hospital for individuals in rural areas with serious mental disorders. The new treatment involves individual sessions with clients and family members via computer-based video chat to educate them about the medication and other supports Donna will need. Discuss the informed consent and confidentiality procedures that Dr. Mizaki will need to ethically implement this new treatment approach.

Susan is completing her clinical internship at an outpatient clinic of a veterans hospital and is supervised by the director of the clinic. She has been treating Alan, a 30-year-old military officer who fought in Afghanistan, for posttraumatic stress disorder (PTSD). After 4 sessions, she believes she sees some reduction in Alan's sleep disturbance and symptoms of anxiety. She has noticed that he is often in the waiting room on days in which he does not have a scheduled appointment. At least twice during the past 2 weeks, she has also noticed him outside the café where she gets coffee every morning. She raises this during the next session, and he responds very angrily, telling her that he needs to see her more than once a week. Given his progress, she believes that the once-weekly frequency of sessions is sufficient and encourages him to discuss what he believes would be the advantages of additional sessions. He has difficulty explaining why he wants more sessions and kicks the door as he leaves the office. Susan discusses the situation with her supervisor, who suggests some interventions, but these are met with increased anger by Alan, along with reports of increased PTSD symptoms. In addition, Alan is now waiting outside the café every morning when Susan gets her coffee. Discuss the ethical challenges raised by this scenario and solutions that Susan and her supervisor might consider.

APPENDIX A

Case Studies for Ethical Decision Making

Case 1. Assessment of Intellectual Disability and Capital Punishment: A Question of Human Rights?

Dr. Eduardo Romaro, a clinically trained forensic psychologist, has been retained by the prosecution to evaluate the intellectual competence of John Stone, a 50-year-old man convicted of first-degree murder of a guard during a bank robbery. John claimed throughout the trial that he was innocent. In the state in which the trial was conducted, individuals convicted of first-degree murder face the death penalty. John's attorney has challenged the death penalty option for his client, claiming that the defendant is intellectually disabled. The US Supreme Court ruled in *Atkins v. Virginia* (2002) that the execution of those with mental retardation (currently termed *intellectual developmental disorder* in the *DSM-5*) is unconstitutional. Dr. Romaro has worked with the prosecution before on intellectual disability cases, but this is the first time he has been retained for a capital punishment case. He is personally ambivalent about whether states should implement the death penalty.

The psychologist meets John in a private room in the prison and administers a battery of intellectual and adaptive behavior tests with proven psychometric validity for determining forensically relevant intellectual ability. Just as he ends the formal test administration, John becomes distraught and appears to be experiencing an anxiety attack. The psychologist hears the prisoner in his distress repeatedly asking God for forgiveness for killing the guard and for murdering another person, whom he keeps calling "the boy waiting for the bus." The psychologist shifts into an emergency crisis intervention mode to help calm the defendant and rings for assistance. Dr. Romaro was shocked to hear John "confess" not only to the bank murder but also to the murder of a "boy waiting for a bus."

The *DSM-5* (APA, 2013) diagnosis of intellectual developmental disorder (IDD) requires that individuals demonstrate significantly subaverage intellectual functioning and impairments in adaptive functioning and that these conditions *must begin during the developmental period.* Similarly, in the state where John was convicted, the standard for intellectual disability includes a developmental history of intellectual impairment. Prior to testing John, Dr. Romaro had asked the prosecutor for all available childhood mental health or school records to determine whether John meets these criteria. No formal educational or psychological evaluations were included in the materials he received. The records indicated that John had a poor academic record, was retained in fifth grade, was suspended several times for coming to school drunk, and left school when he was 15. State criteria also include an IQ score less than 70 and poor adaptive skills.

That evening Dr. Romaro scores the test battery. John's IQ score is 71, and his performance on other cognitive tests falls close to the IDD cutoff score (some scores above, some below). His adaptive functioning score is a standard deviation below average. However, given the prisoner's age, without a more detailed set of childhood records, it is difficult to clearly conclude that he meets the *DSM-IV-TR* or state legal criteria for intellectual disability. Dr. Romaro has not been asked to administer assessments for mood, schizophrenia, or other psychotic disorders that might impair intellectual and adaptive performance.

Ethical Dilemma

Dr. Romaro is not sure what forensic opinion to give regarding whether or not John meets the legal criteria for intellectual developmental disorder. Without evidence of intellectual disability in his youth, a diagnosis of intellectual disability may not be possible and, thus, could not be used to support John's death penalty appeal. Dr. Romaro is also unsure whether he has an ethical responsibility to include in his report John's "confession" as informing the "ultimate issue" before the court or to include John's statement about the "boy waiting for a bus."

Discussion Questions

1. Why is this an ethical dilemma? Which APA Ethical Principles help frame the nature of the dilemma?
2. Who are the stakeholders, and how will they be affected by how Dr. Romaro resolves this dilemma?
3. How might Dr. Romaro's ambivalence toward the death penalty influence his decision to offer a forensic diagnosis of intellectual developmental disorder? How might John's "confession" or John's comment about the "boy waiting for the bus" influence the decision? To what extent should these factors play a role in Dr. Romaro's report?
4. How are APA Ethical Standards 2.01f, 3.06, 4.04, 4.05, 5.01, 9.01a, and 9.06 relevant to this case? Which other standards might apply?
5. Does this dilemma raise issues regarding Dr. Romaro's involvement in justifying or defining a violation of John's human rights? (See also, Standard 1.02

and the Hot Topic in Chapter 4 "Human Rights and Psychologists' Involvement in Assessments Related to Death Penalty Cases.")

6. What are Dr. Romaro's ethical alternatives for resolving this dilemma? Which alternative best reflects the Ethics Code aspirational principles and enforceable standards, legal standards, and Dr. Romaro's obligations to stakeholders? Can you identify the ethical theory (presented in Chapter 3) guiding your decision?
7. What steps should Dr. Romaro take to ethically implement his decision and monitor its effect?

Suggested Readings

Gillespie, L. K., Smith, M. D., Bjerregaard, B., & Fogel, S. J. (2014). Examining the impact of proximate culpability mitigation in capital punishment sentencing recommendations: The influence of mental health mitigators. *American Journal of Criminal Justice, 39,* 698–715.

Glaser, J., Martine, K. D., & Kan, K. B. (2015). Possibility of death sentence has divergent effect on verdicts for Black and White defendants. *Law & Human Behavior, 39,* 539–546.

Kalmbach, K. C., & Lyons, P. M. (2006). Ethical issues in conducting forensic evaluations. *Applied Psychology in Criminal Justice, 2*(Spec. Iss.), 261–290.

Macvaugh, G. S., III, & Cunningham, M. D. (2009). *Atkins v. Virginia:* Implications and recommendations for forensic practice. *Journal of Psychiatry & Law, 37,* 131–184.

Wood, S. E., Packman, W., Howell, S., & Bongar, B. (2014). A failure to implement: Analyzing state responses to the Supreme Court's directives in *Atkins v. Virginia* and suggestions for a national standard. *Psychiatry, Psychology, & Law, 21,* 16–45.

Case 2. Cultural Values and Competent Mental Health Services to Minors

Irina, a 13-year-old girl of Arabic cultural heritage living in Boston, Massachusetts, was brought by her parents to a hospital emergency room after an assault by a stranger. Based on her injuries, the hospital staff suspected that the attacker had also sexually assaulted the girl, but she and her parents refused medical evaluations for rape. The family received a referral to see Janet Matthews, a clinical psychologist specializing in adolescent trauma. During their initial meeting with Dr. Matthews, the parents asked the psychologist not to discuss any sexual aspects of the assault with their daughter but to treat the psychological trauma from the assault in general. They told the psychologist that admitting a rape had taken place would cast a stigma on their daughter and make her ineligible to be married to men in their closely knit ethnic community. When asked in private, the girl also requested that sexual issues not be discussed for the same reason.

Ethical Dilemma

Dr. Matthews does not know whether she should agree to the parents' and child's request.

Discussion Questions

1. Why is this an ethical dilemma? Which APA Ethical Principles help frame the nature of the dilemma?
2. Who are the stakeholders, and how will they be affected by how Dr. Matthews resolves this dilemma?
3. How might Irina's age and her parents' involvement in the referral affect how Dr. Matthews can resolve this dilemma? How might state law on treatment of minors and HIPAA rules on access of guardians to a minor's health care records influence Dr. Matthew's decision? (See "A Word About HIPAA" in the preface of this book; the section on parental rights under Standard 3.10b, Informed Consent, in Chapter 6; and the Hot Topic at the end of Chapter 7, "Confidentiality and Involvement of Parents in Mental Health Services for Children and Adolescents.")
4. What attitudes, knowledge, and skills are required to develop a culturally competent treatment plan for Irina (see the Hot Topic in Chapter 5, "Multicultural Ethical Competence")?
5. Is Irina likely to benefit from the treatment if the possibility of sexual aspects to the trauma is not explored?
6. How are APA Ethical Standards 2.01a, b, and c; 2.04; 3.04; 3.06; 4.01; 4.02; and 10.10a relevant to this case? Which other standards might apply?
7. What are Dr. Matthews's ethical alternatives for resolving this dilemma? Which alternative best reflects the Ethics Code aspirational principles and enforceable standards, legal standards, and Dr. Matthews's obligations to stakeholders? Can you identify the ethical theory (presented in Chapter 3) guiding your decision?
8. What steps should Dr. Matthews take to ethically implement her decision and monitor its effect?

Suggested Readings

American Psychological Association. (2003). Guidelines on multicultural education, training, research, practice, and organizational change for psychologists. *American Psychologist, 58*, 377–402.

American Psychological Association. (2007). Guidelines for psychological practice with girls and women. *American Psychologist, 62*, 949–979.

Arredondo, P., & Toporek, R. (2004). Multicultural counseling competencies = ethical practice. *Journal of Mental Health Counseling, 26*(1), 44–55.

Gallardo, M. E., Johnson, J., Parham, T. A., & Carter, J. A. (2009). Ethics and multiculturalism: Advancing cultural and clinical responsiveness. *Professional Psychology: Research and Practice, 40,* 425–435.

Vasquez, M. (2012). Social justice and civic virtue. In S. Knapp, M. Gottlieb, M. Handelsman, & L. VandeCreek (Eds.), *Handbook of ethics in psychology* (Vol. 1, pp. 75–98). Washington, DC: American Psychological Association.

Zerr, A., & Pina, A. (2014). Predictors of initial engagement in child anxiety mental health specialty services. *Child & Youth Care Forum, 2,* 151–164.

Case 3. Request for Services Following Termination

Dr. Howard Lightfoot, a psychologist in independent practice, works in a small, rural town in New Mexico. He treated Mary for a year, helping her with depression and anxiety related to her conflicting feelings about her lesbian sexual orientation. At the time of treatment termination, Mary's depression and anxiety were reduced, and she had begun to have positive dating experiences with other women.

Three years after termination of the therapy, Dr. Lightfoot receives a voice mail from Mary. She states that a month ago Allison, her partner of 2 years, was diagnosed with breast cancer. At that time, Mary became depressed and anxious again and started psychotherapy with another therapist because Dr. Lightfoot was no longer on the list of health providers covered by her insurance plan. She then ended the therapy because the new therapist appeared to have no understanding of the real-world challenges faced by lesbian couples.

Mary tells Dr. Lightfoot that Allison has also begun to experience a great deal of anxiety and would like to begin psychotherapy with someone she can trust is sensitive to lesbian issues. Since Allison's insurance plan would cover Dr. Lightfoot's services for individual therapy and Mary's participation as caretaker and collateral support, she is calling to ask whether he would consider treating Allison.

Ethical Dilemma

Based on his previous professional relationship with Mary and Allison's current personal relationship with Mary, Dr. Lightfoot is unsure whether or not he should agree to see Allison for psychotherapy.

Discussion Questions

1. Why is this an ethical dilemma? Which APA Ethical Principles help frame the nature of the dilemma?
2. Who are the stakeholders, and how will they be affected by how Dr. Lightfoot resolves this dilemma?
3. How should the nature of Mary's mental health problems when she was in treatment with Dr. Lightfoot, the amount of time that has passed since

termination of his treatment with her, and Mary's current mental health and treatment status influence how this dilemma might be resolved?

4. What ethically relevant issues are raised by Allison's relationship with Mary, her breast cancer, her concern about a therapist sensitive to lesbian issues, and the small-town setting?
5. How are APA Ethical Standards 2.01a, b, and d; 3.05a; 3.09; 6.04; and 10.04 relevant to this case? Which other standards might apply?
6. What are Dr. Lightfoot's ethical alternatives for resolving this dilemma? Which alternative best reflects the Ethics Code aspirational principles and enforceable standards, legal standards, and obligations to stakeholders? Can you identify the ethical theory (presented in Chapter 3) guiding your decision?
7. What steps should Dr. Lightfoot take to implement his ethical decision and monitor its effect?

Suggested Readings

American Psychological Association. (2012). Guidelines for psychological practice with lesbian, gay and bisexual clients. *American Psychologist, 67,* 10–42.

Barnett, J. E., Lazarus, A. A., Vasquez, M. J. T., Moorehead-Slaughter, O., & Johnson, W. B. (2007). Boundary issues and multiple relationships: Fantasy and reality. *Professional Psychology: Research and Practice, 38,* 401–410.

Green, R. J., & Mitchell, V. (2002). Gay and lesbian couples in therapy: Homophobia, relational ambiguity, and social support. In A. S. Gurman & N. S. Jacobson (Eds.), *Clinical handbook of couple therapy* (pp. 536–568). New York, NY: Guilford Press.

Shapiro, E. L., & Ginzberg, R. (2003). To accept or not to accept: Referrals and the maintenance of boundaries. *Professional Psychology: Research & Practice, 34,* 258–263.

Younggren, J. N., & Gottlieb, D. (2004). Managing risk when contemplating multiple relationships. *Professional Psychology: Research and Practice, 35,* 255–260.

Case 4. Research on Intimate Partner Violence and the Duty to Protect

Dr. Daniela Yeung, a health psychologist, has been conducting a federally funded ethnographic study of couples in which the male partner has been paroled following conviction and imprisonment for intimate partner violence (IPV). Over the course of a year, she has had individual monthly interviews with 25 couples while one partner was in jail and following their release. Aiden is a 35-year-old male parolee convicted of seriously injuring his wife. He and his wife, Maya, have been interviewed by Dr. Yeung on eight occasions. The interviews have covered a range of personal topics including Aiden's problem drinking, which is marked by blackouts and threatening phone calls made to his wife when he becomes drunk, usually in the evening. To her knowledge, Aiden has never followed through on these threats. Dr. Yeung has the impression both Aiden and Maya feel a sense of social support when discussing their life with Dr. Yeung. One evening Dr. Yeung checks her answering machine and finds a message from Aiden. His words are slurred and angry: "Now that you know the truth about what I am you know that there is nothing you can do to help the evil inside me. The bottle is my savior and I will end this with them tonight." She calls both Aiden's and Maya's cell phone numbers, but no one answers.

Ethical Dilemma

Dr. Yeung has Aiden's address, and after 2 hours, she is considering whether or not to contact emergency services to suggest that law enforcement officers go to Aiden's home or to the homes of his parents and girlfriend.

Discussion Questions

1. Why is this an ethical dilemma? Which APA Ethical Principles help frame the nature of the dilemma?

2. Who are the stakeholders, and how will they be affected by how Dr. Yeung resolves this dilemma?

3. Does this situation meet the standards set by the *Tarasoff* decision's "duty to protect" statute (see Chapter 7)? How might whether or not Dr. Yeung's state includes researchers under such a statute influence Dr. Yeung's ethical decision making? How might the fact that Dr. Yeung is a research psychologist without training or licensure in clinical practice influence the ethical decision?

4. In addressing this dilemma, should Dr. Yeung consider how her decision may affect the completion of her research (e.g., the confidentiality concerns of other participants)?

5. How are APA Ethical Standards 2.01f, 3.04, 3.06, 4.01, 4.02, 4.05, and 8.01 relevant to this case? Which other standards might apply?

6. What are Dr. Yeung's ethical alternatives for resolving this dilemma? Which alternative best reflects the Ethics Code aspirational principles and enforceable standards, legal standards, and obligations to stakeholders? Can you identify the ethical theory (discussed in Chapter 3) guiding your decision?

7. What steps should Dr. Yeung take to implement her decision and monitor its effect?

Suggested Readings

Appelbaum, P., & Rosenbaum, A. (1989). *Tarasoff* and the researcher: Does the duty to protect apply in the research setting? *American Psychologist, 44*(6), 885–894.

Fisher, C. B. (2011). Addiction research ethics and the Belmont principles: Do drug users have a different moral voice? *Substance Use & Misuse, 46*(6), 728–741.

Gable, L. (2009). Legal challenges raised by non-intervention research conducted under high-risk circumstances. In D. Buchanan, C. B. Fisher, & L. Gable (Eds.). *Research with high-risk populations: Balancing science, ethics, and law* (pp. 47–74). Washington, DC: American Psychological Association.

Paavilainen, E., Lepisto, S., & Flinck, A. (2014). Ethical issues in family violence research in healthcare settings. *Nursing Ethics, 21,* 43–52.

Case 5. Web-Based Advertising for a Community Program Development and Evaluation Consulting Service

Dr. Martin Lux, an applied developmental psychologist, has created his own community consultation and program evaluation business. He specializes in helping communities and service organizations set up day care programs for children aged 1 to 3 years. He wants to advertise his services on the Internet and is beginning to develop the following plan:

a. To gain maximum exposure on search engines like Google, he will name the website "SuccessfulDayCarePrograms.org."

b. As a service to potential community clients, he will put links on his website to other online information about infant mental health and social and legal services available in different communities where he might find clients.

c. He is currently under contract with a city agency. He helped the agency design a day care program for children of employees and is now in the process of evaluating its first year of implementation. He would like to ask a few parents whose children go to the day care program to endorse his new consultation service. He would use a picture of the parent and place the endorsement in quotes under the picture.

d. The website will include a question-and-answer blog. Individuals can post questions to the blog about their preschool child's development (e.g., toilet training, language development, social development, "terrible twos," etc.), and he will post answers.

Ethical Dilemma

Dr. Lux is aware that he will have to ensure his website and blog have appropriate firewalls and other privacy and security safeguards. Beyond the technical aspects of implementation, however, he is unsure whether his plan requires additional ethical considerations.

Discussion Questions

1. Identify an ethical challenge for each element (a–d) of Dr. Lux's advertising plan. Which APA Ethical Principles best help understand why these elements may create ethical problems?

2. Who are the stakeholders in the advertising plan, and how will they be affected by how Dr. Lux handles each of the advertising elements?
3. Is the name of Dr. Lux's website potentially misleading? What ethical responsibilities does he have when he creates the website and sets up links to other service websites?
4. Will the parents of children in the city day care center feel free to refuse Dr. Lux's invitation to provide a testimonial? What professional risks and ethical problems might Dr. Lux have when answering parents' questions on his blog?
5. How are APA Ethical Standards 2.01b, 2.04, 3.05a, 3.06, 3.08, 5.01, 5.04, and 5.05 relevant to this case?
6. For each aspect of the plan (a–d), generate ethical alternatives for creating an effective website to advertise Dr. Lux's new community consultation service. Which alternative best reflects the Ethics Code aspirational principles and enforceable standards, legal standards, and obligations to stakeholders? Can you identify the ethical theory (discussed in Chapter 3) guiding your decision?
7. What steps should Dr. Lux take to ethically implement his advertising plan and monitor its effect?

Suggested Readings

Heinlen, K., Welfel, T., Reynolds, E., Richmond, E., & O'Donnell, M. S. (2003). The nature, scope, and ethics of psychologists' e-therapy Web sites: What consumers find when surfing the Web. *Psychotherapy: Theory, Research, Practice, Training, 40,* 112–124.

McGarrah, N. A., Baker, A., Martinem, J. N., & Haldeman, D. C. (2009). In the public eye: The ethical practice of media psychology. *Professional Psychology: Research and Practice, 40,* 172–180.

Schenker, Y., Arnold, R. M., & London, A. J. (2014). The ethics of advertising for health care services. *American Journal of Bioethics, 14,* 34–43.

Shaw, H. E., & Shaw, S. H. (2006). Critical ethical issues in online counseling: Assessing current practices with an ethical intent checklist. *Journal of Counseling & Development, 84,* 41–53.

Case 6. Fees and Financial Arrangements: Referring Clients/Patients to Members Within a Group Practice

Dr. Naila Ambrose, a clinical psychologist, is a partner in a group practice that has a waiting room and suite of offices in a building in a small suburb. For the past 3 months, Dr. Ambrose has been providing therapy to Kenneth Nishakawa, a patient with diagnosed bipolar disorder. She works collaboratively with Dr. Pill, one of her partners in the group. Dr. Pill, a psychiatrist, is responsible for prescribing and monitoring the physical effects of Kenneth's use of the medication lithium. The group practice has a capitation contract with Ken's health insurer. Given the severity of his disorder, the actual cost of his treatment is greater than the fixed (capitated) amount of dollars the group is allocated for each patient.

Over several sessions, Kenneth has told Dr. Ambrose about the difficulties his family is having with his illness and that he is particularly worried about how it is affecting his daughter's schoolwork. He asks Dr. Ambrose if she would see his wife and daughter for a few family sessions. Dr. Ambrose is worried that holding these family sessions would increase the negative monetary effect of Kenneth's treatment on the group practice. Jim Taylor, a licensed clinical social worker, is also a member of the practice group. Jim Taylor's session rates are lower than Dr. Ambrose's. If she refers the family therapy component to Jim, the practice group may be able to make up for the overcost of Kenneth's individual treatment.

Ethical Dilemma

Dr. Ambrose does not know whether it is ethical to refer Kenneth, his wife, and daughter to her social work partner for the family sessions.

Discussion Questions

1. Why is this an ethical dilemma? Which APA Ethical Principles help frame the nature of the dilemma?
2. Who are the stakeholders, and how will they be affected by how Dr. Ambrose resolves this dilemma?
3. Which aspects of Kenneth's individual treatment and family treatment needs are important for Dr. Ambrose to consider? To what extent should the issue of group finances play a role in Dr. Ambrose's decision?
4. To what extent, if any, should Dr. Ambrose consider Jim Taylor's status as a clinical social worker?
5. What role should Kenneth's preferences for who conducts the family treatment play in the decision?
6. How are APA Ethical Standards 2.01a, 3.04, 3.05a, 3.06, 3.08, 6.04b, 6.07, 10.02 a and b, and the Hot Topic in Chapter 9, "Managing the Ethics of Managed Care," relevant to this case? Which other standards might apply?
7. What are Dr. Ambrose's ethical alternatives for resolving this dilemma? Which alternative best reflects the Ethics Code aspirational principles and enforceable standards, legal standards, and obligations to stakeholders? Can you identify the ethical theory (discussed in Chapter 3) guiding your decision?
8. What steps should Dr. Ambrose take to implement her decision and monitor its effect?

Suggested Readings

Kielbasa, A. M., Pomerantz, A. M., Krohn, E. J., & Sullivan, B. F. (2004). How does clients' method of payment influence psychologists' diagnostic decisions. *Ethics & Behavior, 14,* 187–195.

Shapiro, E. L., & Ginzberg, R. (2003). To accept or not to accept: Referrals and the maintenance of boundaries. *Professional Psychology: Research & Practice, 34,* 258–263.

Wilcoxon, S., Magnuson, S., & Norem, K. (2008). Institutional values of managed mental health care: Efficiency or oppression? *Journal of Multicultural Counseling and Development, 36,* 143–154.

Woody, R. H. (2011). The financial conundrum for mental health practitioners. *American Journal of Family Therapy, 39,* 1–10.

Case 7. Handling Disparate Information for Evaluating Trainees

Rashid Vaji, PhD, a member of the school psychology faculty at a midsize university, serves as a faculty supervisor for students assigned to externships in schools. The department has formalized a supervision and evaluation system for the extern program. Students have weekly individual meetings with the faculty supervisor and biweekly meetings with the on-site supervisor. The on-site supervisor writes a mid-year (December) and end of academic year (May) evaluation of each student. The site evaluations are sent to Dr. Vaji, and he provides feedback based on the site and his own supervisory evaluation to each student. The final grade (fail, low pass, pass, high pass) is the responsibility of Dr. Vaji.

Dr. Vaji also teaches the spring semester graduate class Health Disparities in Mental Health. One of the course requirements is for students to write weekly thought papers, in which they take the perspective of therapy clients from different ethnic groups in reaction to specific session topics. Leo Watson, a second-year graduate student, is one of Dr. Vaji's externship supervisees. He is also enrolled in the Health Disparities course. Leo's thought papers often present ethnic-minority adolescents as prone to violence and unable to grasp the insights offered by school psychologists. In a classroom role-playing exercise, Leo plays an ethnic-minority student client as slumping in his chair, not understanding the psychologist, and giving angry retorts. In written comments on these thought papers and class feedback, Dr. Vaji encourages Leo to incorporate more of the readings on racial/ethnic discrimination and multicultural competence into his papers and to provide more complex perspectives on clients.

One day during his office hours, three students from the class come to Dr. Vaji's office to complain about Leo's behavior outside the classroom. They describe incidents in which Leo uses derogatory ethnic labels to describe his externship clients and brags about "putting one over" on his site supervisors by describing these clients in "glowing" terms just to satisfy his supervisors' "stupid do-good" attitudes. They also report an incident at a local bar at which Leo was seen harassing an African American waitress, including by using racial slurs.

After the students have left his office, Dr. Vaji reviews his midyear evaluation and supervision notes on Leo and the midyear on-site supervisor's report. In his own evaluation report, Dr. Vaji had written, "Leo often articulates a strong sense of duty to help his ethnic minority students overcome past discrimination but needs additional growth and supervision in applying a multicultural perspective to his clinical work." The on-site supervisor's evaluation states that

> Leo has a wonderful attitude toward his student clients. . . . Unfortunately, evaluation of his multicultural treatment skills is limited because Leo has had fewer cases to discuss than some of his peers, since a larger than usual number of ethnic minority clients have stopped coming to their sessions with him.

It is the middle of the spring semester, and Dr. Vaji still has approximately 6 weeks of supervision left with Leo. The students' complaints about Leo are consistent with what Dr. Vaji has observed in Leo's class papers and role-playing exercises. However, these complaints are very different from Leo's presentation during on-site supervision. If Leo has been intentionally deceiving both supervisors, then he may be more ineffective or harmful as a therapist to his current clients than either supervisor has realized. In addition, purposeful attempts to deceive the supervisors might indicate a personality disorder or lack of integrity that, if left unaddressed, might be harmful to adolescent clients in the future.

Ethical Dilemma

Dr. Vaji would like to meet with Leo to discuss, at a minimum, ways to retain adolescent clients and to improve his multicultural treatment skills. He does not know to what extent his conversation with Leo and final supervisory report should be influenced by the information provided by the other graduate students.

Discussion Questions

1. Why is this an ethical dilemma? Which APA Ethical Principles help frame the nature of the dilemma?
2. Who are the stakeholders, and how will they be affected by how Dr. Vaji resolves this dilemma?
3. What additional information might Dr. Vaji collect to get a more accurate picture of Leo's multicultural attitudes and professional skills? What are reasons for and against contacting Leo's site supervisor for more information? Should he request that Leo's sessions with clients be electronically taped or observed?
4. Is Dr. Vaji in a potentially unethical multiple relationship as both Leo's externship supervisor and his teacher in the Health Disparities class. Why or why not?

5. To what extent, if any, should Dr. Vaji consider Leo's own ethnicity in his deliberations? Should he address the dilemma differently if Leo self-identifies as non-Hispanic White than as Hispanic or non-Hispanic Black?
6. Once the dilemma is resolved, should Dr. Vaji have a follow-up meeting with the students who complained?
7. How are APA Ethical Standards 1.08, 3.04, 3.05, 3.09, 7.04, 7.05, and 7.06 and the Hot Topics "Ethical Supervision of Trainees in Professional Psychology Programs" (Chapter 10) and "Multicultural Ethical Competence" (Chapter 5) relevant to this case? Which other standards might apply?
8. What are Dr. Vaji's ethical alternatives for resolving this dilemma? Which alternative best reflects the Ethics Code aspirational principles and enforceable standards, legal standards, and obligations to stakeholders? Can you identify the ethical theory (discussed in Chapter 3) guiding your decision?
9. What steps should Dr. Vaji take to implement his decision and monitor its effect?

Suggested Readings

Allen, J. (2007). A multicultural assessment supervision model to guide research and practice. *Professional Psychology: Research and Practice, 38,* 248–258.

Barnett, J. E., & Molzon, C. H. (2014). Clinical supervision of psychotherapy: Essential ethics issues for supervisors and supervisees. *Journal of Clinical Psychology: In Session, 70*(11), 1051–1061. doi:10.1002/jclp.22126

Boysen, G. A., & Vogel, D. L. (2008). The relationship between level of training, implicit bias, and multicultural competency among counselor trainees. *Training and Education in Professional Psychology, 2,* 103–110.

Dailor, A. N. (2011). Ethically challenging situations reported by school psychologists: Implications for training. *Psychology in the Schools, 48,* 619–631.

Gilfoyle, N. (2008). The legal exosystem: Risk management in addressing student competence problems in professional psychology training. *Training and Education in Professional Psychology, 2,* 202–209.

Case 8. Using Deception to Study College Students' Willingness to Report Threats of Violence Against Female Students

College drinking has become a serious public health issue that has been associated with violence against women on college campuses. Although some programs to prevent violence against women appear promising when empirically tested, most have small effect sizes and have not been replicated on other campuses. Rachel Cohen, a first-year faculty member in an applied developmental psychology program at a large research institution, was asked to join a group of other scientists in an application to the National Institute for Alcohol Abuse and Alcoholism to conduct a two-phase multisite study. The senior investigator is well-known, and Dr. Cohen was flattered that she had been invited to join the project. The long-term goal of the study is to develop a peer-oriented prevention program that encourages freshmen living in campus housing to contact their resident director (RD) if an inebriated student is making comments suggesting an intent to commit violence against female dorm residents. To help inform the final design of the prevention program, the first phase of the study will experimentally test conditions under which students are more or less likely to report a threatening incident.

For this first phase, the lead investigator on the project suggests a design that uses deception to control conditions under which reporting of an incident may or may not occur. The design would test the following hypotheses: (a) Freshmen are more likely to call an RD if an inebriated student mentions a potential victim by name, and (b) students are more likely to contact an RD if another student suggests doing so. To test these hypotheses across different dorms and campuses, the study would use research confederates acting as students.

A 10:00 p.m. Pizza Study Break would be advertized through posters and held in a small meeting room in the freshman dorm. One confederate would walk into the room at the start of the break, pretending she was there for the pizza. Once there were at least 10 students in the room, the confederate acting as the inebriated student would enter the room, and both confederates would act out one of the following four conditions:

Condition A1B1: The "inebriated" student actor speaks threateningly about an *unnamed* female student; the second student actor *does not* encourage anyone to call.

Condition A2B1: The "inebriated" student actor speaks threateningly about and *names* a (fictitious) female student; the second student actor *does not* encourage anyone to call.

Condition A1B2: The "inebriated" student actor speaks threateningly about an *unnamed* female student; the second student actor says, "*Shouldn't someone call the RD?*"

Condition A2B2: The "inebriated" student actor speaks threateningly about and *names* a (fictitious) female student; the second student actor says, "*Shouldn't someone call the RD?*"

The RDs in each dorm would be informed of the study and participate by coming to remove the "inebriated" confederate from the premises if called by students. If after a given period of time RDs were not contacted, they would tell the students they had heard loud noises and take the confederate to their office.

Ethical Dilemma

Dr. Cohen believes that violence against women on college campuses is an important issue to address and that to do so requires understanding the conditions that increase students' willingness to report other students who threaten to harm females on campus. She also believes the deceptive research design adequately tests important hypotheses that may lead to the design of effective peer intervention studies. However, she is uncomfortable with the idea of deceiving the students and worries that the deception might harm them in some way. She does not know how to respond to the invitation to participate in the multisite research.

Discussion Questions

1. Why is this an ethical dilemma? Which APA Ethical Principles help frame the nature of the dilemma?
2. Who are the stakeholders, and how will they be affected by how Dr. Cohen resolves this dilemma?
3. Could exposure to the experimental conditions cause serious emotional harm to students unknowingly exposed to the different conditions?
4. Could these hypotheses be adequately and realistically tested without using deception?
5. Should informed consent be required for this study if the researchers do not record the names or other identifying information about the students who are exposed to each condition? Why or why not?
6. If the study were conducted, what ethical issues would be involved in deciding whether and how to explain the deception to students when the study was over (debriefing/dehoaxing)?
7. How are APA Ethical Standards 1.04, 3.04, 3.06, 8.05, 8.07, and 8.08 relevant to this case? Which other standards might apply?
8. Are there equally valid but nondeceptive research methods that Dr. Cohen could suggest to test the hypotheses? If not, could modifications to the deception method minimize participant harms and maximize research benefits?
9. What are the ethical alternatives for Dr. Cohen's participation in the study, and which best reflects the Ethics Code aspirational principles and enforceable standards, legal standards, and obligations to stakeholders? Can you identify the ethical theory (discussed in Chapter 3) guiding your decision?
10. What steps should Dr. Cohen take to implement her decision and monitor its effect?

Suggested Readings

Benjamin, L. T., & Simpson, J. A. (2009). The power of the situation: The impact of Milgram's obedience studies on personality and social psychology. *American Psychologist, 64*, 12–19.

Fisher, C. B., & Fyrberg, D. (1994). Participant partners: College students weigh the costs and benefits of deceptive research. *American Psychologist, 49,* 417–427.

Kimmel, A. J. (2012). Deception in research. In M. Gottlieb, M. Handelsman, L. VandeCreek, & S. Knapp (Eds.), *APA handbook of ethics in psychology: Vol. 2. Practice, teaching, and research* (pp. 401–421). Washington, DC: American Psychological Association.

Oczak, M., & Niedzwienska, A. (2007). Debriefing in deceptive research: A proposed new procedure. *Journal of Empirical Research on Research Ethics, 2,* 49–59.

Pascual-Leone, A., Singh, T., & Scoboria, A. (2010). Using deception ethically: Practical research guidelines for researchers and reviewers. *Canadian Psychology, 51,* 241–248.

Case 9. Competence Assessment for an Assisted Suicide Request

Santosh Patel is a neuropsychologist affiliated with a hospital located in a state with a voter-approved Death With Dignity Act. Under this law, the hospital may approve a dying patient's wish to receive a lethal prescription if a physician corroborates a 6-month terminal diagnosis. If the physician believes competence to be an issue, a psychologist or psychiatrist evaluates the patient to determine competence to make the decision to end life.

A physician requests a psychological evaluation for a 62-year-old Jewish woman with 6-month terminal cancer who has requested the lethal prescription. The physician questions the patient's competence because it appears that her decision to end her life now is motivated by the fact that her health care benefits have run out and her adult children have been complaining about the financial burden of providing the potent pain medications and hospice care she needs.

Dr. Patel administers standard tests for mental health disorders (the Minnesota Multiphasic Personality Inventory) and cognitive functioning (the Wechsler Adult Intelligence Scale). The patient's scores do not meet clinical cutoffs for any mental disorder, and her cognitive scores are in the normal range. During the clinical interview, the patient states that her primary reason for seeking the lethal prescription is to ease the financial burden and conflict among her children. Her reasoning process flows logically, and she understands and appreciates the personal implications of the procedure and her own medical condition. She has spoken to her rabbi and believes God will forgive her for this decision. Although the standardized assessment does not provide evidence of mental impairment, the psychologist believes that while the patient's decision may be rational, it is not truly voluntary but a result of pressure from the patient's children. The psychologist knows that in general, this type of end-of-life decision-making process is emotionally taxing for the patient, the patient's family members, and the health care team. He also realizes that whatever his assessment, it may be challenged in court by the patient's or family's legal representative.

Ethical Dilemma

Dr. Patel does not know whether or not he should place a constraint on the patient's decision by recommending a waiting period for psychotherapeutic intervention in the hope that treatment may shift the patient's concerns from her children's welfare to her own.

Discussion Questions

1. Why is this an ethical dilemma? Which APA Ethical Principles help frame the nature of the dilemma?
2. Who are the stakeholders, and how will they be affected by how Dr. Patel resolves this dilemma?
3. To what extent, if any, should Dr. Patel's personal moral attitudes toward assisted suicide play a role in his decision? To what extent is it professionally responsible to draw conclusions beyond the cognitive capacities measured by the assessment instruments?
4. Is it "irrational" for terminally ill patients to be concerned about the financial burden of their care on family members? Can Dr. Patel obtain a valid assessment of whether family members' financial concerns are or are not "coercive"?
5. What role should the patient's age, gender, and religious beliefs play in Dr. Patel's selection of tests and interpretation of the patient's responses?
6. How are APA Ethical Standards 2.01b, 2.01f, 2.04, 3.01, 3.04, 9.01a, 9.01b, 9.02b, 9.06, and 9.10 related to this case? Which other standards might apply?
7. What are Dr. Patel's ethical alternatives for resolving this dilemma? Which alternative best reflects the Ethics Code aspirational principles and enforceable standards, legal standards, and obligations to stakeholders? Can you identify the ethical theory (discussed in Chapter 3) guiding your decision?
8. What steps should Dr. Patel take to implement his decision and monitor its effect?

Suggested Readings

American Psychological Association. (2009). *APA resolution on assisted suicide.* Retrieved from http://www.apa.org/about/policy/assisted-suicide.aspx

Baeke, G., Wils, J., & Broeckaert, B. (2011). "We are (not) the master of our body": Elderly Jewish women's attitudes towards euthanasia and assisted suicide. *Ethnicity & Health, 16,* 259–278.

King, D. A., Kim, S. Y. H., & Conwell, Y. (2000). Family matters: A social systems perspective on physician-assisted suicide and the older adult. *Psychology, Public Policy, and Law, 6,* 434–451.

Niederjohn, D. M., & Rogers, D. T. (2009). Objectivity in evaluations for assisted suicide: Appreciating the role of relational and intrapsychic components. *Journal of Forensic Psychology Practice, 9,* 70–81.

Rosenberg, T., & Speice, J. (2013). Integrating care when the end is near: Ethical dilemmas in end-of-life care. *Families, Systems & Health, 31*, 75–83.

Werth, J. L., Lewis, M. M., & Richmond, J. M. (2009). Psychologists' involvement with terminally ill individuals who are making end-of-life decisions. *Journal of Forensic Psychology Practice, 9*, 82–91.

Case 10. Handling Unexpected Disruptive Member Behavior During Group Therapy

Esther Hernandez, PhD, a specialist in the psychology of addictions, conducts group therapy sessions for patients treated at a local methadone clinic funded by Medicaid. She has been meeting with a group of 12 women on a weekly basis for 2 months and has been pleased that, for the most part, members attend the meetings regularly. Although the women take methadone as a substitute for heroin, many also take other illicit drugs. At the initial session, Dr. Hernandez and group members agreed on a rule that members should not come to a session if they are high or intoxicated. The rule has been enforced several times during the past 2 months.

At the beginning of the most recent session, Angela, one of the group members, walks in late and is obviously intoxicated. Dr. Hernandez reminds Angela about the rule, noting that Angela must leave but will be welcome back at the next meeting if she is sober. Angela starts crying and begs to stay. Dr. Hernandez expresses sympathy and then restates the rule. Angela stands up and states that a drug dealer to whom she owes money has found out where she lives and she is afraid for her life. Then as she rushes out of the building, she tells the group, "You will all be sorry when I'm dead."

The other group members are obviously shaken by Angela's behavior. Some in the group feel Dr. Hernandez should end the group meeting and try to find Angela to make sure she is OK. Others think Dr. Hernandez should call the police. Still others in the group believe that Angela was trying to manipulate Dr. Hernandez into permitting her to break the rule. They note that in the past, she has tried to get around other group rules.

Ethical Dilemma

Dr. Hernandez does not know how best to handle this situation.

Discussion Questions

1. Why is this an ethical dilemma? Which APA Ethical Principles help frame the nature of the dilemma?
2. Who are the stakeholders, and how will they be affected by how Dr. Hernandez resolves this dilemma?
3. Does Dr. Hernandez have a professional responsibility for Angela's safety outside the group therapy context?

4. How should Dr. Hernandez immediately address the group members' concerns, keeping in mind that group members have voiced different opinions about the situation?
5. From a treatment perspective, how important is it for Dr. Hernandez to uphold the group's self-generated and agreed-upon rules regarding attendance while intoxicated? Do group members have the same confidentiality obligations as Dr. Hernandez?
6. What legal concerns should Dr. Hernandez consider?
7. How are APA Ethical Standards 2.01a, 2.01e, 4.01, 4.05, 4.06, 10.03, and 10.10 and the *Clinical Practice Guidelines for Group Psychotherapy* relevant to this dilemma? Which other standards might apply?
8. What are Dr. Hernandez's ethical alternatives for resolving this dilemma? Which alternative best reflects the Ethics Code aspirational principles and enforceable standards, legal standards, and obligations to stakeholders? Can you identify the ethical theory (discussed in Chapter 3) guiding your decision?
9. Is Angela's current situation one that Dr. Hernandez should have anticipated when she established group therapies designed to treat addiction and substance dependence? What steps should Dr. Hernandez take to ensure she is better prepared to ethically address similar situations in the future?

Suggested Readings

American Psychological Association. (2007). Guidelines for psychological practice with girls and women. *American Psychologist, 62*, 949–979.

Bernard, H., Burlingame, G., Flores, P., Greene, L., Joyce, A., Kobos, J. C., . . . American Group Psychotherapy Association. (2008). Clinical practice guidelines for group psychotherapy. *International Journal of Group Psychotherapy, 58*(4), 455–542.

Brabender, V. (2006). The ethical group psychotherapist. *International Journal of Group Psychotherapy, 56*(4), 395–414.

Lasky, G. B., & Riva, M. T. (2006). Confidentiality and privileged communication in group psychotherapy. *International Journal of Group Psychotherapy, 56*(4), 455–476.

Vannicelli, M. (2001). Leader dilemmas and countertransference considerations in group psychotherapy with substance abusers. *International Journal of Group Psychotherapy, 51*(1), 43–62.

References

Aardoom, J. J., Dingemans, A. E., Spinhoven, P., & Van Furth, E. F. (2013). Treating eating disorders over the Internet: A systematic review and future research directions. *International Journal of Eating Disorders, 46*(6), 539–552. doi: 10.1002/eat.22135

Accurso, E. C., Taylor, R. M., & Garland, A. F. (2011). Evidence-based practices addressed in community-based children's mental health clinical supervision. *Training and Education in Professional Psychology, 5*(2), 88–96.

Acuff, C., Bennett, B. E., Bricklin, P. M., Canter, M. B., Knapp, S. J., & Moldawsky, S. (1999). Considerations for ethical practice in managed care. *Professional Psychology: Research and Practice, 30*, 563–565.

Adkins, D. C. (1952). Proceedings of the sixteenth annual business meeting of the American Psychological Association, Inc., Washington, DC. *American Psychologist, 7*, 645–670.

Age Discrimination in Employment Amendments of 1996, Pub. L. No. 104-208, div. A, title I, §101(a) [title I, §119], 110 Stat. 3009 (1996).

Akins, C. K., & Panicker, S. (2012). Ethics and regulation of research with nonhuman animals. In H. Cooper, P. M. Camic, D. L. Long, A. T. Panter, D. Rindskopf, & K. J. Sher (Eds.), *APA handbook of research methods in psychology: Vol. 1. Foundations, planning, measures, and psychometrics* (pp. 75–82). Washington, DC: American Psychological Association.

Alderson, P., Sutcliffe, K., & Curtis, K. (2006). Children's competence to consent to medical treatment. *Hastings Center Report, 36*, 25–34.

Alleman, J. R. (2002). Online counseling: The Internet and mental health treatment. *Psychotherapy: Theory, Research, Practice, Training, 39*, 199–209.

Allen, A. (2013). Ethics in correctional and forensic psychology: Getting the balance right. *Australian Psychologist, 48*, 47–56.

Allen, P. D., Cherry, K. E., & Palmore, E. (2009). Self-reported ageism in social work practitioners and students. *Journal of Gerontological Social Work, 52*(2), 124–134.

Althouse, R. (2000). Standards for psychological services in jails, prisons, correctional facilities, and agencies. *Criminal Justice & Behavior, 27*, 433–494.

Ambwani, S., Cardi, V., & Treasure, J. (2014). Mobile self-help interventions for anorexia nervosa: Conceptual, ethical, and methodological considerations for clinicians and researchers. *Professional Psychology: Research and Practice*. doi:10.1037/a0036203

American Academy of Clinical Neuropsychology. (2001). Policy statement on the presence of third party observers in neuropsychological assessments. *The Clinical Neuropsychologist, 15*, 433–439.

American Academy of Clinical Neuropsychology. (2003). Official position of the American Academy of Clinical Neuropsychology on ethical complaints made against clinical neuropsychologists during adversarial proceedings. *The Clinical Neuropsychologist, 17*, 443–445.

American Educational Research Association, American Psychological Association, & National Council on Measurement in Education. (2014). *Standards for educational and psychological testing.* Washington, DC: American Educational Research Association.

American Psychiatric Association. (2003). *Practice guidelines for the assessment and treatment of patients with suicidal behavior.* Washington, DC: Author.

American Psychiatric Association. (2013). *Diagnostic and statistical manual of mental disorders* (5th ed.). Washington, DC: Author.

American Psychiatric Association & American Psychological Association. (1985). *Against torture: Joint resolution of the American Psychiatric Association and the American Psychological Association.* Retrieved from https://www.apa.org/news/press/statements/joint-resolution-against-torture.pdf

American Psychological Association. (1947). Committee on training in clinical psychology: Recommended graduate training program in clinical psychology. *American Psychologist, 2*(12), 539–558.

American Psychological Association. (1993). Guidelines for providers of psychological services to ethnic, linguistic, and culturally diverse populations. *American Psychologist, 48,* 45–48.

American Psychological Association. (1994). Guidelines for child custody evaluations in divorce proceedings. *American Psychologist, 49,* 677–680.

American Psychological Association. (2000). Guidelines for psychotherapy with lesbian, gay, & bisexual clients. *American Psychologist, 55,* 1440–1451.

American Psychological Association. (2001). *The death penalty in the United States.* Retrieved from http://www.apa.org/about/policy/death-penalty.aspx

American Psychological Association. (2002a). Criteria for evaluating treatment guidelines. *American Psychologist, 57,* 1052–1059.

American Psychological Association. (2002b). Ethical principles of psychologists and code of conduct. *American Psychologist, 57,* 1060–1073.

American Psychological Association. (2003). Guidelines on multicultural education, training, research, practice, and organizational change for psychologists. *American Psychologist, 58,* 377–402.

American Psychological Association. (2006). *Editor's handbook: Operating procedures and policies for APA publications.* (Available by request from http://www.apa.org/about/division/officers/handbook/index.aspx?item=9)

American Psychological Association. (2007a). Guidelines for education and training at the doctoral and postdoctoral levels in consulting psychology/organizational consulting psychology. *American Psychologist, 62,* 980–992.

American Psychological Association. (2007b). Guidelines for psychological practice with girls and women. *American Psychologist, 62,* 949–979.

American Psychological Association. (2007c). Recordkeeping guidelines. *American Psychologist, 62,* 992–1004.

American Psychological Association. (2007d, August 16). *Resolution on religious, religion-based, and/or religion-derived prejudice.* Retrieved from https://www.apa.org/about/policy/religious-discrimination.pdf

American Psychological Association. (2009). *Report of the task force on appropriate therapeutic responses to sexual orientation.* Washington, DC: American Psychological Association. https://www.apa.org/pi/lgbt/resources/therapeutic-response.pdf

American Psychological Association. (2010a). *American Psychological Association amends ethics code to address potential conflicts among professional ethics, legal authority and organizational demands.* Retrieved from http://www.apa.org/news/press/releases/2010/02/ethics-code.aspx

American Psychological Association. (2010b). *Comprehensive search guide: PsycINFO® search fields on PsycNET®*. (No longer available online; see http://www.apa.org/pubs/databases/psycinfo/index.aspx)

American Psychological Association. (2010c). *Ethical principles of psychologists and code of conduct with the 2010 amendments.* Retrieved from http://www.apa.org/ethics/code/

American Psychological Association. (2010d). Guidelines for child custody evaluations in family law proceedings. *American Psychologist, 65*(9), 863–867.

American Psychological Association. (2010e). *Publication manual of the American Psychological Association* (5th ed.). Washington, DC: Author.

American Psychological Association. (2011a). Practice guidelines regarding psychologists' involvement in pharmacological issues. *American Psychologist, 66,* 835–849.

American Psychological Association. (2011b). *Revised benchmarks competencies.* Retrieved from https://www.apa.org/ed/graduate/revised-competency-benchmarks.doc

American Psychological Association. (2012a). Guidelines for assessment of and intervention with persons with disabilities. *American Psychologist, 67,* 43–62.

American Psychological Association. (2012b). *Guidelines for ethical conduct in the care and use of nonhuman animals in research.* Retrieved from http://www.apa.org/science/leadership/care/care-animal-guidelines.pdf

American Psychological Association. (2012c). Guidelines for psychological practice with lesbian, gay and bisexual clients. *American Psychologist, 67,* 10–42.

American Psychological Association. (2012d). Guidelines for the evaluation of dementia and age-related cognitive change. *American Psychologist, 67,* 1–9.

American Psychological Association. (2012e). Guidelines for the practice of parenting coordination. *American Psychologist, 67,* 63–71.

American Psychological Association (2012f). *A practical guidebook for the competency benchmarks.* Washington, DC: APA Books.

American Psychological Association (2013a). *Competencies for psychological practice in primary care: Report of the Interorganizational Work Group on Competencies for Primary Care Psychology.* Retrieved from https://www.apa.org/ed/resources/competencies-practice.pdf

American Psychological Association. (2013b). Guidelines for psychological evaluations in child protection matters. *The American Psychologist, 68*(1), 20–31. doi:10.1037/a0029891

American Psychological Association (2013c). Guidelines for psychological practice in health care delivery systems. *American Psychologist, 68,* 1–6.

American Psychological Association (2013d). *Guidelines for the practice of telepsychology.* Retrieved from http://www.apapracticecentral.org/ce/guidelines/telepsychology-guidelines.pdf

American Psychological Association. (2013e). Specialty guidelines for forensic psychology. *American Psychologist, 68,* 7–19.

American Psychological Association. (2014). Guidelines for prevention in psychology. *American Psychologist, 69*(3), 285–96. doi:10.1037/a0034569

American Psychological Association. (2015a, November 25). *APA journals Internet posting guidelines.* Retrieved from http://www.apa.org/pubs/authors/posting.aspx

American Psychological Association. (2015b). *Guidelines for psychological practice with transgender and gender nonconforming people.* Retrieved from http://www.apa.org/practice/guidelines/transgender.pdf

American Psychological Association. (2015c). *Just the facts about sexual orientation & youth.* Retrieved from http://www.apa.org/pi/lgbt/resources/just-the-facts.aspx

American Psychological Association. (2015d). *Report to the special committee of the Board of Directors of the American Psychological Association: Independent review relating to the APA Ethics Guidelines, national security interrogations, and torture*. Retrieved from http://www.apa.org/independent-review/APA-FINAL-Report-7.2.15.pdf

American Psychological Association. (2015e). *Standards of accreditation for health service psychology*. Retrieved from http://www.apa.org/ed/accreditation/about/policies/standards-of-accreditation.pdf

American Psychological Association Committee on Animal Research and Ethics. (2012). *Guidelines for ethical conduct in the care and use of animals* [Brochure]. Retrieved from http://www.apa.org/science/anguide.html

American Psychological Association Committee on Colleague Assistance. (2006). *Advancing colleague assistance in professional psychology*. Retrieved from http://www.apa.org/practice/resources/assistance/monograph.pdf

American Psychological Association Committee on Legal Issues. (2006). Strategies for private practitioners coping with subpoenas or compelled testimony for client records or test data. *Professional Psychology: Research and Practice, 37*, 215–222.

American Psychological Association Council of Representatives. (1986). *American Psychological Association resolution against torture*. Retrieved from http://www.apa.org (no longer available online)

American Psychological Association Council of Representatives. (2006). *The resolution against torture and other cruel, inhuman, and degrading treatment or punishment*. Retrieved from http://www.apa.org/about/policy/torture-2006.aspx

American Psychological Association Data Sharing Working Group. (2015). *Data sharing: Principles and considerations for policy development*. Retrieved from http://www.apa.org/science/leadership/bsa/data-sharing-report.pdf

American Psychological Association Education Directorate (2013, July) *Preparing professional psychologists to serve a diverse public*. Retrieved from http://www.apa.org/ed/graduate/diversity-preparation.aspx

American Psychological Association Practice Organization. (2013). *Guidelines for the practice of telepsychology*. Retrieved from http://www.apa.org/practice/guidelines/telepsychology.aspx

American Psychological Association Presidential Task Force. (2005, February). *The report of the Presidential Task Force on Psychological Ethics and National Security (PENS)*. Washington, DC: American Psychological Association. Retrieved from https://www.apa.org/pubs/info/reports/pens.pdf

American Statistical Association. (1999). *Ethical guidelines for statistical practice*. Retrieved from http://www.amstat.org/about/ethicalguidelines.cfm

American Telemedicine Association. (2014). *Core operational guidelines for telehealth services involving provider-patient interactions*. Retrieved from http://www.americantelemed.org/docs/default-source/standards/core-operational-guidelines-for-telehealth-services.pdf?sfvrsn=6

American Veterinary Medical Association. (2007). *AVMA guidelines on euthanasia*. Retrieved from https://grants.nih.gov/grants/olaw/Euthanasia2007.pdf

Americans with Disabilities Act of 1990, Pub. L. No. 101-336, 104 Stat. 327, 42 U.S.C. §12101 *et seq*. (1990).

Anderson, B., & Simpson, M. (2007). Ethical issues in online education. *Open Learning, 22*, 129–138.

Anderson, E. E., Solomon, S., Heitman, E., Dubois, J. M., Fisher, C. B., Kost, R. G., . . . Friedman Ross, L. (2012). Research ethics education for community engaged research: A review and research agenda. *Journal of Empirical Research on Human Research Ethics, 7*, 3–19.

Anderson, S. K., & Handelsman, M. M. (2010). *Ethics for psychotherapists and counselors: A proactive approach.* Malden, MA: Wiley-Blackwell.

Anderson, S. K., & Handelsman, M. M. (2013). A Positive and Proactive Approach to the Ethics of the First Interview. *Journal of Contemporary Psychotherapy, 43*(1), 3–11. doi:10.1007/s10879-012-9219-3

Anderson, S. K., & Kitchener, K. S. (1996). Nonromantic, nonsexual posttherapy relationships between psychologists and former clients: An exploratory study of critical incidents. *Professional Psychology: Research and Practice, 27*, 59–66.

Anderson, S. K., Williams, P., & Kramer, A. L. (2012). Life and executive coaching: Some ethical issues. In M. Gottlieb, M. Handelsman, L. VandeCreek, & S. Knapp (Eds.), *Handbook of ethics in psychology* (Vol. 2, pp. 169–182). Washington, DC: American Psychological Association.

Andersson, L., King, R., & Lalande, L. (2010). Dialogical mindfulness in supervision role-play. *Counselling & Psychotherapy Research, 10*(4), 287–294.

Andover, M. S., Primack, J. M., Gibb, B. E., & Pepper, C. M. (2010). An examination of non-suicidal self-injury in men: Do men differ from women in basic NSSI characteristics? *Archives of Suicide Research, 14*(1), 79–88.

Anno, B. J. (2001). National correctional health standards. In J. B. Ashford, B. D. Sales, & W. H. Reid (Eds.), *Treating adult and juvenile offenders with special needs* (pp. 31–49). Thousand Oaks, CA: Sage.

Appelbaum, P. S. (2009). Decisional versus peformative capacities: Not exactly a new idea. *American Journal of Bioethics, 9*, 31–42.

Appelbaum, P. S., & Grisso, T. (2001). *MacArthur Competence Assessment Tool for Clinical Research (MacCAT-CR).* Sarasota, FL: Professional Resource Press.

Appelbaum, P. S., Lidz, W. L., & Grisso, T. (2004). Therapeutic misconception in clinical research: Frequency and risk factors. *IRB: Ethics & Human Research, 26*, 1–8.

Appelbaum, P. S., & Rosenbaum, A. (1989). *Tarasoff* and the researcher: Does the duty to protect apply in the research setting? *American Psychologist, 44*(6), 885–894.

Appelbaum, P. S., Roth, L. H., & Lidz, C. (1982). The therapeutic misconception: Informed consent in psychiatric research. *International Journal of Law and Psychiatry, 5*, 319–329.

Aronson, H. (2006). Treating "the poor": Classism or a rigid loyalty to theory? Comment. *American Psychologist, 61*(4), 335–336.

Arredondo, P. (1999). Multicultural competencies as tools to address oppression and racism. *Journal of Counseling and Development, 77*, 102–108.

Arredondo, P., & Toporek, R. (2004). Multicultural counseling competencies = ethical practice. *Journal of Mental Health Counseling, 26*(1), 44–55.

Atkins v. Virginia, 536 U.S. 304 (2002).

Austin, W. G., Kirkpatrick, H. D., & Flens, J. R. (2011). The emerging forensic role for work product review and case analysis in child access and parenting plan disputes. *Family Court Review, 49*(4), 737–749.

Backhaus, A., Agha, Z., Maglione, M. L., Repp, A., Ross, B., Zuest, D., & Thorp, S. R. (2012). Videoconferencing psychotherapy: A systematic review. *Psychological Services, 9*, 111–131. doi:10.1037/a0027924

Baeroe, K. (2010). Patient autonomy, assessment of competence and surrogate decision-making: A call for reasonableness in deciding for others. *Bioethics, 24*(2), 87–95.

Baier, A. (1985). What do women want in a moral theory? *Nous, 19*, 53–63.

Baird, B. N. (2014). *The internship, practicum, and field placement handbook: A guide for the helping professions* (7th ed.). New York, NY: Routledge.

Baker, D. C., & Bufka, L. F. (2011). Preparing for the telehealth world: Navigating legal regulatory reimbursement, and ethical issues in an electronic age. *Professional Psychology: Research and Practice, 42*(6), 405–411.

Baker, S. C., & Serdikoff, S. L. (2013). Addressing the role of animal research in psychology. *Controversy in the psychology classroom: Using hot topics to foster critical thinking,* 105–112. doi:10.1037/14038-007

Bamonti, P. M., Keelan, C. M., Larson, N., Mentrikoski, J. M., Randall, C. L., Sly, S. K., . . . McNeil, D. W. (2014). Promoting ethical behavior by cultivating a culture of self-care during graduate training: A call to action. *Training and Education in Professional Psychology, 8*(4), 253–260.

Barak, A., & English, N. (2002). Prospects and limitations of psychological testing on the Internet. *Journal of Technology in Human Services, 19,* 65–89.

Barenbaum, N. B., & Winter, D. G. (2013). Personality. In D. K. Freedheim & I. B. Weiner (Eds.), *Handbook of psychology: Vol. 1. History of psychology* (pp. 198–223). New York, NY: Wiley.

Barlow, D. H. (2010). Negative effects from psychological treatments: A perspective. *American Psychologist, 65*(1), 13–20.

Barnett, J. E. (2008). Impaired professionals: Distress, professional impairment, self-care, and psychological wellness. In M. Herson & A. M. Gross (Eds.), *Handbook of clinical psychology* (Vol. 1, pp. 857–884). New York, NY: John Wiley.

Barnett, J. E., Baker, E. K., Elman, N. S., & Schoener, G. R. (2007). In pursuit of wellness: The self-care imperative. *Professional Psychology: Research and Practice, 38*(6), 603–612. doi:10.1037/0735-7028.38.6.603

Barnett, J. E., & Cooper, N. (2009). Creating a culture of self-care. *Clinical Psychology: Science and Practice, 16*(1), 16–20.

Barnett, J. E., Cornish, J. A. E., Goodyear, R. K., & Lichtenberg, J. W. (2007). Commentaries on the ethical and effective practice of clinical supervision. *Professional Psychology: Research and Practice, 38,* 268–275.

Barnett, J. E., & Hillard, D. (2001). Psychologist distress and impairment: The availability, nature, and use of colleague assistance programs for psychologists. *Professional Psychology: Research and Practice, 32,* 205–210.

Barnett, J. E., & Molzon, C. H. (2014). Clinical supervision of psychotherapy: Essential ethics issues for supervisors and supervisees. *Journal of Clinical Psychology: In Session, 70*(11), 1051–1061. doi:10.1002/jclp.22126

Barnett, J. E., & Walfish, S. (2011). *Billing and collecting for your mental health practice.* Washington, DC: American Psychological Association.

Barnett, J. E., & Walfish, S. (2012). The ethics of billing, collecting, and financial arrangements: A working framework for clinicians. In J. E. Barnett & S. Walfish (Eds.), *Billing and collecting for your mental health practice* (pp. 7–25). Washington, DC: American Psychological Association.

Barnett, J. E., Zimmerman, J., & Walfish, S. (2014) *The ethics of private practice: A practical guide for mental health clinicians.* New York, NY: Oxford University Press.

Barry, C. T., Golmaryami, F. N., Rivera-Hudson, N., & Frick, P. J. (2013). Evidence-based assessment of conduct disorder: Current considerations and preparation for DSM-5. *Professional Psychology: Research and Practice, 44*(1), 56–63. doi:10.1037/a0029202

Bartol, C. R., & Bartol, A. M. (2014). *Current perspectives in forensic psychology and criminal behavior* (4th ed.). Thousand Oaks, CA: Sage.

Baumrind, D. (1964). Some thoughts on ethics of research: After reading Milgram's "Behavioral study of obedience." *American Psychologist, 26,* 887–896.

Baumrind, D. (1985). Research using intentional deception: Ethical issues revisited. *American Psychologist, 40,* 165–174.

Beach, S. H., Lei, M., Brody, G. H., Simons, R. L., Cutrona, C., & Philibert, R. A. (2012). Genetic moderation of contextual effects on negative arousal and parenting in African-American parents. *Journal of Family Psychology, 26*(1), 46–55.

Bearse, J. L., McMinn, M. R., Seegobin, W., & Free, K. (2013). Barriers to psychologists seeking mental health care. *Professional Psychology: Research and Practice, 44*(3), 150–157. doi:10.1037/a0031182

Beauchamp, T. L., & Childress, J. F. (2001). *Principles of biomedical ethics* (5th ed.). New York, NY: Oxford University Press.

Beck, A. T., Steer, R. A., & Brown, G. K. (1996). *The Beck Depression Inventory second edition (BDI-II).* San Antonio, TX: Psychological Corporation.

Beebe, L. H., & Smith, K. (2010). Describing research informed consent in persons with schizophrenia spectrum disorders (SSDs): Responses and correlates. *Nursing Ethics, 17,* 425–434.

Begley, A. M. (2006). Facilitating the development of moral insight in practice: Teaching ethics and teaching virtue. *Nursing Philosophy, 7,* 257–265.

Behnke, S. (2007). Ethics and the Internet: Requesting clinical consultations over listservs. *Monitor on Psychology, 38*(7), 62. Retrieved from http://www.apa.org/monitor/julaug07/ethics.aspx

Belar, C. D. (2014). Reflections on the health service psychology education collaborative blueprint. *Training and Education in Professional Psychology, 8,* 3–11. http://dx.doi.org/10.1037/tep0000027

Belsky, J., & Pluess, M. (2009). Beyond diathesis stress: Differential susceptibility to environmental influences. *Psychological Bulletin, 135*(6), 885–908.

Benjamin, L. T., & Simpson, J. A. (2009). The power of the situation: The impact of Milgram's obedience studies on personality and social psychology. *American Psychologist, 64,* 12–19.

Bennett, B. E., Bricklin, P. M., Harris, E., Knapp, S., VandeCreek, L., & Younggren, J. N. (2006). *Assessing and managing risk in psychological practice: An individualized approach.* Rockville, MD: The Trust.

Ben-Porath, Y. S. (1994). The ethical dilemma of coached malingering research. *Psychological Assessment, 6,* 14–15.

Berenson, R. A., & Rich, E. C. (2010). US approaches to physician payment: The deconstruction of primary care. *Journal of General Internal Medicine, 25*(6), 613–618.

Berke, D. M., Rozell, C. A., Hogan, T. P., Norcross, J. C., & Karpiak, C. P. (2011). What clinical psychologists know about evidence-based practice: Familiarity with online resources and research methods. *Journal of Clinical Psychology, 67*(4), 329–339.

Bernat, J. L. (2013). Ethical and quality pitfalls in electronic health records. *Neurology, 80*(11), 1057–1061.

Berry, D. T. R., Lamb, G. L., Wetter, M. W., Baier, R. A., & Widiger, T. A. (1994). Ethical considerations in research on coached malingering. *Psychological Assessment, 6,* 16–17.

Bersoff, D. N. (1976). Therapists as protectors and policemen: New roles as a result of *Tarasoff? Professional Psychology: Research and Practice, 7,* 267–273.

Bersoff, D. N. (1994). Explicit ambiguity: The 1992 ethics code as an oxymoron. *Professional Psychology: Research and Practice, 25,* 382–387.

Bersoff, D. N., DeMatteo, D., & Foster, E. E. (2012). Assessment and testing. In M. Gottlieb, M. Handelsman, L. VandeCreek, & S. Knapp (Eds.), *Handbook of ethics in psychology* (Vol. 2, pp. 45–74). Washington, DC: American Psychological Association.

Beskow, L. M., & Burke, W. (2009). Ethical issues in genetic epidemiology. In S. S. Coughlin, T. L. Beauchamp, & D. L. Weed (Eds.), *Ethics and epidemiology* (2nd ed., pp. 182–103). New York, NY: Oxford University Press.

Beskow, L. M., Dame, L., & Costello, J. (2008). Certificates of confidentiality and the compelled disclosure of research data. *Science, 14,* 1054–1055. doi:10.1126/science.1164100

Bethea, M. S., & McCollum, E. E. (2013). The disclosure experiences of male-to-female transgender individuals: A systems theory perspective. *Journal of Couple and Relationship Therapy, 12,* 89–112.

Beutler, L. E., Blatt, S. J., Alimohamed, S., Levy, K. N., & Angtuaco, L. (2006). Participant factors in treating dysphoric disorders. In L. G. Castonguay & L. E. Beutler (Eds.), *Principles of therapeutic change that work* (pp. 13–63). New York, NY: Oxford University Press.

Bike, D. S., Norcross, J. C., & Schatz, D. (2009). Processes and outcomes of psychotherapists' personal therapy: Replication and extension 20 years later. *Psychotherapy: Theory, Research, Practice, Training, 46*(1), 19–31.

Bioethics Advisory Committee. (2005). *Genetic testing and genetic research.* Singapore: The Bioethics Advisory Committee. Retrieved from http://www.bioethics-singapore.org/images/uploadfile/55211%20PMGT%20Research.pdf

Birgden, A., & Perlin, M. L. (2009). "Where the home in the valley meets the damp dirty prison": A human rights perspective on therapeutic jurisprudence and the role of forensic psychologists in correctional settings. *Aggression and Violent Behavior, 14*(4), 256–263.

Bixler, R., & Seeman, J. (1946). Suggestions for a code of ethics for consulting psychologists. *Journal of Abnormal Psychology, 41,* 486–490.

Bloom, J. R., Wang, H., Kang, S., Wallace, N. T., Hyun, J. K., & Hu, T. (2011). Capitation of public mental health services in Colorado: A five-year follow-up of system-level effects. *Psychiatric Services, 62*(2), 179–185.

Bluebond-Langner, M., DiCicco, A., & Belasco, J. (2005). Involving children with life-shortening illnesses in decisions about participation in clinical research: A proposal for shuttle diplomacy and negotiation. In E. Kodish (Ed.), *Ethics and research with children: A case-based approach* (pp. 323–343). New York, NY: Oxford University Press.

Bongar, B., Beutler, L., Zimbardo, P., Breckenridge, J., Brown, L., Sullivan, G., & Crawford, E. (2002). *Behavioral emergencies update: Psychology & terrorism.* Retrieved from http://topmdi.com/cerita/war/Psychology.of.Terrorism.pdf

Bordnick, P. S., Elkins, R. L., Orr, T. E., Walters, P., & Thyer, B. A. (2004). Evaluating the relative effectiveness of three aversion therapies designed to reduce craving among cocaine abusers. *Behavioral Interventions, 19,* 1–24.

Brabeck, K., Lykes, M. B., Sibley, E., & Kene, P. (2015). Ethical ambiguities in participatory action research with unauthorized migrants. *Ethics & Behavior, 25*(1), 21–36.

Brabeck, M. (Ed.). (2000). *Practicing feminist ethics in psychology.* Washington, DC: American Psychological Association.

Brabeck, M. M., & Brabeck, K. M. (2012). Feminist and multicultural ethics in counseling psychology. In E. N. Williams & C. Z. Enns (Eds.), *The Oxford handbook of feminist multicultural counseling psychology.* New York, NY: Oxford University Press.

Brabender, V., & Fallon, A. (2009). *Group development in practice: Guidance for clinicians and researchers on stages and dynamics of change.* Washington, DC: American Psychological Association.

Branaman, T. F., & Gottlieb, M. C. (2013). Ethical and legal considerations for treatment of alleged victims: When does it become witness tampering? *Professional Psychology: Research and Practice, 44*(5), 299–306. doi:10.1037/a0033020

Braun, S. A., & Cox, J. A. (2005). Managed mental health care: Intentional misdiagnosis of mental disorders. *Journal of Counseling and Development, 83,* 425–433.

Brey, P. (2006). Social and ethical dimensions of computer-mediated education. *Journal of Information, Communication and Ethics in Society, 41,* 91–101.

Brodsky, S. L. (2013). Knowing when to fold them. In *Testifying in court: Guidelines and maxims for the expert witness* (2nd ed., pp. 107–110). Washington, DC: American Psychological Association. doi:10.1016/S0026-0576(08)80337-6

Brodsky, S. L., & Galloway, V. A. (2003). Ethical and professional demands for forensic mental health professionals in the post-Atkins era. *Ethics & Behavior, 13,* 3–9.

Brodsky, S. L., & Gutheil, T. G. (2016). Ethics in expert testimony. In S. L. Brodsky & T. G. Gutheil (Eds.), *The expert expert witness: More maxims and guidelines for testifying in court* (2nd ed., pp 44–48). Washington, DC: American Psychological Association.

Brodsky, S. L., & Titcomb, C. (2013). Treating reluctant and involuntary clients. In G. P. Koocher, J. C. Norcross, & B. A. Greene (Eds.), *Psychologist's desk reference* (3rd ed., pp. 197–202). New York, NY: Oxford University Press.

Brody, G. H., Chen, Y., Beach, S. R. H., Philibert, R. A., & Kogan, S. M. (2009). Participation in a family-centered prevention program decreases genetic risk for adolescents' risky behaviors. *Pediatrics, 124*(3), 911–917.

Broome, M. E., Kodish, E., Geller, G., & Siminoff, L. A. (2003). Children in research: New perspectives and practices for informed consent. *IRB: Ethics & Human Research, 25*(Suppl. 5), S20–S25.

Brotman, L. E., Liberi, W. P., & Wasylyshyn, K. M. (1998). Executive coaching: The need for standards of competence. *Consulting Psychology Journal: Practice and Research, 50,* 40–46.

Brown v. Board of Education, 347 U.S. 483 (1954).

Brownlee, K. (1996). Ethics in community mental health care: The ethics of non-sexual dual relationships; A dilemma for the rural mental health profession. *Community Mental Health Journal, 32,* 497–503.

Bruzzese, J. M., & Fisher, C. B. (2003). Assessing and enhancing the research consent capacity of children and youth. *Applied Developmental Science, 7,* 13–26.

Buchanan, T. (2002). Online assessment: Desirable or dangerous? *Professional Psychology: Research and Practice, 33,* 138–154.

Bull, R. (2015). The impact of personal expectations and biases in preparing expert testimony. In R. J. Sternberg & S. T. Fiske (Eds.), *Ethical challenges in the behavioral and brain sciences: Case studies and commentaries* (pp. 200–201). Cambridge, UK: Cambridge University Press.

Burian, B. K., & Slimp, A. O. (2000). Social dual-role relationships during internship: A decision-making model. *Professional Psychology: Research and Practice, 31,* 332–338.

Burkholder, D., & Burkholder, J. (2014). Reasons for ethical misconduct of counseling students: What do faculty think? *Journal of Counselor Preparation and Supervision, 6*(2), 35–51.

Burnette, A. T., & Padmanabhan, S. (2014). Tips and tactics for transmitting PHI by email. *AHLA Connections,* 16–21.

Burns, M. K., Parker, D. C., & Jacob, S. (2013). Legal issues in school psychological assessments. In K. F. Geisinger (Ed.), *APA handbook of testing and assessment in psychology* (pp. 259–277). Washington, DC: American Psychological Association.

Bush, S. S. (2006). Neurocognitive enhancement: Ethical considerations for an emerging subspeciality. *Applied Neuropsychology, 13,* 125–136.

Bush, S. S. (2010). Determining whether or when to adopt new versions of psychological and neuropsychological tests: Ethical and professional considerations. *The Clinical Neuropsychologist, 24,* 7–16.

Bush, S. S., Connell, M. A., & Denney, R. L. (2006). *Ethical practice in forensic psychology: A systematic model for decision-making.* Washington, DC: American Psychological Association.

Butcher, J. N. (2000). Revising psychological tests: Lessons learned from revisions of the MMPI. *Psychological Assessment, 12,* 263–271.

Butcher, J. N., Dahlstrom, W. G., Graham, J. R., Tellegen, A., & Kaemmer, B. (2002). *Minnesota Multiphasic Personality Inventory (MMPI-2): Manual for administration, scoring, and interpretation* (Rev. ed.). Minneapolis: University of Minnesota Press.

Butcher, J. N., Hass, G. A., Greene, R. L., & Nelson, L. D. (2015). Importance of assessing response attitudes in forensic evaluations. In J. N. Butcher, G. A. Hass, R. L. Greene, & L. D. Nelson (Eds.), *Using the MMPI-2 for forensic assessment* (pp. 27–47). Washington, DC: American Psychological Association.

Byczkowski, T. L., Kollar, L. M., & Britto, M. T. (2010). Family experiences with outpatient care: Do adolescents and parents have the same perceptions? *Journal of Adolescent Health, 47*(1), 92–98.

Call, J. A., Pfefferbaum, B., Jenuwine, M. J., & Flynn, B. W. (2012). Practical legal and ethical considerations for the provision of acute disaster mental health services. *Psychiatry, 75*(4), 305–22. doi:10.1521/psyc.2012.75.4.305

Callahan, D. (1982). Should there be an academic code of ethics? *Journal of Higher Education, 53,* 335–344.

Campbell, L. F. (2014). Ethical implications of complexities in diversity: Response to Hancock. *Psychology of Sexual Orientation and Gender Diversity, 1*(2), 112–113.

Candilis, P. J., & Neal, T. M. S. (2014). Not just welfare over justice: Ethics in forensic consultation. *Legal and Criminological Psychology, 19,* 19–29.

Canter, M. B., Bennett, B. E., Jones, S. E., & Nagy, T. F. (1994). *Ethics for psychologists: A commentary on the APA ethics code.* Washington, DC: American Psychological Association.

Carey, B. (2012, May 19). Psychiatry giant sorry for backing gay "cure." *The New York Times,* pp. 1, 3.

Carone, D. A., Bush, S. S., & Iverson, G. L. (2013). Providing feedback on symptom validity, mental health, and treatment in mild traumatic brain injury. In D. A. Carone & S. S. Bush (Eds.), *Mild traumatic brain injury: Symptom validity assessment and malingering* (pp. 101–117). New York, NY: Springer.

Carpenter, W. R., Gold, J. M., Lahti, A. C., Queern, C. A., Conley, R. R., Bartko, J. J., . . . Appelbaum, P. S. (2000). Decisional capacity for informed consent in schizophrenia research. *Archives of General Psychiatry, 57*(6), 533–538.

Carr, M. L., Goranson, A. C., & Drummond, D. J. (2014). Stalking of the mental health professional: Reducing risk and managing stalking behavior by patients. *Journal of Threat Assessment and Management, 1,* 4–22.

Cassidy, B. (2013). Uncovering values-based practice: VBP's implicit commitment to subjectivism and relativism. *Journal of Evaluation in Clinical Practice,* 19, 547–552.

Castonguay, L. G., Boswell, J. F., Constantino, M. J., Goldfried, M. R., & Hill, C. E. (2010). Training implications of harmful effects of psychological treatments. *American Psychologist, 65*(1), 34–49.

Cea, C., & Fisher, C. B. (2003). Health care decision-making by adults with mental retardation. *Mental Retardation, 41,* 78–87.

Cellini, N., & Parma, V. (2015). Commentary: Olfactory aversive conditioning during sleep reduces cigarette smoking behavior. *Frontiers in Psychology, 6,* 13.

Centers for Disease Control and Prevention. (2015). *Elimination of mother-to-child HIV transmission (EMCT) in the United States.* Retrieved from http://www.cdc.gov/hiv/group/gender/pregnantwomen/emct.html

Cervantes, R. C., Goldbach, J. T., Varela, A., & Santisteban, D. A. (2014). Self-harm among Hispanic adolescents: Investigating the role of culture-related stressors. *Journal of Adolescent Health, 55,* 633–639.

Chafetz, M. D. (2010). Symptom validity issues in the psychological consultative examination for Social Security Disability. *The Clinical Neuropsychologist, 24*(6), 1045–1063.

Cheng, S., & Powell, B. (2015). Measurement, methods, and divergent patterns: Reassessing the effects of same-sex parents. *Social Science Research, 52,* 615–616.

Chenneville, T. (2000). HIV, confidentiality, and duty to protect: A decision-making model. *Professional Psychology: Research and Practice, 31,* 661–670.

Chenneville, T., Sibille, K., & Bendell-Estroff, D. (2010). Decisional capacity among minors with HIV: A model for balancing autonomy rights with the need for protection. *Ethics & Behavior, 20*(2), 83–94.

Child Abuse Prevention and Treatment Act of 1976, Pub. L. No. 93-247.

Childs, R. A., & Eyde, L. D. (2002). Assessment training in clinical psychology doctoral programs: What should we teach? *Journal of Personality Assessment, 78,* 130–144.

Christopher, J., Christopher, S. E., Dunnagan, T., & Schure, M. (2006). Teaching self-care through mindfulness practices: The application of yoga, meditation, and qigong to counselor training. *Journal of Humanistic Psychology, 46*(4), 494–509.

Christopher, J., & Maris, J. A. (2010). Integrating mindfulness as self-care into counselling and psychotherapy training. *Counselling & Psychotherapy Research, 10*(2), 114–125.

Civil Rights Act of 1964, Pub. L. No. 88-352, 42 U.S.C. § 2000d (1964).

Cohen, D. J., & Cicchetti, D. (2006). *Developmental psychopathology.* New York, NY: John Wiley.

Colbow, A. J. (2013). Looking to the future: Integrating telemental health therapy into psychologist training. *Training and Education in Professional Psychology, 7*(3), 155–165. doi:10.1037/a0033454

Coleman, E., Bockting, W., Botzer, M., Cohen-Kettenis, P., DeCuypere, G., et al. (2012). Standards of care for the health of transsexual, transgender, and gender nonconforming people, 7th version. *International Journal of Transgenderism, 13,* 165–232.

Combs, D. R., Penn, D. L., & Fenigstein, A. (2002). Ethnic differences in subclinical paranoia: An expansion of norms of the Paranoia Scale. *Cultural Diversity & Ethnic Minority Psychology, 8,* 248–256.

Condie, L., & Koocher, G. P. (2008). Clinical management of children's incomplete comprehension of confidentiality limits. *Journal of Child Custody: Research, Issues, and Practices, 5*(3–4), 161–191.

Consolidated Appropriations Act, 2008, Pub. L. No. 110-161, § 218 (2008).

Cooper, S. E., & Cody, N. (2015). Consultants' use of telepractice: Practitioner survey, issues, and resources. *Consulting Psychology Journal: Practice & Research, 67,* 85–89.

Corely, M. C. (2002). Nurse moral distress: A proposed theory and research agenda. *Nursing Ethics, 9,* 636–650.

Cornell University Law School, Legal Information Institute. (2007). *Employment discrimination.* Retrieved from http://www.law.cornell.edu/wex/index.php/Employment_discrimination/

Cornish, J. A. E., & Monson, S. P. (2014). Supervision and disabilities. In C. A. Falender, E. P. Shafranske, & C. J. Falicov (Eds.), *Multiculturalism and diversity in clinical supervision: A competency-based approach* (pp. 163–180). Washington, DC: American Psychological Association.

Costanzo, M., & Krauss, D. (2012). *Forensic and legal psychology: Psychological science applied to law.* New York, NY: Worth.

Council of National Psychological Associations for the Advancement of Ethnic Minority Interests. (2000). *Guidelines for research in ethnic minority communities.* Washington, DC: American Psychological Association.

Courtois, C. A. (2015). First, do no more harm: Ethics of attending to spiritual issues in trauma treatment. In D. F. Walker, C. A. Courtois, & J. D. Aten (Eds.), *Spiritually oriented psychotherapy for trauma* (pp. 55–75). Washington, DC: American Psychological Association. doi:10.1037/14500-000

Cramer, R. J., Golom, F. D., LoPresto, C. T., & Kirkley, S. M. (2008). Weighing the evidence: Empirical assessment and ethical implications of conversion therapy. *Ethics & Behavior, 18,* 93–114.

Crowley, J. D., & Gottlieb, M. C. (2012). Objects in the mirror are closer than they appear: A primary prevention model for ethical decision making. *Professional Psychology: Research and Practice, 43*(1), 65–72.

Cunningham, M. D., & Reidy, T. J. (2002). Violence risk assessment at federal capital sentencing: Individualization, generalization, relevance and scientific standards. *Criminal Justice and Behavior, 29*(5), 512–537.

Cunningham, M. D., & Tassé, M. J. (2010). Looking to science rather than convention in adjusting IQ scores when death is at issue. *Professional Psychology: Research and Practice, 41*(5), 413–419.

Dailor, A. N., & Jacob, S. (2011). Ethically challenging situations reported by school psychologists: Implications for training. *Psychology in the Schools, 48*(6), 619–631.

D'Amico, E., & Julien, D. (2012). Disclosure of sexual orientation and gay, lesbian, and bisexual youths' adjustment: Associations with past and current parental acceptance and rejection. *Journal of GLBT Family Studies, 8*(3), 215–242. doi:10.1080/1550428X.2012.677232

D'Amour, D., & Oandasan, I. (2005). Interprofessionality as the field of interprofessional practice and interprofessional education: An emerging concept. *Journal of Interprofessional Care, 19*(Suppl. 1), 8–20.

D'Andrea, M., & Daniels, J. (2010). Promoting multiculturalism, democracy, and social justice in organizational settings: A case study. In J. G. Ponterotto, J. M. Casas, L. A. Suzuki, & C. M. Alexander (Eds.), *Handbook of multicultural counseling* (3rd ed., pp. 165–188). Thousand Oaks, CA: Sage.

Daniels, D., & Jenkins, P. (2010). *Therapy with children: Children's rights, confidentiality and the law* (2nd ed.). Thousand Oaks, CA: Sage.

Daniels, J. A., & Larson, L. M. (2001). The impact of performance feedback on counseling self-efficacy and counselor anxiety. *Counselor Education & Supervision, 41,* 120–130.

Dar-Nimrod, I., & Heine, S. J. (2011). Genetic essentialism: On the deceptive determinism of DNA. *Psychological Bulletin, 137*(5), 800–818.

Daubert v. Merrell Dow Pharmaceuticals, Inc., 509 U.S. 579 (1993).

David, E. J. R., Okazaki, S., & Giroux, D. (2014). A set of guiding principles to advance multicultural psychology and its major concepts. *APA Handbook of Multicultural Psychology: Vol. 1. Theory & Research* (pp. 85–104). Washington, DC: APA Books.

Davis, D. D., & Younggren, J. N. (2009). Ethical competence in psychotherapy termination. *Professional Psychology: Research and Practice, 40*(6), 572–578.

Davis, D. M., & Hayes, J. A. (2011). What are the benefits of mindfulness? A practice review of psychotherapy-related research. *Psychotherapy, 48*(2), 198–208.

de Montjoye, Y. A., Radaelli, L., Singh, V. K., & Pentland, A. (2015). Unique in the shopping mall: On the reidentifiability of credit card metadata. *Science, 347*(6221), 536–539.

Deidan, C., & Bush, S. S. (2002). Addressing perceived ethical violations by colleagues. In S. S. Bush & M. L. Drexler (Eds.), *Ethical issues in clinical neuropsychology* (pp. 81–305). Lisse, Netherlands: Swes & Zeitlinger.

DeLeon, P. H., Sells, J. R., Cassidy, O., Waters, A. J., & Kasper, C. E. (2015). Health policy: Timely and interdisciplinary. *Training and Education in Professional Psychology, 9*(2), 121–127. doi:10.1037/tep0000077

DeMatteo, D., Murrie, D. C., Anumba, N. M., & Keesler, M. E. (2011). *Forensic mental health assessments in death penalty cases.* New York, NY: Oxford University Press.

Denney, R. L. (2012). Criminal responsibility and other criminal forensic issues. In G. Larrabee (Ed.), *Forensic neuropsychology: A scientific approach* (2nd ed., pp. 473–500). New York, NY: Oxford University Press.

Denney, R. L., & Wynkoop, T. F. (2000). Clinical neuropsychology in the criminal forensic setting. *Journal of Head Trauma Rehabilitation, 15,* 804–828.

Denny, R. T. (2014). Abuse hotline does not create a duty to victim. *Litigation News, 39*(4), 25.

Department of Health and Human Services. (2009). *HIPAA Administrative Simplification: Enforcement 5 CFR Part 160.* Washington, DC: Government Printing Office, author. Retrieved from http://www.hhs.gov/sites/default/files/ocr/privacy/hipaa/administrative/enforcementrule/enfifr.pdf

Department of Health and Human Services. (2009). *Title 45 Public Welfare, Part 46, Code of Federal Regulations, Protection of Human Subjects.* Washington, DC: Government Printing Office. Retrieved from http://www.hhs.gov/ohrp/policy/ohrpregulations.pdf

Department of Health and Human Services. (2013). *Omnibus rule.* Washington, DC: Government Printing Office, author. Retrieved from http://www.hhs.gov/news/press/2013pres/01/20130117b.html

Department of Health and Human Services. (2014). *Draft guidance on disclosing reasonably foreseeable risks in research evaluating standards of care.* Washington, DC: Government Printing Office, author. Retrieved January 5, 2015, from http://www.hhs.gov/ohrp/newsroom/rfc/comstdofcare.html

Department of Health and Human Services Secretary's Advisory Committee on Human Research Protections (SACHRP). (2013). *Attachment B: Considerations and recommendations concerning Internet research and human subjects research regulations with revisions.* Washington, DC: Government Printing Office, author. Retrieved from http://www.hhs.gov/ohrp/sachrp/commsecbytopic/Internet%20Research/may20,2013,attachmentb.html

Derry, S. J., Pea, R. D., Barron, B., Engle, R. A., Erickson, F., Goldman, R., . . . Sherin, B. L. (2010). Conducting video research in the learning sciences: Guidance on selection, analysis, technology, and ethics. *Journal of the Learning Sciences, 19*(1), 3–53.

Devereaux, R. L., & Gottlieb, M. C. (2012). Record keeping in the cloud: Ethical considerations. *Professional Psychology: Research and Practice, 43*(6), 627–632. doi:10.1037/a0028268

Dewsbury, D. A. (1990). Early interactions between animal psychologists and animal activists and the founding of the APA committee on precautions in animal experimentation. *American Psychologist, 45*(3), 315–327.

Dickens v. Johnson County Board of Education, 661 F. Supp. 155 (E.D. Tenn. 1987).

Dickert, N., & Sugarman, J. (2005). Ethical goals of community consultation in research. *American Journal of Public Health, 95*(7), 1123–1127.

Diedrich, R. C. (2008). Still more about coaching. *Consulting Psychology Journal: Practice and Research, 60*, 4–6.

Dieter, R. C. (2011). *United Nations Human Rights Day is December 10th, 2011*. Retrieved from www.deathpenaltyinfo.org/Oxfordpaper.pdf

Dillon, S. (2010, January 31). Obama to seek sweeping change in "No Child" law. *The New York Times*. p. A1.

Dimeff, L. A., Rizvi, S. L., Contreras, I. S., Skutch, J. M., & Carroll, D. (2011). The mobile revolution and the DBT coach. *The Behavior Therapist, 34*(6), 104–110.

Dimidjian, S., & Hollon, S. D. (2010). How would we know if psychotherapy were harmful? *American Psychologist, 65*(1), 21–33.

Dobmeyer, A. C. (2013). Primary care behavioral health: Ethical issues in military settings. *Families, Systems, & Health: The Journal of Collaborative Family Health Care, 31*(1), 60–68.

Doka, K. (2008). Disenfranchised grief in historical and cultural perspective. In M. Stroebe, R. Hansson, H. Schut, & W. Stroebe (Eds.), *Handbook of bereavement research and practice* (pp. 223–240). Washington, DC: American Psychological Association.

Doll, B., Strein, W., Jacob, S., & Prasse, D. P. (2011). Youth privacy when educational records include psychological records. *Professional Psychology: Research and Practice, 42*(3), 259–268.

Dombo, E. A., Kays, L., & Weller, K. (2014). Clinical social work practice and technology: Personal, practical, regulatory, and ethical considerations for the twenty-first century. *Social Work in Health Care, 53*, 900–919. doi:10.1080/00981389.2014.948585

Dovidio, J. F., & Gaertner, S. L. (2004). Aversive racism. In M. P. Zanna (Ed.), *Advances in experimental social psychology* (Vol. 36, pp. 1–52). San Diego, CA: Elsevier Academic Press.

Drogin, E. Y., Connell, M., Foote, W. E., & Sturm, C. A. (2010). The American Psychological Association's revised "Record Keeping Guidelines": Implications for the practitioner. *Professional Psychology: Research and Practice, 41*(3), 236–243.

DuBois, J., Baily-Church, B., Bustillos, D., Campbell, J., Cottler, L., Fisher, C. B., . . . Stevenson, R. D. (2011). Reviewing the ethical, regulatory and scientific case for engaging communities in mental health and drug addiction research. *Current Opinions in Psychiatry, 24*, 208–214.

Duffy, M. (2010). Writing about clients: Developing composite case material and its rationale. *Counseling and Values, 54*(2), 135–153.

Dunn, L. B., Nowrangi, M. A., Palmer, B. A., Jeste, D. V., & Saks, E. R. (2006). Assessing decisional capacity for clinical research or treatment: A review of instruments. *American Journal of Psychiatry, 163*, 1323–1334.

Dworkin, R. (1977). *Taking rights seriously*. Cambridge, MA: Harvard University Press.

Education for All Handicapped Children Act of 1975, Pub. L. No. 94-142 (1975).

Edwards, L. M., & Sullivan, A. L. (2014). School psychology in rural contexts: Ethical, professional, and legal issues. *Journal of Applied School Psychology, 30*, 254–277. doi:10.1080/15377903.2014.924455

Eisner, D. A. (2010). Expert witness mental health testimony: Handling deposition and trial traps. *American Journal of Forensic Psychology, 28*(1), 47–65.

Ellis, E. M. (2012). When are MMPI-2 test results considered "outdated" for use in a child custody case? *Journal of Forensic Psychology Practice, 12*, 48–56.

Elrod, L. D., & Spector, R. G. (2004). A review of the year in family law: Children's issues remain the focus. *Family Law Quarterly, 37*, 527–578.

Emam, K., & Moher, E. (2013). Privacy and anonymity challenges when collecting data for public health purposes. *Journal of Law and Medical Ethics, Suppl. 1*, 37–41.

Emanuel, E. J. (2005). Undue inducement: Nonsense on stilts? *American Journal of Bioethics, 5*(5), 9–13.

English, A., & Kenney, K. E. (2003). *State minor consent laws: A summary* (2nd ed.). Chapel Hill, NC: Center for Adolescent Health and the Law.

Equal Employment Opportunity Act of 1972, Pub. L. No. 92-261 (1972).

Etengoff, C., & Daiute, C. (2014). Family members' uses of religion in post-coming-out conflicts with their gay relative. *Psychology of Religion and Spirituality, 6*, 33–43.

Everington, C., & Olley, J. (2008). Implications of *Atkins v. Virginia*: Issues in defining and diagnosing mental retardation. *Journal of Forensic Psychology Practice, 8*(1), 1–23.

Everly, G. S., Flannery, R. B., & Mitchell, J. T. (2000). Critical incident stress management (CISM): A review of the literature. *Aggressive Violent Behavior, 5*, 23–40.

Everson, M. D., & Faller, K. (2012). Base rates, multiple indicators, and comprehensive forensic evaluations: Why sexualized behavior still counts in assessments of child sexual abuse allegations. *Journal of Child Sexual Abuse, 21*(1), 45–71.

Everson, M. D., & Sandoval, J. (2011). Forensic child sexual abuse evaluations: Assessing subjectivity and bias in professional judgements. *Child Abuse & Neglect, 35*(4), 287–298.

Exec. Order No. 11246, 3 C.F.R. 339 (1964–1965 Compilation).

Eysenbach, G., & Till, J. (2001). Ethical issues in qualitative research on Internet communities. *BMJ: British Medical Journal (International Edition), 323*(7321), 1103.

Falender, C. A., Collins, C. J., & Shafranske, E. P. (2009). "Impairment" and performance issues in clinical supervision: After the 2008 *ADA Amendments Act*. *Training and Education in Professional Psychology, 3*(4), 240–249.

Falender, C. A., Cornish, J. A., Goodyear, R., Hatcher, R., Kaslow, N. J., Leventhal, G., Grus, C. (2004). Defining competencies in psychology supervision: A consensus statement. *Journal of Clinical Psychology, 60*, 771–787.

Falender, C. A., & Shafranske, E. P. (2007). Competence in competency-based supervision practice: Construct and application. *Professional Psychology: Research and Practice, 38*, 232–240.

Falender, C. A., Shafranske, E. P., & Falicov, C. J. (2014) Diversity and multiculturalism in supervision. In C. A. Falender, E. P. Shafranske, & C. J. Falicov (Eds.), *Multiculturalism and diversity in clinical supervision: A competency-based approach* (pp. 3–28). Washington, DC: American Psychological Association.

Faller, K. C., & Everson, M. D. (2012). Contested issues in the evaluation of child sexual abuse allegations: Why consensus on best practice remains elusive. *Journal of Child Sexual Abuse, 21*(1), 3–18.

False Claims Amendments Act, 31 U.S.C. § 3701 (1986).

Falzon, L., Davidson, K. W., & Bruns, D. (2010). Evidence searching for evidence-based psychology practice. *Professional Psychology: Research and Practice, 41*(6), 550–557.

Family and Medical Leave Act of 1993, Pub. L. No. 103-3 (1993).

Family Educational Rights and Privacy Act, 20 U.S.C. § 1232g; 34 C.F.R. Part 99 (1974). Retrieved from http://www2.ed.gov/policy/gen/guid/fpco/ferpa/index.html

Farah, M. J., Hutchinson, J. B., Phelps, E. A., & Wagner, A. D. (2014). Functional MRI-based lie detection: Scientific and societal challenges. *Nature Publishing Group, 15*(2), 123–131. doi:10.1038/nrn3665

Farmer, P. (2003). *Pathologies of power: Health, human rights, and the new war on the poor*. Berkeley: University of California Press.

Federal Register (2015). *Proposed changes: Federal policy for the protection of human subjects*. Retrieved from https://www.federalregister.gov/articles/2015/09/08/2015-21756/federal-policy-for-the-protection-of-human-subjects/

Fedewa, A. L., Prout, S. M., & Prout, H. T. (2015). Ethical and legal issues in psychological interventions with children and adolescents. In H. T. Prout & A. L. Fedewa (Eds.), *Counseling and psychotherapy with children and adolescents* (pp. 25–59). New York, NY: John Wiley & Sons.

Ferreri, S. J., Tamm, L., & Wier, K. G. (2006). Using food aversion to decrease severe pica by a child with autism. *Behavior Modification, 30,* 456–471.

Field, M. J., & Behrman, R. E. (Eds.). (2004). *Ethical conduct of clinical research involving children.* Washington, DC: National Academies Press.

Fields, A. J. (2010). Multicultural research and practice: Theoretical issues and maximizing cultural exchange. *Professional Psychology: Research and Practice, 41*(3), 196–201.

Fine, M. A., & Kurdek, L. A. (1993). Reflections on determining authorship credit and authorship order on faculty-student collaborations. *American Psychologist, 48,* 1141–1147.

Fisher, C. B. (1995). American Psychological Association's (1992) ethics code and the validation of child abuse in day-care settings. *Psychology, Public Policy, & Law, 1,* 461–478.

Fisher, C. B. (1999). Relational ethics and research with vulnerable populations. In National Bioethics Advisory Commission (Ed.), *Reports on research involving persons with mental disorders that may affect decision-making capacity* (Vol. 2, pp. 29–49). Rockville, MD: National Bioethics Advisory Commission.

Fisher, C. B. (2000). Relational ethics in psychological research: One feminist's journey. In M. Brabeck (Ed.), *Practicing feminist ethics in psychology* (pp. 125–142). Washington, DC: American Psychological Association.

Fisher, C. B. (2002a). A goodness-of-fit ethic of informed consent. *Urban Law Journal, 30,* 159–171.

Fisher, C. B. (2002b). Respecting and protecting mentally impaired persons in medical research. *Ethics & Behavior, 12,* 279–284.

Fisher, C. B. (2003a). Adolescent and parent perspectives on ethical issues in youth drug use and suicide survey research. *Ethics & Behavior, 13,* 302–331.

Fisher, C. B. (2003b). *Decoding the ethics code: A practical guide for psychologists.* Thousand Oaks, CA: Sage.

Fisher, C. B. (2003c). A goodness-of-fit ethic for informed consent to research involving persons with mental retardation and developmental disabilities. *Mental Retardation and Developmental Disabilities Research Reviews, 9,* 27–31.

Fisher, C. B. (2004). Ethics in drug abuse and related HIV risk research. *Applied Developmental Science, 8,* 90–102.

Fisher, C. B. (2005a). Deception research involving children: Ethical practice and paradox. *Ethics & Behavior, 15,* 271–287.

Fisher, C. B. (2005b). SES, ethnicity and goodness-of-fit in clinician-parent communication during pediatric cancer trials. *Journal of Pediatric Psychology, 30,* 219–229. PMID: 15784919

Fisher, C. B. (2006). Privacy and ethics in pediatric environmental health research: Part I. Genetic and prenatal testing. *Environmental Health Perspectives, 114,* 1617–1621.

Fisher, C. B. (2009). *Decoding the ethics code: A Practical guide for psychologists* (2nd ed.). Thousand Oaks, CA: Sage.

Fisher, C. B. (2010). Enhancing HIV vaccine trial consent preparedness among street drug users. *Journal of Empirical Research on Human Research Ethics, 5,* 65–80.

Fisher, C. B. (2011). Addiction research ethics and the Belmont principles: Do drug users have a different moral voice? *Substance Use & Misuse, 46*(6), 728–741.

Fisher, C. B. (2014). Multicultural ethics in professional psychology practice, consulting, and training. In F. T. L. Leong (Ed.), *APA handbook of multicultural psychology, Vol. 2* (pp. 35–58). Washington, DC: American Psychological Association.

Fisher, C. B. (2015). Enhancing the responsible conduct of sexual health prevention research across global and local contexts: Training for evidence-based research ethics. *Ethics & Behavior, 25*(2). doi:10.1080/10508422.2014.948956

Fisher, C. B., Arbeit, M., Dumont, M., Macapagal, E., & Mustanski, B. (in press). Self-consent for HIV prevention research involving sexual and gender minority youth: Reducing barriers through evidence-based ethics. *Journal of Research on Human Research Ethics.*

Fisher, C. B., Brunnquell, D. J., Hughes, D. L., Liben, L. S., Maholmes, V., Plattner, S., . . . Susman, E. J. (2013). Preserving and enhancing the responsible conduct of research involving children and youth: A response to proposed changes in federal regulations. *Social Policy Report, 27*(1), 1–23.

Fisher, C. B., Busch-Rossnagel, N. A., Jopp, D. S., & Brown, J. (2012). Applied developmental science, social justice and socio-political well-being. *Applied Developmental Science, 16,* 54–64.

Fisher, C. B., Cea, C. D., Davidson, P. W., & Fried, A. L. (2006). Capacity of persons with mental retardation to consent to participation in randomized clinical trials. *American Journal of Psychiatry, 163,* 1813–1821.

Fisher, C. B., Fried, A. F., & Feldman, L. (2009). Graduate socialization in the responsible conduct of research: A national survey on the research ethics training experiences of psychology doctoral students. *Ethics & Behavior, 19*(6), 496–518.

Fisher, C. B., & Fyrberg, D. (1994). Participant partners: College students weigh the costs and benefits of deceptive research. *American Psychologist, 49,* 417–427.

Fisher, C. B., & Goodman, S. J. (2009). Goodness-of-fit ethics for non-intervention research involving dangerous and illegal behaviors. In D. Buchanan, C. B. Fisher, & L. Gable (Eds.), *Research with high-risk populations: Balancing science, ethics, and law* (pp. 25–46). Washington, DC: American Psychological Association.

Fisher, C. B., Hatashita-Wong, M., & Isman, L. (1999). Ethical and legal issues. In W. K. Silverman & T. H. Ollendick (Eds.), *Developmental issues in the clinical treatment of children and adolescents* (pp. 470–486). Needham Heights, MA: Allyn & Bacon.

Fisher, C. B., Hoagwood, K., Boyce, C., Duster, T., Frank, D. A., Grisso, T., . . . Zayas, L. H. (2002). Research ethics for mental health science involving ethnic minority children and youths. *American Psychologist, 57*(12), 1024–1040.

Fisher, C. B., Hoagwood, K., & Jensen, P. S. (1996). Casebook on ethical issues in research with children and adolescents with mental disorders. In K. Hoagwood, P. S. Jensen, & C. B. Fisher (Eds.), *Ethical issues in mental health research with children and adolescents* (pp. 135–238). Mahwah, NJ: Lawrence Erlbaum.

Fisher, C. B., Kornetsky, S. Z., & Prentice, E. D. (2007). Determining risk in pediatric research with no prospect of direct benefit: Time for a national consensus on the interpretation of federal regulations. *American Journal of Bioethics, 7,* 5–10.

Fisher, C. B., & Masty, J. K. (2006). A goodness-of-fit ethic for informed consent to pediatric cancer research. In R. T. Brown (Ed.), *Comprehensive handbook of childhood cancer and sickle cell disease: A biopsychosocial approach* (pp. 205–217). New York, NY: Oxford University Press.

Fisher, C. B., & McCarthy, E. L. H. (2013). Ethics in prevention involving genetic testing. *Prevention Science, 14,* 310–318.

Fisher, C. B., & Mustanski, B. (2014). Reducing health disparities and enhancing the responsible conduct of research involving LGBT youth. *Hastings Center Report, 5,* 28–31. PMID 25231783

Fisher, C. B., & Oransky, M. (2008). Informed consent to psychotherapy: Protecting the dignity and respecting the autonomy of patients. *Journal of Clinical Psychology, 64,* 576–588.

Fisher, C. B., Oransky, M., Mahadevan, M., Singer, M., Mirhej, G., & Hodge, G. D. (2009). Do drug abuse researchers have a duty to protect third parties from HIV transmission? Moral perspectives of street drug users. In D. Buchanan, C. B. Fisher, & L. Gable (Eds.), *Research with high-risk populations: Balancing science, ethics, and law* (pp. 189–206). Washington, DC: American Psychological Association.

Fisher, C. B., & Ragsdale, K. (2006). A goodness-of-fit ethics for multicultural research. In J. Trimble & C. B. Fisher (Eds.), *The handbook of ethical research with ethnocultural populations and communities* (pp. 3–26). Thousand Oaks, CA: Sage.

Fisher, C. B., True, G., Alexander, L., & Fried, A. L. (2013). Moral stress, moral practice, and ethical climate in community-based drug use research: Views from the front line. *American Journal of Bioethics: Primary Research, 4*(3), 27–38.

Fisher, C. B., & Vacanti-Shova, K. (2012). The responsible conduct of psychological research: An overview of ethical principles, APA ethics code standards, and federal regulations. In M. Gottlieb, M. Handelsman, L. VandeCreek, & S. Knapp (Eds.), *Handbook of ethics in psychology* (Vol. 2, pp. 335–370). Washington, DC: American Psychological Association.

Fisher, C. B., & Wallace, S. A. (2000). Through the community looking glass: Re-evaluating the ethical and policy implications of research on adolescent risk and psychopathology. *Ethics & Behavior, 10*(2), 99–118. PMID: 11841105

Fisher, C. B., & Whiting, K. A. (1998). How valid are child sexual abuse validations? In S. J. Ceci & H. Hembrooke (Eds.), *Expert witnesses in child abuse cases: What can and should be said in court* (pp. 159–184). Washington, DC: American Psychological Association.

Fisher, C. B., & Younggren, J. (1997). The value and utility of the APA ethics code. *Professional Psychology: Research and Practice, 28,* 582–592.

Fisher, M. A. (2014). Why "Who is the client?" is the wrong ethical question. *Journal of Applied School Psychology, 30*(3), 183–208. doi: 10.1080/15377903.2014.888531

Flanagan, J. C. (1954). The critical incident technique. *Psychological Bulletin, 54,* 327–358.

Flynn, J. R. (1984). The mean IQ of Americans: Massive gains 1932 to 1978. *Psychological Bulletin, 95,* 29–51.

Foster, D. F. (2010). Worldwide testing and test security issues: Ethical challenges and solutions. *Ethics & Behavior, 20*(3–4), 207–228.

Fouad, N. A., & Chavez-Korell, S. (2014). Considering social class and socioeconomic status in the context of multiple identities: An integrative clinical supervision approach. In C. A. Falender, E. P. Shafranske, & C. J. Falicov, (Eds.). *Multiculturalism and diversity in clinical supervision: A competency-based approach* (pp. 145–161). Washington DC: American Psychological Association.

Fowers, B. J. (2012). Placing virtue and the human good in psychology. *Journal of Theoretical and Philosophical Psychology, 32*(1), 1–9.

Fowers, B. J., & Davidov, B. J. (2006). The virtue of multiculturalism: Personal transformation, character, and openness to the other. *American Psychologist, 61*(6), 581–594.

Fox, R. E., DeLeon, P. H., Newman, R., Sammons, M. T., Dunivin, D. L., & Baker, D. C. (2009). Prescriptive authority and psychology: A status report. *American Psychologist, 64,* 257–268.

Frankel, M. S. (1996). Developing ethical standards for responsible research: Why? Form? Functions? Process? Outcomes? *Journal of Dental Research, 75,* 832–835.

Freedman, B. (1987). Equipoise and the ethics of clinical research. *New England Journal of Medicine, 317*(3), 141–145. doi:10.1056/NEJM198707163170304

Frerich, E. A., Garcia, C. M., Long, S. K., Lechner, K. E., Lust, K., & Eisenberg, M. R. (2012). Health care reform and young adults' access to sexual health care: An exploration of potential confidentiality implications of the *Affordable Care Act. American Journal of Public Health, 102,* 1818–1821.

Fried, A. L. (2015). Professional boundaries in your backyard: The ethics of practice in embedded communities. *The Clinical Psychologist, 68*(Summer), 21–23.

Fried, A. L., & Fisher, C. B. (2008). The ethics of informed consent for research in clinical and abnormal psychology. In D. McKay (Ed.), *Handbook of research methods in abnormal and clinical psychology* (pp. 5–22). Thousand Oaks, CA: Sage.

Fried, A. L., & Fisher, C. B. (in press). Moral stress and job burnout among frontline staff conducting clinical research on affective and anxiety disorders. *Professional Psychology: Research and Practice.*

Friedland, L., & Kaslow, F. (2013). Interacting with the media. In G. P. Koocher, J. C. Norcross, & B. A. Greene (Eds.), *Psychologist's Desk Reference* (3rd ed., pp. 721–726). New York, NY: Oxford University Press.

Friedman Ross, L., Loup, A., Nelson, R. M., Botkin, J. R., Kost, R., Smith, G. R., & Gehlert, S. (2010). Human subjects protections in community-engaged research: A research ethics framework. *Journal of Empirical Research on Human Research Ethics, 5*(1), 5–17.

Friedrich, J., & Douglass, D. (1998). Ethics and persuasive enterprise of teaching psychology. *American Psychologist, 53,* 549–562.

Frye v. United States, 293 F. 1013 (54 App. D.C. 1923).

Gallardo, M. E., Johnson, J., Parham, T. A., & Carter, J. A. (2009). Ethics and multiculturalism: Advancing cultural and clinical responsiveness. *Professional Psychology: Research and Practice, 40,* 425–435.

Gallo, F. J., & Halgin, R. P. (2011). A guide for establishing a practice in police preemployment postoffer psychological evaluations. *Professional Psychology: Research and Practice, 42*(3), 269–275.

General Electric Co. v. Joiner, 522 U.S. 136 (1997).

Genetic Information Nondiscrimination Act of 2008, 42 USC §§ 101–301(2008).

Ghormley, C., Basso, M., Candlis, P., & Combs, D. (2011). Neuropsychological impairment corresponds with poor understanding of informed consent disclosures in persons diagnosed with major depression. *Psychiatry Research, 187*(1–2), 106–112.

Gibson, B. E., Stasiulis, E., Gutfreund, S., McDonald, M., & Dade, L. (2011). Assessment of children's capacity to consent for research: A descriptive qualitative study of researchers' practices. *Journal of Medical Ethics: Journal of the Institute of Medical Ethics, 37*(8), 504–509.

Gillespie, L. K., Smith, M. D., Bjerregaard, B., & Fogel, S. J. (2014). Examining the impact of proximate culpability mitigation in capital punishment sentencing recommendations: The influence of mental health mitigators. *American Journal of Criminal Justice, 39,* 698–715.

Ginsberg, K. R., Winn, R. J., Rudy, B. J., Crawford, J., Zhao, H., & Schwarz, D. (2002). How to reach sexual minority youth in the health care setting: The teens offer guidance. *Journal of Adolescent Health, 31,* 407–416.

Gizara, S. S., & Forest, L. (2004). Supervisors' experiences of trainee impairment and incompetence in APA-accredited internship sites. *Professional Psychology: Research and Practice, 3,* 131–140.

Glaser, J., Martin, K. D., & Kahn, K. B. (2015). Possibility of death sentence has divergent effect on verdicts for Black and White defendants. *Law & Human Behavior, 39,* 539–546.

Glass, T. A. (1998). Ethical issues in group therapy. In R. M. Anderson, T. L. Needels, & H. V. Hall (Eds.), *Avoiding ethical misconduct in psychology specialty areas* (pp. 95–126). Springfield, IL: Charles C Thomas.

Glosoff, H. L., Herlihy, S. B., Herlihy, B., & Spence, E. B. (1997). Privileged communication in the psychologist-client relationship. *Professional Psychology: Research and Practice, 28,* 573–581.

Godine, N., & Barnett, J. E. (2013). The use of telepsychology in clinical practice: Benefits, effectiveness, and issues to consider. *International Journal of Cyber Behavior, Psychology, and Learning, 3,* 70–83.

Goel, V. (2014, July 3). Privacy group complains to F.T.C. about Facebook emotion study. *The New York Times,* Retrieved from: http://bits.blogs.nytimes.com/2014/07/03/privacy-group-complains-to-f-t-c-about-facebook-emotion-study/

Gold, A., & Appelbaum, P. S. (2011). Unconscious conflict of interest: A Jewish perspective. *Journal of Medical Ethics: Journal of the Institute of Medical Ethics, 37*(7), 402–405.

Goldman, J., & Choy, A. (2001). *Privacy and confidentiality in health research.* Paper commissioned by the National Bioethics Advisory Commission. Retrieved August 26, 2008, from http://govinfo.library.unt.edu/nbac/human/overv012.html

Gonsiorek, J. C., Richards, P., Pargament, K. I., & McMinn, M. R. (2009). Ethical challenges and opportunities at the edge: Incorporating spirituality and religion into psychotherapy. *Professional Psychology: Research and Practice, 40*(4), 385–395.

Gonzales, M. H., Pederson, J. H., Manning, D. J., & Wetter, D. W. (1990). Pardon my gaffe: Effects of sex, status, and consequence severity on accounts. *Journal of Personality and Social Psychology,* 57, 610–621.

Goodie, J. L., Kanzler, K. E., Hunter, C. L., Glotfelter, M. A., & Bodart, J. J. (2013). Ethical and effectiveness considerations with primary care behavioral health research in the medical home. *Families, Systems, & Health, 31*(1), 86–95.

Gormley-Fleming, L., & Campbell, A. (2011). Factors involved in young people's decisions about their health care. *Nursing Children and Young People, 23,* 19–22.

Goss v. Lopez, 419 U.S. 565 (1975).

Gostin, L. O. (2007). Biomedical research involving prisoners: Ethical values and legal regulation. *Journal of the American Medical Association, 297,* 737–740.

Gottlieb, M. C. (1993). Multiple-role dilemmas for military mental health care providers: Avoiding exploitative dual relationships; A decision-making model. *Psychotherapy, 30,* 41–48.

Gottlieb, M. C., & Coleman, A. (2012). Ethical challenges in forensic psychology practice. In S. J. Knapp, M. C. Gottlieb, M. M. Handelsman, & L. VandenCreek (Eds.), *APA Handbook of ethics in psychology: Vol. 2. Practice, teaching, and research* (Vol. 2, pp. 91–123). Washington, DC: American Psychological Association. doi:10.1037/13272-006

Gottlieb, M. C., Robinson, K., & Younggren, J. N. (2007). Multiple relations in supervision: Guidance for administrators, supervisors, and students. *Professional Psychology: Research and Practice, 38,* 241–247.

Grady, C. (2005). Payment of clinical research subjects. *Journal of Clinical Investigation,* 115, 1681–1687. doi:10.1172/JCI25694

Graham, T. A. (2001). Teaching child development via the Internet: Opportunities and pitfalls. *Teaching Psychology, 28,* 67–71.

Grandjean, P., & Sorsa, M. (1996). Ethical aspects of genetic predisposition to environmentally-related disease. *Science of the Total Environment, 184,* 37–43.

Green, R. J., & Mitchell, V. (2002). Gay and lesbian couples in therapy: Homophobia, relational ambiguity, and social support. In A. S. Gurman & N. S. Jacobson (Eds.), *Clinical handbook of couple therapy* (pp. 536–568). New York, NY: Guilford Press.

Greenberg, S. A., & Shuman, D. W. (1997). Irreconcilable conflict between therapeutic and forensic roles. *Professional Psychology: Research and Practice, 28,* 50–57.

Greene, A. H. (2012). HIPAA compliance for clinician texting. *Journal of AHIMA, 83,* 34–36.

Greenwald, A. G. (2009). What (and where) is the ethical code concerning researcher conflict of interest? *Perspectives on Psychological Science, 4*(1), 32–35.

Gregg v. Georgia, 428 U.S. 153 (1976).

Griffith, D. M., Mason, M., Yonas, M., Eng, E., Jeffries, V., Plihcik, S., & Parks, B. (2007). Dismantling institutional racism: Theory and action. *American Journal of Community Psychology, 39*(3–4), 381–392.

Griggs v. Duke Power, 401 U.S. 424 (1971).

Grisso, T. (2003). *Evaluating competencies* (2nd ed.). New York, NY: Plenum Press.

Grisso, T., & Appelbaum, P. S. (1998). *Assessing competence to consent to treatment: A guide for physicians and other health professionals.* New York, NY: Oxford University Press.

Grohol, J. H. (2001). *Best practices in e-therapy: Clarifying the definition.* Retrieved from http://www.psychcentral.com/best/best3.htm

Grove, W. M., & Barden, R. C. (1999). Protecting the integrity of the legal system: The admissibility of testimony from mental health experts under *Daubert/Kumho* analyses. *Psychology, Public Policy, and Law, 5,* 224–242.

Grove, W. M., Barden, R. C., Garb, H. N., & Lilienfeld, S. O. (2002). Failure of Rorschach-comprehensive-system-based testimony to be admissible under the *Daubert-Joiner-Kumho* standard. *Psychology, Public Policy, and Law, 8,* 216–234.

Gubi, P. M. (2001). An exploration of the use of Christian prayer in mainstream counseling. *British Journal of Guidance and Counseling, 29,* 425–434.

Gutheil, T. G., & Gabbard, G. O. (1993). The concept of boundaries in clinical practice: Theoretical and risk-management dimensions. *American Journal of Psychiatry, 150,* 188–196.

Gutheil, T. G., & Simon, R. L. (2004). Avoiding bias in expert testimony. *Contemporary Psychiatry, 34,* 260–270.

Guyatt, G., Rennie, D., Meade, M., & Cook, D. (Eds.). (2008). *Users' guides to the medical literature: A manual for evidence-based clinical practice* (2nd ed.). New York, NY: McGraw-Hill Professional.

Haas, L. J., & Cummings, N. A. (1991). Managed outpatient mental health plans: Clinical, ethical, and practical guidelines for participation. *Professional Psychology: Research and Practice, 22,* 45–51.

Hadjistavropoulos, T., & Bieling, P. (2001). File review consultation in the adjudication of mental health and chronic pain disability claims. *Consulting Psychology Journal: Practice and Research, 53,* 52–63.

Haldeman, D. C. (1994). The practice and ethics of sexual orientation conversion therapy. *Journal of Consulting and Clinical Psychology, 62,* 221–227.

Haldeman, D. C. (2004). When sexual and religious orientation collide. *Counseling Psychologist, 32,* 691–715.

Hall, C. C. I. (2014). The evolution of the revolution: The successful establishment of multicultural psychology. In F. T. L. Leong (Ed.), *APA handbook of multicultural psychology: Vol. 1. Theory & research* (pp. 3–18). Washington, DC: APA Books.

Hall, G. C. N., & Yee, A. H. (2014). Evidence-based practice. In F. T. L. Leong (Ed.), *APA handbook of multicultural psychology: Vol. 2. Applications and training* (pp. 59–80). Washington, DC: APA Books.

Hall, R. C. W., & Hall, R. C. W. (2007). A profile of pedophilia: Definition, characteristics of offenders, recidivism, treatment outcomes, and forensic issues. *Mayo Clinic Proceedings, 82,* 457–471.

Hall v. Florida, 572 (U.S. 2014). Last visited March 11, 2016 https://supreme.justia.com/cases/federal/us/572/12-10882/

Hamilton, C. J., & Mahalik, J. R. (2009). Minority stress, masculinity, and social norms predicting gay men's health risk behaviors. *Journal of Counseling Psychology, 56*(1), 132–141.

Hancock, K. A. (2014). Student beliefs, multiculturalism, and client welfare. *Psychology of Sexual Orientation and Gender Diversity, 1*(1), 4–9. doi:10.1037/sgd0000021

Handelsman, M. M., Gottlieb, M. C., & Knapp, S. (2005). Training ethical psychologists: An acculturation model. *Professional Psychology: Research and Practice, 36*(1), 59–65. doi:10.1037/0735-7028.36.1.59

Haney-Caron, E., & Heilbrun, K. (2014). Lesbian and gay parents' determination of child custody: The changing landscape and implications for policy and practice. *Psychology of Sexual Orientation and Gender Diversity, 1,* 19–29.

Hanson, S. L., & Kerkoff, T. R. (2011). The APA ethical principles as a foundational competence: Application to rehabilitation psychology. *Rehabilitation Psychology, 56,* 219–230.

Hathaway, W. (2013). Ethics, religious issues, and clinical child psychology. In D. F. Walker and W. L. Hathaway (Eds.), *Spiritual interventions in child and adolescent psychotherapy* (pp. 17–39). Washington, DC: American Psychological Association.

Hauerwas, S. (1981). *A community of character.* Notre Dame, IN: University of Notre Dame Press.

Haworth, C. M. A., & Plomin, R. (2012). Genetics and education: Toward a genetically sensitive classroom. In K. Harris, S. Graham, & T. Urdan (Eds.), *APA educational psychology handbook: Vol. 1. Theories, constructs and critical issues* (pp. 529–599). American Psychological Association. doi:10.1037/13273-018

Hayes, J. A., & Erkis, A. J. (2000). Therapist homophobia, client sexual orientation, and source of client HIV infection as predictors of therapists' reactions to clients with HIV. *Journal of Counseling Psychology, 47,* 71–78.

Hayes v. Unified School District No. 377, 877 F. 2d 809, 811 (10th Cir. 1989).

Health Insurance Portability and Accountability Act of 1996, Pub. L. No. 104-191, 110 Stat. 1936 (1996).

Health Research Extension Act of 1985, Pub. L. No. 99-158 (1985).

Health Service Psychology Education Collaborative. (2013). Professional psychology in health care services: A blueprint for education and training. *American Psychologist, 68,* 411–426. http://dx.doi.org/10.1037/a0033265

HealthIT.gov. (2014). *Your mobile device and health information privacy and security.* Retrieved from http://www.healthit.gov/providers-professionals/your-mobile-device-and-health-information-privacy-and-security/

Hecker, L. L., & Edwards, A. B. (2014). The impact of HIPAA and HITECH: New standards for confidentiality, security, and documentation for marriage and family therapists. *The American Journal of Family Therapy, 42*(2), 95–113.

Heilbrun, K. (2001). *Principles of forensic mental health assessment.* New York, NY: Kluwer Academic/Plenum Press.

Heilbrun, K., Grisso, T., & Goldstein, A. (2009). *Foundations of forensic mental health assessment.* New York, NY: Oxford University Press.

Heilbrun, K., & LaDuke, C. D. (2015). Foundational aspects of forensic mental health assessment. In B. L. Cutler & P. A. Zapf (Eds.). *APA handbook of forensic psychology* (Vol. 1, pp. 3–18). Washington, DC: American Psychological Association.

Heilferty, C. (2011). Ethical considerations in the study of online illness narratives: A qualitative review. *Journal of Advanced Nursing, 67*(5), 945–953.

Hein, I. M., De Vries, M. C., Troost, P. W., Meynen, G., Van Goudoever, J. B., & Lindauer, R. J. L. (2015). Informed consent instead of assent is appropriate in children from the age of twelve:

Policy implications of new findings on children's competence to consent to clinical research. *BMC Medical Ethics, 16*(76). doi: 10.1186/s12910-015-0067-z

Heinlen, K., Welfel, E. R., Richmond, E. N., & O'Donnell, M. D. (2003). The nature, scope, and ethics of psychologists' e-therapy web sites: What consumers find when surfing the Web. *Psychotherapy, Theory, Research Practice, Training, 40,* 112–124.

Hellkamp, D., & Lewis, J. (1995). The consulting psychologist as an expert witness in sexual harassment and retaliation cases. *Consulting Psychology Journal: Practice and Research, 47,* 150–159.

Helms, J. E. (1993). I also said White racial identity influences White researchers. *The Counseling Psychologist, 21,* 240–243.

Helms, S. W., & Prinstein, M. J. (2014). Risk assessment and decision making regarding imminent suicidality in pediatric settings. *Clinical Practice in Pediatric Psychology, 2*(2), 176–193. doi:10.1037/cpp0000048

Henderson, G. E. (2008). Introducing social and ethical perspectives on gene–environment research. *Sociological Methods & Research, 37,* 251–276.

Hennan, M. R., Dornbusch, S. M., Herron, M. C., & Herting, J. R. (1997). The influence of family regulation, connection, and psychological autonomy on six measures of adolescent functioning. *Journal of Adolescent Research, 12,* 34–67.

Hennessy, K. D., & Green-Hennessy, S. (2011). A review of mental health interventions in SAMHSA's National Registry of Evidence-Based Programs and Practices. *Psychiatric Services, 62*(3), 303–305.

Hess, A. K. (1998). Accepting forensic case referrals: Ethical and professional considerations. *Professional Psychology: Research and Practice, 29,* 109–114.

Hill, J. K. (2013). Partnering with a purpose: Psychologists as advocates in organizations. *Professional Psychology: Research and Practice, 44*(4), 187–192. doi:10.1037/a0033120

Hobbs, N. (1948). The development of a code of ethical standards for psychology. *American Psychologist, 3,* 80–84.

Hoop, J., DiPasquale, T., Hernandez, J., & Roberts, L. (2008). Ethics and culture in mental health care. *Ethics & Behavior, 18*(4), 353–372.

Hoyt, T. (2013). Limits to confidentiality in U.S. Army treatment settings. *Military Psychology, 25*(1), 46–56. doi:10.1037/h0094756

Hulse, G. K. (2013). Improving clinical outcomes for naltrexone as a management of problem alcohol use. *British Journal of Clinical Pharmacology, 76,* 632–541.

Iltis, A. S., Misra, S., Dunn, L. B., Brown, G. K., Campbell, A., Earll, S. A, . . . Dubois, J. M. (2013). Addressing risks to advance mental health research. *JAMA Psychiatry, 70*(12), 1363–71. doi:10.1001/jamapsychiatry.2013.2105

Individuals with Disabilities Education Improvement Act of 2004, Pub. L. No. 108-446, 118 Stat. 2647 (2004).

Institute of Medicine. (2006). *Improving the quality of health care for mental and substance-use conditions.* Washington, DC: Author.

Institute of Medicine. (2012). *Crisis Standards of Care: A Systems Framework for Catastrophic Disaster Response.* Washington, DC: The National Academies Press.

Institute of Medicine. (2015, December). Ethical review and oversight issues in research involving standard of care interventions: A workshop. Meeting held in Washington, DC. Retrieved from http://www.iom.edu/standardofcareWIB/

International Association for Correctional and Forensic Psychology. (2010). Standards for psychology services in jails, prisons, correctional facilities, and agencies: International Association for Correctional and Forensic Psychology (formerly American Association for Correctional Psychology). *Criminal Justice and Behavior, 37*(7), 749–808. doi:10.1177/0093854810368253

International Union of Psychological Science. (2008). *Universal declaration of ethical principles for psychologists.* Retrieved from http://www.iupsys.net/about/governance/universal-declaration-of-ethical-principles-for-psychologists.html

Iverson, G. L. (2006). Ethical issues associated with the assessment of exaggeration, poor effort and malingering. *Applied Neuropsychology, 13,* 77–90.

Ivey, G. (2014). The ethics of mandatory personal psychotherapy for trainee psychotherapists. *Ethics & Behavior, 24,* 91–108.

Jackson, S. W. (2001). Presidential address: The wounded healer. *Bulletin of the History of Medicine, 75,* 1–36.

Jacob, B., Vijayakumar, C., & Jayakaran, R. (2008). *A collaborative practice case study describing the College of Nursing Community Health Programme in India.* Vellore, India: Christian Medical College.

Jacob, S., Decker, D. M., & Hartshorne, T. S. (2011). *Ethics and law for school psychologists* (6th ed.). Hoboken, NJ: John Wiley.

Jacob, S., & Hartshorne, T. S. (2007). *Ethics and law for school psychologists* (5th ed.). New York, NY: John Wiley.

Jacobs, D., Qian, Z., Carmichael, J. T., & Kent, S. L. (2007). Who survives on death row: An individual and contextual analysis. *American Sociological Review, 72,* 610–632.

Jansen, L. A. (2014). Mindsets, informed consent, and research. *The Hastings Center Report, 44,* 25–32. doi:10.1002/hast.237

Jelicic, M., Ceunen, E., Peters, M. V., & Merckelbach, H. (2011). Detecting coached feigning using the Test of Memory Malingering (TOMM) and the Structured Inventory of Malingered Symptomatology (SIMS). *Journal of Clinical Psychology, 67*(9), 850–855.

Jerome, L. W. (1998). *Seclusion and restraint: Avoiding ethical misconduct in psychology specialty areas.* Springfield, IL: Charles C Thomas.

Jeste, D. V., & Saks, E. (2006). Decisional capacity in mental illness and substance use disorders: Empirical database and policy implications. *Behavioral Sciences and the Law, 24,* 607–628.

Jobes, D. A. (2012). The Collaborative Assessment and Management of Suicidality (CAMS): An evolving evidence-based clinical approach to suicidal risk. *Suicide and Life Threatening Behavior, 42,* 640–653. doi:10.1111/j.1943-278X.2012.00119.x

Joffe, S., Fernandez, C. V., Pentz, R. D., Ungar, D. R., Matthew, N. A., Alessandri, A. J., . . . Kodish, E. (2006). Guidelines for involving children in decision-making about research participants. *Journal of Pediatrics, 149*(6), 862–868.

Johnson, J. (2009). Ethics and multiculturalism: Merging not colliding. *Professional Psychology: Research and Practice, 40,* 430–432.

Johnson, K. F., & Freeman, K. L. (2014). Integrating interprofessional collaboration and education competencies (IPEC) into mental health counselor education. *Journal of Mental Health Counseling, 36*(4), 328–344.

Johnson, R. (2013). Using the *DSM-5* and *ICD-11* in forensic and clinical applications with children across racial and ethnic lines. In G. P. Koocher, J. C. Norcross, & B. A. Greene (Eds.). *Psychologist's desk reference* (3rd ed., pp. 58–64). New York, NY: Oxford University Press.

Johnson, W. B., Bacho, R., Heim, M., & Ralph, J. (2006). Multiple-role dilemmas for military mental health care providers. *Military Medicine, 171,* 311–315.

Johnson, W. B., & Barnett, J. E. (2011). Preventing problems of professional competence in the face of life-threatening illness. *Professional Psychology: Research and Practice, 42,* 285–293.

Johnson, W. B., Barnett, J. E., Elman, N. S., Forrest, L., & Kaslow, N. J. (2013). The competence constellation model: A communitarian approach to support professional competence. *Professional Psychology: Research and Practice, 44*(5), 343–354. doi:10.1037/a0033131

Johnson, W. B., Bertschinger, M., Snell, A. K., & Wilson, A. (2014). Secondary trauma and ethical obligations for military psychologists: Preserving compassion and competence in the crucible of combat. *Psychological Services, 11*(1), 68–74. doi:10.1037/a0033913

Johnson, W. B., Grasso, I., & Maslowski, K. (2010). Conflicts between ethics and law for military mental health providers. *Military Medicine, 175*(8), 548–553.

Johnson, W. B., Johnson, S. J., Sullivan, G. R., Bongar, B., Miller, L., & Sammons, M. T. (2011). Psychology in extremis: Preventing problems of professional competence in dangerous practice settings. *Professional Psychology: Research and Practice, 42*(1), 94–104.

Johnson, W. B., & Kennedy, C. H. (2010). Preparing psychologists for high-risk jobs: Key ethical considerations for military clinical supervisors. *Professional Psychology: Research and Practice, 41*(4), 298–304.

Johnson, W. B., Redley, C. R., & Nielson, S. L. (2000). Religiously sensitive rational emotive behavior therapy: Elegant solutions and ethical risks. *Professional Psychology: Research and Practice, 31,* 14–20.

Jones, J. H. (1993). *Bad blood: The Tuskegee syphilis experiment* (Rev. ed.). New York, NY: Free Press.

Jordan, A. E., & Meara, N. M. (1990). Ethics and the professional practice of psychologists: The role of virtues and principles. *Professional Psychology: Research and Practice, 21,* 107–114.

Josephson Institute of Ethics. (1999). *Making ethical decisions.* Marina del Rey, CA: Author.

Kabat-Zinn, J. (1993). Mindfulness meditation: Health benefits of an ancient Buddhist practice. In D. Goleman & J. Gurin (Eds.), *Mind/body medicine* (pp. 259–276). New York, NY: Consumer Reports Books.

Kaiser Family Foundation. (2001). *Generation Rx.com: How young people use the Internet for health information.* Retrieved from http://www.kaisernetwork.org/health_cast/hcast_index.cfm

Kampa-Kokesch, S., & Anderson, M. Z. (2001). Executive coaching: A comprehensive review of the literature. *Consulting Psychology Journal: Practice and Research, 53,* 205–228.

Kandler, C., Bleidorn, W., & Riemann, R. (2012). Left or right? Sources of political orientation: The roles of genetic factors, cultural transmission, assortative mating, and personality. *Journal of Personality and Social Psychology, 102*(3), 633–645.

Kangas, J. L., & Calvert, J. D. (2014). Ethical issues in mental health background checks for firearm ownership. *Professional Psychology: Research and Practice, 45*(1), 76–83. doi:10.1037/a0035632

Kant, I. (1959). *Foundations of the metaphysics of morals.* Indianapolis, IN: Bobbs-Merrill. (Original work published 1785)

Kanzler, K. E., Goodie, J. L., Hunter, C. L., Glotfelter, M. A., & Bodart, J. J. (2013a). Ethical and effectiveness considerations with primary care behavioral health research in the medical home. *Families, Systems, & Health, 31*(1), 86–95. Retrieved from http://psycnet.apa.org/journals/fsh/31/1/86/

Kanzler, K. E., Goodie, J. L., Hunter, C. L., Glotfelter, M. A., & Bodart, J. J. (2013b). From colleague to patient: Ethical challenges in integrated primary care. *Families, Systems, & Health, 31*(1), 41–48.

Karraker v. Rent-a-Center, 411 F. 3d 831 (7th Cir., 2005).

Kaslow, F. W., Patterson, T., & Gottlieb, M. (2011). Ethical dilemmas in psychologists accessing Internet data: Is it justified? *Professional Psychology: Research and Practice, 42*(2), 105–112.

Kaslow, N. J., Falender, C. A., & Grus, C. L. (2012). Valuing and practicing competency-based supervision: A transformational leadership perspective. *Training and Education in Professional Psychology, 6*(1), 47–54.

Kaslow, N. J., Rubin, N. J., Forrest, L., Elman, N. S., Van Horne, B. A., Jacobs, S. C., . . . Thorn, B. E. (2007). Recognizing, assessing, and intervening with problems of professional competence. *Professional Psychology: Research and Practice, 38*(5), 479–492.

Kaufman, P. M. (2011). Admissibility of expert opinions based on neuropsychological evidence. In G. Larabee (Ed.), *Forensic neuropsychology: A scientific approach* (pp. 70–100). New York, NY: Oxford University Press.

Kaup, A. R., Dunn, L. B., Saks, E. R., Jeste, D. V., & Palmer, B. W. (2011). Decisional capacity and consent for schizophrenia research. *IRB: Ethics & Human Research, 33*(4), 1–9.

Kazuko, M., & Shimanouchi, S. (2014). The decision-making and communication capacities of older adults with dementia: A population-based study. *Open Nursing Journal, 8,* 17–24.

Keenan, J. (1995). Proposing cardinal virtues. *Theological Studies, 56,* 709–729.

Kendler, K. S. (2005). "A gene for . . . ": The nature of gene action in psychiatric disorders. *American Journal of Psychiatry, 162,* 1243–1252.

Kennedy, C. H., & Johnson, W. B. (2009). Mixed agency in military psychology: Applying the American Psychological Association ethics code. *Psychological Services, 6*(1), 21–31.

Kessler, L. E., & Waehler, C. A. (2005). Addressing multiple relationships between clients and therapists in lesbian, gay, bisexual and transgender communities. *Professional Psychology: Research & Practice, 36,* 66–72.

Kitchener, K. S. (1984). Intuition, critical evaluation and ethical principles: The foundation for ethical decisions in counseling psychology. *The Counseling Psychologist, 12,* 43–55.

Kitchener, K. S., & Anderson, S. K. (2011). *Foundations of ethical practice, research, and teaching in psychology and counseling* (2nd ed.). New York, NY: Routledge/Taylor & Francis Group.

Kirschner, K., Braspenning, J., Maassen, I., Bonte, A., Burgers, J., & Grol, R. (2010). Improving access to primary care: The impact of a quality-improvement strategy. *Quality & Safety in Health Care, 19,* 248–251.

Klee, C. H., & Friedman, H. J. (2001). Neurolitigation: A perspective on the elements of expert testimony for extending the *Daubert* challenge. *NeuroRehabilitation, 16,* 79–85.

Klonsky, E. D. (2011). Non-suicidal self-injury in United States adults: Prevalence, sociodemographics, topography and functions. *Psychological Medicine, 41*(9), 1981–1986.

Knapp, S., Gottlieb, M., Berman, J., & Handelsman, M. M. (2007). When laws and ethics collide: What should psychologists do? *Professional Psychology: Research and Practice, 38,* 54–59.

Knapp, S., Handelsman, M. M., Gottlieb, M. C., & VandeCreek, L. D. (2013). The dark side of professional ethics. *Professional Psychology: Research and Practice, 44*(6), 371–377. doi:10.1037/a0035110

Knapp, S., Lemoncelli, J., & VandeCreek, L. (2010). Ethical responses when patients' religious beliefs appear to harm their well-being. *Professional Psychology: Research and Practice, 41,* 405–412.

Knapp, S., & VandeCreek, L. (1997). *Jaffee v. Redmond:* The Supreme Court recognizes a psychotherapist-patient privilege in federal courts. *Professional Psychology: Research and Practice, 28,* 567–572.

Knapp, S., & VandeCreek, L. (2003). Legal and ethical issues in billing patients and collecting fees. *Psychotherapy: Theory Research, Practice, Training, 30,* 25–31.

Knapp, S., & VandeCreek, L. D. (2007). When values of different cultures conflict: Ethical decision making in multicultural context. *Professional Psychology: Research & Practice, 38,* 660–666.

Knapp, S., VandeCreek, L. D., Handelsman, M. M., & Gottlieb, M. (2013). Professional decisions and behaviors on the ethical rim. *Professional Psychology: Research and Practice, 44*(6), 378–383. doi:10.1037/a0035108

Knauss, L. K., & Knauss, J. W. (2012). Ethical issues in multiperson therapy. In M. Gottlieb, M. Handelsman, L. VandeCreek, & S. Knapp (Eds.), *Handbook of ethics in psychology* (Vol. 2, pp. 29–44). Washington, DC: American Psychological Association.

Knoppers, B., Joly, Y., Simard, J., & Durocher, F. (2006). The emergence of an ethical duty to disclose genetic research results: International perspectives. *European Journal of Human Genetics, 14*(12), 1170–1178.

Kocsis, R. N. (2011). *The Structured Interview of Reported Symptoms*, 2nd edition (SIRS-2): The new benchmark towards the assessment of malingering. *Journal of Forensic Psychology Practice, 11*(1), 73–81.

Koelch, M., Singer, H., Prestel, A., Burkert, J., Schulze, U., & Fegert, J. M. (2009). "... because I am something special" or "I think I will be something like a guinea pig": Information and assent of legal minors in clinical trials—assessment of understanding, appreciation and reasoning. *Child and Adolescent Psychiatry and Mental Health, 3*(1), 2.

Koenig, A. M., & Richeson, J. A. (2010). The contextual endorsement of sexblind versus sexaware ideologies. *Social Psychology, 41*, 186–191.

Koh, H. K., & Sebelius, K. G. (2010). Promoting prevention through the Affordable Care Act. *New England Journal of Medicine, 363*, 1296–1299.

Koocher, G. P., & Henderson Daniel, J. (2012). Treating children and adolescents. In S. J. Knapp, M. C. Gottlieb, M. M. Handelsman, & L. D. VandeCreek (Eds.), *APA handbook of ethics in psychology: Vol. 2. Practice, teaching, and research* (pp. 3–14). Washington, DC: American Psychological Association.

Koocher, G. P., & Keith-Spiegel, P. (2008). *Ethics in psychology and the mental health professions: Standards and cases* (3rd ed.). New York, NY: Oxford University Press.

Koocher, G. P., & Keith-Spiegel, P. (2013). Dealing with licensing board and ethics complaints. In G. P. Koocher, J. C. Norcross, & B. A. Greene (Eds.), *Psychologist's desk reference* (3rd ed., pp. 551–554). New York, NY: Oxford University Press.

Korchin, S. J. (1980). Clinical psychology and minority problems. *American Psychologist, 35*, 262–269.

Kosinski, M., Matz, S. C., Gosling, S. D., Popov, V., & Stillwell, D. (2015). Facebook as a research tool for the social sciences: Opportunities, challenges, ethical considerations, and practical guidelines. *American Psychologist, 70*, 543–556.

Kramer, A. D. I., Guillory, J. E., & Hancock, J. T. (2014). Experimental evidence of massive-scale emotional contagion through social networks. *Proceedings of the National Academy of Sciences of the United States of America, 22*(111), 8788–8790.

Krauss, D. A., & Sales, D. B. (2000). Legal standards, expertise and experts in the resolution of contested child custody cases. *Psychology, Public Policy, and Law, 6*, 843–879.

Krauss, D., & Lieberman, J. (2007). Expert testimony on risk and future dangerousness. In M. Costano, D. Krauss, & K. Pezdek (Eds.), *Expert psychological testimony for the courts* (pp. 227–250). Mahwah, NJ: Lawrence Erlbaum.

Kremen, W. S., Panizzon, M. S., Xian, H., Barch, D. M., Franz, C. E., Grant, M. D., ... Lyons, M. J. (2011). Genetic architecture of context processing in late middle age: More than one underlying mechanism. *Psychology and Aging, 26*(4), 852–863.

Kuehnle, K., & Sparta, S. N. (2006). Assessing child sexual abuse allegations. In S. N. Sparta & G. P. Koocher (Eds.), *Forensic mental health assessment of children and adolescents* (pp. 129–148). New York, NY: Oxford University Press.

Kumho Tire Co., Ltd. v. Carmichael, 119 S. Ct. 1167 (March 23, 1999); 119 S. Ct. 1167; 143 L. Ed. 2d 238 (1999).

Lakes, K., Vaughan, E., Jones, M., Burke, W., Baker, D., & Swanson, J. (2012). Diverse perceptions of the informed consent process: Implications for the recruitment and participation of diverse communities in the National Children's Study. *American Journal of Community Psychology, 49*(1–2), 215–232.

Lamb, D. H., & Catanzaro, S. J. (1998). Sexual and nonsexual boundary violations involving psychologists, clients, supervisees, and students: Implications for professional practice. *Professional Psychology: Research and Practice, 29,* 498–503.

Lambert, M. J. (2013). Outcome in psychotherapy: The past and important advances. *Psychotherapy. 50,* 42–51. doi:10.1037/a0030682

Landwher, D. N., & Llorente, A. M. (2012). Forensic issues in neuropsychological assessment: Culture and language. In E. M. S. Sherman & B. L. Brooks (Eds.), *Pediatric forensic neuropsychology* (pp. 162–181). New York, NY: Oxford University Press.

Lang, S. (1993). Questions of scientific responsibility: The Baltimore case. *Ethics & Behavior, 3,* 3–72.

Larrabee, G. J. (2007). *Assessment of malingered neuropsychological deficits.* New York, NY: Oxford University Press.

Latane, B., & Darley, J. M. (1970). *The unresponsive bystander: Why doesn't he help?* New York, NY: Appleton-Century-Crofts.

Lease, S. H., Horne, S. G., & Noffsinger-Frazier, N. (2005). Affirming faith experiences and psychological health for Caucasian lesbian, gay and bisexual individuals. *Journal of Counseling Psychology, 52,* 378–388.

Lebow, J. (2014). *Couple and family therapy: An integrative map of the territory* (pp. 207–219). Washington, DC: American Psychological Association.

Lee, J., Lim, N., Yang, E., & Lee, S. (2011). Antecedents and consequences of three dimensions of burnout in psychotherapists: A meta-analysis. *Professional Psychology: Research and Practice, 42*(3), 252–258.

Lefkowitz, J. (2012). Ethics in industrial-organizational psychology. In S. Knapp, M. Gottlieb, M. Handelsman, & L. VandeCreek (Eds.), *Handbook of ethics in psychology* (Vol. 2, pp. 149–168). Washington, DC: American Psychological Association.

Lehavot, K., Barnett, J. E., & Powers, D. (2010). Psychotherapy, professional relationships, and ethical considerations in the MySpace generation. *Professional Psychology: Research and Practice, 41*(2), 160–166.

Leigh, I. W. (Ed.). (2010). *Psychotherapy with Deaf clients from diverse groups.* Washington, DC: Gallaudet University Press.

Lemoire, S. J., & Chen, C. P. (2005). Applying person-centered counseling to sexual minority adolescents. *Journal of Counseling & Development, 83,* 146–154.

Lewis, N. (2004). Red Cross president plans to visit Washington on question of detainees' treatment. *The New York Times.* Retrieved from http://www.nytimes.com/2004/12/01/politics/red-cross-president-plans-visit-to-washington-on-question-of-detainees-treatment.html.

Lieberman, R., Toste, J. R., & Heath, N. L. (2008). Prevention and intervention in the schools. In M. K. Nixon & N. Heath (Eds.), *Self-injury in youth: The essential guide to assessment and intervention.* New York, NY: Routledge.

Lilienfeld, S. O. (2007). Psychological treatments that cause harm. *Perspectives on Psychological Science, 2,* 53–70.

Lippman, A. (1991). Prenatal genetic testing and screening: Constructing needs and reinforcing inequities. *American Journal of Law and Medicine, 17,* 15–50.

Liptak, A. (2011, November 3). Justices weigh judges' duties to assess reliability of eyewitness testimony. *The New York Times* (New York Edition), p. A20.

Lowman, R. L. (Ed.). (2006). *The ethical practice of psychology in organizations* (2nd ed.). Washington, DC: American Psychological Association and the Society for Industrial and Organizational Psychology.

Luo, J. S. (2009). The Facebook phenomenon: Boundaries and controversies. *Primary Psychiatry, 16*(11), 19–21.

Lyon, A. R., & Cotler, S. (2007). Toward reduced bias and increased utility in the assessment of school refusal behavior: The case for diverse samples and evaluations of context. *Psychology in the Schools, 44,* 551–565.

MacIntyre, A. (1984). *After virtue* (2nd ed.). Notre Dame, IN: University of Notre Dame Press.

MacIntyre, A. (1989). *Whose justice? Which rationality?* Notre Dame, IN: University of Notre Dame Press.

Macklin, R. (1981). "Due" and "undue" inducements: On paying money to research subjects. *Ethics and Human Research, 3,* 1–6.

Macklin, R. (1999). *Against relativism: Cultural diversity and the search for ethical universals in medicine.* New York, NY: Oxford University Press.

Magaldi-Dopman, D., & Park-Taylor, J. (2010). Sacred adolescence: Practical suggestions for psychologists working with adolescents' religious and spiritual identity. *Professional Psychology Research and Practice, 41*(5), 382–390.

Maheu, M. M. (2001). *Exposing the risk, yet moving forward: A behavioral e-health model.* Retrieved from http://www3.interscience.wiley.com/cgi-bin/fulltext/120837826/HTMLSTART

Maheu, M. M., & Gordon, B. L. (2000). Counseling and therapy on the Internet. *Professional Psychology: Research and Practice, 31,* 484–489.

Maheu, M. M., Pulier, M. L., Wilhelm, F. H., McMenamin, J., & Brown-Connolly, N. (2005). *The mental health professional and the new technologies: A handbook for practice today.* Mahwah, NJ: Lawrence Erlbaum.

Mahoney, E. B., & Morris, R. J. (2012). Practicing school psychology while impaired: Ethical, professional, and legal issues. *Journal of Applied School Psychology, 28*(4), 338–353. doi:10.1080/15377903.2012.722180

Mailloux, S. L. (2014). The ethical imperative: Special considerations in the trauma counseling process. *Traumatology: An International Journal, 20*(1), 50–56.

Mailloux, S. L., Scholar, I., & Isidore, S. (2014). The ethical imperative: Special considerations in the trauma counseling process. *Traumatology: An International Journal, 20*(1), 50–56. doi:10.1177/1534765613496649

Maltzman, S. (2011). An organizational self-care model: Practical suggestions for development and implementation. *The Counseling Psychologist, 39*(2), 303–319.

Mangione, L., Forti, R., & Iacuzzi, C. M. (2007). Ethics and endings in group psychotherapy: Saying good-bye and saying it well. *International Journal of Group Psychotherapy, 57,* 25–40.

Mantzari, E., Vogt, F., & Marteau, T. M. (2015). Financial incentives for increasing uptake of HPV vaccinations: A randomized control trial. *Health Psychology, 34,* 160–171.

Marachi, R., Astor, R. A., & Benbenishty, R. (2007). Effects of teacher avoidance of school policies on student victimization. *School Psychology International, 28*(4), 501–518.

Margolin, G. (1982). Ethical and legal considerations in marital and family therapy. *American Psychologist, 37,* 788–801.

Martelli, M. F., Bush, S. S., & Sasler, N. D. (2003). Identifying, avoiding, and addressing ethical misconduct in neuropsychological medicolegal practice. *International Journal of Forensic Psychology, 1,* 26–44.

Martindale, D. A. (2004). Integrity and transparency: A commentary on record keeping in child custody evaluations. *Journal of Child Custody: Research, Issues, and Practices, 1*(1), 31–40.

Masty, J., & Fisher, C. B. (2008). A goodness-of-fit approach to parent permission and child assent pediatric intervention research. *Ethics & Behavior, 18*, 139–160.

Matfield, M. (2002). Animal experimentation: The continuing debate. *Nature Reviews Drug Discovery, 1*(2), 149–152.

Matthews, C. H., & Salazar, C. F. (2012). An integrative, empowerment model for helping lesbian, gay & bisexual youth negotiate the coming-out process. *Journal of LGBT Issues in Counseling, 6*(2), 96–117.

May, W. F. (1984). The virtues in a professional setting. *Soundings, 67*, 245–266.

Mayworm, A. M., & Sharkey, J. D. (2014). Ethical considerations in a three-tiered approach to school discipline policy and practice. *Psychology in the Schools, 51*(7), 693–704.

McAllister, P. H. (1991). Overview of state legislation to regulate standardized testing. *Educational Measurement: Issues and Practice, 10*, 19–22.

McCambridge, J., Kypri, K., Bendtsen, P., & Porter, J. (2013). The use of deception in public health behavioral intervention trials: A case study of three online alcohol trials. *The American Journal of Bioethics: AJOB, 13*(11), 39–47. doi:10.1080/15265161.2013.839751

McCarthy, M. A. (2012). Sexual orientation: Toward a biological understanding. In R. E. Landrum & M. A. McCarthy (Eds.), *Teaching ethically: Challenges and opportunities* (pp. 181–190). Washington, DC: American Psychological Association.

McCollum, E. E., & Gehart, D. R. (2010). Using mindfulness meditation to teach beginning therapists therapeutic presence: A qualitative study. *Journal of Marital & Family Therapy, 36*(3), 347–360.

McCrickerd, J. (2010). Sudden discontinuation and the subjective character of experience: A reason to resist psychotropic neuroenhancements. *AJOB Neuroscience, 1*(1), 23–25.

McDaniel, S. H., Belar, C. D., Schroeder, C., Hargrove, D. S., & Freeman, E. L. (2002). A training curriculum for professional psychologists in primary care. *Professional Psychology: Research and Practice, 33*(1), 65–72. doi:10.1037//0735-7028.33.1.65

McGarrah, N. A., Alvord, M. K., Martin, J. N., & Haldeman, D. C. (2009). In the public eye: The ethical practice of media psychology. *Professional Psychology: Research and Practice, 40*(2), 172–180.

McGivern, J. E., & Walter, M. J. (2014). Legal and ethical issues related to treatment integrity in psychology and education. In L. M. H. Sanetti & T. R. Katochwill (Eds.), *Treatment integrity: A foundation for evidence-based practice in applied psychology* (pp. 229–254). Washington, DC: American Psychological Association. doi: 10.1037/14275-002

McGourty, A. J., Farrants, J., Pratt, R., & Cankovic, M. (2010). Taking your participants home: Self-care within the research process. *Counselling Psychology Review, 25*(4), 65–72.

McKeown, J., Clarke, A., Ingleton, C., & Repper, J. (2010). Actively involving people with dementia in qualitative research. *Journal of Clinical Nursing, 19*(13–14), 1935–1943.

McNulty, N., Ogden, J., & Warren, F. (2013). "Neutralizing the patient": Therapists' accounts of sexual boundary violations. *Clinical Psychology & Psychotherapy, 20*(3), 189–198. doi:10.1002/cpp.799

McShane, K. E., Davey, C. J., Rouse, J., Usher, A. M., & Sullivan, S. (2014). Beyond ethical obligation to research dissemination: Conceptualizing debriefing as a form of knowledge transfer. *Canadian Psychology/Psychologie Canadienne*, 1–8. doi:10.1037/a0035473

Meharg, S. S., & Bush, S. S. (2010). Notation of professional qualifications and affiliations: Avoiding puffery and deception. *Applied Neuropsychology, 17*(3), 205–209.

Meier, M. H., Slutske, W. S., Heath, A. C., & Martin, N. G. (2011). Sex differences in the genetic and environmental influences on childhood conduct disorder and adult antisocial behavior. *Journal of Abnormal Psychology, 120*(2), 377–388.

Melchert, T. P. (2015). Ethical foundations of behavioral health care. In *Biopsychosocial practice: A science-based framework for behavioral health care* (pp. 61–95). Washington, DC: American Psychological Association. doi:10.1037/14441-004

Melton, G. (1990). Ethical dilemmas in playing by the rules: Applied developmental research and the law. In C. B. Fisher & W. W. Tryon (Eds.), *Ethics in applied developmental psychology: Emerging issues in an emerging field* (pp. 145–161). Norwood, NJ: Ablex.

Mendenhall, A. N., Frauenholtz, S., & Conrad-Hiebner, A. (2014). Provider perceptions of mental health literacy among youth. *Child Adolescent Social Work Journal, 31,* 281–293.

Mental Health and Developmental Disabilities Confidentiality Act of 1979, 740 Ill. Comp. Stat. 110/1 et seq. (1979).

Milgram, S. (1963). Behavioral study of obedience. *Journal of Abnormal and Social Psychology, 7,* 371–378.

Mill, J. S. (1957). *Utilitarianism.* New York, NY: Bobbs-Merrill. (Original work published 1861)

Miller, F. G., & Emanuel, E. J. (2008). Quality-improvement research and informed consent. *New England Journal of Medicine, 358,* 765–767.

Miller, F. G., Gluck, J. P., Jr., & Wendler, D. (2008). Debriefing and accountability in deceptive research. *Kennedy Institute of Ethics Journal, 18,* 235–251.

Miller, V. A., Drotar, D., & Kodish, E. (2004). Children's competence for assent and consent: A review of empirical findings. *Ethics & Behavior, 14*(3), 255–295.

Millum, J. (2014). The foundation of the child's right to an open future. *Journal of Social Philosophy, 45*(4), 522–538.

Mitchell, C. W., Disque, J. G., & Robertson, P. (2002). When parents want to know: Responding to parental demands for confidential information. *Professional School Counseling, 6,* 156–161.

Mittal, D., Palmer, B. W., Dunn, L. B., Landes, R., Ghormley, C., Beck, C., . . . Jeste, D. V. (2007). Comparison of two enhanced consent procedures for patients with mild Alzheimer disease or mild cognitive impairment. *American Journal of Geriatric Psychiatry, 15,* 163–168.

Moffett, L. A., Becker, C. J., & Patton, R. G. (2014). Fostering the ethical sensitivity of beginning clinicians. *Training and Education in Professional Psychology, 8*(4), 229–235.

Mohatt, G. V., & Thomas, L. R. (2006). "I wonder, why would you do it that way?" Ethical dilemmas in doing participatory research with Alaska Native communities. In J. E. Trimble & C. B. Fisher (Eds.), *The handbook of ethical research with ethnocultural populations and communities* (pp. 93–116). Thousand Oaks, CA: Sage.

Monshi, B., & Zieglmayer, V. (2004). The problem of privacy in transcultural research: Reflections on an ethnographic study in Sri Lanka. *Ethics & Behavior, 14,* 305–312.

Montalto, M. (2014). The ethical implications of using technology in psychological testing and treatment. *Ethical Human Psychology and Psychiatry: An International Journal of Inquiry, 16,* 127–136.

Morales, E., & Norcross, J. C. (2010). Evidence-based practices with ethnic minorities: Strange bedfellows no more. *Journal of Clinical Psychology: In Session, 66*(8), 821–829.

Morris, R. J., & Mather, N. (Eds.). (2007). *Evidence-based interventions for students with learning and behavioral challenges.* Oxford, UK: Taylor & Francis.

Morris, S. E., & Heinssen, R. K. (2013). Informed consent in the psychosis prodrome: Ethical, procedural, and cultural considerations. *Philosophy, Ethics, & Humanities in Medicine, 9,* 2–19.

Moye, J., Marson, D. C., & Edelstein, B. (2013). Assessment of capacity in an aging society. *The American Psychologist, 68*(3), 158–171. doi:10.1037/a0032159

Muehlenkamp, J. J., & Gutierrez, P. M. (2004). An investigation of differences between self-injurious behavior and suicide attempts in a sample of adolescents. *Suicide & Life-Threatening Behavior, 34*, 12–23.

Munsey, C. (2006). Helping colleagues to help themselves. *Monitor on Psychology, 37*(7), 35.

Murphy, J., Scott, J., Kaufman, D., Geller, G., LeRoy, L., & Hudson, K. (2008). Public expectations for return of results from large-cohort genetic research. *American Journal of Bioethics, 8*(11), 36–43.

Musci, R. J., Bradshaw, C. P., Maher, B., Uhl, G. R., Kellam, S. G., & Ialongo, N. S. (2013). Reducing aggression and impulsivity through school-based prevention programs: A gene by intervention interaction. *Prevention Science, 15*(6), 831–840. doi:10.1007/s11121-013-0441-3

Myer, R. A., Williams, R. C., Haley, M., Brownfield, J. N., McNicols, K. B., & Pribozie, N. (2014). Crisis intervention with families: Assessing changes in family characteristics. *Educational Psychology and Special Services, 22*(2), 179–185.

Nagy, T. F. (2011). *Essential ethics for psychologists: A primer for understanding and mastering core issues*. Washington, DC: American Psychological Association.

Nash, J. M., Khatri, P., Cubic, B. A., & Baird, M. A. (2013). Essential competencies for psychologists in patient centered medical homes. *Professional Psychology: Research and Practice, 44*(5), 331–342. doi:10.1037/a0033106

National Academy of Neuropsychology Policy and Planning Committee. (2000). Presence of third party observers during neuropsychological testing: Official statement of the National Academy of Neuropsychology. *Archives of Clinical Neuropsychology, 15*, 379–380.

National Academy of Neuropsychology Policy and Planning Committee. (2003). *Test security: An update*. Official statement of the National Academy of Neuropsychology. Retrieved from https://www.nanonline.org/docs/PAIC/PDFs/NANTestSecurityUpdate.pdf

National Academy of Sciences. (1995). *On being a scientist: Responsible conduct in research*. Washington, DC: National Academy Press.

National Association of School Psychologists (NASP). (2010). *Principles for professional ethics*. Retrieved from http://www.nasponline.org/Documents/Standards%20and%20Certification/Standards/1_%20Ethical%20Principles.pdf

National Association of School Psychologists (NASP). (2015). *School violence prevention* [Position statement]. Retrieved from https://www.nasponline.org/assets/Documents/Research%20and%20Policy/Position%20Statements/SchoolViolence.pdf

National Bioethics Advisory Committee. (2001). *Ethical and policy issues in international research: Clinical trials in developing countries* (Vol. 1). Rockville, MS: Author.

National Instant Criminal Background Check System. (2006). *2006 operations report*. Washington, DC: Federal Bureau of Investigation.

National Institutes of Health. (1979). *The Belmont report: Ethical principles and guidelines for the protection of human subjects of research*. Washington, DC: Government Printing Office.

National Institutes of Health. (2011, October 1). *NIH grants policy statement*. Retrieved from http://grants.nih.gov/grants/policy/nihgps_2011/index.htm

National Research Council. (2003). *Protecting participants and facilitating social and behavioral sciences research*. Washington, DC: National Academies Press.

National Research Council. (2014). *Proposed revisions to the Common Rule for the protection of human subjects in the behavioral and social sciences*. Washington, DC: National Academies Press.

Nedopil, N. (2002). The boundaries of courtroom experience. *Journal of Forensic Psychiatry & Psychology, 13*, 494–498.

Needleman, H. M. (1993). Reply to Ernhart, Scarr, and Geneson. *Ethics & Behavior, 3*, 95–101.

Neoh, J., & Mellor, D. (2009). Professional issues related to allegations and assessment of child sexual abuse in the context of family court litigation. *Psychiatry, Psychology and Law, 16*(2), 303–321.

Neumark, D. (2009). The Age Discrimination in Employment Act and the challenge of population aging. *Research on Aging, 31*(1), 41–68.

Newman, J. L., Gray, E. A., & Fuqua, D. R. (1996). Beyond ethical decision making. *Consulting Psychology Journal: Practice and Research, 48*, 230–236.

Newport-Mesa Unified School District v. State of California Department of Education, 371 F. Supp. 2d 1170 (C.D. Cal. 2005).

Nicholson, I. R. (2011). New technology, old issues: Demonstrating the relevance of the Canadian code of ethics for psychologists to the ever-sharper cutting edge of technology. *Canadian Psychology, 52*(3), 215–224.

Nicolaidis, C., Timmons, V., Thomas, M. J., Waters, A. S., Wahab, S., Mejia, A., & Mitchell, S. R. (2010). "You don't go tell white people nothing": African American women's perspectives on the influence of violence and race on depression and depression care. *American Journal of Public Health, 100*(8), 1470–1476.

No Child Left Behind Act of 2001, Pub. L. No. 107-110, 115 Stat. 1425 (2001).

Nock, M. K., Joiner, T. E., Gordon, K. H., Lloyd-Richardson, E., & Prinstein, M. J. (2006). Non-suicidal self-injury among adolescents: Diagnostic correlates and relation to suicide attempts. *Psychiatry Research, 144*(1), 165–172.

Noddings, N. (1984). *Caring: A feminine approach to ethics and moral education*. Berkeley: University of California Press.

Noe, T. D., Manson, S. M., Croy, C. D., McGough, H., Henderson, J. A., & Buchwald, D. S. (2006). In their own voices: American Indian decisions to participate in health research. In J. E. Trimble & C. B. Fisher (Eds.), *Handbook of ethical research with ethnocultural populations and communities* (pp. 93–116). Thousand Oaks, CA: Sage.

Norcross, J. C. (2005). The psychotherapist's own psychotherapy: Educating and developing psychologists. *American Psychologist, 60*(8), 840–850. doi:10.1037/0003-066X.60.8.840

Nordal, K. C. (2012). Healthcare reform: Implications for independent practice. *Professional Psychology: Research and Practice, 43*, 535–544. doi:10.1037/a0029603

Norris, D. M., Gutheil, T. G., & Strasburger, L. H. (2003). This couldn't happen to me: Boundary problems and sexual misconduct in the psychotherapy relationship. *Psychiatric Services, 54*, 517–522.

Nuremberg Code. (1949). In A. Mitscherlich & F. Mielke (Eds.), *Doctors of infamy: The story of the Nazi medical crimes* (pp. xxiii–xxv). New York, NY: Schuman.

Nutting, P. A., Crabtree, B. F., Miller, W. L., Stange, K. C., Stewart, E., & Jaen, C. (2011). Transforming physician practices to patient-centered medical homes: Lessons from the National Demonstration Project. *Health Affairs, 30*(3), 439–445. doi:10.1377/hlthaff.2010.0159

Oberlander, S. E., & Barnett, J. E. (2005). Multiple relationships between graduate assistants and students: Ethical and practical considerations. *Ethics & Behavior, 15*, 49–63.

O'Brien, J. M. (2011). Wounded healer: Psychotherapist grief over a client's death. *Professional Psychology: Research and Practice, 42*(3), 236–243.

O'Connell, M., Boat, T., & Warner, K. (Eds.). (2009). *Preventing mental, emotional, and behavioral disorders among young people: Progress and possibilities*. Washington, DC: National Academies Press.

O'Connor, M. F. (2001). On the etiology and effective management of professional distress and impairment among psychologists. *Professional Psychology: Research and Practice, 32,* 345–350.

Oczak, M., & Niedz′wien′ska, A. (2007). Debriefing in deceptive research: A proposed new procedure. *Journal of Empirical Research on Human Research Ethics, 2*(3), 49–59.

O'Donohue, W. T., Beitz, K., & Tolle, L. (2009). Controversies in child custody evaluations. In J. Skeem, K. Douglas, & S. Lilienfeld (Eds.), *Psychological science in the courtroom: Consensus and controversy* (pp. 284–308). New York, NY: Guilford Press.

O'Donohue, W. T., & Engle, J. L. (2013). Errors in psychological practice: Devising a system to improve client safety and well-being. *Professional Psychology: Research and Practice, 44*(5), 314–323.

Oetzel, K. B., & Scherer, D. G. (2003). Therapeutic engagement with adolescents in psychotherapy. *Psychotherapy: Theory, Research, Practice, Training, 40,* 215–225.

Office for Protection from Research Risks, Department of Health and Human Services, National Institutes of Health. (1993). *Protecting human research subjects: Institutional review board guidebook.* Washington, DC: Government Printing Office.

Office of the President of the United States. (2013). *Now is the time: The president's plan to protect our children and our communities by reducing gun violence.* Retrieved from http://www.whitehouse.gov/sites/default/files/docs/wh_now_is_the_time_full.pdf

Olafson, E. (2012). A call for field-relevant research about child forensic interviewing for child protection. *Journal of Child Sexual Abuse: Research, Treatment, & Program Innovations for Victims, Survivors, & Offenders, 21,* 109–129.

Olivieri, N. (2003). Patients' health or company profits? The commercialization of academic research. *Science & Engineering Ethics, 9,* 29–41.

Olson, B., Soldz, S., & Davis, M. (2008). The ethics of interrogation and the American Psychological Association: A critique of policy and process. *Philosophy, Ethics, and Humanities in Medicine, 3,* 3. Retrieved from http://www.peh-med.com/content/3/1/3/

Oransky, M., Fisher, C. B., Mahadevan, M., & Singer, M. (2009). Barriers and opportunities for recruitment for non-intervention studies on HIV risk: Perspectives of street drug users. *Substance Use & Misuse, 44,* 1642–1659.

Orme, D. R., & Doerman, A. L. (2001). Ethical dilemmas in the U.S. Air Force clinical psychologists: A survey. *Professional Psychology: Research and Practice, 32,* 305–311.

Orszag, P. R., & Emanuel, E. J. (2010). Health care reform and cost control. *New England Journal of Medicine, 363,* 601–603.

Ossorio, P., & Duster, T. (2005). Race and genetics: Controversies in biomedical, behavioral, and forensic sciences. *American Psychologist, 60*(1), 115–128.

Otto, R. K., DeMier, R., & Boccaccini, M. (2014). *Forensic reports and testimony: A guide for effective communication for psychologists and psychiatrists.* New York, NY: Wiley.

Otto, R. K., & Martindale, D. A. (2007). The law, process, and science of child custody evaluation. In M. Costanzo, D. Krauss, & K. Pezdek (Eds.), *Expert psychological testimony for the courts* (pp. 251–275). Englewood Cliffs, NJ: Lawrence Erlbaum.

Pachter, W. S., Fox, R. E., Zimbardo, P., & Antonuccio, D. O. (2007). Corporate funding and conflicts of interest: A primer for psychologists. *American Psychologist, 62,* 1005–1015.

Page, M. J. L., Lindahl, K. M., & Malik, N. M. (2013). The role of religion and stress in sexual identity and mental health among lesbian, gay, and bisexual youth. *Journal of Research on Adolescence, 23*(4), 665–677.

Palma, T. V., & Iannelli, R. J. (2002). Therapeutic reactivity to confidentiality with HIV positive clients: Bias or epidemiology? *Ethics & Behavior, 12,* 353–370.

Panetti v. Quarterman, 127 S. Ct. 2482 (2007).

Panter, A. T., & Sterba, S. K. (2011). *Handbook of ethics in quantitative methodology.* New York, NY: Taylor & Francis/Routledge.

Pargament, K. I., Murray-Swank, N. A., Magyar, G. M., & Ano, C. G. (2005). Spiritual struggle: A phenomenon of interest to psychology and religion. In W. R. Miller & H. D. Delaney (Eds.), *Judeo-Christian perspectives on psychology: Human nature, motivation, and change* (pp. 245–268). Washington, DC: American Psychological Association.

Parham v. J. R., 442 U.S. 584 (1979).

Parry, G., Roth, A. D., & Kerr, I. B. (2005). Brief and time limited psychotherapy. In G. O. Gabbard, J. S. Beck, & J. Holmes (Eds.), *Oxford textbook of psychotherapy* (pp. 507–521). New York, NY: Oxford University Press.

Pascual-Leone, A., Singh, T., & Scoboria, A. (2010). Using deception ethically: Practical research guidelines for researchers and reviewers. *Canadian Psychology/Psychologie Canadienne, 51*(4), 241–248.

Patient Protection and Affordable Care Act, 42 U.S.C. § 18001 (2010).

Patterson, C. J. (2006). Children of lesbian and gay parents. *Current Directions in Psychological Science, 15,* 241–244.

Patterson, D. R., & Hanson, S. L. (1995). Joint Division 22 and ACRM guidelines for postdoctoral training in rehabilitation psychology. *Rehabilitation Psychology, 40,* 299–310.

Pearson, C. R., Parker, M., Fisher, C. B., & Moreno, C. (2014). Capacity building from the inside out: Development and evaluation of a CITI ethics certification training module for American Indian and Alaska Native community researchers. *Journal of Empirical Research on Human Research Ethics, 9*(1), 46–57. PMCID: 24572083

Peisah, C., Sorinmade, O. A., Mitchell, L., & Hertogh, C. M. (2013). Decisional capacity: Toward an inclusionary approach. *International psychogeriatrics, 25,* 1571–1579.

Pellegrino, E. D. (1989). Can ethics be taught? An essay. *Mount Sinai Journal of Medicine, 56,* 490–494.

Pellegrino, E. D. (1995). Toward a virtue-based normative ethics for the health professions. *Kennedy Institute Journal of Ethics, 5,* 253–278.

Perlin, M. L., & McClain, V. (2009). "Where souls are forgotten": Cultural competencies, forensic evaluations, and international human rights. *Psychology, Public Policy & Law, 15,* 257–277.

Perry, J. L., & Dess, N. K. (2012). Laboratory animal research ethics: A practical, educational approach. In S. J. Knapp, M. C. Gottlieb, M. M. Handelsman, & L. D. VandeCreek (Eds.), *APA handbook of ethics in psychology: Vol. 2. Practice, teaching, and research* (pp. 423–440). Washington, DC: American Psychological Association.

Peterson, D. B. (2007). Executive coaching in cross-cultural context. *Consulting Psychology Journal: Practice and Research, 59,* 261–271.

Pettifor, J., McCarron, M. E., Schoepp, G., Stark, C., & Stewart, D. (2011). Ethical supervision in teaching, research, practice, and administration. *Canadian Psychology/Psychologie Canadienne, 52*(3), 198–205.

Pettifor, J., Sinclair, C., & Falender, C. A. (2014). Ethical supervision: Harmonizing rules and ideals in a globalizing world. *Training and Education in Professional Psychology, 8*(4), 201–210. doi:10.1037/tep0000046

Phillips, S. B. (2011). Up close and personal: A consideration of the role of personal therapy in the development of a psychotherapist. In R. Klein, H. S. Bernard, & V. L. Schermer (Eds.), *On Becoming a Psychotherapist* (pp. 144–164). New York, NY: Oxford University Press.

Phillips, T. (2011). Exploitation in payments to research subjects. *Bioethics, 25*(4), 209–219.

Pierce, R. (2010). Complex calculations: Ethical issues in involving at-risk healthy individuals in dementia research. *Journal of Medical Ethics, 36*(9), 553–557.

Pietrzak, E., Pullman, S., Campbell, L., & Cotea, C. (2010). *Effectiveness of electronically delivered therapies for depression, anxiety disorders and alcohol abuse: A systemic review.* Herston, Australia: University of Queensland Centre for Military and Veterans' Health.

Pillay, N. (2012). *Keynote address by Ms. Navi Pillay, United Nations High Commissioner for Human Rights at the 30th International Congress of Psychology.* Retrieved from http://www.ohchr.org/en/NewsEvents/Pages/DisplayNews.aspx?NewsID=12417&LangID=E

Pipes, R. B., Holstein, J. E., & Aguirre, M. G. (2005). Examining the personal–professional distinction ethics codes and the difficulty of drawing a boundary. *American Psychologist, 60*(4), 325–334.

Plante, T. G. (2007). Integrating spirituality and psychotherapy: Ethical issues and principles to consider. *Journal of Clinical Psychology, 63,* 891–902.

Plante, T. G. (2014). Four steps to improve religious/spiritual cultural competence in professional psychology. *Spirituality in Clinical Practice, 1*(4), 288–292.

Plante, T. G., & Sherman, A. C. (Eds.). (2001). *Faith and health: Psychological perspectives.* New York, NY: Guilford Press.

Plomin, R., & Davis, O. S. P. (2009). The future of genetics in psychology and psychiatry: Microarrays, genome-wide association, and non-coding RNA. *Journal of Child Psychology and Psychiatry, 50*(1–2), 63–71.

Polanin, M., & Vera, E. (2013). Bullying prevention and social justice. *Theory Into Practice, 52,* 303–310.

Pomerantz, A. M. (2005). Increasingly informed consent: Discussing distinct aspects of psychotherapy at different points in time. *Ethics & Behavior, 15,* 351–360.

Ponterotto, J. G. (2014). Best practices in psychobiographical research: Ethical considerations and publishing; Supplement. *Qualitative Psychology, 1*(1), 77–90. http://dx.doi.org/10.1037/qup0000005

Ponterotto, J. G., Casas, J. M., Suzuki, L. A., & Alexander, C. M. (Eds.). (2001). *Handbook of multicultural counseling* (2nd ed.). Thousand Oaks, CA: Sage.

Pope, K. S. (2013). Managing sexual feelings for patients in psychotherapy. In G. P. Koocher, J. C. Norcross, & B. A. Greene (Eds.), *Psychologist's desk reference* (3rd ed., pp. 242–246). New York, NY: Oxford University Press.

Pope, K. S., Keith-Spiegel, P., & Tabachnick, B. G. (2006). Sexual attraction to clients: The human therapist and the (sometimes) inhuman training system. *Training and Education in Professional Psychology, S*(2), 96–111.

Pope, K. S., & Vasquez, M. J. T. (2007). *Ethics in psychotherapy and counseling: A practical guide* (3rd ed.). New York, NY: John Wiley.

Pratt, B., & Loff, B. (2011). Justice in international clinical research. *Developing World Bioethics, 11*(2), 75–81.

Pregnancy Discrimination Act, Pub. L. No. 95-555, 92 Stat. 2076, 42 U.S.C. 2000e(k) (1978).

Presidential Commission for the Study of Bioethical Issues. (2014). *Gray matters: Integrative approaches for neuroscience, ethics, and society* (Vol. 1). Washington, DC: Presidential Commission for the Study of Bioethical Issues. Retrieved from http://www.bioethics.gov/sites/default/files/Gray%20Matters%20Vol%201.pdf

Prilleltensky, I. (1997). Values, assumptions, and practices: Assessing the moral implications of psychological discourse and action. *American Psychologist, 52,* 517–535.

Protection of Pupil Rights Amendment of 2004, 20 U.S.C. § 1232–34 C.F.R. pt. 98 (2004). Retrieved from http://www2.ed.gov/policy/gen/guid/fpco/ppra/index.html

Public Health Service Act 3.01(d), 42 U.S.C. § 241(d) (1946). Retrieved from https://history.nih.gov/research/downloads/PL79-725.pdf

Quattrocchi, M. R., & Schopp, R. F. (2005). Tarasaurus Rex: A standard of care that could not adapt. *Psychology, Public Policy & Law, 11,* 109–137.

Racine, S. E., Burt, S., Iacono, W. G., McGue, M., & Klump, K. L. (2011). Dietary restraint moderates genetic risk for binge eating. *Journal of Abnormal Psychology, 120*(1), 119–128.

Rada, R. (2003). *HIPAA in 24 hours: Small healthcare entity HIPAA manual.* Liverpool, England: Hypermedia Solutions Limited.

Raiya, H. A., & Pargament, K. I. (2010). Religiously integrated psychotherapy with Muslim clients: From research to practice. *Professional Psychology: Research and Practice, 41,* 181–188.

Ramsey, P. (2002). *The patient as person: Explorations in medical ethics* (2nd ed.). New Haven, CT: Yale University Press.

Randsdell, S. (2002). Teaching psychology as a laboratory science in the age of the Internet. *Behavior Research Methods, Instruments & Computers, 34,* 145–150.

Rappo, P. D. (2002). Coding for mental health and behavioral problems: The arcane elevated to the ranks of the scientific. *Pediatrics, 110,* 167–169.

Ravitsky, V., & Wilfond, B. S. (2006). Disclosing individual genetic results to research participants. *American Journal of Bioethics, 6*(6), 8–17.

Reddy, M., Borum, R., Berglund, J., Vossekuil, B., Fein, R., & Modzeleski, W. (2001). Evaluating risk for targeted violence in schools: Comparing risk assessment, threat assessment and other approaches. *Psychology in the Schools, 38,* 157–172.

Rest, J. (1983). Morality. In P. H. Mussen (Series Ed.), J. Flavell, & E. Markham (Vol. Eds.), *Handbook of child psychology: Vol. 4. Cognitive development* (pp. 520–629). New York, NY: John Wiley.

Richards, P. S., & Bergin, A. E. (2005). *A spiritual strategy for counseling and psychotherapy* (2nd ed.). Washington, DC: American Psychological Association.

Richards, P. S., & Potts, R. W. (1995). Using spiritual interventions in psychotherapy: Practices, successes, failures, and ethical concerns of Mormon psychotherapists. *Professional Psychology: Research and Practice, 26,* 163–170.

Ridley, C. R., Liddle, M. C., Hill, C. K. L., & Li, L. C. (2001). Ethical decision making in multicultural counseling. In J. G. Ponterotto, J. M. Casas, L. A. Suzuki, & C. M. Alexander (Eds.), *Handbook of multicultural counseling* (2nd ed., pp. 165–188). Thousand Oaks, CA: Sage.

Riggle, E. B., Rostosky, S. S., & Horne, S. G. (2010). Psychological distress, well-being, and legal recognition in same-sex couple relationships. *Journal of Family Psychology, 24*(1), 82–86.

Risen, J. (2014). *Pay any price: Greed, power, and the endless war.* New York, NY: Houghton Mifflin Harcourt.

Ritzler, B., Erard, R., & Pettigrew, G. (2002). Protecting the integrity of Rorschach expert witnesses: A reply to Grove and Barden (1999) Re: The admissibility of testimony under *Daubert/Kumho* analyses. *Psychology, Public Policy, and Law, 8,* 201–215.

Roberts, L. W. (1999). Ethical dimensions of psychiatric research: A constructive, criterion-based approach to protocol preparation; The research protocol ethics assessment tool (RePEAT). *Biological Psychiatry, 46,* 1106–1119.

Rodolfa, E., Bent, R., Eisman, E., Nelson, P., Rehm, L., & Ritchie, P. (2005). A cube model for competency development: Implications for psychology educators and regulators. *Professional Psychology: Research and Practice, 36,* 347–354.

Roeher Institute. (1996). *Building bridges: Inclusive postsecondary education for people with intellectual disabilities*. North York, Ontario, Canada: Author.

Romney, P. (2008). Consulting for diversity and social justice: Challenges and rewards. *Consulting Psychology Journal: Practice and Research, 60*(2), 139–156.

Rose, E. M., Westefeld, J. S., & Ansley, T. N. (2008). Spiritual issues in counseling: Clients' beliefs and preferences. *Psychology of Religion and Spirituality, S1,* 18–33.

Rosenberg, T., & Speice, J. (2013). Integrating care when the end is near: Ethical dilemmas in end-of-life care. *Families, Systems, & Health, 31*(1), 75–83.

Rosenfeld, G. W. (2011). Contributions from ethics and research that guide integrating religion into psychotherapy. *Professional Psychology: Research and Practice, 42,* 192–199.

Rozensky, R. H. (2014a). Implications of the Affordable Care Act for education and training in professional psychology. *Training and Education in Professional Psychology, 8,* 83–94.

Rozensky, R. H. (2014b). Implications of the *Patient Protection and Affordable Care Act*: Preparing the professional psychology workforce for primary care. *Professional Psychology: Research and Practice, 45*(3), 200–211. doi:10.1037/a0036550

Rozensky, R. H., Celano, M., & Kaslow, N. (2013). Implications of the Affordable Care Act for the practice of family psychology. *Couple and Family Psychology: Research and Practice, 2,* 163–178.

Rudd, M. D., Cordero, L., & Bryan, C. J. (2009). What every psychologist should know about the FDA black box warning label for antidepressants. *Professional Psychology: Research and Practice, 40,* 321–326.

Rudd, M. D., Joiner, T., Brown, G. K., Cukrowicz, K., Jobes, D. A., Silverman, M., & Cordero, L. (2009). Informed consent with suicidal patients: Rethinking risks in (and out of) treatment. *Psychotherapy 46*(4), 459–468.

Russell, C. S., & Peterson, C. M. (1998, December). The management of personal and professional boundaries in marriage and family therapy training programs. *Contemporary Family Therapy, 20,* 457–470.

Saks, M. J., & Lanyon, R. I. (2007). Pitfalls and ethics of expert testimony. In M. Costanzo, D. Krauss, & K. Pezdek (Eds.), *Expert psychological testimony for the courts* (pp. 277–296). Mahwah, NJ: Lawrence Erlbaum.

Sales, B. D., & Shuman, D. W. (2007). Science, experts and law: Reflections on the past and the future. In M. Costanzo, D. Krauss, & K. Pezdek (Eds.), *Expert psychological testimony for the courts* (pp. 9–30). Mahwah, NJ: Lawrence Erlbaum.

Salter, D. S., & Salter, B. R. (2012). Competence with diverse populations. In S. Knapp, M. Gottlieb, M. Handelsman, & L. VandeCreek (Eds.), *Handbook of ethics in psychology* (Vol. 1, pp. 217–241). Washington, DC: American Psychological Association.

Sanders, R. K., Swenson, J., & Schneller, G. R. (2011). Beliefs and practices of Christian psychotherapists regarding non-sexual multiple relationships. *Journal of Psychology and Theology, 39*(4), 330–344.

Sanjari, M., Bahramnezhad, F., Fomani, F. K., Shoghi, M., & Chiraghi, M. A. (2014). Ethical challenges of researchers in qualitative studies: The necessity to develop a specific guideline. *Journal of Medical Ethics and History of Medicine, 7,* 1–6.

Sarason, S. B. (1984). If it can be studied or developed, should it? *American Psychologist, 39,* 477–485.

Scarr, S. (1988). Race and gender as psychological variables: Social and ethical issues. *American Psychologist, 43,* 56–59.

Schenker, Y., Arnold, R. M., & London, A. J. (2014). The ethics of advertising for health care services. *American Journal of Bioethics, 14,* 34–43.

Scherer, M. J. (2010). *Rehabilitation psychology*. New York, NY: John Wiley.

Schlomer, G. L., Cleveland, H. H., Vandenbergh, D. J., Fosco, G. M., & Feinberg, M. E. (2015). Looking forward in candidate gene research: Concerns and suggestions. *Journal of Marriage and Family, 77*(2), 351–354. doi:10.1111/jomf.12165

Schuck, S., & Kearney, M. (2006). Capturing learning through student-generated digital video. *Australian Educational Computing, 21*, 15–20.

Schultz, D. S., & Loving, J. L. (2012). Challenges since Wikipedia: The availability of Rorschach information online and Internet users' reactions to online media coverage of the Rorschach–Wikipedia debate. *Journal of Personality, 94*, 73–81.

Schur, G. M. (1982). Toward a code of ethics for academics. *Journal of Higher Education, 53*, 319–334.

Schwartz, A., Rodríguez, M., Santiago-Rivera, A. L., Arredondo, P., & Field, L. D. (2010). Cultural and linguistic competence: Welcome challenges from successful diversification. *Professional Psychology: Research and Practice, 41*(3), 210–220.

Schwartz, L., Hunt, M., Redwood-Campbell, L., & de Laat, S. (2014). Ethics and emergency disaster response. Normative approaches and training needs for humanitarian healthcare providers. In D. P. O. Mathuna, B. Gordijn, & M. Clarke (Eds.), *Disaster bioethics: Normative issues when nothing is normal.* New York, NY: Springer Science and Business Media Dordrecht.

Schwartz, T. J., & Lonborg, S. (2011). Security management in telepsychology. *Professional Psychology: Research and Practice, 42*, 419–425.

Scott, P. A. (2003). Virtue, nursing, and the moral domain of practice. In V. Tschudin (Ed.), *Approaches to ethics* (pp. 25–32). London, UK: Butterworth Heinemann.

Sechrest, L., & Coan, J. A. (2002). Preparing psychologists to prescribe. *Journal of Clinical Psychology, 58*, 649–658.

Sechzer, J., & Rabinowitz, V. C. (2008). Feminist perspectives on research methods. In F. L. Denmark & M. A. Paludi (Eds.), *Psychology of women: Handbook of theories and issues.* Westport, CT: Praeger.

Secretary's Advisory Committee on Human Research Protections (SACHRP). (2013). *Considerations and recommendations concerning internet research and human subjects research regulations, with revisions.* Retrieved from http://www.hhs.gov/ohrp/sachrp/mtgings/2013 March Mtg/internet_research.pdf

Section 504 of the Rehabilitation Act of 1973, as amended 29 U.S.C. § 794 (1993).

Sedlander, E., Brindis, C. D., Bausch, S. H., & Tebb, K. P. (2015). Options for assuring access to confidential care for adolescents and young adults in an explanation of benefits environment. *Journal of Adolescent Health, 56*, 7–9.

Seitz, J., & O'Neill, P. (1996). Ethical decision-making and the code of ethics of the Canadian Psychological Association. *Canadian Psychology, 37*, 23–30.

Serfaty, V. (2004). *The mirror and the veil: An overview of American online diaries and blogs.* New York, NY: Rodopi.

Sgroi, S. M. (Ed.). (1982). *Handbook of clinical intervention in child sexual abuse.* Lexington, MA: Lexington Books.

Shafranske, E. P., & Sperry, L. (2005). Addressing the spiritual dimension in psychotherapy: Introduction and overview. In L. Sperry & E. P. Shafranske (Eds.), *Spiritually oriented psychotherapy* (pp. 11–29). Washington, DC: American Psychological Association.

Shallcross, R. L., Johnson, W. B., & Lincoln, S. H. (2010). Supervision. In M. Herson (Ed.), *Handbook of clinical psychology competencies*. New York, NY: Springer-Verlag.

Shapiro, D. E., & Schulman, C. E. (1996). Ethical and legal issues in e-mail therapy. *Ethics & Behavior, 6*, 107–124.

Shapiro, E., & Ginzberg, R. (2003). To accept or not to accept: Referrals and the maintenance of boundaries. *Professional Psychology: Research and Practice, 34,* 258–263.

Shapiro, S. L., Brown, K. W., & Biegel, G. M. (2007). Teaching self-care to caregivers: Effects of mindfulness-based stress reduction on the mental health of therapists in training. *Training and Education in Professional Psychology, 1,* 105–115.

Shead, N. W., & Dobson, K. S. (2004). Psychology for sale: The ethics of advertising professional services. *Canadian Psychology, 45,* 125–136.

Sherman, M. D., & Thelen, M. H. (1998). Distress and professional impairment among psychologists in clinical practice. *Professional Psychology: Research and Practice, 29,* 79–85.

Sherry, A., Adelman, A., & Whilde, M. R. (2010). Quick, Daniel: Competing selves; Negotiating the intersection of spiritual and sexual identities. *Professional Psychology: Research & Practice, 41*(2), 112–119.

Shipman, D., Hooten, J., & Roa, M. (2011). Is managed care an oxymoron? *Nursing Ethics, 18*(1), 126–128.

Shore, P., & Lu, M. (2015). Patient safety planning and emergency management. In P. W. Tuerk & P. Shore (Eds). *Clinical videoconferencing in telehealth: Program development and practice* (pp. 167–201). Gewerbestrasse, Switzerland: Springer International.

Shpigel, M. S., Belsky, Y., & Diamond, G. M. (2015). Clinical work with non-accepting parents of sexual minority children: Addressing causal and controllability attributions. *Professional Psychology: Research and Practice, 46,* 46–54.

Shuman, D. W., & Greenberg, S. A. (2003). The expert witness, the adversarial system, and the voice of reason: Reconciling impartiality and advocacy. *Professional Psychology: Research and Practice, 34,* 219–224.

Shumway, B., & Waldo, M. (2012). Client's religiosity and expected working alliance with their psychotherapists. *Psychology of Religion and Spirituality, 4*(2), 85–92.

Sieber, J. E. (1982). Kinds of deception and the wrongs they may involve. *IRB: A Review of Human Subjects Research, 4,* 1–5.

Sieck, B. C. (2012). Obtaining clinical writing informed consent versus using client disguise and recommendations for practice. *Psychotherapy, 49*(1), 3–11.

Simmons, J., & Koester, K. (2003). Hidden injuries of research on social suffering among drug users. *Practicing Anthropology, 25*(3), 53–57.

Simons, L. K., Leibowitz, S. F., & Hidalgo, M. A. (2014). Understanding gender variance in children and adolescents. *Pediatric Annals, 43*(6). doi: 00904481-20140522

Sinclair, C., Poizner, S., Gilmour-Barrett, K., & Randall, D. (1987). The development of a code of ethics for Canadian psychologists. *Canadian Psychology, 28,* 1–8.

Singer, M., Marshall, P., Trotter, R., Schensul, J., Weeks, M., Simmons, J. E., & Radda, K. E. (1999). Ethics, ethnography, drug use and AIDS: Dilemmas and standards in federally funded research. In P. Marshall, M. Singer, & M. Clatts (Eds.), *Cultural, observational, and epidemiological approaches in the prevention of drug abuse and HIV/AIDS* (pp. 198–222). Bethesda, MD: National Institute on Drug Abuse.

Singer, M., Stopka, T., Siano, C., Springer, K., Barton, G., Khoshnood, K., . . . Heimer, R. (2000). The social geography of AIDS and hepatitis risk: Qualitative approaches for assessing local differences in sterile-syringe access among injection users. *American Journal of Public Health, 90,* 1049–1056.

Singh, A. L., D'Onofrio, B. M., Slutske, W. S., Turkheimer, E. E., Emery, R. E., Harden, K. P., . . . Martin, N. G. (2011). Parental depression and offspring psychopathology: A children of twins study. *Psychological Medicine: A Journal of Research in Psychiatry and the Allied Sciences, 41*(7), 1385–1395.

Singh, I., & Kelleher, K. J. (2010). Neuroenhancement in young people: Proposal for research, policy, and clinical management. *AJOB Neuroscience, 1*(1), 3–16.

Sireci, S. G., & Parker, P. (2006). Validity on trial: Psychometric and legal conceptualizations of validity. *Educational Measurement: Issues and Practice, 25,* 27–34.

Smith, A. (2014). Managing dual relationships for rehabilitation professionals who work with clients who are deaf or hard of hearing. *Journal of the American Deafness & Rehabilitation Association, 49,* 41–52.

Smith, P. L., & Burton Moss, S. (2009). Psychologist impairment: What is it, how can it be prevented, and what can be done to address it? *Clinical Psychology Science and Practice, 16*(1), 1–15.

Smith, P. L., Constantine, M. G., Graham, S. V., & Dize, C. B. (2008). The territory ahead for multicultural competence: The "spinning" of racism. *Professional Psychology: Research and Practice, 39,* 337–345.

Smith, R. D., Cornish, J. A. E., & Riva, M. T. (2014). Contracting for group supervision. *Training and Education in Professional Psychology, 8,* 236–240.

Snyder, K. D., & Doss, B. D. (2005). Treating infidelity: Clinical and ethical directions. *Journal of Clinical Psychology: In Session, 61,* 1383–1391.

Sommers-Flanagan, R. (2012). Boundaries, multiple roles and the professional relationship. In S. Knapp, M. Gottlieb, M. Handelsman, & L. VandeCreek (Eds.), *Handbook of ethics in psychology* (Vol. 1, pp. 241–278). Washington, DC: American Psychological Association.

Sood, J. R., Fisher, C. B., & Sulmasy, D. (2006). Religious coping and mental health outcomes in family members making DNR decisions. *Research in the Social & Scientific Study of Religion, 16,* 221–243.

Sorensen, J., & Cunningham, M. D. (2010). Conviction offense and prison violence: A comparative study of murderers and other offenders. *Crime & Delinquency, 56*(1), 103–125.

Spanierman, L. B., Poteat, V. P., Wang, Y. F., & Oh, E. (2008). Psychosocial costs of racism to White counselors: Predicting various dimensions of multicultural counseling competence. *Journal of Counseling Psychology, 55,* 75–88.

Sprague, R. L. (1993). Whistleblowing: A very unpleasant avocation. *Ethics & Behavior, 3,* 103–134.

Staal, M. A., & King, R. E. (2000). Managing a multiple relationship environment: The ethics of military psychology. *Professional Psychology: Research and Practice, 31,* 698–705.

Stanton, M., & Welsh, R. (2011). *Specialty competencies in couple and family psychology.* New York, NY: Oxford University Press.

State of New Jersey v. Margaret Kelly Michaels, 625 A.2d 489 (N.J. Superior A.D. 1993).

State of North Carolina v. Bradley (2006) 179 NC App 551, 634 SE2d 258.

Steele, K. D., & Morlin, B. (2007). Spokane psychologists linked to CIA: Congress probes role in controversial interrogations. *The Spokesman-Review.* Retrieved from http://www.spokesmanreview.com/news/archives.asp

Steensma, T. D., McGuire, J. K., Kreukels, B. P., Beekman, A. J., & Cohen-Kettenis, P. T. (2013). Factors associated with desistence and persistence of childhood gender dysphoria: A quantitative follow-up study. *Journal of the American Academy of Child and Adolescent Psychiatry, 52,* 582–590.

Steinbock, B., Arras, J. D., & London, A. J. (Eds.). (2003). *Ethical issues in modern medicine.* New York, NY: McGraw-Hill.

Stern, B. H. (2001). Admissibility of neuropsychological testimony after *Daubert* and *Kumho*. *NeuroRehabilitation, 16,* 93–101.

Stratton, J. S., & Smith, R. D. (2006). Supervision of couples cases. *Psychotherapy: Theory, Research, Practice, Training, 43,* 337–348.

Striefel, S. S. (2007). Ethical practice issues in treating pain. *Biofeedback, 35,* 44–47.

Stuart, R. B. (2004). Twelve practical suggestions for achieving multicultural competence. *Professional Psychology: Research and Practice, 35*(1), 3–9.

Substance Abuse and Mental Health Services Administration (SAMHSA). (2015). *Ending conversion therapy: Supporting and affirming LGBTQ youth* (HHS Publication No. [SMA] 15-4928). Rockville, MD: Substance Abuse and Mental Health Services Administration. Retrieved from http://store.samhsa.gov/product/SMA15-4928

Sue, D. W. (2008). Multicultural organizational consultation: A social justice perspective. *Consulting Psychology Journal: Practice and Research, 60,* 157–169.

Sue, D. W., Capodilupo, C. M., Torino, G. C., Bucceri, J. M., Holder, A. M. B., Nadal, K. L., & Esquilin, M. (2007). Racial microaggressions in everyday life: Implications for clinical practice. *American Psychologist, 62,* 271–286.

Sue, D. W., & Sue, D. (2003). *Counseling the culturally diverse.* New York, NY: John Wiley.

Sue, S. (1999). Science, ethnicity, and bias: Where have we gone wrong? *American Psychologist, 54*(12), 1070–1077.

Summit, R. C. (1983). The child sexual abuse accommodation syndrome. *Child Abuse & Neglect, 7,* 177–193.

Supady, A., Voelkel, A., Witzel, J., Gubka, U., & Northoff, G. (2011). How is informed consent related to emotions and empathy? An exploratory neuroethical investigation. *Journal of Medical Ethics, 37*(5), 311–317.

Svendsen, M. N., & Koch, L. (2006). Genetics and prevention: A policy in the making. *New Genetics & Society, 25*(1), 51–68.

Tamura, L. J. (2012). Emotional competence and well-being. In S. J. Knapp, M. C. Gottlieb, M. M. Handelsman, & L. D. VandeCreek (Eds.), *APA handbook of ethics in psychology: Vol. 1. Moral foundations and common themes* (pp. 175–215). Washington, DC: American Psychological Association.

Tan, S. (2003). Integrating spiritual direction into psychotherapy: Ethical issues and guidelines. *Journal of Psychology & Theology, 31,* 14–23.

Tarasoff v. Regents of the University of California (Tarasoff II), 17 Cal. 3d 425, 551 P.2d 334 (Cal. 1976).

Tarbox, S. I., & Pogue-Geile, M. F. (2011). A multivariate perspective on schizotypy and familial association with schizophrenia: A review. *Clinical Psychology Review, 31*(7), 1169–1182.

Taube, D. O., & Olkin, R. (2011). When is differential treatment discriminatory? Legal, ethical, and professional considerations for psychology trainees with disabilities. *Rehabilitation Psychology, 56*(4), 329–339.

Taylor, L., & Adelman, H. S. (1989). Reframing the confidentiality dilemma to work in children's best interests. *Professional Psychology: Research and Practice, 20,* 79–83.

Taylor, L., McMinn, M. R., Bufford, R. K., & Chang, K. B. T. (2010). Psychologists' attitudes and ethical concerns regarding the use of social networking sites. *Professional Psychology: Theory, Research, and Practice, 41,* 153–159.

Taylor, R. E., & Gazda, G. M. (1991). Concurrent individual and group therapy: The ethical issues. *Journal of Group Psychotherapy, Psychodrama, and Sociometry, 44,* 51–59.

Thapar v. Zezulka, 994 S.W.2d 635 (Tex. 1999).

Thoburn, J. W., Bentley, J. A., Ahmad, Z. S., & Jones, K. C. (2012). International disaster psychology ethics: A social justice model imbedded in a systems paradigm. *Traumatology, 18*(4), 79–85. doi:10.1177/1534765612444880

Thompson, J., Baird, P., & Downie, J. (2001). *The Olivieri Report: The complete text of the report of the independent inquiry commissioned by the CAUT.* Toronto, Ontario, Canada: James Lorimer.

Tishelman, A. C., Kaufman, R., Edwards-Leeper, L., Mandel, F. H., Shumer, D. E., & Spack, N. P. (2015). Serving transgender youth: Challenges, dilemmas, and clinical examples. *Professional Psychology: Research and Practice, 46,* 37–45.

Tjeltveit, A. C., & Gottlieb, M. C. (2010). Avoiding the road to ethical disaster: Overcoming vulnerabilities and developing resilience. *Psychotherapy: Theory, Research, Practice, Training, 47*(1), 98–110.

Tolman, A. O., & Rotzien, A. L. (2007). Conducting risk evaluations for future violence: Ethical practice is possible. *Professional Psychology: Research and Practice, 38,* 71–79.

Trestman, R. L. (2014). Ethics, the law, and prisoners: Protecting society, changing human behavior and protecting human rights. *Bioethical Inquiry, 11,* 311–318.

Trimble, J. E. (2009). The principled conduct of counseling research with ethnocultural populations: The influence of moral judgments on scientific reasoning. In J. Ponterotto, J. M. Casas, L. Suzuki, & C. M. Alexander (Eds.), *Handbook of multicultural counseling* (3rd ed.). Thousand Oaks, CA: Sage.

Trimble, J. E., & Fisher, C. B. (Eds.). (2006). *The handbook of ethical research with ethnocultural populations & communities.* Thousand Oaks, CA: Sage.

Trimble, J. E., Scharrón-del Rio, M., & Casillas, D. (2013). Ethical matters and contentions in the principled conduct of research with ethnocultural communities (pp. 59–82). In F. T. L. Leong, L. Comas-Dias, G. N. Hall, V. McLloyd, & J. E. Trimble (Eds.), *Handbook of multicultural psychology.* Washington, DC: American Psychological Association.

Trimble, J., Trickett, E., Fisher, C. B., & Goodyear, L. (2012). A conversation on multicultural competence in evaluation. *American Journal of Evaluation, 31*(1), 112–123.

Turchik, J. A., Karpenko, V., Hammers, D., & McNamara, J. R. (2007). Practical and ethical assessment issues in rural, impoverished, and managed care settings. *Professional Psychology: Research and Practice, 38,* 158–168.

Tynan, W., & Woods, K. E. (2013). Emerging issues: Psychology's place in the primary care pediatric medical home. *Clinical Practice in Pediatric Psychology, 1*(4), 380–385. doi:10.1037/cpp0000042

Unguru, Y. (2011). Making sense of adolescent decision-making: Challenge and reality. *Adolescent Medicine: State of the Art Reviews, 22*(2), 195–206, vii–viii.

Uniformed Services Employment and Reemployment Rights Act of 1994, 38 U.S.C. §§ 4301–4333 (1994).

United Nations. (1948). *Universal declaration of human rights.* Retrieved from http://www.un.org/en/documents/udhr/

United Nations. (1966). *International covenant on economic, social and cultural rights.* Retrieved from http://www.ohchr.org/EN/ProfessionalInterest/Pages/CESCR.aspx (Entry into force 1976)

United Nations. (1984). *Convention against torture and other cruel, inhuman or degrading treatment or punishment.* Retrieved from http://legal.un.org/avl/ha/catcidtp/catcidtp.html

United Nations Educational, Scientific and Cultural Organization. (1997). *Universal declaration on the human genome and human rights.* Paris, France: Author. Retrieved from http://www.unesco.org/new/en/social-and-human-sciences/themes/bioethics/human-genome-and-human-rights/

United Nations General Assembly. (1989, December 12). *UN Convention on the Rights of the Child* (Document A/RES/44/25).

US Department of Defense. (1997a). *Mental health evaluations of members of the armed forces* (DoD Directive 6490.1). Washington, DC: Government Printing Office.

US Department of Defense. (1997b). *Requirements for mental health evaluations of members of the armed forces* (DoD Instruction 6490.4). Washington, DC: Government Printing Office.

van Emmerik, A. A. P., Kamphuis, J. H., Hulsbosch, A. M., & Emmelkamp, P. M. G. (2002). Single session debriefing after psychological trauma: A meta-analysis. *Lancet, 360,* 766–771.

Vance, S. R., Jr., Ehrensaft, D., & Rosenthal, S. M. (2014). Psychological and medical care of gender nonconforming youth. *Pediatrics, 134*(6), 1184–1192.

VandeCreek, L. (2013). Assessing and responding to aggressive and threatening clients. In G. P. Koocher, J. C. Norcross, & B. A. Greene (Eds.), *Psychologist's desk reference* (3rd ed., pp. 616–619). New York: Oxford University Press.

VandenBos, G. R. (2001). *Disguising case material for publication.* Unpublished manuscript. Available from American Psychological Association, 750 First Street, NE, Washington, DC 20002-4242.

VanderWalde, A., & Kurzban, S. (2011). Paying human subjects in research: Where are we, how did we get here, and now what? *Journal of Law, Medicine & Ethics, 39*(3), 543–558.

Vasquez, M. (2012). Social justice and civic virtue. In S. Knapp, M. Gottlieb, M. Handelsman, & L. VandeCreek (Eds.), *Handbook of ethics in psychology* (Vol. 1, pp. 75–98). Washington, DC: American Psychological Association.

Vasquez, M. J. T. (2009). Ethics in multicultural counseling practice. In J. G. Ponterotto, L. A. Suzuki, J. M. Casas, & C. M. Alexander (Eds.), *Handbook of multicultural counseling* (3rd ed., pp. 127–145). Thousand Oaks, CA: Sage.

Vieten, C., Scammell, S., Pilato, R., Ammondson, I., Pargament, K. I., & Lukoff, D. (2013). Spiritual and religious competencies for psychologists. *Psychology of Religion and Spirituality, 5*(3), 129–144. doi:10.1037/a0032699

Vitacco, M. J., Gonsalves, V., Tomony, J., Smith, B. E. R., & Lishner, D. A. (2012). Can standardized measures of risk predict inpatient violence? Combining static and dynamic variables to improve accuracy. *Criminal Justice and Behavior, 39,* 589–606.

Volicer, L., & Ganzine, L. (2003). Health professional views on standards for decision-making capacity regarding refusal of medical treatment in mild Alzheimer's disease. *Journal of the American Gerontological Association, 51,* 1270–1274.

Voss Horrell, S. C., Holohan, D. R., Didion, L. M., & Vance, G. (2011). Treating traumatized OEF/OIF veterans: How does trauma treatment affect the clinician? *Professional Psychology: Research and Practice, 42*(1), 79–86.

Waldman, K. (2014). *Facebook's unethical experiment.* Retrieved from http://www.slate.com/articles/health_and_science/science/2014/06/facebook_unethical_experiment_it_made_news_feeds_happier_or_sadder_to_manipulate.html

Walsh, B. (2008). Strategies for responding to self-injury: When does the duty to protect apply? In J. L. Werth, E. R. Welfel, & G. A. H. Benjamin (Eds.), *The duty to protect: Ethical, legal, and professional considerations for mental health professionals* (pp. 181–193). Washington, DC: American Psychological Association.

Walzer, M. (1983). *Spheres of justice: A defense of pluralism and equality.* New York, NY: Basic Books.

Wang, J. Y., & Kitsis, E. A. (2013). Tangling the web: Deception in online research. *The American Journal of Bioethics, 13*(11), 59–61. doi:10.1080/15265161.2013.840868

Wang, S., & Kim, B. S. K. (2010). Therapist multicultural competence, Asian American participants' cultural values, and counseling process. *Journal of Counseling Psychology, 57,* 394–401.

Wang, Z., Hart, S. A., Kovas, Y., Lukowski, S., Soden, B., Thompson, L. A., Plomin, R., McLoughlin, G., Bartlett, C. W., Lyons, I. M., & Petrill, S. A. (2014). Who is afraid of math? Two sources of genetic variance for mathematical anxiety. *Journal of Child Psychology & Psychiatry, 55*(9), 1056–1064.

Ward v. Polite. (2012). 667 F. 3d 727 (U.S. Ct. App., 6th Cir. 2012).

Wards Cove Packing Company v. Antonio, 490 U.S. 642, Certiorari to the United States Court of Appeals for the Ninth Circuit, No. 87-1387 (1989).

Wasserman, R. (2013). Ethical issues and guidelines for conducting data analysis in psychological research. *Ethics & Behavior, 23*(1), 3–15. doi:10.1080/10508422.2012.728472

Webb, C., & Orwig, J. (2015). Expanding our reach. Telehealth and licensure implications for psychologists. *Journal of Clinical Psychology in Medical Settings, 22,* 243–250.

Webb, K. B. (2011). Care of others and self: A suicidal patient's impact on the psychologist. *Professional Psychology: Research and Practice, 42*(3), 215–221.

Wechsler, D. (1991). *Wechsler Intelligence Scale for Children* (3rd ed., *WISC-III*). San Antonio, TX: Psychological Corporation.

Weijer, C., & Emanuel, E. J. (2000). Ethics: Protecting communities in biomedical research. *Science, 289*(5482),1142–1144.

Weijer, C., & Miller, P. B. (2004). When are research risks reasonable in relation to anticipated benefits? *Nature Medicine, 10*(6), 570–573. doi:10.1038/nm0604-570

Weinberger, L. E., & Sreenivasan, S. (2003). Ethical principles of correctional psychology. In W. O'Donohue & K. Ferguson (Eds.), *Handbook of professional ethics for psychologists* (pp. 359–375). Thousand Oaks, CA: Sage.

Weiner, R. L., & Bornstein, B. H. (2011). *Handbook of trial consulting.* New York, NY: Springer.

Weinfeld, J. M., & Finkelstein, K. (2005). How to answer your clinical questions more efficiently. *Family Practice Management, 12,* 37–41.

Weisz, J. R., & Hawley, K. M. (2002). Developmental factors in the treatment of adolescents. *Journal of Consulting and Clinical Psychology, 70,* 21–43.

Weithorn, L. A. (2006). The legal contexts of forensic assessment of children and families. In S. N. Sparta & G. P. Koocher (Eds.), *Forensic mental health assessment of children and adolescents* (pp. 11–19). New York, NY: Oxford University Press.

Werth, J. L., Hastings, S. L., & Riding-Malon, R. (2010). Ethical challenges of practicing in rural areas. *Journal of Clinical Psychology, 66*(5), 537–548.

Wertheimer, A., & Miller, F. G. (2008). Payment for research participation: A coercive offer? *Journal of Medical Ethics, 34,* 389–392.

Wester, S. R., Danforth, L., & Olle, C. (2013). Social networking sites and the evaluation of applicants and students in applied training programs in psychology. *Training and Education in Professional Psychology, 7*(3), 145–154. doi:10.1037/a0032376

Whealin, J. M., & Ruzek, J. (2008). Program evaluation for organizational cultural competence in mental health practices. *Professional Psychology: Research and Practice, 39*(3), 320–328.

Wilcoxon, A., Remley, T. P., & Gladding, S. T. (2012). *Ethical, legal, and professional issues in the practice of marriage and family therapy* (5th ed.). Upper Saddle River, NJ: Pearson Education.

Williams, B. E., Pomerantz, A. M., Segrist, D. J., & Pettibone, J. C. (2010). How impaired is too impaired? Ratings of psychologist impairment by psychologists in independent practice. *Ethics & Behavior, 20*(2), 149–160.

Wisconsin v. Yoder, 406 U.S. 205 (1972).

Wise, E. H., & Cellucci, T. (2014). Using the ethical context to enhance practicum training. *Training and Education in Professional Psychology, 8*(4), 221–228.

Wise, E. H., Nutt, R. L., Schaffer, J. B., Sturm, C. A., Rodolfa, E., & Webb, C. (2010). Life-long learning for psychologists: Current status and a vision for the future. *Professional Psychology: Research and Practice, 41*(4), 288–297.

Wise, R. A., King, A. R., Miller, J. C., & Pearce, M. W. (2011). When HIPAA and FERPA apply to university training clinics. *Training and Education in Professional Psychology, 5*(1), 48–56.

Wolf, L. E., Dame, L. A., Patel, M. J., Williams, B. A., Austin, J. A., & Beskow, L. M. (2012). Certificates of confidentiality: Legal counsels' experiences with and perspectives on legal demands for research data. *Journal of Empirical Research on Human Research Ethics, 7*(4), 1–9. doi:10.1525/jer.2012.7.4.1

Wong, M. L., Chan, R., Tan, H. H., Yong, E., Lee, L., Cutter, J., . . . Koh, D. (2012). Sex work and risky sexual behaviors among foreign entertainment workers in urban Singapore: Findings from Mystery Client Survey. *Journal of Urban Health, 89*, 1031–1044.

Wong, T. M. (2000). Neuropsychological assessment and intervention with Asian Americans. In E. Fletcher-Janzen, T. L. Strickland, & C. R. Reynolds (Eds.), *Handbook of cross-cultural neuropsychology* (pp. 43–53). New York, NY: Kluwer Academic/Plenum Press.

Wong, T. M., Strickland, T. L., Fletcher-Janzen, E., Ardila, A., & Reynolds, C. R. (2000). Theoretical and practical issues in the neuropsychological assessment and treatment of culturally dissimilar patients. In E. Fletcher-Janzen, T. L. Strickland, & C. R. Reynolds (Eds.), *Handbook of cross-cultural neuropsychology* (pp. 3–18). New York, NY: Kluwer Academic/Plenum Press.

Wood, S. E., Packman, W., Howell, S., & Bongar, B. (2014). A failure to implement: Analyzing state responses to the Supreme Court's directives in *Atkins v. Virginia* and suggestions for a national standard. *Psychiatry, Psychology, & Law, 21*, 16–45.

Woody, R. (2009). Ethical considerations of multiple roles in forensic services. *Ethics & Behavior, 19*(1), 79–87.

Woody, R. (2011). The financial conundrum for mental health practitioners. *American Journal of Family Therapy, 39*(1), 1–10.

World Health Organization. (2003). *Genetic databases: Assessing the benefits and the impact on human and patient rights.* Geneva, Switzerland: World Health Organization. Retrieved from http://www.who.int/genomics/publications/en/index5.html

World Health Organization. (2010). *Framework for action on interprofessional education and collaborative practice.* Retrieved from http://whqlibdoc.who.int/hq/2010/WHO_HRH_HPN_10.3_eng.pdf

World Medical Association. (2008). World Medical Association Declaration of Helsinki: Ethical principles for medical research involving human subjects. Retrieved from http://www.wma.net/en/30publications/10policies/b3/

Wylie, M. S. (1995, May–June). The power of *DSM-IV*: Diagnosing for dollars. *Family Therapy Networker,* 23–33, 65–69.

Yell, M. L. (1994). Timeout and students with behavior disorders: A legal analysis. *Education and Treatment of Children, 17*, 293–301.

Younggren, J. N. (2009). Who is your patient? *The National Psychologist,* pp. 18, 19.

Younggren, J. N. (2011). Three-prong approach to risk prevention. *Ethics & Behavior, 21*(1), 88–90.

Younggren, J. N., Fisher, M., Foote, W. E., & Hjelt, S. E. (2011). A legal and ethical review of patient responsibilities and psychotherapist duties. *Professional Psychology: Research and Practice, 42*(2), 160–168.

Younggren, J. N., & Gottlieb, D. (2004). Managing risk when contemplating multiple relationships. *Professional Psychology: Research and Practice, 35*, 255–260.

Younggren, J. N., & Gottlieb, M. C. (2008). Termination and abandonment: History, risk, and risk management. *Professional Psychology: Research and Practice, 39*(5), 498–504.

Yuen, E. K., Goetter, E. M., Herbert, J. D., & Forman, E. M. (2012). Challenges and opportunities in Internet-mediated telemental health. *Professional Psychology: Research and Practice, 43,* 1–8.

Zavos, H. S., Gregory, A. M., & Eley, T. C. (2012). Longitudinal genetic analysis of anxiety sensitivity. *Developmental Psychology, 48*(1), 204–212.

Zeranski, L., & Halgin, R. P. (2011). Ethical issues in elder abuse reporting: A professional psychologist's guide. *Professional Psychology: Research and Practice, 42*(4), 294–300.

Zur, O., Williams, M. H., Lehavot, K., & Knapp, S. (2009). Psychotherapist self-disclosure and transparency in the Internet age. *Professional Psychology: Research and Practice, 40*(1), 22–30.

Index